m H

Fodo

India

// *"When it comes to information on regional history, what to see and do, and shopping, these guides are exhaustive."*

—*USAir Magazine*

"Usable, sophisticated restaurant coverage, with an emphasis on good value."

—Andy Birsh, *Gourmet Magazine* columnist

"Valuable because of their comprehensiveness."

—*Minneapolis Star-Tribune*

"Fodor's always delivers high quality...thoughtfully presented...thorough."

—*Houston Post*

"An excellent choice for those who want everything under one cover."

—*Washington Post* **//**

915.4
F

Fodor's Travel Publications, Inc.
New York • Toronto • London • Sydney • Auckland
http://www.fodors.com/

Fodor's India

Contributors: Rob Andrews, Kathleen Cox, Smita Patel, Vikram Singh, Peter Soparkar, Dinah Spritzer, Julie Tomasz

Editor: Nancy van Itallie

Editorial Contributors: Robert Blake, Fionn Davenport, Rebecca Miller, Linda Schmidt, M. T. Schwartzman (Gold Guide editor)

Creative Director: Fabrizio La Rocca

Cartographer: David Lindroth

Cover Photograph: Lindsay Hebberd/Woodfin Camp

Design: Between the Covers

Copyright

First Edition

ISBN 0–679–02725–4

Special Sales

Fodor's Travel Publications are available at special discounts for bulk purchases for sales promotions or premiums. Special editions, including personalized covers, excerpts of existing guides, and corporate imprints, can be created in large quantities for special needs. For more information, contact your local bookseller or write to Special Markets, Fodor's Travel Publications, 201 East 50th Street, New York, NY 10022. Inquiries from Canada should be directed to your local Canadian bookseller or sent to Random House of Canada, Ltd./Marketing Dept., 1265 Aerowood Drive, Mississauga, Ontario L4W 1B9. Inquiries from the United Kingdom should be sent to Fodor's Travel Publications, 20 Vauxhall Bridge Road, London, England SW1V 2SA.

PRINTED IN THE UNITED STATES OF AMERICA

10 9 8 7 6 5 4 3 2 1

CONTENTS

Maps

ON THE ROAD WITH FODOR'S

A GOOD TRAVEL GUIDE is like a wonderful traveling companion. It's charming, it's brimming with sound recommendations and solid ideas, it pulls no punches in describing lodging and dining establishments, and it's consistently full of fascinating facts that make you view what you've traveled to see in a rich new light. In the creation of *Fodor's India*, we at Fodor's have gone to great lengths to provide you with the very best of all possible traveling companions— and to make your trip the best of all possible vacations.

About Our Writers

The information in these pages is the result of the collaboration of a number of extraordinary writers.

Kathleen Cox coordinated the text of the whole book and wrote the introduction, Chapter 4, Delhi, the essay "The Religions of India," and parts of several other chapters. She is the author of *Fodor's The Himalayan Countries* and has written about the subcontinent for numerous American and Indian publications, including *Travel and Leisure, Harper's Bazaar, Vogue,* the *Wall Street Journal,* the *Los Angeles Times,* and the *Times of India.* A former columnist for the *Village Voice* and *Playboy,* she was the cowriter and coproducer of the documentary comedy film, *Gizmo!* Since 1991 she has lived in Delhi, where she is a business consultant.

Smita Patel was responsible for parts of Chapter 2, Special-Interest Travel in India; Chapter 5, Rajasthan; and the Agra and Khajuraho sections of Chapter 6. She was born in India and, though raised in the United States, has traveled extensively in the country of her birth. Trained as a journalist, she has written for the *Modesto Bee* and *The Oregonian.*

Vikram Singh researched and wrote the Varanasi, Calcutta, Kerala, and Tamil Nadu chapters, as well as parts of Chapter 2, Special-Interest Travel in India. A freelance writer from California, he has lived and traveled extensively in India. He has worked on the Fodor's Berkeley Guides series and currently teaches English in California.

Julie Tomasz has toiled for Fodor's on just about every side of the editorial desk— as an editor in the New York office, as an updater and revisor in Budapest, Hungary, and now as a writer-from-scratch for this new book. With the unfaltering help of research partner **Peter Soparkar** and his relatives in Ahmedabad and Bombay, she scoured six states of the subcontinent with her Fodor's tools, only once losing her cool during a run-in with a cranky wild elephant.

We'd like to thank Alka Kohli and Vikas Rustagi of the Government of India Tourism Department, and the state and national tourism departments of the Andaman Islands, Goa, Karnataka, Kerala, Madhya Pradesh, Maharashtra, Orissa, Rajasthan, Tamil Nadu, and Uttar Pradesh, as well as Shona Adhikari, Rajen Bali, Pankaj Baliga, B. S. Banerjee, Indira Banerji, Zaffer Boktoo, G. S. Chahal, Biswanath Chatterjee, P. G. Chunekar, R. P. Dabhade, A. K. Davé, Sushil Dubey, S. M. Gani, Anil Goswami, M. K. Shankaralinge Gowda, Robert Hubner, Syed Iqbal, Sulaiman Jadwet, Alok Jain, U. D. Kamat, Param Kannampilly, Prem Kumar, Ehrlich Lobo, Chandni Luthra, R. Mathur, Dev Mehta, Raj Menon, U. Mishra, Mohadin, J. Mohanty, Raji Muralidharan, Mustafa, Devika Nanda, A. Padhi, Lalit K. Panwar, Balendu Sing Parmar, Arlindo Pereira, Alpana Rathore, Ranjeet Rathore, C. Ruthnaswamy, Anil Sachdev, Seema Shahi, D. D. Singh, Kesri Singh, Maya Singh, Nishit Srivastav, Subramani, Minal Talim, Rozina Tharakan, Reji Thomas, P. J. Varghese, Mac Vaz, Nanette Vaz, D. M. Yadav, Tower Air, and the many others in India's travel industries who provided invaluable help in making this book possible.

We gratefully acknowledge Delta Airlines for their crucial help and superior service.

What's New

A New Design

If this is not the first Fodor's guide you've purchased, you'll immediately notice our new look. More readable and easier to use than ever? We think so—and we hope you do, too.

And in India

India's **economic reforms,** which began in 1991, pried open the country's formerly closed economy and triggered a stream of foreign trade delegations and potential investors that became a flood in late 1994. New policies *are* changing the face of India, but the government is still struggling over the degree of liberalization, especially in the massive public sector, which controls much of the country's inadequate infrastructure. The bottom line: Consider India a mixed-bag destination with good news and bad news for any visitor.

As newly arriving conglomerates and expanding domestic companies demand more electrical power, telephone connections, and water, the country's dismal infrastructure will remain stretched beyond capacity for years to come. This may add unwanted problems to your trip. Most **roads** are a mess. City **traffic** is hideous during work hours, and **pollution** is breathtakingly awful. India did, however, introduce unleaded gas in April 1995 in Delhi, Bombay, Calcutta, and Madras, but most cars aren't fitted with catalytic converters, and long-distance trips are out for cars that require unleaded gas.

The **hotel** sector suffers from an extreme **shortage** of government-approved rooms, as well as intermittent electrical and telephone breakdowns. In cities where business-oriented travelers outnumber vacationers, room prices have increased significantly in the swankiest properties, and managers gloat over waiting lists. The only bright note in the tariff structure is that the government has **halved** the **expenditure tax** on rooms that cost over Rs. 1200 (about $40) from 20% to 10%. Hoteliers are campaigning to get the tax completely removed.

Major international **hotel chains,** including Howard Johnson, are racing into the country to fill the hotel-room gap. India's own chains are also creating new properties. The majority of these new facilities will be in the moderate price range.

Economic liberalization has also opened India's skies to **private domestic air carriers,** which have proved that competition can lead to improved service, including that offered by Indian Airlines. The speed with which these new airlines start, dissolve, and expand makes it impossible for us to provide detailed information on their schedules and destinations.

The Palace on Wheels, Rajasthan's luxury train, is also now just one of many **upscale tourist trains** that are scheduled to chug along popular tourist circuits in India. Already, the Royal Orient, a joint venture between Gujarat's tourism corporation and the Indian Railways, is carrying passengers in gold-embossed saloon cars to popular destinations in Rajasthan and Gujarat. Private-sector companies will concentrate on other good circuits. Cunard, in partnership with an Indian firm, plans to start **luxury cruises** docking at Indian ports. Maharashtra's tourism corporation is starting up **floating restaurants** off the coast of Bombay. A **catamaran service** now ferries passengers between Goa and Bombay. **New destinations** have also opened up to foreigners in Ladakh, Himachal Pradesh, Sikkim, and other remote areas.

Another windfall for the international visitor is an **attractive foreign exchange rate** that helps, marginally, to ameliorate the rise in the cost of nearly everything connected with a trip in India. The cost of liquor served in upscale hotels and resorts has skyrocketed. Airfares are also increasing, along with the cost of travel by train and car with hired driver. Getting around this vast country, however, costs far less than what you would pay in Europe or the United States. And when it comes to **shopping,** India still has fabulous buys.

Finally, disturbances continue to beset the lovely state of Jammu and Kashmir. If you want to visit this area, speak with your state department and the Indian tourist office in your country before booking your trip.

How To Use this Guide

Organization

Up front is the **Gold Guide,** comprising two sections on gold paper that are chock-full of information about traveling within

India and traveling in general. Both are in alphabetical order by topic. **Important Contacts A to Z** gives addresses and telephone numbers of organizations and companies that offer destination-related services and detailed information or publications. Here's where you'll find information about how to get to India from wherever you are. **Smart Travel Tips A to Z,** the Gold Guide's second section, gives specific tips on how to get the most out of your travels, as well as information on how to accomplish what you need to in India.

Chapters in *Fodor's India* are arranged geographically in a rough triangle around the country, starting with Delhi, going west to Rajasthan, then east, south, and north to finish in Bombay. Each chapter covers exploring, shopping, sports, dining, lodging, and arts and nightlife, and ends with a section called Essentials, which tells you how to get there and get around and gives you important local addresses and telephone numbers.

At the end of the book you'll find **Portraits,** with a wonderful essay about in religion in India, followed by suggestions for pre-trip reading, both fiction and nonfiction. Here we also recommend videos you can rent to get you in the mood for your travels. In addition, you'll find a glossary of food terms that will surely enrich your Indian dining experience.

Stars

Stars in the margin are used to denote highly recommended sights, attractions, hotels, and restaurants.

Restaurant and Hotel Criteria and Price Categories

Restaurants and lodging places are chosen with a view to giving you the cream of the crop in each location and in each price range. In all restaurant price charts, costs are per person, excluding drinks, tip, and tax. In hotel price charts, rates are for standard double rooms, excluding city and state sales taxes. Price categories are as follows:

For restaurants (except Delhi):

CATEGORY	MAJOR CITIES	OTHER AREAS*
$$$$	Over $15/ Rs.450	over $10/ Rs. 300
$$$	$10–$15/ Rs. 300– Rs. 450	$6–$10/ Rs. 200– Rs. 300
$$	$5–$10/ Rs. 150– Rs.300	$3–$6/ Rs. 100– Rs. 200
$	under $5/ under Rs. 150	under $3/ Rs. 100

Per person for a three-course meal, excluding drinks, service, and sales tax.

For hotels:

CATEGORY	MAJOR CITIES*	OTHER AREAS*
$$$$	over $200	over $100
$$$	$125–$200	$70–$100
$$	$50–$125	$40–$70
$	under $50	under $40

All prices are for a standard double room, excluding taxes and service charge.

Hotel Facilities

Note that in general you incur charges when you use many hotel facilities. We wanted to let you know what facilities a hotel has to offer, but we don't always specify whether or not there's a charge, so when you're planning a vacation that entails a stay of several days, it's wise to ask what's included in the rate.

Dress Code in Restaurants

Look for an overview in the Packing for India section of **Smart Travel Tips A to Z** in the Gold Guide pages at the front of this book. The **What to Wear** section at the beginning of the individual chapters' dining sections tells you what's most common in that area. In general, we note a dress code only when men are required to wear a jacket or a jacket and tie.

Credit Cards

The following abbreviations are used: **AE,** American Express; **DC,** Diners Club; **MC,** MasterCard; and **V,** Visa. Discover is not accepted outside the United States.

Please Write to Us

Everyone who has contributed to *Fodor's India* has worked hard to make the text accurate. All prices and opening times are based on information supplied to us at press time, and the publisher cannot accept responsibility for any errors that may have occurred. The passage of time will bring changes, so it's always a good idea to call ahead and confirm information when it matters—particularly if you're making a detour to visit specific sights or attractions. When making reservations at a hotel or inn, be sure to speak up if you have a disability or are traveling with children, if you prefer a private bath or a certain type of bed, or if you have specific dietary needs or any other concerns.

Were the restaurants we recommended as described? Did our hotel picks exceed your expectations? Did you find a museum we recommended a waste of time? We would love your feedback, positive and negative.

If you have complaints, we'll look into them and revise our entries when the facts warrant it. If you've happened upon a special place that we haven't included, we'll pass the information along to the writers so they can check it out. So please send us a letter or postcard (we're at 201 East 50th Street, New York, NY 10022). We'll look forward to hearing from you. And in the meantime, have a wonderful trip!

Karen Cure
Editorial Director

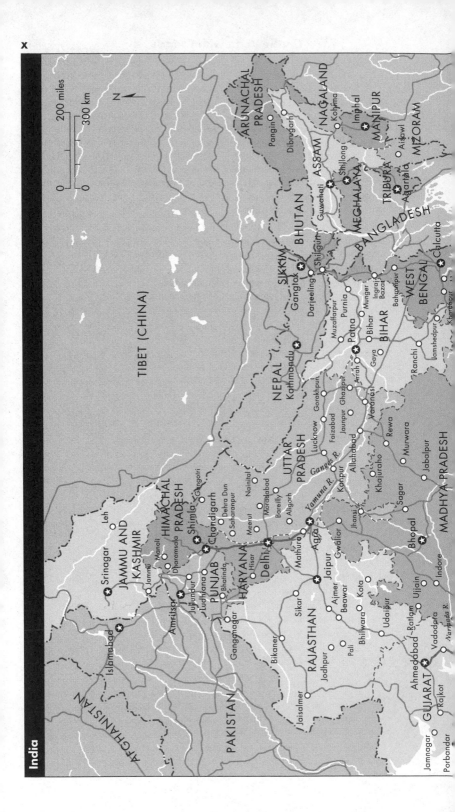

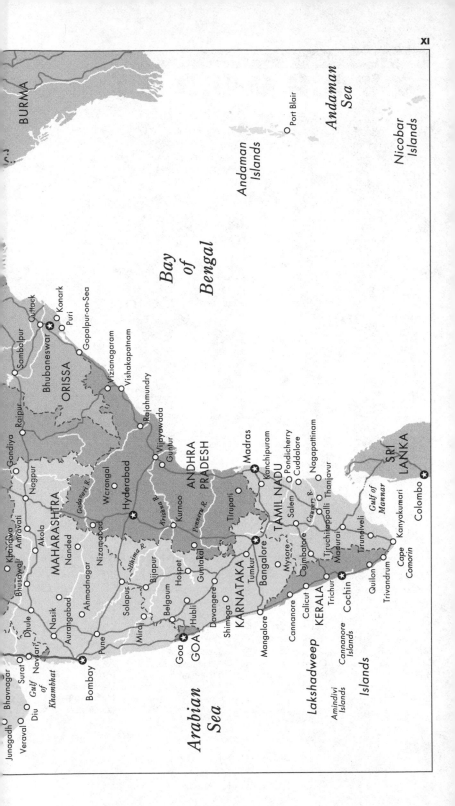

World Time Zones

Numbers below vertical bands relate each zone to Greenwich Mean Time (0 hrs.).
Local times frequently differ from these general indications,
as indicated by light-face numbers on map.

Algiers, **29**	Berlin, **34**	Delhi, **48**	Istanbul, **40**
Anchorage, **3**	Bogotá, **19**	Denver, **8**	Jerusalem, **42**
Athens, **41**	Budapest, **37**	Djakarta, **53**	Johannesburg, **44**
Auckland, **1**	Buenos Aires, **24**	Dublin, **26**	Lima, **20**
Baghdad, **46**	Caracas, **22**	Edmonton, **7**	Lisbon, **28**
Bangkok, **50**	Chicago, **9**	Hong Kong, **56**	London
Beijing, **54**	Copenhagen, **33**	Honolulu, **2**	(Greenwich), **27**
	Dallas, **10**		Los Angeles, **6**
			Madrid, **38**
			Manila, **57**

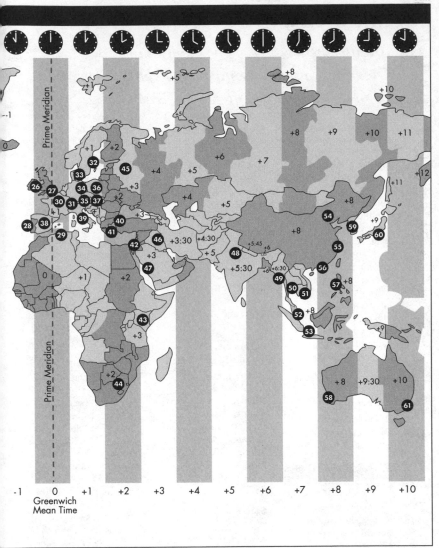

THE GOLD GUIDE / IMPORTANT CONTACTS

IMPORTANT CONTACTS A TO Z

*An Alphabetical Listing of Publications,
Organizations, and Companies That Will Help You
Before, During, and After Your Trip*

No single travel resource can give you every detail about every topic that might interest or concern you at the various stages of your journey—when you're planning your trip, while you're on the road, and after you get back home. The following organizations, books, and brochures will supplement the information in FODOR'S INDIA. For related information, including both basic tips on visiting India and background information on many of the topics below, study Smart Travel Tips A to Z, the section that follows Important Contacts A to Z.

A

AIR TRAVEL

The major gateways to India include **Indira Gandhi International Airport** in New Delhi (☎ 11/329–5434) and **Bombay International Airport** (☎ 22/836–6767). Flying time is 16 hours from New York, 18 hours from Chicago, and 20 hours from Los Angeles.

CARRIERS

Delta Airlines (☎ 800/221–1212) offers daily flights to and from Bombay through its Frankfurt hub. Other carriers serving India include **Air Canada** (☎ 800/776–3000),

Air India (☎ 212/751–6200), **Northwest Airlines** (☎ 800/447–4747), **Tower Air** (☎ 800/344-8693 or 718/553–8500), and **United Airlines** (☎ 800/241–6522).

Carriers from the U.K. include **Air Canada** (☎ 0181/7592636), **Air India** (☎ 01753/684828), **British Airways** (☎ 0345/222–111), and **Thai Airways** (☎ 0171/491–7953).

COMPLAINTS

To register complaints about charter and scheduled airlines, contact the U.S. Department of Transportation's **Office of Consumer Affairs** (400 7th St. NW, Washington, DC 20590, ☎ 202/366–2220 or 800/322–7873).

CONSOLIDATORS

Established consolidators selling to the public include **UniTravel** (Box 12485, St. Louis, MO 63132, ☎ 314/569–0900 or 800/325–2222). **FLY-ASAP** (3824 E. Indian School Road, Phoenix, AZ 85018, ☎ 800/359–2727) isn't a discounter, but gets good deals from among published fares and discount tickets from consolidators.

PUBLICATIONS

For general information about charter carriers, ask for the Office of

Consumer Affairs' brochure **"Plane Talk: Public Charter Flights."** The Department of Transportation also publishes a 58-page booklet, **"Fly Rights"** ($1.75; Consumer Information Center, Dept. 133B, Pueblo, CO 81009).

For other tips and hints, consult the Consumers Union's monthly **"Consumer Reports Travel Letter"** ($39 a year; Box 53629, Boulder, CO 80322, ☎ 800/234–1970) and the newsletter **"Travel Smart"** ($37 a year; 40 Beechdale Rd., Dobbs Ferry, NY 10522, ☎ 800/327–3633); *The Official Frequent Flyer Guidebook,* by Randy Petersen ($14.99 plus $3 shipping; 4715-C Town Center Dr., Colorado Springs, CO 80916, ☎ 719/597–8899 or 800/487–8893); *Airfare Secrets Exposed,* by Sharon Tyler and Matthew Wonder (Universal Information Publishing; $16.95 plus $3.75 shipping; Sandcastle Publishing, Box 3070-A, South Pasadena, CA 91031, ☎ 213/255–3616 or 800/655–0053); and *202 Tips Even the Best Business Travelers May Not Know,* by Christopher McGinnis ($10 plus $3 shipping; Irwin Professional Publishing, 1333 Burr Ridge Pkwy.,

Burr Ridge, IL 60521, ☎ 800/634–3966).

WITHIN INDIA

Indian Airlines is the national domestic carrier. A number of private airlines are starting operations, but financial turbulence may force many of them out of business. Contact your travel agent, tour operator, or the Government of India Tourist Offices for the latest details.

B

BETTER BUSINESS BUREAU

For local contacts in the home town of a tour operator you may be considering, consult the **Council of Better Business Bureaus** (4200 Wilson Blvd., Arlington, VA 22203, ☎ 703/276–0100).

BUS TRAVEL

WITHIN INDIA

Bus travel is not recommended within India.

C

CAR RENTAL

The only major international car-rental company represented in India is **Hertz** (☎ 800/654–3001, 800/263–0600 in Canada, 0181/679–1799 in the U.K.). Rates in New Delhi begin at $45 a day and $300 a week for an economy car with unlimited mileage.

CHILDREN AND TRAVEL

FLYING

Look into **"Flying With Baby"** ($5.95 plus $1 shipping; Third Street Press, Box 261250, Littleton, CO 80126, ☎ 303/595–5959), cowritten by a flight attendant. **"Kids and Teens in Flight,"** free from the U.S. Department of Transportation's Office of Consumer Affairs, offers tips for children flying alone. Every two years the February issue of *Family Travel Times* (*see* Know-How, *below*) details children's services on three dozen airlines.

GAMES

Game meister Milton Bradley has games to help keep little (and not so little) children from getting fidgety while riding in planes, trains, and automobiles. Try packing the *Travel Battleship* sea battle game ($7), *Travel Connect Four,* a vertical strategy game ($8), the *Travel Yahtzee* dice game ($6), the *Travel Trouble* dice and board game ($7), and the *Travel Guess Who* mystery game ($8).

KNOW-HOW

Family Travel Times, published four times a year by Travel With Your Children (TWYCH, 45 W. 18th St., New York, NY 10011, ☎ 212/206–0688; annual subscription $40), covers destinations, types of vacations, and modes of travel.

The *Family Travel Guides* catalog ($1 postage; ☎ 510/527–5849) lists about 200 books and articles on family travel. *Traveling with Children—And Enjoying It,* by Arlene K. Butler ($11.95 plus $3 shipping; Globe Pequot Press, Box 833, 6 Business Park Rd., Old Saybrook, CT 06475, ☎ 203/395–0440 or 800/243–0495, 800/962–0973 in CT) helps plan your trip with children, from toddlers to teens. Also check *Take Your Baby and Go! A Guide for Traveling with Babies, Toddlers and Young Children,* by Sheri Andrews, Judy Bordeaux, and Vivian Vasquez ($5.95 plus $1.50 shipping; Bear Creek Publications, 2507 Minor Ave., Seattle, WA 98102, ☎ 206/322–7604 or 800/326–6566).

CUSTOMS

U.S. CITIZENS

The **U.S. Customs Service** (Box 7407, Washington, DC 20044, ☎ 202/927–6724) can answer questions on duty-free limits and publishes a helpful brochure, "Know Before You Go." For information on registering foreign-made articles, call 202/927–0540.

CANADIANS

Contact **Revenue Canada** (2265 St. Laurent Blvd. S, Ottawa, Ontario K1G 4K3, ☎ 613/993–0534) for a copy of the free brochure **"I Declare/Je Déclare"** and for details on duties that exceed the standard duty-free limit.

U.K. CITIZENS

HM Customs and Excise (Dorset House, Stamford St., London SE1 9NG, ☎ 0171/202–4227) can answer questions about U.K. customs regulations and publishes **"A Guide for Travellers,"** detailing standard procedures and import rules.

D

FOR TRAVELERS WITH DISABILITIES

COMPLAINTS

To register complaints under the provisions of the Americans with Disabilities Act, contact the U.S. Department of Justice's **Public Access Section** (Box 66738, Washington, DC 20035, ☎ 202/514–0301, TTY 202/514–0383, FAX 202/307–1198).

ORGANIZATIONS

For Travelers with Hearing Impairments➤ Contact the **American Academy of Otolaryngology** (1 Prince St., Alexandria, VA 22314, ☎ 703/836–4444, FAX 703/683–5100, TTY 703/519–1585).

For Travelers with Mobility Problems➤ Contact the **Information Center for Individuals with Disabilities** (Fort Point Pl., 27–43 Wormwood St., Boston, MA 02210, ☎ 617/727–5540, 800/462–5015 in MA, TTY 617/345–9743); **Mobility International USA** (Box 10767, Eugene, OR 97440, ☎ and TTY 503/343–1284, FAX 503/343–6812), the U.S. branch of an international organization based in Belgium (*see below*) that has affiliates in 30 countries; **MossRehab Hospital Travel Information Service** (1200 W. Tabor Rd., Philadelphia, PA 19141,

☎ 215/456–9603, TTY 215/456–9602); the **Society for the Advancement of Travel for the Handicapped** (347 5th Ave., Suite 610, New York, NY 10016, ☎ 212/447–7284, FAX 212/725–8253); the **Travel Industry and Disabled Exchange** (TIDE, 5435 Donna Ave., Tarzana, CA 91356, ☎ 818/344–3640, FAX 818/344–0078); and **Travelin' Talk** (Box 3534, Clarksville, TN 37043, ☎ 615/552–6670, FAX 615/552–1182).

For Travelers with Vision Impairments➤ Contact the **American Council of the Blind** (1155 15th St. NW, Suite 720, Washington, DC 20005, ☎ 202/467–5081, FAX 202/467–5085) or the **American Foundation for the Blind** (15 W. 16th St., New York, NY 10011, ☎ 212/620–2000, TTY 212/620–2158).

IN THE U.K.

Contact the **Royal Association for Disability and Rehabilitation** (RADAR, 12 City Forum, 250 City Rd., London EC1V 8AF, ☎ 0171/250–3222) or **Mobility International** (Rue de Manchester 25, B1070 Brussels, Belgium, ☎ 00–322–410–6297), an international clearinghouse of travel information for people with disabilities.

PUBLICATIONS

Several free publications are available from the U.S. Information Center (Box 100, Pueblo, CO 81009, ☎ 719/948–3334): **"New Horizons for the Air Traveler with

a Disability"** (address to Dept. 355A), describing legally mandated changes; the pocket-size **"Fly Smart"** (Dept. 575B), good on flight safety; and the Airport Operators Council's worldwide **"Access Travel: Airports"** (Dept. 575A).

The 500-page *Travelin' Talk Directory* ($35; Box 3534, Clarksville, TN 37043, ☎ 615/552–6670) lists people and organizations who help travelers with disabilities. For specialist travel agents worldwide, consult the *Directory of Travel Agencies for the Disabled* ($19.95 plus $2 shipping; Twin Peaks Press, Box 129, Vancouver, WA 98666, ☎ 206/694–2462 or 800/637–2256).

TRAVEL AGENCIES AND TOUR OPERATORS

The Americans with Disabilities Act requires that travel firms serve the needs of all travelers. However, some agencies and operators specialize in making group and individual arrangements for travelers with disabilities, among them **Access Adventures** (206 Chestnut Ridge Rd., Rochester, NY 14624, ☎ 716/889–9096), run by a former physical-rehab counselor. In addition, many general-interest operators and agencies (*see* Tour Operators, *below*) can arrange vacations for travelers with disabilities.

For Travelers with Hearing Impairments➤ One agency is **International Express**

(7319-B Baltimore Ave., College Park, MD 20740, ☎ TTY 301/699–8836, FAX 301/699–8836), which arranges group and independent trips.

FOR TRAVELERS WITH MOBILITY IMPAIRMENTS➤ A number of operators specialize in working with travelers with mobility impairments, including **Hinsdale Travel Service** (201 E. Ogden Ave., Suite 100, Hinsdale, IL 60521, ☎ 708/325–1335 or 800/303–5521), a travel agency that will give you access to the services of wheelchair traveler Janice Perkins; and **Wheelchair Journeys** (16979 Redmond Way, Redmond, WA 98052, ☎ 206/885–2210), which can handle arrangements worldwide.

FOR TRAVELERS WITH DEVELOPMENTAL DISABILITIES➤ Contact the nonprofit **New Directions** (5276 Hollister Ave., Suite 207, Santa Barbara, CA 93111, ☎ 805/967–2841), as well as general-interest operators (*see* Tour Operators, *below*).

DISCOUNT CLUBS

Options include **Entertainment Travel Editions** (fee $28–$53, depending on destination; Box 1068, Trumbull, CT 06611, ☎ 800/445–4137), **Great American Traveler** ($49.95 annually; Box 27965, Salt Lake City, UT 84127, ☎ 800/548–2812), **Moment's Notice Discount Travel Club** ($25 annually, single or family; 163 Amsterdam Ave., Suite 137, New York, NY 10023, ☎ 212/486–0500), **Privilege Card** ($74.95 annually; 3391 Peachtree Rd. NE, Suite 110, Atlanta, GA 30326, ☎ 404/262–0222 or 800/236–9732), **Travelers Advantage** ($49 annually, single or family; CUC Travel Service, 49 Music Sq. W, Nashville, TN 37203, ☎ 800/548–1116 or 800/648–4037), and **Worldwide Discount Travel Club** ($50 annually for family, $40 single; 1674 Meridian Ave., Miami Beach, FL 33139, ☎ 305/534–2082).

PASSES

See Rail Travel and Air Travel, *below*.

E

ELECTRICITY

Send a self-addressed, stamped envelope to the **Franzus Company** (Customer Service, Dept. B50, Murtha Industrial Park, Box 142, Beacon Falls, CT 06403, ☎ 203/723–6664) for a copy of the free brochure "Foreign Electricity Is No Deep Dark Secret."

EMERGENCIES

HOSPITALS

Contact the **East West Medical Center** (38 Golf Links, New Delhi 110003, ☎ 11/462–3738, 11/469–9229, 11/469–0955, or 11/469–8865; FAX 11/469–0428 or 11/463–2382). East West can provide a referral list of doctors, dentists, opticians, chemists, and lawyers throughout India. It is also the only clinic in India (so far) recognized by most international insurance companies. Patients, however, pay for services and are reimbursed by their own company or can arrange for payment through S.O.S. East West accepts major cards and is open 24 hours. It also provides 24-hour emergency medical services (including medivac) anywhere in India.

G

GAY AND LESBIAN TRAVEL

ORGANIZATIONS

The **International Gay Travel Association** (Box 4974, Key West, FL 33041, ☎ 800/448–8550), a consortium of 800 businesses, can supply names of travel agents and tour operators.

PUBLICATIONS

The premier international travel magazine for gays and lesbians is *Our World* ($35 for 10 issues; 1104 N. Nova Rd., Suite 251, Daytona Beach, FL 32117, ☎ 904/441–5367). The 16-page monthly *"Out & About"* ($49 for 10 issues; ☎ 212/645–6922 or 800/929–2268) covers gay-friendly resorts, hotels, cruise lines, and airlines.

TOUR OPERATORS

Toto Tours (1326 W. Albion, Suite 3W, Chicago, IL 60626, ☎ 312/274–8686 or 800/565–1241) has group tours worldwide.

TRAVEL AGENCIES

The largest agencies serving gay travelers are **Advance Travel** (10700 Northwest Fwy., Suite 160, Houston, TX

THE GOLD GUIDE / IMPORTANT CONTACTS

77092, ☎ 713/682–2002 or 800/695–0880), **Islanders/Kennedy Travel** (183 W. 10th St., New York, NY 10014, ☎ 212/242–3222 or 800/988–1181), **Now Voyager** (4406 18th St., San Francisco, CA 94114, ☎ 415/626–1169 or 800/255–6951), and **Yellowbrick Road** (1500 W. Balmoral Ave., Chicago, IL 60640, ☎ 312/561–1800 or 800/642–2488). **Sky-link Women's Travel** (746 Ashland Ave., Santa Monica, CA 90405, ☎ 310/452–0506 or 800/225-5759) works with lesbians.

H
HEALTH ISSUES

FINDING A DOCTOR

For members, the **International Association for Medical Assistance to Travellers** (membership free; IAMAT, 417 Center St., Lewiston, NY 14092, ☎ 716/754–4883; 40 Regal Rd., Guelph, Ontario N1K 1B5, ☎ 519/836–0102; 1287 St. Clair Ave., Toronto, Ontario M6E 1B8, ☎ 416/652–0137; 57 Voirets, 1212 Grand-Lancy, Geneva, Switzerland) publishes a worldwide directory of English-speaking physicians meeting IAMAT standards.

MEDICAL-ASSISTANCE COMPANIES

Contact **International SOS Assistance** (Box 11568, Philadelphia, PA 19116, ☎ 215/244–1500 or 800/523–8930; Box 466, Pl. Bonaventure, Montréal,

Québec H5A 1C1, ☎ 514/874–7674 or 800/363–0263), **Medex Assistance Corporation** (Box 10623, Baltimore, MD 21285, ☎ 410/296–2530 or 800/573–2029), **Near Travel Services** (Box 1339, Calumet City, IL 60409, ☎ 708/868–6700 or 800/654–6700), and **Travel Assistance International** (1133 15th St. NW, Suite 400, Washington, DC 20005, ☎ 202/331–1609 or 800/821–2828). Because these companies also sell death-and-dismember-ment, trip-cancellation, and other insurance coverage, there is some overlap with the travel-insurance policies sold by the companies listed under Insurance, *below.*

PUBLICATIONS

The Safe Travel Book, by Peter Savage ($12.95 plus $2 postage; Lexington Books, 866 3rd Ave., 22nd Floor, New York, NY 10022, ☎ 212/702–4771 or 800/223–23485, FAX 212/605–4872), and *Traveler's Medical Resource,* by William W. Forgey ($19.95; ICS Books, Box 10767, Merrillville, IN 45410, ☎ 219/769–0585 or 800/541–7323), are authoritative.

WARNINGS

The **National Centers for Disease Control** (Center for Preventive Services, Division of Quarantine, Traveler's Health Section, 1600 Clifton Rd., MSE03, Atlanta, GA 30333, automated hot line 404/332–4559) provides information on health risks abroad and vaccination require-

ments and recommen-dations.

I
INSURANCE

Travel insurance cover-ing baggage, health, and trip cancellation or interruption is available from **Access America** (Box 90315, Richmond, VA 23286, ☎ 804/285–3300 or 800/284–8300), **Carefree Travel Insurance** (Box 9366, 100 Garden City Plaza, Garden City, NY 11530, ☎ 516/294–0220 or 800/323–3149), **Near** (Box 1339, Calumet City, IL 60409, ☎ 708/868–6700 or 800/654–6700), **Tele-Trip** (Mutual of Omaha Plaza, Box 31716, Omaha, NE 68131, ☎ 800/228–9792), **Travel Insured International** (Box 280568, East Hartford, CT 06128–0568, ☎ 203/528–7663 or 800/243–3174), **Travel Guard International** (1145 Clark St., Stevens Point, WI 54481, ☎ 715/345–0505 or 800/826–1300), and **Wallach & Company** (107 W. Federal St., Box 480, Middleburg, VA 22117, ☎ 703/687–3166 or 800/237–6615).

IN THE U.K.

The **Association of British Insurers** (51 Gresham St., London EC2V 7HQ, ☎ 0171/600–3333; 30 Gordon St., Glasgow G1 3PU, ☎ 0141/226–3905; Scottish Provident Bldg., Donegall Sq. W, Belfast BT1 6JE, ☎ 01232/249176; and other locations) gives advice by phone and publishes the free **"Holi-day Insurance,"** which sets out typical policy provisions and costs.

L
LODGING

HOTELS

The major hotel chains in India include **Ashok Hotels** (reservations must be made through a travel agent or Ashok Sales Office, Jeevan Vihar, 3rd Floor, 3 Sansad Marg, New Delhi 110001, ☎ 11/353557, FAX 11/311459), **Best Western** (☎ 800/528–1234; ☎ 4481/541–0033 in the U.K.; ☎ 11/332–5579, FAX 11/332–5045 in India), **Choice Hotels International** (☎ 800/424–6423; ☎ 800/444444 in the U.K.; ☎ 11/611–8434, FAX 11/611–2427 in India), **Clarks** (for reservations contact U.P. Hotels, 1101 Surya Kiran, 19 Kasturba Gandhi Marg, New Delhi 110001, ☎ 11/331–2367 or 11/372–2596, FAX 11/3312990), **Holiday Inn** (☎ 800/465–4329; ☎ 800/89712 in the U.K.), **Hyatt Regency** (☎ 800/233–1234; ☎ 171/580–8197 in London, ☎ 345/581666 elsewhere in the U.K.), **Oberoi Hotels International** (☎ 800/562–3764; ☎ 800/515517 in the U.K.), **Taj Group** (☎ 800/458–8825 or 212/972–6830; ☎ 800/282699 or 0171/828–5909 in the U.K.), **Welcomgroup** (reserve through Welcomgroup Maurya Sheraton, ☎ 11/301–0101 in New Delhi; ☎ 171/828–8386 in the U.K.), and **Welcomgroup Sheraton** hotels (☎ 800/325–3535;

☎ 800/353535 in the U.K.).

M
MONEY MATTERS

CURRENCY EXCHANGE

If your bank doesn't exchange currency, contact **Thomas Cook Currency Services** (41 E. 42nd St., New York, NY 10017, or 511 Madison Ave., New York, NY 10022, ☎ 212/757–6915 or 800/223–7373 for locations) or **Ruesch International** (☎ 800/424–2923 for locations).

WIRING FUNDS

Funds can be wired via **American Express MoneyGram**^{SM} (☎ 800/926–9400 from the U.S. and Canada for locations and information) or **Western Union** (☎ 800/325–6000 for agent locations or to send using MasterCard or Visa, 800/321–2923 in Canada).

P
PASSPORTS
AND VISAS

U.S. CITIZENS

For fees, documentation requirements, and other information, call the **Office of Passport Services** information line (☎ 202/647–0518).

CANADIANS

For fees, documentation requirements, and other information, call the Ministry of Foreign Affairs and International Trade's **Passport Office** (☎ 819/994–3500 or 800/567–6868).

U.K. CITIZENS

For fees, documentation requirements, and to get an emergency passport, call the **London passport office** (☎ 0171/271–3000).

PHONE MATTERS

The country code for India is 91. For local access numbers abroad, contact **AT&T USA Direct** (☎ 800/874–4000), **MCI** Call USA (☎ 800/444–4444), or **Sprint** Express (☎ 800/793–1153).

PHOTO HELP

The **Kodak Information Center** (☎ 800/242–2424) answers consumer questions about film and photography.

R
RAIL TRAVEL

DISCOUNT PASSES

To purchase the Indrail Pass outside India, contact your travel agent or the Government of India Tourist Office for the name of a designated General Sales Agent. Fares, which range from second class to air-conditioned first class, are: one-day pass, $15 to $78; seven-day pass, $70 to $270; 15-day pass, $80 to $330; 21-day pass, $90 to $400; 30-day pass, $110 to $500; 60-day pass, $165 to $720; 90-day pass, $210 to $960.

You can also purchase the pass in India at railway offices in major cities, international airports, and through government-recognized travel agents in Bombay, Calcutta, Delhi, and Madras. The pass must be purchased in

U.S. dollars, U.S. dollar traveler's checks, or in pounds sterling.

S
SENIOR CITIZENS

EDUCATIONAL TRAVEL

The nonprofit **Elderhostel** (75 Federal St., 3rd Floor, Boston, MA 02110, ☏ 617/426–7788), for people 60 and older, has offered inexpensive study programs since 1975. The nearly 2,000 courses cover everything from marine science to Greek myths and cowboy poetry. Fees for two- to three-week international trips—including room, board, and transportation from the United States—range from $1,800 to $4,500.

ORGANIZATIONS

For discounts on lodgings, car rentals, and other travel products, along with magazines and newsletters, contact the **National Council of Senior Citizens** (membership $12 annually; 1331 F St. NW, Washington, DC 20004, ☏ 202/347–8800) and **Mature Outlook** (subscription $9.95 annually; 6001 N. Clark St., Chicago, IL 60660, ☏ 312/465–6466 or 800/336–6330).

PUBLICATIONS

The 50+ Traveler's Guidebook: Where to Go, Where to Stay, What to Do, by Anita Williams and Merrimac Dillon ($12.95; St. Martin's Press, 175 5th Ave., New York, NY 10010, ☏ 212/674–5151 or 800/288–2131), offers many useful tips. **"The Mature Traveler"** ($29.95; Box 50400, Reno, NV 89513, ☏ 702/786–7419), a monthly newsletter, covers travel deals.

STUDENTS

HOSTELING

Contact **Hostelling International–American Youth Hostels** (733 15th St. NW, Suite 840, Washington, DC 20005, ☏ 202/783–6161) in the United States, **Hostelling International–Canada** (205 Catherine St., Suite 400, Ottawa, Ontario K2P 1C3, ☏ 613/237–7884) in Canada, and the **Youth Hostel Association of England and Wales** (Trevelyan House, 8 St. Stephen's Hill, St. Albans, Hertfordshire AL1 2DY, ☏ 01727/855215 or 01727/845047) in the United Kingdom. Membership ($25 in the U.S., C$26.75 in Canada, and £9 in the U.K.) gets you access to 5,000 hostels worldwide that charge $7–$20 nightly per person.

I.D. CARDS

To get discounts on transportation and admissions, get the **International Student Identity Card** (ISIC) if you're a bona fide student or the **International Youth Card** (IYC) if you're under 26. In the United States, the ISIC and IYC cards cost $16 each and include basic travel accident and illness coverage, plus a toll-free travel hot line. Apply through the Council on International Educational Exchange *(see* Organizations, *below).* Cards are available for $15 each in Canada from Travel Cuts (187 College St., Toronto, Ontario M5T 1P7, ☏ 416/979–2406 or 800/667–2887) and in the United Kingdom for £5 each at student unions and student travel companies.

ORGANIZATIONS

A major contact is the **Council on International Educational Exchange** (CIEE, 205 E. 42nd St., 16th Floor, New York, NY 10017, ☏ 212/661–1450) with locations in Boston (729 Boylston St., Boston, MA 02116, ☏ 617/266–1926), Miami (9100 S. Dadeland Blvd., Miami, FL 33156, ☏ 305/670–9261), Los Angeles (1093 Broxton Ave., Los Angeles, CA 90024, ☏ 310/208–3551), 43 college towns nationwide, and the United Kingdom (28A Poland St., London W1V 3DB, ☏ 0171/437–7767). Twice a year, it publishes *Student Travels* magazine. The CIEE's Council Travel Service is the exclusive U.S. agent for several student-discount cards.

Campus Connections (325 Chestnut St., Suite 1101, Philadelphia, PA 19106, ☏ 215/625–8585 or 800/428–3235) specializes in discounted accommodations and airfares for students. The **Educational Travel Centre** (438 N. Frances St., Madison, WI 53703, ☏ 608/256–5551) offers rail passes and low-cost airline tickets, mostly for flights departing from Chicago. For air travel only, contact **TMI Student Travel** (100 W. 33rd St., Suite 813, New York, NY 10001, ☎ 800/245–3672).

In Canada, also contact **Travel Cuts** *(see above)*.

T

Among the companies selling tours and packages to India, the following have a proven reputation, are nationally known, and offer plenty of options.

GROUP TOURS AND PACKAGES

Super-deluxe escorted tours of India are available from **Abercrombie & Kent** (1520 Kensington Rd., Oak Brook, IL 60521, ☎ 708/954–2944 or 800/323–7308) and **Travcoa** (Box 2630, Newport Beach, CA, 92658, ☎ 714/476–2800 or 800/992–2003). For deluxe programs, try **Cox & Kings** (511 Lexington Ave., Suite 335, New York, NY 10017, ☎ 212/935–3935 or 800/999–1758).

First-class and first-class superior programs are sold by **Asian Pacific Adventures** (826 S. Sierra Bonita Ave., Los Angeles, CA 90036, ☎ 213/935–3156 or 800/825–1680), **Big Five Tours and Expeditions** (819 S. Federal Hwy., Stuart, FL 34994, ☎ 407/287–7995 or 800/445–7002), **General Tours** (☎ 800/678–7942), **Himalayan Travel** (112 Prospect St., Stamford, CT 06901, ☎ 203/359–3711 or 800/225–2380), **India Tours/Exotic Journeys** (230 N. Michigan Ave., #2230,

Chicago, IL 60601, ☎ 312/726–2223 or 800/554–6342), and **InnerAsia Expeditions** (2627 Lombard St., San Francisco, CA 94123, ☎ 415/922–0448 or 800/777–8183). These operators also sell independent vacation packages.

FROM THE U.K.

Among the companies offering packages to India from Great Britain are: **Abercrombie & Kent** (Sloane Square House, Holbein Pl., London SW1W 8NS, ☎ 0171/730–9600); **American Express** (19–20 Berners St., London W1P 4AE, ☎ 0171/637–8600); and **Cox & Kings** (St. James Court, 45 Buckingham Gate, London SW1E 6AF, ☎ 0171/873–5005).

IN INDIA

Two firms stand out: **Great India Tour Company** (Mullassery Towers, Vanross Junction, Trivandrum 695039, Kerala, ☎ 471/331516, FAX 471/330579) and **RBS Travels** (Shop G, Connaught Palace Hotel, 37 Shaheed Bhagat Singh Marg, Delhi, ☎ 11/373–3950).

THEME TRIPS

See Chapter 2, Special-Interest Travel in India.

ORGANIZATIONS

The **National Tour Association** (546 E. Main St., Lexington, KY 40508, ☎ 606/226–4444 or 800/755–8687) and **United States Tour Operators Association** (USTOA, 211 E. 51st St., Suite 12B, New York, NY 10022,

☎ 212/750–7371) can provide lists of member operators and information on booking tours.

PUBLICATIONS

Consult the brochure **On Tour** and ask for a current list of member operators from the National Tour Association *(see* Organizations, *above)*. Also get a copy of the **"Worldwide Tour & Vacation Package Finder"** from the USTOA *(see* Organizations, *above)* and the Better Business Bureau's **"Tips on Travel Packages"** (publication No. 24-195, $2; 4200 Wilson Blvd., Arlington, VA 22203).

For names of reputable agencies in your area, contact the **American Society of Travel Agents** (1101 King St., Suite 200, Alexandria, VA 22314, ☎ 703/739–2782).

U

The U.S. Department of State's Overseas Citizens Emergency Center (Room 4811, Washington, DC 20520; enclose SASE) issues **Consular Information Sheets,** which cover crime, security, political climate, and health risks as well as embassy locations, entry requirements, currency regulations, and other routine matters. (Travel Warnings, which counsel travelers to avoid a country entirely, are issued in extreme cases.) For the latest information, stop in at any U.S. passport office, consulate, or embassy; call the interactive hot line (☎ 202/647–5225 or fax 202/647-3000); or, with your PC's modem, tap into the Bureau of Consular Affairs' computer bulletin board (☎ 202/647–9225).

V
VISITOR
INFORMATION

Contact the **Government of India Tourist Office** in the U.S. at 30 Rockefeller Plaza, Room 15, North Mezzanine, New York, NY 10112, ☎ 212/586–4901, FAX 212/582–3274; 3550 Wilshire Blvd., Suite 204, Los Angeles, CA 90010, ☎ 213/380–8855, FAX 213/380–6111; in Canada at 60 Bloor St. W, Suite 1003, Toronto, Ontario M4W 3B8, ☎ 416/962–3787, FAX 416/962–6279; or in the U.K. at 7 Cork St., London, W1X 2AB, ☎ 0171/437–3677, FAX 0171/494–1048.

W
WEATHER

For current conditions and forecasts, plus the local time and helpful travel tips, call the **Weather Channel Connection** (☎ 900/932–8437; 95¢ per minute) from a touch-tone phone.

SMART TRAVEL TIPS A TO Z

Basic Information on Traveling to and in India and Savvy Tips to Make Your Trip a Breeze

The more you travel, the more you know about how to make trips run like clockwork. To help make your travels hassle-free, Fodor's editors have rounded up dozens of tips from our contributors and travel experts all over the world, as well as basic information on visiting India. For names of organizations to contact and publications that can give you more information, *see* Important Contacts A to Z, *above*.

A
AIR TRAVEL

If time is an issue, **always look for nonstop flights,** which require no change of plane. If possible, **avoid connecting flights,** which stop at least once and can involve a change of plane, although the flight number remains the same; if the first leg is late, the second waits.

CUTTING COSTS

The Sunday travel section of most newspapers is a good source of deals.

MAJOR AIRLINES➤ The least-expensive airfares from the major airlines are priced for round-trip travel and are subject to restrictions. You must usually **book in advance and buy the ticket within 24 hours** to get cheaper fares. The lowest fare is subject to availability, and only a small percentage of the plane's total seats are sold at that price. It's good to **call a number of airlines, and when you are quoted a good price, book it on the spot**—the same fare on the same flight may not be available the next day. Airlines generally allow you to change your return date for a $25 to $50 fee, but most low-fare tickets are nonrefundable. However, if you don't use it, you can apply the cost toward the purchase price of a new ticket, again for a small charge.

CONSOLIDATORS➤ Consolidators, who buy tickets at reduced rates from scheduled airlines, sell them at prices below the lowest available from the airlines directly—usually without advance restrictions. Sometimes you can even get your money back if you need to return the ticket. Carefully read the fine print detailing penalties for changes and cancellations. If you doubt the reliability of a consolidator, **confirm your reservation with the airline.**

ALOFT

AIRLINE FOOD➤ If you hate airline food, **ask for special meals when booking.** These can be vegetarian, low cholesterol, or kosher, for example; commonly prepared to order in smaller quantities than standard catered fare, they can be tastier.

JET LAG➤ To avoid this syndrome, which occurs when travel disrupts your body's natural cycles, try to maintain a normal routine. At night, **get some sleep.** By day, move about the cabin to **stretch your legs, eat light meals, and drink water—not alcohol.**

SMOKING➤ Smoking is banned on all flights within the United States of less than six hours' duration and on all Canadian flights; the ban also applies to domestic segments of international flights aboard U.S. and foreign carriers. Delta has banned smoking system-wide. On U.S. carriers flying to India and other destinations abroad, a seat in a no-smoking section must be provided for every passenger who requests one, and the section must be enlarged to accommodate such passengers if necessary as long as they have complied with the airline's deadline for check-in and seat assignment. If smoking bothers you, request a seat far from the smoking section.

Foreign airlines are exempt from these rules but do provide no-smoking sections; some nations have banned smoking on all domestic flights, and others may

THE GOLD GUIDE / SMART TRAVEL TIPS

ban smoking on some flights. Talks continue on the feasibility of broadening no-smoking policies.

WITHIN INDIA

The entry of privately owned domestic carriers into the market has forced Indian Airlines to improve its service, but Indian Airlines flights are still subject to delays, and some scheduled departures are canceled without explanation. Many of the new carriers are struggling to survive. **Check with your travel agent, tour operator, or the Government of India Tourist Office for the latest information on the private carriers and flight schedules.** Currently, the fares for all carriers, including Indian Airlines, are about 40% to 50% higher than air-conditioned first class tickets on trains to the same destinations, but travel by air is much more comfortable.

For domestic flights, **get your tickets when you purchase your international ticket to the subcontinent if possible.** Some carriers are not allowed to sell their tickets outside India. **Be certain tickets and not just reservations are confirmed.** Indian Airlines is notorious for overbooking to important destinations, and you can be stranded with no recourse. **Never schedule back-to-back flights;** plan enough time for unexpected delays.

It is vital to **reconfirm your flights at least 72**

hours before departure. Since there are rigid security procedures, **check in no later than 60 minutes before flight time,** and expect tight security at all airports. Do not pack a pocketknife in your hand luggage. Even golf clubs are not allowed as hand luggage. Also remove the batteries from your camera or any electronics (except your computer) and pack them into your checked-in luggage. If you hand carry a computer, you will usually be asked to turn it on during the security check. For many flights, checked-in luggage must be identified on the tarmac before boarding.

DISCOUNT PASSES⟩ Private airlines are not permitted to offer special flight discounts to foreigners, but Indian Airlines does have concessional fare packages: "Discover India," which allows unlimited travel for 21 days within India for $400 and "India Wonderfare," which allows a week of unlimited travel within either the north, east, west, or south of India for $200. There's a surcharge of $100 for Port Blair in the Andaman Islands if you choose the east or south sector. Payment must be made in foreign currency.

Students age 12 to 26, with valid student identity card, and children under 12 qualify for discounts on most airlines.

B
BUS TRAVEL

Bus travel is not recommended in India.

BUSINESS HOURS

India has numerous national and religious holidays when the commercial world shuts down. Most government and private banks are open Monday through Friday 10 to 2 and Saturday 10 to noon; they are closed on government holidays. International airports and some luxury hotels have 24-hour money-changing facilities. The major offices of American Express that offer check-cashing facilities also have extended hours. Western-style hotels will also change money for their guests. Post offices are generally open Monday through Saturday 10 to 5 and are closed on government holidays. Most museums are closed on Mondays and site museums (near archaeological monuments) are normally closed on Fridays. Museums are also closed on government holidays. As business hours of shops, markets, and bazaars vary in India, hours are noted in each chapter.

C
CAMERAS,
CAMCORDERS,
AND COMPUTERS

Dust is a problem in India for sensitive electronic equipment. Keep delicate equipment under wraps when it's not in use.

LAPTOPS

Before you depart, **check your portable computer's battery,** because you may be asked at security to turn on the computer to prove that it is what it appears to be. At the airport, you may prefer to **request a manual inspection,** although security X-rays do not harm hard-disk or floppy-disk storage. Also, **register your foreign-made laptop with U.S. Customs.** If your laptop is U.S.-made, call the consulate of the country you'll be visiting to find out whether or not it should be registered with local customs upon arrival. You may want to **find out about repair facilities at your destination** in case you need them. You should also consider bringing a spare battery: New batteries may be hard to find in India. Never plug your computer into any socket before asking about surge protection. Some hotels do not have built-in current stabilizers, and the extreme electrical fluctuations and surges can short your adapter or even destroy your computer.

PHOTOGRAPHY

If your camera is new or if you haven't used it for a while, **shoot and develop a few rolls of film** before you leave. Always **store film in a cool, dry place**—never in the car's glove compartment or on the shelf under the rear window.

Every pass through an X-ray machine increases film's chance of clouding. To protect it, carry it in a clear plastic bag and **ask for hand inspection at security.** Such requests are virtually always honored at U.S. airports, but rarely accommodated in India. Don't depend on a lead-lined bag to protect film in checked luggage—the airline may increase the radiation to see what's inside.

Carry some change for those people who demand money for the privilege of taking their picture. If someone asks you to send a copy of the photo, don't say yes unless you intend to keep the promise. Most Indians are good-natured about posing for a picture, but some women and tribal people may object. **Ask before you shoot.** Remember, too, that photography is not permitted in airports or at sensitive military sites, including some bridges, and at some religious sites and events.

VIDEO

Before your trip, **test your camcorder, invest in a skylight filter to protect the lens, and charge the batteries.** (Airport security personnel may ask you to turn on the camcorder to prove that it's what it appears to be.) The batteries of most newer camcorders can be recharged with a universal or worldwide AC adapter charger (or multivoltage converter), usable whether the voltage is 110 or 220. All that's needed is the appropriate plug.

Videotape is not damaged by X-rays, but it may be harmed by the magnetic field of a walk-through metal detector, so **ask that videotapes be hand-checked.** Videotape sold in India is based on the PAL standard, which is different from the one used in the United States. You will not be able to view your tapes through the local TV set or view movies bought here in your home VCR. Blank tapes bought in India can be used for camcorder taping, but they are pricey. Some U.S. audiovisual shops convert foreign tapes to U.S. standards; contact an electronics dealer to find the nearest.

CANTONMENTS

Cantonments are the sections of many Indian cities where the British established their garrisons. The streets are usually wider and more regularly laid out.

CHILDREN AND TRAVEL

BABY-SITTING

For recommended local sitters, **check with your hotel desk.**

DRIVING

Indians don't use seat belts, much less infant seats.

FLYING

Always **ask about discounted children's fares.** On international flights, the fare for infants under age 2 not occupying a seat is generally either free or 10% of the accompanying adult's fare; children ages 2 through 11 usually pay half to two-thirds of the adult fare. On domestic flights, children under 2 not occupying a seat travel free, and older children currently travel on the lowest applicable adult fare.

A trip to India is a long flight. Be sure to **bring a bag of amusements**—books, coloring books and crayons.

BAGGAGE➤ In general, the adult baggage allowance applies for children paying half or more of the adult fare. Before departure, **ask about carry-on allowances,** if you are traveling with an infant. In general, those paying 10% of the adult fare are allowed one carry-on bag, not to exceed 70 pounds or 45 inches (length + width + height) and a collapsible stroller; you may be allowed less if the flight is full.

SAFETY SEATS➤ According to the Federal Aviation Administration (FAA), it's a good idea to **use safety seats aloft.** Airline policy varies. U.S. carriers allow FAA-approved models, but airlines usually require that you buy a ticket, even if your child would otherwise ride free, because the seats must be strapped into regular passenger seats. Foreign carriers may not allow infant seats, may charge the child's rather than the infant's fare for their use, or may require you to hold your baby during takeoff and landing, thus defeating the seat's purpose.

FACILITIES➤ When making your reservation, **ask for children's** **meals or freestanding bassinets** if you need them; the latter are available only to those with seats at the bulk-head, where there's enough legroom. If you don't need a bassinet, **think twice before requesting bulkhead seats**—the only storage for in-flight necessities is in the inconveniently distant overhead bins.

LODGING

Most hotels allow children under a certain age to stay in their parents' room at no extra charge, while others charge them as extra adults; be sure to **ask about the cut-off age.** Luxury hotels usually have swimming pools, but they don't have life guards. Most health clubs do not admit children under 14.

CUSTOMS
AND DUTIES

IN INDIA

If you are bringing dutiable articles or unaccompanied baggage or high-value articles into India with you, they must be entered on a Tourist Baggage Re-Export Form (TBRE). These articles must be re-exported at the time of departure. Failure to re-export anything listed on the TBRE means you'll have to pay a duty levied for each missing item.

You can bring in the following duty-free: personal effects (clothes and jewelry); cameras and up to five rolls of film; binoculars; a portable musical instrument: a radio or portable tape recorder, a tent and camping equipment: sports equipment (fishing rod, a pair of skis, two tennis rackets); 200 cigarettes or 50 cigars; .95 liters of liquor; and gifts not exceeding a value of Rs. 600 (about $20). You may not bring in dangerous drugs or firearms, gold coins, gold and silver bullion and silver coins not in use, Indian currency, or live plants. Depending on the attitude of the custom's official, you may or may not have to enter a portable computer on a TBRE form.

BACK HOME

Rupees are not allowed out of India. You must exchange them before you depart. Banking facilities for the conversion of rupees into foreign currency are usually located in the same airport hall as the check-in counters. You have no access to these facilities once you pass through immigration.

All animal products, souvenirs, and trophies are subject to the protected list under the Wildlife (Protection) Act, 1972. The export of skins made from protected wildlife species is not allowed, and India is becoming increasingly rigorous in its monitoring of such exports. Such items cannot be imported into many countries, including the United States. As a general rule, avoid any souvenir made of wild animal skins (except crocodile leather goods). Ivory, unless it can be proved to be old, is also not allowed in the United States, although it is widely available for purchase. Help stop the poaching, which is reducing elephant herds: Don't buy ivory products.

Generally, items more than 100 years old cannot be exported without a permit from the Archaeological Survey. It has offices in many cities, including Delhi, Bombay, Madras, Calcutta, Bangalore, and Bhubaneswar. Reputable shops will provide you with the required permit or help you procure it. Items without permits will be detained by Indian Customs if they are believed to be over 100 years old.

IN THE U.S.➤ You may bring home $400 worth of foreign goods duty-free if you've been out of the country for at least 48 hours and haven't already used the $400 exemption, or any part of it, in the past 30 days.

Travelers 21 or older may bring back 1 liter of alcohol duty-free, provided the beverage laws of the state through which they reenter the United States allow it. In addition, 100 non-Cuban cigars and 200 cigarettes are allowed, regardless of your age. Antiques and works of art more than 100 years old are duty-free.

Duty-free, travelers may mail packages valued at up to $200 to themselves and up to $100 to others, with a limit of one parcel per ad-

dressee per day (and no alcohol or tobacco products or perfume valued at more than $5); outside, identify the package as being for personal use or an unsolicited gift, specifying the contents and their retail value. Mailed items do not count as part of your exemption.

IN CANADA➤ Once per calendar year, when you've been out of Canada for at least seven days, you may bring in C$300 worth of goods duty-free. If you've been away less than seven days but more than 48 hours, the duty-free exemption drops to C$100 but can be claimed any number of times (as can a C$20 duty-free exemption for absences of 24 hours or more). You cannot combine the yearly and 48-hour exemptions, use the C$300 exemption only partially (to save the balance for a later trip), or pool exemptions with family members. Goods claimed under the C$300 exemption may follow you by mail; those claimed under the lesser exemptions must accompany you.

Alcohol and tobacco products may be included in the yearly and 48-hour exemptions but not in the 24-hour exemption. If you meet the age requirements of the province through which you reenter Canada, you may bring in, duty-free, 1.14 liters (40 imperial ounces) of wine or liquor *or* 24 12-ounce cans or bottles of beer or ale. If

you are 16 or older, you may bring in, duty-free, 200 cigarettes, 50 cigars or cigarillos, and 400 tobacco sticks or 400 grams of manufactured tobacco. Alcohol and tobacco must accompany you on your return.

An unlimited number of gifts valued up to C$60 each may be mailed to Canada duty-free. These do not count as part of your exemption. Label the package "Unsolicited Gift— Value under $60." Alcohol and tobacco are excluded.

IN THE U.K.➤ From countries outside the European Union (EU), including India, you may import duty-free 200 cigarettes, 100 cigarillos, 50 cigars or 250 grams of tobacco; 1 liter of spirits or 2 liters of fortified or sparkling wine; 2 liters of still table wine; 60 milliliters of perfume; 250 milliliters of toilet water; plus £136 worth of other goods, including gifts and souvenirs.

D

DINING

Dry days, when alcohol is not available in India, are observed on January 26, August 15, and October 2. Some states observe additional dry days, while other states only allow the consumption of beer. Gujarat and Andhra Pradesh observe prohibition. In fact a prohibition movement is underway throughout India. In Andhra Pradesh, out-of-state visitors can purchase a drinking permit through their hotel for about Rs. 100 per day. Foreign travelers may apply to the Gujarat Tourism Development Corporation for a permit that allows you to purchase alcohol in the state. The Government of India Tourist Offices abroad also issue a three-month liquor permit allowing you to carry liquor into Gujarat.

In major cities, restaurants normally stay open until 11 PM or midnight. In other areas expect an earlier dinner unless you're staying in a Western-style hotel. Some Indian states observe a weekly meatless day, when no slaughtering is done and no red meat is sold or served in most restaurants.

FOR TRAVELERS
WITH DISABILITIES

India has a large population of people with disabilities, but in a country with so many problems, the needs of these people are not a high priority. If you use a wheelchair or walker, luxury hotels have ramps, but few bathrooms are designed for use by people with disabilities. Except for a couple of international airports, disembarkation from a plane is by stairs. Be aware, too, that there are very few sidewalks in India. There is no such thing as the pedestrian right-of-way in India: When pedestrians cross the street, they are considered fair game.

When discussing accessibility with an operator

or reservations clerk, **ask hard questions.** Are there any stairs, inside *or* out? Are there grab bars next to the toilet *and* in the shower/tub? How wide is the doorway to the room? To the bathroom? For the most extensive facilities, meeting the latest legal specifications, **opt for newer facilities,** which more often have been designed with access in mind. Be sure to **discuss your needs before booking.**

DISCOUNT CLUBS

Travel clubs offer members unsold space on airplanes, cruise ships, and package tours at as much as 50% below regular prices. Membership may include a regular bulletin or access to a toll-free hot line giving details of available trips departing from three or four days to several months in the future. Most also offer 50% discounts off hotel rack rates. Before booking with a club, **make sure the hotel or other supplier isn't offering a better deal.**

DRIVING

Driving in India is a nightmare. Traffic in India moves on the left side of the road. There is no general speed limit for cars apart from the 30 MPH limit in the cities, which is normally ignored. Slow-moving cyclists, bullock carts, and occasional elephants or camels share the road with dare-devil long-distance trucks and buses. Speeds vary according to road conditions. The horn is used as a warning

before a vehicle passes. It's also used to warn pedestrians to get out of the way. In fact, the horn can create a deafening racket. **Bring earplugs.** Remember that for Hindus, cows are considered sacred; for them, drivers slow down and use their horn.

Many roads, except for a very few trunk roads, can be a mess, especially during monsoons. In rural areas, roads are also often a novel extension of farms, with food grains laid out to dry or sisal rope strung over the pavement so that passing vehicles tamp it down.

Hiring a car with a driver or a tourist taxi is a better alternative than driving yourself.

HIRED CARS AND JEEPS WITH DRIVERS

This is the best way to travel in India if you intend to concentrate on a particular state or region. A car with driver is reasonably priced by Western standards. At press time, the cost, which varies from state to state, is determined by the number of hours and a specified number of kilometers. You will pay extra if you exceed the time or kilometer allotment. **Establish the surcharge in advance.** In general, figure that the cost will work out to about Rs. 8 to Rs. 10 per kilometer for a non-air-conditioned Ambassador, a delightful car designed by the British in the 1940s. Toyotas, mini-vans, and Mercedes Benzes are also available at a higher rate. Also expect to pay a halt charge of Rs. 100 to Rs. 200 per night. To go by road in some areas requires a Jeep. **Hire a car or Jeep with driver only from a government-approved and licensed operator** (*see* Travel Agencies *in each chapter*).

G

GAY AND LESBIAN TRAVEL

Although India is a sexually conservative society, there is a growing awareness and acceptance of homosexuality and lesbianism in major cities. Still, gay or lesbian visitors to this country should keep their sexual preference to themselves. No hotel will object to two people of the same sex sharing a bedroom; **but don't openly display your affection in public.**

H

HEALTH CONCERNS

BEFORE YOU GO

For entry into India from the United States, Canada, or the United Kingdom, no vaccination certificate or inoculations are required. Although immigration officials don't normally ask to see an International Health Certificate, it's smart to have one: The certificate contains valuable information in case you need medical attention. See your doctor about obtaining one, and **talk to your doctor about vaccinations three months before departure.**

SHOTS AND MEDICATION➤ According to the Centers for Disease Control (CDC), there is a limited risk of malaria, hepatitis B, dengue, and a number of other diseases in most parts of India. If you plan to visit remote regions or stay for more than six weeks, **check with the CDC's International Travelers Hotline.** In areas with malaria and dengue, which are both carried by mosquitoes, take mosquito nets, wear clothing that covers the body, apply repellent containing DEET, and use a spray against flying insects in living and sleeping areas. The hot line recommends chloroquine (analen) as an antimalarial agent; no vaccine exists against dengue.

It is advisable to **bring a medical kit** containing mosquito repellent with at least 95% DEET (N. diethyl toluamide), adhesive bandages, plastic strip thermometer, water-purification tablets, aspirin or its equivalent, diarrhea medication, antibiotics, and an antiseptic skin cleanser.

WITHIN INDIA

In India, a major health risk is posed by the contamination of drinking water, fresh fruit, and vegetables by fecal matter, which causes the intestinal ailment known variously as Montezuma's Revenge and traveler's diarrhea. To prevent it, **watch what you eat.** Stay away from ice, uncooked food, and unpasteurized milk and milk products, and **drink only water that has been bottled or boiled** for at least 20 minutes. Also **turn down offers of "filtered" water;** water is often filtered to take out particles, but this doesn't mean it has been purified to kill off parasites. Buy bottled water from a reputable hotel or shop, and **check the cap to make sure it has not been tampered with:** Bottles are sometimes refilled with tap water and sold to unknowing tourists.

Always keep at least one bottle of water in your hotel room for brushing teeth and late-night drinks. India's heat can cause dehydration, and the dust may irritate your throat, so you will need to **drink more liquids** than usual. Dehydration will make you weak and more susceptible to other health problems, so when you're walking around town, remind yourself to stop for a drink.

Mild cases of intestinal distress may respond to Imodium (known generically as loperamide) or Pepto-Bismol (which is not as strong), both of which can be purchased over the counter; paregoric, another antidiarrheal agent, requires a doctor's prescription in India. Get plenty of purified water or tea—chamomile is a good folk remedy for diarrhea. In severe cases, rehydrate yourself with a salt-sugar solution (½ tsp. salt and 4 tbsp. sugar per quart/liter of water).

A little bit of personal hygiene can also go a long way in preventing stomach upsets: Remember to wash your hands before you eat anything, even snacks. Carry premoistened towelettes with you, and use them when soap and water are not available. They are also a welcome refreshment on hot afternoons.

IN CITIES➤ All cities in India are heavily polluted. Pollution-control regulations and devices were introduced in 1995, but the majority of India's vehicles continue to use leaded gas or diesel. People with breathing problems, especially asthma, should **carry appropriate respiratory remedies.**

OUTSIDE CITIES➤ If you travel into forested areas during or right after the monsoon, **protect yourself against leeches.** Cover your legs and carry salt. Don't wear sandals. When a leech clings to your clothing or skin, dab it with a pinch of salt, and the leech will fall off. If itching persists, apply an antiseptic; infection rarely occurs. For bedbugs, buy a bar of Dettol soap (available throughout India) and use it when you bathe. It relieves itching and discomfort. At all times, **treat any scratches, cuts, or blisters at once.** If you're trekking, bring bottled water and save the bottle and cap so that you can refill it with water that you prepare with purification tablets.

High altitude sickness, an adverse reaction to low oxygen pressure, can be deadly. If your urine turns bright yellow, you're not drinking enough water. Eat foods that are high in carbohydrates and cut back on salt. Stop and rest immediately if you develop any of the following symptoms: nausea, loss of appetite, extreme headache or lightheadedness, unsteady feet, sleeplessness. If resting doesn't help, head for lower ground immediately.

IN RESTAURANTS➤ You should **avoid raw vegetables and fruit** that have been peeled before they are brought to you. At many restaurant buffets and salad bars the vegetables are imported or presoaked in an iodine preparation to kill parasites, but be sure to ask the waiter before you indulge. When in doubt, eat something else. **Peel your own fruit,** choosing varieties with thick skins. Pork products should be avoided; make certain that other meats are thoroughly cooked. Some people find it best to stick to a vegetarian diet, but that would mean missing out on some very delicious dishes. Choose restaurants with care and eat hot foods while they're hot and you should not have any trouble.

When choosing a restaurant keep in mind that very often the locally popular restaurant that looks worn around the edges offers the safest food. A small restaurant that can't afford refrigeration cooks food acquired that day. This isn't always true with the upscale hotels. As electricity can be temperamental and some chefs buy in bulk, the hotel's refrigeration can be a repository for more than foodstuffs. Keep in mind, however, that stomach upsets often are due as much to the richness of Indian food as to the lack of hygiene. Many hotel restaurants tend to cook Indian dishes especially with a large amount of oil, which can trigger Delhi Belly. Ask the chef to use less oil. Fried foods from street vendors often look delicious, but check the oil: If it looks as old as the pot, it could be rancid and lead to trouble. It's safest to resist the temptation.

ON TRAINS➤ If you travel by train, never accept any food or beverage from another passenger. At press time, some foreigners who had accepted such generosity received tea or food that was drug-laced and were robbed once the drug took effect.

IN THE SUN➤ The sun can be intense in India. Beware of overexposure even on overcast days. To avoid sunburn, **use a sunscreen** with a sun protection factor of at least 24. Play it safe and also **wear a wide-brimmed hat.** If you plan to travel higher than 3,048 meters (10,000 feet), also use zinc oxide or lip balm with sun block and keep your eyes protected behind sunglasses that block ultraviolet rays. When you're in snow, remember that UV rays reflect from below.

I
INSURANCE

Travel insurance can protect your investment, replace your luggage and its contents, or provide for medical coverage should you fall ill during your trip. Most tour operators, travel agents, and insurance agents sell specialized health-and-accident, flight, trip-cancellation, and luggage insurance as well as comprehensive policies with some or all of these features. Before you make any purchase, **review your existing health and home-owner policies** to find out whether they cover expenses incurred while traveling.

BAGGAGE

Airline liability for your baggage is limited to $1,250 per person on U.S. domestic flights. On international flights, the airlines' liability is $9.07 per pound or $20 per kilogram for checked baggage (roughly $640 per 70-pound bag) and $400 per passenger for unchecked baggage. Insurance for losses exceeding the terms of your airline ticket can be bought directly from the airline at check-in for about $10 per $1,000 of coverage; note that it excludes a rather extensive list of items, shown on your airline ticket.

FLIGHT

You should **think twice before buying flight insurance.** Often purchased as a last-minute impulse at the airport, it pays a lump sum when a plane crashes, either to a beneficiary if the insured dies or sometimes to a surviving passenger who loses eyesight or a limb. Supplementing the airlines' coverage described in the limits-of-liability paragraphs on your ticket, it's expensive and basically unnecessary. Charging an airline ticket to a major credit card often automatically entitles you to coverage and may also embrace travel by bus, train, and ship.

HEALTH

If your own health insurance policy does not cover you outside the U.S., **consider buying supplemental medical coverage.** It can provide from $1,000 to $150,000 worth of medical and/or dental expenses incurred as a result of an accident or illness during a trip. These policies also may include a personal-accident, or death-and-dismemberment, provision, which pays a lump sum ranging from $15,000 to $500,000 to your beneficiaries if you die or to you if you lose one or more limbs or your eyesight, and a medical-assistance provision, which may either reimburse you for the cost of referrals, evacuation, or repatriation and other services, or may automatically

enroll you as a member of a particular medical-assistance company. *(See* Health Issues *in* Important Contacts A to Z, *above.)*

FOR U.K. TRAVELERS

You can buy an annual travel-insurance policy valid for most vacations during the year in which it's purchased. If you go this route, make sure it covers you if you have a preexisting medical condition or are pregnant.

TRIP

Without insurance, you will lose all or most of your money if you must cancel your trip due to illness or any other reason. Especially if your airline ticket, cruise, or package tour is nonrefundable and cannot be changed, it's essential that you **buy trip-cancellation-and-interruption insurance.** When considering how much coverage you need, look for a policy that will cover the cost of your trip plus the nondiscounted price of a one-way airline ticket should you need to return home early. Read the fine print carefully, especially sections defining "family member" and "preexisting medical conditions." Also **consider default or bankruptcy insurance,** which protects you against a supplier's failure to deliver. However, such policies often do not cover default by a travel agency, tour operator, airline, or cruise line if you bought your tour and the coverage directly from the firm in question.

THE GOLD GUIDE / SMART TRAVEL TIPS

L

LANGUAGE

Hindi is the national language and many states have their own mother tongue, but English is widely spoken.

LODGING

India has confusing room classifications. With each lodging, we describe a typical standard room. But many luxury hotels in metropolitan cities offer a mind-boggling range of room options. Some hotels call their least expensive rooms superior, with deluxe rooms more expensive; others call their least expensive rooms deluxe, with superior rooms more expensive. Many deluxe hotels also have different categories of rooms on exclusive floors. When you make a reservation, **ask for a complete description of the room's classification** to be certain that you get what you want.

India's Tourism Department also approves and classifies hotels based on a star rating system from five stars (the fanciest) to no star (no-frills). Some excellent hotels and inns, which prefer to maintain an Eastern or old-world ambience, choose not to be classified, as the rating is based exclusively on the number of facilities and the hotel and bedroom size. The system does not take into account service or other important intangibles that can add up

to charm. Still, many tour agents will provide the hotel's star rating when you book a room, so it is handy to **know what the stars represent.** A five-star hotel has a large lobby and large bedrooms, numerous restaurants, and a full range of facilities from swimming pool to extensive shopping arcade. A four-star hotel usually has the same size bedroom as a five-star bedroom, but a smaller lobby. It is not required to have more than two restaurants and will normally have fewer shops; but it will have a swimming pool. A three-star hotel isn't required to have a swimming pool. Its bedrooms are smaller and less luxurious. Also expect fewer shops and facilities. Two-star hotels and below are very simple by Western standards with limited facilities. As the star classification can often be misleading and also excludes many viable options, we don't include the ratings in our hotel descriptions.

Hotel room rates are skyrocketing in business-oriented cities such as Bangalore, Bombay, Calcutta, Delhi, and Madras. In other areas, hotels may even be seeking guests; you may be able to negotiate your room price.

Travelers should also **ask about additional taxes,** such as service charges, that increase the quoted room price. At press time, India has a 10% expenditure tax

added to any room that costs more than Rs. 1200 (about $35). Some states also levy a luxury tax and sales tax. The hotel industry recognizes that these surcharges are a powerful deterrent and is lobbying for changes. Currently, taxes on a hotel room can easily increase the cost by 30%.

The prudent visitor to India should **secure all room reservations before arrival,** especially during the peak season from September to March. Metropolitan hotels rarely have off-season discounts; however, some international chains do have special incentive programs for frequent guests (see Hotels *in* Important Contacts A to Z, *above*).

When complimentary breakfast is included with the room, it is mentioned in the individual listing.

CAMPING

Some areas, such as the beautiful Maharashtra coastline, have camping sites set up with roomy safari-style tents that are available at reasonable cost.

GOVERNMENT LODGING

The Government of India, individual state governments, the Public Works Department (PWD), and the Forestry Department provide inexpensive accommodation throughout India. But most of these facilities are poorly maintained. Government employees and officials also receive priority booking. If you have a reservation, you could be thrown out if an unexpected V.I.P. arrives. You're better off camping.

HERITAGE HOTELS

The Hotel Classification Committee of the Government of India has initiated an excellent incentive program that encourages owners of traditional *havelis* (old mansions), forts, and palaces to convert their properties into hotels or to make restorations on already-converted hotels to bring them up to government standards. These properties are called Heritage Hotels. In them, the architecture and the interiors evoke the East, not the West. If this sounds appealing to you, **contact the Government of India Tourist Office abroad for a list of Heritage Hotels.** They are also noted in the lodging listings in each chapter. Room prices usually range from $$ to $$$$.

INDIAN-STYLE HOTELS

An Indian-style hotel is less luxurious, less costly, and often comes with a bathroom that has an open shower (the water runs all over the floor), instead of a western shower/bathtub. Rooms have the basic necessities, which may include air-conditioning and television; but **don't expect opulent furnishings in Indian-style hotels.** Some of these properties accept credit cards; some take

traveler's checks, all accept rupees.

M
MAIL

The cost of an airmail letter (weighing 10 grams) to the United Kingdom, Europe, Canada, and the United States is Rs. 11.50. Aerograms cost Rs. 6.50. Air mail postcards are Rs. 6.

RECEIVING MAIL

To receive mail in India, **have letters or packages sent to a local branch office of American Express.** Mail is held for thirty days before it's returned to the sender. It can also be forwarded for a nominal fee. To retrieve your mail, you show your American Express card or American Express Travelers Checks, plus one piece of identification, preferably a passport. It's a free service to Amex travelers check or card holders; non-card holders pay a fee.

MEDICAL ASSISTANCE

No one plans to fall ill while traveling, but it happens, so **consider signing up with a medical assistance company.** These outfits provide referrals, emergency evacuation or repatriation, 24-hour telephone hot lines for medical consultation, dispatch of medical personnel, relay of medical records, cash for emergencies, and other personal and legal assistance. For more information, *see* Health Concerns, *above.*

MONEY AND EXPENSES

The units of Indian currency are the *rupee* and the *paisa* (100 paise equal one rupee). Paper money comes in denominations of 1, 2, 5, 10, 20, 50, 100, and 500 rupees; a 1,000-rupee note may be available soon. Coins are in denominations of 5, 10, 20, 25, and 50 paise, one rupee, two rupees, and five rupees. The rate of exchange, which fluctuates, is approximately U.S.$1 = Rs. 34; £1 = Rs. 52; C$1 = Rs. 21.

EXCHANGING CURRENCY

India has strict rules against importing or exporting its currency. International airports have currency exchange booths that are always open for arriving or departing overseas flights. When you change money, remember to get a certain amount in small denominations. Also **reject torn bills.** Many merchants, hotels, and restaurants won't accept worn or tattered bills, and it's a hassle to go to a bank to get them exchanged.

Always **change money from an authorized money-changer and insist on receiving an encashment slip.** Some banks now charge a nominal fee for this slip, which is necessary if you plan to pay hotel bills or travel expenses in rupees. The encashment slip is also required if you need to reconvert rupees into your own currency at departure. Do not be lured by illegal street hawkers who offer you a higher exchange rate.

India's state-run banks can take forever to cash traveler's checks. Save time and use American Express Traveler's Service. Otherwise, cash the check at the foreign exchange counter at your hotel. Rates will be slightly lower, but you will save irritation and time.

COSTS

India is less expensive than most destinations when it comes to shopping, staying in budget Western-style hotels, and eating in independent restaurants. Travel, which used to be a bargain, is still reasonable; but the increasing cost of gasoline has led to fare-hikes of about 50% for planes, trains, hired cars with drivers, taxis, and auto-rickshaws. These prices are still lower than those in many other world destinations. Rates for a hired car with driver, taxis, auto-rickshaws also vary from state to state. Costs for deluxe hotels in major cities (Bangalore, Bombay, Calcutta, Delhi, Madras) are skyrocketing, and deluxe resorts in Goa are more expensive than in the rest of India. Many luxury hotels also have a dollar tariff rate for foreigners that is higher than the rupee tariff for Indian nationals.

A cup of tea from a stall costs about 10 cents. In luxury hotels, it can cost over $1 before

taxes. A chicken burger with french fries costs about $2 without taxes. A 650-ml bottle of beer costs $4 without taxes. A 5-kilometer (about 3-mile) taxi ride in Delhi costs about $1.

TAXES

AIRPORT➤ Visitors must pay an airport departure tax when they leave India. If you're heading for Bhutan, Nepal, Pakistan, or other neighboring countries, the tax is Rs. 150; for other international destinations the tax is Rs. 300.

HOTEL➤ At press time, hotels with double rooms that cost above Rs. 1200 (about $35) per night levy a 10% expenditure tax on the room and food and beverage bills. Hoteliers are lobbying the government to abolish this tax, so it might be gone by the time you arrive. You should also expect an additional sales tax on food and beverages; the percentage varies from state to state.

TRAVELER'S CHECKS

Whether or not to buy traveler's checks depends on where you are headed; **take cash to rural areas and small towns, traveler's checks to cities.** The most widely recognized are American Express, Citicorp, Thomas Cook, and Visa, which are sold by major commercial banks for 1% to 3% of the checks' face value—it pays to **shop around.** Both American Express and Thomas Cook issue checks that can be

countersigned and used by you or your traveling companion. So you won't be left with excess foreign currency, **buy a few checks in small denominations** to cash toward the end of your trip. Record the numbers of the checks, cross them off as you spend them, and keep this information separate from your checks.

WIRING MONEY

You don't have to be a cardholder to send or receive funds through MoneyGram^{SM} from American Express. Just go to a MoneyGram agent, located in retail and convenience stores and in American Express Travel Offices. Pay up to $1,000 with cash or a credit card, anything over that in cash. The money can be picked up in the form of U.S. dollar traveler's checks or local currency at the nearest Money-Gram agent, or, abroad, the nearest American Express Travel Office. There's no limit, and the recipient need only present photo identification. The cost runs from 3% to 10%, depending on the amount sent, the destination, and how you pay.

You can also send money using Western Union. Money sent from the United States or Canada will be available for pickup at agent locations in 100 countries. Once the money is in the system, it can be picked up at any one of 25,000 locations. Fees range from 4% to 10%, depending on the amount you send.

P
PACKAGES
AND TOURS

A package or tour to India can make your vacation less expensive and more convenient. Firms that sell tours and packages purchase airline seats, hotel rooms, and rental /cars in bulk and pass some of the savings on to you. In addition, the best operators have local representatives to help you out at your destination.

A GOOD DEAL?

The more your package or tour includes, the better you can predict the ultimate cost of your vacation. Make sure you know exactly what is included, and **beware of hidden costs.** Are taxes, tips, and service charges included? Transfers and baggage handling? Entertainment and excursions? These can add up.

Most packages and tours are rated deluxe, first-class superior, first class, tourist, and budget. The key difference is usually accommodations. Remember, tourist class in the U.S. might be a comfortable chain hotel, while in India you might share a bath and do without hot water. If the package or tour you are considering is priced lower than in your wildest dreams, **be skeptical.** Also, **make sure your travel agent knows the hotels** and other services. Ask about location, room size, beds, and whether it has a pool, room service, or programs for children, if you care about these. Has your agent been there or sent others you can contact?

BUYER BEWARE

Each year consumers are stranded or lose their money when operators go out of business—even very large ones with excellent reputations. If you can't afford a loss, take the time to **check out the operator**—find out how long the company has been in business, and ask several agents about its reputation. Next, **don't book unless the firm has a consumer-protection program.** Members of the United States Tour Operators Association and the National Tour Association are required to set aside funds exclusively to cover your payments and travel arrangements in case of default. Nonmember operators may instead carry insurance; look for the details in the operator's brochure—and the name of an underwriter with a solid reputation. Note: When it comes to tour operators, **don't trust escrow accounts.** Although there are laws governing those of charter-flight operators, no governmental body prevents tour operators from raiding the till.

Next, **contact the local Better Business Bureau and the attorney general's office** in both your own state and the operator's; have any complaints been filed? Last, **pay with a major credit card.** Then you can cancel payment, provided that you can document your complaint. Always **consider trip-cancellation insurance** (*see* Insurance, *above*).

BIG VS. SMALL➤ An operator that handles several hundred thousand travelers annually can use its purchasing power to give you a good price. Its high volume may also indicate financial stability. But some small companies provide more personalized service; because they tend to specialize, they may also be experts on an area.

USING AN AGENT

Travel agents are an excellent resource. In fact, large operators accept bookings only through travel agents. But it's good to **collect brochures from several agencies,** because some agents' suggestions may be skewed by promotional relationships with tour and package firms that reward them for volume sales. If you have a special interest, **find an agent with expertise in that area;** the American Society of Travel Agents can give you leads in the United States. (Don't rely solely on your agent, though; agents may be unaware of small niche operators, and some special-interest travel companies only sell direct.)

SINGLE TRAVELERS

Prices are usually quoted per person, based on two sharing a room. If traveling solo, you may be required to pay the full double-occupancy rate. Some operators eliminate this surcharge if you agree to be matched up with a roommate of the same sex, even if one is not found by departure time.

PACKING
FOR INDIA

In India, delicate fabrics do not stand up well to laundering facilities except at deluxe hotels. While dry cleaning is available at all deluxe hotels in major cities, the cleaning fluid can be harsh. If you bring clothing that requires dry cleaning, it's wise to have them cleaned back home. Plain cottons or cotton/synthetic blends are the most practical and the coolest in summer. It's best to **avoid synthetic fabrics that don't "breathe."**

The sun is strong in India. To protect yourself from overexposure, **bring a hat with a wide brim.** If you travel during the monsoon, bring a collapsible umbrella. During the winter months, bring a sweater or light-weight jacket if you travel in the plains or the south; and if you intend to go north, bring warm clothes, as it can be wintry cold and many accommodations don't have central heating. Rooms can be chilly.

India is not a dressy society. If you attend a fancy function, men can wear a business suit and women can wear a dress or skirt and blouse with flats or low heels.

Travelers should also **remember that what is appropriate in the West isn't necessarily appropriate in the East.** Only children can get away with short shorts. Men should dress in comfortable jeans or long shorts. A t-shirt is not offensive; but the topless look should be left to the wandering *sadhu* (Hindu holy man). If it's warm, women should stick to skirts or lightweight slacks. While shorts are acceptable in the West and many foreign women wear them in the mountains or coastal areas, women in cities who reveal bare legs under even a conservative pair of shorts may attract undesired attention. To enter a holy shrine, women should wear a below-the-knee skirt or dress or neat pants. To go braless is mindless. Any woman wearing a top with a scooped or plunging neckline must be prepared for wandering eyes and unflattering remarks. Travel in a Muslim community calls for even more discretion. Women should consider wearing a *salwar kameez*, the local loose pants and long blouse, inexpensive and very flattering. Bathing suits should be conservative. Topless and nude bathing have become serious issues in India and not just for the individuals who leave themselves exposed. Many men assume that all foreign women, irrespective of their swimming attire, are fair game for aggressive pursuit.

If you go to the Himalayas, it can be cold in the extreme altitudes by day as well as night. The trick to assembling your wardrobe is triple layering. The layer next to your skin (long johns) should be made of synthetic fabrics or silk that carry moisture away from the skin to the outer surface of the garment. Cotton soaks up perspiration and will make you wet. For the second layer wool, fleece, or a synthetic fabric knitted into thick pile, like Polar Plus, is best. Choose a down vest if you anticipate extremely cold weather. Comfortable jeans or lightweight Polar Plus trousers are good choices. For the third layer, bring a well-made, generously sized windbreaker or lightweight parka insulated with a small amount of down and made of Gore-Tex (or an equivalent fiber like Zepel or VersaTech), which not only allows moisture to escape but is waterproof, not merely water-repellent. Bulky down parkas are advisable only for winter excursions or a climb into higher mountains. Bring a pair of lined Gore-Tex overpants—indispensable in the rain and cold or when you're thrashing through wet underbrush.

Most adventure-travel companies supply sleeping bags for their clients. If you're roughing it on your own and need a sleeping bag, choose one with an outer shell that will keep you dry. As for the weight, you don't need a bag designed for an assault on a mountain peak unless that's the trip you've planned. A down bag guaranteed to keep you warm at 15°F (a fairly cold temperature during the Himalayan trekking season) is adequate. If you plan to travel overnight on trains, it's useful to carry a sleeping-bag liner.

Trekkers or visitors going on any outdoor adventure should bring a day pack that will hold a sweater, camera, and plastic quart-size water bottle (a must for excursions). Consider bringing along a good pair of binoculars and sunglasses that block out ultraviolet rays.

Bring the following indispensable extras: strong sunblock, sewing kit, pre-moistened towelettes, pocket knife with can opener, lock and key for each duffel or bag, high-power impact-resistant flashlight, spare batteries (unless they're a popular size). Good sanitary napkins are now available, but tampons are substandard. Sports enthusiasts should bring their own tennis or golf balls, which are expensive in India.

Bring an extra pair of eyeglasses or contact lenses in your carry-on luggage, and if you have a health problem, **pack enough medication** to last the trip or have your doctor write a prescription using the drug's generic name, because brand names vary from country to country (you may then need a prescription from a doctor in India,

although most drugs are available here without a prescription). In case your bags go astray, **don't put prescription drugs or valuables in luggage to be checked.** To avoid problems with customs officials, carry medications in original packaging. Also don't forget the addresses of offices that handle refunds of lost traveler's checks.

ELECTRICITY

To use your U.S.-purchased electric-powered equipment, **bring a converter and an adapter.** The electrical current in India is 220 volts, 50 cycles alternating current (AC); wall outlets take plugs with two round prongs.

If your appliances are dual voltage, you'll need only an adapter. Hotels sometimes have 110-volt outlets for low-wattage appliances marked "For Shavers Only" near the sink; don't use them for high-wattage appliances like blow-dryers. If your laptop computer is older, carry a converter; new laptops operate equally well on 110 and 220 volts, so you need only an adapter. **Check with your hotel to see if stabilizers are functioning in your room before you plug in your computer.** Adaptors can't survive an Indian-style surge in electricity, which is a daily event.

LUGGAGE

Free airline baggage allowances depend on the airline, the route, and the class of your ticket; ask in advance.

In general, on domestic flights and on international flights between the United States and foreign destinations, you are entitled to check two bags—neither exceeding 2 inches, or 158 centimeters (length + width + height), or weighing more than 70 pounds (32 kilograms). A third piece may be brought aboard; its total dimensions are generally limited to less than 45 inches (114 centimeters), so it will fit easily under the seat in front of you or in the overhead compartment. In the United States, the FAA gives airlines broad latitude to limit carry-on allowances and tailor them to different aircraft and operational conditions. Charges for excess, oversize, or overweight pieces vary.

If you are flying between two foreign destinations, note that baggage allowances may be determined not by piece but by weight—generally 88 pounds (40 kilograms) in first class, 66 pounds (30 kilograms) in business class, and 44 pounds (20 kilograms) in economy. If your flight between two cities abroad *connects* with your transatlantic or transpacific flight, the piece method still applies.

SAFEGUARDING YOUR LUGGAGE➤ Before leaving home, **itemize your bags' contents** and their worth and label the bags with your name, address, and phone number. (If you use your home address, cover the label so that potential thieves can't see it.) Inside your bag, **pack a copy of your itinerary.** At check-in, **make sure that your bag is correctly tagged** with the airport's three-letter destination code. If your bags arrive damaged or not at all, file a written report with the airline before leaving the airport. Finding and then retrieving lost luggage in India is a nightmare that can go on for days. **Check all tickets and baggage numbers before you let the baggage out of your sight.**

PASSPORTS AND VISAS

If you don't already have one, **get a passport.** While traveling, **keep one photocopy of the data page** separate from your wallet and leave another copy with someone at home. If you lose your passport, promptly call the nearest embassy or consulate, and the local police; having the data page can speed replacement.

You must **arrive in India within six months of the date your visa is issued.** If you need to extend your visa, visit the Foreigners' Regional Registration Office in the major cities or any of the Offices of the Superintendent of Police in the District Headquarters.

Foreigners can now visit newly opened northern areas previously restricted to Indian nationals. You

must travel with a government-recognized tour operator and be in a group with a minimum of four people. You must also obtain a Restricted Area or Inner-line permit (the names are interchangeable), which your tour operator will help you secure. Although these permits can be arranged in about a week, play it safe and make arrangements for your trip at least two months in advance. At press time, foreign nationals need permits to travel in these new destinations: Spiti and Kinnaur districts in Himachal Pradesh; Pangong Tso, Tso Moriri, Nubra Valley, and the Drogpa villages in Ladakh; Sikkim; the Andaman and Nicobar Islands; and Lakshadweep. To visit these islands, however, you do not have to go as part of a group. All these areas offer excellent adventures or terrific beaches (*see* Chapter 2, Special-Interest Travel in India).

U.S. CITIZENS

All U.S. citizens, even infants, need a valid passport and a visa to enter India for stays of up to one year. New and renewal passport application forms are available at any of the 13 U.S. Passport Agency offices and at some post offices and courthouses. Passports are usually mailed within four weeks; allow five weeks or more in spring and summer. Visas can be obtained from the Indian embassy or

consulates or through travel agencies. The cost is $40 for 3 months, $60 for 6 months, and $70 for one year.

CANADIANS

You need a valid passport and a visa to enter India for stays of up to five years. Passport application forms are available at 28 regional passport offices as well as post offices and travel agencies. Whether for a first or a subsequent passport, you must apply in person. Children under 16 may be included on a parent's passport but must have their own to travel alone. Passports are valid for five years and are usually mailed within two to three weeks of application. Visas can be obtained from the Indian embassy or consulates or through travel agencies. The cost is $30 for 3 months, $55 for 6 months, $70 for 1 year, and $140 for 5 years.

U.K. CITIZENS

Citizens of the United Kingdom need a valid passport and a visa to enter India for stays of up to 6 months. Applications for new and renewal passports are available from main post offices as well as at the passport offices, located in Belfast, Glasgow, Liverpool, London, Newport, and Peterborough. You may apply in person at all passport offices, or by mail to all except the London office. Children under 16 may travel on an accompanying parent's passport. All passports are valid for 10 years. Allow a

THE GOLD GUIDE / SMART TRAVEL TIPS

month for processing. Visas can be obtained from the Indian embassy or consulates or through travel agencies. The cost starts at £13 for three months.

PERSONAL SECURITY AND COMFORT

Never leave an unlocked suitcase in a hotel room. Never leave suitcases unattended in airports or train stations. Women traveling alone should never get into a taxi or rickshaw if there's a second man accompanying the driver. Women should also chain lock their door when they are in their hotel room; room boys love to knock and barge in. Everyone should be alert in crowds for pickpockets. Wear a money belt; women should keep their pocketbook close to the body and securely closed. Be careful when you use your credit cards. Many people when eating out insist that the machine be brought to the dining table to make certain that the card isn't used to make an impression on more than one form.

R
RAIL TRAVEL

DISCOUNT PASSES

To save money, **look into rail passes** (see Important Contacts A to Z, above). Try to **purchase the pass at least two months before your journey.** Provide your travel agent or the rail pass agent with your complete rail itinerary to insure seat confirmation before you depart. Every overseas Government of India Tourist Office should have copies of the Tourist Railway Timetable. Otherwise, get a copy of Thomas Cook's International Railway Timetable. *Travel Links* and *Travel Hour*, which list plane and some train schedules, are available in India. But be aware that if you don't plan to cover many miles, you may come out ahead by buying individual tickets.

Many travelers assume that rail passes guarantee them seats on the trains they wish to ride. Not so. You need to **book seats ahead even if you are using a rail pass.** You will also need a reservation if you purchase overnight sleeping accommodations.

If your trip plans are flexible, you can also try to get reservations once you arrive. To save a lot of time, use a local agent, who may need to borrow your passport, or head to the railway station and prepare for lines and long waits while you make the arrangements yourself. At the time of travel, **be sure you arrive at the station with enough time to find your seat**—the sleeper and seat numbers are displayed on the platform and on each carriage, along with a list of passengers' names and seat assignments.

Indian trains have numerous classes of accommodations: first-class air-conditioned (private compartments with two or four sleeping berths), ordinary first-class (non-air-conditioned private compartments with two or four sleeping berths), second-class air-conditioned sleeper (only available on some trains), second-class two-tier sleeper (padded berths), and ordinary second class (always crowded and never comfortable).

Many new trains designated "Superfast," such as the Shatabadi and Rajdhani Expresses, have "air-conditioned chair cars" where the seats recline. These expresses link more and more important destinations and should be your choice if time is a factor.

The next fastest trains are called "Mail" trains. "Passenger" trains, which usually offer only second-class accommodations, make numerous stops and are crowded. Trains that run on broad-gauge tracks are much faster than those on meter-gauge or narrow-gauge tracks. Even on the best trains, lavatories are less than pleasant and seats can be very well worn.

Still, some daily trains are worth considering. The Shatabadi Express and the Taj Express travel between Delhi and Agra. Both trains leave early in the morning from Delhi; the Shatabadi takes about two hours and the Taj Express 2½. They allow for a full day of sightseeing before returning to Delhi. The Pink Express, which travels between Delhi and Jaipur, takes six hours and allows for about five hours of sightseeing before returning to Delhi. Another convenient Shatabadi Express connects Bombay and Delhi with departures in the late afternoon and arrivals early in the morning in both directions. An overnight Rajdhani Express also connects Delhi and Calcutta (Howrah Station).

LUXURY TRAINS

At press time, the following two luxury train journeys were in operation: The Rajasthan Tourism Development Corporation's **Palace on Wheels** and the Gujarat State Tourism Development Corporation's **Royal Orient.**

RELIGION

HOLY SITES

Visiting a religious monument demands respect. With all sects, you must **remove your shoes before entering a shrine,** even if it seems in ruins (in some places, such as the Taj Mahal, cloth overshoes are provided for a small charge). All religions ask that you **do not smoke or drink alcoholic** beverages on the premises or speak in a raised voice. Some structures are off-limits to visitors who don't practice the faith; **don't try to bribe your way inside.** Women should always be properly dressed (see Packing for India, above) and should cover the head before entering a Sikh

gurdwara (temple) or a mosque.

When you enter a mosque, you are supposed to step right foot first over the threshold into the courtyard. Some Hindu and Jain temples prohibit all leather products inside a shrine—shoes, belts, handbags, camera cases. Many temples also expect you to purify yourself by washing your hands and feet in a nearby tap or tank before you enter. No visitor in a gurdwara should point his or her feet toward the Holy Book or step over any one sitting in prayer or meditation. In general, play it safe; if you decide to sit on the floor of a Hindu or Sikh temple, sit cross-legged or with your feet tucked beneath you. In some religious shrines, sexes are separated. Look around before you sit, and let the situation govern what you do.

Many well-meaning tourists commit an unforgivable sacrilege when they visit a Buddhist monastery. You're perfectly welcome to spin any prayer wheel, but just as you must circumambulate the interior and exterior of a monastery, stupa, or mani wall in a clockwise direction, you must follow this rule when you spin a prayer wheel. Inside the monastery, interior cushions and chairs are reserved for lamas (monks). Sit on the steps outside or on the floor. If you have the opportunity to meet a

rimpoche (head lama) or a respected monk, it's polite not to turn your back on him when you leave. Also remove your hat and lower an umbrella within the confines of a monastery. This courtesy is also observed in the presence of a lama.

HOME VISITS

If you are welcomed into a house, try to **observe the rules governing the seating.** Often men sit separate from women. If in doubt, ask. There are numerous other customs associated with food and the partaking of meals. In many households, you arrive, you sit and talk, and then the food is served. After you eat, the evening is over. Don't be surprised if the woman of the house serves her guests but doesn't join the gathering. Don't protest, don't follow her into the kitchen (frequently in orthodox Hindu homes the kitchen is off-limits). Just accept her behavior as the tradition of this particular home. When you eat in villages or remote areas, you may not be given utensils; use your right hand (the left is considered unclean). If you want second helpings or if you are buying openly displayed food, don't help yourself with your hands, especially in a Hindu society; this act pollutes the food. Let your host or vendor serve you.

SACRIFICES

With any trip planned around a Hindu or Muslim festival, remember that many celebrations involve animal sacrifice, which may upset you or your child (see Festivals and Seasonal Events, above). In general, regional dances, especially Kathakali performances, and Buddhist celebrations, with their ritualized dancing, colorful costumes, and elaborate masks, are a safe bet and great fun.

RENTING A CAR

INSURANCE

In the event you must drive a rented car in India, you are generally responsible for any damage or personal injury that you cause as well as damage to the vehicle. Before you rent, see what coverage you already have by means of your personal auto-insurance policy and credit cards. For about $14 a day, rental companies sell insurance, known as a collision damage waiver (CDW), that eliminates your liability for damage to the car; it's always optional and should never be automatically added to your bill.

REQUIREMENTS

In India your own driver's license is not acceptable. An International Driver's Permit, available from the American or Canadian Automobile Association, is necessary.

S
SHOPPING

Above all, be alert when shopping. Don't let taxi drivers take you to their favorite shops—they get a commission and you pay a higher price. Don't buy wild animal skins or ivory; it is illegal, but poaching is decimating India's wildlife. Before you purchase any item that a shopkeeper claims is 100 years old, ask for an export permit. A reputable shopkeeper will have the permit or help you procure it. Otherwise, the item is a fake or, if it's old, it has not been approved by the government for export. Check goods after paying, and count your change.

In bazaars, bargaining is expected, offer a third of the stated price; settle for 60%.

STUDENTS ON THE ROAD

To save money, look into deals available through student-oriented travel agencies. To qualify, you'll need to have a bona fide student I.D. card. Members of international student groups also are eligible. See Students in Important Contacts A to Z, above.

T
TELEPHONES

A local phone call in India normally costs between Rs. 1 and Rs. 5, depending on where you make the call. Some deluxe hotels have coin-operated public phones that take a Rs. 5 coin or a token purchased at the hotel reception desk. To use a public phone, dial the number, then deposit the required coin once the connection has been made. There is a three-minute time limit that can be extended to six minutes. If you use an International Subscriber Dialing/Subscriber Trunk Dialing (ISD/STD; see Long-Distance, below) facility, a meter will record the duration of your conversation, and you pay the proprietor the required amount. The dial tone sounds, but often after you dial the number, you hear a pulsing tone for some seconds before the ring cuts in.

Domestic long-distance calls are expensive and can be made quickly through a computer system called Subscriber Trunk Dialing (STD), which is available in most hotels, through specially designated public phones, and at private ISD/STD offices, which are easily spotted by their bright yellow signs. When you dial a long distance number in India, add 0 before each area code listed in this book.

When using a public STD booth check the meter reading before you pay, to see that the time on the slip matches the actual time used on the phone and that the number recorded on the slip matches the number you dialed. Rates decrease by 50% after 6 PM and 75% after 9 PM.

If you are unable to find an STD facility, you must book long-distance calls through an operator. To reach the operator, dial 180.

LONG-DISTANCE

The long-distance services of AT&T, MCI, and Sprint make

THE GOLD GUIDE / SMART TRAVEL TIPS

calling home relatively convenient and may let you avoid hotel surcharges (check before you make your call); typically, you dial a local number. Before you go, **find out the local access codes** for your destinations.

International telecommunications can be subject to long delays outside major cities, but most hotels, airports, and post offices are connected to the computerized International Subscriber Dialing (ISD) system, which eliminates the need to book a call through an operator. With ISD, you just dial 00, followed by the country code, the area code, and the number. There is no surcharge for using the ISD system, but most hotels will add their own surcharge, which can be extremely high. Check before you use the hotel facility. To avoid the surcharge, make your calls at ISD/STD offices. Even then, the price will be around three dollars a minute to most places in the world. At press time, India does not offer reduced-rate calling hours.

OPERATORS AND INFORMATION

If you are unable to find an ISD facility, you must book long-distance calls through an operator. To reach an international operator, dial 186.

For local telephone number information, dial 197. For domestic long-distance telephone number information, dial 183. Speak slowly,

but don't be surprised if the operator just hangs up on you. India is modernizing its phone system, and the operator may not even have the latest number. Also remember that throughout India and even within cities, the number of digits in phone numbers varies.

TIPPING

Most major hotels include a service charge of 10%. Waiters, room service boys, housekeepers, porters, and doormen all expect to be tipped. You won't go wrong if you tip your room waiter Rs. 10 per night. Bellboys and bell captains should be paid Rs. 5 per bag. For room service, tip Rs. 10–Rs. 20. Tip the concierge about Rs. 5 if he gets you a taxi. Railroad porters should be paid Rs. 5–Rs. 10 per bag, depending on the weight. Set the rate before you let him take your bags. Taxi drivers don't expect tips unless they go through a great deal of trouble to get to your destination; but if you hire a car with a driver, tip him about Rs. 50–Rs. 100 per day, depending on the distance traveled. If you hire a local guide, tip him or her Rs. 40 for four hours, Rs. 80 for a full day.

W
WHEN TO GO

The peak tourist season in India runs from mid-September through March—the ideal time to visit the plains and the South. India is a

year-round destination as long as you pay attention to the weather. Temperatures in the north remain comfortable during May and June. Ladakh, Lahaul, and Spiti, where the mountains usually hold back the monsoon, are a great escape from the torrential July and August rains that inundate the rest of the north. Travelers should realize that the monsoon can disrupt plane schedules, phone systems, and electricity. Heavy rains can also wash away roads or bury them in landslides.

During the peak season at popular destinations, you should expect crowds. Make all reservations well in advance. This is obligatory for trips to Goa, Kerala, and Rajasthan in the winter months and trips to Manali and Ladakh in summer.

If you go to a popular festival, that, too, will be crowded with other tourists and villagers. For a complete list of events, *see* Festivals and Seasonal Events, *in* Chapter 1, Destination: India.

India does not have enticing off-season bargains. Prices at many resorts will be lower during the monsoon, but the rain will restrict your time on the beach.

CLIMATE

India's climate is monsoon-tropical with local variations depending on where in the subcontinent you are. Cool weather lasts from October to the end of February, and really hot and muggy weather in the south of India from the beginning of April to the beginning of June, at which point the mon-soon brings rain-laden clouds that move north, watering nearly every part of India until September. In the far north, the Himalayas and Sikkim can be extremely cold in winter, when many mountain passes and valleys are closed because of deep snow.

The following are average daily maximum and minimum tempera-tures for key Indian cities.

Climate in India

AGRA

Jan.	72F	22C	May	107F	42C	Sept.	92F	33C
	45	7		81	27		77	25
Feb.	79F	26C	June	106F	41C	Oct.	92F	33C
	50	10		85	29		66	19
Mar.	90F	32C	July	95F	35C	Nov.	85F	29C
	61	16		81	27		54	12
Apr.	101F	38C	Aug.	92F	33C	Dec.	75F	24C
	72	22		79	26		46	8

BOMBAY

Jan.	88F	31C	May	92F	33C	Sept.	86F	30C
	61	16		79	26		76	24
Feb.	90F	32C	June	90F	32C	Oct.	90F	32C
	63	17		79	26		74	23
Mar.	92F	33C	July	86F	30C	Nov.	92F	33C
	68	20		77	25		68	20
Apr.	92F	33C	Aug.	85F	29C	Dec.	90F	32C
	76	24		76	24		65	18

CALCUTTA

Jan.	79F	26C	May	97F	36C	Sept.	90F	32C
	54	12		79	26		79	26
Feb.	85F	29C	June	94F	34C	Oct.	88F	31C
	59	15		79	26		75	24
Mar.	94F	34C	July	90F	32C	Nov.	85F	29C
	68	20		79	26		64	18
Apr.	97F	36C	Aug.	90F	32C	Dec.	81F	27C
	76	24		79	26		55	13

DELHI

Jan.	70F	21C	May	106F	41C	Sept.	93F	34C
	45	7		81	27		77	25
Feb.	93F	34C	June	104F	40C	Oct.	95F	35C
	50	10		84	29		66	19
Mar.	86F	30C	July	95F	35C	Nov.	84F	29C
	59	15		81	27		54	12
Apr.	97F	36C	Aug.	93F	34C	Dec.	73F	23C
	70	21		79	26		46	8

GANGTOK

Jan.	57F	14C	May	72F	22C	Sept.	73F	23C
	39	4		57	14		61	16
Feb.	59F	15C	June	73F	23C	Oct.	72F	22C
	41	5		61	16		54	12
Mar.	66F	19C	July	73F	23C	Nov.	66F	19C
	48	9		63	17		48	9
Apr.	72F	22C	Aug.	73F	23C	Dec.	59F	15C
	54	12		63	17		43	6

MADRAS

Jan.	84C	29C	May	100F	38C	Sept.	93F	34C
	68	20		82	28		77	25
Feb.	88F	31C	June	99F	37C	Oct.	90F	32C
	70	21		82	28		75	24
Mar.	91F	33C	July	95F	35C	Nov.	84F	29C
	73	23		79	26		73	23
Apr.	95F	35C	Aug.	95F	35C	Dec.	82F	28C
	79	26		79	26		70	21

SHIMLA

Jan.	48F	9C	May	73F	23C	Sept.	68F	20C
	36	2		59	15		57	14
Feb.	50F	10C	June	75F	24C	Oct.	64F	18C
	37	3		61	16		50	10
Mar.	57F	14C	July	70F	21C	Nov.	59F	15C
	45	7		61	16		45	7
Apr.	66F	19C	Aug.	68F	20C	Dec.	52F	11C
	52	11		59	15		39	4

TRIVANDRUM

Jan.	88F	31C	May	88F	31C	Sept.	86F	30C
	72	22		77	25		73	23
Feb.	90F	32C	June	84F	29C	Oct.	86F	30C
	73	23		75	24		73	23
Mar.	91F	33C	July	84F	29C	Nov.	86F	30C
	75	24		73	23		73	23
Apr.	90F	32C	Aug.	84F	29C	Dec.	88F	31C
	77	25		72	22		73	23

1 Destination: India

COSMIC CHAOS

BACK IN 1986 I made my first trip to India, prepared for a country that good friends (or were they doomsayers?) insisted was overrun with people, poverty, and far too many methane-gas-producing cows. Be careful about what you eat and touch, I was warned. Take lots of Handi Wipes, toilet paper, water purification tablets, and antibiotics, and get yourself inoculated against cholera, typhoid, meningitis, polio, tetanus, diphtheria, measles, mumps—and rabies, for good measure.

Years have passed. I have succumbed to India's mysticism and her inscrutable spell. India has become my second home. During this time I learned that the more distant the destination, the less we know; the more foreign a culture, the more foolish our assumptions. India has oodles of toilet paper, plenty of Handi Wipes, and yes, lots of sacred cows and lots and lots of religion. In fact, it has so many revered gods and goddesses that I take issue with Mark Twain, who wrote in *Following the Equator:* "In religion all other countries are paupers, India is the only millionaire." India is a billionaire. Hinduism alone accounts for 330,000,000 deities. Wherever you travel in this spiritual land, you come across monuments that pay homage to the faith they commemorate: the Taj Mahal with its carefully inlaid Quranic verses; the Khajuraho temples with their astonishing exteriors carved with intricate Hindu sculptures; the Ajanta Caves with their serene murals of the Buddha; the Catholic churches in Goa with their Hindu-influenced images of Jesus; the Jain temples with their Tirthankaras (perfect souls) whose poses and features resemble those of the Buddha.

My introduction to all of India's faiths taught me another truth about this country that you can discover when you prowl any of her streets. In India, religion is no one-day-a-week affair: it's a way of life—the force that moves the country. It governs the mind, defines most behavior, sets much of the country's agenda and calendar. It can even become a personal lullaby or alarm clock, with Hindu chanting at nighttime and the Muslim muezzin calling the faithful to prayer in the morning.

India is also fusion and contrast. Throughout this country, where the earliest remnants of a civilization date from at least 3200 BC, you see the effect of repeated invasions on India's culture and heritage. Some claim that India's ability to adapt is the source of her strength and resilience. British bungalows adorn hill stations and line thoroughfares in major cities. Persian-influenced Islamic tombs add delicacy to urban skylines. Cuisines, adopted mother tongues, dance and music styles, and artwork and handicrafts change from region to region. You won't find an American-style homogeneity in India. It's a country of surprises as diverse as its landscape.

India is a destination veiled in mysteries, many of which are difficult for a Westerner to understand. I've always wondered why, for example, India's urban cows prefer to chew on newspaper rather than on rotting garbage (in plentiful supply) or random patches of grass in a field. Even Aldous Huxley noticed their strange dietary preference in *Jesting Pilot,* a record of his journey to India in the early 1900s. "Outside one of the doors of a building stood a row of brimming waste-paper baskets, and from these, as from mangers, two or three sacred bulls were slowly and majestically feeding. When the baskets were empty, officious hands from within replenished them with a fresh supply of torn and scribbled paper. The bulls browsed on; it was a literary feast."

Explanations for this peculiar behavior and answers to many other questions about this country are often misleading or beyond my Western-oriented grasp. This gives rise to another truth I've discovered about India. It's a destination where opinions formed in the morning (but don't waste your time) are usually thrown out by nightfall. India is an unending paradox.

India can also be exasperating and exhausting—a difficult place for people accustomed to efficiency and a Western work ethos. To enjoy your visit to India, surrender, take it slow, and don't plan too much in one trip. Prepare to give in to the laissez-faire attitude that seems a natural extension of India's belief in fatalism. Accept that what happens is meant to be or is the will of some supreme authority (frequent Indian responses). If your plane is canceled, the phone doesn't work, or the fax won't go through, don't go into a rage. When the slow-motion pace of workers in a public-sector bank or post office is about to drive you crazy, remember that this lack of value attached to time will have an appealing effect when you travel into rural areas or villages. There, time's insignificance induces a dreamlike state. You can sit for hours and watch the simplest routines: village women drawing water from a well or a man tilling the soil with a crude wooden plow. You can lose yourself in all sorts of thoughts as you walk around a deserted ancient city such as Fatehpur Sikri, or as you watch the Hindu devout in Varanasi go through their purification or cremation rituals. During these moments, and they occur frequently in this country, you will at least understand why the art of meditation evolved here. A lack of obsession with time allows other concerns to take precedence. Arrive with the determination to experience India, and don't make quick assumptions. Otherwise, this country that has a strong love-it-or-hate-it effect on all its visitors could have a negative impact on you.

It helps to be forgiving about elements of India's inefficiency and overstretched infrastructure. When this country gained independence in 1947, the new democracy chose nonalignment, opted for a large nationalized public sector, and instituted government regulations that kept out most foreign products and virtually led to economic isolationism. The first prime minister, Jawaharlal Nehru, believed these policies would make India self-reliant and would ultimately bring about an improved standard of living, especially for the impoverished.

The policies did move India toward self-reliance; but lack of competition stifled India's own development. Its captive market had to accept indigenous products that were often substandard or old-fashioned. Until recently, the dominant car on India's roads was a copy of a British design from the 1940s, the Ambassador, with its curvaceous yet bulky chassis, which symbolized the automobile of 50 years ago—a nostalgic gas-guzzler.

Then in 1991, a severe debt crisis and shortage of foreign exchange forced the government to initiate economic reforms that have been nothing short of astonishing to witness and experience. This country, which studiously fended off foreign companies, is suddenly encouraging them to accept investment opportunities. Even McDonald's could be serving its fare (beefless) in Delhi and Bombay in 1996.

India's stirring has profound implications that already affect her once-rigid lifestyle. While many Indian women continue to wear their exquisite saris, some now rush off to their corporate jobs dressed in the latest Western designs (a rare sight just a few years ago). Many men have become label-conscious as well—on everything from the shirts they wear to the foreign liquor they drink. An increasing number of individuals who work in the private sector complain about a new problem: business-related stress.

Children dress in clothes from the local Benetton. Teenagers listen to the *Billboard* top-10 Western hits on recently privatized FM stations. Coca-Cola and Pepsi are staging a war on new turf. Sanyo. Panasonic. Ford. Ray-Bans. Even Barbizon has arrived to teach models how to saunter down the catwalk and executives how to master foreign etiquette so as to seal the deal with a partner who was so recently kept out of this land.

Cable TV is also changing India. British, American, French, Pakistani, and Chinese commentators relay their own view of the news on satellite channels. Oprah Winfrey and Phil Donahue expose America's lifestyles to wide-eyed viewers. Reruns of *Dynasty* and *The Bold and the Beautiful* show steamy romances to a people whose Bollywood movies made in Bombay were not even permitted to show a kiss until a few years back.

If you've never been to India before, remember this Westernization is recent; when you're frustrated, understand that everyone from villagers to wealthy urbanites is equally annoyed by lousy services and impatient for a quality infrastructure that most Americans and other Westerners take for granted. But while frustration exists, so does a sense of concern. Many Indians lament the arrival of the foreign competitor to solve their problems. They worry about the increasing disparity between the haves and have-nots as a result of reforms that have pushed up inflation. They wonder whether the benefits will really trickle down to the masses. Others wonder if India will succumb to an economic form of colonization that will rob them of their identity.

All these questions add a thought-provoking dimension to any trip to India. You are visiting a country in profound transition. Today's India is now more than its thousands of monuments; more than the home of 400 tribes; more than the land of festivals and fairs; more than the birthplace of Hinduism, Buddhism, Jainism, and Sikhism. India is taking its first steps toward becoming an economic giant. With a population of over 912,000,000 people in 1995, it is a country that can't be ignored.

—*Kathleen Cox*

WHAT'S WHERE

India, which is in the Northern Hemisphere, is the world's seventh-largest country, with a total land area of 3,287,000 square kilometers (1,261,000 square miles) and a coastline 6,100 kilometers (3,535 miles) long. In the north, the Himalayas separate India from Nepal and China. To the east is Bhutan, which is still closely connected to India by a special treaty. More mountains separate India from Myanmar (Burma) on the eastern border. Also to the east lies Bangladesh, wedged between the Indian states of Assam, Meghalaya, Tripura, and West Bengal. In the northwest, Pakistan borders India. Just off the southeastern tip of the subcontinent lies the independent nation of Sri Lanka, separated from the mainland by 50 kilometers (31 miles) of water, the Palk Straits. Conversely, the Lakshadweep Islands in the Arabian Sea and the Andaman and Nicobar islands in the Bay of Bengal, much farther away, are part of the Indian Union.

The Himalayas (*hima* meaning snow; *laya*, abode), the wall of mountains that sweeps 3,200 kilometers (1,984 miles) across north India, are divided into distinct ranges. Among them to the north are the Greater Himalayas, or Trans-Himalayas, a crescendo of peaks (many above 20,000 feet) that includes some of the world's highest massifs. In Ladakh, the lunar-landscape Karakorams merge into the northwestern edge of the Greater Himalayas. In these two ranges massive glaciers cling to towering peaks; rivers, chilled with melting snow and ice, rage through deep gorges; wild blue sheep still traverse craggy cliffs.

Below the Himalayas is the densely populated Indo-Gangetic Plain. Mountains and hills separate numerous plateaus, and the basins of the Ganges and Brahmaputra rivers make the land rich and productive. This is particularly true in the Punjab, India's greenbelt. The enormous plain also includes the Thar Desert, which extends across the western half of Rajasthan (southwest of Delhi). Most of its terrain, except when the vegetation from irrigated fields is lush after the monsoon, is marked by scrub, cactus, and low rocky hills. The desert's vibrancy emerges in the rich culture of its inhabitants, many of whom still travel by camel, and in the brilliant colors of its sari-clad women. The unusual Rann of Kutch, a wide salt flat, is in the state of Gujarat, southwest of Rajasthan. Just a few feet above sea level, this strange land mass, which floods during the monsoon, is home to former nomads dependent on camels and a meager income from their exquisite handicrafts.

More mountains cut through India's peninsula and follow its contour. The Eastern Ghats mark off a broad coastal strip next to the Bay of Bengal. On the opposite side of the peninsula, the Western Ghats define a narrower coast off the Arabian Sea. These two low ranges merge near the southern tip of India in the Nilgiri Hills. In the more remote areas of these ghats and plateaus, such as in the states of Madhya Pradesh and Orissa, numerous tribes continue to share forested land with wild animals.

India's south is tropical, with paddy fields, coffee plantations, and forests that shade spice crops. The southwestern state of Kerala and part of neighboring Karnataka also have exquisite waterways that thread inland from the Arabian Sea through a natural network of canals connecting palm-fringed fishing villages.

Agra, Khajuraho, Varanasi

Agra and Varanasi are in southern Uttar Pradesh, and Khajuraho is in northern Madhya Pradesh. These destinations, which form a triangle southeast of Delhi, provide tremendous insight into India's spirituality and offer a glimpse of the country's stellar monuments. **Agra,** dusty and crowded, offers the glorious Taj Mahal and exquisite, jewel-like smaller tombs. Southeast of Agra, in the sleepy village of **Khajuraho,** some of India's finest Hindu temples celebrate an ancient vision of earthly life and the glories of the hereafter. Crowds of Hindus descend on the holy city of **Varanasi,** northeast of Khajuraho, to purify themselves in the sacred River Ganga (Ganges).

Bombay

Bombay, the capital of Maharashtra, facing the Arabian sea, is also known as Bollywood because it outranks Hollywood as the world's largest producer of films. Bombay is urbane, jazzy, and as hip as India can get. But beneath its Westernizing exterior, Indian preferences still reign. Sheiks mingle with members of the Western and Indian business community in swank hotel lobbies or classy restaurants, while next door you'll see slums.

Bhubaneswar

The capital of the eastern state of Orissa, Bhubaneswar is an easygoing temple city with 500 ancient shrines—many off-limits to non-Hindus. Tiny and reasonably peaceful, Bhubaneswar is also a town of artisans. On palm-sheltered side streets sculptors chisel beautiful statues from stone, weavers create gorgeous silk or cotton hand-loomed fabrics, and painters create *patta-chitra* (finely wrought temple paintings) and *talapatra* (palm-leaf art).

Calcutta

The city is a dynamo—exhausting and exhaustive, and essential if you want to claim that you've experienced India. It's India's best city for walkers, with streets that tell stories: Old mansions, dripping with moss and spotted with mildew, remind us of its affluent history tied to cultures and people—Armenians, Bengalis, the British, and Marwari merchants from Rajasthan; vast bazaars reveal clues to today's Bengali culture; and the pavement dwellers show the daily rhythm and rigors of their own difficult lives. Calcutta's resilience may yet surprise the world and make it one of India's most productive centers.

Delhi

India's capital city is huge. In it, a succession of capitals, built in different locations over the centuries, have left behind hundreds of monuments that reflect diverse influences: from Hinduism to Islam to British-turned-secular independent India. Divide Delhi into manageable sections, then go out and explore. If you want the hurly-burly of crowds, get lost in Old Delhi's Chandni Chowk; for the feel of Old Delhi without the masses, head to the infrequently visited Nizamudin and see Hazrat Nizamudin Aulia, a Sufi tomb in an old-style Muslim district. Go shopping: Delhi is one big emporium offering all of India's handicrafts and art forms. Enjoy great meals—the capital has restaurants that offer Indian and non-Indian cuisines. And save time each day to unwind in a tranquil park such as Lodi Gardens, with its historic tombs.

Karnataka

The capital of the southwestern state of Karnataka is tropical-looking Bangalore, surrounded by India's Silicon Valley. Outside Bangalore, once a favorite British city, green dominates, and village life transports you to an earlier time. Mysore, once the capital of a Hindu dynasty, is a city of palaces; the former maharaja's palace is an architectural tour de force. Near Mysore are Belur and Halebid villages, with their meticulously wrought 12th-century temples. Karnataka also has one of India's most enjoyable game parks, the Nagarhole Wildlife Sanctuary (*see* Chapter 2, Special-Interest Travel in India).

Kerala

The best way to explore this southern state is slowly, from the deck of an indigenous boat as it moves through picturesque backwater canals past palm-shrouded fishing villages. Cochin, the state's port city, is congested, but its historic district sells good curios. Kerala's excellent game park, Lake Periyar (*see* Chapter 2, Special-Interest Travel in India), is best visited by boat to sight wildlife, especially elephants. Finally, you can enjoy a secluded beach resort set in a cove on the Arabian Sea near Kovalam (*see* Chapter 2, Special-Interest Travel in India), a few kilometers south of the small capital of Trivandrum.

Rajasthan

In spirit, the great cities of Rajasthan—Jaipur, Jodhpur, Jaisalmer, and Udaipur—are the legendary land of the Rajput (martial warrior). Forts and palaces (many of them delightful hotels), lakes and gardens, even the wildlife sanctuaries that were once the exclusive hunting grounds of royalty (*see* Chapter 2, Special-Interest Travel in India), are steeped in romance and chivalry.

Tamil Nadu

Madras, the capital of Tamil Nadu and the fourth-largest city in India, sits on the Bay of Bengal. At two famous temple cities—Tiruchirapalli and Madurai—the devout crowd into the enormous shrines, and you experience Hindu temple life, dominated by fascinating rituals. You can also relax at beach resorts south of Madras in Mamallapuram, with its historic cave carvings and a shore temple.

POSITIVE TOURISM

India has numerous distinct cultures and religions and an intense regional pride. Come prepared to respect mores that are often quite different from your own. Because India is essentially conservative, try to follow the advice about appropriate attire (*see* Clothing *in* What to Pack *in* the Gold Guide).

Begging

There's no denying the presence of beggars in India. Unfortunately for the traveler with a pocketful of rupees, it's hard to resist a plea, especially from a child. Travelers are encouraged to visit a local school or medical clinic and make a contribution through a responsible adult.

Environmental Respect

Do not litter India's environment with plastic (bottles or polyethylene bags) or other nonbiodegradable refuse. Try to take back to your own country whatever nonbiodegradable items you bring into India. Trekkers should also pack out their nonbiodegradable garbage and bury biodegradable refuse away from water sources. Use a trekking agency that carries kerosene for cooking.

Illegal Substances

Marijuana, hashish, heroin, and other recreational drugs are illegal in India.

PLEASURES & PASTIMES

Beaches

Good beach resorts are attracting new visitors to India's western coastline; foreigners are also "discovering" the Andaman Islands in the Andaman Sea and the Lakshadweep Islands in the Arabian Sea, with coral reefs that are ideal for snorkeling (*see* Beaches *in* Chapter 2, Special-Interest Travel in India).

Dining

Indian dishes, which vary from region to region, are elevated to high art. Meat, seafood, vegetables, lentils, and grains proliferate in splendid combinations—subtle and enticing. The word curry is a British corruption of the Hindi word *kari,* the aromatic leaf of the kari plant; typical "curries" are dishes with *masala* (a spicy gravy). Over the centuries, each invading force introduced new cooking techniques, new products, and new dishes that continue to appear on the restaurant table. The Mughals (Moguls), above all, did much to revolutionize Indian cooking, especially in the north, introducing *biriyanis, kormas, kebabs, kofta, dum pukht* dishes, and the tandoori method of food preparation. (*See* the Dining Glossary *in* Chapter 13, Portraits, for definitions.) The British introduced simple puddings and custards. The Tibetans who emigrated to India brought *momo* (steamed dumplings), *kothay* (fried dumplings), and hearty noodle soups called *thukpa.* In the northeast, the Bengalis and Assamese took advantage of the nearby waters and created dishes with an emphasis on fish. Gujaratis, Rajasthanis, and Hindus from the south, who all tend to shun meat, developed India's vegetarian cuisine.

South Indian coffee has a caramel tang and is inexpensive. In much of India, however, expect instant coffee. Tea is excellent; it is frequently brewed Indian-style with milk and sugar. In Buddhist areas, you find butter tea; the salty flavor helps ward off dehydration, and the butter keeps your lips from cracking. India produces excellent beer, and its Riviera brand wine is reasonably good. Luxury hotels also import spirits that are available at luxury prices. Sikkim manufactures good rum, brandies, and *paan* liqueur. *Chang* (local wine), made from distilled barley or rice, is available in many mountain destinations. Goa has tasty sweet wines and *feni* (a potent liquor made from cashew nuts).

Local restaurants offer great meals at bargain rates in an Indian or a lingering British-Raj setting that makes you feel far from home. Street stalls, cooking up simple specialties, can satisfy an eating urge at almost no cost. In many cities, eating out at a locally favorite restaurant can be a special culinary adventure. Don't be afraid to ask your hotel for the name of a popular restaurant that draws a crowd. At all times, however, do pay attention to food precautions (*see* Staying Healthy *in* the Gold Guide).

For food terms, *see* the Dining Glossary *in* Chapter 13, Portraits.

Performing Arts

DANCE➤ India's folk dances derive from various sources, but the origin of its classical dances is the temple. The four main dance forms are Bharata Natyam in the south, particularly in Tamil Nadu; Kathakali in Kerala; Manipur in the northeast; and Kothak in the north.

Bharata Natyam is a dynamic, precise dance style. The dancer wears anklets of bells that emphasize the rhythm. In many south Indian temples, one can see Bharata Natyam dance poses in sculpture. **Kathakali,** developed during the 16th and 17th centuries, was inspired by the heroic myths and legends of Hindu religious writings and involves phenomenal body control right

down to synchronized movements of the eyeballs. Boys ages 12 to 20 are trained for six years in this dance form. Kathakali makeup is an elaborate process, with characters classified into distinct types according to the color of their makeup and costumes. **Manipur** dances are vigorous when performed by men and lyrical when performed by young women. They revolve around episodes in the life of Vishnu. The women's costumes are picturesque and richly embroidered. **Kathak** is exciting and entertaining—the most secular of all the classical dance forms. The footwork is fast, clever, expressive, and accentuated by bands of bells worn around the dancers' ankles. The great masters of all these dance forms are accorded great respect in India. They have studied for years to perfect their artistry, and age is a factor only when the dancer decides to put away his or her costumes.

Buddhist dances are as stylized as classical Hindu dance forms, except that the movements of the costumed and masked monks are more ritualized and usually work from a slow pace up to a whirl in which the flowing skirts of costumes become a blur of color. The accompanying music, usually dominated by long horns and cymbals, adds an eerie counterpoint to the deliberate footwork of the monks. The dances are also usually enactments of important Buddhist legends or are performed to ward off demons.

MUSIC➤ As with classical dance, the beginnings of classical Indian music can be traced to the Hindu Vedas (sacred writings). Over time, this music, an adjunct to worship, developed definite laws of theory and practice. It also evolved into two broadly divided forms—Carnatic in south India and Hindustani in the north. North Indian music uses a wide range of beautiful instruments such as the sitar and the flute. In the south, the forms of music are stricter, with little improvisation. In both schools, ragas, based on a twelve-tone system unusual, at first, to the Western ear, became the form of musical expression. At a concert of **ragas** or **bhajans** (Hindu devotional songs with lyrics), the audience will participate with comments or gestures, expressing enthusiasm over the skill of tonal expression.

The arrival of the Moguls in the 12th century led to a new form of northern music incorporating the Persian *ghazal* (rhyming couplets expressing love). In the ghazal, however, the object of devotion can be a woman or the divine or even one's state. Part of the joy in hearing ghazals, at least for those who understand Urdu, comes from deciphering oblique references that give layers of meanings to a single line and are attributed to the skill of the poet and even the singer. At a ghazal performance the audience shows its appreciation by mirroring a hand motion of the musician or singer or by speaking out in praise over a turn of phrase.

Years of concentrated study lead to revered status for musicians. The finest performers and singers are well over the age of 30 and frequently in their 60s.

Shopping

Every region specializes in its own products and makes them available at unbeatable prices. Villages still exist where the majority of the residents are weavers, painters, or sculptors. Similar artisan districts remain within the old bazaars of many cities. India holds annual handicraft *melas* (fairs) in popular tourist destinations, where the visitor can shop and watch the artist or weaver at work (*see* Festivals and Seasonal Events, *below*).

India has the world's largest **rug** industry. Tibetan refugees and the Sikkimese make superb carpets with Buddhist themes. Also consider India's dhurries (cotton or wool rugs), with charming folk or tribal motifs. Particularly fine dhurries come from Rajasthan and Madhya Pradesh.

India (especially Delhi, Rajasthan, and Karnataka) has wonderful **silver work,** including old ethnic and tribal jewelry. In many cases the silver is not pure, so ask when you're negotiating the price. **Gold jewelry** is another smart purchase. In many cities (Bombay, Calcutta, Delhi, Jaipur, and Madras) you'll find jewelers who can quickly design to order. The price per gram is determined by the world rate, but the cost for the workmanship is a bargain. **Precious and semiprecious stones,** beautifully cut and highly polished, are another good investment, with great savings. In particular, Jaipur has wonderful gems that can be bought separately or fashioned into exquisite jewelry. Jaipur also sells intricately worked **enamelware,** as does

Madhya Pradesh. In Hyderabad, the center of India's pearl trade, **pearls** of every shape and hue are polished and sold according to quality (sheen, smoothness, and uniformity of roundness).

Beautiful **brass and copper work** are available everywhere, but Tamil Nadu has especially fine sculptures and temple ornaments. Tribal areas in Orissa and Madhya Pradesh specialize in metal **figurines.** Hyderabad and Aurangabad produce jet and silver **bidriware** boxes and bangles. Sculptors chisel **stone** into delightful **statues** in Orissa, Tamil Nadu, and Rajasthan. Artisans in Agra create exquisite **marble inlay** work, carrying on a tradition that began with the Moguls. Jewels are sliced petal thin and embedded in the marble with such precision that the joints are imperceptible even with a magnifying glass.

Wherever you find people living in wooden dwellings, you find **products in teak, ebony, cedar, sandalwood,** or **walnut.** Rajasthan is known for objects covered with enchanting thematic paintings: from doors and furniture to small boxes and figurines. Orissa and Andhra Pradesh create charming painted toys. **Lac** turnery is an Indian art form in which layers of color are added to wood and then polished. The best lac products—bangles, toys, boxes—come from Jaipur and Gujarat. Kashmir specializes in carved walnut items: boxes, tables, gorgeous screens. Kerala and Karnataka are known for finely wrought carvings in sandalwood.

You can watch artists paint intricate Mogul- and Rajput-style **miniatures** or work on cloth to make **batik** wall hangings in Rajasthan. You can see artists create **patachitra** and **tala patra** in Orissa. In every Indian state, weavers work designs into **cotton** or **silk** (sometimes threaded with gold or silver). Indeed, Indian **fabrics** are a fabulous buy. Beautiful brocades and crepe silk come from Varanasi. The finest heavy silks are made in Tamil Nadu's Kanchipuram. Bangalore and Mysore are also important centers for silk weaving. *Himru* (cotton and silk brocade) is woven in Aurangabad. *Jamdani* weaving, a cotton fabric brocaded with cotton and *zari* (silver) thread comes from West Bengal. Orissa is famous for *ikat,* a weave that creates a brushstroke effect to color borders on silk or cotton. Gujarat and Rajasthan create marvelous tie-dyed and embroidered fabrics. To see a good selection of all these products, visit one of the fixed-price, government-run Central Cottage Industries Emporiums in Bangalore, Bombay, Calcutta, Delhi, Hyderabad, or Madras.

Sports and the Outdoors

Luxury hotels have swimming pools, health clubs, and occasionally tennis courts. Most of these facilities, however, are reserved for hotel guests and members. Many cities have golf courses and some allow visitors to use their greens for a fee. In major cities you can check the daily newspaper or with your hotel to see if there's the chance to watch cricket, polo, or horse racing—the country's most popular spectator sports. India also offers a wide range of terrific outdoor adventures (*see* Adventure Travel *in* Chapter 2, Special-Interest Travel in India).

FODOR'S CHOICE

No two people will agree on what makes a perfect vacation, but it's fun and helpful to know what others think. We hope you'll have a chance to experience some of Fodor's Choices yourself while visiting India. For detailed information about each entry, refer to the appropriate chapters within this guidebook.

Adventures

★ **Ice trek through the Zanskar Gorge, Ladakh.** This unforgettable trip takes you through narrow windswept gorges on the frozen Zanskar River, with nights spent in caves and nearby villages. (Chapter 2)

★ **Kanchenjunga trek, Sikkim.** In the spring, this trek takes you from lush jungles with orchids and rhododendrons to vistas of the Himalayas and into the rugged high terrain. (Chapter 2)

★ **Nagarhole Wildlife Sanctuary, Karnataka.** Here you can watch wild elephants roam the Karapur Forest, along with deer, wild dogs, wild bison, and crocodiles. (Chapter 2)

★ **Shimla–Kinnaur–Spiti–Lahaul–Leh–Nubra–Leh by Jeep, Himachal Pradesh.** This Jeep adventure takes you to the best of India's newly opened and, therefore, most culturally pure destinations in the northwestern Himalayas and the Karakorams. (Chapter 2)

Monumental Monuments

★ **Cave temples of Ellora and Ajanta.** These 2,000-year-old monolithic temples were hewn from solid rock faces and decorated with lavishly painted frescoes and statues profusely carved to breathtaking detail. (Chapter 12)

★ **Five Rathas, Mamallapuram, Tamil Nadu.** These freestanding 8th-century chariot temples are among the treasures the Pallava dynasty left in the port city. (Chapter 9)

★ **Pemayangtse Monastery, Sikkim.** A spectacular rhododendron trek leads you to the most important monastery in the region. (Chapter 2)

★ **Sun Temple, Konark.** This 13th-century masterpiece was built in the shape of the sun god's chariot, complete with 24 giant wheels and 7 pulling horses, every surface encrusted with elaborate carvings— some of the finest in India. (Chapter 8)

★ **Taj Mahal, Agra.** At sunrise or sunset, this graceful marble monument to the love of a shah for his wife takes on an especially piercing beauty. (Chapter 6)

★ **Temples, Khajuraho.** These 11th-century temples decorated with erotic sculptures represent central-Indian temple architecture at its best, while the combination of structure and sculpture give them a unique feeling of completeness and exuberance. (Chapter 6)

Nature's Greatest Displays

★ **Coral reefs, Andaman Islands.** The magnificently clean waters of the Andaman Sea reveal colors so varied and vibrant they don't seem possible. (Chapter 2)

★ **Lunar landscape, Ladakh.** The barren moonscape, sparsely littered with carved stones and ghostly *chortens* (memorial stupas or shrines for relics) is profoundly moving. (Chapter 2)

★ **Lush backwater canals, Kerala.** On a cruise through these inland waterways you can see both people and nature. (Chapter 10)

★ **Mt. Kanchenjunga, Sikkim.** At sunrise or sunset, Sikkim's guardian deity, the world's third highest peak, appears most godlike. (Chapter 2)

★ **Wild elephant herds in an approaching storm, Nagarhole Wildlife Sanctuary.** If you're lucky enough to catch a sudden, late-spring storm, you may happen upon large groups of wild elephants, afraid of the thunder(!), huddled nervously at the edge of the forest under a darkening purple sky. (Chapter 2)

Restaurants

★ **Vishalla, Ahmedabad.** Snake charmers, folk musicians, and flickering lantern shadows cast an aura of magic at this famous outdoor restaurant, a recreated Gujarati village, where guests sit on straw mats and feast on superb local fare served on banana leaves. (Chapter 3.) *$$$$*

★ **Bukhara, Delhi.** Among Delhi's most popular restaurants, it serves northwest frontier cuisine (kebabs and marinated leg of lamb) so delicious that the uncomfortable seats are a novel form of crowd management. *$$–$$$*

★ **Fort Cochin, Cochin, Kerala.** In a courtyard furnished with wicker and old lanterns, giving it the feel of a Keralan village, you dine on the day's fresh catch, chosen from a wooden cart wheeled before you. *$$*

★ **Mahesh Lunch Home, Bombay.** It may not appear fancy, but this modest eatery serves some of the freshest, most succulent seafood in Bombay. Locals pack in at lunchtime for hefty portions of steaming tandoori crab or fish. *$*

★ **Pumpernickel Bakery, Mamallapuram, Tamil Nadu (Dec.–Apr.); Leh, Ladakh (May–Oct.).** This small cafe is run by a German expat and serves cheesecake, cappuccino, fresh fruit juices, and hot baked goods. It moves seasonally—employees, blenders, yak cheese, and all. (Chapters 9, 2.) *$*

Inns and Hotels

★ **Taj Mahal Hotel, Bombay.** India's most famous hotel is steeped in the magic of its grand past as the favored haunt of Mark Twain and other luminaries. Its elegant Victorian stone building is a Bombay landmark in its own right. *$$$$*

★ **Welcomgroup Bay Island, Andaman Islands.** Perched on a steep hill, this well-run resort commands lovely views out to sea and a balanced blend of first-rate service and island informality. (Chapter 2.) *$$$$*

★ **Bangaram Island Resort, Bangaram Island, Lakshadweep.** Feel like Robinson Crusoe at this simple resort (the only one on a small atoll) where the world recedes with the aqua tide, and time is marked by swaying palm fronds. (Chapter 2.) *$$$*

★ **Hyatt Regency, Delhi.** This Delhi hotel knows how to appease the harried Western visitor (especially the business client) with its emphasis on an environment that allows you to unwind in excellent workout facilities and a great outdoor pool while also offering efficient service right down to E-mail correspondence. *$$$*

★ **Taj Holiday Village, Goa.** Upscale but informal, this tropical beach resort offers a wealth of facilities and activities, excellent service, and elegantly rustic rooms in tileroof cottages. (Chapter 2.) *$$$*

★ **Surya Samudra, Kovalam, Kerala.** On a lush hillside above two idyllic beaches, you live in traditional Keralan houses designed for beauty and comfort, and you bask in a full range of ayurvedic treatments. (Chapter 2.) *$$–$$$*

Palaces, Forts, and Havelis (Mansions)

★ **Chapslee, Shimla, Himachal Pradesh.** Every object in this private home of a prince is sumptuous and in keeping with the elegant service, which makes this Heritage Inn a splurge worth even the trip to crowded Shimla. (Chapter 2.) *$$$$*

★ **Neemrana Fort Palace, Rajasthan.** When you want a getaway from Delhi, you don't need to stay in the fanciest rooms to fall in love with this carefully renovated fort that has set the standard for India's Heritage Hotels. (Chapter 4.) *$–$$$$*

GREAT ITINERARIES

Classic Subcontinent

This tour is a broader version of the over-done Golden Triangle trip that normally concentrates on **Jaipur, Agra,** and **Delhi.** To have a more comprehensive and meaningful experience in India, we suggest including **Khajuraho** and **Varanasi,** which add a spiritual dimension, and five overnights for relaxation: three nights at architecturally rich yet lesser known destinations; two nights at a game park. Since air travel is unreliable, we organize most of the tour by car with driver, which also allows for impromptu stops along the way.

DURATION➤ 17 days

GETTING AROUND➤ Travel by car and driver from Delhi to Khajuraho, then fly to Varanasi and fly back to Delhi.

THE MAIN ROUTE➤ **Three days: Delhi to Jaipur.** Drive 122 kilometers (76 miles) from Delhi to Rajasthan's Neemrana Fort Palace, located just off the main highway between Delhi and Jaipur. This restored palace, set on a bluff, affords great views and allows for complete relaxation or delightful short walks in the afternoon. The next day, it's about three hours to Jaipur, where you can stay at a choice of converted palaces or Heritage Hotels while you explore Jaipur's old bazaars and city monuments.

Two days: Bharatpur. From Jaipur, head to Bharatpur, 176 kilometers (109 miles) to the northeast and India's most famous bird sanctuary, with more than 300 species in its marshlands and forests.

Three days: Fatehpur Sikri and Agra. Head 30 kilometers (19 miles) from Bharatpur toward Agra and visit the ancient and deserted Mogul capital, Fatehpur Sikri, with its splendid architecture. Then proceed to Agra, where you'll find the world-famous Taj Mahal and other architecturally powerful tombs and a fort.

Two days: Gwalior and Orchha. Drive 118 kilometers (73 miles) to Gwalior, the capital of a former princely state, which has stunning palaces and a fort. Take an optional excursion to Orchha, a 17th-century city of palaces.

Two days: Khajuraho. Drive about 160 kilometers (100 miles) to Khajuraho and spend two days enjoying the wonderful Chandela Dynasty 10th- and 11th-century temples and the surrounding pastoral villages that cling vigorously to an agrarian lifestyle.

Two days: Varanasi. Fly from Khajuraho to Varanasi. Take a peaceful morning cruise on the Ganges River to witness Hindu rituals performed by the devout on the ghats and in the sacred waters. Visit its temples, silk and carpet emporiums, and nearby Sarnath, imbued with Buddhist significance.

Three days: Delhi. Fly to Delhi. Explore the old and new capitals. Don't miss the Red Fort, Jama Masjid, Chandni Chowk, and the Charity Bird Hospital—all in Old Delhi. Enjoy the crafts museum and save time for last minute shopping in Delhi's wonderful shops.

INFORMATION➤ *See* Chapter 6, Agra, Khajuraho, and Varanasi; Chapter 4, Delhi; and Chapter 2, Special-Interest Travel in India.

Southern Idyll

Experience the tropical south in a journey in **Tamil Nadu** that includes historic cities and temple-cities that follow the rhythm of Hindu rituals. Relax at seaside resorts and in indigenous Keralan boats as you cruise through **Kerala**'s lush backwaters. Search for wildlife at the excellent **Lake Periyar** sanctuary. Add one more cultural dimension—a Kathakali dance performance—and some personal indulgence—soothing ayurvedic massages to chase away any stress.

DURATION➤ 13–14 days

GETTING AROUND➤ Hire a car with driver for excursions from Tamil Nadu's Madras, then fly from Madras to Madurai. Hire a car with a driver, proceed to Lake Periyar in Kerala (140 kilometers or 87 miles), on to Cochin (210 kilometers or 130 miles), and then enjoy a boat cruise. Drive on to Kovalam (160 kilometers or 99 miles), ending the tour at nearby Trivandrum.

THE MAIN ROUTE➤ **Four days: Madras and Mamallapuram.** Spend two days in Madras, originally developed by the Portuguese and the British, but now decidedly south Indian with delightful bazaars, colorful Hindu temples, and a thriving film center. Then take a leisurely two-day excursion to Mamallapuram via Kanchipuram, a silk center with excellent bargains and the site of more than 200 temples. At Mamallapuram on the Bay of Bengal, see the exquisite cave sculptures and shore temple left behind by the Pallava Dynasty (6th to 10th centuries). Catch some sun and surf during a two-night stay at a relaxing resort. Return to Madras.

Two days: Madurai. Fly to Madurai and spend two days exploring the temple city and its astonishing Meenakshi Temple with its marvelous architecture that includes towering *gopurams* (gateways) and a prominent display of rituals. Comb through the bazaars tucked around the temple complex and visit silk emporiums.

Two days: Lake Periyar. Drive from Madurai in Tamil Nadu across the Western Ghats to Kerala's Lake Periyar (136 kilometers or 84 miles), where boat rides provide the means for a safari to search for wild elephants and other animals that roam the banks of this lovely preserve.

Two days: Cochin. Proceed northwest by car to Cochin and take two days to see the port city that is admittedly crowded but affords appealing escapes: into its old district with its small synagogue and numerous good curios shops; to a Kathakali performance where you also see how the dancers apply the complicated makeup before they mesmerize you with their talent.

One or two days: Alleppey and Back-water Cruise. In the early morning, drive to Alleppey (64 kilometers or 40 miles) and take a cruise through the backwaters of Kerala past charming villages to Changanacherry village or extend the trip with an overnight backwater cruise. Transfer back to a car and continue to a delightful resort just south of Kovalam (170 kilometers or 105 miles).

Two days: Kovalam Beach. Stay two days at a special beach resort tucked away in a cove on the Arabian Sea. Swim, then plan to recover from your "exercise" with soothing ayurvedic massages. You can also learn yoga and meditation—skills to carry home with you after this tour. Fly out from nearby Trivandrum's airport.

INFORMATION➤ *See* Chapter 10, Kerala; Chapter 9, Tamil Nadu; and Chapter 2, Special-Interest Travel in India.

FESTIVALS AND SEASONAL EVENTS

India, deeply imbued with spirituality, holds religious celebrations year-round, along with numerous fairs and cultural festivals. As the specific dates of many celebrations each year are determined by the lunar calendar, check with the Government of India Tourist Office or your travel agent for details.

Dec.➤ **Rajasthan: The Shekhawati Festival** honors the frescoes on the town's havelis, as well as other local arts, traditional music and dance, and regional cuisine. At **Shilp Darshan Mela** near Udaipur, master craftsmen show how they create award-winning handicrafts, which are also for sale; dancers and musicians perform daily.

Jan.➤ **Countrywide: Republic Day** on the 26th commemorates India's adoption of its constitution with a big parade in Delhi and celebrations elsewhere. **Kerala:** The four-day **Great Elephant March** features caparisoned elephants, snakeboat races, and cultural events staged each day in a different location. **Rajasthan:** The two-day **Camel Festival** in Bikaner celebrates the ship of the desert with parades, races, and dancing. **Makar Sankranti** in Jaipur has inhabitants engaging in kite duels from rooftops. **Tamil Nadu: Pongal**, a

colorful three-day festival at the close of the harvest season gives thanks to the rain god, the sun god, and the cow, with bonfires, bulls and cows adorned with beads and garlands, games, and dancing.

Jan.–Feb.➤ **Calcutta:** During **Gangasagar Mela**, the festival of the Ganges River, pilgrims from all over India celebrate the most important natural element in their mythology—the river, source of life, purifier, destroyer, and nurturer. **Rajasthan: Nagaur** (135 kilometers or 84 miles from Jodhpur) holds an enormous cattle, camel, and horse **fair** with cultural programs and camel races. The five-day **Desert Fair,** Jaisalmer's gala, includes traditional Rajasthani music and dances, a display of handicrafts, camel caravans, camel races, and turban-tying events.

Feb.➤ **Bombay:** During the three-day **Elephanta Festival of Music and Dance,** artists perform nightly on a platform near the caves. **Delhi:** The **Surajkund Crafts Mela** draws crowds to an ethnic-style village near Delhi to watch traditional dances, puppeteers, magicians, and acrobats and shop for the goods of artisans from every state. **Sikkim:** On **Losar,** the Buddhist New Year, costumed lamas (monks) perform dances at monasteries in Sikkim. **Tamil Nadu:** During **Tirumala Nayak,** the temple city of Madurai holds a spectacular procession of decorated floats, which carry

sacred idols, around the temple tanks.

Feb.–Mar.➤ **Countrywide:** On the first night of **Holi,** the festival of spring, Hindu devotees light a bonfire in which a demoness goes up in flames, demonstrating the destruction of evil; on the second day, kids throw colored water on each other and you. On **Id-ul-Fitr,** the Muslim holiday that concludes Ramadan, a monthlong period of daytime fasting to commemorate the descent of the Quran from heaven, the devout give alms to the poor, offer prayers, and feast and rejoice. The **Kumbh Mela,** India's largest religious festival, a celebration of immortality, is held once every three years in one of these four sacred cities: Allahabad, Haridwar, Nasik, or Ujjain. The next Khumb Mela is at Haridwar in 1998. **Madhya Pradesh:** The three-day **Orchha Festival** has cultural shows and a handicraft fair. **Uttar Pradesh:** The two-week **Taj Mahotsav** handicraft and cultural mela in Agra focuses on traditional heritage.

Mar.➤ **Ellora:** India's best performers entertain under the moonlight, with the historic Kailasa Temple as a backdrop, during the three-day **Ellora Festival of Classical Music and Dance.** **Khajuraho:** The

Khajuraho Dance Festival presents classical Indian dance performed by India's best dancers on an outdoor stage with the temples in the background. The **Lok Ranjan Festival** offers nightly performances of tribal and folk dances as well as regional music. **Rajasthan:** Pachyderms have their day in Jaipur when the **Elephant Festival** sets off processions, races, and even elephant polo.

MAR.–APR.➤ Goa: **Carnival,** the Mardi Gras held three days before Lent, is a big party with masked dancers, floats, and good eating. **Rajasthan:** The **Gangaur Festival** in Jaipur and Udaipur honors the goddess Parvati with processions of young girls and images of the goddess and, in Udaipur, fireworks, dancing, and a boat procession.

APR.➤ Bhubaneswar: Honoring Lord Jagannath, the 21-day **Chandan Yatra** features processions with devotees who carry images of deities to sacred tanks where they're rowed around in decorated boats.

APR.–MAY➤ Kerala: At **Puram,** a major temple festival in Trichur, elephants sporting gorgeous gold-plated mail carry Brahmins with ceremonial umbrellas and the temple deity, Vadakkunathan (Shiva), in a procession to the beat of temple drums. **Tamil Nadu:** The spectacular 10-day **Chitra Festival** celebrates the marriage of goddess Meenakshi to Lord Shiva at Madurai's Meenakshi Temple.

MAY➤ Countrywide: Buddhists celebrate **Buddha Jayanti**—the birthday

of Sakyamunni (Historic Buddha), his enlightenment, and death—with rituals and chanting at monasteries. Special celebrations are held in Sikkim and major Buddhist pilgrimage centers, such as Sarnath near Varanasi and Bodhgaya in Bihar. On **Muharram,** Shiite Muslims commemorate the martyrdom of the Prophet Mohammed's grandson Hussain, who died at the battle of Karbala; participants' intense self-flagellation may discourage the squeamish. On **Bakrid** or **Id-ul-Zuha,** celebrating the sacrifice of Harrat Ibrahim, who willingly killed his son at the behest of God, Muslims solemnly sacrifice one animal per family or group of families and conclude with a feast and joyous celebration.

SUMMER

JUNE–JULY➤ Bhubaneswar: Puri's seven-day **Rath Yatra,** honoring Lord Krishna, is Orissa's most sacred festival and draws big crowds. **Ladakh:** The two-day **Hemis Festival** at the state's largest monastery commemorates the birthday of Guru Padmasambhava with masked lamas performing ritual *chaams* (dances) and haunting music.

JULY–AUG.➤ Rajasthan: In Jaipur, women and girls observe **Teej,** celebrating the arrival of the monsoon, dedicating the festivities to the goddess Parvati.

AUG.➤ Countrywide: **Independence Day,** on the 15th, commemorates the country's independence from British rule in 1947.

AUG.–SEPT.➤ Bombay: **Ganesha Chaturthi,** a 10-day festival, celebrated in nearby Puna as well, marks the birthday of the Hindus' elephant-headed god; clay images of Ganesh are paraded through streets, installed on platforms, and worshipped. **Kerala: Onam** celebrates the harvest season with dancing, singing, and exotic snakeboat races in Alleppey, Aranmula, and Kottayam. **Sikkim: Pang Lhabsol** offers thanks to Mt. Kanchenjunga, Sikkim's guardian deity, and honors Yabdu, the great warrior who protects the mountain.

AUTUMN

SEPT.–OCT.➤ Countrywide: For **Dussehra** or **Durga Puja,** a 10-day festival honoring the Hindu goddesses Durga, Lakshmi, and Saraswati, Calcutta turns into one giant festival. Mysore holds concerts and cultural events in Durbar Hall, and the palace's treasures and the maharaja himself come out in full regalia for the traditional procession.

OCT.➤ Delhi: On the 2nd, **Gandhi Jayanti,** Mahatma Gandhi's birthday, pilgrims visit the Raj Ghat, where Gandhi was cremated. **Rajasthan:** The **Marwar Festival** in Jaipur brings to life myth and folklore in Marwari culture, music, and dance.

OCT.–NOV.➤ **Country-wide: Diwali/Deepavali,** the most important Hindu festival in India, celebrates the day the Hindu God Rama (Vishnu) ended a 14-year exile, as well as the start of the New Year; Hindus worship Lakshmi, the goddess of prosperity; oil lamps flicker in most homes symbolizing the victory of truth (light) over ignorance (darkness); cities crackle with the explosion of fireworks; and Bengalis worship Kali (the black goddess of destruction).

NOV.➤ **Orissa:** During the five-day **Konark Dance Festival,** you can watch Odissi (classical Orissan dances) performed at the Sun Temple and attend a crafts fair. **Rajasthan:** At the **Pushkar Festival** in a small village near Ajmer, nomads assemble with their camels and gaily festooned cattle in a carnival atmosphere.

NOV.–DEC.➤ **Goa: International Seafood Festival** at Miramar Beach near Panaji offers three to five days of good eating; music; and Indian, Western, and local folk dances.

2 Special-Interest Travel in India

*India's antiquity and diversity make it
a great destination for an adventure or
culture-oriented experience that can
stir your body and your soul.*

By Kathleen
Cox

INDIA'S ANTIQUITY AND DIVERSITY make it a great destination for an adventure or culture-oriented experience that can stir your body and your soul. You can plan a trip around India's art and archaeology, her festivals, or some of her 400 tribes. You can concentrate on villages where artisans create handicrafts or weave traditional designs in cotton or silk. You can go on a photo or culinary tour.

Join a research expedition and help scholars, or enroll in a scholastic program and study in the field. You can practice yoga with well-known gurus or discover the spiritual side of India by embarking on a pilgrimage or staying at a Hindu ashram or Buddhist retreat. You can even become a volunteer and experience India by doing some good while having fun.

You can move slowly on an elephant through India's sanctuaries and search for wildlife. Go on a camel or horse safari. You can travel by jeep into the Himalayas. Put on hiking boots and trek through parts of southern India or in much of the north. Scale a mountain, ski, join a bike trip, raft on rivers. Surf along India's coastline or snorkel in coral reefs near exquisite islands. Cruise in an indigenous fishing craft down the Ganga (Ganges) River or through the backwaters of Kerala. Or just pamper yourself on beaches backed by palm trees or coconut groves.

Whatever your interest, you can contact the recommended tour operators for details (*see* Tour Operators, *below* and under each special-interest category). Many of them can design a special trip just for you, whatever your budget or age, and age is usually no barrier. For most trips, you should make arrangements at least two months in advance.

Tour Operators

United States

Above the Clouds Trekking (Box 398, Worcester, MA 01602, ☎ 508/799–4499 or 800/233–4499) offers excellent treks in Ladakh and unique treks in Sikkim. For a no-frills adventure in India with an international mix of independent-minded travelers, contact **Adventure Center** (1311-ST 63rd St., Suite 200, Emeryville, CA 94608, ☎ 510/654–1879 or 800/227–8747). **All Adventure Travel** (5589 Arapahoe No. 208, Boulder, CO 80303, ☎ 800/537–4025), which represents more than 80 tour operators, can satisfy virtually any special interest in India. **American Museum of Natural History** (Central Park W at 79th St., New York, NY 10024–5192, ☎ 212/769–5700 or 800/462–8687) offers tours to Ellora and Ajanta, the new Royal Orient Express train journey, and visits to Agra, Khajuraho, and Varanasi in its Discovery Tours program. To sample the best of Indian cooking, try a tour from the **Annemarie Victory Organization** (136 E. 64th St., New York, NY 10021, ☎ 212/486–0353). **Archaeological Tours** (271 Madison Ave., Suite 904, New York, NY 10016, ☎ 212/986–3054) sponsors excellent scholar-led tours, with a special emphasis on archaeology and history. **Asian Pacific Adventures** (826 S. Sierra Bonita Ave., Los Angeles, CA 90036, ☎ 213/935–3156 or 800/825–1680) runs a complete program of special-interest tours; topics range from folk-art festivals to trekking to solar eclipses. A **Culinary Tour of India with Julie Sahani** (101 Clark St., Brooklyn, NY 11201, ☎ 718/625–3958), led by an Indian cookbook author, hits tourist centers while exploring where spices are grown and the cuisines of different regions. **Distant Horizons** (619 Tremont St., Boston, MA 02118, ☎ 617/267–5343 or 800/333–1240) conducts cultural tours led by Asian scholars. To stay in some of India's royal residences, contact **EastQuest** (1 Union Sq. W, Suite 606, New York, NY 10003, ☎ 212/741–1688 or 800/638–3449), which custom designs exotic itineraries for independent travelers. You can ride horseback from palace to palace in Rajasthan with **Equitour** (Box 807, Dubois, WY 82513, ☎ 800/545–0019). **Himalayan Travel** (112 Prospect St., Stamford, CT 06901, ☎ 203/359–3711 or 800/225–2380) arranges both independent and escorted general and adventure tours throughout India. **Himalayan Trekking and Wilderness Expeditions** (1900 8th St., Berkeley, CA 94710, ☎ 510/540–8040 or 800/777–8735) offers trips in many parts of India, from Goa, Khajuraho, Agra, to Ladakh, Manali Sikkim, and Himachal Pradesh. **InnerAsia** (2627 Lombard St., San Francisco, CA 94123, ☎ 415/922–0448 or 800/777–8183) sponsors cultural trips in southern India, treks in Himachal Pradesh and Ladakh, a Rajasthan camel safari, a kayaking adventure around the Andaman Islands, and a wildlife-emphasis tour. **International Expeditions** (1 Environs Park, Helena, AL 35080, ☎ 205/428–1700 or 800/633–4734), which organizes trips for leading zoological societies, offers natural history trips to major Indian sanctuaries. **Mountain Travel-Sobek** (6420 Fairmount Ave., El Cerrito, CA 94530, ☎ 510/527–8100 or 800/227–2384), a pioneer in outdoor adventure, offers a cultural tour and moderately easy trek in Ladakh that concentrates on monastery visits, and a cross-cultural exchange program in Ladakh. **Overseas Adventure Travel** (625 Mount Auburn St., Cambridge, MA 02138, ☎ 617/876–0533 or 800/221–0814) conducts a 13-day cultural tour to Varanasi, Khajuraho, Orchha, and Agra. **Photo Adventure Tours** (2035 Park St., Atlantic Beach, NY 11509, ☎ 516/371–0067 or 800/821–1221) conducts tours for photographers in the Himalayas, southern India, Rajasthan, Gujarat, and the Andaman Islands. Access Adventure Tours, its subsidiary at the same address, offers treks and trips throughout India. **Safaricentre International** (3201 N. Sepulveda Blvd., Manhattan Beach, CA 90266, ☎ 310/546–4411 or 800/233–6046) is a leader in adventure travel. **Snow Lion Expeditions** (Oquirrh Pl., 350 S. 400 East, Suite G-2, Salt Lake City, UT 84111, ☎ 801/355–6555 or 800/525–8735) offers mountain expeditions, treks, and/or vehicular journeys in Ladakh, Himachal Pradesh, northern Uttar Pradesh, and Sikkim. **Wilderness Travel** (801 Allston Way, Berkeley, CA 94710, ☎ 510/548–0420 or 800/368–2794) sponsors treks, camel safaris, and wildlife safaris. **Wildland Adventures** (3516 N.E. 155th St., Seattle, WA 98155, ☎ 206/365–0686 or 800/345–4453) conducts treks and/or vehicular tours in Sikkim, Himachal Pradesh, and Ladakh, plus safaris in wildlife sanctuaries.

Great Britain

Exodus Adventure (9 Weir Rd., London SW12 0LT, ☎ 0181/675–5550) offers vehicular trips to Ladakh, Himachal Pradesh, West Bengal, Sikkim, Assam, Orissa, Rajasthan, and the south, including a mini-coach visit to the entire southern half of India, plus treks in Sikkim. **Pettitts India** (14 Lonsdale Gardens, Tunbridge Wells, Kent, TN1 1NU, ☎ 01892/515966) concentrates on personalized trips for individuals, couples, or families. It can arrange traditional rice barge trips in Kerala, tribal or handicraft tours, wildlife safaris, and treks. **Trans Indus** (Northumberland House, Popes Lane, Ealing, London W5 4NG, ☎ 0181/566–2729) offers comprehensive tours of southern India, some timed with festivals; numerous trips to Rajasthan; special interest tours that concentrate on history or wildlife; beach holidays; pilgrimages to sacred destinations; tours in India's luxury trains; and camel safaris in the Thar Desert.

India

Discover Tours (463 Lewis Rd., Bhubaneswar, Orissa, ☎ 674/57377) offers textile and tribal tours to villages in Orissa. **Distant Frontiers** (U-9 Green Park Extension, New Delhi 110016, India, ☎ 11/6858857 or 11/685072, FAX 11/6875553) creates customized trips that focus on museums, regional cuisines, photography, crafts, and textiles. **EMPL Tours** (282 Sant Nagar, New Delhi 110065, ☎ 11/642–8310, FAX 11/642–8311 or 11/644–7982) offers bicycling in Karnataka, Kerala, and Tamil Nadu; wildlife trips in sanctuaries; camel safaris in Rajasthan; boat cruises on the Ganga (Ganges); Jeep trips to Spiti and Ladakh; and trekking in Ladakh. **Exotic Journeys** (26 Sector 2 Market, R. K. Puram, New Delhi 110022, ☎ 11/670221 or 11/6875320, FAX 11/676377) offers village stays, photo safaris, and novel in-depth regional visits by Jeep that include a guide and camping (equipment provided) or stays in hotels, inns, or palaces. **Himalayan Adventurers** (Opposite Tourist Information Center, The Mall, Manali 175131, Himachal Pradesh, ☎ 1901/2182 or 3050, FAX 1901/2182, or C-489, Sheikh Sarai, Phase-1, New Delhi 110017, ☎ and fax 11/6421358) offers great treks in Himachal Pradesh, Ladakh, and northern Uttar Pradesh, as well as winter treks, mountain expeditions, and Jeep safaris. **Himalayan River Runners** (F-5 Hauz Khas Enclave, 1st Floor, New Delhi 110016, ☎ 11/685–2602, FAX 11/463–1747) is the best rafting company in India, with imported equipment and professional crews. It sponsors fixed departure trips or customized runs, plus a kayaking and rafting training camp at Rishikesh in Uttar Pradesh (February–April and September–November). **Ibex Expeditions** (G-66, east of Kailash, New Delhi 110065, ☎ 11/691–2641 and 11/682–8479, FAX 11/684–6403) offers mountaineering and trekking holidays in Himachal Pradesh, Ladakh, Uttar Pradesh, and Sikkim; wildlife tours in most important parks; camel and horse safaris in Rajasthan; elephant safaris in Kerala and Uttar Pradesh; mountain biking; angling tours; Jeep and camel safaris; and golf tours. **Paddy's Treks** (Box 32, Manali 175131, Himachal Pradesh, ☎ 1901/2490; or U-9, Green Park Extension, New Delhi 110016, ☎ 11/685–5072 or 685–8857, FAX 11/687–5553) organizes treks in Himachal Pradesh, the Garhwals in Uttar Pradesh, and Sikkim; as well as walking holidays in Himachal Pradesh and the Nilgiris in South India; fishing trips; bird-watching tours; and expeditions for photographers and artists. **Swosti Travels** (103 Janpath, Bhubaneswar, Orissa, ☎ 674/407470, 674/408738, FAX 674/407524) offers a cultural and wildlife tour to Orissan artisan villages and sanctuaries, plus tribal tours.

Research Programs

Center for Himalayan Research and Studies (CHRS, 14600 S.E. Aldridge Rd., Portland OR 97236-6518, ☎ 800/225–4666 or 503/658–6600) is a nonprofit organization that creates minicourses in the Himalayas and other areas of India for participants at least 20 years old and physically fit, as well as Elderfolk programs for individuals at least 55 years old. Courses focus on themes such as traditional culture, history, religion, arts and crafts, women in society, and health care. Programs include on-site visits, trekking, and wildlife safaris (*see* Students *in* the Gold Guide). **Earthwatch** (Box 403, 680 Mt. Auburn St., Watertown, MA 02272, ☎ 800/776–0188 or 617/926–8200), **Foundation for Field Research** (Box 2010, Alpine, CA 91903, ☎ 619/450–3460), and **University Research Expedition Programs** (University of California, Berkeley, CA 94720-7050, ☎ 510/642–6586) occasionally sponsor trips to India in which participants work with researchers on a specific project.

Spiritual Journeys

Footsteps of the Buddha (c/o Aura Wright, Holistic Resources Foundation, Suite 207, 3439 N.E. Sandy Blvd., Portland, OR 97232, ☎ 503/335–0794; in U.K., c/o Vivien Bell, 22 Bourne Way, Midhurst, West Sussex, GU 29 9HZ, ☎ 730/812362; in India, c/o Shantum Seth, 309-B, Sector 15A, Noida, near Delhi, 201301, ☎ or FAX 11/892–1520) offers two- and three-week programs that include primary Buddhist sites in India and Nepal guided by a respected Buddhist scholar. **Great India Tour Company** (*see* Tour Operators, *above*) offers a 10-day ayurvedic package in Kerala, specially designed for each participant by a physician and including specific herbal massages, yoga, and meditation. **Insight Travel** (602 S. High St., Yellow Springs, OH 45387, ☎ 800/688–9851 or 513/767–1102) offers pilgrimages to India that include visits with Buddhist and/or Hindu scholars, meditation, and group discussions. Alternative life-style magazines, such as *East West* or the *Yoga Journal,* list overseas offices for Hindu and Buddhist sects with an international following. Contact them for details about programs in India that are open to foreigners. Most Hindu ashrams and Buddhist retreats are extremely inexpensive; expect rigid schedules and rules that must be followed if you choose to participate in their programs. Lodging in most ashrams, in particular, is modest and at times spartan; food is typically vegetarian but nutritious. Many facilities also expect their visitors to abstain from smoking, alcohol, and sex. Check the rules before you sign up. Contact the facility that interests you months in advance. Most are open year round.

Volunteer Vacations

Habitat for Humanity International (121 Habitat St., Americus, GA 31709-3498, ☎ 912/924-6935) sponsors home-construction projects in Kerala, Karnataka, Maharashtra, Haryana, Andhra Pradesh, and Tamil Nadu. **Indian Volunteers for Community Service** (12 Eastleigh Ave., Harrow, HA2 OUF, U.K., ☎ 081/864–4740) oversees volunteer projects in different parts of India that are open to individuals over 18.

ADVENTURE TRAVEL

Contact a tour operator who is familiar with the area in which you want to trek. Play safe: don't set out on any route without a guide. Travelers in high-altitude areas should heed warnings about the sun and high-altitude sickness (*see* Health Concerns *in* the Gold Guide). Even if you're in a Jeep, bring high-altitude pills, powerful UVA/UVB sunblock, a wide-brimmed hat, and sunglasses that block ultraviolet rays. Also plan to acclimatize yourself the first three days. In remote areas, bring water purification tablets, a quart-size canteen, and energy-producing snacks.

Inner Line Permit. At press time (summer 1995), foreigners must obtain an Inner Line Permit and travel with at least four persons and a government-recognized tour operator in order to visit the following areas: Spiti and Kinnaur in Himachal Pradesh; and Pangong Tso, Tso Moriri, Nubra Valley, and the Drogpa villages in Ladakh. You also need to be in a recognized group for trekking in Sikkim (*see below*). Most tour operators can help you secure the permit (*see* Tour Operators, *above,* and Tour Operators listed under these destinations, *below*).

Himachal Pradesh

Place five mountain ranges across the northwestern state of Himachal Pradesh like fingers on an open hand: the Siwalik, Dhauladhar, Pir Panjal, Great Himalayas, and Zanskar; thread them with rivers; dot them with lakes. This is Himachal Pradesh—about the size of Indiana. Except for the capital, Shimla, and the overpopulated destinations of Dharamsala in the district of Kangra and Manali in the district of Kulu, Himachal is a state of villages.

It's also home to diverse cultures, including two distinct seminomadic tribes, the Gaddi and Gujjar, who still follow many of their old traditions. The Gaddi, who travel with sheep, goats, and cattle, are Hindu and believe in evil spirits that are appeased by animal sacrifices and animist rituals. Gaddi men wear a *chola* (a white thigh-length woolen coat) over *sutthan* (tight woolen trousers), held in place by a *dora* (a black rope of sheep's wool) coiled around the waist. The women wear a *luanchari* (a long, colorful dress) with a woven dora tied around the waist and lots of jewelry for good luck and to indicate wealth.

The Muslim Gujjar travel with buffalo and make their living by selling fresh milk and ghee (clarified butter). The men are usually bearded and wear turbans and long robes. The women wear the traditional Muslim dress: a *kameez* (a long blouse) and *salwar* (loose pants)—often somber in color and accentuated by paisley scarves and chunks of silver jewelry worn around the neck and wrists and dangling from their ears.

Visitors to the capital, **Shimla,** the gateway to the newly opened district of Kinnaur, be warned. The charms of Kipling's city have faded; paint peels on Victorian structures, and mortar is left to crumble. Also be prepared for a city that's habitually crowded. **Manali,** 280 kilometers (174 miles) due north and the gateway to Lahaul and Spiti, has a splendid backdrop of jagged peaks, but a hotel explosion and the presence of hippies "stoned" on hemp have destroyed its isolation. Crowds swarm here from May until September, and the traffic jams rival those in Manhattan. **Dharamsala,** the district capital of Kangra Valley, 253 kilometers (157 miles) west of Manali, is home to the exiled Dalai Lama, who fled Tibet. Devastated by an earthquake in 1905, Dharamsala now suffers from an infusion of ugly hotels and too many visitors who disturb the tranquility that should surround the home of His Holiness.

Adventures present themselves throughout the state. References to the Kangra Valley, nestled in the pine-covered Dhauladhar Range, date back 3,500 years to the age of the Hindu *Vedas*. Today, the valley, with its tropical and alpine terrain backed by snow-topped mountains and intersected by rivers, is a popular destination for good treks, fishing, and horseback riding.

Buddhists also live in the remote and high-altitude districts of Lahaul, Spiti, and Kinnaur. Most practice a Tibetan form of tantric Buddhism. The women twist their hair into numerous long pigtails held in place by a silver ornament. Many men wear a long overcoat (usually maroon or brown). As with most Buddhist communities, men and women share all tasks, from raising a family to working in the fields, where they grow crops of barley, buckwheat, and potatoes.

Lahaul, which offers good treks and Jeep safaris, begins 51 kilometers (32 miles) north of Manali on the far side of the 3,978-meter (13,048-foot) Rohtang Pass. Though it is much smaller than Ladakh (*see below*) and offers fewer and less-ornate *gompas* (monasteries), similarities between the two, such as the mingling of religion and nature, abound.

Mountains bear in from all directions, and windswept passes throw preconceived notions of beauty into disarray. Glaciers look icy and somber, and an occasional lake sparkles under the hot sun. Prayer flags or a rare green valley beckon with their unexpected displays of color, as do the gompas. But Lahaul is experiencing an influx of trekkers. To avoid crowds, ask your tour operator to choose your route carefully.

You can raft, day hike, trek, and travel by Jeep in **Spiti Valley,** a sensitive border area on the far side of Kunzum Pass (4,590 meters or 15,055 feet) southeast of Lahaul. Spiti's landscape is more arid, its mountains, split by the raging Spiti River, steeper than Lahaul's, and it is more thoroughly Buddhist, with the 11th-century Tabo Gompa, one of the holiest monasteries for Tibetan Buddhists.

Kinnaur is south of Spiti and more fertile. This newly opened district offers great day hikes, treks, and Jeep excursions. Sliced by the Sutlej River, it is nestled in the towering Kinnaur Kailash mountains, a part of the Himalayas. Like Spiti, it has wonderful old monasteries.

At press time, foreigners visiting Spiti or Kinnaur need an Inner Line Permit (*see* Inner Line Permit, *above*).

Tour Operators
Many good outfits, especially in India, offer great trips in Himachal Pradesh (*see* Tour Operators, *above*).

Adventures
FISHING
Fish for trout in the Pabar River near Rohru, a daylong excursion from Shimla, and in the Beas River near Manali, or try for *mahseer* (Himalayan river fish) on the Beas near Dharamsala. Contact Himalayan Adventurers or Paddy's Treks (*see* Tour Operators, *above*), who can help procure the appropriate license and take you to good fishing spots in each district. There is no bag limit for mahseer; but with trout, conservation dictates that you keep only what you can eat. Fishing seasons are March–April and mid-April–October.

JEEP SAFARIS
Manali–Leh. Many companies offer this trip; the route can be crowded with vehicles. Take time—five days—to enjoy the show-shopping vistas as you head over four passes, across high-altitude plains, and through valleys. You can also visit the Suraj Tal (lake) in Lahaul beneath the Baralacha Pass (4,883 meters or 16,016 feet) that leads to Ladakh. (Mid-July to mid-September or when passes are clear of snow.)

★ **Shimla–Kinnaur–Spiti–Lahaul–Leh–Nubra–Leh.** This 24-day adventure offers stellar Himalayan vistas and great opportunities to explore remote villages in Himachal and Ladakh. From Shimla, you drive to Sarahan, with its 1,500-year-old Bhimakali Temple, and enter Kinnaur via the lush Sangla Valley. You visit Kamroo castle in Baspa Valley's highest village and Kalpa, the district capital, beneath Mt. Kinnaur Kailash (6,500 meters or 21,320 feet). Then you drive to Ribba village, with its 1,000-year-old monastery, and Nako village, with its high-altitude lake and 10th-century monastery. Next is rugged Spiti, with narrow river valleys and high mountains that are often topped by monasteries and villages. You visit Tabo, the district's most important monastery with 8th-century murals; the Pinn Valley, known for its wildlife, where you see Guling village, with its 1,000-year-old Ningma-pa monastery; and Dhankar village, with its 6th-century monastery. After you visit the Kye and Kibber monasteries, you cross a pass into Lahaul and proceed to Leh in Ladakh, where you see more monasteries. Finally, you head southeast of Leh and visit Buddhist villages in lush fertile valleys and see exquisite high-altitude lakes and stunning mountain vistas. (July–September.) Contact **Himalayan Adventurers** (*see* Tour Operators, *above*).

PONY SAFARIS

★ **Kangra Valley.** Experienced riders can explore the Kangra Valley, with its lovely Himalayan views, on high-spirited polo ponies owned by the family of the former maharaja of Kashmir. You gallop through meadows and forests and visit Kangra villages and a Tibetan monastery. Each night you tent at idyllic campsites. A fixed-departure, five-day trip is usually scheduled in May, but customized trips can be arranged April through June and mid-September through October. Contact **Taragarh Palace Hotel** (*see* Dining and Lodging, *below*).

RAFTING

★ **Spiti River.** This 12-day adventure from Manali to Shimla includes a three-day run on the scenic Spiti River, surrounded by mountains, and vehicular sightseeing trips and day hikes to historic monasteries and old villages. You can join a fixed-departure 16-day trip: Delhi–Manali–Lahaul–Spiti–Kinnaur–Shimla–Delhi. Customized trips are also available. No experience is required, but you must be physically fit for the high altitude. (July–August.) Contact **Himalayan River Runners** (*see* Tour Operators, *above*).

TREKKING

Kulu–Shimla. This eight-day trek, with lots of up- and downhill walking, heads through mountain forests and alpine valleys and into enchanting Gaddi villages, where you get a good glimpse of the culture. From Manali, you drive to Banjar village, the trailhead. The route climbs past lakes bordered by modest wood temples. You cross the Jalori Pass (3,424 meters or 11,230 feet), with views of Spiti and Kinnaur peaks. At the old Hindustan Tibet Road and Margi village, a vehicle takes you to Shimla. (Mid-April–June and September–October; easy.) Contact **Himalayan Adventurers** or **Paddy's Treks** (*see* Tour Operators, *above*).

Lahaul–Spiti–Kinnaur. Many tour operators offer this popular 17-day trip with a 13-day trek that starts once you drive from Manali across the Rohtang Pass (3,978 meters or 13,048 feet) into Lahaul to Patseo village. You head over Baralacha Pass (4,883 meters or 16,016 feet), with its astonishing panorama of mountains. Cross Kunzum Pass (4,590 meters or 15,055 feet) and enter Spiti, where you follow the Spiti River to Losar and Hansa villages. You visit La-Darcha, the site of a popular trade fair attended by Tibetans and Ladakhis and then head to Kibber village (4,130 meters or 13,546 feet), the highest Asian village accessible by road. You follow a mountain ridge and visit monasteries. Then you drive through the Pinn Valley and visit more important villages and monasteries, including Tabo, before continuing to Kinnaur then Shimla. (May–mid-October; moderate, but high-altitude terrain.)

★ **Manali–Bir.** This 14-day trek takes you from Kulu Valley into Kangra Valley along a lesser-known high-altitude route. From Manali, you enter evergreen forests that lead to the Manaslu Valley, where you follow icy streams, cross alpine meadows, and catch great views of Kulu Valley en route. You cross the Kaliheyni Pass (4,726 meters or 15,500 feet), where the landscape changes to patches of snow and glacier moraines, and see distant views of Buddhist Lahaul. You traverse a glacier and

Northwest Trekking

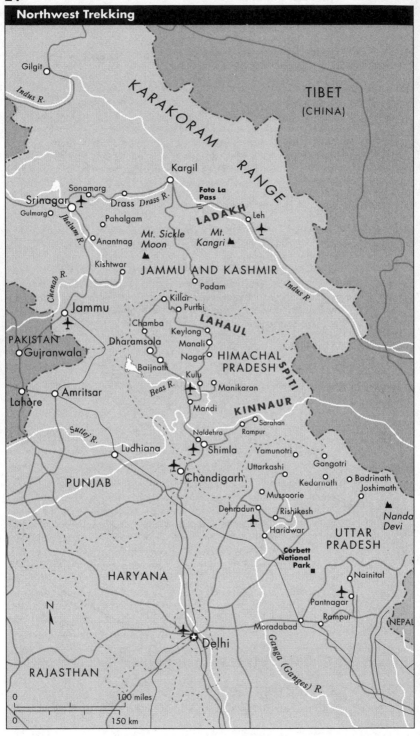

Gilgit

Indus R.

KARAKORAM RANGE

TIBET
(CHINA)

Kargil

Srinagar
Sonamarg
Gulmarg
Drass *Drass R.*
Pahalgam
Jhelum R.
Anantnag
Kishtwar
Mt. Sickle Moon
Foto La Pass
LADAKH
Leh
Mt. Kangri

JAMMU AND KASHMIR

Chenab R.

Padam

Indus R.

Jammu

Killar
Purthi
Chamba
LAHAUL
Keylong
PAKISTAN
Dharamsala
Gujranwala
Manali
Nagar
HIMACHAL PRADESH
SPITI
Baijnath
Kulu
Amritsar
Beas R.
Manikaran
Lahore
Mandi
KINNAUR
Sutlej R.
Naldehra
Sarahan
Rampur
Ludhiana
Shimla
Yamunotri
Gangotri
Uttarkashi
Kedarnath
Badrinath
Joshimath
Chandigarh
Mussoorie
PUNJAB
Dehradun
Rishikesh
Nanda Devi
Haridwar
UTTAR PRADESH

Corbett National Park

HARYANA

Nainital

N

Pantnagar
Rampur
NEPAL

Moradabad
Delhi

Ganga (Ganges) R.

RAJASTHAN

0   100 miles
0   150 km

enter Sunni River Valley, with its meadows and gorges. A snow bridge leads to forests and the isolated valley home of the Gaddi shepherds in Barabangal village. The next destination is the base of Thamser Pass (4,802 meters or 15,750 feet). From here, you travel through meadows and pass lakes and waterfalls until you enter Kangra Valley and the Tibetan settlement in Bir. (June and September; moderate to strenuous.) Contact **Himalayan Adventurers** (*see* Tour Operators, *above*).

Manali–Leh. This extremely popular 10- or 20-day trek starts after a drive across the Rohtang Pass (3,978 meters or 13,048 feet) and the descent into Lahaul. Expect to ford snow-fed streams, cross a high-altitude pass into Ladakh's Zanskar district, visit ancient monasteries and typical Buddhist villages, and experience a panoramic lunar landscape. You can take a Jeep from Padam, the district headquarters in Zanskar, or continue trekking to Leh, the capital of Ladakh. The most rigorous route includes four more passes. Each version is rugged but stunning, with multihued mountains, jagged glaciers, and green village oases. You're apt to see traders with their horses laden with goods, and you will see *many* trekkers. (Mid-July–mid-September; strenuous.)

★ **Sangla Trek.** This 11-day trek in Kinnaur starts after a drive from Shimla to Sarahan and gives you a chance to see the Kinnauri culture. You walk through forests, cross streams and old bridges, follow a mountain ridge with great views, and see ancient temples steeped in Kinnauri mythology. Count on plenty of up- and downhill walking and a steep climb over the Shibaling Pass (3,980 meters or 12,975 feet). Also expect forest or meadow campsites near streams and visits to typical villages, such as Sangla and Chitkul (the highest village in the valley), where many residents work on hand looms creating exquisite Kinnauri shawls. (May–October; moderate.) Contact **Himalayan Adventurers** (*see* Tour Operators, *above*).

Dining and Lodging

For price categories, *see* the charts for Other Areas *in* On the Road with Fodor's.

BAIJNATH

$ **Taragarh Palace Hotel.** This former palace from the 1930s is now a
★ Heritage Hotel owned by a member of the Kashmir Hindu royalty. You can swim in a Victorian pool and then relax in the foyer and lounge furnished with Art Deco furniture and photos galore of the family. The teak-paneled dining room has an exquisite fireplace and smoked-glass windows. The fixed menu is Indian. Bedrooms are not opulent and contain eclectic furnishings from the family's estate; the rooms in the back are more spacious. You can also stay at the adjoining Jungle Camp in a fruit grove. Electrified safari-style tents have hand-blocked interior walls, mat floors, and attached bathrooms with hot water by the bucket. ⌑ *P.O. Taragarh, Kangra Valley 176081, H.P.,* ☎ *Baijnath 3034 or reserve through Yasho Travel & Tours, Delhi,* ☎ *11/463–1124,* ☒ *11/343703 or 11/463–1124. 14 rooms, 3 suites, 6 tents. Restaurant, lounge, pool, tennis court, horseback riding and safaris, trekking and tour arrangements. No credit cards.*

DHARAMSALA

$ **Glenmoor Cottages.** At this secluded hideaway, a half-hour walk from
★ Mcleod Ganj, the owners live in a British bungalow that has been in their family since the 1940s and has two simple suites. Separate cottages offer more privacy and spectacular mountain and valley views. A modest concrete and wood-trim exterior conceals a charming interior where crisp white walls accentuate modern spruce and pine fur-

nishings. Each cottage also has a kitchenette and modern bathroom with shower. Sumptuous fixed-menu Indian and Continental meals are served for guests. ☎ *Upper Dharamsala 176219, H.P., ☎ 1892/25010 or 1892/23355, FAX 1892/23374. 2 suites, 5 cottages. Dining room, lounge, travel services. No credit cards.*

$ **Hotel Tibet Restaurant.** The Tibetan Administration Welfare Society runs this hotel restaurant, which has a parquet floor and simple modern decor. Unfortunately, its windows overlook garbage and slum dwellings. Concentrate on the distant Himalayas, the old black-and-white Tibetan photographs on the walls, or the food: Japanese, Chinese, Continental (including grilled meat dishes), and authentic Tibetan. ✕ *Bagsunagh Rd., Mcleod Ganj, ☎ 1892/2587. No credit cards.*

MANALI

$ **John Bannon's Guest House.** Although this isn't Manali's most beautiful lodge, it has a garden and an orchard, and John Bannon is a delightful host who ensures a pleasant stay. The upstairs rooms in this inn, built in 1934, with a new block added in the 1980s, have good orchard and mountain views. The old block has the advantage of a sweeping veranda on either floor. All the rooms have fireplaces, clean, simple furnishings, and showers. Meals are included. ☎ *Manali Orchards, Manali 175131, H.P., ☎ 1901/2335 or 1901/3077, FAX 1901/2392. 10 rooms. Restaurant, travel services. No credit cards.*

$ **Mount View Restaurant.** Chinese lanterns hang from the ceiling, but this tiny eatery is definitely dedicated to Tibet. Photos of the Dalai Lama and Lhasa decorate the wall. Booths and tables are informally crammed into the narrow room. The Tibetan chef creates Chinese, Tibetan, and Japanese cuisines. For the tasty *gyako* (meat, fish, vegetables mixed into a broth and cooked at the table in a brass mizutaki pot), place your order six hours in advance. It serves four people. Mount View also has good dumplings, soups with homemade noodles, and spicy Szechuan dishes. ✕ *The Mall, opposite taxi stand, no phone. No credit cards.*

$ **Negi's May Flower Guest House.** Up the road from central Manali, this
★ charming two-story inn with a rustic wood-and-stone exterior has verandas on each floor. The new wing, built in 1989, has impeccably clean rooms with polished wide-plank floors, pine ceilings and furniture, fireplaces, and modern bathrooms with tubs. Some new rooms have enclosed balconies that overlook a protected forest. The rooms in the old wing, which are less expensive, are simple, but clean, with fireplaces and showers. Indian and Continental fare are served from a fixed menu. ☎ *Manali 175131, H.P, ☎ 1901/2104. 21 rooms. Restaurant, travel services. No credit cards.*

SHIMLA

$$$ **Chapslee.** When you walk onto the small lawn, golden retrievers greet
★ you and a gray parrot jabbers "coochy coo." But step inside this ivy-covered old manor house, now a Heritage Hotel, and opulence surrounds you: Gobelin tapestries, European wallpaper, rare textiles and furnishings from the Doge's palace in Venice, Persian carpets, blue pottery from the subcontinent. The formal dining room, which seats about 12 guests, has exquisite imported wallpaper and furnishings worthy of a museum. Expect a hot water bottle slipped into your bed at night, afternoon tea, and sumptuous fixed-menu Indian cuisine at lunch and Continental dishes at night. Meals are included; nonguests may dine here by reservation only. ☎ *Lakkar Bazar, Shimla 171001, H.P., ☎ 177/77319 or 177/202542, FAX 177/77567 (attention: Chapslee). 6 rooms. Dining room, travel services. DC, MC, V.*

$$ Quality Inn Hotel Springfields. A short walk through a typical English garden leads to a former maharaja's bungalow recently converted into a small hotel. An attached front cottage has a cozy sitting room and spacious bedroom. The rooms with the best view are in the back of this two-story retreat. Banks of Tudor-style windows overlook a garden in the foreground and the Himalayas in the distance. Every bedroom has a double bed, overhead fans, a working fireplace, a polished wide-plank or parquet floor, and modest Victorian and Art Deco furnishings. Unfortunately, the walls don't absorb the sounds of the recently installed TVs. ⌧ *Opposite Tibetan School, Chotta Shimla, Shimla 171002, H.P.,* ☎ *177/3609,* ⛶ *in Delhi: 11/606390, or reserve through Choice Hotels International. 11 rooms. Restaurant, lounge, travel services. AE, MC, V.*

Ladakh

By Vikram Singh

Tucked between the world's two highest ranges, the Karakoram and the Great Himalayas, Ladakh, about twice the size of Switzerland, is for the traveler who wants an adventure in the world of Mahayana Buddhism. Called Little Tibet, Ladakh is now more culturally pure than its namesake, although tourists in the capital are diluting the Buddhist culture. Still, Ladakh's gompas are splendid, with beautiful interior frescoes and statues that are as breathtaking as the ethereal landscape. This high-altitude desert, with gray barren crags, an occasional green valley, jewellike waterways, and mountains of different hues deepened by the sharp sun, is punctuated by colorful prayer flags and scattered *chortens* (memorial stupas or shrines for relics).

Leh, Ladakh's capital, is built into the base of the snow-covered Karakoram range at over 3,500 meters (11,500 feet). An important Buddhist center since the 3rd century BC, Leh has also been a major commercial hub on the Silk Route in central Asia. The 20th century has turned Leh into an important Indian military base and tourist boomtown. The palace and, above it, the Temple of the Guardian Deities are both in disrepair. Still, Leh lends itself to walks and relaxation. The narrow lanes behind the main bazaar have tempting little shops, but everything here is overpriced. On your way out of town to the south, stop at the **Tibetan Refugee Handicraft Center** in Choglamsar. The beautiful handicrafts here include handwoven rugs and thick woolens. It's open weekdays 9 to 5.

Outside this "urban center," you can travel up and down Ladakh's windswept terrain seeing little human life. The 150,000 residents of Ladakh appear in the most surprising places, generally alongside the reminders of Buddhist culture that sprinkle the countryside. On the most deserted stretch of road you will find stones stacked into little chortenlike piles and *mani* walls of beautifully engraved stones that the inhabitants have erected to protect the land from demons and evil spirits. The walls are enticing, but don't touch or remove the stones because they are sacred to the people who put them there.

Zanskar, south of Leh, is a wide, high-altitude valley. Parts of the district are rocky desert punctuated by bits of green. The Zanskar River races along its deep gorge. The bases of barren slopes are barricaded by sand and shaped by the wind and the water into oversized ramparts. The valley is vast, with sweeping panoramas ending at soft-hued mountains. Zanskar men in robes gallop by on their handsome ponies. **Padam,** the former capital of the Kingdom of Zanskar, is set in a wide valley, ringed by mountains, with the **Karsha Gompa** perched on a nearby cliff. Within this sparsely populated district, the dominant sounds come from chattering birds or the wind that grows intense by late day, rustling the wheat, barley, and countless prayer flags. The arrival of tourists, especially trekkers, has begun to alter Zanskar's lifestyle. The men, who worked alongside the women in the fields and helped with the household chores and children, now look for jobs as porters. The women sell crafts. The preference for money and western goods is altering a society accustomed to bartering. Old Buddhist traditions are also under threat.

Recently, several new areas have opened up in Ladakh, making it more attractive than ever to visitors. The brackish **Pangong Tso** and **Tso Moriri** (*tso* means lake) in the eastern district of Changthang are astonishing alpine seas. Pangong, at an elevation of 4,270 meters (14,500 feet) is over 150 kilometers (90 miles) long—two-thirds of it lying in China. Tso Moriri is a pearl-shaped lake rich in mineral deposits, giving it a mysterious range of colors against the barren mountains. It is 240 kilometers (150 miles) southeast of Leh at an elevation of 4,575 meters (15,000 feet). Both lakes are accessible by road from Leh between late May and October. North of Leh, Ladakh's "Valley of Flowers," the **Nubra Valley,** is now open to visitors. Getting to this richly vegetated area around the Shayok and Siachen rivers requires a journey over Khardungla Pass—the world's highest drivable road, at 5,606 meters (18,383 feet). From here, you descend through the towering peaks to the villages of Nubra, which were important stops for rations along the Silk Route to central Asia. The trekking possibilities here lie along virtually unexplored routes. Camel safaris and river rafting are available, and the hot spring that warmed weary travelers at Panamik village is still steaming. The last of the new treasures in Ladakh are the **Drogpa villages** to the west of Leh, where the Dard people still inhabit the shimmering Indus valley. Isolated from the modern world, the people remain Buddhist farmers, eking a living from the rugged mountainsides. Overnight stays can be arranged in Khaltsi, where the main road forks off toward Kargil, and in new tourist bungalow in the Dard village of Biama.

Travelers who plan to visit Ladakh should read about high-altitude sickness (*see* Health Concerns *in* the Gold Guide) and follow the precautions suggested above. Also carry a flashlight for viewing poorly lit gompas.

Most travel in Ladakh is fairly unrestricted, but to visit any of the new areas discussed above, foreigners need an inner-line permit (*see* Inner Line Permit *in* Adventure Travel, *above*).

Tour Operators
Many outfits offer great trips to Ladakh (*see* Tour Operators, *above*). In Leh itself, some excellent tour operators are **Adventure North Tours and Travels** (☎ 1982/3820 or at the Dragon Hotel, 1982/2339), **Gypsy's World Treks and Tours** (☎ 1982/3935, FAX 1932/3835), and **Silk Route Travels** (☎ 1982/2503). You can write to any of these agencies in Leh, Ladakh 194101, Jammu and Kashmir, India.

Adventures
JEEP AND CAMEL SAFARI
★ **Nubra Adventure.** This special eight-day adventure, which requires an Inner Line Permit, explores the newly opened Nubra Valley, a high-altitude area north of Leh that is home to Buddhists and Muslims and the double-humped Bactrian camel. Nubra, which means garden, is sublime: a heady mixture of cultivated fields set in an arid desert surrounded by the Karakoram range and sliced by rivers. From Leh, a Jeep takes

you across the Khardungla Pass, at 5,606 meters (18,383 feet), with
its exquisite valley and mountain vistas. Once you enter Nubra, you
proceed to Disket village, your camping base. You visit its 500-year-
old village monastery and nearby Hunder village with its monastery.
Then you begin a four-day safari by Bactrian camel, an intrepid trans-
porter that leads you through the ethereal high-altitude valley, with
overnight stays at Panamik village, where you enjoy hot springs, and
at Samtanling village with its old monastery. At the safari's conclusion,
you drive back to Leh. Contact **Ibex Expeditions** (*see* Tour Operators,
above). (Mid-July–mid-October.)

JEEP SAFARIS

Manali–Leh (*see* Jeep Safaris *in* Himachal Pradesh, *above*).

Newly opened areas. Travel agents offer Jeep trips through Ladakh,
particularly to the newly opened areas that can often be combined with
trekking. One extended Jeep safari is run by **Adventure North** (*see* Tour
Operators, *above*). From Manali, you make a two-week odyssey
through all the newly opened areas before reaching Leh (or returning
to Manali).

★ **Pang Gong Lake.** This six-day journey begins in Leh and heads across
the Chang Pass, 5,400 meters (17,604 feet), to the Pang Gong Lake,
which straddles the border of Ladakh and Tibet. Surrounded by mountains and resting at an altitude of 4,300 meters (14,018 feet), Pang Gong
is one of the world's largest glacier-fed lakes and dazzles the eye with
its vibrant blue-and-green hues. An area newly opened to foreigners
that requires an Inner Line Permit, the Pang Gong Lake has long been
the summer haunt of migratory waterbirds who come to nest and the
summer home of shepherds, with their pashmina goats, who cultivate
barley and peas in fields near their small villages along the lake's border. Contact **Ibex Expeditions** (*see* Tour Operators, *above*). (Mid-
July–mid-October.)

JEEP SAFARIS AND TREKKING

Manali–Leh (*see* Himachal Pradesh, *above*).

RAFTING

Only experienced rafters should attempt Ladakh's challenging rivers,
which offer runs generally in July and August. Make sure your outfit
has all the right equipment and expertise.

★ **Zanskar–Indus River.** Plan a 15-day Leh-to-Leh adventure that starts
with short hikes and vehicular journeys to important monasteries and
great vistas. On the eighth day, you raft from Padam to Saspul villages,
beginning a six-day trip with five days of rafting and a spectacular day
hike in the Markha Valley. For two days you are locked in a gorge—
a rough, fantastic journey that is rated classes 2–4. Experience is required. Fixed departures are available, but book well in advance.
Contact **Himalayan River Runners** (*see* Tour Operators, *above*).
(July–September, depending on weather.)

TREKKING

★ **Ice Trek through the Zanskar Gorge.** No doubt it will be cold by night,
but the days can be warm during this incredible 20-day winter adventure.
After an acclimatization in Leh that includes visits to monasteries, you
go by Jeep along the Indus River to its confluence with the Zanskar
River and then to Chilling village, the trailhead. From here, you walk
five days on the frozen river, the traditional winter route between
Padam, the district capital of Zanskar, and Leh. The unusual "trail"
takes you inside a gorge with towering peaks overhead; by night you

sleep in caves or in nearby village homes. Besides encountering local inhabitants on the move, you may also spot ibex or a snow leopard. After leaving the gorge and river, you follow a land-based trail through the open plain and Zanskari villages to Padam, with its lovely old monastery. After a day's rest, you repeat the journey back to Leh. (January–February. Strenuous.) Contact **Ibex Expeditions** (*see* Tour Operators, *above*).

Lamayuru–Chilling. Starting at Lamayuru (an immense monastery built in the 11th century), this trek leads through rugged terrain to an area of Ladakh famous for its copper work. Lamayuru hasn't lost its ancient feel, and the diligence of the monks here makes it one of Ladakh's most vibrant monasteries. From here, you walk down the valley and then climb up to the village of Sumdahchenmo, from where you can look toward the Zanskar River. Farther on you can either follow the Zanskar route to Chilling (10 days) or head back toward the Indus and **Alchi** (5 days). This exquisite 11th-century gompa is in the Indus Valley at one of Ladakh's pristine hidden villages. From Chilling it is possible to trek up to Leh via Hemis. (Moderate–difficult.)

★ **Manali–Leh** (*see* Treks *in* Himachal Pradesh, *above*). Trekking from Manali allows for safer acclimatization.

Nubra Trek. This seven-day trek starts after a drive from Leh to Sabu village in Nubra Valley, with its apple and apricot orchards and unexpected fertile spots. You hike up to Polu Digar, a summer grazing pasture for yaks and sheep, then climb over the Digar La Pass, at 5,500 meters (18,040 feet), and descend to Digar village. The next day you follow a river to Khungru village. From here, you visit yet another typical Buddhist village before you retrace the route back to Sabu. After visiting its monastery, you drive back to Leh. (July–September. Easy, but high altitude.) Contact **Himalayan Adventurers** (*see* Tour Operators, *above*).

Dining and Lodging

Leh is well organized for tourists, and hotels are divided into uniformly priced categories. The most expensive (A Class) are around $50 per night including meals. The cheapest you'll find are the economy-class guest houses, which are less than Rs. 100 per night. The tourist office hands out lists at the airport and main office. Ask what the current price should be. During slow times, negotiation is possible. All the restaurants are small and informal. Try the standards: *momos* (Tibetan dumplings) and *thugpa* (noodle soup).

For price categories, *see* the charts for Other Areas *in* On the Road with Fodor's.

LEH

$$ **Hotel Dragon.** This hotel makes up for being a little farther from town with its traditional decor and excellent food. The white building is adorned with hand-carved wooden awnings and borders. Every room has carved furniture and a Ladakhi feel. ⌕ *Leh 194101,* ☎ *1982/2339. 26 rooms with bath. Restaurant, travel services. No credit cards.*

$$ **Hotel Kanghri.** Like all hotels in Leh, this one has great views. It is also the *only* hotel in Leh open year-round. The rooms have good heaters to keep you warm (and your skin dry) during the frigid winter. Pipes in Ladakh don't thaw before mid-May, so although winter here is gorgeous, it means no plumbing. ⌕ *Leh 194101,* ☎ *1982/2251. 32 rooms with bath. Restaurant, travel services. AE, MC.*

$$ **Hotel Lha-Ri-Mo.** A short walk from the markets and nestled behind
★ an attractive garden, this is the loveliest hotel in Leh. The Ladakhi look
of the exterior is continued in the lobby and the restaurant, which also
has intricately hand-painted beams. Rooms are simple, with western
toilets and hot and cold showers. ⌧ *Leh 194101, Ladakh,* ☎ *1982/2301.
30 rooms with bath. Restaurant, travel services. AE. Closed Nov.–Apr.*

STOK

$$ **Hotel Highland.** Up the road from the Ladakh Sarai near the Stok
monastery, this new two-story hotel, with a lovely back lawn, has a
Ladakhi-style exterior (white with black-and-red trim) and modern,
comfortably furnished rooms. Cultural performances are arranged on
request. Fixed-menu meals with some Ladakhi dishes, airport transfer, and mountain bikes are included in the price. ⌧ *Stok, Leh 194101;
reservations, c/o EMPL Tours, 108 Vishal Bhawan, 95 Nehru Pl.,
New Delhi 110019,* ☎ *11/642–8310,* 𝙵𝙰𝚇 *11/642–8311. 12 rooms with
bath. Restaurant, bar, travel services. AE, DC, MC, V. Closed Dec.–May.*

$$ **Ladakh Sarai.** Here, you stay in a yurt (tent) in a meadow below the
Stok Gompa, 15 kilometers (9 miles) from Leh. The large circular tents
are attractively furnished and use lantern and candlelight. Each clus-
ter of four tents has a small, private solar-heated building with a mod-
ern Western-style toilet and a shower. The separate lobby is Lakdakhi
style with comfortable low platforms and a little shrine. Meals, included
in the price, are normally served outside. Sightseeing is also included.
⌧ *Stok, Leh 194101; reservations, c/o Mountain Travel India, Pvt.
Ltd. 1/1, Rani Jhansi Rd., New Delhi 110055,* ☎ *11/752–5032,* 𝙵𝙰𝚇
*11/777–7483. 15 tents. Restaurant, bar. AE, DC, MC, V. Closed Oct.
15–May 15.*

Rajasthan

By Smita Patel A thick layer of tourist-trap gloss has settled over much of Rajasthan
since its rise as one of India's most popular tourist destinations. To find
the real Rajasthan, just step off the beaten track—on foot, on a bike,
on the back of a horse or camel. You can explore the state's rugged
beauty or the many little villages, the last bastions of indigenous arts
and crafts. You can spend a romantic night under the desert sky or take
a longer trip with stops at fort or palace hotels. The best season is from
October to March, when Rajasthan temperatures are most comfort-
able. While many hotels now offer short tours to nearby villages, the
quality of these "safaris" varies widely. Some are excellent but many
feel trite and tired. Most of the organizations listed below can help you
tailor your own safari. Make all arrangements well in advance.

Tour Operators

Alternative Travels (Nawalgarh 333042, Shekhawati, Rajasthan, ☎
1594/22129, 𝙵𝙰𝚇 1592/32280 offers terrific artisan village stays, spe-
cial trips focusing on music and dance, and treks and bicycling, Jeep,
horse, and camel safaris in Shekhawati and other parts of the state.
Historic Resort Hotels (Shikarbadi, Udaipur 313001 ☎ 294/83200) of-
fers several *shaan* (horse) safaris around the Udaipur area, including
the Ranakpur temples and the Kumbalgarh Wildlife Sanctuary, with
night halts in tented camps or other hotels. **Rajasthan Mounted Sports
Association** (c/o Dundlod House, Hawa Sarak, Civil Lines, Jaipur
302006, Rajasthan, ☎ 141/366276, 𝙵𝙰𝚇 141/366276) provides horse-
back riding and polo lessons in Jaipur; elephant, horse, and camel day
trips in Shekhawati; and horse and Jeep safaris that may include stays
at palaces and forts. **Rajasthan Safaris and Treks** (Birendra Singh Tan-
war, Bassai House, Purani Ginani, Bikaner, 334001 Rajasthan, ☎ 151/

28557, FAX 151/24321 offers less luxurious but more authentic camel, camel-cart, or Jeep safaris out of Bikaner; while food (traditional desert fare) and water are provided, you're on your own as far as toilet facilities go. **Roop Nivas Safaris** (c/o Roop Nivas Palace, Nawalgarh, Dist. Jhunjhunu, Shekhawati 333702, ☎ 15941/22008; Jaipur, ☎ 141/46949 or 141/351511) offers a Shekhawati Brigade Horse Safari around the colorful painted towns of Shekhawati and longer safaris from Nawalgarh to Pushkar or Bikaner. Nights are spent in tents with bathroom facilities or at palace and fort hotels. **Royal Safari** (Royal Safari, Box 23, Nachna Haveli, Gandhi Chowk, Jaisalmer 345001, Rajasthan; ☎ 2992/52538 or 53202) offers treks, camel safaris and nights in the desert around Bikaner, Jodhpur, and Jaisalmer, as well as visits to ethnic villages, homes of craftspeople, little-known fairs, and ashrams.

Sikkim

By Vikram
Singh

Lepchas, the first known inhabitants of Sikkim, aptly called their mountain home paradise. The last *chogyal* (king), who ruled over Sikkim until it became India's 22nd state in 1975, was an avid conservationist who protected his Buddhist kingdom. Today, the capital, Gangtok, is overbuilt and crowded. Once you escape its boundaries, you're surrounded by tropical forests rich with 600 species of orchids and 46 varieties of rhododendron. Waterfalls splash down mountains and power prayer wheels. Tidy hamlets with prayer flags flapping in the breeze and cultivated terraced fields occupy idyllic valleys. Sikkim's guardian deity, Mount Kanchenjunga (also known as Mount Khangchendzonga)—the world's third-highest peak, at 8,586 meters (28,162 feet)—is still revered by all who live in its shadow.

Three distinct ethnic groups live in Sikkim. The Lepchas, or Rongkup (Children of Rong), originally lived in seclusion in north Sikkim, where they developed a harmonious relationship with the environment to ensure their survival. Although most Lepchas converted to Buddhism, many still worship aspects of their physical surroundings: rainbows, clouds, rivers, and trees. Village priests still preside over elaborate rituals, including animal sacrifices, to appease their animist deities.

Bhutias from Tibet came into Sikkim with the first chogyal in the 17th century. Buddhism governs Bhutia life, with the monastery and the lama accorded tremendous influence over daily activities. Every village has its prayer flags and chortens; most families have one relative who has joined a monastery or convent. Every home has an altar room. Buddhism even works its way into weavings, handwoven rugs, *thang-kas* (religious scrolls), statues, and delicately carved *choktses* (tables). The Bhutias' culture dominates Sikkim, right down to the women's national dress: the traditional *kho* or *bhoku,* the epitome of elegance, worn over a *wanju* (blouse), with the *pangden* (apron), the final colorful touch, restricted to married women and formal occasions.

Also sharing Sikkim are the Nepalese, responsible for the introduction of terrace farming to the region. Although most Nepalese are Hindu, you see few Hindu temples in Sikkim, and their faith often incorporates Buddhist beliefs and practices as it does in Nepal. The Nepalese are dominant in business, and theirs is the language heard most in Sikkim.

Because of Sikkim's sensitive border location, foreigners need a **Restricted-Area Permit** (RAP) to visit. The general permit is good for 15 days but does not allow trekking (or even driving) in much of north and west Sikkim. All trekking here takes place in west Sikkim from the base camp in Yuksam, and the trekking permit is good for 15 days. There is no trekking in north Sikkim, and to visit the beautiful Valley of Flowers at Yumthang, foreigners must obtain yet another permit, good for four days and three nights. For anything other than the basic RAP, you must be in a group of at least four people and travel with a government-recognized tour operator (*see* Tour Operators, *above* and *below*). From Delhi, you can get the basic RAP from the **Sikkim Tourist Information Centre** (14 Panchshel Marg, Chanakyapuri, New Delhi 110021, ☎ 11/301–5346).

Tour Operators

Sikkim World Expeditions (Zero Point, NH 31A, Gangtok, Sikkim 737101; ☎ 3592/23494, FAX 3592/24195) is Gangtok's oldest tour operator and runs the Yakshi Resort in Lachung, near Yumthang. **Tashila Tours and Travels** (31-A National Hwy., PB No. 70, Gangtok, Sikkim, 737101; ☎ 3592/22979, FAX 3592/22155) leads the way in river rafting on the beautiful Teesta and Rangeet rivers. **Kanchenjunga Treks and Tours** (1 D.B. Giri Rd., Darjeeling, West Bengal, ☎ 354/3058 or 3408) is run by Dhamey and Jamling Tenzing, the sons of Norgay Tenzing, who climbed Mt. Everest with Sir Edmund Hillary. The company offers treks in western Sikkim, including flora treks. It conducts vehicular tours in the newly opened north and cultural tours to monasteries and can arrange stays in villages.

Adventures

Yak safaris are currently available from Dzongri, and kayaking on the Teesta or Rangeet rivers can be arranged for special groups. Contact a tour operator (*see* Tour Operators, *above*).

RAFTING

Rafting on the **Teesta** and **Rangeet** rivers offers everything from gentle rides through amazing mountain views and lush canyon vegetation to white-water for the experienced rafter only. A trip on the Teesta will probably take you from Makha to Rongpo, while adventures down the Rangeet go from Sikip to Melli. (October–November.) Contact **Tashila Tours and Travels** (*see above*).

TREKKING

Trekking in Sikkim (available March–May and October–December) means frigid nights and warm, tiring days. In the spring you may face some nasty rain, as well. The spring (April–May) is best for flowers (orchids, rhododendrons), and the winter is best for alpine vistas (the Himalayas). Contact a tour operator (*see above*) if you want a customized trek.

★ **Kanchenjunga Trek.** Because this 7–10-day trek demands considerable up- and downhill walking, you should be physically fit. You hike from Yuksam in western Sikkim through forests of rhododendron, orchids, pine, and magnolia to Bakhim village. The next day's tough walk passes through a village populated by gentle yak-herding Tibetans to Dzongri outpost, at an altitude of 4,030 meters (13,218 feet), with its views of Mt. Kanchenjunga. Here you can ride a yak, hike up to Thangsing (3,930 meters or 12,890 feet), at the base of Jopino Peak, and climb to Zimathang (4,500 meters or 14,760 feet). (Moderate.)

Rhododendron Trek. From the Soreng village in western Sikkim, in four or five days you climb up to Bershay, at 3,600 meters (12,000 feet), in the forested Singalila Range, which is known as the rhododendron belt and has about 40 different varieties of flowering trees, as well as numerous birds. From here, you descend to Dentam village, inhabited

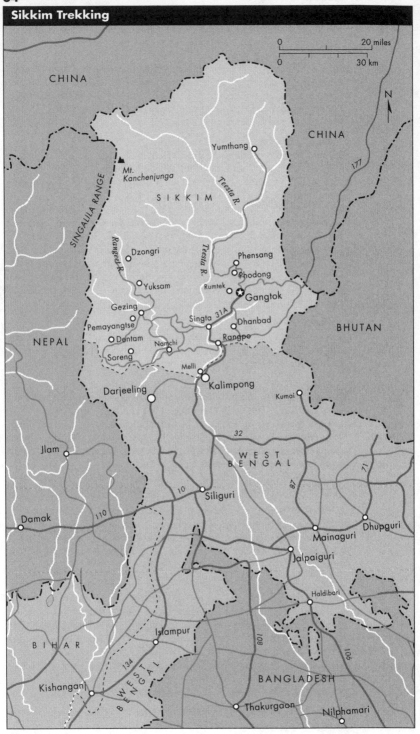

★ mainly by Subba tribal people, and continue down to the historic **Pemayangtse Monastery**. (March–May; easy.)

Dining

Try Sikkimese sautéed ferns (in season), sautéed bamboo shoots, nettle soup, and roast pork. If you like momo (Tibetan dumplings), order beef or vegetable—pork is risky if undercooked. Sikkim also makes good local brews: Cherry or musk brandy, wine, Teesta River white rum, juniper gin, *paan* (mixed nuts and leaves) liquor, and *chang* (fermented millet wine) are worth trying (particularly the last two). All hotel restaurants are open to the public, except for Norkhill. With Norkhill, call first to see if it can accommodate you. Also, for traditional Sikkimese meals, restaurants require advance notice and generally ask for parties of four or more. If you're solo, make some friends; it's worth it.

For price categories *see* the chart for Other Areas *in* On the Road with Fodor's.

GANGTOK

$ **Blue Poppy.** This delightful Sikkimese-style restaurant, with star cutouts on its blue ceiling, views of the mountains, and live music in season, serves good steaks, as well as Chinese, Indian, Sikkimese, and Continental fare. Food is also served upstairs and, in good weather, on the sun deck. ✗ *Hotel Tashi Delek, Mahatma Gandhi Marg,* ☎ *03592/22038. Reservations advised. AE, DC, MC, V.*

$ **House of Bamboo.** This dark little upstairs restaurant is very informal,
★ very Tibetan, and very cheap. Try *sha bhalay* (Tibetan meat paddies), *gyathak* (noodle soup), and momos. You can also choose Chinese dishes. Try for one of the three window booths. ✗ *M.G. Marg. No credit cards. Closed full moon, half-moon, and Tibetan New Year.*

$ **Shangrila Restaurant.** This small, elegant dining room, in an old royal guest house, serves good Indian, Continental, and Sikkimese food. The furnishings are simple, and the ambience is low key. ✗ *Hotel Norkhill, Gangtok,* ☎ *03592/22386. Reservations required. AE, DC, MC, V.*

$ **Snow Lion.** This peaceful restaurant is run by the Dalai Lama's Char-
★ itable Trust. In softly lit, loud Tibetan decor, it serves Tibetan, Japanese, Chinese, Continental, and Indian food. Try the unusual *menyak polo* (slightly sweet, cheese-filled steamed dumplings). ✗ *Hotel Tibet, Paljor Namgyal Stadium Rd.,* ☎ *3592/22523. AE, DC, MC.*

Lodging

For price categories, *see* the chart for Other Areas *in* On the Road with Fodor's.

GANGTOK

$ **Hotel Mayur.** This hotel, with knotty pine ceilings and trim, has func-
★ tional furniture (lots of vinyl and simulated wood grain) and provides good service. The rooms have modern bathrooms with either tubs or showers. Ask for a mountain view. ▨ *Paljor Namgyal Stadium Rd., Gangtok 737101, Sikkim,* ☎ *3592/22825. 25 rooms with bath. Restaurant, bar, travel services. No credit cards.*

$ **Hotel Norkhill.** Gangtok's oldest hotel sits on a quiet ridge below the city. The former royal guest house has lovely gardens and excellent views. Its public rooms and exterior accentuate Sikkimese architecture with colorful carvings. The rooms are simple, with discreet Buddhist and Sikkimese details such as traditional carpets and religious artwork. Ask for a room with view. ▨ *Gangtok 737101, Sikkim,* ☎ *3592/23186,* FAX *3592/22707. 25 rooms with bath. Restaurant, bar, travel services. AE, DC, MC, V.*

$ **Hotel Tashi Delek.** The Sikkimese decor in the entrance, lobby, and pub-
★ lic rooms is bright enough to warrant sunglasses. Though pleasant and
clean, the bedrooms are simple by comparison. Ask for a mountain
view. ⌕ *M.G. Marg, Gangtok 737101,* ☏ *3592/22038,* ℻ *03592/
22363. 45 rooms with bath. Restaurant, bar, travel services. AE, DC,
MC, V.*

$ **Hotel Tibet.** Run by the Dalai Lama Charitable Trust, this central hotel
★ has a wonderful Tibetan ambience, with thang-kas and peaceful Buddhist artifacts. The modest rooms have either a tub or shower. Ask for
a mountain view. ⌕ *Paljor Namgyal Stadium Rd., Gangtok 737101,
Sikkim,* ☏ *3592/22523. 28 rooms with bath. Restaurant, bar, travel
services. AE, DC, MC, V.*

PEMAYANGTSE

$ **Hotel Mount Pandim.** This government-run bungalow stands on a hill
with great views and an attractive garden. The modestly furnished rooms
are large; ask for one with a view. The staff sometimes needs prodding
to provide good service; meals are included. ⌕ *Pemayangtse, Pelling,
West Sikkim, 737113,* ☏ *3593/50756. 25 rooms with bath. Restaurant. No credit cards.*

Uttar Pradesh

By Kathleen
Cox

The Himalayan stretch of Uttar Pradesh, also called Uttarakhand, is
locked in by Himachal Pradesh, Tibet, and Nepal. Uttarakhand, which
figures prominently in revered Hindu books, is considered the mythological abode of the Hindu pantheon. Every year thousands of pilgrims
make *yatras* (Hindu pilgrimages) to the Garhwal mountains and the
sacred Char Dhams (four temples)—Yamunotri, Gangotri, Kedarnath,
and Badrinath—the homes of the Hindu gods Vishnu and Shiva and
the source of the holy Yamuna and Ganges rivers.

Uttarakhand's Garhwal mountains, with more than 100 peaks towering above 6,000 meters (20,000 feet), draw the peripatetic climber,
especially Mt. Nanda Devi, 7,817 meters (26,056 feet). Trekkers are
drawn to its sanctuaries, such as Nanda Devi and the Valley of Flowers, strewn with wild blossoms and surrounded by glaciers and white-
capped mountains. Few foreigners, however, are aware of other good
treks through equally sublime Himalayan vistas to mountain villages
and the revered Char Dhams and other hallowed shrines. For rafters
searching for serious white water, Uttarakhand's runs, ranked with Asia's
best, are swift, long, and away from the mainstream.

Tour Operators
Excellent outfits offer adventures in this state (*see* Tour Operators, *above*).

Adventures
RAFTING
For the following trips, make advance arrangements with **Himalayan
River Runners** (*see* Tour Operators, *above*).

Alakananda River. Take a five-day run on the Alakananda from
Rudraprayag to Rishikesh. Expect good rapids, historic temples, good
vistas of the Himalayas, campsites on secluded beaches, and class 3
and 4 rapids. (November–mid-December and February–April.)

★ **Bhagirathi River.** This six-day run goes from Tehri to Rishikesh in the
Himalayas and is one of India's greatest rafting adventures. You move
through at least two gorges and river valleys and even maneuver a small
waterfall. (November–mid-December and February–April.)

Ganges River. Enjoy an easy one-to-three-day rafting trip from Deoprayag to Rishikesh in the lower Himalayas. (October–mid-December and February–June.)

<u>TREKKING</u>

★ **Gangotri–Gaumukh.** This nine-day trek heads to the source of the sacred Ganga (Ganges), with its trailhead at Gangotri Temple in northern Uttar Pradesh. Gangotri and Gaumukh are also popular abodes of sadhus, Hindu holy men. You pass through forests and a valley and follow the pilgrim route that climbs above the tree line to Bhijbasa and its solitary ashram. You cross flowering meadows backed by towering peaks and camp on the wide, sandy beach of the Gaumukh, where the holy Ganga emerges from the Gangotri Glacier. The trail weaves through moraine, then cuts across the glacier, and climbs steeply up grassy slopes to Tapovan Valley, with vast meadows that brush against the base of Shivling Peak. You camp at Tapovan and take day hikes to Kirti Bamak glacier, the base of Kedarnath Dome and Kirti, and Meru glacier and the base of Mt. Meru (believed by Hindus to be the center of the universe). From Tapovan, you make an excursion across the moraine-covered Gangotri glacier to Nandanvan at the confluence of the Chaturangi and Gangotri glaciers. You camp in a meadow set against the Bhagirathi Massif, which is home to bharal (blue sheep), then follow a grassy ridge that runs parallel to the Chaturangi Glacier to the Vaski Tal (lake) before retracing the route back to Nandanvan and Gangotri. (April–June and September–October; moderate, but high-altitude terrain.)

Mandakini Valley. This nine-day trek concentrates on Garhwali village lifestyle and great views of the central and western Garhwal Himalayas. The trek usually begins after a drive from Mussoorie to Bhagirathi Valley and Malla village, the trailhead. You climb to picturesque Shilla village, pass through forests and alpine pastures, follow a mountain ridge, then traverse the northern slopes of Mt. Kushkalyan with its great vistas. The trail passes through alpine pastures to the high-altitude land of 1,000 lakes, including the lovely Shastrutal Lake. Next, you follow a stream that empties into the Bhilangana River, which takes you to Kalyani village and then to the confluence with the Kundgad River. You climb to a ridge that takes you through forests and down to the Trijuginarayan township, with numerous important Hindu temples. (April–June; strenuous.) Contact **Himalayan Adventurers** (*see* Tour Operators, *above*).

Dining and Lodging

<u>MUSSOORIE</u>
See Excursions *in* Chapter 4, Delhi.

BEACHES

From October to March, a visitor in India can spend a few days or an entire holiday on a superb beach in a deluxe resort, a beach cottage, or even a delightful safari-style tent. Some of India's beaches are backed by palm or coconut groves and sand dunes. If you head for the Andaman Islands in the Andaman Sea or Lakshadweep Islands in the Arabian Sea, you can snorkel around coral reefs.

Andaman and Nicobar Islands

By Julie Tomasz   Rising out of turquoise waters speckled a darker blue, where coral beds spread out from white sandy beaches, the Andaman Islands, which were originally mountains, could become one of India's most beautiful vacation spots. Of the some 300 islands in the chain, only about 30 are inhabited, many only by tribal groups who have lived in chosen seclusion. In the late 19th century, the British established a penal colony in Port Blair, the capital, primarily for Indian freedom fighters who struggled for independence before the British left. The Cellular Jail, just north of the Aberdeen Jetty, is now a national memorial to these imprisoned fighters.

The inaccessibility of the tribal population, preserved for so long by their unwillingness to have contact with outsiders, is now preserved by the Indian government. Of the islands's six tribes, five have control over their traditional habitation areas, which have been set aside by the government as "Special Primitive Tribal Reserve Areas."

★ Although only a few islands are open to foreign tourists, those that are offer some of the world's best **coral reefs,** guaranteed to satisfy even experienced divers. These reefs also support spectacular underwater marine life. From close to shore, you can snorkel out to the coral-covered seafloor and come across darting schools of fish, including the vibrantly colored parrot fish, the shy clownfish hiding in poisonous sea anemones, and the fragile angelfish. Any of the recommended hotels and travel agencies can help arrange day trips to good coral beds at Jolly Buoy and Redskin islands, which are uninhabited and open to foreigners specifically for snorkeling. Another plea for preservation: Don't touch anything; corals are not only incredibly fragile, they are also extremely sharp! If you just want to relax or swim, head to Corbyn's Cove, a miniature but lovely white sandy beach at the eastern end of Port Blair, where tall palms, which ring the crescent-shaped beach, cast long shadows across the sands in the late afternoon.

Note: Foreign citizens need a permit to visit the Andamans; the Nicobar Islands are off-limits. Though you can obtain a permit from the Indian mission or consular offices in your home country, permits are easily obtainable on landing at Port Blair by filling out a short form. These permits, good for 30 days, allow visits to the Port Blair municipal area, Mount Harriet, and Madhuban on South Andaman Island; Mayabunder and Rangat on Middle Andaman; Diglipur on North Andaman; and the islands of Jolly Buoy, Redskin, Cinque, Neil, Havelock, and Long. Overnight stays are not permitted on Jolly Buoy, Redskin, and Cinque islands.

Also, all visits to the tribes are controlled by the government and, for the most part, are prohibited. Don't be lured into going to a tribal island with a nonofficial who offers—the tribal cultures are increasingly fragile and can be saved only if they are not interfered with.

For information on the islands, contact these government offices: **The Andaman and Nicobar Tourist Information Center** (Secretariat, Port Blair, ☎ 3192/20694 or 3192/20380), open Monday through Friday, 8:15 to 12:30 and 1 to 4:45; the **airport** information counter (☎ 3192/20414), open with arriving flights; and the **Government of India Tourist Office** (189 VIP Rd. 2nd Floor, Super Shoppe Bldg., Junglighat, Port Blair, ☎ 3192/21006), open Monday through Friday, 8:30 to 5.

Tour Operators
Island Travels (Aberdeen Bazaar, Port Blair, ☎ 3192/21358 or 3192/21034, FAX 3192/30109; in Welcomgroup Bay Island Hotel, Marine Hill, Port Blair, ☎ 3192/20881) rents cars and drivers and snorkeling equipment, operates guided tours and charter boats, and arranges private guides and trips. Other outfits also offer adventures in the Andamans (*see* Tour Operators, *above*).

Beaches

Most Andamans beaches are thin crescents of fine sand fringed with thick palm groves, gently sloping into calm, impossibly clear water. So far they are only sparsely peopled. The sun here is strong even before and after the usual peak tanning hours. Apply a good UVA/UVB **sunscreen** before heading to the beach. Bring along extra sunscreen for reapplications. When snorkeling, you may want to wear a t-shirt to protect your back and shoulders, which remain completely exposed to the sun. Carry lots of **bottled water;** the sun and saltwater are dangerously dehydrating. For immediate refreshment, you can always buy from a street vendor a fresh coconut full of sweet coconut milk, which, if the shell is hacked open in front of you, is guaranteed by nature itself to be germ-free.

CORBYN'S COVE

This is not only the most popular beach on the main island near Port Blair, it's basically the *only* beach. It's surprisingly small—only about 200 yards in length, 50 yards wide—and is embraced by towering palm trees. Warm, gentle waters make it great for safe, easy swimming—even into the night, when the beach is illuminated by a floodlight (good for swimming, not so good for stargazing). If you're a strong swimmer, you can swim out to tiny, nearby Snake Island, which is encircled by lovely, less-known coral reefs; bring a snorkeling mask and tube for a look. Before you go, consult the staff at the Andaman Beach Resort (across the street) about seasonal currents and safety precautions. Corbyn's Cove is about 6 kilometers (3½ miles) south of downtown Port Blair.

CHIDIYATAPU

This is the southernmost tip of South Andaman Island—a good hour's drive from central Port Blair. To reach the beach, you must take a roughly 1½-kilometer (1 mile) path through a forest bird sanctuary that leads to the shore. Walk to the cove beach, which is small but secluded, with calm, shallow waters. Don't forget to begin your return walk before the sun goes down. In the village where you arrive, numerous fishermen are willing to take tourists out in their noisy boats to the beach or just for a ride. The boats have no seats, but it's a good adventure if you don't mind roughing it a bit. Fix the price, a few dollars (in rupees, though) per person; and don't pay until you're back where you started.

JOLLY BUOY ISLAND

This tiny, uninhabited island, in the Mahatma Gandhi Marine National Park, is blessed with a gorgeous belt of coral reefs that offer excellent snorkeling. A 1½-hour boat ride from Wandoor Beach past empty islands (strictly off-limits) anchors you just offshore. For a break from the sun, set up camp under one of the several bamboo-thatched umbrellas or retreat into the shade of the dense palm forest, but don't explore too deeply—king cobras and other local creatures may not appreciate the visit. Just a few meters from the shore, you enter the spectacular world of parrot fish nibbling at coral; fat sea cucumbers lolling on the sandy floor; and the sun streaming through tiny opalescent fish. Don't touch anything—you'll help preserve the reef and avoid getting hurt. You can change in a few thatched-roof huts just inside the forest. Snorkel equipment can be rented as you buy your ticket from the men operating the boat. As the equipment is used by different people every day, it's a good idea to rinse it thoroughly and wipe off the mouthpiece with antiseptic wipes. Snorkels can also be rented from the travel agencies listed above or from your hotel. Boats to Jolly

Buoy leave daily except Monday at 10 AM from Wandoor Beach, about 29 kilometers (18 miles) or a one-hour drive south of Port Blair. They usually return to Wandoor by 3:30 PM. Get to Wandoor at least half an hour early to ensure a spot on the boat. Avoid Sundays.

REDSKIN

If you're lucky, you may have this island all to yourself. The boat to Jolly Buoy (*see above*), which makes a stop here on the way if requested, leaves you on an ivory sand beach with swaying palms, the eternally blue sky, and the transparent sea. The beach strip is bordered by tangles of trees and shrubbery, but explorers can seek out more beach by swimming or wading around. Redskin, too, has gorgeous coral reefs with, in fact, a larger variety of marine life than at Jolly Buoy. Ask the boat staff to point out which way the reefs are. The boat trip takes roughly one hour each way.

FARTHER OUT

Some of the best beaches open to tourists are on islands that take hours to reach. Most of the areas listed below involve long, tedious journeys. Within a few years, however, high-speed boat service is planned. Accommodations are in very basic government structures.

By boat, **Cinque Island** is about 3½ hours south of Port Blair, and overnight stays are not permitted. The only way to get to this island's beautiful beach and fantastic coral reefs is to charter a boat (at least $500) from a travel agency (*see above*). About three hours northeast of Port Blair, **Neil Island** has two designated beaches, at Bharatpur and Silapur. A small, cheap government guest house is due for completion in 1996. **Havelock Island,** a five-hour boat trip, has two beaches and a fairly comfortable small government guest house. **Long Island,** an eight-to nine-hour boat journey, has a lovely beach at Lalaji Bay, but as yet, the accommodations here are limited. You can reach **Rangat** in six to seven hours by sea or by road with the help of two ferries. **Mayabunder,** on the northeastern tip of Middle Andaman, is another three to four hours by road or by boat from Rangat. Beaches are in Cuthbert Bay, near Rangat, and around Mayabunder. Both areas have small government guest houses that are frequently used by officials. A new one in Mayabunder, just for tourists, is scheduled for 1996. **Diglipur** on North Andaman Island requires a 15-hour journey from Port Blair. The government plans to open a much-needed guest house in 1996. The beaches are in Lamia Bay in Kalipur, southeast of Diglipur.

All transport among these islands is very cheap; the shorter trips cost under $1, the longer ones around $2. The no-frills boats leave from Phoenix Bay Harbour in Port Blair. For schedule information, inquire at the tourist office or your hotel, or contact the Shipping Directorate (Phoenix Bay, ☎ 3192/20725). Sailing schedules are also printed in the local newspaper.

Scuba Diving and Water Sports

The Andaman and Nicobar Scuba Diving Society (c/o Welcomgroup Bay Island Resort, Marine Hill, Port Blair, ☎ 3192/20881, FAX 3192/21389) offers diving trips in the Marine National Park and in more distant, deep-water locations, as well as PADI certification courses. Book early. **The Andaman Water Sports Complex** (Aberdeen Rd., at old Aberdeen Jetty, Port Blair, ☎ 3192/30799) rents nonmotorized boats and offers windsurfing, parasailing, waterskiing, and water scootering. **Snorkeling equipment** can be rented for a small sum from your hotel, from travel agencies, and from the ticket sellers at Wandoor Beach (for trips to Jolly Buoy or Redskin). **Boat charters** can be arranged through your hotel and through the travel agencies listed above.

Dining

There's plenty of fresh seafood in the Andamans. Most other food, however, even green chilies, is shipped from the mainland: the result is high food prices by Indian standards. Your best dining options are in the major resort restaurants, with the finest food at the **Welcomgroup Bay Island,** followed by the **Andaman Beach Resort.** Both serve buffets as well as Indian, Chinese, and Continental food à la carte; the average price is about 200 rupees (a bit more at the Welcomgroup). For an out-of-hotel adventure, try the **China Room** in downtown Port Blair, where you can eat fresh Chinese seafood dishes on a cozy, candlelit outdoor terrace; ask your hotel to reserve you a table at dinner; it's small and popular. An average meal here costs about 100 rupees.

For price categories, *see* the chart for Other Areas *in* On the Road with Fodor's.

Lodging

Only a few Andaman Islands hotels and guest houses are up to international standards. Unless mentioned otherwise, hotels have air-conditioning and foriegn exchange facilities.

For price categories, *see* the chart for Other Areas *in* On the Road with Fodor's.

$$$$ **Welcomgroup Bay Island.** Classy yet informal, this handsome resort,
★ on a hill overlooking Ross Island and just above the downtown area, was designed by the renowned Indian architect Charles Correa. Breezeways connect the large, open lobby with the rooms, which have rich *padouk* (a wood) floors and inlaid furniture with bamboo and shell accents. Request a room with a sea-facing balcony—the views are fantastic. The resort posts signs and brochures throughout the hotel and Port Blair offering tips and information on preserving the surroundings. Also expect a friendly, well-informed staff. ⌖ *Marine Hill, Port Blair 744101, Andaman and Nicobar Islands,* ☏ *3192/20881,* ℻ *3192/21389. 48 rooms with bath. Restaurant, bar, refrigerators, room service, saltwater pool, Ping-Pong, snorkeling, scuba diving, fishing, bicycles, dry cleaning, laundry service, meeting room, travel services, airport shuttle. AE, DC, MC, V.*

$$$ **Andaman Beach Resort.** Across the road from the island's only sandy beach, 7 kilometers (4 miles) from the downtown area, this is a laid-back resort. The 35 acres of grounds include palm trees and flowering hedges, providing tropical seclusion. The cozy lobby is full of rustic, beachy decor: low teak rafters, wicker chairs, and hanging chains of seashells. The rooms are clean and simple, with teak furniture and stone floors. All rooms have balconies. ⌖ *Corbyn's Cove, Box 21, Port Blair 744101, Andaman and Nicobar Islands,* ☏ *3192/21462,* ℻ *3192/21463. 47 rooms with bath, 4 cottages. Restaurant, bar, Ping-Pong, beach, scuba diving, snorkeling, recreation room, laundry service, meeting room, travel services, airport shuttle. AE, DC, V.*

$$ **Sinclairs Bay View.** This white, five-story resort, opened in 1991, has been under reconstruction for years but has a prime location on a hill over looking the sea, halfway between Corbyn's Cove and Marine Hill. The rooms have modern decor and balconies that face the ocean. ⌖ *South Point, Port Blair 744101, Andaman and Nicobar Islands,* ☏ *3192/ 21159 or 3192/20937. 30 rooms with bath. Restaurant, dry cleaning, laundry service, meeting room, travel services. DC, V.*

$ **Megapode Nest.** In this government-run facility on a hilltop near Phoenix Bay Jetty, expect a clean room with simple, modern decor and a small balcony. The bathrooms have open showers (no curtains or separate stall). Some rooms are air-conditioned, and some have ocean views. For about $10 more (still a low price), you can stay in an adorable, secluded octagonal hut built into the hillside, bright and cheery with mauve carpeting, floral curtains, and lots of windows affording lovely views. Both huts have private balconies and modern bathrooms with athtubs. ☎ *Tourist Home Rd., Haddo, Port Blair 744102, Andaman and Nicobar Islands,* ☎ *3192/20207 or 3192/203880,* FAX *3192/ 21227. 25 rooms with bath, 2 huts. Restaurant. No credit cards.*

Goa

By Julie Tomasz

India's most famous beach destination is the former Portuguese colony of Goa. With the exception of the monsoon season (June to September), the temperature and weather stay high and dry. Silvery beaches are never more than a short walk away from Goa's charming villages. The wide, palm-bordered rivers move lazily down to the Arabian Sea. The towns are a pleasing blend of Portuguese and Indian. Houses gleam with a light wash of color set off by brightly painted pillared front porches and trim.

Closest to Panaji, Goa's capital, are Miramar and Dona Paula beaches, both city beaches written up in tourist brochures. Avoid them. At Miramar, the swimming is marred by a strong undertow and the view is marred by broken glass and garbage littering the sand, plus architectural eyesores. The Dona Paula beach is a glorified cement dock crowded with vendors.

For the most seclusion, head far north to or around Arambol Beach, cloistered in cliffs (and popular with European hippies), or far south, to the less-developed beaches below Colva Beach, like Palolem.

Along most of the Goan coast, surfers have to wait for the monsoon for giant waves.

Integral to the Goan beach experience are the beach vendors. You're approached constantly by men and women offering "Pineapples?" "Cheese?" "Sandwiches?" "Cold drink?" "Massage?" Their persistence can drive you into the water. Nomadic Lambani women dressed in vibrant-colored costumes and silver jewelry set up blankets cluttered with great handicrafts, jewelry, embroideries, and quilts. What they sell is often beautiful, and by the end of a Goan vacation, most foreigners have bought something.

For a slice of Goan life, visit a weekly market. On Wednesday, vendors sell mostly Indian and Tibetan crafts and artifacts on Anjuna Beach. Friday is the big market day at Mapusa, the main town of the Bardez district. Here, people from adjoining villages sell everything from vegetables to handicrafts. Also, devote at least half a day to visit some of Goa's beautiful old churches and the historic Old Town.

Tour Operators

For sightseeing, contact any of these agencies for organized tours and car and driver hire: **The Goa Tourism Development Corporation** (Trionara Apartments, Dr. Alvares Costa Rd., Panaji, ☎ 832/226515), the **Directorate of Tourism** (Government of Goa, Tourist Home, Pato Bridge, Panaji, ☎ 832/225583 or 832/224757), **Trade Wings** (6 Mascarenhas Bldg., Alfonso de Albuquerque Rd., Panaji, ☎ 832/42430). You can hire a private guide from the **Government of India Tourist Of-**

fice (Communidade Bldg., Church Sq., Panaji, ☎ 832/43412). Other outfits also offer adventures in Goa (*see* Tour Operators, *above*).

Beaches

The state is divided into 11 districts (*talukas*); the location given at the end of each beach entry below includes the name of the district.

All beaches have official lifeguards theoretically on duty every day from 6 AM to 6 PM, but their chairs are often empty.

Numbers in the margin correspond to beaches on the Beaches, Bombay–Goa map.

★ ➏ **Arambol Beach.** Goa's northernmost beach (also known as Harmal) is ruggedly beautiful. You enter through a lively but slow-paced hippie colony, where young foreigners live in small huts. The best beach is 20 minutes' walk to the right beyond the ragged food and drink shacks. Here, a freshwater pond nestles at the base of the hillside just 50 yards from the crashing surf below. The scenery is spectacular: the ocean foams around dark rocks rising just offshore. The sea is rougher here than at other beaches, still good for swimming but a bit more fun for surf seekers. It can be crowded in season, but if you walk beyond the pond you'll find tide-dependent inlets and rock ledges. *Pernem district.*

➑ **Baga Beach.** This small beach north of (and technically part of) Calangute Beach is a lively place known for its hopping "shack life," with popular food and drink joints, including the favorites St. Anthony's for seafood and Tito's Bar for nighttime revelry. The beach drops steeply to the water where fishing canoes make use of the good boat-launching conditions and provide rides for tourists, often to the Wednesday market at Anjuna Beach just around the bend—15 minutes away by sea, but significantly farther by road. There are more open, less crowded areas farther down the beach to the left of the entrance where you can spread your towel for sunbathing. *Bardez district, about 15 km (12 mi) north of Panaji.*

⓫ **Bogmalo Beach.** Picturesque and rarely overcrowded, this tiny crescent of fine sand is perfect for swimming and sunning. It's overlooked by a low, verdant hill topped by a few modern buildings on one side and the Bogmalo Beach Resort on the other. You can gaze out at two tiny islands about 10 kilometers (6 miles) into the sea. For the most privacy, walk down to the far right, where there are fewer fishing boats, shacks, and people. Another of Bogmalo's assets is its boating and water sports facilities. **Watersports Goa** (☎ 8345/512305 after 7 PM), operating out of a shack on the beach, offers instruction, excursions to nearby islands, and water sports. Trips to the islands (book in advance) are also offered by the experienced young staff of the **Sandy Treat** snack shack (the first one that juts out on the right). For a lunch break, the **Seagull**, a simple, thatched-roof shack right on the beach, serves some of the best prawn curry rice in Goa. *Bardez district.*

➒ **Calangute Beach.** Stretching some 16 kilometers (10 miles) from Sinquerim Beach in the south, near Fort Aguada, up through Vagator Beach in the north, it covers several separate subbeaches, including Baga and Anjuna. The smaller, main part of Calangute Beach, about two thirds of the way down, just south of Baga Beach, is an open stretch of sand reached by a set of cement steps. Some palm trees provide patchy shade. There's a fairly strong undertow; a sign warns that swimming is dangerous. Calangute is bustling: its entrance area is crammed with stalls and shops. The government-run Calangute Tourist Resort (☎ 832/

Beaches, Bombay to Goa

Bordi ❶
Dahanu
Tarapur
Palghar
Nasik
Shirdi

Vasai
Thane
Kalyan

Bombay ✯
Matheran

Elephanta
Pen
Karli

Alibag

Murud
Pune

Mahad

Mahabaleshwar

Harihareshwar ❷
MAHARASHTRA

Murud-Harnai ❸
Dapoli

Guhagar
Chiplun

Jaigarh

Arabian Sea

Ganapatipule ❹

Ratnagiri

Bhatye ❺

Miraj

Rajapur
Kolhapur

Vijayadurg
Nippani

Malwan

Belgaum

Arambol Beach ❻
Vagator Beach ❼
Mapusa

Baga Beach ❽
Panaji

Greater Calangute Beach
Calangute Beach ❾
GOA

Sinquerim Beach ❿

Bogmalo Beach ⓫
Margao

Colva Beach ⓬

Palolem Beach ⓭

KARNATAKA

N

0 ___ 30 miles
0 ___ 45 km

276024) offers general tourist information and changes money and travelers' checks. *Bardez district.*

⑫ **Colva Beach.** This is the most crowded beach in the south, about 6 kilometers (3½ miles) west of Margao. Its large parking and entrance areas are crowded with shacks selling souvenirs and snacks and young men offering their mopeds for rental. The first 300 meters of beach feel hectic—busy with fishing boats, cows, and vendors–but the sand stretches in both directions, backed by palm groves and offering less-trafficked spots to settle down. The water is good for swimming, with only nominal waves. The row of restaurant and bar shacks focus nightlife for the whole region. Colva officially stretches nearly the entire length of the Salcete district, but it is broken up into smaller beach sections. The tourism department's Tourist Cottages reception desk (☎ 834/222287) serves as an information center. *Salcete district.*

★ ⑬ **Palolem Beach.** For seclusion and idyllic scenery, Goa's southernmost beach, nicknamed "Paradise Beach," is a dream. Palolem receives only those nature devotees and privacy-seekers who are willing to make the rugged, two-hour drive from the nearest resort (Leela Beach). Palolem is a long, curving stretch of white sand backed by palm groves and low, green mountains. Depending on the tides, you can wander past secluded coves and nooks sheltered by rocks. All the way on the right, the beach ends in a rugged, rocky point teeming with crabs. The water is shallow and warm, with very little surf. Shacks sell refreshments near the main entrance. An occasional vendor sells pineapples and bananas from a weathered basket on his head. Local men sell rides in wooden canoes to look for dolphins. *Canacona district.*

⑩ **Sinquerim Beach.** This, like Bogmalo Beach, is one of the few beaches where you can rent windsurfers, waterskis, and other water toys without having to be a guest at a hotel. Stretching in front of the three Taj resorts, this small sandy beach gets fairly crowded with tourists and vendors. The water is warm and clean, with slightly higher waves good for bodysurfing. *Bardez district.*

⑦ **Vagator Beach.** At the north end of Calangute Beach, this tiny, semicircular getaway is backed by high palms. To the right and behind, Fort Chapora's dark red walls rise above a low hill. To the left, a rock jetty juts out into the sea topped by a striking white cross. This picturesque setting makes Vagator a popular lunch break spot on organized sightseeing tours. The surf is gentle and good for swimming. Some shacks sell food just beyond the rocky, somewhat polluted rise on the right. *Bardez district; entrance beyond Mahalaxmi Bar and Restaurant.*

Water Sports
Many of the big hotels have water sports centers available only to guests. You can find private facilities open to the public on Bogmalo and Sinquerim Beach. On most beaches, you'll find fishermen happy to take you out for a boat ride for a negotiated price.

Dining
Portuguese dishes have been adapted with a Goan touch: a healthy pinch of red chili tempered with coconut milk. Typical local dishes include zesty-sweet prawn curry rice, *chouris pao* (sausage bread) and chicken *cafreal* (amply seasoned with ginger, garlic, green chilies, lime, and more). Goa's seafood is superb: fresh crabs, pomfret, squid, lobster, and prawns. Try pomfret in a red or green sauce or tiger prawns *baffad* (spicy Goan style). For calorie-hunters, *bebinka* is a sinfully rich layered pastry dense with butter, egg yolk, and coconut. And no Goan experience is truly complete without at least a taste of *feni,* the potent

local brew made of either palm sap or cashew fruit; both pack a hard punch. Prices are wonderfully low, except for the tiger prawns.

For price categories, *see* the chart for Other Areas *in* On the Road with Fodor's.

WHAT TO WEAR

Goan life is decidedly casual, with a focus on comfort. Except for the most elegant dining rooms of the most expensive resorts, casual dress is acceptable for dining out. Many tourists wear shorts and t-shirts, but in restaurants it's most appropriate to keep lengths conservative and tops not too cut-out.

$$$$ **Banyan Tree.** You cross a small footbridge to enter this Thai-style restaurant, named for the centuries-old banyan tree in its yard. You can dine on excellent Thai and Chinese cuisine on the tile-covered veranda or in the air-conditioned room indoors. Specialties include *gaeng kiaw waan goong* (king prawns cooked in green curry) and *phad Thai* (noodles tossed with bean sprouts and garnished with peanuts). ✕ *Taj Holiday Village, Sinquerim, Bardez,* ☏ *832/7514. Dinner reservations advised. AE, DC, MC, V.*

$$ **Cajueiro.** From the day it opened in 1993, Cajueiro ("cashew tree" in
★ Goa's local language) has been a favorite of locals and tourists for its tasty Goan cuisine and its great atmosphere. You eat outdoors on a raised platform under a large straw-thatched roof supported by long betel nut tree trunks. Candles and rustic burlap and wood lanterns provide soft lighting at night—the best time to come, when the highway nearby is less visible. The menu is bound in heavy teakwood and features seafood specialties such as pomfret fillets stuffed with prawns, as well as hearty mutton dishes and Goan sausage. It all goes down smoothly, preceded by a Palm Beach pineapple cocktail spiked with potent palm feni. ✕ *Mapusa Hwy., Alto Betim, Bardez,* ☏ *832/217375. Reservations advised. MC, V.*

$$ **Coconut Inn.** This Goan house, now a restaurant, is nestled in palm trees and lush green gardens. The atmosphere is casual and very friendly. Eat on a softly lit veranda surrounded by antiques or in a statue-filled garden strung with blue lights and paper lanterns. The chef serves Goan-, general Indian-, and Continental-style dishes, including tandoori items cooked outdoors in the tandoor oven in the yard and seafood, which you pick from the day's catch displayed on a tray of ice at the entrance. ✕ *Marquis Vaddo, next to Shanta Durga Temple, Candolim, Bardez,* ☏ *832/276169. Dinner reservations advised. AE.*

$$ **O Coqueiro.** This eatery established in 1970 won an award for its Goan
★ and Portuguese cuisine from the London-based International Wine and Food Society in 1986, but didn't find out until 1992, when an official finally made the trip to Goa. The extensive, well-worn menu features fresh prawn curries, hearty Goan sausages, and other local dishes. Guests dine at rustic wood tables in a large open-air, thatch-roof room with ceiling fans or in enclosed back rooms. The chef will be happy to cook up something you don't see on the menu. ✕ *Alto Porvorim, Bardez,* ☏ *832/217271. Reservations advised. AE, DC, MC, V.*

$ **Florentine Bar and Restaurant.** A long, dirt driveway leads to this simple eatery. It's low on atmosphere and far from elegant, but the well-informed know it has tasty, fresh Goan fare at rock-bottom prices. You can eat inside in a small, basic white room or outdoors in a dirt yard set up with green metal folding chairs and a table under a floppy straw roof. Try the house specialty, chicken cafreal, or a large, steaming plate of vegetable fried rice. ✕ *Chogm Rd., Saligao, Bardez,* ☏ *832/ 278249. No credit cards.*

$ White House. With bare wood tables, plastic chairs, and a few potted plants for decor, this low-frills eatery has a panoramic harbor view. To reach the restaurant, in a simple white house at the top of a high hill near the Cidade de Goa (*see* Lodging, *below*), you climb a flight of stairs in what appears to be someone's living room. Try a plate of vegetable fried rice or some typical Goan chicken cafreal. ✗ *Dona Paula, Tiswadi,* ☏ *832/221239. No credit cards.*

Lodging

Goa has accommodations for every preference: fancy resort hotels, small intimate hotels, and ethnic-style villages. The tourism department has also initiated a bed-and-breakfast–style option so visitors can stay in private, traditional homes. For seclusion, pick your destination carefully. The peak months (December–February) bring huge crowds. Lodging prices also vary drastically according to the season.

For most major hotels, the rates are the highest from mid-December through early to mid-January and then drop by $20 to $30 for mid-January and February and even more for the months following. During monsoon season——May through October—many hotels cut their room prices by more than 50%. During the peak season, you must book your room months in advance.

Unless mentioned otherwise, hotels have central air-conditioning, room service, doctors on call, and foreign-exchange facilities, and rooms have cable TV and bathrooms with tubs.

For price categories, *see* the chart for Major Cities and Resorts *in* On the Road with Fodor's.

$$$$ **Aguada Hermitage.** If you crave seclusion and luxury—and you can
★ afford it—stay at this Taj property. On a hill overlooking Sinquerim Beach and the Arabian Sea, units in these Goan-style villas are like separate, elegant homes. Expect one or two bedrooms and several other rooms (including two bathrooms), and dark wood furniture; each has a large terrace with upholstered garden furniture. A regular car service shuttles you down the hill to the nearby Taj Fort Aguada Beach Resort, with which it shares the lobby and all facilities (*see below*). Facilities of the Taj Holiday Village, just next door, are also open to guests. ▣ *Sinquerim, Bardez, Goa 403515,* ☏ *832/87507,* ℻ *832/276044. 15 villas.* (See *Taj hotels,* below). *AE, DC, MC, V.*

$$$$ **Leela Beach.** You are welcomed with a coconut drink and a map, which you need to explore this 60-acre resort with its gorgeous secluded beach. The salmon-colored, two-story cement villas arranged along a winding man-made lagoon could very well be in a condo colony in southern Florida. Rooms have cool tile floors, dark-wood furniture, well-appointed bathrooms, and a private balcony. "Pavilion" rooms in the villas are better and just slightly more expensive than the standard rooms in the larger block buildings. Power outages can be frequent depending on the season, and service can be slow and impersonal. Not all bathrooms have tubs. ▣ *Mobor Cavelossim, Salcete, Goa 403731,* ☏ *834/246363,* ℻ *834/246352. 219 rooms, 21 suites. 5 restaurants, bar, 9-hole golf course, 3 tennis courts, pool, barbershop, beauty salon, outdoor hot tub, sauna, steam room, exercise room, horseback riding, Ping-Pong, squash, beach, snorkeling, windsurfing, boating, jet skiing, parasailing, waterskiing, fishing, bicycles, dance club, children's play center, dry cleaning, laundry service, business services, meeting rooms, travel services, airport shuttle. AE, DC, MC, V.*

$$$ **Taj Fort Aguada Beach Resort.** Within the ramparts of a 17th-century fort, this hotel's dark exterior blends well with its dramatic surroundings. The view from the chic, open-air lobby—of the fort, sea, and beach—is gorgeous. All rooms face the sea and have contemporary Goan-style dark wood and cane furnishings and tile floors. You can also stay in intimate, tile-roofed cottages (two units per cottage). Facilities of the resort's sister Taj properties just next door are shared among the three resorts. ☎ *Sinquerim, Bardez 403515, Goa, ☎ 832/276201, ℻ 832/276044. 106 rooms, 24 suites. 3 restaurants, bar, pool, barbershop, beauty salon, tennis court, health club, beach, windsurfing, boating, parasailing, waterskiing, baby-sitting, travel services, airport shuttle. AE, DC, MC, V.*

$$$ **Taj Holiday Village.** Designed like a ritzy Goan village, this delightful trop-
★   ical resort has tile-roof cottages scattered around gardens and extensive lawns that face Sinquerim Beach. Equally upscale but less formal than its neighbor, the Fort Aguada Resort, the Taj Village is a great place for kids and for adults who want an informal experience. All rooms have private terraces and are elegantly rustic, most with attractive rattan furniture and wall-to-wall straw floor mats. The staff is friendly, helpful, and effective. Just slightly more expensive two-room villas are recommended. Some rooms (less expensive) do not have air conditioning. Facilities of the adjoining Taj properties are shared among the three resorts. ☎ *Sinquerim, Bardez 403519, Goa, ☎ 832/276201, ℻ 832/276045. 137 rooms, 5 suites. 4 restaurants, bar, pool, beauty salon, 5-hole golf course, tennis courts, health club, Ping-Pong, squash, volleyball, beach, windsurfing, boating, jetskiing, parasailing, waterskiing, baby-sitting, dry cleaning, laundry service, business services, meeting room, travel services, airport shuttle. AE, DC, MC, V.*

$$ **Cidade de Goa.** Built into a hillside near Panaji and modeled after a Portuguese hill town, this stylish resort is good if you want a more urban, less rustic-beachy atmosphere and if you want to be near Panaji and Old Goa. Designed by Indian architects Charles Correa and Rubina D'Souza, the building has open, multi-level corridors and public areas full of flat matte surfaces painted with contrasting oranges, geometric tile floors, and murals depicting the travels of Vasco da Gama. The rooms offer two distinct decors: *Damao* rooms have a Gujarati ambience with terracotta, mirrorwork, and a sleeping platform; *Casa* rooms are faintly Iberian with white walls, blue tiles, and wicker furniture. Request a terrace and a sea view. ☎ *Vainguinim Beach, Dona Paula, Tiswadi 403004, Goa, ☎ 832/221133, ℻ 832/223303. 205 rooms, 5 suites. 5 restaurants, 2 bars, pool, beauty salon, massage, sauna, 2 tennis courts, exercise room, volleyball, beach, windsurfing, boating, jet skiing, parasailing, waterskiing, baby-sitting, dry cleaning, laundry service, meeting rooms, travel services, airport shuttle. AE, DC, MC, V.*

$$ **Dona Sylvia.** Cute, little whitewashed cottages with red-tile roofs and doors painted pastel colors house the guest rooms at this south Goa resort. Rooms—two per cottage—are snug and slightly worn, decorated with white tile and stone and simple wood furniture. Worn stone paths lead through verdant grounds bursting with colorful hibiscus blooms to the open-air lobby and restaurant buildings, clustered around a large pool. A good beach is a short walk across the garden. ☎ *Cavelossim Beach, Salcete, Goa 403731, ☎ 834/246321, ℻ 834/246320. 174 rooms. Restaurant, 3 bars, pool, beauty salon, tennis court, beach, laundry service, travel services. AE, DC, MC, V.*

$$ **Holiday Inn Resort.** This friendly southern Goa resort has an intimate, down-to-earth ambience. The open-air lobby has white pillars, arches, and comfortable cane furniture and is alive with plants and ebullient birds. The rooms, in a two-story white stucco building, have red stone floors, standard modern teak furnishings, thick pastel drapes, and balconies. Paths lead through lovely grounds to an excellent secluded beach.

⊡ *Mobor Beach, Cavelossim, Salcete 403731, Goa, ☎ 834/246303,* FAX *834/246333. 138 rooms, 1 suite. 2 restaurants, bar, refrigerators, pool, tennis court, exercise room, Ping-Pong, beach, baby-sitting, dry cleaning, laundry service, business services, meeting room, travel services. AE, DC, MC, V.*

$$ **Majorda Beach Resort.** Facing Majorda Beach, this resort bears a modern Portuguese influence in its decor, a refreshing change from the standard chain-hotel look of many of its peers. Its large, open lobby, filled with marble, tile, and various Goan and Indian artifacts, has a swimming pool under the roof on its lower level. Rooms in the main, three-story red stone building are spacious, with white tile floors, teak or cane furnishings, and terraces. Built in 1984, the resort is beginning to show its age, but the rooms and lobby are gradually being refurbished while retaining their Goan flavor. You can also stay in villas (up to four units per villa) that have similar decor, plus a veranda or porch. ⊡ *Majorda, Salcete 403713, Goa, ☎ 834/220025,* FAX *834/220212. 106 rooms, 4 suites, 10 villas. 2 restaurants, 2 bars, coffee shop, indoor pool, outdoor pool, beauty salon, sauna, steam room, tennis court, exercise room, beach, baby-sitting, meeting rooms, travel services, airport shuttle. AE, DC, MC, V.*

$$ **Sterling Holiday Resort.** This secluded, Goan-style complex of white, tile-roof cottages is in a palm grove just 40 meters (43 yards) from the high-tide line on pretty Vagator Beach. Taken over by the Sterling Resorts time-share group in late 1993, all the rooms were exhaustively renovated and uniformly decorated with pale gold-colored stone floors, geometric-print upholsteries, painted wood furniture, and some decorative local artifacts. The swimming pool, on a hill behind the main enclave, is shared with the time-share cottages nearby. At the lower end of its price category, this is a good deal. ⊡ *Vagator, Bardez, Goa, ☎ 832/262918. 38 rooms. 2 restaurants, 2 bars, pool, beach, travel services. AE, DC, MC, V.*

$ **Estrela Do Mar Beach Resort.** Fuchsia blossoms spill over the top of the small iron gate to this cozy red Goan house nestled in an exuberant garden lush with brilliant-colored flowers. Standard rooms have no private telephone, no television, no air-conditioning, and no frills, but they offer peaceful seclusion within easy walking distance of the beach. All are minimally furnished and have ceiling fans and private verandas; bathroom sinks have only cold water. For a bit more money, request a popular new, air-conditioned suite in a separate cottage. ⊡ *Cobra Wado, Calangute, Baga, Bardez 403516, ☎ and fax 832/276014. 12 rooms, 2 suites. Restaurant, bar, beach, laundry service. No credit cards. Closed June–Sept.*

Kerala

By Vikram Singh

India's sun-drenched, palm-fringed southern paradise, Kerala has some of the world's best beaches and resorts. Resorts here offer a unique blend of getting away from it all and invigorating Ayurvedic health programs. You can undergo intensive treatments with a doctor, simply enjoy an occasional massage or yoga session, or even just laze around on the sand with a good book and a cool drink.

Just 10 kilometers (6 miles) south of Trivandrum are Kovalam's sandy beaches, lined with palm-fringed lagoons and rocky coves. Lungi (colorful cloth wrap)-clad fishermen drag in nets filled with the day's catch, then push their slender wooden fishing boats out again with a Malayalam "heave ho." You can spend your days on warm sand or exploring rocky outcroppings. You can enjoy the sunset and spend your evenings watching the dim lights of distant fishing boats. Even with tremendous development, Kovalam retains a mellow atmosphere. This has become the place for Ayurvedic treatment. Many hotels offer complete health and revitalization packages (of anywhere from two days to two weeks) in which Ayurvedic doctors, masseurs, and yoga and meditation instructors team up to optimize your physical and spiritual well-being (*see* Lodging, *below*). The Great India Tour Company also offers a good health tour in Kerala (*see* Tour Operators, *above*).

DINING

Thanks to a large tourist population, Kovalam is filled with restaurants, most of which serve fresh, delicious seafood.

For price categories, *see* the chart for Other Areas *in* On the Road with Fodor's.

$ Nalukettu. This 70-year-old traditional Nair family house with a pitched tile roof has numerous dining rooms. The air-conditioned one is best, but walk around and see the interior *nalukettu* (courtyard). You can also eat outside at night. The chef prepares dishes from many cuisines, including Kerala dishes. Try the mutton or chicken coconut fry (a curry dish prepared with chopped coconut, coconut milk, and masala spices). ✕ *Opposite Trivandrum Club, Vellayambalam,* ☎ *471/69287. Reservations advised. AE, DC, MC, V.*

$ Rockholm Hotel Restaurant. Though you can eat indoors, the best ambience is on the delightful terrace set on the bluff with the ocean pounding below. Kovalam's best chef prepares excellent multicuisine dishes, including the day's catch. Try the seasonal fish dishes, such as grilled pomfret, fried mussels, or prawns served Kerala style. ✕ *Light House Rd.,* ☎ *471/480607. AE, DC, MC, V.*

LODGING

For price categories, *see* the chart for Other Areas *in* On the Road with Fodor's.

$$$ ★ Kovalam Ashok Beach Resort. Built in tiers into a bluff overlooking the Arabian sea, this resort lacks great character and warmth, but it has a good beach. The rooms in the main block have modern furnishings and private verandas; ask for an unobstructed sea view. Cottages, with tile floors and a cozier feel, offer sea views and privacy. 🏨 *Kovalam, Vizhinjam, Trivandrum 695527, Kerala,* ☎ *471/68010,* FAX *471/62522. 125 rooms with bath, 2 suites. Restaurant, bar, pool, massage, health club, tennis court, travel services. AE, DC, MC, V.*

$$–$$$ ★ Surya Samudra Beach Resort. Overlooking the sea 10 kilometers (6 miles) south of Kovalam, this resort on eight acres is secluded, with an exquisite beach. Fastidiously designed, it offers a range of accommodations from simple cottages with interiors that blend modern and ethnic touches and have a shared bath to stunningly restored Kerala-style wooden homes, called *nallakettus,* with intricate carvings on the exterior, domed wooden ceilings, and pleasing understated modern decor. All cottages offer privacy and ocean views. No loud noise is permitted, and there are no TVs in the rooms. Full Ayurvedic treatments, complete with two doctors and several technicians/masseurs, are available for guests. Food is prepared daily without the use of preservatives and served in a delightful open-air restaurant with a Kerala-style design. Book well in advance. 🏨 *Pulinkudi, Mullur, Trivandrum 695521, Kerala,* ☎ *471/480413,* FAX *471/481124. 14 rooms, 8 with air-conditioning. Restaurant, bar, saltwater pool, beach, travel services. MC, V. Closed June and July.*

$$ Somatheeram. This ayurvedic beach resort has consciously attempted to preserve its natural setting. Guests stay in traditional houses or simple cottages along twisting paths on 13 lush acres above the sea. With two doctors, eight technicians, and a yoga master, Somatheeram is well prepared for stressed-out westerners. Various traditional treatment programs (normally 14-day sessions) are available, as well as one-time treatments (massage, medicated steam bath). Rooms have no air-conditioning or TV. ⊞ *Chowara, near Kovalam, Trivandrum 695501, Kerala,* ☎ *471/480600,* ⅢX *471/481600. 25 rooms. Restaurant, ayurvedic treatment, yoga, meditation, beach, travel services. AE, DC, MC, V.*

$ **Hotel Rockholm.** This small seaside hotel in the thick of things overlooks Kovalam's main beach. The rooms are spacious and clean, with modest contemporary furnishings and verandas. All rooms have overhead fans. ⊞ *Light House Rd., Kovalam, Trivandrum 695521, Kerala,* ☎ *471/480306,* ⅢX *471/480607. 17 rooms. Restaurant, travel services. AE, DC, MC, V.*

Lakshadweep

Of the 36 or so coral atolls that make up Lakshadweep, about 250 kilometers (160 miles) off the coast of Kerala, about 10 are inhabited by devout Sunni Muslims. Tourism here is severely restricted to protect the fragile islands and traditional people from the impact of tourism. At press time, only one island, Bangaram, was open to foreigners. Casino Hotels operates *the* resort on this isolated paradise. Flights leave from Cochin a couple of times a week.

Tours

Some outfits offer holidays in Lakshadweep (*see* Tour Operators, *above*). This is such a popular destination, you must make arrangements well in advance.

Dining and Lodging

For price categories, *see* the charts for Other Areas *in* On the Road with Fodor's.

$$$$ **Bangaram Island Resort.** The only place to stay in Bangaram, it is a
★ true paradise of simple thatched cottages (two or four rooms to a unit) with terra-cotta floors and Western furnishings. The emphasis is on the preservation of the environment, with minimal construction. The water sports (particularly snorkeling) are unbeatable. Meals are included. ⊞ *Lakshadweep; reservations, Casino Hotel, Willingdon Island, Cochin 682003, Kerala,* ☎ *484/668221,* ⅢX *484/668001. 27 rooms, 3 2-bedroom bungalows. Restaurant, bar, snorkeling, windsurfing, fishing. AE, DC, MC, V.*

Maharashtra

By Julie Tomasz   The Maharashtra coastline north of Goa may become the most beautiful resort area in India. Some of the region's many 17th-century forts are actually built on tiny off-shore islands that are dwarfed by the ramparts. The coastline offers wide panoramas without any encroachment of the modern world. You pass traditional villages that are usually the home of Kolis, one of the original fishing tribes. The women walk with a fine stride, saris worn Marathi fashion, skintight between their legs. The men master the waves and bring back the fish, which is then cooked in a zesty cuisine called Konkan.

In the early 1990s, the state enacted a plan to control the growth of resorts, protect valuable marshlands, and restore at least one coastal fort. No upscale accommodations exist today, but you can travel from Bombay south to Goa and spend nights under rustling palm fronds in idyllic coves and harbors at enjoyable, yet simple, tented beach resorts set up by the Maharashtra State Tourism Development Corporation (MTDC; Tours and Reservation Office, opposite L.I.C. Bldg., Madame Cama Rd., Bombay 400020, Maharashtra, ☎ 22/202–6713, FAX 22/202–4521).

Beaches and Tented Resorts

Because these areas are still only minimally developed, the beaches at or near the tented resorts are your best bets for sun and sand; the resorts and beaches are thus grouped together below. At each resort, you can choose a walk-in, two- or four-bed tent. Tents have windows, front and back entrances, and plenty of interior space. They come with comfortable cots, clean linen, electricity, fans, and filtered drinking water. Each tented resort also has separate bathrooms and shower facilities in clean, but unappealing concrete buildings—the only drawback. The resorts also have restaurants; many are thatch covered and in the open air. They usually serve Indian (sometimes Konkan) and limited Continental cuisines that may include the catch of the day. All these resorts are closed June 15 to October 1. They are restricted to couples and families; each tent costs about 300 rupees per day, double occupancy. MTDC also has a rent-a-tent scheme that allows you to choose your own private beach hideaway.

To get to these resorts, you can hire a car and driver from Bombay (*see* Tourist Information *in* Chapter 12, Bombay and the Ellora and Ajanta Caves).

Numbers in the margin correspond to beaches on the Beaches, Bombay–wGoa map.

❺ **MTDC Bhatye Beach Tented Resort.** This complex stands on a sandy hill overlooking a secluded beach near coconut groves and casuarina trees. Water sports facilities offer windsurfing, kayaking, waterscooters, and pedal boats. ⊞ *Ratnagiri district, 356 km (221 mi) south of Bombay. 15 4-bed tents with shared bath.*

❶ **MTDC Bordi Beach Tented Resort.** This small seaside town, north of Bombay, is a favorite holiday spot for escaping Bombay residents. Tents are on an isolated beach stretch backed by casuarina trees. ⊞ *Thane district, 130 km (81 mi) north of Bombay. 5 tents with shared bath.*

❹ **MTDC Ganapatipule Beach Tented Resort.** Nestled in a coconut grove, this complex also has a good restaurant. The tents have views onto the white sand beach, offering plenty of privacy. Because this is an important Hindu pilgrimage site, liquor is not available or allowed. ⊞ *Ratnagiri district, 375 km (233 mi) south of Bombay. 20 2-bed and 25 4-bed tents with shared bath.*

❷ **MTDC Harihareshwar Beach Tented Resort.** Set on an inlet and backed by hills, this delightful complex stands near two beaches. The more secluded beach is preferable. Authentic Konkan fare is served in a rustic restaurant, often followed by a crackling campfire. ⊞ *Raigad district, 230 km (143 mi) south of Bombay. 10 2-bed and 10 4-bed tents.*

❸ **MTDC Murud-Harnai Tented Resort.** This complex, set on a palm-fringed beach, also offers good local Konkan cuisine. ⊞ *Ratnagiri district, 247 km (153 mi) south of Bombay. 5 4-bed tents with shared bath.*

Tamil Nadu

Just south of Madras, you can spend time at the Taj Fisherman's Cove Resort in Covelong, a hideaway nestled in a lovely fishing village. You can also head south to Mamallapuram, where beach resorts are near famous temple ruins (*see* Excursions from Madras *in* Chapter 9, Tamil Nadu).

Dining and Lodging

For dining and lodging, *see* Madras and Mamallapuram *in* Chapter 9, Tamil Nadu.

WILDLIFE PARKS

India has 59 national parks and over 250 sanctuaries, in which more than 350 different mammals and 1,200 birds live. Many of these creatures are unique to the subcontinent: the white tiger, the royal Bengal tiger, the Asian lion, the lion-tailed macaque, the Andaman teal, the great Indian bustard, and the monal pheasant.

Before 1947 India did not protect its wildlife. By 1952, 13 species had been endangered, and today the list has multiplied to 70 species of mammals, 16 species of reptiles, and 36 species of birds. Tigers, the symbolic mascot of India, were killed so frequently that by 1970, only 1,500 remained. In 1972, the Indian government finally passed the Wildlife Act, which preserves natural parks and sanctuaries and provides for the protection of wildlife, particularly endangered species. Three years later, Corbett National Park became India's first tiger reserve, part of a large-scale enterprise, Project Tiger, cosponsored by India's Department of Wildlife and the World Wildlife Fund. Under Project Tiger, the government banned killing and set up 10 reserves. The total number of tigers has risen to over 1,800, but now poachers are a serious threat that may finish off this rare animal.

India is also attempting to re-cover a third of its landmass with forests— a daunting task that requires more than saplings. The rural poor will need viable fuel sources to replace wood, and a humane initiative must be mandated to control the movement of foraging livestock, including the sacrosanct cow.

Still, for admirers of wildlife, many of India's parks and sanctuaries are enchanting. Visitors should remember that many of India's animals are elusive and move in small packs at daybreak and in the evening or at night. You're lucky if you spot a tiger, an Asian lion, or a leopard. Come with the proper expectations and you will see many animals: numerous species of deer, wild boar, langur of all descriptions, and spectacular birds. Keep your camera and binoculars ready. Shooting, of course, is prohibited, but the hunter's loss is the photographer's gain. Just be sure to bring enough film when you visit any park. Wear neutral-color clothes so you blend into the forest.

Also, remember that if you plan to stay overnight *inside* a sanctuary, you must arrive before it closes at sunset. Expect to pay a nominal charge for entrance and often a small fee to use your still or video camera. All fees are paid at park entrances. The Government of India Tourist Office in Delhi has good information on wildlife parks (*see* the Gold Guide, *above*).

Bandhavgarh National Park

By Smita Patel On the northern side of the Satpura range in Madhya Pradesh, Bandhavgarh was once the private hunting preserve of the royal family of Rewa. Its ancient hills are weathered and gnarled, and the park (343 square kilometers or 137 square miles) is covered with a blanket of mixed forest dominated by sal and bamboo and riddled with streams that occasionally broaden into marshland. Bandhavgarh is rich in wildlife, especially the magnificent sambar (spotted deer) and the ugly but sturdy wild boar. You also have the chance to see foxes, sloth bears, and the massive gaur, or Indian ox. Tiger sighting, though still common, is no longer a certainty. If you see a tiger in Bandhavgarh now, it is due to your luck and the tracking skills of your guide. While you scan the surrounding trees for signs of animals, don't forget to look up. Bandhavgarh also has a rich collection of birds, including the vulture, ibis, spoonbill, Malabar hornbill, steppe eagle, and blue-bearded bee eater.

The park is open from sunrise to about 11 AM and then from 4 PM to sunset, the best times for seeing wildlife. It is closed during the monsoons (approximately June through August). Jeep rental is available at the park (Rs. 400 per round); some of the jungle camps include rounds of the park in their charges. You can go on elephant, but you cover much less ground.

For park information and reservations in government-run accommodations, contact the Madhya Pradesh State Tourism Development Corporation (MPSTDC, Gangotri, 4th Floor, T. T. Nagar, Bhopal 462003, M.P., ☎ 755/554340, 554341, or 554342).

Dining and Lodging

For price categories, *see* the charts for Other Areas *in* On the Road with Fodor's.

$$ Bandhavgarh Jungle Lodge. These mud huts are the real thing; there's no concrete under their thatched roofs. The rooms are decorated in colorful ethnic prints, and pottery set up outside gives this place a village feel. The lodge stands right near the park entrance. The restaurant serves fixed-menu meals from a variety of cuisines. ☷ *Tiger Resorts Pvt. Ltd., Suite 206, Rakesh Deep Bldg., Gulmohar Enclave, New Delhi 110049, ☎ 11/666770, ℻ 11/686–5212. 12 rooms with bath. Restaurant, travel services. No credit cards.*

$ Tiger Trails Resort. These clean and comfortable brick cottages with tile roofs and fireplaces are furnished in cane and jute. The dining room is lovely, mostly open brick with a tiled roof. The restaurant offers a fixed menu with a variety of cuisines. ☷ *Bandhavgarh. Reserve through Indian Adventures, 257 S. V. V. Rd., Bandra (W), Bombay 50, ☎ 22/640–8742 or 22/643–3622, ℻ 22/640399. 12 rooms. Restaurant, travel services. No credit cards.*

Bharatpur

It was once the duck-hunting forest of the local maharajas. Now people come from all over to see birds, and birds come from all over to be seen. Founded by the Jat ruler Suraj Mal in 1733, the city of Bharatpur is famous for the **Keoladeo National Park,** a water-bird sanctuary that is the winter home of hundreds of species. Only 55 kilometers (34 miles) from Agra, and just across the state border from Fatehpur Sikri, this park is an ornithologist's treat—packed into 29 square kilometers (12 square miles) of forests and wetlands.

The main artery of the park is a blacktop road that runs from the entrance gate to the center. Surrounded by marshlands but screened by bushes, this road is the most convenient place from which to watch the birds. This is also the route for the cycle rickshaws (Rs. 25), a horse and buggy, and the park's electric bus. The rickshaw drivers are trained by the forest department and are fairly good at finding and pointing out birds. You can also walk or hire a bicycle (about Rs. 20) and head into the less-traveled areas of the park. (Apart from the blacktop, the roads are unpaved and can make for a bumpy bicycle ride.) You can explore by boat in a limited boating area. Excellent guides at the gate (Rs. 35 per hour), who are familiar with the haunts of the birds, can also point out and identify birds.

The park is also home to mammals and reptiles, including the ungainly blue bull, the spotted deer, a few otters, and Indian rock pythons, which can be seen, in winter, basking outside their burrows during the day.

Don't forget to take a bird guide book (Salim Ali's *The Birds of India* is a good choice; he's a member of the former royal family.) The best season is November to February; by the end of February, many birds start heading home. The best time to see the birds is early in the morning or late in the evening. Be sure to stick around the park at sunset, when the water takes on a mirrorlike stillness and the air is filled with the calls of day birds settling down and night birds stirring.

Dining and Lodging

Given the park's popularity, there's often a rush during the season, especially on weekends, so book early.

For price categories, *see* the charts for Other Areas *in* On the Road with Fodor's.

$$ Ashok Bharatpur Forest Lodge. Inside the sanctuary, this ivy-covered
★ bungalow offers clean, comfortable rooms, some with decorative interior swings. All rooms have balconies, and you may see spotted deer nibbling the grass outside your window. The Indian and Continental food served in the hotel's buffet-style restaurant is excellent. ☎ *Bharatpur, Rajasthan 321001,* ☎ *5644/22760,* FAX *5644/22864. 17 rooms with bath. Restaurant, bar. AE, DC, MC, V.*

$ Laxmi Vilas Palace Hotel. The home of the former maharaja's uncle,
★ it's even called *Kakaji ki kothi* (uncle's house). Recently converted into a Heritage Hotel by the family, the two-story *haveli* (mansion) was built at the turn of the century. The rooms are all different, but many contain old brass beds and antique furniture. The more expensive rooms have the original tiles and painted walls and fireplaces. The less expensive rooms are smaller and have newer furniture, but they are still pleasant. The dining room offers meals from a variety of cuisines. The family, who still reside in the house, also offer excursions to surrounding areas, such as Deeg, Agra, and Fatehpur Sikri. ☎ *Kakaji Ki Kothi, Bharatpur, Rajasthan 321001,* ☎ *5644/25259 or 5644/253523,* FAX *5644/25265. 25 rooms with bath. Restaurant. No credit cards.*

Corbett National Park

By Kathleen Cox

India's oldest wildlife sanctuary (started in 1936), Corbett National Park in Uttar Pradesh is named after Jim Corbett, the fearless hunter and author of *Man-Eaters of Kumaon* who became a conservationist. Corbett grew up in these hills, and the local people, a number of whom he saved from tigers at the risk of his own life, revered him. Corbett hunted tigers, but came to regret the sport as he saw the turn-of-the-century population of up to 40,000 tigers drastically reduced. But it wasn't until his death in Kenya in 1956 that India honored him by renaming the Hailey National Park after this well-liked man.

The park, with elephant grass, sal forests, and the Ramganga River slicing through its entire length, covers 1,318 square kilometers (527 square miles). You can explore the park on the back of an elephant as it sways quietly through the jungle brush. You can sit in an open Jeep as it rolls along miles of tracks; or you can just peer into the vast vista from the top of a stationary watchtower and listen to the sounds of the park inhabitants. This is a great park worthy of Corbett's memory. You will see many species of deer, monkeys, and birds. If you're lucky, you may spot wild elephants, tigers, leopards, black bear, wild boar, snakes (including the python), and crocodiles.

The best viewing time is December through April. Corbett is closed from June 15 to November 15. Day visitors (only 100 are allowed inside per day) are not allowed in Dhikala, near the core area (closed to tourists) or to enter by Dhangarhi Gate. Day visitors who are not staying at a nearby private lodge must get an entry permit from the Ramnagar Reception (open in season daily 8–1 and 3–5) to enter by the Amdanda Gate and can make excursions into the Bijrani area (7–11 and 2:30–4:30 in winter and 5:30–9:30 and 4–7 in spring). If you stay at a private lodge, it will make excursion arrangements. A guide, available at the park, must accompany each vehicle. Jeeps for excursions are for hire at nearby Ramnagar. Elephant safaris can be arranged inside the park. If you stay in the park, excursions at Dhikala are from 7 to 11 and 3 to 5 in winter and 5 to 9 and 4 to 7 in spring. The Uttar Pradesh Tourist Office in Delhi (U.P. Tourism, Chandralok Building, 36 Janpath, New Delhi 110001, ☎ 11/332–2251) has good information on the park. Corbett is just a six-hour drive from Delhi, which makes it a popular getaway.

Dining and Lodging

Both private lodges offer package stays that can include a night in a Corbett Park rest house, where the private lodge provides the linen and a cook prepares the food.

For price categories, *see* the charts for Other Areas *in* On the Road with Fodor's.

$$ Claridges Corbett Hideaway. This resort in a mango orchard offers an intimate ambience. Claridges is on the banks of the Kosi River and not far from the park. Pebbled walkways lead to about 12 cottages with *chaprel* (baked-tile roofs), stone tile floors, woven bamboo mat ceilings, and working fireplaces. An ethnic decor incorporates rattan and jute furniture. Each cottage has an interior sitting area, a modern bathroom with a shower, and a covered front veranda. You can enjoy fixed-menu meals from a variety of cuisines in an open-air thatched hut or in a new lodge with a deck overlooking the river. ☎ *Zero Garjia, Dhikuli, Ramnagar, Nainital district, Uttar Pradesh,* ☎ *5945/85959; or Claridges, New Delhi,* ☎ *11/301–0211,* FAX *11/301–0625. 28 rooms. 2 restaurants, bar, hiking. AE, DC, MC, V.*

$$ Tiger Tops Corbett Lodge. Not affiliated with the international Tiger
★ Tops organization, this resort has a classy atmosphere. Its location on the banks of the Kosi lets you hear the rush of the river. The two-story lodge is built with marble, stone, and slate. Each spacious room, with a large picture window, has an attractive stone wall and a bamboo-and-tile ceiling and a modern bathroom with a shower. The private balconies overlook a mango grove, the river, and mountains. Tiger Tops also has an attractive circular lounge, where you can eat, drink, and relax inside or on the deck, and a gorgeous outdoor swimming pool. Meals and activities are included. ☎ *Dhikuli, Ramnagar, Nainital district, Uttar Pradesh, 224715,* ☎ *5946/85279,* FAX *5946/85380; or Khatau International, N/37 Panchshila Park, New Delhi 110017,* ☎ *11/644–4016,* FAX *11/644–7564; or Bombay,* ☎ *22/262–2649,* FAX *22/262–1723. 24 rooms. Restaurant, bar, pool, elephant and Jeep safaris, hiking, travel services. AE, DC, MC, V.*

$ Corbett National Park Government Lodging. For all reservations inside the park (reservations can be hard to obtain because preference is given to VIPs), contact the following well in advance. ✉ *Field Director, Project Tiger, Corbett National Park, Ramnagar 244715, Uttar Pradesh,* ☎ *5946/85489 or 5946/85322; or the Uttar Pradesh Tourist Office in New Delhi. No credit cards.*

Bijrani Rest House. In an open area at the southern end of the park, this older one-story lodge was popular with Rajiv Gandhi. Rooms are good sized, but not electrified. The menu is Indian and Continental. ✉ *6 rooms with bath (hot water by the bucket). Cafeteria, elephant safaris.*

Dhikhala Forest Rest House Complex. The rooms are in two lodges and an annex. The old lodge, which is a large bungalow, has spacious rooms, old pictures on the walls, and an appealing ambience that fits the environment. The new lodge and annex lack character, but the rooms are clean. The restaurant serves Indian and Continental food. ✉ *About 23 rooms with simple bathrooms containing showers. Restaurant, elephant safaris, travel services.*

Khinanauli, Gairal, and Sarapduli rest houses. More secluded within the forest, these rest houses are rustic and not electrified, but they provide great getaways for the wildlife enthusiast. Expect simple rooms and a no-frills kitchen. Bring a sleeping bag or your own linen and all food provisions. ✉ *2–6 rooms per rest house with bath (water by the bucket).*

Kanha National Park

By Smita Patel

In southeastern Madhya Pradesh, Kanha, now a Project Tiger reserve, ranks as one of India's finest sanctuaries. Kipling set his *Jungle Book* in this vicinity, and its characters (Baloo, Bagheera, and Sher Khan) still hang out here. Declared a national park in 1955, Kanha is one of India's largest sanctuaries, with 940 square kilometers (376 square miles) plus a 1,000-square-kilometer buffer zone extending across plateaus of forests, meadows, and grasslands threaded with rivers. More than 22 species of mammals roam the park, including the tiger, *barasingha* (subspecies of swamp deer unique to this park), barking deer, gaur, *dhole* (wild dog), leopard, jungle cat, sloth bear, hyena, and, of course, the ubiquitous spotted deer. You're also apt to spot numerous birds: gray hornbills, black ibis, white-necked crane, hoopoe, shrike, stork, heron, and painted snipe.

Though Kanha is considered a sal forest, these large trees are liberally interspersed with meadows and bamboo. The park's expanse gives the animals ample room to hide from prying eyes, so you may come away having seen nothing. Stay long enough to make several rounds in the jungle and increase your chance for success.

The park is open from sunrise to about 11 AM and then from 4 PM to sunset, which are also the best times for seeing wildlife. The park closes down during the monsoons (approximately June through August). Jeep rides are available at the park (Rs. 400 per round); some of the jungle camps include Jeep safaris in their charges.

Dining and Lodging

For price categories, *see* the charts for Other Areas *in* On the Road with Fodor's.

$$ Kipling Camp. The cottages of this nonprofit lodge are scattered in a grove. Some huts have mud floors and bamboo roofs; others are white-washed brick structures. The camp's best feature is its charming restaurant (serving a variety of cuisines) and bar, which is illuminated by candlelight in the evening. All rooms have attached baths, most have showers. Between jungle rounds, you can help bathe the resident elephant. ☎ *Kisli. Reserve through Mr. R. H. White, Tollygunge Club, 120 D. P. Sasmal Rd., Calcutta 700033; ☎ 33/473–3306 or 33/473–1430, FAX 33/472–0484. 16 rooms. Restaurant, travel services. No credit cards.*

$$ Wild Chalet Resort. This charming complex of tile-roof cottages on the
★ banks of the Banjar River is the lodging farthest (10 kilometers, 6 miles) from the park entrance, but the location is beautiful, and animals come to the river to drink. The rooms have jute mats on the floor and cane furniture. The restaurant serves a variety of cuisines from a fixed menu. ☎ *Kisli. Reserve through Indian Adventures, 257 S. V. Rd., Bandra (W), Bombay 50; ☎ 22/640–8742, FAX 22/640–6399. 12 rooms. Restaurant, travel services. No credit cards.*

$ Kanha Safari Lodge. Set at the Mukki entrance to the park, this small hotel has a charming lobby with a huge fireplace in the center and stairs leading up to a spacious dining room with huge windows overlooking the river. Run by MPSTDC, it offers simple but clean rooms with verandas; some rooms have air-conditioning. The hotel stands on the banks of the river surrounded by a forest. The restaurant offers Indian, Chinese, and a few Continental dishes. This is the only hotel here that is open year-round. ☎ *Mukki. Reserve through MPSTDC (see address in Bandhavgarh National Park, above). 30 rooms. Restaurant, travel services. No credit cards.*

Lake Periyar Wildlife Sanctuary

By Vikram
Singh

Kerala's Lake Periyar, with its many fingers that wind around low-lying hills, is the heart of the 777-square-kilometer (300-square-mile) wildlife sanctuary. Periyar offers one of the most sybaritic ways of seeing big game. Here, forget exhausting treks or long safaris. You lounge in a motor launch as it drifts around a bend and comes upon elephants or deer or bison drinking at the shores of the lake. During the dry season, when water holes in the forest are empty, leopards and tigers also pad up to the water. One word of advice: Either bribe the Indian children to be quiet—they love to scream and shout at a sighting—or hire a private launch (about Rs. 500). Elephant herds are so accustomed to *quiet* visitors that they hardly notice the intrusion. Elephants with their young graze beside deer, gaur (wild oxen), and sambar (large Asiatic deer); you may even glimpse tigers and bears. The best viewing time is October through May. Admission to the park is Rs. 50, or about $1.75, and video cameras are Rs. 100.

Dining and Lodging

For price categories, *see* the charts for Other Areas *in* On the Road with Fodor's.

$$–$$$$ Hotel Lake Palace. This former maharaja's hunting lodge, on an island inside the sanctuary, is run by the Kerala Tourism Development Corporation (KTDC) and is scheduled for renovation. The ambience is idyllic. The best rooms open onto a sweeping porch with good views. Meals at the multicuisine, fixed-menu restaurant are included. ☎ *Thekkady, Idukki district 685536, Kerala, ☎ 4869/2023; reserve through KTDC (see Kerala Essentials in Chapter 10, Kerala). 8 rooms with bath. Restaurant, boating, travel services. AE, DC. MC, V.*

$$$ Spice Village. This charming resort is just outside the sanctuary on the edge of a small village. Tiers of thatch-roof cottages are built into the side of a hill. The interiors are rustic modern: lots of knotty pine furnishings and trim, white walls, red-tile floors, and plaid upholstery and bedspreads. Lush plantings, including spice trees, add fragrance and privacy. The restaurant serves Indian and Continental food. ▣ *Kummily Rd., Thekkady 685536,* ☎ *4869/2314; reserve through Casino Hotel, Willingdon Island, Cochin 682003, Kerala,* ☎ *484/668221,* FAX *484/668001. 37 rooms with bath. Restaurant, bar, pool, travel services. AE, DC, V.*

Nagarhole Sanctuary

By Julie Tomasz   In Karnataka many years ago, an infamous practice called *khedda* (wild elephant roundup) was common. The big pachyderms of the region were in great demand among maharajas and princes, circuses, zoos, and people wanting working beasts for construction projects. The arena for these roundups was in the Karapur forest, with swarms of skilled tribesmen pitted against a herd of trumpeting elephants. Today, the kheddas have stopped, and instead of animals in terror, you can watch wild elephants—untrapped and untamed—moving around the same forests, which now comprise the Nagarhole Sanctuary, established in 1954.

From Kabini River Lodge (*see* Dining and Lodging, *below*) you can take fantastic game-viewing tours led by Colonel Wakefield and his excellent staff, who are skillful at stalking the wild beasts. You may spot dholes (wild dogs), the massively muscular Indian gaur, sambars, barking deer, sloth bears, crocodiles, and families of elephants (mothers, calves, "aunt" elephants, and tuskers), and if you're lucky, maybe an elusive leopard or tiger. You can also glide around in a coracle, a round, basket-shaped boat lined with buffalo hide. Coracles are so slow and quiet that you can approach very close to wild animals and the abundance of birdlife (over 225 different species). The best viewing times are early morning and evening from October through March. Nagarhole is also home to some of India's tribes (the Jenu Kurubas and the Betta Kurubas).

Dining and Lodging

For price categories, *see* the charts for Other Areas *in* On the Road with Fodor's.

$$$ **Kabini River Lodge.** Once the vice-regal and maharaja's hunting lodge, this resort in the sanctuary is run by wildlife expert Colonel Wakefield and his staff, who are gracious and knowledgeable. Chances are you will see wildlife nearby. The ambience is peaceful, with a languid daily routine: long Jeep safaris or coracle boating on the river, broken up by morning and afternoon tea sessions on the veranda and hearty open-air meals from a variety of cuisines (included; drinks are extra) overlooking the river. At night, before dinner, you gather in the common room with the other guests to share the day's animal stories and watch a video about wildlife. The basic rooms have overhead fans, simple stone floors, and a rustic dark-wood decor. You can also stay in two-bed safari-style tents. ▣ *Karapur, Karnataka; reservations through Jungle Lodges & Resorts Limited, 2nd Floor, Shrungar Shopping Centre, M. G. Rd., Bangalore 560001,* ☎ *80/558–6163 or 80/559–7021,* FAX *80/ 558–6163. 14 rooms with bath, 6 cottages. Restaurant, bar, jeep and elephant safaris. AE, DC, MC, V.*

Sariska National Park

By Smita Patel   Sariska was once the exclusive game preserve of the rulers of the princely state of Alwar. Today, this sanctuary nestled in the Arvalli Range provides a great weekend escape from Delhi, which is just 200 kilometers (124 miles) away. The terrain is mostly scrub interspersed with lush stands of forest and grasslands. Peacocks abound here, as do monkeys, blue bulls, spotted deer, and wild boars. There are tigers and leopards too, but their nocturnal habits make sighting rare. However, you do have a good chance of seeing langurs and other monkeys, porcupines, hyenas, and numerous species of deer (including the *chowsingha,* or four-horned deer—unique to India) and a great variety of birds.

Keeping the animals company in Sariska are a number of historic monuments. Within the park is the Pandupol, a huge hole in the rock supposedly made by Bhim, one of the five Pandava brothers who are celebrated in the Hindu epic *Mahabharata.* Outside the sanctuary, but still close by, are the Neelkanth Mahadev, which contains bits and pieces of about 300 Hindu and Jain temples, including some beautiful sculptures, and a lovely Shiva temple that is still standing, as well as the ruins of the Kankwari Fort, perched high on a hill (a good picnic spot). The tiger, never one for respecting other people's boundaries, is often seen by villagers living at the base of the hill. Other sights include a ruined ghost town and ruins of Jain and Buddhist temples.

The best viewing time at Sariska is early morning or evening from November through June (but it starts getting hot by March). Jeeps are available. Wear neutral colors and take a jacket in winter.

Dining and Lodging
For price categories, *see* the charts for Other Areas *in* On the Road with Fodor's.

$$ **Sariska Palace Hotel.** This former palace and royal hunting lodge on the edge of the Sariska National Park was built by the maharaja of Alwar for the visit of Queen Victoria's son, the duke of Connaught. Its architecture is a blend of French regal with eastern detailing, and it is now a Heritage Hotel. The interior is not opulent, but it does have some Louis XIV and Art Deco furniture, along with wicker chairs and Victoriana. The rooms and suites are gigantic (with the typical high ceilings) and clean, with phones but no TV; some are air-conditioned. The lovely flower-bedecked grounds are encircled by a large wall to keep out the animals, though they often find their way in. You may see wildlife while relaxing on the terrace. The dining room serves Continental and Indian (including Rajasthani) cuisine. ⚏ *Alwar district, Rajasthan,* ☎ *14441/322; reservations through Shebawheels, 4/1 D. B. Gupta Rd., Paharganj, New Delhi,* ☎ *11/739712 or 11/732365. 40 rooms with bath, 5 suites. Restaurant, bar, pool, tennis court, travel services. AE, DC, MC, V.*

Fishing

By Julie Tomasz   Karnataka's rivers teem with fish and an occasional crocodile. Fishing expeditions for visitors are becoming an important part of the state's tourist industry.

Tour Operators
Jungle Lodges & Resorts Limited (Shrungar Shopping Center, 2nd Floor, M.G. Rd., Bangalore 560001, ☎ 80/5597021, ℻ 80/5586163), the outdoor-activity branch of the Karnataka Tourism Department, has rustic facilities in the state's protected wild areas, where professional guides take guests on wildlife-viewing jeep tours or to fish-rich rivers.

Adventures

FISHING

The mammoth mahseer fish swim in the **Cauvery River** near Bhimeswari, about 100 kilometers (60 miles) south of Bangalore and 75 kilometers (46 miles) east of Mysore. Anglers regularly hook mahseers weighing upwards of 50 pounds here, as well as smaller Carnatic carp, pink carp, and the catfish. Catch can be weighed and photographed for proof but must be returned to the river. You can fish from the shore or go out in a round, basket-like boat called a coracle for midstream casting. You share the forest with elephants, sambar deer, wild boars, and four-horned antelopes. (December–March.)

Dining and Lodging

For price categories, *see* the charts for Other Areas *in* On the Road with Fodor's.

$$ Cauvery Fishing Camp. This peaceful camp is on the bank of the Cauvery River. Guests sleep overlooking the river in simple twin-bedded tents with attached bathrooms; wholesome meals are served in an open-air dining area around a campfire. Trained guides take you to the prime angling spots in Jeeps or coracle boats; fishing equipment is not provided. Meals are included. Reserve far in advance; accommodations are limited and popular. ⊠ *Bhimeswari, Karnataka; reservations through Jungle Lodges & Resorts Limited* (see above). *6 tents. AE, DC, MC, V.*

3 Business Travel in India

India has opened its doors to the international market, but doing business in India requires thorough research before you board a plane for the subcontinent. Do as much as you can in advance; come armed with patience.

DOING BUSINESS IN INDIA

By Kathleen
Cox

INDIA HAS OPENED ITS DOORS to the international market, creating opportunities from infrastructural development projects to export or import collaborations. But doing business in India requires thorough research before you board a plane for the subcontinent. To save time and avoid bureaucratic hurdles, contact your government's appropriate departments, such as the India desks at the U.S. State Department and the Commerce Department, to get the latest rules and regulations governing investment, the export of goods, and the import of goods or services. Also contact the nearest Indian consulate or embassy for the names of bilateral trade organizations in your home country that can offer useful advice and current information on India's ongoing reforms.

If you are visiting Delhi, try to arrange a meeting with the commercial affairs department attached to your embassy or high commission (*see* Delhi Essentials *in* Chapter 4, Delhi). This department may be able to put you in touch with helpful officials in the Indian government and appropriate parties in the country's private sector. The department can also provide a list of Indian business organizations, such as the Chamber of Commerce and the Confederation of India Industries, and the names of their officers. With memberships that include leading business executives and industrialists, these organizations have tremendous clout.

Try to fix most of your appointments before you leave, and don't plan a trip close to a major holiday, such as Diwali or Republic Day, when business slows to a crawl for days. Remember that, in the best circumstances, doing business in India takes time. Do as much as you can in advance and assume that everything will take twice as long once you arrive. For this reason, come armed with patience.

Also understand that India still has mixed feelings about the arrival of multinationals and foreign businesses. Some politicians and industrial houses fear the onslaught of international consumer goods that they believe will destroy indigenous companies or have no intrinsic value for the country. A popular slogan in India is "computer chips, not potato chips." Consequently, liberalization has been subject to hiccups, and reforms are moving at an uneven pace. Some deals are approved quickly; others become stuck in bureaucratic red tape. If you want to enter India and actually set up shop, investigate which states are more aggressive in the pursuit of foreign investments, because it could save you time and money in the long run. Some multinationals have had to abort projects after they've sunk money and even acquired land in a state that is mired in protest over the arrival of outsiders.

Also understand that by nature, Indians want to be obliging and find it hard to say no. Often they communicate a negative response by endless stalling. Although you must arrive with patience and not be too aggressive, you must also set a realistic time frame. If you can't get a solid yes or if you experience repeated delaying tactics, take this as a signal that the parties with whom you are negotiating aren't interested. Also get all commitments on paper with a minimum of ambiguity, such as targeted dates for the next stage of negotiations. If you can't get anything of substance in writing, this is the time to put negotiations on ice.

When you go to India, bring business cards—lots of them! They're your passport to get past the clerk who guards the room of an important government official and the receptionist who controls access to anyone highly placed in the private sector. Also bring some of your business letterheads. As for appropriate clothing, business women should dress for "business" and wear a conservative skirt, dress, or suit to meetings. Power clothes do give women power and respect in India. Men can be casual and even get away without a suit jacket, although evening events may require a jacket and tie.

Americans, in particular, should speak slowly because many Indians find it difficult to understand American English, especially on the phone. You should use the phone the first morning you arrive to re-confirm all your appointments, especially appointments with members of the government. Because of stringent security, entry into ministries or any government building housing the offices of senior officials is usually prohibited unless your name appears on an appointment list or is cleared with the clerk or secretary.

Be prompt for appointments, but don't be surprised if you end up waiting to see ministers or senior government bureaucrats. Also don't be surprised if other people are in the room when you are ushered in to conduct your business. Often they are also waiting for their moment with the official. You may have to wait your turn, or your meeting may take precedence. Don't attach any significance to this situation. Expect tea or coffee; relax and enjoy it. If you expect to launch immediately into your reason for sitting in the room, you will end up frustrated. Also expect frequent interruptions: Bureaucrats or clerks will walk in with files or letters that need urgent attention, and desk phones will ring every minute.

If your meeting is with a woman, don't offer your hand to her unless she extends hers to you. Many Indian women tend to follow the custom that governs their religion. A Hindu woman may hold her hands together in the traditional "namaste" greeting, which you should do in return. A Muslim woman may just nod and say hello. But don't think that these forms of reserve translate into limited business authority. Many women in India have considerable power in the private and government sectors.

When you discuss yourself and your business needs, speak with a comfortable yet quiet authority. American men are often considered aggressive, so don't come on strong. Present yourself as a professional who is respectful of the person sitting across from you. In general, most first meetings in India are "feelers" during which the establishment of rapport is the primary agenda; don't hope for much more. This rapport, however, is invaluable in the long term.

It's also unwise to criticize India when you are with Indian business associates. The elevator you take or the stairwell that you climb to an office may be filthy, but keep the observation to yourself. India is proud and sensitive about foreigners' critical comparisons. Tact will score you points. If your Indian host is confronted with an awkward moment—say, the phone doesn't work or the air-conditioner malfunctions and turns everyone hot under the collar—keep your cool. It will be appreciated.

During meetings, take notes. Then provide a written summation of what has been agreed and what still needs to be discussed and resolved. This is one good reason to take letterheads with you. These summations will be useful if your meetings ultimately lead to a memorandum of understanding (MOU) prepared by the associates with whom you want to do business. They become an invaluable source of reference and help assure that the MOU accurately reflects any verbal agreement.

Many foreigners doing business in India have also discovered that casual discussions held during a game of golf, after tennis, or over lunch or dinner have a winning effect. The point to remember is that whom you know in the business and government hierarchy is part of the game, how well you get along will make the difference, and gaining trust helps seal the deal. For this reason, feel comfortable about accepting non-business-oriented or nonbusiness-hour invitations. India is a land of the joint family tradition, and this concept flows into the business arena. To be treated like family is an honor and can win you more than a new friend.

SPECIAL HINTS FOR BUSINESS TRAVELERS

Most luxury hotels in India's major cities have special floors designed for business travelers. The Hyatt and the New Delhi Hilton in Delhi and many of the Taj and Welcomgroup Sheraton properties throughout the country have floors that include business-oriented or exclusive facilities, such as a private lounge with complimentary breakfast and afternoon snacks and beverages, a private business center, a legal library, private seminar rooms, and computer on-line business services like Knight Ridder. The bedrooms on many of these floors also have voice-mail machines and computer hookups.

Some of these hotels, including the Oberoi chain (which doesn't have designated business floors), have private dining rooms that are perfect for daylong meetings or discreet business luncheons or dinners. If you think you will need specific business amenities, find out what facilities are provided before you book a hotel. Room classifications in a hotel can also be confusing. Be sure that you understand the differences and, especially, the difference in price.

Even if you don't stay on a special business floor, many luxury hotels, such as the Hyatt and the New Delhi Hilton in Delhi and city-located Oberoi, Taj, and Welcomgroup Sheraton properties throughout India, offer reasonably sophisticated business services. Typically, these business services are available 24 hours and include private offices, seminar and small conference rooms with audiovisual equipment (charged by the day), modems and computers for hire, and fax and photocopying services, as well as secretaries, translators, and interpreters on request. The Hyatt in Delhi also has e-mail; many other hotels will probably have this service by 1996. Other hotels, such as the international-franchise budget chains and Ashok, provide less elaborate business services. Expect fax and photocopying services and secretaries and translators.

Private fax and computer services are also available in nearly every city. The prices are often more competitive than those at hotels, but your hotel may provide more reliable service. When you send a fax, make certain that you receive a transmission record and that it indicates that the fax went through without an error. Many fax facilities charge for unsuccessful transmissions and insist that the error message is wrong. Don't believe this; before sending a fax, ask how charges are determined, especially in the event of faulty transmissions. For information on long-distance domestic or international telephone calls, *see* Telephones *in* the Gold Guide. For information about traveling with a computer, *see* Traveling with Cameras, Camcorders, and Computers *in* the Gold Guide.

The three cities below are important business destinations that are not described elsewhere in the book. Bangalore, Bombay, Calcutta, Delhi, and Madras also receive many business travelers. For descriptions of these destinations, *see* the appropriate chapters.

AHMEDABAD

By Julie
Tomasz

Ahmedabad, the principal city of Gujarat, blends the glorious past and a vibrant present. For architects, it is a remarkable repository of architectural styles—from the early Indo-Saracenic of the 15th-century Muslim sultans to the experimental modern forms of Le Corbusier and contemporary Indian architects Charles Correa and Louis Kahn.

Founded in AD 1411 by the Muslim Sultan Ahmed Shah, Ahmedabad flourished under the Gujarat dynasty and subsequently became the seat of the Mogul governors of Gujarat—Jahangir, Shah Jahan, and Aurangzeb, all of whom later became emperors.

At one time it was said that Ahmedabad hung on three threads: gold, silk, and cotton. Today, the city is once again the Manchester of the East, with dozens of mills that employ thousands of workers and produce about one-third of India's total textiles. Although textiles used to be *the* industry in Ahmedabad, today the city is also a booming business center for the minerals, power, agribusiness, petroleum chemicals, scientific development, and pharmaceuticals industries, thriving on massive international as well as domestic participation. It's an important cargo port as well, as the Ahmedabad Airport is an official "all goods custom clearance" airport, where all types of goods can be easily imported and exported.

Ahmedabad has benefited enormously from being situated at the head of the 500-kilometer industrial belt that stretches south to Bombay. The city is also home to several of India's premier educational institutions, such as the Indian Institute of Management and the National Institute of Design.

Ahmedabad is divided into old and new by the Sabarmati River; most of the new development is on the west side of the river. The pace and scope of the development are amazing: Brand-new towering office buildings and complexes, designed by well-known Indian architects, are going up everywhere, particularly along C. G. Road, the up-and-coming business and shopping strip where real estate prices already challenge those of Bombay.

In some ways, Ahmedabad doesn't quite yet look the part of a major international business hub. Ashram and C. G. roads, the city's main streets, lined with exclusive shopping complexes and office buildings, are perpetually under construction, with deep, dusty shoulders instead of sidewalks and a constant crowd of camels, cows, and monkeys. But this is likely to change as development continues.

Exploring

If you have some time off from meetings, have a look at these important Ahmedabad sights.

★ **Calico Museum.** Considered one of the world's best textile museums, this vast collection is a rich way to experience the lavish colors and textures of Ahmedabad's age-old primary industry: textiles. Housed in a *haveli* (traditional Gujarati carved mansion) estate, the museum buildings are connected by paths through lush gardens of shady trees and exotic flowers. Thick gold brocade royal costumes, silver gilt and silk-embroidered battle scenes, 12-foot-long Banarasi silk cummerbunds, 17th-century painted prayer cloths: The museum is filled with beautiful examples of the myriad varieties of embroidery, dyeing, weaving, and other textile traditions from all over India. The rooms are dimly lit to preserve the cloths; and because of strict security and preservation precautions, first-time visitors are required to adhere to what may be the most rigid visiting schedule anywhere. A sign on the wall bears an apologetic explanation. You must go on a guided tour, provided free at the entrance. The tour of the first section, the religious textiles gallery, begins promptly at 10:30 and ends at 11:30, when part two, the tour of the larger historical exhibit, commences. It, too, lasts one hour. The same two-part tour sequence begins again at 2:45 PM. If you miss the time, you can't enter until the next tour begins. *Retreat Bungalow, near Shahibaug overpass,* ☎ *79/868172.* ☛ *Free.* ☉ *Mon., Tues., and Thurs.–Sun. 10:30–12:30 and 2:30–5.*

Hatheesing Jain Temple. This elaborately carved white marble temple dedicated to Dharmanath, the 15th Jain apostle, took 25 years to complete and is the finest example of Ahmedabad's beautiful Jain temples. Every surface of every pillar and arch is intricately carved with dancing figures and curling ornaments. Just pick a spot and allow yourself to get lost in the details. The main structure is surrounded by 52 miniature temples. The magnificent stone lattice screens of the second-floor windows appear to be woven of stone threads. A few restrictions: Photography of gods or goddesses is prohibited, and menstruating women are theoretically banned from entry. *By Delhi Gate, Balvantrai Mehta Rd.* ☛ *Free.* ☉ *Daily 5:30–1 and 3:30–7:30.*

Sabarmati Ashram. Born in Gujarat, Mahatma Gandhi established his simple retreat, the Insistence on Truth, here in 1915, at a tranquil spot on the bank of the Sabarmati River just outside the rush of the heart of the city. This ashram, where Gandhi and his followers meditated and worked to change the world, became the nerve center of the Indian independence movement. It was from here in 1930 that Gandhi and 79 followers began the 389-kilometer (241-mile) march to the seacoast at Dandi to protest the British salt tax, the event that launched the "Quit India" movement that brought an end to British rule. The main, open-air building houses exhibits, including a moving photo display documenting the major points of Gandhi's life and work. As one strolls along the ashram's paths, the grounds seem blessed by Gandhi's spirit—soothed by river breezes and shady trees, brightened by exuberant birdsong and fluttering green parrots. You can visit the humble cottage where Gandhi lived. When you sign the register, your name will share the pages with those of Nelson Mandela and other foreign dignitaries and peaceworkers who come and pay homage to the father of India. *Sabarmati River.* ☛ *Free.* ☉ *Daily 8:30–6:30. Sound-and-light show in English, Wed., Sat., and Fri. 8:30; tickets, Rs. 5, sold beginning at 2 at box office.*

Shopping

Ahmedabad is a great place to buy authentic Gujarati handicrafts, famous throughout India. The textiles are outstanding; from fine-woven silk *patola* fabrics and *bhandej* tie-dyed materials to elaborately embroidered vests, purses, wall hangings, slippers, and bedspreads from the Kutch desert and Saurashtra in northwestern and western Gujarat. Also look for *moti-kaam* beadwork textiles and figures and copper, brass, and bronze metalwork. Mobiles and chains of small stuffed parrots of various sizes and lengths make inexpensive, colorful decorative accents or cheerful baby toys. Most shops are open Monday through Saturday, 10 to 6 or 7. Some stores accept credit cards.

The Law Garden Market (Netaji Rd.) gets going only at around 7 or 8 every night, when the road is transformed into a bustling, vibrantly colored scene as vendors from the desert known as the Rann of Kutch and elsewhere in Gujarat, as well as from other states, line both sides of the street with stalls hung with exquisitely embroidered wall hangings, shirts, vests, bedspreads, and more, studded with tiny mirrors; bargain like mad. **Manek Chowk** (off Ramanlal Jani and Desai Rds.) is a chaotic, colorful bazaar in the old city where crowded, narrow streets are packed with stalls and small shops selling excellent fabrics and ready-made clothing of all textures and colors.

Gurjari, also known as the Gujarat State Handicrafts Emporium (opposite La-Gajjar Chamber, Ashram Rd., ☎ 79/409–505), a fixed-price government shop with low prices, no taxes, and guaranteed quality, offers an impressive variety of brightly embroidered dresses, hand-woven wall hangings, beaded tribal jewelry, brass figures, traditional silver and brass *pataris* (jewelry boxes), and other examples of Gujarat state craftwork. **Kapasi Handicrafts Emporium** (105 B.K. House, C. G. Rd., near Stadium Circle, ☎ 79/421092) has a good selection of handicrafts, particularly metal- and brass-work.

Dining

Gujarati cuisine is known for its wholesome, almost strictly vegetarian dishes. Gujarati meals, known as *thali,* have numerous small portions of a variety of foods scooped into individual stainless steel cups placed on a large stainless steel tray along with hot puffs of *puri* and several other types of breads. Try not to miss having a meal at a thali dining hall, a Gujarati experience in which you are served *more* than all you can eat.

Note that Gujarat is a dry state: Alcohol is served only in a few hotels, and only to those people who have obtained a permit from their hotels. Permits and alcohol are available at hotels with a "permit room" (*see below*).

Restaurants tend to be closed for two or three hours in the late afternoon.

For price categories, *see* the chart for Other Areas *in* On the Road with Fodor's.

What to Wear
Westerners can dress neatly and casually (with the obvious exception of shorts and other scantier clothes), but should scale it up for the more elegant hotel restaurants.

$$$$ **Vishalla.** No matter how tight your schedule, try to visit this famous
★ outdoor restaurant—a recreated Gujarati village—a few kilometers outside Ahmedabad. When you arrive, you are welcomed with a flower garland, and a *bindi* (colored dot) is placed on your forehead. Once you've placed your order at the entrance (someone will help you), you can try a sugarcane aperitif from the village-style juice bar, a thatch-roof hut where a young boy cranks a giant cog-and-wheel contraption that mashes and squeezes the sweet juice out of the sugarcane stalks. You can stroll on worn dirt paths lit by candles and lanterns and dis-

cover a Rajasthani puppet show performed under a palm tree or wander into a clearing where musicians sing Indian folk songs. When your order is ready—they run around calling your name until they find you——you sit on straw mats at low, rough wood tables while turbaned young waiters serve an exceptional, authentic thali meal on banana leaves. Come hungry and prepare to eat with your hand. For optimal comfort, bring insect repellent. ✗ *Vasana Tol Naka,* ☎ *272/403375. Reservations advised. No credit cards.*

$$$ **Tomato's.** The theme at this trendy downstairs eatery is a 1950s–1960s-style American diner. From the standard posters of Elvis and Marilyn Monroe and the neon Rock & Roll sign to a rusty Michigan license plate and a single woman's gold high-heeled pump, the room is crammed with American pop paraphernalia, with no decorative detail left out. The menu offers Mexican, Chinese, Punjabi Indian, and Continental food—including coleslaw and apple pie. The decor outdoes most of the food, which is fresh but far from the real thing; your best bet is to go with the Indian offerings. ✗ *Mardia Plaza, off C. G. Rd.,* ☎ *79/441198. No credit cards.*

$$$ **The Waterfall.** Named for the trio of simulated waterfalls cascading
★ behind a glass window in the back of the dining room, the Holiday Inn's restaurant is one of the most popular in Ahmedabad. The dining room is intimate and elegant, with candlelight and waiters dressed in black ties. The menu offers an impressive variety of excellent Indian and Continental cuisine as well as authentic Chinese items. Specialties include Kerala kebab (a moist, smoky-spicy chicken leg stuffed with dried fruits and nuts and paneer and baked in a tandoor oven) and *kadai* chicken (boneless chicken chunks in tangy brown sauce named for and served in the traditional Indian wok-like pot in which it is cooked). ✗ *Holiday Inn Ahmedabad, Khanpur,* ☎ *79/350105. Reservations required. AE, DC, MC, V.*

$$ **"10."** As its numerical name implies, this classy restaurant strives for
★ perfection. Special touches, such as heated plates, complimentary bottled mineral water served immediately, and linen napkins embroidered with the names of the restaurant's many regular customers reflect the management's mission of personalized service and attention to detail. Whitewashed walls accented with wood trim set the tone for tables covered with white linens and adorned with fresh flowers. The chef prepares top-notch Punjabi, Continental, and Chinese fare. Try the paneer *khada masala* (cheese chunks in a spicy clove and nutmeg gravy) with some floppy *methi* garlic *naan* bread. Save room for the excellent desserts. ✗ *Urja House, Swastik Char Rasta,* ☎ *79/445070. Reservations advised weekdays. AE, MC, V.*

$ **South-Indian Restaurant.** In the hotel pocket on the east side of the Sabarmati River, this tiny, simple eatery bustles at lunch with neighborhood businesspeople and hotel staff enjoying large portions of tasty, cheap south-Indian vegetarian fare, served promptly and efficiently. Choose from among the nearly 30 varieties of *dosas* (stuffed Indian crepes), or try the fixed thali menu. ✗ *Opposite Ministry Chambers, near Cama Hotel, Khanpur,* ☎ *79/301343. No credit cards.*

$ **Toran Dining Hall.** This Ahmedabad institution is a great place to get
★ the full experience of a Gujarati thali meal. Barefoot waiters, dressed in plain gray uniforms, swarm around the dining room, from the kitchen window in the back to your table, tossing handfuls of chapati and puri bread and spooning refills of the many different vegetarian concoctions, chutneys, and condiments into your stainless steel thali bowls and onto the tray. Each waiter carries just one garnish or type of food. Come hungry and abandon any eating shyness you may have—the waiters will hover over you throughout the meal, replen-

ishing your tray before you can eat the last bite. The large, simple room is cool and dark—strongly air-conditioned—with pale gray walls, dim lighting, and dark mirrors inset in pillars. ✗ *Opposite Sales India, Ashram Rd.,* ☎ *79/462197. No credit cards. No Mon. dinner.*

Lodging

To accommodate the rapidly growing number of business travelers coming to Ahmedabad, new hotels are popping up left and right. Caught up in the boom, some are thrown together too quickly, looking fancy on the surface of the lobby, but in fact poorly constructed from cheap materials that are easily worn and broken. Room prices are extremely low compared with those in other Indian cities. Hotels with alcohol permits are indicated below.

Unless noted otherwise, hotels have central air-conditioning, room service, doctors on call, and foreign exchange facilities, and rooms have cable TV and bathrooms with tubs.

For price categories, *see* the chart for Other Areas *in* On the Road with Fodor's.

\$\$ Cama Hotel. Once the only high-standard hotel in town, the 40-year-old Cama now faces stiff competition from new properties, but it still has the loveliest grounds in the city. The green lawns, palm trees, chirping birds, and small swimming pool of its back garden offer the hotel's many business guests a peaceful break after a hectic day. The interior has an old, slightly worn Indian elegance, with wide, cold hallways and a faded white marble lobby decorated with Gujarati handicrafts and antiques. The standard rooms have modern, mediocre-quality furnishings, with pale floral bedspreads and curtains and light painted-wood furniture. The Cama's views of the Sabarmati River are also the best in town—request a room with a river exposure. ⊞ *Khanpur, Ahmedabad 380001,* ☎ *272/305281,* ⅎ⅏ *272/305285. 46 rooms, 5 suites. Restaurant, coffee shop, pool, dry cleaning, laundry service, business services, meeting rooms, travel services. Alcohol-permit room. AE, DC, MC, V.*

\$\$ Holiday Inn Ahmedabad. A pair of glass capsule elevators glides up
★ and down the soaring atrium lobby of Ahmedabad's classiest hotel. The lobby, gleaming with polished marble and glass, hosts a hushed bustle of local and international businesspeople. The rooms are contemporary-elegant, with occasionally clashing fabric colors and furniture styles. Set on the east bank of the Sabarmati River, the hotel is slightly removed from the city center—a short trip across the Nehru Bridge. West-facing rooms offer river views with a tragic twist of modern Indian paradox: Just below the towering white hotel building, a dense stretch of a cardboard box-like slum village lines the shore. ⊞ *Chand Suraj Estate, Khanpur, Ahmedabad 380001,* ☎ *79/350105,* ⅎ⅏ *79/272359. 61 rooms, 2 suites. 2 restaurants, coffee shop, patisserie, baby-sitting, dry cleaning, laundry service, business services, meeting rooms, travel services, free parking. AE, DC, MC, V.*

\$\$ Inder Residency. This promising young hotel joined the ranks of Ahmedabad's upmarket business hotels in late 1994. Between Ashram and C. G. roads, its central location is a prime selling point. The lobby has low ceilings, white-painted pillars, and a kitschy rainbow-colored water sculpture on the back wall. With clean white walls, modern blond wood furniture, aqua carpeting, and coordinating geometric-pattern fabrics, the rooms feel cool and bright. All face the pool on the front terrace. The rates run in the lowest end of this price category. ⊞ *Opposite Gujarat College, Ellisbridge, Ahmedabad 380006,* ☎ *79/425050* or 79/402202, FAX 79/400407. *74 rooms, 5 suites. Restaurant, coffee shop, patisserie, pool, dry cleaning, laundry service, business services, meeting rooms. AE, DC, MC, V.*

$$ **Quality Suites Shalin.** Designed for business travelers, all the rooms in this hotel opened in 1991 are technically suites, each with a tiny sitting and working area and a small bedroom separated by a sliding, glass-paneled door. The standard rooms are uniformly decorated with modern, functional furnishings and coordinating mauve or light blue carpeting, bedspreads, and curtains. Whereas the rooms tend to show signs of wear and tear quickly, the sleek lobby is immaculate, sparkling with marble and teakwood and flooded with light from large banks of windows that overlook the small garden and pool. Pool-facing rooms have the best view; for less street noise, request an upper-floor or back-side room. The Shalin's location, near the new stock-exchange building and busy M. G. Road, is convenient for business travelers. ⊡ *Gujarat College Cross Rds., Ellisbridge, Ahmedabad 380006, ☎ 272/ 426967 or 272/425590, FAX 272/460022. 70 suites. 2 restaurants, pool, dry cleaning, laundry service, business services, meeting rooms, travel services. Alcohol-permit room. AE, DC, MC, V.*

$$ **The Trident.** This new Oberoi chain property opened in summer 1995 on 2½ acres a half-kilometer from the Ahmedabad Airport. In addition to its excellent location for meet-and-run business trips, the hotel offers the Oberoi's signature sleek rooms, efficient service, and special attention to the business traveler. ⊡ *Airport Cross Rd., Hansol, Ahmedabad 382475, ☎ 79/786–4444, FAX 79/786–4454. 86 rooms, 3 suites. Restaurant, coffee shop, pool, beauty salon, dry cleaning, laundry service, business services, meeting rooms, travel services, airport shuttle, free parking. AE, DC, MC, V.*

$ **Rivera Hotel.** This reliable seven-story hotel, on the east bank of the Sabarmati River, was built in the early 1980s. The lobby with its low ceiling and the echoing hallways give the public areas a somewhat dark, somber feel. The rooms are small and clean, with basic furnishings in moss green and brown tones; the deluxe rooms, slightly more expensive, are roomier and more cheerful. Ask for a river view. Only one-third of the rooms have bathtubs; request one if it's important to you. ⊡ *Khanpur, Ahmedabad 380001, ☎ 79/304201 or 79/305220, FAX 79/302327. 61 rooms, 8 suites. Restaurant, dry cleaning, laundry service, airport shuttle, free parking. Alcohol-permit room. AE, DC, MC, V.*

$ **Rock Regency.** A giant red neon sign blazes above this new white, four-story hotel, just off C. G. Road. Polished gray granite floors and white twisting pillars give the lobby a stylish, contemporary look. Pea-green floral upholstered chairs and headboards with white wooden frames give rooms a garden feeling. ⊡ *Law Garden Rd., Navrangpura, Ahmedabad 380006, ☎ 79/409333, FAX 79/465588. 37 rooms, 2 suites. Restaurant, coffee shop, dry cleaning, laundry service, meeting rooms, travel services. AE, DC, MC, V.*

Ahmedabad Essentials

Arriving and Departing
BY PLANE
Indian Airlines (☎ 79/303061) flies from Bombay, Delhi, Bangalore, and Madras to Ahmedabad. Contact your travel agent or the Government of India Tourist Office in your home country for the latest details about other domestic carriers serving this city. Flights operate into and out of Ahmedabad Airport, 15 kilometers (9 miles) from downtown.

Between the Airport and Downtown. You'll find plenty of taxis outside the terminal. Insist that the driver use his meter and show you the tariff revision card, or agree on a fare before setting out. The trip to center city should cost roughly Rs. 150 to Rs. 200.

Getting Around

Ahmedabad's traffic is chaotic. Expect camels, donkeys, buffalo, goats, and, amidst it all, the omnipresent holy cow. Lanes exist but are often overlooked. Getting around on foot in busy areas is tricky because there are no sidewalks to speak of—just dirt. Practice defensive pedestrianism. Traffic will hurtle toward you from every conceivable direction. Look everywhere.

BY AUTO RICKSHAW

It's not the most luxurious way to go, but in congested traffic, a savvy rickshaw driver can reach your destination faster than a taxi or car. At press time, fares were about 1 Rs. per kilometer, with a starting charge of about 4 Rs. But rates change as fuel prices increase; fares are theoretically calculated by matching up the meter amount with the adjusted rate on the driver's tariff card. If the driver refuses to show you the tariff card, either get another rickshaw or agree on a fare. Ask your hotel or a passerby what an appropriate fare would be.

BY CAR WITH DRIVER

With a car and driver at your disposal, you can move from meeting to meeting without the added stress of sparring over fares with rickshaw and taxi drivers. Air-conditioned car rates start at around 6 Rs. per kilometer, usually with a minimum of 250 kilometers per day. Your hotel can arrange a car and driver for you, but hotels tend to charge more than do the travel agencies listed below.

BY TAXI

You can catch a taxi in town or at most hotels and the airport. Insist that the driver turn on his meter and show you the latest revised tariff card (with which you can calculate the final fare), or agree on a flat price before you get going.

Important Addresses and Numbers

BUSINESS INFORMATION

These organizations are good sources for important general business information: **Indian Institute of Mangement** (Vastrapur, ☏ 79/407242); **Ahmedabad Management Association** (Opposite Punjabi Hall, Navrangpura, ☏ 79/466158); **Gujarat Industrial Extension Bureau** (Nanalal Chambers, ☏ 79/423398); **Gujarat Chamber of Commerce and Industry** (Near Natraj Cinema, Ashram Rd., ☏ 79/402301 or 79/402302); **Gujarat State Export Corporation** (Gujarat Chambers Bldg., Ashram Rd., ☏ 79/402341 or 79/402344); **Gujarat Agro Industries Corporation** (Khet-Udyog Bhavan, opposite High Court, Navrangpura, ☏ 79/460272).

CHANGING MONEY

Nearly all hotels exchange foreign currency for their guests. You may get nominally better rates at the state banks in town, but the hassle of waiting in line may not make it worth it. Try a branch of the **State Bank of India** or the **Bank of Baroda** on Ashram Road (☏ 79/447598), open weekdays 10 to 2 and Saturdays until noon.

EMERGENCIES

Police, ☏ 100; fire, ☏ 101; ambulance, ☏ 102; or contact your hotel, your embassy in Delhi, or the East-West Clinic (*see* Chapter 5, Delhi).

EXPRESS MAIL/COURIER SERVICES
The following agencies offer domestic and international express mail services: **Blue Dart** (FedEx affiliate; ☎ 79/467760 or 79/656360); **DHL Worldwide** (☎ 79/400211, 79/400212, or 79/400218); **Elbee Express** (UPS affiliate; ☎ 79/407364).

TRAVEL AGENCIES
If you need help with travel arrangements or hiring a car and driver, these agencies can take care of you. **Alka Travel Service** (Ashish Complex, C. G. Rd., near Swastik Cross Rds, ☎ 79/446300), **United Car Hire** (6 Sampanna, opposite Havmor, near Navrangpura bus stop, ☎ 79/460524) or the **Travel Corporation of India** (Ashram Rd., behind Handloom House, ☎ 79/407603).

VISITOR INFORMATION
Tourism Corporation of Gujarat, Ltd. (H. K. House, Ashram Rd., ☎ 79/449683 or 79/449172, FAX 79/428183), the government tourist office, provides information, organizes sightseeing tours, and arranges car and chauffeur hire. The office is open Monday through Saturday, 10:30 to 1:30 and 2 to 6; it's closed the fourth Saturday of the month. *The Choice is Yours,* a free bimonthly publication, provides invaluable, up-to-date tourist and business information about Ahmedabad and its environs. It's available at major hotels and travel agencies and from domestic airlines.

BHOPAL

By Smita Patel

Dominated by two lakes, dotted with gardens, and surrounded by hills, Bhopal, surprisingly clean for its size, is one of the most beautiful Indian cities and the capital of Madhya Pradesh. Founded in the 11th century by Raja Bhoja, Bhopal was actually brought to life by the Afghan General Dost Mohammed Khan, who made it a center of art and culture in the early 18th century. Under the hand of several wise Muslim rulers (including a number of women), the city became a refuge for artists and museums. Today Bhopal has a split personality: a vibrant old city still strongly influenced by its history and a new, well-organized and thriving business center.

Bhopal was the site of the Union Carbide gas leak in 1984 that killed hundreds of people and has gone down as one of the worst industrial disasters in history. But little evidence of that disaster remains visible today. Though few industries are actually located in Bhopal itself, the city acts as the administrative center for Madhya Pradesh and is headquarters for most of the state's expanding industries, which range from textiles to oil extraction and automobiles.

Exploring

There's plenty to see in this city, including massive mosques and a state museum packed with ancient relics.

The Chowk. In the main square of the old city is the old bazaar, one of the chief shopping areas of Bhopal. Its small shops offer a fascinating collection of treasures. Here you'll also find mosques and havelis (mansions) that evoke Bhopal's glory days. *Off Sultana Rd., Old City.*

Jama Masjid. This mosque, nestled in the heart of the Chowk, was built in 1837 by Qudsia Begum. Its tall, dark minarets are crowned with golden spikes. *The Chowk.* ☛ *Free.* ☉ *Dawn–sunset.*

Museum of Man. At this huge open-air museum, called the Tribal Habitat, a village is filled with authentic replicas of tribal houses from around the country. You can also see ancient cave paintings in the rock shelters on the museum campus. *Rashtria Manhav Sanghralya, D5 Arrera Colony,* ☏ *755/62250.* ☛ *Free.* ☉ *Sept.–Feb., Tues.–Sun. 1–6; Mar.–Aug., 2–7.*

Taj-ul-Masajid. Started in 1887 by Shah Jehan Begum, one of Bhopal's great woman rulers, this mammoth pink mosque with white domes is still not completed. The towering minarets and gates were added after 1971. *Hamida Rd.* ☛ *Free.* ☉ *Dawn–sunset;* Namaz *(prayer), daily,* 2 PM.

Shopping

Artisans in Madhya Pradesh have kept alive skills hundreds of years old, and in Bhopal's shops you can find a wealth of handicrafts, such as beautiful embroidery and beadwork, silver figurines, and jewelry and lacquer bangles. The state is also renowned for its muslin and brocade from the northern town of Chanderi.

In the **Chowk** (off Sultana Rd., Old City), you have to bargain. The state-run **Mrignayanee Emporium** (9 New Market, T. T. Nagar, ☏ 755/551462; Hamida Rd., ☏ 755/536313) offers a wide selection of handicrafts at fixed prices. The government **Roopmati** (32 Bhad Bhada Rd., New Market, T. T. Nagar) emporium offers fixed prices and specializes in handlooms and textiles, particularly brocade and muslin from Chanderi.

Dining

The cuisine in Bhopal harkens back to its Mogul past. Here you'll find spicy kebabs and a variety of tandoori specialties (meat marinated and baked in a clay tandoor oven). And, of course, Bhopal offers up the bounty of its lakes in a rich variety of fish dishes.

For price categories, *see* the chart for Other Areas *in* On the Road with Fodor's.

What to Wear
Casual dress is acceptable; short shorts and tank tops are not advised.

$$$ **Shahanama.** Here you can enjoy an elegant buffet lunch of excellent
★ Indian, Chinese, and Continental dishes accompanied by a well-stocked salad bar. In the evenings the hotel's large courtyard garden hosts a barbecue. Try the *methi ghost* (mutton curry spiced with fenugreek). ✗ *Jehan Numa Palace Hotel, 157 Shamla Hills, Bhopal,* ☏ *755/540100. Reservations advised. AE, DC, MC, V.*

$$ **Harsingar.** Right in the middle of Bhopal's business district, this popular restaurant is decorated in muted yellow and browns with brocade upholstery. The locals value it for its good Indian, Chinese, and Continental food, especially the fish dishes. Try the chicken soup and the baked fish with chips and vegetables. ✗ *Hotel Palash, near 45 Bungalows, T. T. Nagar, Bhopal-3,* ☏ *755/553006. Reservations advised. DC, MC, V.*

$$ **Kinara.** This popular restaurant offers a beautiful view of the lake and good Indian, Chinese, and Continental fare. Try the kebabs and the specialty: fish Bhopali (tandoori fish in spinach sauce). ✗ *Hotel Lake View Ashok, Shamla Hills, Bhopal,* ☏ *755/541601. Reservations advised. AE, DC, MC, V.*

Lodging

For price categories, *see* the chart for Other Areas *in* On the Road with Fodor's.

$$ Hotel Lake View Ashok. This Western-style red-stone hotel is run jointly by Ashok and MPSTDC. It sits on a hill overlooking the lake. The spacious rooms have modern decor and private balconies that offer good views. ⊠ *Shamla Hills, Bhopal 462003, Madhya Pradesh,* ☎ *755/541601,* FAX *755/541606. 45 rooms, 4 suites. Restaurant, bar, baby-sitters, business services, meeting rooms, travel services. AE, DC, MC, V.*

$$ Jehan Numa Palace Hotel. Once the secretariat of a Muslim nawab,
★ this two-story building with a new, architecturally similar wing is now a Heritage Hotel. The marble lobby (where a stuffed tiger stands guard) opens into an interior courtyard. The two upper-floor rooms are best, with spacious private verandas and period furniture. In the other rooms, which have modernish furnishings, you'll lose all sense of the palace once you close your door. Near the pool and health club is an annex that offers smaller, cheaper rooms. ⊠ *157 Shamla Hills, Bhopal 462003, Madhya Pradesh,* ☎ *755/540100,* FAX *755/540720. 60 rooms, 6 suites. Restaurant, bar, pool, miniature golf, 2 tennis courts, health club, jogging, Ping-Pong, business services, meeting room, travel services. AE, DC, MC, V.*

Bhopal Essentials

Arriving and Departing

BY PLANE

Indian Airlines (☎ 755/550480 or 755/550636) has flights between Delhi and Bhopal and from Bombay. Check with your travel agent for current schedules of other domestic airlines.

Between the Airport and Downtown. The Bhopal airport is about 15 kilometers (9 miles) from the city center. A taxi into town costs between Rs. 150 and Rs. 200.

Getting Around

Bhopal is a well-planned city with wide, spacious streets, particularly in the newer districts. Traffic tends to become congested in the older parts of Bhopal but is nothing like the traffic in Delhi or Ahmedabad.

BY HIRED CAR WITH DRIVER

If you have to move around much, this comfortable option may be worth the cost. Rates for an air-conditioned car start at about Rs. 8 per kilometer with a 90-kilometer minimum through the **MPSTDC** (*see* Visitor Information, *below*). Cars without air-conditioning are considerably cheaper and are fine for the winter months. Hire a car from one of the travel agencies recommended below.

BY TAXI

Taxis and auto-rickshaws are easily available in Bhopal and charge by the meter. Rates are determined by fare cards carried by drivers. It's always a good idea to find out the approximate rates from someone at your hotel.

Opening and Closing Times

Banks in Bhopal are open from 10 to 2. Most businesses are open from 10 to 5 with a lunch break from 1 to 1:30.

Important Addresses and Numbers

CHANGING MONEY

You can change money at most Western-style hotels or at a branch of the State Bank of India (main branch: T. T. Nagar, ☎ 755/554300).

EMERGENCIES

Contact your hotel, your embassy in Delhi, or East-West Clinic (*see* Chapter 4, Delhi).

EXPRESS MAIL/COURIER SERVICES

Blue Dart (Maharana Pratap Nagar, ☎ 755/552922) and **DHL** (Maharana Pratap Nadar, ☎ 755/562084) offer domestic and international express mail services.

TRAVEL AGENCIES

For car hire, hotel bookings, airline and train reservations, or guides, contact the **MPSTDC** (*see* Visitor Information, *below*) or **Radiant Travels** (Plot 5, Zone 2, M. P. Nagar, Bhopal (☎ 755/555460 or 555461).

VISITOR INFORMATION

The **Madhya Pradesh State Tourism Development Corporation (MPSTDC)** (4th Floor, Gangotri, T. T. Nagar, ☎ 755/554340, 554341, 554342) has information on sight-seeing tours, local events, airline and train schedules, car hire, and MPSTDC hotel bookings.

HYDERABAD

By Vikram Singh

Hotel keepers in Hyderabad will tell you that 90% of their clients are in town on business; modern industries such as software and telecommunications as well as traditional textile and jewelry trades thrive here. That is lucky for the business community and unfortunate for tourists, who are missing an Indian treasure. Hyderabad is the capital of Andhra Pradesh, a state full of influences as varied as Buddhism in Ashoka's time and the Mogul influx of the 14th century. Only 400 years old, Hyderabad reflects most dramatically its Mogul and Telugu heritage. Set on rolling hills around the beautiful Husain Sagar Lake, the city's minarets pierce the clear blue sky. Here you can shop for pearls and bangles, enjoy the terrific food, and watch the colorful city go by. If you have the chance, much of Andhra Pradesh is worth exploring; it offers tropical beaches and rain forests, national parks, and ancient ruins.

Exploring

Hyderabad is actually two cities, Secunderabad, north of the lake, and Hyderabad to the south.

Charminar. South of the Musi River near the impressive Osmania Hospital and High Court buildings, you enter the Charkaman area between four (*Char*) great gates (*kaman*). Within these gates you'll find not only Hyderabad's famed pearl and bangle markets, but also the striking Charminar, an imposing granite edifice built by Sultan Quli Qutub Shah in 1591 to appease the forces of evil and protect this new city from plague and epidemic. The arches, domes, and minarets show Islamic influence while much of the ornamentation is Hindu in style. *Charkaman center.* ☛ *Free (50 paise to go up into towers).* ☺ *daily.*

Falaknuma Palace. At press time (winter 1995) no decision had been made on whether or not this stunning late 19th-century palace built by a Paigah noble would be open to the public. If it is, don't miss the chance to see the peaceful Japanese gardens, opulent stained glass windows, carved ceilings, and fine Italian marble staircases that took nine years to build. Bought by the 6th nizam (ruler) in 1897, the palace has served as a royal getaway and hosted European royalty. Plans are in the works to turn it into a luxury hotel. *Sardar Patel Rd. Ask tourist office (see Visitor Information in Hyderabad Essentials, below) for information.*

Golconda Fort. A clap at the gate of the fort echoes clearly up to the Summer Palace, high on the hill. Even if you don't feel like clapping, someone else will test these amazing acoustics during your visit. These are the ruins of what was once not only a capital; it often sheltered whole communities under siege for months, and though tremendously worn by time and war, it tells you stories in crumbling stone. An excellent English-language sound and light show takes place at the fort every Wednesday and Sunday. *6 km (3.7 mi) west of city (contact Yatri Nivas tourist office, ☎ 40/843931). ☞ Free. ⊙ Tues.–Sun. sunrise–end of light show; light show, Nov.–Feb., daily 6:30; Mar.–Oct., daily 7.*

Mecca Masjid. India's second largest mosque is in the Charkaman area south of the Charminar (*see above*). Non-Muslims are welcome except at prayer time. Some bricks here were made with earth brought from Mecca in 1618. *Kishan Prasad Rd., southwest of Charminar, no phone. Open to visitors except during services.*

Shopping

Hyderabad is a gathering center for the many handicrafts of Andra Pradesh. Look for Nirmal toys (delightfully colorful, lightweight wooden toys), Bidriware (a gunmetal-like alloy used for bangles, cufflinks, bowls, and other items), and Ikat textiles—tie-dyed and woven fabric. Here you'll also find silk, woolen, and cotton carpets from the Warangal district. The omnipresent glass bangles worn throughout the country are produced in great quantities here. Hyderabad is also the center of India's pearl trade; pearls from southeast Asia are sent here for polishing, sorting, and piercing. For pearls, the most exciting place is the **Charminar Market,** particularly just north of the Charminar itself. The market bustles with everything one might want to buy, from textiles and handicrafts to bangles (west of the Charminar).

At **Mangatrai Pearls** (Bashirbagh, opposite Hotel Nagarjuna, ☎ 40/235728; 22-6-191 Pathergatti, near Charminar, ☎ 40/521405) you will get high quality and good service. **Sanchay** (Shops 21 and 22, Babukhan Estate, Basheerbagh; ☎ 40/599738) has a fine selection of high-quality handloomed silks. The **Lepakshi Handicrafts Emporium** (94 Minerva Complex, Gunfoundry, ☎ 40/235028) has a good variety.

Dining

Hyderabad is famous for food. The most mouthwatering treats are the rich dishes that can only be called pure Hyderabad, though the Mogul influence is obvious. Some of these include *haleem* (a slow-cooked treat of pounded wheat, mutton, and spices), Hyderabadi *biriyani* (a baked meat and rice dish), and *bagare baingan* (eggplant in a spicy poppy and seasame seed sauce). Some of the best haleem is found in the old town around the Mecca Masjid, though it is also available in classy restaurants.

For price categories, *see* the chart for Other Areas *in* On the Road with Fodor's.

$$$ **Firdaus.** This restaurant evokes the elegance of the nizams, with waiters dressed in *sherwanis* (long Nehru-style jackets), *punka* fans gently swaying from the ceiling, and live *ghazal* (classical Indian vocal music) performances nightly, except Tuesday. The chef serves regal Hyderabadi cuisine. Try the *achar gosht* (lamb cooked in pickled tomato masala paste) and *nizami handi* (vegetable and cottage-cheese curry) or *bagare baingan* (eggplant in a spicy poppyseed and sesame sauce). ✕ *Krishna Oberoi, Banjara Hills, Rd. No. 1, ☎ 40/393323. Reservations advised. AE, DC, MC, V.*

$$$ **Kabab-E-Bahar.** Outdoors on the edge of the lake, set on a lovely lawn, this restaurant serves excellent Hyderabadi cuisine buffet style or à la carte. Try the very good kebabs and barbecue items. ✕ *Taj Gateway Hotel on Banjara Hill, Banjara Hills, ☎ 40/222222. Reservations advised. DC, MC, V.*

$$$ **Lambadi.** The walls are white, with handsome paintings and dark wood pillars. Upholstered chairs and settees are intimately placed around the room. The chef serves good Andhra Pradesh and Deccan region specialties. This is a good place to order haleem. ✕ *Taj Gateway Hotel on Banjara Hill, Banjara Hills, ☎ 40/222222. Reservations advised. AE, DC, MC, V.*

$$$ **Szechuan Garden.** Overlooking beautiful waterfalls and surrounded by a Chinese rock garden, this restaurant offers tasty Szechuan cuisine. Try the honey spareribs, chicken in lotus leaves, or prawns in oyster sauce. ✕ *Krishna Oberoi, Banjara Hills, Rd. No. 1, ☎ 40/222121. Reservations advised. AE, DC, MC, V.*

$$ **Palace Heights.** This upper-floor restaurant in a modern high-rise offers a great city view and elegant surroundings. Pictures of former nizams decorate the walls; antiques add a refined touch. Ask for a table by a window and choose from Continental, Chinese, and Indian cuisine. ✕ *Triveni Complex, Abid Rd., ☎ 40/232898. DC, MC, V.*

Lodging

Hyderabad has more hotel rooms than it can fill, and new construction is everywhere. New business hotels offer services and amenities very close to those of the old luxury hotels for about half the price. Unless noted otherwise, hotels have central air-conditioning, room service, doctors on call, and foreign exchange facilities, and rooms have cable TV and bathrooms with tubs.

For price categories, *see* the chart for Other Areas *in* On the Road with Fodor's.

$$$ **Holiday Inn (Krishna).** If open space could be oppressive, this hotel's lobby would crush you. Bold relief work adorns the high walls around the lobby lounge. The rooms are decorated in standard five-star style. ⌂ *Rd. No. 1, Banjara Hills, Hyderabad 500034, Andhra Pradesh, ☎ 40/223347, ℻ 40/222684. 141 rooms with bath, 9 suites. 2 restaurants, bar, no-smoking floor, pool, health club, business services, travel services. AE, DC, MC, V.*

$$$ **Krishna Oberoi.** Set on nine acres overlooking Lake Husain Sagar, the hotel is a striking blend of modern architecture tempered by strong Mogul influences. Beautiful fountains and formal gardens ornament its front lawn. The rooms are elegant, with soft pastel decor. ⌂ *Rd. No. 1, Banjara Hills, Hyderabad 500034, Andhra Pradesh, ☎ 842/222121, ℻ 842/223079. 262 rooms, 14 suites. 3 restaurants, bar, pool, health club, nightclub, business services, travel services. AE, DC, MC, V.*

$$ **Taj Residency.** This modern high-rise on Banjara Hills overlooks its own small lake. The lobby is spacious marble, and the contemporary rooms are comfortable. The best rooms are on upper floors with lake views. ⌖ *Rd. No. 1, Banjara Hills, Hyderabad 500034, Andhra Pradesh,* ☏ *40/399999,* FAX *40/392218. 121 rooms, 5 suites. 2 restaurants, coffee shop, bar, no-smoking floor, tennis court, pool, business meeting rooms, travel services. DC, MC, V.*

$ **Green Park.** Close to the airport, this hotel has a marble lobby and comfortable rooms with modern decor. The best rooms overlook the garden. It's an excellent value for business travelers. ⌖ *Greenlands Area, Begumpet Rd., Hyderabad 500016, Andhra Pradesh,* ☏ *842/291919,* FAX *842/291900. 151 rooms, 4 suites. Restaurant, coffee shop, bar, concierge floor, business services. AE, DC, MC, V.*

$ **Viceroy.** This new hotel, already being expanded, stands conveniently
★ between Hyderabad and Secunderabad with stunning views over Husain Sagar Lake. Glass elevators and terraced balconies overlook the open lobby; all the facilities are modern. The best rooms have views of the lake and spectacular sunsets. ⌖ *Tankbund Rd., Hyderabad, 500380, Andhra Pradesh,* ☏ *40/618383,* FAX *40/618797. 137 rooms with bath or shower. Restaurant, coffee shop, pool, health club, business services, travel services. AE, DC, MC, V.*

Hyderabad Essentials

Arriving and Departing

BY PLANE
Hyderabad is served by frequent flights from throughout India. **Indian Airlines** (☏ 40/599333 or 140, 141 for reservations, 142 for recorded flight information) has flights between Hyderabad and Bangalore, Bombay, Calcutta, Delhi, and Madras. **Air India** (☏ 40/232747) also has service to Bombay. Check with travel agents for current schedules of other domestic airlines.

The airport is just north of Husain Sagar Lake on Sardar Patel Road in Secunderabad. You can get a prepaid taxi from the airport terminal; depending on your destination, the fare can range from Rs. 50 to Rs. 300.

Getting Around
The city is quite manageable on foot once you reach a particular district. To do that, auto rickshaws or cycle rickshaws are your best bet. Taxis are overpriced and more trouble in traffic, which does become unbearable at rush hour. Only a cryptologist can understand most addresses here, so landmarks and patience serve you well.

Important Addresses and Numbers

BUSINESS INFORMATION
The major hotels have business facilities for their guests (though they can be a bit pricey). Wherever you see large yellow and black signs reading S.T.D., I.S.D., FAX, you're likely to find a better deal. Translation services are available from **Hyderabad Translation Bureau** (1-7-143 Kancharla Towers, 409 Rama Krishna Land, Golconda X; ☏ and FAX 40/613355) and **Alliance Francaise de Hyderabad** (Adarshnagar, ☏ 40/236646). Both **Airtravels** (1005 Babkhan Estate, 10th Floor, Basheerbagh, ☏ 40/224321, FAX 40/831247) and **Europcar** (Karan Apartments, Begumpet, ☏ 40/842023, FAX 40/847146) offer cars for hire (with driver) 24 hours a day.

CHANGING MONEY
All the major hotels change money for their guests. You can also visit **Thomas Cook** (6-1-57 Nasir Arcade, Saifabad, ☏ 40/231988).

EMERGENCIES

Police, ☎ 100; fire, ☎ 101; ambulance, ☎ 102; or contact your hotel, your embassy in Delhi, or East-West Clinic (*see* Chapter 4, Delhi).

EXPRESS MAIL/COURIER SERVICES

Blue Dart Express (1-2-61/62 Siddamsetty Complex, Park La., ☎ 40/812746 or 40/812907) is associated with FedEx and can get packages just about anywhere.

TRAVEL AGENCIES

In addition to the tourist office or agents in hotels, you can use the following for any travel plans: **Jubilee Travels and Tours** (6-3-1090/B/A Somajiguda Raj Bhavan Rd., ☎ 40/312379); **Sita World Travels** (Sita house, 3-5-874 Hyderguda, 40/233628); or **Mercury Travels** (92–93 Suryakiran Bldg., S. D. Rd., ☎ 40/812194).

VISITOR INFORMATION

The **Andhra Pradesh Tourism Development Corporation** (APTDC, 5th Floor, Gangan Vihar, M. J. Rd., ☎ 40/557531) is open daily 9:30 to 5:30 and has counters in both train stations. The **Government of India Tourist Office** (Sandozi Bldg., Himayat Nagar, ☎ 40/66887) is a bit tough to find, but helpful for planning onward journeys. The monthly pamphlet *Channel 6* has excellent information about happenings in the city, and APTDC's *Glimpses of Hyderabad* gives good general information.

4 Delhi

If you want the hurly-burly of crowds, get lost in Old Delhi's Chandni Chowk; for the feel of Old Delhi without the masses, head to Hazrat Nizamudin Aulia, a Sufi tomb in an old-style Muslim district. Go shopping: Delhi is one big emporium offering all of India's handicrafts. Enjoy great meals—the capital has restaurants that offer Indian and non-Indian cuisines. Save time each day to unwind in a tranquil park, such as Lodi Gardens, with its historic tombs.

MANHATTAN APARTMANSIONS—WORLD-CLASS HOMES NOW IN YOUR PART OF THE WORLD. This billboard in India's capital says it all. Delhi is changing and expanding fast. Residential enclaves are cropping up everywhere, along with new commercial centers, and many Delhi-ites are suffering from a new headache: the suburban commute. But their commute bears little resemblance to a morning drive into a busy Western city. More cows stand in Delhi's streets than traffic police, and the absence of police and discipline is largely responsible for all the chaos on the roads. Vehicles swerve between lanes, around cows, or play "chicken" with a speeding bus as it barrels down from the opposite direction.

Still, Delhi's expansion is part of the continuum of history. By the mid-1600s, Delhi was already flourishing in magnificent pomp—the 450-year-old capital of a string of empires. Each new power created its own new Delhi, with each successive capital (there were eight) pushing farther north until the British shifted their center of power from Calcutta to Delhi in 1911. While the British were building their district, called the Civil Lines, on this northerly route, they hit marshy flood-prone land. They then reversed direction and put the bulk of their capital, the Imperial City, to the south.

The impetus for Delhi's most recent growth, however, is different. Villagers from rural areas have descended on the capital to seek their fortune. They move into small open fields, narrow strips along the road, or an unused neighborhood pocket and build shanties that turn into overcrowded slums. Sadly, the "fortune" most villagers make is barely enough to survive. Foreign companies are arriving and setting up shop. Land prices have skyrocketed, yet the market gobbles up every available square foot. Land is so pricey that many home owners find it cheaper to add extensions to their houses rather than buy another plot. As a result, many lawns in Delhi are razor-thin patches of grass.

Something else that happened in Delhi before the 1990s still has an impact today. When the British switched to Delhi, they introduced Western architecture, specifically the bungalow. Over time, the bungalow became more elaborate and hierarchical—the more important the British resident, the more lavish the house and the larger the property. Bungalows, concentrated in the Civil Lines and in Central Delhi, became a class symbol, and their interior amenities became the new definition of the preferred lifestyle, even to many upper-class Indians. When the British quit India, some of their bungalows were bought by Delhi's elite, but most were taken over by embassies and the Indian government for its ministers and senior bureaucrats. To this day, the old hierarchy remains—the more important the individual, the better the bungalow.

With Independence, Delhi's architecture changed again. Wealthy families, especially the nouveau riche, exhibited a preference for more ostentatious Western designs. In residential enclaves or right next door to an old bungalow, you see Indianized European-style villas that make no attempt to conceal their owners' wealth. The Delhi Development Authority, meanwhile, has for decades poured money and cement into dreary public housing. Its characterless apartment buildings, their facades musty with mildew, have cropped up like weeds all over the city.

This hodgepodge usually overwhelms the first-time visitor. Harmonious lines of old monuments and ruins, frequently in the midst of new neighborhoods, accentuate the inferiority of much of Delhi's post-

Independence architecture. Still, the city has its rewards, such as more than 1,000 monuments and two old capitals that are first-class achievements—Mogul emperor Shah Jahan's architectural tour de force in Old Delhi and the present seat of the government designed by the British in New Delhi. The city also has a surprising number of appealing gardens and parks, such as the peaceful Lodi Gardens, with solemn gray tombs that pay homage to the past, and a golf course where Muslim monuments share the fairways with peacocks.

Slightly more subtle aspects of Delhi also distinguish it from other Indian cities. Of course, it is the nation's capital, but Delhi is an unusual capital. It has absorbed the land of former villages, but village life still flourishes in every part of the city, along with a curious mixture of the East and the West. Cows and pigs forage in garbage heaps near upscale houses with satellite dishes. Turbaned shepherds lead goats and sheep through ravines in the remaining open fields and near the city's airports. Eunuchs sashay past shops that sell Western products on Connaught Place. Rajasthani women in bright saris and men in *lungis* (skirtlike wraps) work with outdated tools on construction sites while executives exercise on computerized equipment in chic health clubs. At night, hotel discos are packed with the affluent, and during the day, temples are crowded with the devout. Sadhus (Hindu holy men) in simple garb and often carrying tridents walk along the streets, while young men zoom on their motorcycles with their heads concealed in Darth Vader-style helmets.

Even the world of politics has its own character here. When Parliament is in session, fierce discussions frequently turn proceedings into a circus. Members often lose control—flinging shoes at one another—and storm out of the august chamber. Many Delhi cynics refer to Parliament as a *tamasha*, which, loosely translated, means an outlandish party. Heavy security for political bigwigs or wannabe bigwigs often disrupts daily life. Senior bureaucrats and politicians travel in a cavalcade of cars in which the lead vehicle, with its blaring siren, forces traffic to the side of the road or completely closes off a thoroughfare. When the car with the official screeches to a halt, sten-toting security forces scramble around the VIP, VVIP, or VVVIP as he or she moves through an open door. In this respect, Delhi hasn't changed at all in its hundreds of years as a center of power. Political big shots dominate this city, and their decisions and behavior are the talk of the town.

EXPLORING

Numbers in the margin correspond to points of interest on the Delhi map.

For the first-time visitor, Delhi is complicated because the sites worth seeing (and there are many) are scattered around the enormous capital. **Old Delhi,** about 6 kilometers (4 miles) north of the city center, is in a state of decay. Its old *havelis* (mansions), which line the *gullis* (side lanes) of Chandni Chowk, the main thoroughfare that cuts through this old district, are architecturally stunning but cry out for repair. The entire area is also extremely crowded. Still, Old Delhi's monuments—the Lal Qila (Red Fort) and the Jama Masjid (mosque)—are magnificent, and Chandni Chowk is wonderful fun to explore.

The geographic center of Delhi is **Connaught Place,** which is similarly crowded. South of Old Delhi, it was the commercial hub of the British Raj. Every attempt to spruce up this district seems to grind to a halt. The old buildings that encircle the green traffic circle are getting a face-

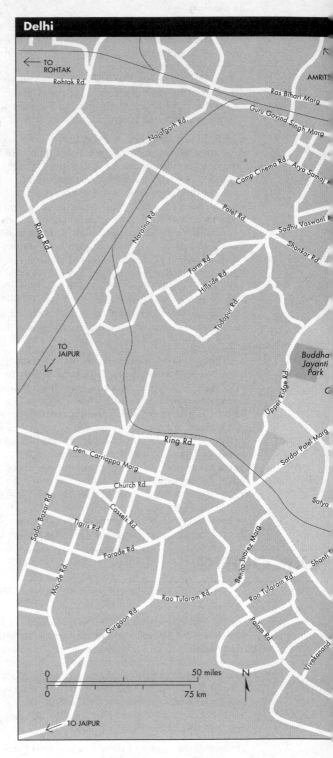

Delhi

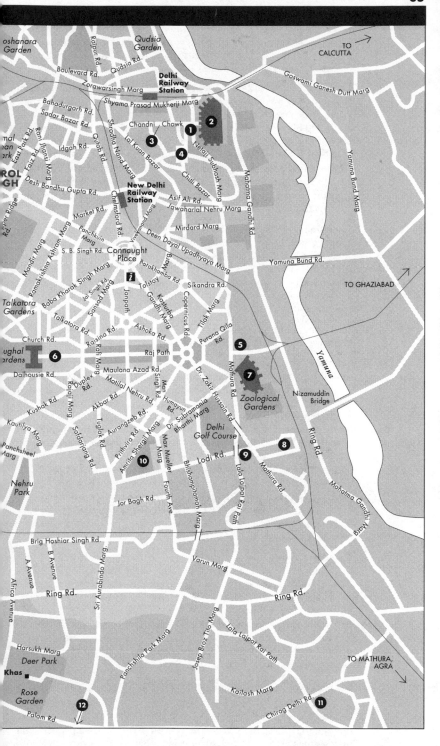

lift, but you still find lots of trash and not a single trash basket. It's also a haunt of beggars, unlicensed money changers, and other people engaging in dubious pursuits. Street hawkers sell essentially second-rate merchandise on the pavement, and touts try to lure you into their shops. The inner circle is a mess—dominated by auto-repair shops.

About 3 kilometers (2 miles) south of Connaught Place is the **Imperial City,** designed by the British architect Sir Edwin Lutyens: Rashtrapati Bhavan (the Presidential Palace), the North and South Secretariats, and the Sansad Bhavan (Parliament House). The Diplomatic Enclave is south-west of this area; to the east is India Gate, another convenient point of reference. Southeast of India Gate and not far from the Oberoi Hotel are the Purana Qila (Old Fort) and Humayun's Tomb; almost due south of India Gate is Lodi Gardens. The entire area surrounding these land-marks is filled with tree-lined boulevards, lovely old bungalows, and affluent residential neighborhoods.

South Delhi, which begins about 6 kilometers (4 miles) south of Con-naught Place, is less lush, with fewer trees. Its numerous enclaves are already crowded with houses—many of them lavish. South Delhi also has its share of monuments that date back centuries, such as the Qutab Minar, and numerous Muslim tombs, in particular, that lie abandoned in the center of a field or stand in a cluster of contemporary houses and apartments. Eastern South Delhi has the handsome new Bahai Temple.

Telephone numbers are included below only when someone is likely to answer the phone or speak English.

★ ⑪ **Bahai Temple.** The Bahai Temple celebrates the lotus, symbol of pu-rity throughout India, and the number nine, which represents the high-est digit and unity in the Bahai faith. The nine pools on the elevated platform signify the green leaves of the lotus and cool the stark, ele-gant interior. The sleek structure has two layers of nine white marble-covered petals that point to heaven and a lower level of nine petals that conceal the portals. The temple, completed in 1986, was designed by Fariburz Sahba, an Iranian-born Canadian architect. The temple's contours resemble a fantastic work of origami rising out of the earth. The interior conforms to that of all Bahai temples: There are no reli-gious icons, just copies of the Holy Scriptures and sleek wooden pews. *Bahapur, Kalkaji (9 km, or 5.6 mi, southeast of Connaught Pl., near Nehru Pl.), South Delhi.* ☛ *Free.* ☉ *Apr.–Sept., Tues.–Sat. 9–7; Oct.– Mar., Tues.–Sat. 9:30–5:30.*

★ ❸ **Chandni Chowk.** Chandni Chowk was the former imperial avenue, where the Mogul emperor Shah Jahan once rode at the head of his lavish cav-alcade. Today, bullock carts, taxis, private cars, dogs, cows, auto rick-shaws, bicycles, bicycle rickshaws, horse-drawn tongas, and pedestrians plow indiscriminately through the congested thoroughfare. If you suf-fer from claustrophobia, you're in trouble; if not, you're in for an ad-venture. On Chandni Chowk, strange aromas fill the air: pungent oriental spices and the stench of garbage. As in the days of the Moguls, astrologers set up their mysterious charts on the pavement. Shoemak-ers squat and repair sandals and other leather articles, blithely ignor-ing the human swirl around them. Sidewalk photographers with old box cameras happily take your picture for a small fee. Medicine booths conceal doctors attending patients. Oversized teeth grin from the win-dows of the offices of local dentists. If you peer through a portico, you may see men getting shaved, silver being weighed, plus every other con-ceivable form of commerce, while outside a cow lies complacently on the street.

The twisting labyrinth of streets begs you to meander, to lose yourself, though you're never really lost. Indeed, have some fun, and turn this gigantic haunt into a treasure hunt. Look for **Dariba Kalan** (Silver Street) and bargain for jewelry, turn down **Kinari Wali Gulli** (Street of Trimmings)—aglitter with bridal accessories and saris, and have a vegetarian snack on **Paratha Walan** (Street of Bread Sellers). If you're lucky, you may stumble on a picturesque lane of painted row houses and find peace and quiet in the exquisite **Jain Sweitamna Temple** at the far end. Here's a clue: The lane is off Kinari Wali Gulli. The entrance to the stunning temple is through the brass doors on the left. Another restful place is **Sisganj Gurdwara**, a Sikh shrine near the police station on the central Chandni Chowk thoroughfare. It marks the site where Aurangzeb beheaded Guru Teg Bahadur in 1675 when the guru refused to convert to Islam. Women must cover their heads; all visitors must remove their shoes. *6 km (3.7 mi) north of Connaught Pl. Most shops closed Sun. Jain temple open Oct.–Mar., daily 6 AM–1 PM and 6 PM–7 PM; Apr.–Sept., daily 5:30–12:30 and 7–8. Gurdwara open daily 24 hours.*

⑤ Crafts Museum. Designed by the architect Charles Correa, this charming ethnic-style complex houses more than 20,000 artifacts and handicrafts from throughout the country. Near the Purana Qila, it's also a great respite from Delhi's crowds and intensity. Terra-cotta sculptures from Tamil Nadu dot its spacious grounds. The Folk and Tribal Art Gallery—a delightful mix of village and tribal India—has objects constructed from locally available materials that highlight the mythology, ingenuity, and whimsy that exists in so much of India's folk art. A wooden temple car stands in an open courtyard that leads to more buildings, including a lavishly decorated two-story Gujarat-style haveli. The Courtly Crafts section displays the luxurious lifestyle of India's royalty. An upper floor celebrates the country's superb saris and textiles—brocades, embroideries, mirror work, and appliqués. In the village complex, with its replicas of rural homes, artisans demonstrate their skills and sell their products. There's also a museum shop and snack bar. *Pragati Bhavan, Mathura Rd.,* ☏ *11/331–7641.* ☛ *Rs. 5.* ☉ *Tues.–Sun. 10–5. Crafts demonstrations, weather permitting.*

★ ⑨ Hazrat Nizamuddin Aulia's Tomb. Here you can enjoy one of Delhi's best treats—the chance to hear Sufi devout sing qawwalis, which are hypnotically intense religious songs of ecstasy. Follow the twisting narrow lanes in Nizamuddin, an old neighborhood about 6 kilometers (3½ miles) southeast of Connaught Place that is a smaller version of Chandni Chowk. You pass open-air stalls selling Islamic religious objects, butchers chopping buffalo meat with the knife often held between dexterous toes, small restaurants cooking simple Indian meals and *paratha* (unleavened Indian bread) that is given away to the poor at day's end, and tiny shops selling audiotapes (many by famous qawwali singers). When you see vendors selling flowers and garlands, you're close to Hazrat Nizamuddin Aulia's tomb. Buy a couple of garlands (about Rs. 10) to donate to the memorial for this Sufi saint who died in 1325. When you are finally asked to remove your shoes, you've arrived at the tomb's entrance.

Within the small courtyard, considered extremely sacred, you see three small mausoleums. The saint's tomb has a white, onion-shaped dome with thin black stripes. It will also have the largest crowd of visitors. A mosque and the graves of other important Muslims, including a daughter of the Mogul emperor Shah Jahan and a relative of the emperor Akbar, the 16th-century conqueror and reformer, surround these tombs.

Chisti Hazrat Nizamuddin Aulia was born in Bukhara and came to Delhi, where he became an important Sufi mystic who inspired a dedicated following. His white mausoleum was constructed in 1562 after the destruction of two earlier tombs. Architecturally, the structure is modest: a little jewel that becomes prettier the longer you study its inlay work and the carved parapet above the verandas. Evenings from around 5 to 7 (especially Thursdays), the Sufi saint's male followers often sing their songs of ecstasy. Performances aren't guaranteed. You sit in the courtyard as the singers wail and gesture lovingly with their hands. *Old Nizsamuddin Bazaar (5 km/3.1 mi southeast of Connaught Pl.). Visitors must remove shoes. Women should cover heads.* ☛ *Free; make charitable donation and request that it be used to feed the poor; give small offering to musicians if you hear them perform.* ☉ *Daily 24 hours.*

★ ⑧ **Humayun's Tomb.** This tomb, erected in the middle of the 16th century by the wife of the Mogul emperor Humayun, launched a new architectural era that culminated in the Mogul masterpieces in Agra and Fatehpur Sikri. The Moguls, who brought to India their love of gardens and fountains, produced harmonious structures, such as this mausoleum, that fuse symmetry with Oriental splendor.

Reminiscent of Persian architecture, the exquisite red sandstone-and-marble tomb rests on a raised podium amid gardens intersected by water channels and enclosed by walls. The design represents the first "tomb-in-a-garden" complex in India. The marble dome, covering the actual tomb, is also a first in India: a dome within a dome (the interior dome is set inside the soaring dome seen from the exterior), a style that was later used in the Taj Mahal.

Besides Humayun, seven other important Moguls are buried here, along with Humayun's wife, Haji Begum, and possibly his barber. As you enter or leave the square, blue-domed structure, stand a moment before the gateway to enjoy the view of the entire monument framed in the arch. The building's serenity belies the fact that many of the dead buried inside were murdered princes, victims of foul play. *Off Mathura Rd. (5 km/3.1 mi southeast of Connaught Pl.).* ☛ *Sat.–Thurs. Rs. 1, free Fri.* ☉ *Daily sunrise–sunset.*

★ ④ **Jama Masjid.** An exquisite statement in red sandstone and marble, the Jama Masjid, India's largest mosque, was completed in 1656 by 5,000 laborers who worked for six years. The mosque is also the last monument commissioned by the Mogul emperor Shah Jahan. Three sets of broad steps lead to double-story gateways and a magnificent courtyard with an ablution tank in the center. The entire space is enclosed by pillared corridors with domed pavilions in each corner. In this courtyard, thousands gather to pray, especially on Friday, which is why the Jama Masjid is also called the Friday Mosque.

The mosque is characteristically Mogul, with its onion-shaped dome and tapering minarets. But Shah Jahan added an innovation: Note the novel stripes running up and down the well-proportioned marble domes. The whole structure breathes peace and tranquillity.

Inside the prayer hall (entered by the devout and the visitor after a ritual purification at the ablution tank), the pulpit is carved from a single marble slab. In one corner is a room where Shah Jahan installed the marble footprints of the Prophet Mohammed. *Old Delhi (6 km/3.7 mi north of Connaught Pl.) across from Lal Qila. Remove your shoes. Women's heads should be covered.* ☛ *Free. Rs. 1 to climb minarets (women must be escorted by a "responsible" man).* ☉ *Daily 7–5 for*

Muslims. On Fri. non-Muslims may visit from 30 minutes after sunrise until noon; otherwise entrance allowed 30 minutes after sunrise until 12:20 PM, 1:45 PM until 20 minutes before asar (afternoon prayer), and 20 minutes after asar until 20 minutes before sunset. Smoking forbidden.

★ ❷ **Lal Qila** (Red Fort). This is the greatest of Delhi's cities, even outdoing Lutyens's Imperial City. Built behind red sandstone walls that gave the fort its name, this is Shah Jahan's 17th-century statement of Mogul power and elegance. Today, you have to reckon with crowds and an ongoing renovation. Try to imagine the imperial elephants swaying by with their *mahouts* (elephant drivers), the royal army of eunuchs, the court ladies hidden in their palanquins, and other vestiges of Shah Jahan's pomp.

The formerly unobstructed view of the main entrance, called the Lahore Gate, flanked by semioctagonal towers and facing Chandni Chowk, is blocked by a barbican (gatehouse), which the paranoid Aurangzeb added for his personal security—much to the grief of Shah Jahan, his father. From his prison, where he was held captive by his power-hungry son, Shah Jahan wrote, "You have made a bride of the palace and thrown a veil over her face."

Once you pass through the main gate, continue along the Chhatta Chowk (Vaulted Arcade), originally the shopping district for the royal harem and now a bazaar that sells less regal goods. The arcade leads to the Naubat Khana (Imperial Bandstand), the main gateway of the palace—a red sandstone structure where music was played five times daily. Beyond this point, everyone but the emperor and princes had to proceed on foot, a rule that was observed until 1857.

A spacious lawn, once a courtyard serving as the boundary at which all but the nobility had to stop, leads to the great **Diwan-i-Am** (Hall of Public Audiences). Now, you've entered the seventh city of Delhi, the Delhi of Shah Jahan, in which marble dominates. The hall, raised on a platform and open on three sides, evokes a time of past glory—like the moment that was described by Bernier, a 17th-century French traveler, who was overwhelmed by the hall's magnificence. Here, the emperor sat on a royal throne studded with decorative panels that sparkled with inlaid precious stones. These panels, stolen by British soldiers after the Indian Mutiny of 1857, were restored 50 years later by Lord Curzon. Watched by throngs of people from the courtyard below, the emperor heard the pleas of his subjects. The rest of the hall, Bernier explained, was reserved for rajas and foreign envoys, all standing with "their eyes bent downwards and their hands crossed." High above them, under a pearl-fringed canopy resting on golden shafts in the royal recess, "glittered the dazzling figure of the Grand Mogul, a figure to strike terror, for a frown meant death."

Behind the Diwan-i-Am, a row of palaces overlooks the distant Yamuna River. To the extreme south is the **Mumtaz Mahal,** now the Red Fort Museum of Archaeology, with relics from the Mogul period and numerous paintings and drawings. Next is the **Rang Mahal** (Painted Palace), once richly decorated with a silver ceiling that was dismantled to pay the bills when the treasury ran low. The palace, which may have been for the royal ladies, contains a marble basin built into the center of a floor that has a water channel—called the Canal of Paradise—that runs through this palace and many of the others.

The third palace is the **Khas Mahal,** the exclusive palace of the emperor, divided into three sections: the sitting room, the dream chamber (for sleeping), and the prayer chamber, all with lavishly decorated walls and painted ceilings still intact. The lovely marble screen is carved with the Scale of Justice—two swords and a scale that symbolize punishment and justice. From the attached octagonal tower, Mutham-man Burj, the emperor would appear before his subjects each morning or watch elephant fights in the nearby fields.

The next palace is the **Diwan-i-Khas** (Hall of Private Audience), the most exclusive pavilion. Here, Shah Jahan would sit on his solid gold Peacock Throne, which was inlaid with hundreds of stones. When Nadir Shah sacked Delhi in 1739, he hauled the throne to Persia. A Persian couplet written in gold above an arch sums up Shah Jahan's sentiments about his city: "If there be a paradise on earth—It is this! It is this! It is this!"

Finally, you reach the **Royal Hammams,** exquisite Mogul baths with inlaid marble floors. The fountain supposedly had rose-scented water. A state-of-the-art steam bath, it could be called a 17th-century sophisticated health club.

From here, a short path leads to the **Moti Masjid** (Pearl Mosque), designed by Aurangzeb for his personal use and that of his harem. The prayer hall is inlaid with *musalla* (prayer rugs) outlined in black marble. Though the mosque has the purity of white marble, some claim that the excessively ornate style reflects the decadence that set in before the end of Shah Jahan's reign. *Old Delhi (6 km/3.7 mi north of Connaught Pl.),* ☎ *11/327–4580.* ☞ *Sat.–Thurs. Rs. 1, free Fri.* ☉ *Daily sunrise–sunset; museum open Sat.–Thurs. Sound-and-light show:* ☞ *Rs. 10–Rs. 20. Purchase tickets 30 min in advance. Show times: Feb.–Apr. and Sept.–Oct., daily 8:30–9:30; May–Aug., daily 9–10; Nov.–Jan. 7:30–8:30, weather permitting.*

🔟 **Lodi Gardens.** After Tamerlane ransacked the city at the end of the 14th century, he ordered the massacre of the entire population—acceptable retribution, he thought, for the murder of some of his soldiers. As if in subconscious response to this horrific act, the subsequent Lodi and Sayyid dynasty built no city, only mausoleums and tombs and a few mosques. Lodi Gardens contains the 15th- and 16th-century tombs of these rulers. Winding walks cut through landscaped lawns with flowers and trees. Near the southern entrance on Lodi Road is the dignified mausoleum of Mohammed Shah, the third ruler of the Sayyid dynasty. This octagon, with its central chamber surrounded by verandas that are carved with arches, is a good example of the architecture of this period. Inside are also housed the graves of other members of this dynasty's family. The smaller, yet equally lovely, octagonal tomb of Sikandar Lodi has an unusual double dome. Surrounded by a garden, it stands in the northwestern corner of the park. *Lodi Rd. (5 km/3.1 mi south of Connaught Pl.).* ☞ *Free.* ☉ *Daily sunrise–sunset.*

6⃝ **Lutyens's Imperial City.** Raj Path—the broadest avenue in Delhi—leads to Delhi's eighth capital: Sir Edwin Lutyens's Imperial City, which was also a symbolically imperialistic design. Starting from India Gate at the lowest and eastern end of Raj Path, nearby land was allocated to numerous princely states, which built small palaces, such as the **Bikaner House** (now the Rajasthan tourism office). One could claim that this placement mirrored the British sentiments toward the princes. During the British Raj, the princes no longer enjoyed the height of their former power or status. Moving up the slowly inclining hill at the western end of the avenue, you also move up the British ladder of power, a concept inherent in the original design. First, you come to the enormous **North and South Secretariats,** facing each other on Raj Path, which reflect the importance of the bureaucracy, a well-entrenched fixture of Indian society since the time of British rule. Identical in design, the two buildings have 1,000 rooms and miles of corridors.

Directly behind the North Secretariat is the **Sansad Bhavan** (Parliament House), a circular building in red-and-gray sandstone with an open colonnade that extends around the circumference. Architecturally, the design is meant to mirror the spinning wheel that was the symbol of Mahatma Gandhi, but the building's placement (off of the main avenue) may suggest the attitude of the British toward the legislative assembly that was made up of Indians: not the ruling force.

At the top of the hill is the former Viceroy's House, now called **Rashtrapati Bhavan** (Presidential Palace), which represents the apex of power. Though it was built in the 20th century, its daunting proportions seem to come from an earlier and more lavish time. Its scale was meant to express British supremacy. The Bhavan contains 340 rooms, and its grounds cover 330 acres. The shape of the central brass dome, the main feature of the palace, copies a Buddhist stupa (shrine). A majestic courtyard bearing the Jaipur Column leads to the yawning Greek portico of the building. The execution of Lutyens's design also has two ironic twists. As you approach the top of the hill, the entire palace was supposed to fill the vista. The gradient, however, is too steep, and only the dome dominates the horizon. In addition, a few years after the Imperial City was completed, the British packed up and went home and it became newly independent India's grand capital. *2 km/1.2 mi south of Connaught Pl. Entrance into Rashtrapati and Parliament requires permission (difficult to obtain) from Government of India Tourist Office.*

❼ Purana Qila (Old Fort). India's sixth capital was the scene of a fierce power struggle between the Afghan Sher Shah and Humayun, the son of the first Mogul emperor Babar. Humayun, who believed deeply in astrology, probably considered himself star crossed. When he started to build his own capital, Dinpanah, on these grounds in the 1530s, Sher Shah forced the emperor to flee for his life. Sher Shah destroyed what existed of Dinpanah to create his own capital, Shergarh. Fifteen years later, Humayun took revenge and seized control, but he died the following year, leaving Sher Shah's city for others to destroy.

Unfortunately, once you enter the massive **Bara Darwaza** (western gate), only two buildings are intact: the **Qila-i-Kunha Masjid,** Sher Shah's private mosque, an excellent example of Indo-Afghan architecture in red sandstone with decorative marble touches, and the two-story octagonal red sandstone and marble tower, the **Sher Mandal,** which ultimately became Humayun's library and his death trap. Hearing the call to prayer, Humayun started down the steep steps, slipped, and fell to his death. *Off Mathura Rd., near Delhi Zoo.* ☛ *Free.* ☉ *Daily sunrise–sunset.*

⓬ Qutab Minar. This 73-meter (234-foot) tower, called the seventh wonder of Hindustan, is the tallest stone tower in India, with 376 steps. Started by the Muslim campaigner Qutab-ud-din-Aibak in 1193 to commemorate his capture of Delhi, it was completed by his son-in-law and successor, Iltutmish, who added the top four stories. This combined effort led to a handsome sandstone example of Indo-Islamic architecture with terra-cotta frills and outbursts of balconies that mark each story. Unfortunately, repairs by a 14th-century ruler destroyed the harmonious lines, adding not only height and marble to the two upper stories, but a silly dose of incongruity. The lower sandstone sections are fluted; the renovation adopted a round motif. Instead of continuing the vertical lines, the 14th-century ruler chose horizontal. He also decided to change the degree of the taper. The decorative bands of intricately carved inscription are Arabic quotations from the Quran.

At the foot of the Qutab Minar lies the **Quwwat-ul-Islam Masjid,** the first Muslim mosque in Delhi and India. It was erected in the 12th century after Muslims defeated the Hindu Chauhan dynasty and created the first capital not far from the mosque. As if to prove their supremacy over the Hindus, the Muslims built their mosque on the site of a Hindu temple and used materials, especially columns, from 27 other demolished Hindu shrines. Hindu and Jain sculptures stand in various parts of the mosque. As the mosque was probably built by Hindu craftsmen, the presence of the large stone screen across the front of the prayer hall may have been intended to block out the strong Hindu influence.

The mosque is also famous for a strange object, a 5th-century iron pillar, which originally stood before a temple of Vishnu and was possibly brought here in the 11th century. This solid shaft of iron, 24 feet high, is inscribed with six lines of Sanskrit. No one knows why the pillar has remained rust free for so many years. According to legend, if you stand with your back to the pillar and can reach around and touch your fingers, any wish you make will come true. *Aurobindo Marg, near Mehrauli (14 km/8.6 mi south of Connaught Pl.).* ☛ *Rs. 1.* ⊙ *Daily sunrise–sunset.*

Off the Beaten Path

❶ **Charity Bird Hospital.** Across from the Lal Qila is a delightful and unusual attraction. It's a hospital—not for humans, but primarily for birds. The Charity Bird Hospital was started by the Jains in 1956. Vegetarian birds (and rabbits) are treated inside on three floors, and nonvegetarian birds and other needy animals are treated in the courtyard. The hospital is modest and shows how tender loving care can stretch limited funds. It even has an intensive-care ward and a research laboratory. Bathed, fed, and given vitamins, the healthy birds refuse to leave. That's how you can spot the building—flocks of birds swirl around its roof. *Nataji Subhash Marg, opposite Lal Qila.* ☛ *Free; donations welcome.* ⊙ *Daily 8–8.*

SHOPPING

Delhi is the marketplace for all India; shopping can be fun, and bargaining is the rule, except at fixed-price shops. Most shops are open six days a week. The day a shop is closed is determined by its location.

Old Delhi

Chandni Chowk and the bazaar inside **Red Fort** are good areas to hunt for bargains. On streets behind the **Jama Masjid,** many shops sell metalware curios and old utensils; on Dariba Kalan (Silver Street), stalls are filled with jewelry, including gold. Except for the Red Fort bazaar, most of Old Delhi shuts down for business on Sunday.

Gems 'n' Jewels (No. 31, Red Fort, ☎ 11/327–0524), a small shop in the Red Fort, has good miniature paintings. It also sells silver jewelry. **Mehra's Art Palace** (No. 35, Red Fort, ☎ 11/328–6953), also in the Red Fort, sells traditional Indian handicrafts, especially wooden objects, tribal work, and brass items. **Ram Parkash Vinod Kumar Jewelers** (Shop No. 107, Dariba Kalan, ☎ 11/326–8583), on "Silver

Street" in Chandni Chowk, has fine old and new silver jewelry sold by the weight with an add-on charge for labor.

Around Connaught Place

This area, closed Sunday, is the former commercial district of the British Raj. Beneath the green park at the center of Connaught Place, you find **Palika Bazaar,** an air-conditioned underground emporium that has the ambience of a Times Square subway station. Still, it has a few great shops. The government emporiums are also near Connaught Place and offer good bargains for visitors with limited time.

Banaras House (N-13 Connaught Pl., opposite Scindia House, ☎ 11/ 331–4751) sells sublime silks from all over India. **Central Cottage Industries Emporium** (Jawahar Vyapar Bhavan, Jan Path, opposite Imperial Hotel, ☎ 11/332–6790), which recently moved to a spacious multistory building, has examples of handicrafts from all over India under its roof. **Gems 'n' Jewels** (*see* Old Delhi, *above*; 9 Jan Path Bhavan, Jan Path, ☎ 11/332–8481) offers more good miniature paintings. **Jewel Mine** (12A Palika Bazaar, Central Hall, Connaught Pl., ☎ 11/ 332–0578), a shop popular with foreign jewelers, specializes in old and new silver jewelry and gems. **Lal Bahari Tandon** (20 Palika Bazaar, Central Hall, Connaught Pl., ☎ 11/332–7327) sells high-quality *chickan* work (hand embroidery) on fine linen and traditional clothing. **Natesans** (GF-2, Suryakiran Bldg., opposite Hindustan Times Bldg., Kasturba Gandhi Marg, ☎ 11/331–2603), with branches throughout India, sells magnificent curios and artifacts. **Real Value** (15 Palika Bazaar, Central Hall, Connaught Pl., ☎ 11/335–3040) offers a good selection of gold jewelry and can custom design special items with a few days' notice. **The Shop** (10 Regal Bldg., Sansad Marg, near Connaught Pl., ☎ 11/310971) sells lovely linen and other home furnishings, some clothing, and high-quality wood products. **State Emporia** (Baba Kharak Singh Marg) are three blocks of state-run shops offering a wonderful collection of regional items.

Diplomatic Enclave

Santushti Shopping Complex, on lovely grounds across the street from the Hotel Samrat, has a collection of shops that sell a range of Indian products, including home furnishings, jewelry, fabrics, leather, and clothing.

Near Lodi Gardens

Sunder Nagar Market, a neighborhood shopping district near the Oberoi Hotel and Delhi Zoo, specializes in jewelry, curios, artifacts, and good artwork.

Kumar Gallery (11 Sunder Nagar, ☎ 11/461–1113) specializes in original tribal statues, old dhurries and Tibetan carpets, miniatures, Tanjore and Mysore paintings, and temple art. **Ladakh Art Gallery** (10 Sunder Nagar, ☎ 11/461–8679) has good-quality silver tribal jewelry and curios. **The Studio** (4 Sunder Nagar Market, ☎ 11/461–9360) has good contemporary silver jewelry.

South Delhi

Dilli Haat (Aurobindo Marg, opposite INA Market; ☛ Rs. 3) is a new food-and-crafts bazaar in South Delhi ("Dilli Haat" means marketplace). Over 60 stalls sell products from different areas of India and 25 stalls offer regional food. Exhibits normally change every 15 days. Also expect open-air cultural performances midafternoon until evening.

Hauz Khas Village (near Deer Park, Hauz Khas) has boutiques and shops that sell handicrafts, curios, old carpets and kilims, and designer clothing (Indian and Western wear) in old converted homes in a neighborhood with narrow alleys.

Lal Bahari Tandon (4 Aurobindo Pl., opposite Green Park Church, Hauz Khas, ☎ 11/656552) offers chickan work (*see also* Around Connaught Place, *above*). **Mehra's Art Palace** (M-1, Main Market, Greater Kalash-II, ☎ 11/641–1194) is the main showroom of the shop in the Red Fort (*see* Old Delhi, *above*). It's gigantic—an entire building filled with lovely merchandise. **Museum Arts** (F-30 Lajpat Nagar II, ☎ 11/345943), in a private home, sells gorgeous old handspun and handwoven woolen Kashmiri shawls, including paisleys (made famous by Napoleon's wife Josephine) and shawls with intricate needlework. Try to have an appointment with Zaffir, who can explain the history and workmanship of each shawl. **Sabah Arts & Crafts** (I-57 Lajpat Nagar-I), also in a private home, has fine embroidered and chain-stitched Kashmiri cushions and rugs in unusual designs. **Wild Orchid** (12 Siri Fort Rd., ☎ 11/644–9347; 10 Southern Rd., Maharani Bagh, ☎ 11/683–2313), with two branches, sells designer ethnic-style clothing in exquisite cotton and silk hand-loomed fabrics and a good selection of Western wear for women.

SPORTS AND FITNESS

Participant Sports

Golf

Play golf against a backdrop of ancient monuments at the 18-hole **Delhi Golf Club** (Dr. Zakir Hussain Marg, ☎ 11/436–2768 or 11/436–2235). Contact the club for reservations and the cost to play.

Health Clubs

Private health clubs are not recommended. As power shortages are frequent in Delhi, you could work up a sweat while you stand around doing nothing. All hotel health clubs are reserved for their guests and private members. The best are at the Hyatt and the Maurya. The Hyatt has a modern unisex gym, plus aerobics and separate facilities for men and women with sauna, Jacuzzi, steam room, cold plunge pool, and massages. Welcomgroup Maurya Sheraton Hotel and Towers offers separate facilities for men and women with a modern exercise room, sauna, steam room, Jacuzzi, cold plunge pool, massages, and yoga classes for men and women.

Swimming

City pools should be avoided; there's no way to judge the water quality. Top hotels have excellent pools open to their guests. The Hotel Samrat has a swimming pool (open daily 8–8) that non-hotel guests can use for a fee (Rs. 200 per day).

Tennis

If your hotel doesn't have a tennis court, reserve one at the **Delhi Lawn Tennis Association** (Africa Ave., ☎ 11/653955). Contact the club for court fees and reservations.

Yoga

If classes aren't conducted at your hotel's health club, contact the **Sivananda Yoga Vedanta Nataraja Center** (52 Commercial Center, east of Kailash, ☎ 11/644–3697), which offers daily classes.

Spectator Sports

Check the newspaper or your hotel for **cricket** and **soccer** matches. Games, in which the rivalry is intense, are popular events; your hotel may be able to get you a ticket. Delhi's polo games (Oct.–Mar.) are another big crowd pleaser. Contact the **President's Estate Polo Club** (President's Estate, Rashtrapati Bhavan, ☎ 11/301–5604).

DINING

A few years ago, most of Delhi's restaurants had limited menus that offered a repetitive choice of Indian, Chinese, and Continental cuisines. That's all changed. Now you can sample good food from different regions of India and beyond the country's borders. Many restaurants, especially in the hotels, import some ingredients and employ foreign chefs who create tasty dishes that satisfy Delhi's new culinary curiosity. Restaurants are generally open daily 12:30–3 for lunch and 7:30–11:30 for dinner unless otherwise noted. Delhi "dry" days are strictly observed in restaurants and bars, with no alcohol available on January 26, August 15, and October 2. When you have liquor in higher-price hotels, expect gigantic taxes. Ask the real cost before you imbibe.

CATEGORY	COST*
$$$$	over $25
$$$	$15–$25
$$	$7.50–$15
$	under $7.50

per person for a three-course meal, excluding drinks, service, and sales tax

What to Wear

Delhi restaurants, unless otherwise indicated, do not observe a strict dress code. Casual and neat attire is just fine.

Chinese

$$$ **Noble House.** Its decor is essentially Western, with pastel silk panel-
★   ing on the walls and heavy gray drapes. Only the large porcelain figures of the five nobles (representations of prosperity, wealth, health, long life, and the Lord Buddha) and stylized brass lamps that resemble inverted roofs of pagodas suggest the Orient. The effect is subdued and elegant, and the Szechuan and Cantonese food is good, as well as the Chinese chef's own recipes. Tasty dishes include pan-fried chicken in honey sauce, spicy prawns in black bean sauce, and any of the dishes cooked in an unusual butter sauce. ✗ *New Delhi Hilton, Barakhamba Ave., Connaught Pl.,* ☎ *11/332–0101. Dinner reservations advised. AE, DC, MC, V.*

$$–$$$ **House of Ming.** This popular Chinese restaurant gets raves for its food and hospitality. The decor is inspired by the Ming Dynasty, which introduced Cantonese cuisine to the West: pale teak lattice-work on the chairs, a pagoda-style ceiling, windows, partitions, and the dynasty's favorite colors—pale blues and the soft sea-green raw silk that covers the walls. Taped Chinese music and soft lighting from brass lanterns reinforce the air of refinement. The chef concentrates on Szechuan and Cantonese cooking. The menu changes frequently, but ask about the

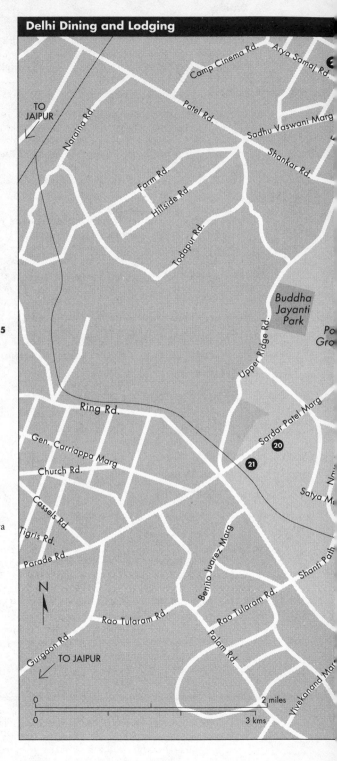

Delhi Dining and Lodging

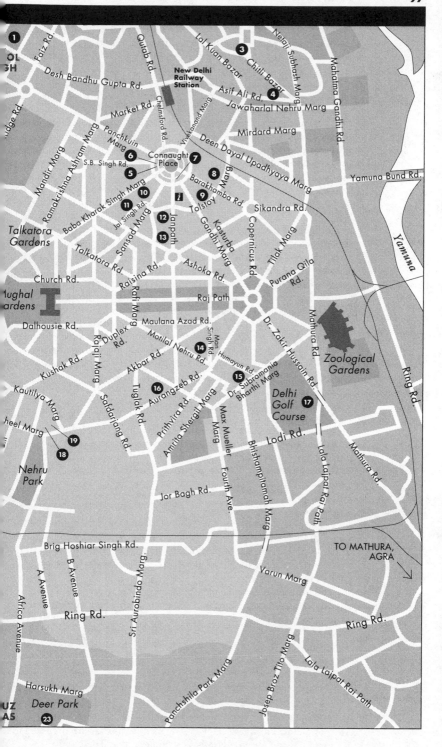

availability of these popular dishes: clear chicken wonton soup with delicately cooked vegetables, tender honey-glazed spareribs, crisp chicken in honey and chili, and spicy slow-fried jumbo prawn with chili bean sauce. And save room for the date-filled pancake with vanilla ice cream. ✕ *Taj Mahal Hotel, 1 Mansingh Rd., ☎ 11/301–6162. Reservations advised. AE, DC, MC, V.*

$$–$$$ **Teahouse of the August Moon.** This teahouse has lots of whimsy, with enormous carved dragons on the ceiling and a narrow bridge built across a goldfish pond that leads to an elevated central pagoda. Brass lanterns create subdued lighting, a full moon is projected onto an upper wall at night, and taped Chinese music adds to the Oriental ambience. Feast on dim sum (the house specialty), served in bamboo steamers at the table, or try the spicy king prawn pepper salt, chicken *tau su* (diced chicken cooked in a black bean-like sauce), spicy shredded lamb *sa cha* (lamb sauteed in seafood-base sauces, garlic, and chili paste). With 24-hour advance notice, the chef will sit with you at a special table and design a customized meal with wine (Rs. 1,000 per person with lobster or duck or Rs. 600 per person with chicken or lamb). ✕ *Taj Palace Inter-Continental, Sardar Patel Marg, Diplomatic Enclave, ☎ 11/301–0404. Reservations advised. AE, DC, M, V.*

$$ **Jewel of the East.** The cuisine at this large restaurant is exclusively
★   Chinese, but the decor underplays the Orient: a few framed silk hangings and water colors, delicate Chinese fans, and clustered modern circular lanterns that hang from domes built into the ceiling. The look of the restaurant is more Victorian: etched-glass windows, dark wood paneling, and upholstered banquettes. You can also kick up your heels on the small dance floor when the Western band plays nightly, except Tuesday. Sonam Choeden, the chef, is Tibetan; he's extremely creative with Beijing cuisine, especially the Mongolian Steamboat, a special soup that is prepared at the table over a flame. A waiter adds fresh vegetables and a variety of meat and seafood to a clear broth; after it's served, he adds three flavorful piquant sauces. Sonam also does a mean honey-coated, deep-fried boneless chicken (if you want it spicy, ask for the red chilies) or honey potatoes (not on the menu). ✕ *Ashok Hotel, 50 B, Chanakyapuri, ☎ 11/600412. Reservations advised. AE, DC, MC, V.*

$ **Fa Yian.** Don't let the dingy location—the middle circle of Connaught
★   Place—keep you from this fine new restaurant. Potted trees spruce up Fa Yian's exterior, where you may have to wait for one of the eight tables that fill the small space. Taped flute music and water spilling into a small fountain are soothing, but the interior decor of this new eatery takes second place to the really good (by Delhi standards) Chinese preparations that are either steamed or stir-fried in a minimum of oil. Many ingredients are imported; condiments and sauces, dumplings and noodles are prepared daily. Try the delicate *sui chiao* (steamed dumplings); *nuek shong ku* (stuffed mushrooms); the stir-fried black bean and chicken chef's special; or any of the good fish dishes, such as steamed fish delight (pomfret prepared with vegetables). ✕ *A block, 25/2 Middle Circle (behind Marina Hotel), Connaught Pl., ☎ 11/332–4603. Reservations advised. No credit cards.*

Continental

$$$$ **Grill Room.** Come to this intimate rooftop restaurant for a panoramic view of Delhi. The chefs emphasize grilled items that are prepared in a show kitchen behind a gleaming wood counter. The banquettes are nestled against low wooden partitions for privacy, and candlelit tables add a romantic touch at night. The menu changes frequently, but try the delicate green herbs soup and crêpes Suzette if they're offered. Prawn, lobster, and a variety of steaks are always available. ✕ *New Delhi Hilton, Barakhamba Ave., Connaught Pl., ☎ 11/332–0101. Dinner reservations advised. AE, DC, MC, V.*

Eclectic

$$ **The Cafe.** Head to the Cafe in the Hyatt's downstairs lobby for Delhi's
★ most extensive buffet. An enormous back-lit teak carving of the Tree of Life is mounted above an exposed kitchen and lots of white-and-green marble. There's the possibility of a good deal of noise other than the waterfall splashing down from the upper lobby. Nightly, except Tuesday, the music from the Western band playing in the upstairs open bar bounces off the walls. But just consider the guitar and drums part of the mood, which is lively, with everyone making repeated trips for food. You can go for the full buffet, which provides Indian, Continental, and some Chinese dishes, or choose just the salad bar or dessert buffet. The salad bar is an enormous spread that usually includes imported items (cheeses, patés, cold cuts, Danish herring, and even flown-in lettuce). Arun Upreti, the confectionery chef, is unrivaled in Delhi. ✕ *Hyatt Regency, Bhikaiji Cama Pl., Ring Rd., ☎ 11/688–1234. No reservations. AE, DC, MC, V.*

French

$$$$ **Orient Express.** Step aboard the Orient Express, an enchanting rail car
★ with handsome teak walls and brass fittings, such as the luggage rack overhead, the softly lit lamps, or the show plate on the table. Most of the 10 intimate tables are separated by beveled glass and wood partitions. A pianist plays in the adjoining bar. Chef Shiva, who's been with the restaurant for ten years, serves French nouvelle cuisine in the form of fixed-price meals that befit the decor. The menu is reviewed every six months; if they're available, try mustard-flavored chicken ragout surrounded by Indian-style fried crisp tarts; or simmered lobster tail; or breast of chicken encased in heart-shaped puff pastry; and the warm soufflé au chocolat. ✕ *Taj Palace Inter-Continental, 2 Sardar Patel Marg, Diplomatic Enclave, ☎ 11/301–0404. Reservations required. Jacket required. AE, DC, MC, V. Closed Sun. lunch.*

$$$ **The Rochelle.** Bernhard Koenig, the new chef, has transformed La Rochelle's cuisine. His classic French dishes are presented like a painting on the plate. As the menu is reviewed every six months and also features cuisine du marché, it's difficult to recommend specific items. But if marinated shrimp is available, it's delicate and flavorful; the lamb, imported from New Zealand, is especially tender; and the flambés are authentic. La Rochelle also has a good fixed-price (Rs. 375) buffet with French and Indian dishes. The restaurant, which has an adjoining bar, was scheduled for renovation at press time. It will have a thematic French decor. ✕ *The Oberoi, Dr. Zakir Hussain Rd., ☎ 11/436–3030. Reservations advised. AE, DC, MC, V.*

Indian

$$$$ **Dum Pukht.** Elegant Nawabi costumes are mounted like artwork on
★ the white walls with their delicate gold-leaf molding. A large window in one corner highlights an exterior waterfall. At night, a pianist plays hit songs from popular films. If the restaurant would only keep the lighting subdued, the ambience would perfectly match the exquisite royal Nawabi cuisine, Dum Pukht, which originated in the former princely state of Avadh in present-day Uttar Pradesh. *Dum* is Persian for

"breathe in," and *pukht* means "to cook." Every dish, with its aromatic herbs and spices, is sealed to retain the flavor and simmered over a slow fire. Come hungry because the cuisine is quite filling. The mutton dishes are the specialty: *kakori kabab* (mutton minced with cloves and cinnamon), *koh-e-Avadh* (shanks of mutton in a delicate curry with saffron), and *biranj-e-kuhna* (basmati rice with mutton). There are also unusual chicken, shrimp, and vegetable dishes. ✕ *Maurya Sheraton Hotel, Diplomatic Enclave,* ☎ *11/301–0101. Reservations required. AE, DC, MC, V.*

$$$ Frontier Room. Dine at wide planked tables in an elaborate fortress with freestanding rough stone walls, arches, and parapets and murals of Indian sepoys on horseback that appear to watch over the spacious room. Electrified copper *mashal* torches emit a fire-like glow, and recessed lights in the dark ceiling twinkle like stars. Nightly except Tuesday a strolling musician plays the *rabab* (similar to a sitar); otherwise expect taped Indian music. You're encouraged to eat the northwestern frontier fare (lots of kebabs and grilled dishes) with your right hand, but waiters in *salwar kameez* (a long loose shirt and baggy trousers) will provide silverware. The chef, Kharak Singh, a fixture at the restaurant, recommends his popular *bannu kabab* (marinated boneless chicken fried in flour and spices, then covered with bread crumbs and cooked in the tandoor) and the *raan aleeshan* (marinated leg of lamb slowly cooked on a hot plate, then sprinkled with rum just before it's done). The *Dal Dera Ishmail Khan* (fried dal) is also one of the best dal preparations in Delhi. ✕ *Ashok Hotel, 50 B, Chanakyapuri,* ☎ *11/600412. Reservations advised. AE, DC, MC, V.*

$$–$$$ Bukhara. This small restaurant with stone walls, mounted Bukhara car-
★ pets, and hanging copper vessels is so packed with patrons that it's hard to hear the taped Indian music. Gleaming wide-plank tables fill the small space, and more tables are set outside near the pool. The banquettes are comfortable, but not the stools on the opposite side of the table. The Bukhara is among Delhi's most popular restaurants; possibly the discomfort keeps diners from lingering. The chef, Mr. Kundan, has prepared his tasty northwest-frontier-province cuisine since the restaurant opened in 1979, and regulars rave over his *tandoori jhinga* (prawns cooked in the tandoor); *murgh malai kabab* (boneless chicken pieces marinated in cheese, cream, and lime); and *Sikandari raan* (leg of lamb marinated in rum and cooked in the tandoor), which serves four people. ✕ *Maurya Sheraton Hotel, Diplomatic Enclave,* ☎ *11/301–0101. No reservations. AE, DC, MC, V.*

$$ Chor Bizarre. Expect a 1927 Fiat roadster for a salad bar, a spiral stair-
★ case that leads nowhere, and an eclectic mix of tables (one created from a four-poster bed and another from an antique sewing-machine table) and a similar mix of chairs—all collected from *chor* (thieves') bazaars around India. Also expect excellent north Indian cuisine, especially Kashmiri dishes. Try *ghazab ka tikka* (tandoori chicken coated with cheddar cheese), *sharabi kababi tikka* (chicken cooked in tomato and onion and served with flaming brandy), or *rohgan josh* (mutton cooked in spicy gravy). ✕ *Hotel Broadway, 4/15 A Asif Ali Rd.,* ☎ *11/327–3821. Reservations advised. AE, DC, MC, V.*

$–$$ Dhaba. Its name refers to a curbside truck stop that serves inexpensive meals. And that's the motif in this small rural-look restaurant: wooden tables, a *lantan* (bamboo) ceiling, a tile floor, and an actual truck body projecting out of the wall behind the display kitchen. Instead of truck drivers, however, an upscale crowd usually waits to enjoy northern Indian cuisine. Popular dishes include chicken *tikka achari* or fish *tikka* (marinated with yogurt and spices, then cooked in the tandoor), *mattar paneer* (cottage cheese and pea curry), and *dal makhan marke* (fried lentils). Also ask about the daily specials. ✕ *Claridges, 12 Aurangzeb Rd.,* ☎ *11/301–0211. Reservations advised. AE, DC, MC, V.*

$ **Amber.** Handsome batik paintings cover the door to this Indian restaurant. Inside, more batik paintings on dark panels simulate Rajasthani-style shutters. Although the decor is not elaborate, the ambience is soothing, with soft lighting emitted from filigree lanterns hanging from the ceiling, and the food is popular. The menu features Muglai dishes; the house specialties are chicken or paneer butter masala (chicken or cheese in a creamy tomato sauce) and *reshmi* chicken *tikka* (boneless chicken pieces cooked in the tandoor). Also try the unusual *Kabul-li-naan,* a bread with a mild sugary taste. ✕ *N-19 Connaught Pl., opposite Scindia House,* ☎ *11/331–2094. Lunch reservations advised. AE, MC, V.*

$ **Coconut Grove.** This cozy restaurant, with cane chairs, bamboo trim, subdued lighting, and taped south Indian classical music, offers the cuisines of Kerala and other southern coastal regions. Try the special *konju thenga* curry (prawns cooked in mildly spicy coconut sauce) and pepper chicken *chettinad* (spicy chicken cooked in a thick pepper gravy). You can also enjoy an outdoor barbecue of south Indian grilled specialties. No liquor is permitted. ✕ *Ashok Yatri Niwas, 19 Ashok Rd.,* ☎ *11/371–3052. Dinner reservations advised. AE.*

$ **Dasaprakash.** Mr. N. P. Rao has been the chef for 15 years at this Delhi branch of Madras's oldest vegetarian restaurant. Twenty-one temple bells (an auspicious number) hang over a garlanded statue of Lord Krishna on the back wall. A circular domed ceiling has inlaid mirrors directly over a brass *gadhashkamba* (a pillar, symbol of Hinduism) positioned on a raised platform. Taped Carnatic classical music plays all the time. The south Indian *dosas* are extremely popular: The butter *dosa masala* is a rice crêpe cooked with pure ghee and butter on top (masala refers to the stuffing: potatoes, onions, or cashews). The onion *rava* masala has a semolina pancake with cooked onions on top. Come hungry if you want to try the *thali* (a platter filled with individual portions of numerous dishes). Available during lunch and dinner, the thali will be refilled until you tell the waiter to stop. ✕ *Ambassador Hotel, Sujan Singh Park, Cornwallis Rd.,* ☎ *11/469–4966. Reservations advised. AE, DC, MC, V.*

$ **Karim.** A sign proclaims that Karim (one of the 100 names for Allah)
★ was "born in 1913," but more than age accounts for the popularity of this Old Delhi establishment. Zainul Abedin, whose grandfather created the restaurant, has built a fourth small dining house on the small compound to accommodate the 1,000 people who come every day to eat his delicious Indian "fast food." The ambience is perfect for its location—off a lane across from the Jama Masjid's southern gate. In one small building, a man sits cross-legged creating *naan* (flat bread) in a tandoor. Nearby, enormous cooking vessels with popular dishes simmer over a low flame. Placards on a wall announce the fare, and the tables and chairs are simple. The fastest moving items are *badam pasanda* mutton (boneless mutton cooked with curd and spices), mutton stew, and chicken or fish tandoori. ✕ *Bazar Matia Mahal, opposite Jama Masjid,* ☎ *11/326–8880. Weekend dinner reservations advised. No credit cards.*

$ **Naivedyam.** This charming new restaurant, meticulously designed by
★ artisans from Tamil Nadu's temple city of Thanjavur, has a polished stone Nandi (Shiva's faithful bull) facing its stained-glass entrance. Three intimate rooms display Tanjore religious paintings chiseled on dark wood pillars and mounted on the clay-look walls. Carnatic instrumental tapes play in the background. The south Indian vegetar-

ian food is visually appealing and tasty: crisp dosas; spicy *oothappas* (Indian pizzas); thalis; unusual *bhaths* (rice concoctions), including the special *bisebele bhath* (rice cooked with tamarind, crunchy pulses, and spices). For dessert, try the *holige* with ghee (a sugary paratha mixed with coconut). ✗ *1 Hauz Khas Village,* ☎ *11/696–0426. No credit cards.*

Italian

$$–$$$
★ **La Piazza.** Finally the capital has excellent pizza, pastas, and a good range of Italian fare. The chef, Hermann Grossbiechler, is Austrian, but previously worked at the Sultan of Brunei's palace creating Italian and Continental dishes. His reputation grew, and he was invited to join the Hyatt in Delhi. Piazza means courtyard, but the restaurant, with an open kitchen and wood-fired ovens, feels more like an informal room in a villa. Dark wooden beams with concealed lights illuminate brick-look tiles in the ceiling. Pale yellow walls and massive pillars, with wall sconces, are delicately fluted and streaked with gold. The antipasto misto (nonvegetarian) is delicious with fresh mozzarella and carpaccio. The assortment of pizzas includes the popular pizza al Piazza with goat cheese, sun-dried tomatoes, roasted garlic, and basil. You can also try fettucine al Gorgonzola and panfried salmon with oregano, sun-dried tomatoes, and extra virgin oil. Finish off with amaretto parfait with red currants. There's also a selection of imported Italian wines and a Sunday lunch buffet. ✗ *Hyatt Regency, Bhikaiji Cama Pl., Ring Rd.,* ☎ *11/688–1234. AE, DC, MC, V.*

Mexican

$ **Rodeo.** The old-fashioned metal-grate elevator to this upstairs restaurant passes walls painted with scenes from American cowboy comics; then you push open saloon doors to enter Rodeo, Delhi's first Tex-Mex eatery. The cuisine is more El Delhi than El Paso, but the booths and wooden tables are usually crowded with a younger crowd. The restaurant is noisy with music videos that don't go with the decor. Stick to the nachos (topped with a carrot, but not bad), burritos, tacos, and enchiladas. Choose chicken or vegetarian; the lamb doesn't suit the cuisine. You can also sit on a saddle-bar stool and enjoy draft beer. ✗ *12-A Connaught Pl.,* ☎ *11/371–3780. Dinner reservations advised. AE, MC, V.*

Thai

$$ **Baan Thai.** The corridor into this traditional Thai *baan* (house) is an Asian art gallery: carved wood statues, "elephant" chairs, a collection of Thai porcelain, and antiques. More statues and exquisite embroidered hangings adorn the interior, where Burmese teak latticework covers the windows, partitions that create private alcoves, and parts of the ceiling. Sit at a traditional Thai *khantok* (floor cushion) on the raised platform or at a table. The chef imports many of the special ingredients to create his authentic Thai cuisine. Try the delicious *miang thai* (stir-fried chicken and water chestnuts) that you roll into fresh greens, a Thai curry, or *poo phad phong karee* (stir-fried crab). The coconut ice cream is home-made and perfect after a spicy meal. There's an adjoining bar. ✗ *The Oberoi, Dr. Zakir Hussain Rd.,* ☎ *11/436–3030. Reservations advised. AE, DC, MC, V.*

LODGING

Unless noted otherwise, hotels have central air-conditioning, and rooms have cable TV, bathrooms with tubs, foreign-exchange services, and room service. Many have a house doctor. In addition, many luxury hotels have executive floors with special privileges or facilities designed for the business traveler (*see* Special Hints for Business Travelers *in* Chapter 3, Business Travel in India). Rooms that cost over Rs. 1,200 are also subject to a 10% expenditure tax.

$$$$ **The Oberoi.** Delhi's first luxury hotel (built in 1965) was completing
★ a renovation at press time. It is perfect for visitors who want elegance and real quiet—an attribute that sets it apart from all other luxury Delhi hotels. You won't find a disco or see a flamboyant Delhi wedding. Even when the hotel is packed, the lobby is peaceful; it's also lovely, with a small marble lotus fountain strewn with rose petals near the entrance, an illuminated carved Tree of Life set in the back wall, and stunning Indian artifacts that catch your eye when you sit and relax. Valuable aquatints and lithographs are also hung in the spacious bedrooms, which have a Western decor and wall-to-wall carpeting. Most rooms have double beds. The best views (the higher the floor, the better) overlook the Delhi Golf Course, where you can usually spot a peacock. ⌨ *Dr. Zakir Hussain Marg, New Delhi 110003,* ☎ *11/436–3030,* ⅢX *11/436– 0758. 300 rooms, 33 suites. 5 restaurants, 3 bars, no-smoking floor, pool, beauty salon, health club, baby-sitting, business services, travel services. AE, DC, MC, V.*

$$$$ **Taj Mahal Hotel.** This jazzy hotel crackles with life—too much life for some visitors. But if you want to be near Connaught Place and surrounded by Delhi's who's who, book a room here. Its lobby has bright Rajasthani-style ceramics mounted on a wall and set in ceiling domes. *Jalis* (marble latticework screens) discreetly cover pool-facing windows and surround a central platform with a bubbling fountain. A quartet plays music at night. Double rooms or executive rooms (the same price, but with a larger writing desk) have wall-to-wall carpeting and twin or double beds, but the undistinguished Western decor doesn't live up to the Taj's reputation. The best rooms are on the upper floors and overlook the pool. At press time, the hotel was creating two exclusive floors for the business traveler. ⌨ *1 Mansingh Rd., New Delhi 110011,* ☎ *11/ 301–6162,* ⅢX *11/301–7299. 299 rooms, 26 suites. 5 restaurants, bar, tea shop, pool, beauty salon, health club, baby-sitting, business services, travel services. AE, DC, MC, V.*

$$$$ **Taj Palace Inter-Continental.** This massive hotel in the Diplomatic Enclave has a curved marble lobby and spacious grounds. Handsome interior *shamianas* (canopies) hang from the ceiling above comfy divans with bolsters. Picture windows overlook a landscaped terrace with a pool. Musicians entertain at night. Larger than the other Taj, it has a more subdued ambience. At press time, the hotel was renovating most of its bedrooms; deluxe doubles (slightly more expensive than standard doubles) are on the upper floors and have better views of the outdoor pool and greenery. All rooms will have wall-to-wall carpeting and upscale Western furnishings. Double and twin beds are available. There are also exclusive floors with amenities for the business traveler. The hotel is midway between the airport and Connaught Place. ⌨ *2 Sardar Patel Marg, Diplomatic Enclave, New Delhi 110021,* ☎ *11/301– 0404,* ⅢX *11/301–1252. 400 rooms, 34 suites. 4 restaurants, bar, pool, beauty salon, health club, nightclub, baby-sitting, business services, travel services. AE, DC, MC, V.*

$$$$ **Welcomgroup Maurya Sheraton Hotel and Towers.** Also in the Diplomatic Enclave and architecturally more dramatic than the neighboring Taj, this gigantic hotel (really two hotels) has the best Indian food in Delhi. Lovely pink *dholpar* stone covers the exterior and the interior lobby walls and pillars. Handsome sitting areas incorporate the colors of a gigantic folk painting set into a massive overhead dome. The grounds are extensive with fountains and landscaped gardens. The least expensive rooms, Executive Club, have a quiet decor with wall-to-wall carpeting and subdued classic Western furnishings. The best views overlook the pool or garden. Sheraton Towers (added in 1982 and much more expensive) has a small private lobby, an exclusive dining room, and posher bedrooms that make this wing extremely popular with corporate clients and distinguished visitors, such as Hillary Clinton and Chelsea during their 1995 Delhi trip. ☒ *Diplomatic Enclave, New Delhi 110021,* ☏ *11/301–0101,* ⓕ*AX 11/301–0908. 444 rooms, 44 suites. 5 restaurants, bar, pool, beauty salon, health club, 2 tennis courts, baby-sitting, business services, travel services. AE, DC, MC, V.*

$$$ **Ashok Hotel.** Near Nehru Park and also in the Diplomatic Enclave, the Ashok's palatial red-and-white sandstone exterior with corner cupolas is an exquisite copy of Indo-Saracenic architecture befitting the country's first government-owned hotel, constructed in 1956, with a new wing added in 1966. A public-sector hotel, it strives to be modern, but it feels a few years behind the times, and the service can be sluggish. Still, the Ashok is popular with VIPs and has a more Indian ambience than its competition. The lobby, with eye-catching artifacts, is also so large that Delhi-ites stroll here evenings during the monsoon. Unless you splurge on an Indian-motif deluxe suite (over $500), the other bedrooms lack memorable details and the Western decor feels a bit dreary. Still, the rooms in the old wing, with double beds, are spacious, and most have a balcony that overlooks the Diplomatic Enclave, Nehru Park, or the swimming pool. The newer rooms have twin beds and are smaller but have the same choice of views. At press time, the hotel was creating a special floor for executives with a private lounge and library. ☒ *50 B Chanakyapuri, New Delhi 110021,* ☏ *11/600121,* ⓕ*AX 11/687–3216. 571 rooms, 112 suites. 7 restaurants, 2 bars, pool, beauty salon, health club, putting green, 2 tennis courts, billiards, dance club, baby-sitting, business services, travel services. AE, DC, MC, V.*

$$$ **Hyatt Regency.** A recent major renovation has made the Hyatt the spiffi-
★ est hotel in town and has pushed its double-room tariff close to very expensive. In South Delhi, a short drive from the Diplomatic Enclave, this hotel offers superb Western food that is popular with embassy staffers and a casual ambience that visitors appreciate. The lobby is bathed in white marble tempered with veined green marble and imbedded mirrors trimmed in brass. A lovely pool, with a statue of a dancing goddess, connects to a waterfall that spills down to the lower lobby. Deluxe doubles are quiet and overlook the outdoor pool and handsome rock garden. Superior doubles, less expensive, offer a view of Ring Road. All doubles, which are not especially large, have attractive miniature paintings, wall-to-wall carpeting, and Victorian-style furniture, including a writing desk and an upholstered chair with a matching hassock. Most rooms have double beds. The Hyatt also has exclusive floors with amenities for the business client. ☒ *Bhikaiji Cama Pl., Ring Rd., New Delhi, 110066,* ☏ *11/688–1234,* ⓕ*AX 11/688–6833. 523 rooms, 27 suites. 4 restaurants, bar, pool, beauty salon, health club, 2 tennis courts, dance club, baby-sitting, business services, travel services. AE, DC, MC, V.*

$$$ New Delhi Hilton. India's Holiday Inn is now India's first Hilton hotel. The 25-story highrise is right behind Connaught Place. Its atrium lobby, with brass-trimmed glass interior elevators, is dominated by cool marble, the sound of a waterfall cascading into a lower lobby, and a delightful painting by Hussain, India's leading modern artist. Although attractive enough, the interior seems like a downscale imitation of the Hyatt and Maurya. The best views (a panorama of distant South Delhi) are on the upper floors. The hotel also has exclusive floors with special amenities for the business client. Its price is crowding the very expensive range. ⌧ *Barakhamba Ave., Connaught Pl., New Delhi 110001,* ☎ *11/332–0101,* ℻ *11/332–5335. 450 rooms, 55 suites. 6 restaurants, bar, 34 no-smoking rooms, pool, beauty salon, health club, dance club, baby-sitting, business services, travel services. AE, DC, MC, V.*

$$ Ambassador Hotel. A new acquisition of the Taj Hotel chain, the Ambassador, built in 1950, was undergoing a face-lift at press time. At a very moderate price, the rooms are a bargain and popular with tourists who are looking for comfort and good value. Not far from Lodi Gardens, the Ambassador is quiet—set back from the road behind its own private garden. The three-story concrete exterior with art-deco-style balconies is extremely modest, but the entrance leads into an enclosed terrace and adjoining lobby with cool marble and attractive banquettes on which you can sit and talk. The huge bedrooms have wall-to-wall carpeting and original teak furnishings that lack elegance but are fine for the price. The best rooms have balconies and overlook the front garden. ⌧ *Sujan Singh Park, Cornwallis Rd., New Delhi 110003,* ☎ *11/463–2600,* ℻ *11/463–2252. 80 rooms, 25 suites. 3 restaurants, bar, baby-sitting, business services. AE, DC, MC, V.*

$$ Claridges. In 1950 a Dutch hotel manager convinced an Indian family to build a hotel with a British name and decor. The family accepted this advice, and to this day, Claridges has a loyal following—many of them fussy, long-term visitors who appreciate the hotel's old-fashioned charm and aim-to-please attitude. The newly renovated lobby is charming: One side has a British "Victorian" decor; the other side evokes an Indian courtyard. The carpeted bedrooms are large and have Victorian furnishings with either twin beds or a double bed. The most popular rooms are on the third floor and have balconies that overlook the pool. The hotel is in the middle of an exclusive residential district not far from Connaught Place. ⌧ *12 Aurangzeb Rd., New Delhi 110011,* ☎ *11/301–0211,* ℻ *11/301–0625. 164 rooms, 11 suites. 4 restaurants, bar, pool, health club, tennis court, business services, travel services. AE, DC, MC, V.*

$$ Hans Plaza. From the outside, this 21-story hotel near Connaught Place resembles a typical Delhi office building. Inside the entrance, the lobby is whistle-clean and cozy, with pleasant sitting areas, plants, and Victorian-style furnishings. The quietest rooms are on the upper floors and overlook Barakhamba Road. The modest rooms are a fair size, with Western decor, including the wall-to-wall carpeting that emphasizes soft neutral tones. At the low end of the moderate scale, this hotel offers good value. ⌧ *15 Barakhamba Rd., Connaught Pl., New Delhi, 110001,* ☎ *11/331–6868,* ℻ *11/331–4830. 70 rooms, 1 suite. Restaurant, bar, business services, travel services. AE, DC, MC, V.*

$$ Hotel Imperial. This Delhi landmark, built in 1933 close to Connaught
★ Place, remains popular with visitors. Its driveway, bordered by palm trees, leads to a portico entranceway. The massively pillared lobby has plush red velvet furniture, old-fashioned etched-glass signboards, and

chandeliers. The rooms in the old wing have a colonial ambience, with delicately stenciled walls, old etchings, and nonfussy period furniture that evokes the British Raj. The bathrooms and tubs are enormous, but the beds are short; six-footers could have a problem. The new section of the hotel has big rooms, with longer beds, but the decor is standard Indian modern-style Western and the magic is gone. The best views in the hotel overlook the spacious lawns and pool. ⚏ *Jan Path, New Delhi 110001,* ☎ *11/332–5332,* ℻ *11/332–4542. 170 rooms, 3 suites. 3 restaurants, bar, pool, health club, 2 tennis courts, baby-sitting, travel services. AE, DC, MC, V.*

$$ Hotel Samrat. Built in 1982, the Samrat is a government-run hotel. The lobby's severe white marble begs for color to add warmth. It feels lifeless (probably because most guests head for the facilities at the Ashok next door). The spacious rooms, however, have wall-to-wall carpeting and decor that evokes the late 1940s and 1950s—pastel walls, built-in furniture with curved moldings, and sleek easy chairs. Most rooms have large double beds. The best rooms overlook the pool. ⚏ *Chanakyapuri, New Delhi 110021,* ☎ *11/603030,* ℻ *11/688–7047. 272 rooms, 15 suites. 2 restaurants, bar, pool, health club, baby-sitting, travel services. AE, DC, MC, V.*

$$ Park Hotel. A five-minute walk from Connaught Place, the hotel has scheduled renovation of public areas and bedrooms for completion by the end of 1995. Currently, the rooms in the 10-story property, which is popular with tour groups, are Western through and through. The quietest rooms overlook the pool or are on the upper floors with a view of Jantar Mantar, an 18th-century astronomical observatory. Guests staying in deluxe rooms on the 10th floor have a private lounge with a library and a dining area that serves a complimentary Continental breakfast. ⚏ *15 Parliament St., New Delhi 110001,* ☎ *11/373–2477,* ℻ *11/373–2025. 230 rooms, 12 suites. 3 restaurants, bar, pool, health club, business services, travel services. AE, DC, MC, V.*

$ Hotel Clark International. On a side street, this five-story hotel with a sea-green stone exterior opened in 1995. It has an unpretentious, cozy lobby and adequate-size bedrooms. Western furnishings include wall-to-wall carpeting, a built-in wardrobe, a sitting area, and beds that unfortunately could cramp a lanky six-footer. The bathrooms have modern bathtubs. The quietest rooms overlook the side street. ⚏ *547 W.E.A., Saraswati Marg, Karol Bagh, New Delhi 110005,* ☎ *11/575–6552,* ℻ *11/575–6551. 32 rooms, 4 suites. Restaurant, refrigerators, travel services. AE, DC, MC, V.*

$ Regent Holiday Home. The lobby of this five-story hotel on a side street has a marble counter, a plastic-look gigantic chandelier, and a sitting area that is amply supplied with daily newspapers. The best rooms have small balconies that overlook a community park. All rooms are on the small side, but clean, with wall-to-wall carpeting and simple Western decor. ⚏ *4/70 W.E.A., Krishna Market, Saraswati Marg, Karol Bagh, New Delhi 110005,* ☎ *11/578–0841 or 11/574–0214,* ℻ *11/573–6405. 38 rooms with showers, 1 suite with tub. Restaurant, bar, refrigerators, travel services. AE, MC, V.*

$ YMCA Tourist Hostel. Just south of the Park Hotel and about a 10-minute walk from Connaught Place, the YMCA has doubles (twin beds) and singles with attached bathrooms (showers) and air-conditioning. There's no carpeting, and the rooms are small with modest furnishings that probably date back to the hostel's construction in the late 1960s. But the linen is clean, water runs from the taps, the hot water geysers work, and you can laze around on your private balcony. Upper floors with rooms facing the back of the hotel are the quietest. Other rooms in the hostel have shared bathrooms (also showers) and overhead fans instead of air-conditioning. None of the rooms has TV. 🖃 *Jai Singh Rd., New Delhi 110001,* ☎ *11/311915,* FAX *11/374–6032. 123 rooms (14 with attached bath), 1 suite. Restaurant, pool, business services, travel services. AE, DC, MC, V.*

THE ARTS AND NIGHTLIFE

The Arts

Well-respected Indian dancers and musicians often perform in the capital. Good Indian films are occasionally shown in better theaters, and many embassies bring in dance troupes or other artists or hold film festivals that highlight their country's culture. To find out what is happening in Delhi, buy the monthly magazine *First City* or the weekly publication *Daily Diary,* which have comprehensive lists of scheduled events in the city.

Dance

Dances of India is a performance of six different folk, tribal, and classical dances that starts at 7 PM (admission, Rs. 75) daily at the Parsi Anjuman Hall (Bahadurshan Zafar Marg, opposite Ambedkar Football Stadium, Delhi Gate, ☎ 11/331–7831 or 11/332–0968 for reservations).

Nightlife

Delhi is dead when it comes to a vibrant nightlife unless you love dancing at discos. Disco fever is the rage, but even these places don't draw crowds until after 11 PM, when the disco regulars—Delhi's smart set—fill the rooms. The typical disco has a small dance floor, with most of the otherwise large room relegated to secluded sitting areas and the bar. The DJs who spin the tunes are considered ministars, and there's fierce competition to create the latest "in" place.

Bars and Lounges

At the **Captain's Cabin** (Taj Mahal Hotel, 1 Mansingh Rd., ☎ 11/301–6162), where the nautical theme is articulated in brass, teak, and old aquatints of seafaring craft, soft lighting and a pianist nightly (except Sunday) make it a quiet mooring for a drink at the bar or in a cozy booth. The **Club Bar** (the Oberoi, Dr. Zakir Hussain Rd., ☎ 11/436–3030) pianist, who needs to update his Western repertoire, plays nightly, except Tuesday, for patrons occupying discreetly positioned clusters of sofas and chairs in an elegant black-paneled room decorated with raw silk and aquatints. The wood-paneled **Polo Lounge** (Hyatt Regency, Bhikaiji Cama Pl., Ring Rd., ☎ 11/688–1234) has a library with newspapers and an odd selection of books, a leather sofa, sports on cable TV, a curved bar, and intimate seating; a Western band draws a crowd except on Tuesdays. In the **Viceroy** (Claridges, 12 Aurangzeb Rd., ☎ 11/301–0211) a brass cannon and old rifles, combined with dark Victorian antiques, set the manly ambience, and a pianist plays nightly (except Tuesday) and quietly, adding to the restful mood.

Discos

These discos supposedly are restricted to members and hotel guests, but if business is slow, you can usually talk and pay your way in. Some charge admission. **Annabelles** (New Delhi Hilton, Barakhamba Ave., Connaught Pl., ☎ 11/332–0101), popular after midnight, has a light show above the small wooden dance floor, a huge bar, and lots of sitting areas. For many years **Ghungroo** (Maurya Sheraton, Diplomatic

Enclave, ☎ 11/301–0101) was the hottest place in town; at press time it was being renovated. With swanky regency decor, **My Kind of Place** (Taj Palace Inter-Continental, Sardar Patel Marg, Diplomatic Enclave, ☎ 11/301–0404), a downstairs nightclub and disco, comes alive after 11 PM. **Oasis** (Hyatt Regency, Bhikaiji Cama Pl., Ring Rd., ☎ 11/688–1234), Delhi's largest and currently most popular disco, has a frosted-glass dance floor suspended over water and surrounded by sofas and casual seating arrangements.

Jazz Clubs

Pictures of jazz greats, such as Miles Davis, Louie Armstrong, and Ella Fitzgerald, share the wall with musical instruments at the **Jazz Bar** (Maurya Sheraton Hotel, Diplomatic Enclave, ☎ 11/301–0101), where you can hear the only live jazz in town.

Excursion to Neemrana

Neemrana Fort Palace, a Heritage Hotel, is in Rajasthan, halfway between Delhi and Jaipur. Perched on a low hill in the Aravalli Range, Neemrana was the capital of a Hindu prince who was killed in battle with invading Muslims in 1192. This 15th-century fort, which was restored and converted into a hotel in 1991, is one of India's finest retreats. Plan to explore the nearby traditional Rajasthani village, with its ancient step-well, an enormous underground well with wrap-around staircases and sitting areas on each level, where people would take refuge during the heat.

Getting There

Hire a car with driver (*see* Travel Agencies *in* Delhi Essentials, *below*). The trip takes around two hours. Expect to pay about Rs. 8 to Rs. 10 per kilometer and a halt charge of Rs. 150 to Rs. 200 per night.

Dining and Lodging

For price categories, *see* the charts for Delhi, *above*.

$–$$$ **Neemrana Fort Palace.** This fort hotel is a gem. The rooms, which vary
★ in size and price, are furnished with antiques and are decorated with Rajput mementos and indigenous handicrafts. The Eastern-palace architecture is characterized by latticed wooden windows or *jalis* (perforated stone screens), cusped arches, gleaming pillars, squinches, and various-sized niches that contain small artifacts collected by the owners. Swatches of the original royal blue pigment have been left untouched, showcased like minimalist paintings. Recovered decorated lintels are mounted on the walls. Forget about room telephones or TVs. Simply relax and watch preening peacocks and swooping parrots from private terraces, balconies, and courtyards; in gardens; or from under a 12-column pavilion. Rajasthani and French fixed-menu meals are served in the restaurant, and breakfast is included in the rate. ☒ *Off National Hwy. 8, (122 km/7 mi from Delhi),* ☎ *1494/6005; reserve through A-58, Nizamuddin East, New Delhi 110013,* ☎ *11/461–8962,* ☒ *11/462–1112. 25 rooms (3 with tubs, 22 with showers), 2 rooms with shared bath, 11 suites. Restaurant, bar, tour services. AE, MC, V.*

Excursion to Mussoorie

In many respects, Mussoorie, which is in the Himalayan foothills of Uttar Pradesh, is like any other former British hill station turned "honeymoon retreat," where the emphasis is on strolling on the pedestrian-only main thoroughfare (called the Mall). As you approach this hill station, you see billboards advertising hotels and cars loaded with young couples. But you can avoid this side of Mussoorie and escape to peaceful nature by booking a room in the Claridges Nabha.

Getting There

Mussoorie is 278 kilometers (172 miles) northeast of Delhi. Hire a car with driver (*see* Travel Agencies *in* Delhi Essentials, *below*). The trip takes around six hours. Expect to pay about Rs. 8 to Rs. 10 per kilometer and a halt charge of Rs. 150 to Rs. 200 per night.

Dining and Lodging

For price categories, *see* the charts for Delhi, *above*.

$$ Claridges Nabha. This summer bungalow, once the property of the former maharaja of Nabha and now owned by Delhi-based Claridges, is the one place in Mussoorie that consciously maintains the ambience of an old-fashioned hill station. Opened in 1994, the small hotel, 2 kilometers (1 mile) from the crowded, polluted, and noisy Mall, provides a peaceful chance to unwind amid natural surroundings. The 1845 main bungalow, with its typical red tin roof, has an enormous foyer, a lounge, a dining room, and a bar that aren't ornate but are absolutely comfy. The best guest rooms, constructed in the 1940s, open onto a veranda and face an interior courtyard. Victorian reproductions and the color schemes, including the area rugs on the gleaming parquet floors, change in each bedroom; the elegance is studiously understated. All the rooms have heaters, ceiling fans, and showers. During your visit, sip tea on the front lawn under a gigantic cypress and enjoy the escapades of langurs jumping through trees; stroll through terraced gardens with lilies and tuber roses and along nature walks in the nearby woods. This inn is also a perfect place to relax before or after a trek or rafting adventure in northern Uttar Pradesh (*see* Adventure Travel *in* Chapter 2, Special-Interest Travel in India). Reserve well in advance for stays from May 15 to July 15. Meals are included. ☎ *Airfield, Barlowganj Rd., Mussoorie 248179, Uttar Pradesh,* ☎ *135/631425 or reserve through Claridges, Delhi,* ☎ *11/301–0211,* FAX *11/301–0625. 22 rooms, 1 suite. Restaurant, tennis court, billiards, travel services. AE, DC, MC, V.*

DELHI ESSENTIALS

Arriving and Departing

By Plane

International flights use the **Indira Gandhi International Airport,** about 23 kilometers (38 miles) southwest of Connaught Place, the city center. Domestic flights use **Palam Airport** (also called the national or domestic airport), which is close to the international airport. Palam has two terminals: the Airbus terminal for Indian Airlines airbuses serving Bangalore, Bombay, Calcutta, Hyderabad, and Madras, and the Boeing terminal for other Indian Airlines flights and private-sector domestic carriers. When you purchase or reconfirm any domestic departure ticket, find out which terminal you should use. For the private-sector domestic carriers, use the extreme right entrance at the Boeing terminal. If you take a taxi to the airport, most drivers are clueless about the appropriate departure terminals. At press time, signs are confusing and don't provide any guidance for passengers using the new airlines.

Reconfirm your flights 72 hours before departure and arrive at the airport 60 minutes before flight time for domestic flights and 3 hours before international flights.

Major international carriers that use Indira Gandhi International Airport include **Air Canada** (☏ 11/372–0014 or 11/372–0043), **Air France** (☏ 11/331–0407 or 11/331–7054), **Air India** (☏ 11/331–1225), **Alitalia** (☏ 11/331–1019), **British Airways** (☏ 11/332–7428), **Cathay Pacific** (☏ 11/332–3332 or 11/331–3777), **Gulf Air** (☏ 11/332–7814 or 11/332–4293), **Japan Airlines** (☏ 11/332–4922 or 11/332–7608), **KLM** (☏ 11/331–747), **Kuwait Airways** (☏ 11/331–4221), **Lufthansa** (☏ 11/332–7609 or 11/332–7268), **Malaysian Airlines** (☏ 11/332–4308), **Qantas** (☏ 11/332–3161), **Singapore Airlines** (☏ 11/332–6373), **Swissair** (☏ 11/332–5511), and **United Airlines** (☏ 11/371–5550 or 11/372–4003).

At press time, India's much-welcomed domestic carriers are going through more than air turbulence. Some airlines are in financial troubles; others are merging. With hope, some will survive. Routes and schedules are just as unsettled. Contact your travel agent or India's Tourist Office in your home country for the latest details.

BETWEEN THE AIRPORT AND CENTER CITY

The trip between Delhi's airports and the city should take about 30 minutes if you arrive before 9 AM or after 8 PM. At other times, traffic near the city center can increase the time to an hour. Most hotels provide complimentary airport transfers if you are staying in a suite or on an executive floor (*see* Special Hints for Business Travelers *in* Chapter 3, Business Travel in India). All hotels, however, will provide airport transfers for about Rs. 200 to Rs. 300, depending on their location.

By Limousine: No Western-style limousines are available in India. If you want a Mercedes Benz to transfer you to and from the airport, make arrangements with your hotel or travel agency. It will cost about Rs. 800 each way.

By Taxi: This is the most convenient way to get to your hotel. As taxi drivers are famous for overcharging and rigging their meters, use the prepaid taxi service offered at each airport. This service is available at a designated counter outside the baggage-claim area and inside the arrival terminal. Your destination and amount of luggage determine the rate, which you pay in advance at this counter. Your receipt includes your taxi's license plate number. When you leave the terminal, drivers and touts will converge on you and offer "assistance." Avoid them and wheel your own baggage cart if you have one to the designated taxi, which is normally waiting in a line near the terminal exit. Taxis are black with yellow tops. If you have trouble locating your taxi, head to the police-assistance booth, which is also near the terminal exit. Once you get into the taxi, don't give the driver the payment slip until you reach your destination. If the driver demands more rupees, complain to the hotel doorman. A taxi from the international airport to the city center should cost about Rs. 200; from the domestic airport, about Rs. 150.

By Train

The **Delhi Railway Station** is about 7 kilometers (4⅓ miles) north of Connaught Place, and the **New Delhi Railway Station** is about 1 kilometer (½ mile) north of Connaught Place. Most trains leave from the New Delhi Railway Station, but check before you set out. For tickets and information, foreigners can save time and energy by using the services of a tour operator (*see* Travel Agencies, *below*). Otherwise, contact the **International Tourist Bureau** (New Delhi Railway Station, ☎ 11/373–4164), which is open Monday–Saturday 7:30 to 5. At this window (for foreigners only), tickets must be purchased in foreign currency, usually dollars or sterling, unless you have a valid encashment slip. If you don't have an encashment slip, you can purchase a ticket in rupees at the general counter at the same location (open daily 9:30–8). Before you board any train, you must have a confirmed ticket and a reservation for a sleeper and berth if you travel overnight (*see* Rail Travel *in* Smart Travel Tips A to Z *in* the Gold Guide).

Getting Around

Only people with steel nerves should drive in and around Delhi. Traffic rules exist, but few drivers observe them and even fewer police enforce them. Every major thoroughfare is congested from 9 AM to 7 PM with bullock carts, rickshaws, tilting overcrowded buses and trucks, bicycles and motorcycles, cows, horses, occasional goats, elephants, and dogs. Major highways (oversize two-lane roads) from Jaipur, Agra, and northern Uttar Pradesh are famous for accidents, with overturned trucks and demolished cars as common as roadside restaurants. Road conditions are subject to the quality of construction (new roads can develop craters overnight). They're also at the mercy of the weather; poorly designed culverts lead to flooding during the monsoon.

Except for the old city's Chandni Chowk, 6 kilometers (3.7 miles) north of Connaught Place, the best way to travel around Delhi is by taxi, hired car with driver, or auto rickshaw. To visit Chandni Chowk, take a motorized vehicle to the Red Fort; then walk or take a bicycle rickshaw through the neighboring crowded district and its maze of narrow lanes.

By Auto Rickshaw
This is the best way to scoot around town. The driver can be surly, can claim that the meter is broken, and can rig the meter to go faster than his rickshaw. But still, rickshaws are fun and cheap. At press time, auto rickshaws charged Rs 4.40 for the first kilometer and Rs. 2.10 per additional kilometer. Rate increases are frequent, and meters usually don't reflect the actual cost. Expect to pay 50% above the reading if the meter starts at Rs. 3.

By Bicycle Rickshaw
In Old Delhi if you're not up to walking, this is the best alternative. A real bargain, it should be cheaper than the auto rickshaw. Ask a local merchant to help you negotiate the fare, but remember, these guys pedal hard for a living.

By Hired Car with Driver
Let an experienced driver chauffeur you around Delhi and to nearby destinations. Expect to pay as much as Rs. 300 to Rs. 400 for four hours or 40 kilometers (24 miles) and Rs. 700 to Rs. 800 for eight hours or 80 kilometers (48 miles) of sightseeing in Delhi in a non-air-conditioned Ambassador car, which is the least expensive vehicle. Larger cars or ones with air-conditioning cost more. Ask in advance about the cost for extra mileage or hours. If you are staying in an upscale hotel, you can often pay less if you arrange for a car from an outside travel agent; shop around, but hire a car from a government-recognized tour operator (*see* Travel Agencies, *below*).

By Taxi
In early 1995, taxis cost Rs. 7.50 for the first kilometer, Rs. 4.50 for each additional kilometer. There was also a 25% surcharge between 10 PM and 5 AM. Since rates frequently increase, the meter reading is

usually inaccurate. Drivers should carry a chart with revised fares; ask to see it before you pay. At press time, fares were 50% above the meter reading if the meter started at Rs. 5. Taxis are available at every hotel, at taxi stands in shopping areas, and in each neighborhood.

Important Addresses and Numbers

Bookstores

Delhi has great book bargains, including lower-priced Indian editions of new titles published abroad. Although better hotels have small bookshops, the best selections are at **Book Worm** (B-29 Connaught Pl.), **New Book Depot** (B-18 Connaught Pl.), **Oxford Book and Stationery** (N Block, Connaught Pl.), and **Piccadilly Book Stall** (Shop 64, Shankar Market, off Connaught Pl.) These stores are open Monday through Saturday 10 to 7. Oxford takes a lunch break from 1:30 to 2:30. Vendors on Parliament Street near Connaught Place also have stacks of books for which you can negotiate the price. Khan Market has excellent bookstores that are open Monday through Saturday 10 to 7.

Changing Money

Most Western-style hotels have foreign-exchange facilities for their guests and will cash traveler's checks with twice the speed and half the hassle of banks. **American Express** (Wenger House, A-Block, Connaught Pl., ☎ 11/332–4149 or 11/332–4119) and **Thomas Cook** (Hotel Imperial, Jan Path, ☎ 11/335–0561 or 11/335–0562 and International Trade Tower, 717–718 Nehru Pl., 7th floor, ☎ 11/642–3035) will cash their own traveler's checks. The **Central Bank of India** (Ashok Hotel, Chanakyapuri, ☎ 11/601848) is open 24 hours daily, except national holidays. You can also cash traveler's checks at **ANZ Grindlays** (5 Kasturba Gandhi Marg, ☎ 11/332–1370), **Bank of America** (15 Hansaslaya,4 Barakhamba Rd., ☎ 11/372–2332), and **Citibank** (124 Connaught Pl., ☎ 11/371–2484).

Embassies

The **United States Embassy** (Shanti Path, Chanakyapuri, ☎ 11/600651) is open weekdays 8:30 to 1 and 2 to 5:30 for consular services. The **Canadian High Commission** (7/8 Shanti Path, Chanakyapuri, ☎ 11/687–6500) is open Monday through Thursday 8:30 to 12:45 and 1:30 to 5:30 and Friday 8:30 AM to 1 PM for consular services. The **British High Commission** (Shanti Path, Chanakyapuri, ☎ 11/687–2161) is open weekdays 9 to 1 and 2 to 5 for consular services. For lost passports or emergencies, a duty officer is available 24 hours a day at each embassy.

Emergencies

For any emergency, contact your embassy or the **East West Clinic** (38 Golf Links, ☎ 11/462–3738, 11/469–9229, 11/469–0955, 11/469–8865, or 11/469–00429; FAX 11/469–0428 or 11/463–2382), which has a 24-hour medical emergency room and can also supply lawyers (*see* Emergencies *in* the Gold Guide). Most hotels also have house physicians and dentists on call.

Late-Night Pharmacies

Most hotels have chemists that are open daily until about 9 PM. The chemist in Super Bazaar on Connaught Place is open 24 hours.

Post Offices

Centrally located post offices are near American Express on Connaught Place and at the Eastern Court Post Office on Jan Path. Hotels have mailing facilities; some sell stamps.

Travel Agencies

Travel agencies are apt to offer different rates for a car with driver, for Delhi tours, for Delhi excursions, and even for hotel rooms. Shop around and ask what's included in the price. Only use government-recognized tour operators or travel agents (ask to see their licenses). **Air Travel Bureau** (M-95 Connaught Pl., New Delhi 110001, ☎ 11/ 371–3204 or 11/371–3205), open daily 9:30 to 7, also offers visa and foreign-exchange services. **American Express** (Wenger House, A-Block, Connaught Pl., ☎ 11/332–4149 or 11/332–4119) is open daily 9:30 to 6 for nonmembers and until 7:30 for card members. **Ashok Travel and Tours** (New Delhi House, 3rd Floor, 27 Barakhamba Rd., ☎ 11/ 331–3233), open Monday–Saturday 10–5:30, has desks open 24 hours at all Ashok hotels. **RBS Travels** (Shop G, Connaught Palace Hotel, 37 Shaheed Bhagat Singh Marg, ☎ 11/373–3950, and 5/47 W.E.A., Saraswati Marg, Karol Bagh, ☎ 11/344952; ☎ 11/461–0596 after hours), which offers extremely competitive rates, is open daily 9– 8:30. **Thomas Cook** (Hotel Imperial, Jan Path, ☎ 11/332–2171) is open Monday through Saturday 9:30 to 6.

Visitor Information

The **Government of India Tourist Office** (88 Jan Path, ☎ 11/332–0005) is open Monday through Friday 9 to 5 and Saturday 9 to 1; its airport counters are open for flight arrivals, and railroad stations have counters that are open 24 hours. At press time, the employees at the **Delhi Tourism and Transportation Development Corporation** were poorly informed; don't waste your time.

5 Rajasthan

In spirit, the great cities of Rajasthan—Jaipur, Jodhpur, Jaisalmer, and Udaipur—are the legendary land of the Rajput, or martial warrior. Forts and palaces, lakes and gardens, even the wildlife sanctuaries that were once the exclusive hunting grounds of the royalty are steeped in romance and chivalry.

By Smita Patel

ONCE CALLED RAJPUTANA ("Abode of Kings"), Rajasthan had more than 22 princely states, each ruled by a Rajput (prince), with borders that shifted like desert sands. Hundreds of forts and palaces stand watch over Rajasthan, historic reminders of tumultuous battles and grand processions. Their architecture, a blend of Rajput and Mogul styles, exudes massive power and a delicate grace. Their perforated stone windows recall the hidden eyes of royal women who accepted a life of concealment and seclusion. Their magnificent halls and chambers sparkle with precious stones.

For centuries, the Hindu Rajput rulers, who were (and still are) great horsemen, and the powerful Moguls passionately fought each other for control of northern India. When they weren't fighting the Muslim rulers, the Rajputs battled each other, and many of their forts and museums today display pillaged treasure. The Rajputs were masterful warriors who held to an unwavering sense of honor and pride. This led to a tradition that demanded the supreme sacrifice when a battle went against them. Dressed in saffron robes of immolation, they went into war prepared to die. If the sign of defeat was displayed on the battlefield, the women in the fortress performed the rite of *sati* and threw themselves into a flaming pyre—far better, they thought, than the indignity of capture.

Following India's independence, the Rajput princes and kings were forced to merge their states into the new country, but they still kept title to their palaces and forts, private lands, jewels, and sumptuous possessions. More recently, the government has begun to take over their lands, palaces, and forts (many of the royal museums existing today were established to avoid this). Without their stipend, many maharajas became hoteliers; others turned their properties over to leading hotel chains. A few are paupers or recluses.

From the kings who still live in splendor to the peasants who still bow to, and even worship, the descendants of their former rulers, Rajasthan retains the spirit of Rajputana. You sense it in the palaces with their magnificent lakes and gardens, at royal hunting grounds that are now wildlife sanctuaries, and in the faces of the Rajasthani people, who retain the chivalry and grace of their past. This explains the state's position as India's most popular tourist destination; the abundance of visitors during the peak season, October through March, is Rajasthan's only downside.

India's second largest state, Rajasthan has deserts and lakes, craggy hills and deep ravines, golden sand dunes that stretch to the horizon and scrubby grasslands alive with antelope and gazelle. Nearly every hilltop is crowned with a fort, a relic of the days when warriors fought for control of this harsh yet beautiful land. The rigors of life in the unfriendly climate have kept Rajasthan from becoming as densely populated as other parts of India, and distances between the major cities are great. Centuries of intermarriages and political alliances between the states have resulted in a web of family ties binding the principalities together. Yet the different regions of Rajasthan vary widely in everything from the color of the sandstone used in their buildings to the style of the local arts and crafts and the languages the locals speak.

For many, Rajasthan conjures up images of deserts and sand dunes, but the pure desert lies mainly around Jaisalmer in the western part of

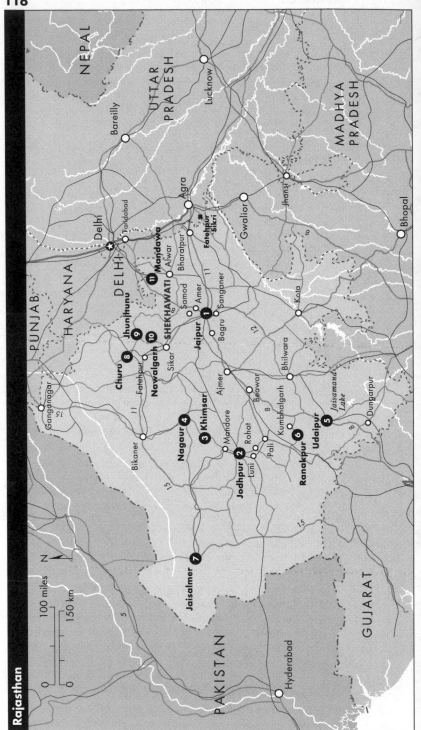

Rajasthan

the state. As you move farther south and east, the sands become increasingly scrubby and are eventually brought up short by the Aravalli hills, highest in the southwestern part of the state. Cradled in the valleys are the city of Udaipur, with its artificial lakes, and the Ranakpur Jain temples.

To help you plan a trip to Rajasthan, this chapter focuses on the three major cities of Jaipur, Jodhpur, and Udaipur, which are well connected by air, as well as by road and rail. From these hubs, you can design your own excursions to other parts of the state.

Numbers in the margin correspond to points of interest on the Rajasthan map.

JAIPUR

Encircled on all but the southern side by the rugged Aravalli hills and under the benevolent watch of weathered fortresses, **Jaipur** is well protected. The city takes its name from Maharaja Jai Singh II, an avid scientist, architect, and astronomer, who conceived and designed the bulk of his new capital in 1727 when he moved from Amber, the ancient rockbound stronghold of his ancestors.

Jaipur today is dusty and crowded with dogs, camels, horses, and people, but head down any of its 33-meter- (108-foot-) wide main roads and you see the symmetry of the exquisite buildings on either side. The city was enclosed within fortified walls 6 meters (20 feet) high and guarded by eight gates. Every aspect of the city—streets, sidewalks, height of the buildings, and number and division of blocks—was based on geometric harmony, sound environmental and climatic considerations, and the intended use of each zone in the city. No detail escaped the king's attention. The city was originally yellow, but was decked out in pink, the color of welcome, for the visit of the Prince of Wales in 1876. Jaipur has been pink since then.

Exploring

Albert Hall Museum. The sandstone-and-marble building, constructed in the late 1800s in the Indo-Saracenic style, is worth seeing just for its architecture. The museum contains folk arts, unexpected exhibits of yoga postures, and convenient visual explanations of Indian culture and traditions. *Ram Niwas Gardens.* ☛ *Weekends and Tues.–Thurs. Rs. 1, free Mon.* ☉ *Sat.–Thurs. 10:30–4:30.*

Amber Palace. For six centuries, this now-uninhabited palace was the capital of the Kachchwah Rajputs. Its construction, started in the early 1700s and completed 100 years later, shows Rajput and Mogul influences. (Amber benefited from Mogul patronage when the Emperor Akbar married a Rajput princess from here.) Surrounded by ramparts, the palace rests on a hill behind the Maota Lake. To reach the palace, you can walk or arrive on a caparisoned elephant.

Inside the palace, the principal hall, the **Hall of Victory**, contains alabaster panels with fine inlay work of the tenderest hues, together with every kind of workmanship for which Jaipur is famous. Typical of the Mogul period, the rooms are small and intimate, while the successive courtyards and narrow passages are particularly Rajput.

From the latticed corridor atop the elegantly carved **Ganesh Pole** or elephant gate, the queen would await the king's return from battle and sprinkle scented water and flowers down upon him. Each room shows some vestige of its former glory, especially the **Sheesh Mahal** (Palace of Mirrors). Step inside, close the doors, strike a match, and watch the ceiling twinkle. Narrow flights of stairs lead up to the royal apartments, which provide the best views of the valley, the palace courtyards, the formal gardens abutting an octagonal pool that edges the lake, and the vast **Jaigarh Fort**, the ancient fortress on the crest of the hill above you.

Also look into the 400-year-old **Kali Temple**, with its silver doors and marble carvings, and exit the palace by the gate near the temple. Just a few minutes down the road, you'll come to the 450-year-old **Jagat Shiromani temple.** This exquisitely carved marble and sandstone temple was built by Raja Mansingh I in memory of his son. *Delhi Rd., 11 km (7 mi) north of Jaipur.* ☛ *Rs. 6.* ۞ *Daily 9–4:30.*

★ **City Palace.** Enter the City Palace through the **Sireh Deorhi Gate,** the principal entrance on the east. This complex, with its pavilions, courtyards, chambers, and palace, was begun by Jai Singh II, with further additions made by later maharajas. Once you're in the outer courtyard, the marble-and-sandstone building directly in front is the **Mubarak Mahal** (guest pavilion), built by Maharaja Madho Singh in the late 1800s. It is now a museum with brocades, silks, and hand-blocked garments and robes, plus musical instruments (all donated by the royal family). Some of the exhibits go back to the 17th century. At the **armory** in the northwest corner of the courtyard you'll see one of India's best collections of arms and weapons, including an 11-pound sword belonging to Akbar's Rajput general. On the 250-year-old painted ceiling some of the paints are said to be made of crushed semi-precious stones.

In the inner courtyard (through the gateway guarded by two stone elephants) is the art gallery housed in the **Diwan-e-Am** (House of Public Audiences). The building, constructed in the late 1700s, is huge, with rows of gray marble columns, the second-largest chandelier in India, and a magnificent 1930s-vintage painted ceiling. The art gallery has a collection of miniatures from the Mogul and various Rajput schools, rare manuscripts, and 17th century carpets that were originally in the Amber Palace. From the inner courtyard, enter the Zenana courtyard on the left. Here you'll see the seven-story **Chandra Mahal** (Moon Palace). Built by Jai Singh II, the cream-hued building is still the official residence of the present maharaja, "Bubbles," or, more formally, Lieutenant Colonel Sawai Bhawani Singh, who lives on the upper floors. The ground floor has sumptuous chandeliers, murals, and a quasi-three-dimensional painting of an old maharaja. *City center.* ☛ *Rs. 20 (cameras extra).* ۞ *Daily 9:30–4:45.*

Hawa Mahal. The Hawa Mahal (Palace of Winds) was built by Maharaja Sawai Pratap Singh in 1799. Designed so the ever-discreet women of the court could enjoy the breeze and watch the activities on the street below, every story has semi-octagonal overhanging windows, each with a perforated screen. The curious five-story pink sandstone structure, which draws its name from the westerly winds that send cool breezes through the windows, is just one room thick. Its delicate honeycomb design glows in the evening light. *Siredeori Bazaar (north of Johari Bazaar).* ☛ *Rs. 20.* ۞ *Sat.–Thurs. 10–5.*

Jantar Mantar. Jai Singh II supervised the design and construction of five remarkable observatories in northern India. The largest and best preserved—the Jantar Mantar—is in Jaipur near the entrance to the City Palace. Built in 1726 of masonry, marble, and brass, it is equipped with futuristic scientific instruments called *yantras.* Jai Singh II, the Newton of the East, was aware of European developments in this field and wanted to create the world's finest observatories. Weirdly beautiful, each yantra is uncannily precise in measuring celestial data. *Tripoliya Bazaar.* ☛ *Rs. 4.* ☉ *Daily 9–4:30.*

Shopping

Rajasthan's craftspeople have been famous for centuries for stonecutting, enameling, setting precious stones, tie-dying textiles, block printing silks and muslin, creating blue pottery, and lacquer and filigree work. When you shop in Jaipur, beware of guides and drivers. They often insist that they know the best shops and bargains, but they usually get a commission on purchases, which increases the price of your "bargain." Also, "government approved" are meaningless words easily painted over a shop door.

The following shops are reliable, provide good service, and sell excellent merchandise. **P. M. Allah Buksh and Son** (M. I. Rd., ☎ 141/40441), established in 1880, still sells the finest hand-engraved, enameled, or embossed brassware, including oversize old trays and historic armory. **Bhorilal Hanuman Sahar** (Shop 131, Tripoliya Bazar, no ☎), a tiny, unpretentious shop, has burlap bags filled with old brass, copper, and bronze pieces that are sold by the weight at great bargains. **Channi Carpets and Textiles** (Mount Rd., opposite Ramgarh Rd. ☎ 141/40414) offers an excellent selection of handwoven merino wool carpets, cotton dhurries, and hand-blocked cotton and silk fabrics; it can also tailor clothes for you in six hours. **Manglam Arts** (Amber Palace Rd., ☎ 141/37170) has floors filled with exquisite old and new fine art, including Hindu *pichwies* (cloth temple hangings), Jain temple art, tantric and folk art, and terra-cotta sculptures, silver furniture, handwoven dhurries, wood carvings, and wonderful old fabrics. **Gem Palace** (M. I. Rd., ☎ 141/37175) has the best gems, jewelry, a small collection of museum-quality curios, and a royal clientele; prices range from $2 to $2 million. At **Rajasthan Small Scale Cottage Industries** (Jagat Shiromani Temple Rd., Amber 303101, ☎ 141/530519), you can get a demonstration of hand-blocked printmaking and browse through a good collection of gems, handicrafts, and textiles; purchases are guaranteed. **Tilak Gitai** (E-5, Gokhle Marg, Ashok Nagar, ☎ 141/372101) is a master craftsman creating miniature paintings on antique paper: Mogul, Rajput, and Pahari ("hilly")-styles. Finally, wander through **Kazana Walon ka Rasta** in the old city and watch stonecutters create wonderful art in marble.

For good hand-blocked fabrics, visit these villages: **Sanganer** (Kota Rd., 10 km/6 mi from Jaipur) and **Bagru** (Ajmer Rd., 30 km/18½ mi from Jaipur). Nearly every family is involved in this craft.

Sports

Polo is a passion in Jaipur. During the polo season (mid-March–end of March and mid-October–end of October) matches are held at the **Rajasthan Polo Club.** For information, call the Rambagh Palace Hotel (☎ 141/381919) or the Jaipur Polo Club (☎ 141/69235). The Rajasthan Mounted Sports Association (☎ 141/366276) also offers polo lessons.

Dining

For price categories, *see* the chart for Major Cities *in* On the Road with Fodor's.

What to Wear

Casual, neat dress is acceptable. Short shorts and tank tops are not advised.

$$$$ **Panghat.** Set in a grove at the Rambagh Palace Hotel, this dinner the-
★ ater offers you an exquisite performance (starting at 8) of traditional Rajasthani dance and music while you sip cocktails in a small open-air amphitheater. After the performance (depending on the season) you sit on cushions or chairs and watch a puppet show, or you can watch women prepare different traditional breads over a wood fire. Dinner is served on a *thali* (steel plate) that comes with a variety of foods in small bowls. You'll also get to try the freshly baked breads. ✕ *Taj Rambagh Palace,* ☎ *141/381919. Dinner reservations advised. AE, DC, MC, V.*

$$$ **Suvarna Mahal.** Once the maharaja's royal banquet hall, this room is so grand, with a high, painted ceiling, handsome drapes and tapestry-covered walls, that it's hard to keep your eyes on the menu, which of-fers Indian, Chinese, and Continental dishes. Regional specialties include *murgh tikka zaffrani* (chicken marinated in yogurt and saffron and cooked in the tandoor) or *dahi ka mass* (lamb cooked in a yogurt-based curry). Piano music is performed during lunch and in the evening. ✕ *Taj Rambagh Palace,* ☎ *141/381919. Dinner reservations advised. AE, DC, MC, V.*

$$ **Niros.** Established in 1949, this Jaipur institution, with marble floors and mirrors set into the walls, is probably the most popular restaurant in town, known mainly for its Continental food that actually tastes like Continental food. It also has excellent Chinese and Indian fare. Specialties include *reshmi kebab* (skewered boned chicken), *paneer tikka* (cottage cheese with skewered tomatoes, onions, and capsicum), or mutton *tikka* masala (tandoori lamb simmered in a spicy tomato-and-butter sauce). ✕ *M. I. Rd.,* ☎ *141/374493 or 141/371874. Dinner reserva-tions advised. AE, DC, MC, V.*

$$ **Shivir.** This rooftop restaurant is cozy with plush carpeting and of-fers a fine city view and good Indian cuisine. Live Indian *ghazals* (songs) set the mood during lunch and dinner. Try *Aloo Bhojpuri* (potato stuffed with cheese) and chicken *lajawaab* (boneless chicken served in a nicely spiced gravy). You can top it off with a creamy dessert of *ras malai* (ricotta cheese in thickened milk flavored with cardamom). ✕ *M. I. Rd., Govt. Hostel Junction,* ☎ *141/378771. Reservations advised. AE, DC, MC, V.*

$ **Chanakya.** Subdued lighting, table linen, and taped Indian classical music create an appealing ambience for terrific vegetarian meals: Indian, Continental, and Chinese. Try the Chanakya special (a tasty mixture of dried fruits, cottage cheese, vegetables, and spices, topped with ed-ible pure silver) or the Rajasthani standard called *gatta* (a spicy dish of graham flour rolled in herbs and spices and cooked in tasty tomato sauce). ✕ *M. I. Rd.,* ☎ *141/378461. Dinner reservations advised. AE, DC, MC, V.*

$ **Chokhi Dhani.** This evening excursion takes you to an ethnic village
★ complex, where you sit on the floor inside a lantern-lit hut and eat (with your hands) Rajasthani vegetarian dishes served on the original dis-posable tableware—plates and bowls made of leaves. Come hungry! You'll be offered large quantities of food. You can also wander around the compound and enjoy traditional dances, singing, puppet shows, and juggling by villagers. It's all included in the cost of the meal, and tipping is discouraged. The temples in the complex are real, and if you're there at sunset, you will see the traditional village *aarti* (prayer cere-mony). Camel and boat rides cost Rs. 5. ✕ *Tonk Rd. (22 km/14 mi from Jaipur),* ☎ *141/550118. Rupees only.*

$ **Handi Restaurant.** This no-frills restaurant, with its thatched roof and
★ bamboo walls, has some of the best nonvegetarian Mogul food in town.
Take one bite of the *kathi* kebab (garlicky mutton kebab wrapped in
a thinly rolled bread with onions and tomatoes) and you'll forget all
about the plastic chairs. Other specialties include a tangy butter
chicken (chicken marinated in yogurt and baked in a tandoor before
being cooked in a tomato curry) and the specialty, *handi* meat (a spicy
mutton dish cooked in a handi, or clay pot). ✕ *Opposite General Post
Office, M. I. Rd.,* ☎ *141/364839. Rupees only.*

Lodging

For price categories, *see* the chart for Other Areas *in* On the Road with
Fodor's.

$$$$ **Taj Rambagh Palace.** Rajasthan's most famous palace hotel was once
★ the home of the maharaja of Jaipur. Now run by the Taj Group, it is
classy, right down to the peacocks that strut across its elegant lawns.
A bedroom in the original palace will surround you with original furnishings, although they won't be opulent. The new wing is done in contemporary decor, but the luxury rooms in this wing have been colorfully
painted in the Shekhawati style or decorated along themes; the safari
suite is furnished in bamboo, and the Kamal Mahal has lotus blooms
painted on the walls and inlaid in the furniture. The hotel is next to
the polo grounds and on the edge of the city. ⊞ *Bhawani Singh Rd.,
Jaipur 302005, Rajasthan,* ☎ *141/381919,* 𝖥𝖠𝖷 *141/381098. 106 rooms,
4 suites. 2 restaurants, bar, refrigerators, indoor pool, beauty salon,
barbershop, 3 tennis courts, badminton, health club, Ping-Pong, squash,
bookstore, astrologer, baby-sitting, business services, meeting rooms,
travel services. AE, DC, MC, V.*

$$$$ **Welcomgroup Rajputana Palace Sheraton.** This sprawling brick struc-
★ ture, designed as a *haveli* (a traditional Rajput mansion with an interior courtyard), has four courtyards and numerous fountains but is more
chic than reminiscent of old Rajputana. The Western-style rooms are
plush and comfortable. The pool, set in the main courtyard along with
an outdoor bar, is lovely. This is the place to be if you value comfort
over nostalgia. ⊞ *Palace Rd., Jaipur 302006, Rajasthan,* ☎ *141/360011,*
𝖥𝖠𝖷 *141/367848; in the U.S.* ☎ *800/325–3535. 220 rooms, 17 suites.
2 restaurants, 2 bars, patisserie, refrigerators, pool, beauty salon, barbershop, health club, jogging, astrologer, business services, travel services. AE, DC, MC, V.*

$$$ **Clarks Amer.** A modern white high-rise, this hotel is close to the air-
port. Although it lacks a Rajasthani ambience, it offers excellent ser-
vice. The spacious rooms have contemporary decor, and the upper floors
offer a nice view. ⊞ *Jawaharlal Nehru Marg, Jaipur 302018, Ra-
jasthan,* ☎ *141/550616 or 141/550701,* 𝖥𝖠𝖷 *141/550013. 202 rooms,
2 suites. 3 restaurants, 2 bars, pool, beauty salon, barbershop, astrologer,
business services, meeting rooms, travel services. AE, DC, MC, V.*

$$$ **Jai Mahal Palace Hotel.** This 250-year-old palace is not as grand as
the maharaja's other ancestral homes and is also farther from the city
center. The elegant white structure does have its charm, though, particularly the lavish Mogul-style garden with its row of fountains and
an enormous chess board with almost life-size plaster-of-paris pieces.
The interior has been restored with Rajasthani handicrafts and heir-
looms. The suites are sumptuous, with priceless antiques and artwork.
The other rooms, all of which have fans as well as air-conditioning and
look out over the lawns or the pool, are Western-style comfortable.
⊞ *Jacob Rd., Civil Lines, Jaipur 302006, Rajasthan,* ☎ *141/371616,*
𝖥𝖠𝖷 *141/365237. 102 rooms, 6 suites. Restaurant, coffee shop, bar, re-*

frigerators, pool, beauty salon, barbershop, astrologer, meeting rooms, travel services. AE, DC, MC, V.

$$$ **Samode Palace.** Set in a narrow valley between red-and-green hills, 45
★ kilometers (28 miles) from Jaipur, this 18th-century palace, built in the shadow of a small fort, towers over its little village. The palace has splendidly painted and enameled public rooms, including a grand 250-year-old audience hall now used for gala dinners. The rooms, which have internal pillars and arches, are furnished with traditional Rajasthani-style chairs and beds with mosquito-net canopies. Though the rooms aren't regal, they are clean and comfortable. There are no telephones and no TVs. 🕾 *Samode, Jaipur district 303806,* ☎ *1423/4114; reserve through Samode House, Gangapole, Jaipur 302002, Rajasthan,* ☎ *141/42407. 35 rooms. Restaurant, bar. AE, MC, V.*

$$ **Alsisar Haveli.** This cheerful yellow haveli is close to the Pink City, but its large lawn shuts out the noise. The 170-year-old bungalow, once the city residence of Shekhawati Rajputs, has been converted into a hotel. It offers elegant rooms with antique carved furniture, bedspreads with traditional Rajasthani prints, tiled floors covered with rugs, and brass-framed mirrors in the bathrooms. The public areas are hung with crystal chandeliers, hunting trophies, and various weapons. You can also take a safari to a nearby village and fort. 🕾 *Sansar Chandra Rd., Jaipur 302001; reserve through Bhandari Royal Hotel and Tourism Finance, Ltd., Bhandari Chambers, M. I. Rd., Jaipur 302001,* ☎ *141/ 370357,* 🅵🅰🆇 *141/363833. 11 rooms. Restaurant. MC, V.*

$$ **Jaipur Ashok.** Although this hotel, built in 1978, lacks historic charm, its exterior has contemporary charm—red sandstone and marble covered with vines. The garden, with its fountain and circular pool, is also a quiet escape from the heat and dust. The rooms, all with twin beds, are modern and decorated in soft pastels. 🕾 *Jai Singh Circle, Bani Park, Jaipur 302016, Rajasthan,* ☎ *141/320091 or 141/320098,* 🅵🅰🆇 *141/313423. 99 rooms, 2 suites. Restaurant, bar, pool, travel services. AE, DC, MC, V.*

$$ **Rajmahal Palace.** Built in 1729 by Maharaja Jai Singh II, the small palace has a world-weary air. This is hardly surprising considering its turbulent history: It was used as a refuge by a queen who feared her son might be in danger from rivals to the throne, became the site of much political activity when the British started taking over, and even served as the residence of the royal family for a time. Now a Heritage Hotel run by the Taj group, this palace offers spacious, but modest, rooms with high ceilings and few windows. The restaurant serves Indian and Continental cuisines. 🕾 *Sardar Patel Marg, Jaipur 302001, Rajasthan,* ☎ *141/381757,* 🅵🅰🆇 *141/371887. 12 rooms, 2 suites. Restaurant, bar, pool. AE, DC, MC, V.*

$$ **Samode Haveli.** Tucked away in a corner of the Pink City, this vanilla-
★ yellow haveli is hidden from the noise and hustle. Now a Heritage Hotel, it was built for a prime minister in the royal court in the mid-19th century. Arranged around two courtyards, the haveli, with its colorful frescoes, still has an air of stately grace. The rooms are simply furnished and spacious. If you want opulence, stay in one of the two sheesh mahals (still moderate in price), which have antique furniture and walls and pillars elaborately inlaid with mirror work. The best view is over the elegant palace gardens. There are no telephones or TVs. Some rooms are air-conditioned; others have coolers. The restaurant serves Indian-buffet cuisine. 🕾 *Samode House, Gangapole, Jaipur 302002, Rajasthan,* ☎ *141/540370,* 🅵🅰🆇 *141/42407. 23 rooms, 3 suites. Restaurant, travel services. AE, MC, V.*

$ **Bissau Palace.** A sweeping drive leads to the veranda of this renovated
★ two-story 1919 bungalow, now a Heritage Hotel, on the outskirts of the
old city. The Bissau's interior has a small Royal Museum, with weapons
that date from the 17th century. Mementoes, paintings, and artifacts are
delightfully placed in its lounge, library, and intimate dining room. The
rooms in the old wing have the original furniture, cotton dhurries on
the floors, and some wall paintings. The new wing is furnished with four-
poster beds and divans and decorated with pieces from the armory.
Though they're not fancy (no telephones or TV), the rooms have Rajasthani touches and are neat and clean. The family also has a farmhouse,
16 kilometers (10 miles) from town, where you can relax by the pool,
spend the night in the quaint two-room bungalow, or take a camel ride
through the surrounding villages. ☎ *Outside Chand Pole, Jaipur 302016,
Rajasthan,* ☎ *141/310371 or 141/320191,* ℻ *141/317628. 36 rooms,
15 suites. Restaurant, pool, tennis court, travel services. AE, MC, V.*

$ **Chokhi Dhani.** Separated by a wall from the restaurant of the same name,
★ this little hotel 19 kilometers (12 miles) from Jaipur lets you stay in
the village, but with modern conveniences. You can opt for a room in
one of the mud huts with wooden doors and carved furniture or live
like a wealthy landowner in the large painted haveli with its marble
floors. The bathrooms are modern. The complex mirrors a village
right down to the swimming pool designed to look like a village water
tank. The vegetarian restaurant, however, does have Western-style tables and chairs. ☎ *Tonk Rd. via Vatika, Jaipur 302015,* ☎ *141/550118
or 141/382034,* ℻ *141/381888. 47 rooms, 8 suites. Restaurant, bar,
pool, meeting room. AE, DC, MC, V.*

$ **Narain Niwas Palace Hotel.** Time stands still in this modest former
★ palace, now a Heritage Hotel, not far from the Rambagh. The public
rooms and higher-priced bedrooms (still inexpensive) have objets d'art,
mementoes, portraits, wall frescoes, and eccentric Victoriana. The
less-interesting standard rooms and garden-cottage rooms have marble floors and simple furnishings. Most rooms are air-conditioned. The
grounds are spacious and peaceful, shaded by mango trees. Only the
suites have TVs. ☎ *Kanota Bagh, Narain Singh Rd., Jaipur 302004,
Rajasthan,* ☎ *141/563448. 28 rooms, 4 suites. Restaurant, bar, pool,
car-rental. AE, DC, MC, V.*

$ **Royal Castle Kanota.** In a quiet village 15 kilometers (9 miles) from
Jaipur, this restored 18th-century fortified palace has thick ramparts
that conceal spacious grounds, including gardens and an orchard. Its
pothikhana (library) is filled with rare books and manuscripts. Its durbar hall (public room), with Victorian furniture, is a portrait gallery
of the royal family. Many exterior and interior walls are delicately painted
with frescoes or simpler designs. There's no air-conditioning. ☎ *Reserve through Narain Niwas Palace Hotel, Kanota Bagh, Narain Singh
Rd., Jaipur 302004, Rajasthan,* ☎ *141/563448. 10 rooms, 1 suite.
Restaurant, bar, library, travel services. AE, MC, V.*

The Arts

Many hotels offer cultural programs for their guests. In addition, you
may want to check out the following: **Rambagh's Panghat Restaurant**
(*see* Dining, *above*) offers an excellent performance of Rajasthani folk
dance, coupled with a traditional Rajasthani meal. The **Choki Dhani
village complex** (*see* Dining, *above*) also offers the opportunity to experience traditional Rajasthani crafts and cuisine. **Ravindra Rang
Manch** (Ram Niwas Garden, ☎ 141/49061) offers occasional cultural
programs.

Nightlife

In terms of nightlife, your best bet is one of the hotel bars, which are usually open from about 11 AM to 3 PM and 7 to 11:30 PM.

Jaipur Essentials

Arriving and Departing

BY CAR

Jaipur is about 261 kilometers (162 miles), a five-hour drive, from Delhi along National Highway (NH) 8, a congested road with a high accident rate. It is safest to travel only during daylight and take your time. (*See also* Rajasthan Essentials, *below*).

BY PLANE

Indian Airlines (Nehru Pl., Tonk Rd., ☎ 141/514500 or 514407) has daily flights connecting Jaipur to Udaipur, Jodhpur, Delhi, Aurangabad, and Bombay. Also contact your travel agent about flights aboard private domestic carriers. (*See also* Rajasthan Essentials, *below*).

Between the Airport and Center City. Sanganer airport is about 13 kilometers (8 miles) from town; a taxi to the city costs about Rs. 125.

BY TRAIN

The Shatabdi, an air-conditioned, chair-car express, travels daily except Sunday from New Delhi to Jaipur and takes about five hours. The Pink City Express to Jaipur from New Delhi takes about six hours.

Getting Around

BY AUTO RICKSHAW

Auto rickshaws are metered, though the meters are often ignored. Insist on going by the meter or set the rate in advance. It should be no more than Rs. 4.50 per kilometer.

BY BICYCLE RICKSHAW

This pleasant option should cost about Rs. 30 per hour. Set rates in advance. You can hire one for the whole day for about Rs. 100.

BY TAXI

Taxis are unmetered here, so be sure to fix a rate before the driver takes you for a ride. Ask your hotel for the current rates.

Important Addresses and Numbers

CHANGING MONEY

Most hotels will change money for their guests, or head to the State Bank of India (Tilak Marg, C-Scheme, ☎ 141/380421).

VISITOR INFORMATION

Rajasthan Tourism Development Corporation (RTDC, Paryatan Bhawan, Government Hostel Campus, ☎ 141/376362) can provide information, travel assistance, and guides. The Government of India has a tourist office at Hotel Khasa Kothi (☎ 141/72200). Many hotels also offer information and travel services.

Look for *Jaipur Vision* and the *Jaipur City Guide,* two periodicals that carry useful tourist information and up-to-date phone numbers. They are available in most hotels.

JODHPUR

❷ **Jodhpur,** the capital of the Marwar kingdom for five centuries, sits at the base of a golden sandstone ridge, guarded by one of the most imposing fortresses of Rajputana. Jodhpur is named after its 15th-century founder Rao Jodha, chief of the Rathore clan of Marwar, which traces its lineage to Lord Rama, hero of the Hindu epic, *The Ramayana*. The city is on the fringe of the Thar Desert; a city wall 9 kilometers (6 miles) in circumference keeps out the desert sands. In Jodhpur, you can visit a great fort, temples, and palaces and wander through the Girdikot and Sardar markets, lined with stalls selling fruit, textiles, and handicrafts. Jodhpur also makes a good starting place for excursions to nearby Heritage properties or the city of Jaisalmer.

Exploring

Jaswant Thada. At this royal crematorium in marble, built in 1899 for Maharaja Jaswant Singh II, you may see people bowing before the image of the king, who is considered to have joined the ranks of the deities. *Near Mehrangarh Fort.* ☛ *Free.* ☉ *Daily 8–6.*

Mandore Gardens. In the old Marwar capital at Mandore, these gardens house the exquisitely sculpted red sandstone *davals* (cenotaphs) of former rulers. The Hall of Heroes depicts 16 colorfully painted heroes and dcities carved from a single piece of stone. The garden also has a small museum displaying sculptures from the 5th to the 9th centuries, as well as ivory and lacquer work. *Mandore (8 km/5 mi north of Jodhpur).* ☛ *Free.* ☉ *Gardens open daily sunrise–sunset, museum open Sat.–Thurs. 10–4.*

Meherangarh Fort. Perched atop a hill, this enormous fort was built in 1459 by Rao Jodha when he shifted his capital from Mandore to Jodhpur. Standing above a perpendicular cliff, the fort has been impregnable—an imposing landmark, especially at night when it is bathed in yellow light. You approach the fort up a steep walkway, passing under no fewer than eight huge gates. The first, the Victory Gate, was built by Maharaja Ajit Singh to commemorate his military successes over the Moguls at the beginning of the 18th century. The other seven gates commemorate victories over other Rajput states. The last gate, as is common in many Rajput forts, displays the palm prints of women who immolated themselves after their husbands were defeated in battle. Delicate latticed windows and pierced screens worked in sandstone are the surprising motifs inside the rugged fort. The palaces—**Moti Mahal** (pearl palace), **Phool Mahal** (flower palace), **Sheesh Mahal** (glass palace), and the other apartments—are exquisitely decorated, with paintings on ceilings, walls, and even floors. The palace museum offers exquisite rooms filled with lavish royal palanquins, thrones, paintings, and even a giant tent. The ramparts provide an excellent city view. At press time, guided tours were included in the admission. *Fort Rd.* ☛ *Rs. 35 (cameras additional).* ☉ *Daily 9–5.*

Umaid Bhawan Palace Museum. Built from 1929 to 1942 by 3,000 workers at the behest of Maharaja Umaid Singh as a public works project during a long famine, this palace is now part museum, part deluxe hotel, and part royal residence. Its art-deco architecture makes it unique in the state. Amazingly, no cement was used in its construction; the palace is made of interlocking blocks of sandstone. Think about that when you stand under the imposing 183-foot-high central dome. The museum has a collection of royal finery, local arts and crafts, miniature paintings, and a large number of clocks. You may also catch a glimpse of the family of the current maharaja, who live in one extensive wing of the palace. *Umaid Bhawan Palace.* ☛ *Rs. 10.* ☉ *Daily 9–5.*

TIME OUT One of the most exquisite places to watch the sunset is the **Pillars,** the restaurant set on the elegant, colonnaded veranda of **Umaid Bhawan Palace.** The veranda offers a view of the immaculately manicured palace gardens, where peacocks strut up the steps and the strains of sitar music fill the air. To discourage day-trippers, the hotel charges nonguests a Rs. 250 minimum.

Shopping

Sardar Bazaar. Jodhpur's vibrant bazaars are worth a visit; one of the best to shop or browse is the old Sardar Bazaar.

Abani Handicrafts (Anand Bhawan, High Court Rd., near Ghoomer Tourist Bungalow, Umaid Bhawan Hotel, ☎ 291/22316) has a wide selection of old and new wood carvings, curios, brass, silver, copper, paintings, and textiles.

Sports

Some hotels offer safaris to outlying villages. A good bet is the horse or camel trip offered by **Rohet Safaris** (☎ 291/31161).

Dining

For price categories, *see* the chart for Other Areas *in* On the Road with Fodor's.

$$$ **Marwar Hall.** A gorgeous palace dining room, Marwar Hall has huge chandeliers hanging from its high, vaulted ceiling. The chef in this buffet-style restaurant prepares very good Continental and Indian food, including tasty Mughlai and regional Marwari dishes. ✕ *Welcomgroup Umaid Bhawan Palace,* ☎ *291/33316. Dinner reservations advised. AE, DC, MC, V.*

$ **Ajit Bhawan.** You can enjoy a buffet of traditional Rajasthani-style food in the cozy flagstone courtyard of this charming hotel. ✕ *Ajit Bhawan,* ☎ *291/37410. Reservations advised. MC, V.*

$ **Midtown Vegetarian Restaurant.** This unpretentious but spotlessly clean Rajasthani-decor restaurant specializes in Rajasthani and south Indian cuisine. It also offers some Chinese and Continental fare. Try their Midtown specials—a *dosa* (Indian-style crêpe), filled with potato, cheese, and cashew nuts, or *kabuli* (rice layered with vegetables, bread, and dried fruits and nuts)—and sample the salad bar. Top off your meal with an unlikely dessert of apple pie and ice cream. ✕ *Hotel Shanti Bhawan, Station Rd.,* ☎ *291/37001 or 291/27266. No credit cards.*

Lodging

For price categories, *see* the chart for Other Areas *in* On the Road with Fodor's.

$$$$ **Welcomgroup Umaid Bhawan Palace.** This magnificent pink sand-
★ stone palace, built in the 1930s in the art-deco style of colonial India, is perhaps the grandest of the palace hotels in Rajasthan. It's also home to the current Jodhpur maharaja. The public rooms are lavish and filled with objets d'art. Many of the rooms, though not opulent, have period decor. The newer standard rooms tend to be small and ordinary. The building is centrally air-conditioned. ▨ *Jodhpur 342006, Rajasthan,* ☎ *291/33316,* ▨ *291/35373. 94 rooms, 30 suites. 3 restaurants, bar, indoor pool, golf privileges, 2 tennis courts, health club, horseback riding, squash, billiards, travel services. AE, DC, MC, V.*

$ **Ajit Bhawan.** For an abundance of charm and less regal display, stay in
★ this enchanting small palace and village complex, designed and owned
by the maharaja's uncle. The rooms in the palace are now suites. Each
cottage is decorated in its own Rajasthani motif. With their painted tables and doors and traditional Rajathani fabrics, the rooms are colorful and quaint. On the grounds, paths wind through greenery and over
little bridges. Stay an extra day, so you can join one of the hotel's excellent village tours. Some rooms are air-conditioned, but there are no
telephones or TVs. ⊞ *Near Circuit House, Jodhpur 324006, Rajasthan,*
☏ *291/37410,* ⅄ *291/37774. 50 rooms, 5 suites. Restaurant, bar,*
pool, golf privileges, tennis court, horseback riding, bicycles, travel ser-
vices. AE, DC, MC, V.

Nearby Resorts

The following hotels are within 100 kilometers (60 miles) of Jodhpur.
Though they are not as conveniently placed for sightseeing in the city,
they are well worth a stopover on your way to or from Jodhpur.

$$$ **Sardarsamand Lake Resort.** The hunting lodge of Jodhpur's former ma-
haraja, which is 60 kilometers (36 miles) southeast of Jodhpur, is now
a resort. Built in 1933, the pink sandstone-and-granite lodge stands
near an artificial lake that attracts migrating birds from October to
March. The air-cooled rooms have art deco-style furnishings and ve-
randas that offer views of the lake and the plains. ⊞ *Sardarsamand*
Lake; reserve through General Manager, Umaid Bhawan Palace, Jodh-
pur 342006, Rajasthan, ☏ *291/33316,* ⅄ *291/35373. 10 rooms.*
Restaurant, pool, tennis court, squash. AE, DC, MC, V.

$ **Fort Chanwa.** This 200-year-old fort, in the dusty village of Luni 58 kilo-
★ meters (36 miles) south of Jodhpur, is now a charming Heritage Hotel.
The imposing fort, with spacious courtyards, has delightful rooms,
complete with small arched windows, old photographs, and Rajasthani-
style furniture and fabrics. Many of the small rooms have stairways lead-
ing to an alcove or the bathroom. The water wheel, now a fountain in
the bar, was originally used to channel water around the fort. The
restaurant has a fixed menu. ⊞ *Luni Village, Jodhpur Rajasthan,* ☏
291/84216; reserve through Dilip Bhawan, House 1, P. W. D. Rd.
Jodhpur, Rajasthan, ☏ *291/32460. 17 rooms. Restaurant, bar, indoor*
pool. No credit cards.

$ **Rohetgarh.** This 17th-century desert fortress, 40 kilometers (25 miles)
★ south of Jodhpur, is now a Heritage Hotel but is still home to its Raj-
put family, whose members tend to their guests. It is a great place to
experience the lifestyle of Rajput nobility. The public rooms are dec-
orated with old paintings and weapons and furnished with traditional
carved furniture. The guest rooms, which are either air-conditioned or
air-cooled, are all different, decorated with carved furniture and col-
orful hand-blocked prints. Some rooms even have swings. None has
a phone or TV. ⊞ *Rohetgarh Village, Pali district,* ☏ *2932/82431;*
reserve through Rohetgarh, Rohet House, P. W. D. Rd., Jodhpur
342001, Rajasthan, ☏ *291/31161. 20 rooms. Restaurant, pool. AE,*
DC, MC, V.

The Arts

Special festivals and exhibits are staged at the Mehrangarh Fort at var-
ious times throughout the year. Inquire at the Tourist Reception Cen-
ter (☏ 291/45083) or your hotel for more information.

Nightlife

Your best bet is one of the hotel bars, which are usually open from 11 AM to 2:30 PM and 6 to 11 PM. The **Trophy Bar** (Umaid Bhawan Palace, ☎ 291/33316), with its richly paneled walls and carpeted floors, offers a regal yet intimate atmosphere.

Excursion to Khimsar and Nagaur

Jodhpur has delightful getaways. The Welcomgroup Royal Castle at **Khimsar,** a three-hour drive, is the 16th-century palace of the local *thakur* (feudal lord). Khimsar is surrounded by a small village, green fields, and sand dunes, and the castle offers a quiet place to relax.

If you come to **Nagaur** during its colorful cattle fair (end of January or beginning of February; see Festivals and Seasonal Events in Chapter 1), you can camp out in royal style at the historic Nagaur Fort. Today its crumbling walls show remnants of beautiful frescoes and an amazing engineering system that supplied the fort with water enough to fill its fountains and royal baths and provide air-conditioning in this otherwise arid land.

Dining and Lodging

For price categories, *see* the charts for Other Areas *in* On the Road with Fodor's.

KHIMSAR

$$ **Welcomgroup Royal Castle.** At this Heritage Hotel, a 16th-century palace, ★ relax and enjoy the fine service. The best rooms are in the original palace. Hidden around enclosed courtyards, they are brightly lit and colorfully decorated with traditional fabrics. The older rooms are large, and some have furniture dating back to the 1920s. None of the rooms has a phone or TV. You can take a jeep safari to see black buck and have tea on the nearby sand dunes. Dinner—Rajasthani or Continental— is served by candlelight in the crumbling ruins of one of the original fort towers. ☎ *P.O. Khimsar, Nagaur district, 341025, Rajasthan,* ☎ *01585/2228 or 01585/2308. 12 rooms, 25 suites. Restaurant, bar, pool, travel services. AE, MC, V.*

NAGAUR

$$$ **Nagaur Fort.** This enormous fort, constructed from the 4th to the ★ 16th century, serves as a backdrop to a royal camp of spacious tents with hand-blocked designs inside, electric lanterns for light, and attached bathrooms with toilets that flush (hot water comes by the bucket). You hang a little red flag outside your door to signal for service. Meals are served in a marble pavilion in what was once a Mogul garden. In the evening, you can drink cocktails and sit back on cushions laid out before a bonfire as you watch a performance of traditional folk dances. The camp is open only during the cattle fair or by special arrangement; book at least 60 days in advance. ☎ *Nagaur; reservations through General Manager, Umaid Bhawan Palace, Jodhpur 342006, Rajasthan,* ☎ *291/33316,* FAX *291/35373. 35 tents. Dining. No credit cards.*

Jodhpur Essentials

Arriving and Departing

BY CAR

Jodhpur is 602 kilometers (373 miles) from Delhi, 332 kilometers (206 miles) from Jaipur, 368 kilometers (229 miles) from Udaipur, and 295 kilometers (183 miles) from Jaisalmer. Roads are rough and the going is slow. Don't expect to average more than 40 kilometers (25 mi) per hour.

BY PLANE

Jodhpur is connected to Jaipur, Udaipur and Delhi, Bombay and Aurangabad by **Indian Airlines** (☎ 291/36757). Also contact your travel agent about flights provided by private domestic carriers. (*See also* Rajasthan Essentials, *below*). The airport (☎ 291/30617) is 5 kilometers (3 miles) from the city center.

Between the Airport and Center City. A taxi into town costs about Rs. 150.

BY TRAIN

The Superfast Jodhpur (railway inquiry, ☎ 291/131 or 291/132) leaves New Delhi at 8 PM and reaches Jodhpur at 5:30 AM. Contact the Tourist Reception Center (☎ 291/45083) for more information. (*See also* Arriving and Departing by Train *in* Rajasthan Essentials, *below.*)

Getting Around

Jodhpur is a fairly small town, and getting around here is easy.

BY AUTO RICKSHAW

Auto rickshaws are unmetered; negotiate!

BY TAXI

Taxis are unmetered, but you can hire one for half a day for about Rs. 175 or a full day for Rs. 275. Contact the Tourist Reception Centre (☎ 291/45083) to arrange a fixed-rate taxi.

Important Addresses and Numbers

CHANGING MONEY

If your hotel doesn't have foreign exchange facilities, head to the State Bank of India (High Court Rd., ☎ 291/45090).

EMERGENCIES

Contact your hotel, consulate, or the East West Clinic (*see* Delhi Essentials *in* Chapter 4, Delhi).

VISITOR INFORMATION

The **Tourist Reception Centre** (RTDC, Hotel Ghoomar, High Court Rd., ☎ 291/45083), run by the RTDC, can provide information and assistance on transportation, guided tours, and guides. **Rajasthan Tours** (Airport Rd., ☎ 291/326940) and **Travel Corporation of India** (Madho Niwas, Airport Rd., ☎ 291/30281) also provide travel services and information.

UDAIPUR

⑤ Cradled in green hills, surrounded by lakes, **Udaipur,** with its marble palaces, is romantic. Once ruled by the Mewar clan, which traces its ancestors to the sun, Udaipur has elaborately planned gardens and island palaces that sparkle on artificial lakes. It was founded in the mid-16th century by Maharana Udai Singh, who, weary of repeated Mogul attacks on his city, fled the old Mewar capital of Chittaur after it was sacked for the third time. The Mewar rulers were among the most determined foes of the Moguls, continuing to fight long after other Rajput rulers had given up. As a result, their kingdom was rather poor by Rajput standards, but they still found the money to build many splendid palaces, temples, and gardens.

Exploring

Though it's one of Rajasthan's larger cities, Udaipur still retains a small-town atmosphere. You can probably see most major sites in one day, but to really appreciate the city, plan on two or three days.

City Palace Museum. The imposing maharana's palace (maharana is the word for maharaja in Udaipur)—the largest in Rajasthan—its white exterior weathered to ivory, stands on a ridge overlooking the lake. Started by Udai Singh and extended by subsequent maharanas, the sprawling structure has preserved its harmonious design, enhanced by massive octagonal towers surmounted by cupolas and connected by a maze of narrow passageways. The fifth-floor courtyard even has a thriving tree in the center. The rooms of the palace contain beautiful paintings, colorful enamel, inlay glasswork, and antique furniture. Each has its own tale to tell; this is one place to have a guide—you can buy one in the bookshop or hire one at the gate. The City Palace is actually one of a complex of palaces, two of which have been converted to hotels and one of which houses the current maharana. *City Palace Complex.* ☞ *Rs. 15.* ◷ *Daily 8–4:30.*

Lake Palaces. Jag Niwas (now the Lake Palace Hotel), seems to float like a white-marble fantasy on the waters of Lake Pichola. Unfortunately, its apartments, courts, fountains, and gardens are off-limits unless you are a guest or have reservations at the restaurant. (If it looks familiar, you probably saw it in the James Bond film *Octopussy.)* The equally lovely **Jag Mandir Palace** occupies another island at the southern end of Lake Pichola. Started in the 17th century, it was added to and embellished during 50 years. Three stories high, of yellow sandstone with an inner lining of marble, it is crowned by an imposing dome. Its interior is decorated with arabesques of colored stones. It was to Jag Mandir that Prince Khurrum (later known as Shah Jahan), son of Emperor Jahangir, came to hide after leading an unsuccessful revolt against his father. *Boats to Jag Mandir run from jetty at base of City Palace. Fare: Rs. 95 round-trip with stopover.* ◷ *Daily 2–5.*

Sahelion Ki Bari (Garden of the Maidens). Udaipur is famous for its gardens. Don't miss this one, with its colorful fountains. Men were forbidden in this 18th-century garden, where the queens and their ladies-in-waiting came to relax, though the king still found his way in. The fountains, with their carved pavilions and monolithic marble elephants, don't have pumps. They were designed to run on water pressure from the lakes, so before you go, make sure the area has had a good monsoon. The garden is depressing during a drought. The pavilion opposite the entrance houses a small children's museum. *Saheli Marg.* ☞ *Rs. 1.* ◷ *Daily 8–7.*

Shilpgram. This rural arts-and-crafts village, 3 kilometers (about 2 miles) from the city, comes alive with the **Shilpgram Utsav** in December, when artists and craftspeople from around the country come to the complex to sell and display their works. The complex is filled with recreations of village huts (authentic down to their toilets) from Rajasthan, Gujarat, Maharashtra, Goa, and Madhya Pradesh. It's well worth seeing even when the fair isn't on. You can also take a camel ride around the complex. *Rani Rd.* ☞ *Rs. 2.* ◷ *Daily 8–5.*

Shopping

You can find interesting handicrafts, such as wooden toys, paintings, and Udaipur and Gujarati-style embroidery here. The main shopping area is Chetak Circle. **Manglam Arts** (Sukhadia Circle, ☎ 294/28239) is a branch of the excellent shop described under Jaipur.

Dining

For price categories, *see* the chart for Other Areas *in* On the Road with Fodor's.

$$$$ **Gallery Restaurant.** The maharana brought over two hostesses from
★ England to oversee the service in this small Continental-style restaurant. Situated in a gallery bordering Fateh Prakash Palace's magnificent durbar hall and overlooking Lake Pichola with its palaces, the restaurant offers Udaipur's most lavish dining experience. The menu keeps changing, but the Continental food is delicious and served in proper English style, accompanied by a selection of imported and local wines and beers. You can also stop by in the afternoon for an English cream tea with all the trimmings. For $10, you can take a guided tour of the crystal gallery above the restaurant. The 200-year-old collection includes everything from wine decanters to tables, chairs and beds made of Birmingham crystal. ✗ *Fateh Prakash Palace, City Palace Complex, Udaipur,* ☎ *294/28239 or 294/528016. Reservations advised. Jacket and tie. AE, DC.*

$$$ **Neelkamal.** Subdued and elegant, with views of a lily pond, this restaurant serves Continental and Indian cuisines, including Rajasthani specialties. Try the *sula chat* (cold, thin strips of mutton in a spicy chutney) and the Rajasthani *besan-ka-gatta* (chunks of gram flour steamed with garlic and served in a spicy curry). Nonhotel guests must call in advance for reservations; the room is small. ✗ *Taj Lake Palace Hotel,* ☎ *294/23241. AE, DC, MC, V.*

$ **Shilpi.** A 15-minute cab ride from the city center, this garden restaurant
★ offers casual dining and good Indian and Chinese fare. You can eat on the huge lawn or under the thatched roof of the dining room. Try the *missi roti* (bread made of gram flour) and the butter chicken (chicken baked in spices and then cooked in rich tomato curry). The restaurant also has an outdoor pool and a bar and is a good place to relax and enjoy the sun. ✗ *Near Shilpgram Village, Rani Rd.,* ☎ *294/ 522475. AE, MC, V.*

Lodging

For price categories, *see* the chart for Other Areas *in* On the Road with Fodor's.

$$$$ **Fateh Prakash Palace.** This small but grand palace, built by Maharana Fateh Singh at the turn of the century, stands next to the City Palace and offers an excellent view of Lake Pichola. The suites are plushly furnished with period furniture (some of it once used by the family), heavy draperies, and brass fixtures but have neither TVs nor air-conditioning. The rooms, which are also luxurious, do have TVs and air-conditioning, as well as black stone and marble floors. ▣ *City Palace Complex; reserve through Manager Reservations, City Palace, Udaipur 313001, Rajasthan,* ☎ *294/528016,* ℻ *294/528006. 9 rooms, 6 suites. Restaurant, bar, pool, health club, horseback riding, Ping-Pong, squash, boating, billiards. AE, DC, MC, V.*

$$$$ **Shivniwas Palace.** Arranged around a large pool like a white crescent
★ moon and adjacent to the City Palace, this palace was once the royal guest house. The standard rooms, set apart from the main palace, have a contemporary decor. The gorgeous suites (starting at $150) are regal, with molded ceilings, canopied beds, and original paintings and fur-

niture; some have private terraces. They offer great privacy and excellent views of Lake Pichola. ☎ *City Palace, Udaipur 313001, Rajasthan,* ☎ *294/528016. 13 rooms, 18 suites. Restaurant, bar, pool, tennis court, health club, boating, billiards, meeting rooms, travel services. AE, DC, MC, V.*

$$$$ **Taj Lake Palace Hotel.** This 250-year-old marble palace sits like a vi-
★   sion in Lake Pichola. The interior public rooms are elegant. If you want regal surroundings, opt for a suite; all other rooms have contemporary decor. Most rooms offer lake views, though some have views of the lily pond or the courtyard. ☎ *Pichola Lake, Udaipur 313001, Rajasthan,* ☎ *294/23241,* FAX *294/25804. 69 rooms, 15 suites. Restaurant, bar, coffee shop, pool, horseback riding, boating, travel services. AE, DC, MC, V.*

$$$ **Laxmi Vilas Palace Hotel.** The nostalgia of earlier times still clings to this former royal guest house, built in 1933. On a hillside above the banks of Fateh Sagar Lake, the hotel offers a lovely view of the lake and the Monsoon Palace from its verandas and gardens. Rooms in the new wing are western-style and modern but lack historic charm. The old wing, though not lavish, has far more atmosphere. ☎ *Sagar Rd., Udaipur 313001, Rajasthan,* ☎ *294/29711,* FAX *294/25536. 54 rooms, 10 suites. Restaurant, bar, pool, travel services. AE, DC, MC, V.*

$$ **Hotel Hilltop Palace.** Perched on a hill overlooking Fateh Sagar Lake, this hotel offers lovely views of the city. With its spacious marble lobby, glass-walled elevator, elegant garden, and many rooftop terraces, this hotel may not take you back in time, but it's an excellent value. The Western-style rooms are simple but clean and have individual balconies. ☎ *5 Ambavgarh, Fateh Sagar, Udaipur 313001, Rajasthan,* ☎ *294/28764 or 294/28765,* FAX *294/525106. 62 rooms. Restaurant, bar, pool, meeting room. AE, DC, MC, V.*

$$ **Hotel Shikarbadi.** Just outside the city, this former hunting lodge of the Udaipur royal family is a lovely, rustic retreat. The rooms are attractive, with tiled ceilings and stone walls. Deer and monkeys come nearly to the door. The hotel has an open-air restaurant that serves traditional Mewari fare. ☎ *Goverdhan Vilas, Udaipur 313001, Rajasthan,* ☎ *294/83200,* FAX *294/83204; reserve through Central Office, Palace Organization, City Palace, Udaipur 313001,* ☎ *294/ 528016. 25 rooms. 2 restaurants, bar, pool, horseback riding, jogging, travel services. AE, DC, MC, V.*

$$ **Jaisamand Island Resort.** Fifty-one kilometers (32 miles) southeast of Udaipur, this newly opened hotel sits on an island on Jaisamand Lake, one of the largest artificial lakes in the world. You take a 15-minute boat ride to reach the large, white multilevel hotel leaning against a brown-and-green slope. The spacious lobby and the bar have granite floors and Rajasthani furniture. The rooms are Western style and comfortable. ☎ *P.O. Jaisamand Lake, Udaipur, Rajasthan,* ☎ *2906/2222,* FAX *294/523898. 20 rooms. Restaurant, bar, boating, fishing, meeting rooms, airport shuttle. AE, DC, MC, V.*

$ **Hotel Rajdarshan.** If you can get past the garish color scheme (the lobby furniture is done in blue and orange), this hotel, just outside the city wall, is quite a good bet. A large wall surrounding the hotel grounds shelters it from the noise and hustle of the city, but you're in the old downtown district of Udaipur almost as soon as you step through the gate. The rooms are simple but clean and have wall-to-wall carpeting. The deluxe rooms have balconies overlooking Udaipur's original city wall. ☎ *18 Pannadhai Marg, Udaipur 313001, Rajasthan,* ☎ *294/ 520661,* FAX *294/524588. 52 rooms. Restaurant, bar, pool, meeting rooms, travel services. AE, DC, MC, V.*

$ Lake Pichola Hotel. This lovely old palace, on the banks of the lake, has a pleasant, old-time ambience and charming Rajasthani decor in its modest bedrooms. All rooms have marble balconies with a lake view. ⌂ *Outside Chandpole, Udaipur 313001, Rajasthan,* ☎ *294/29197, 22 rooms with bath, 2 suites. Restaurant, bar, boating, business services, car rental. AE, MC, V.*

The Arts

Bharatya Lok Kala Mandal, a folk-art museum, has a collection of puppets, dolls, masks, folk dresses, ornaments, musical instruments, and paintings. There is a puppet show every evening. *Near Chetak Circle.* ☛ *Rs. 7 (evening program, Rs. 20).* ☉ *Daily 9–6 (evening program, 6–7).*

Nightlife

For nightlife, your best bet is one of the hotel bars.

Excursions

Ranakpur

➏ About 96 kilometers (60 miles) northwest of Udaipur is **Ranakpur,** the site of a famous Jain temple, nestled in a glen. Legend has it that this 15th-century temple, dedicated to Lord Rishabadeva, appeared in a dream to a minister of the Mewar king, who then had it built.

The three-story temple is surrounded by a wall about 60 meters (200 feet) high, which contains 27 halls supported by 1,114 pillars, each with different carvings. Below the temple are underground chambers where the idols were hidden to protect them from the Moguls. Look for the one pillar that was intentionally warped (just to separate human from god). As you enter, look for the pillar on the left where the minister and the architect provided themselves with front-row seats of worship. Outside are two smaller Jain temples and a shrine dedicated to the sun god (displaying erotic sculptures). ☛ *Free.* ☉ *To non-Jains, daily 11– sunset.*

DINING AND LODGING

For price categories, *see* the chart for Other Areas *in* On the Road with Fodor's.

$ Maharani Bagh Orchard Retreat. This retreat of a 19th-century Jodhpur maharani is perfect for relaxing. The little brick cottages, scattered among huge mango trees, are decorated in traditional style with painted wooden beds and tiled floors. Indian and Rajasthani specialties are served under small thatched shelters to the sound of water rushing through a canal in the middle of the property. The rooms don't have phones and are air-cooled in the summer. ⌂ *Ranakpur,* ☎ *2934/3705 or 2934/3751; or reserve through General Manager, Umaid Bhawan Palace, Jodhpur 342006, Rajasthan,* ☎ *291/33316,* 🖷 *291/35373. 11 rooms. Restaurant, pool. AE, MC, V.*

Udaipur Essentials

Arriving and Departing

BY CAR

Udaipur is on National Highway (NH) 8, which links Bombay and Delhi. Udaipur is 406 kilometers (252 miles) from Jaipur and 275 kilometers (170 miles) from Jodhpur. Don't expect to travel much above 40 kilometers (25 miles) per hour.

BY PLANE

Indian Airlines (outside Delhi Gate, ☎ 294/528999) has daily flights connecting Udaipur with Jaipur, Jodhpur, Delhi, Aurangabad, and Bombay. Also contact your travel agent about flights provided by private domestic carriers. (*See also* Rajasthan Essentials, *below*).

Between the airport and the Center City. Dabok Airport is 25 kilometers (16 miles) from the city center. A taxi to the city will cost about Rs. 185.

BY TRAIN

Udaipur is directly connected by rail to Delhi, Jaipur, Ajmer, Chittaurgarh, Jodhpur, and Ahmedabad. For more information, contact railway inquiry (☎ 294/131) or the Tourist Reception Center (☎ 294/29535).

Getting Around

BY AUTO RICKSHAW

Auto rickshaws are not metered. Set the rate before departing. You can hire one for the day for about Rs. 30 per hour.

BY BICYCLE

You can hire bicycles from some hotels or from shops near the Kajri Tourist Bungalow. Inquire at your hotel for current rates.

BY TAXI

Taxis are not metered, but you can hire a fixed-rate taxi through the Tourist Reception Center (☎ 294/29535). Set the rate before departing.

Guided Tours

The Tourist Reception Center (☎ 294/29535) offers half-day guided tours of Udaipur and environs.

Important Addresses and Numbers

CHANGING MONEY

If you can't hange money at your hotel, head to the **State Bank of India** (Hospital Rd., ☎ 294/28418).

TRAVEL AGENCIES

Rajasthan Tours (Garden Hotel, ☎ 294/25777) and **Travel Corporation of India** (☎ 294/26239) can help in hiring cars and provide other travel services.

VISITOR INFORMATION

The **Tourist Reception Center** (Shastri Circle, ☎ 294/29535) can provide information, travel assistance, and guides. Many hotels also offer travel services.

ELSEWHERE IN THE STATE

Jaisalmer

❼ The golden city of **Jaisalmer** rises up from the surrounding desert like a giant sand castle. Approach it slowly and savor the golden-hued fortress with its carved spires and palaces that jut above its imposing wall. Founded in 1156, this ancient city lies at the extreme western edge of Rajasthan in the heart of the Thar Desert. Jaisalmer began as an important caravan center; remnants of caravansaries still exist (some of them converted into hotels). Right through the 18th century, rulers amassed their wealth from taxes levied on those passing through. Jaisalmer was also a smuggler's paradise, with opium the longtime best-seller. Today it attracts visitors who want to take camel safaris into the desert.

Exploring

The walled city is ideal for long walks that allow you to examine the intricately carved golden buildings, especially its memorable havelis (mansions).

Folklore Museum. At the 12th-century **Gadsisar tank,** outside the walled city, this charming little museum is the perfect place to get a grounding in the local history and culture before you set out exploring. It's made in the style of a traditional house, and its small rooms are filled with historic memorabilia. *Behind main bus stand.* ☛ *Rs.2.* ☯ *Daily 9–noon and 3–6.*

The Fort. Standing guard some 76 meters (249 feet) above the town, the fort is protected by a 9-meter- (30 foot-) high wall. Two great gateways, from east to west, pierce the towered battlements of the 12th-century citadel. Inside its web of tiny lanes are Jain and Hindu temples, palaces, and charming havelis. The seven-story **Juna Mahal** (Old Palace), built around 1500, towers over the other buildings and stands under a vast umbrella of metal that is mounted on a stone shaft. At the **Satiyon-ka-Pagthiya** (Steps of the Satis), a historic spot just before the palace entrance, the royal ladies performed sati, the act of self-immolation, when their husbands were slain. Also within the fort are eight **Jain temples** built from the 12th to the 16th century; they house thousands of carved deities and dancing figures in mythological settings. No photography is allowed here, and you'll have to leave your leather items at the gate. The **Gyan Bhandar** (Jain Library) inside the Jain temple complex contains more than 1,000 old manuscripts—some of them from the 12th century and written on palm leaf with painted wooden covers—and a collection of Jain, pre-Mogul, and Rajput paintings. *Fort. Juna Mahal:* ☛ *Rs. 6;* ☯ *daily 8–1 and 3–5. Jain temples:* ☛ *Free.* ☯ *daily 7–noon. Library:* ☛ *Free;* ☯ *daily 10 AM–11 AM.*

Havelis. Outside the fortress, in a narrow lane with more of the delicate, lacy architecture that shimmers in soft yellow, stand a string of five connected havelis (traditional Rajput mansions) built by the **Patva** brothers in the 1800s. Two of the five are now owned by the government and are open to the public. It's also possible to visit the interior of the others; offer a small fee (not more than Rs. 50) to the current residents. The 19th-century **Nathamal Ki Haveli** was carved by two brothers, each working exclusively on his own half. The haveli's design is remarkably harmonious, though small differences are visible. Here, too, a courteous request may get you inside. The interior of the 17th-century **Salim Singh Ki Haveli** is in sad disrepair. The exterior of the six-story 18th-century haveli, however, is still lovely, with 38 balconies and elaborate carvings.

Shopping

In Jaisalmer you can find woolen carpets, wall hangings, and beautiful embroidery. Take time to browse, avoid touts, and bargain. Visit the **Rajasthali** (Gandhi Chowk) government emporium to get an idea of prices. **Damoder Handicraft Emporium** (Fort, near Rang Prol) has an excellent selection of local handicrafts, especially good old textiles; be sure to bargain.

Sports

Royal Safaris (Gandhi Chowk, ☎ 2992/52538 or 2992/53202) is the recommended camel safari agent. It can tailor a visit to surrounding villages or a night in the desert.

Dining

For price categories, *see* the chart for Other Areas *in* On the Road with Fodor's.

$ **The Trio.** Eat upstairs under the open sky or under a Rajasthani canopy surrounded by ethnic decor. This popular restaurant serves delicious dishes from various cuisines. Try Royal Safari soup (tomato and chicken soup unusually flavored with fenugreek) and the tandoori specialties: cheese naan and chicken *tikkas* (skewered and barbecued). Local performers entertain at night. ✕ *Mandir Palace, near Gandhi Chowk,* ☎ *2992/52733. AE, DC, MC, V.*

Lodging

For price categories, *see* the chart for Other Areas *in* On the Road with Fodor's.

$$$ **Gorbandh Palace.** This new hotel, constructed in golden sandstone, is spacious and elegant. The rooms are arranged in haveli-style blocks around a series of small courtyards with skylights and fountains. The Western-style rooms are comfortable with some Rajasthani touches and lovely, large windows. Some rooms are air-conditioned. 🏠 *1 Tourist Complex, Sam Rd., Jaisalmer 345001, Rajasthan,* ☎ *2992/531112. 67 rooms, 3 suites. Restaurant, bar, pool, travel services. AE, DC, MC, V.*

$$$ **Himmatgarh Palace.** Just opposite the royal cenotaphs, this hotel is about 1 kilometer (½ mile) from the city, but it offers one of the best views in town (especially at sunset). The regular rooms are comfortable and modern, but the small circular *burj* (tower) rooms are the most charming, with marble beds and lights concealed in the nooks of their stone walls. 🏠 *1 Ramgarh Rd., Jaisalmer 345001, Rajasthan,* ☎ *2992/52002,* ☒ *2992/52005. 35 rooms (15 burj rooms). Restaurant, bar, travel services. AE, MC, V.*

$$ **Narayan Niwas Palace.** A former caravansary, this hotel offers perfect rooms for a desert city—unassumingly modern and comfortable. The rooms are furnished with sandstone beds or carved Barmer furniture. Some rooms are air-conditioned; others are air-cooled. The interior courtyard feels like an oasis. 🏠 *Near Malka Prol, Jaisalmer 342006, Rajasthan,* ☎ *2992/52408 or 2992/52801,* ☒ *2992/52101. 38 rooms, 5 suites. Restaurant, bar, health club. AE, DC, MC, V.*

Arriving and Departing

Jaisalmer is 897 kilometers (556 miles) from Delhi—a long drive. If you have time, you can design a delightful trip to Jaisalmer by traveling from Delhi through the district of Shekhawati (*see below*) and Khimsar (*see above*) and spend each night in a charming Heritage Hotel. You can also fly into Jodhpur, which is 285 kilometers (171 miles) from Jaisalmer, and continue by road.

Shekhawati

Shekhawati, a large region in northeastern Rajasthan that lies between Delhi, Jaipur, and Khimsar, takes its name from its 15th-century ruler, Rao Shekhaji. Later, Shekhawati became a cluster of principalities, each with its own ruling family. Home to the Marwaris, the trading community of Rajasthan, which still controls much of the wealth in India, the region flourished through the 19th century, when these traders displayed their wealth by creating huge havelis (traditional Rajput mansions with interior courtyards) and decorating them with colorful frescoes. These paintings are a rich chronicle that reflects the concerns of those days—from religious and mythological themes to new wonders such as trains, gramophones, and the British. The frescoes, made with vegetable dyes, were painstakingly crafted by master artists who drew and painted their designs on the still-wet plaster. Unfortunately, this golden period came to an end in the 1930s with the mass exodus of the Marwari families to places, such as Bombay and Calcutta, that were closer to their businesses. Since then, many of these beautiful mansions and their paintings have fallen into disrepair and succumbed to water damage. Some frescoes have even been whitewashed over or obscured by new construction. A few, however have recently been restored by their owners. Villages with good havelis worth a visit are **Churu, Jhunjhunu, Mandawa,** and **Nawalgarh.** You can drive to Shekhawati from Delhi or Jaipur.

Dining and Lodging

For price categories, *see* the charts for Other Areas *in* On the Road with Fodor's.

$$ Castle Mandawa. This 18th-century castle, now a popular Heritage Hotel, is owned by the descendants of the local thakur. Complete with turrets and terraces, courtyards and narrow passageways, this place retains its castle ambience. All rooms are different and have period furniture. The suites and some rooms are opulent and spacious, though none have phones or TVs. ☎ *Mandawa, Jhunjhunu district, Shekhawati 333702, Rajasthan, ☎ 1593/23124; reserve through Castle Mandawa, 9 Sardar Patel Marg, C-Scheme, Jaipur 302001, Rajasthan, ☎ 141/381906, FAX 141/382214. 47 rooms, 10 suites. Restaurant, bar. AE, MC, V.*

$$ Desert Resort. The interiors of these clay-covered "village huts," set on a large sand dune, sparkle with glass inlaid in their walls and glow with the warmth of traditional Rajasthani fabrics and handicrafts. Even the resort's lounge is made of mud, and the dining room gleams from the bits of glass and cowrie shells adorning its walls. Sit by the pool or in the gardens and enjoy the beautiful view of the surrounding area. ☎ *Mandawa, Jhunjhunu district, Shekhawati 333702, Rajasthan, ☎ 1592/23151; reserve through Castle Mandawa, 9 Sardar Patel Marg, C-Scheme, Jaipur 302001, Rajasthan, ☎ 141/381906, FAX 141/382214. 40 rooms, 1 suite, 12 cottages. Restaurant, bar, pool. AE, MC, V.*

$$ Mukandgarh Fort. Built in 1859, this sprawling yellow fort with flags flying from its ramparts is now a Heritage Hotel. The bar overlooks a courtyard where an outdoor barbecue serves kebabs and curry in the evenings. Rooms have painted walls and ceilings, tie-dyed curtains, and fat-legged beds under patchwork bedspreads, but no TVs. ☎ *Mukandgarh, Jhunjhunu district, Shekhawati 333702, Rajasthan, ☎ 15945/52396 or 15945/52397, FAX 15945/52395. 42 rooms, 4 suites. 2 restaurants, bar, pool, travel services. AE, DC, MC, V.*

$ Dera Dundlod Kila. This 18th-century fort and Heritage Hotel is still owned by the descendants of the former thakur. Its stunning Diwan-e-Khas, with original wall frescoes in shades of yellow and orange and Louis XIV furniture, features a well-stocked library. The clean, simple bedrooms have painted walls but no telephones or TVs. The family has 20 horses and is mainly involved in promoting horse safaris using the hotel as a base. ☎ *P.O. Dundlod, Jhunjhunu district, Shekhawati 333702, Rajasthan, ☎ 15945/2519; reservations through Dundlod House, Civil Lines, Jaipur 302006, Rajasthan, ☎ 141/366276, FAX 141/366276. 25 rooms, 8 suites. Restaurant, bar, horseback riding, palmist. No credit cards.*

$ Hotel Piramel Haveli. Built in 1928, this haveli is painted in the art-deco style of the 1920s and reflects the British influence in Rajasthan; its traditional courtyards are surrounded by colonial-style pillared corridors. Now a small Heritage Hotel, it offers a peaceful getaway. The air-cooled rooms, which face a central courtyard and are decorated along color themes, are furnished with restored period pieces and have stone floors and floral bedspreads. Its restaurant serves traditional, local-style vegetarian food. ☎ *P.O. Baggar, Shekhawati 333023, Rajasthan,* ☎ *1592/22220; reserve through A-58 Nizamuddin, New Delhi 110013,* ☎ *11/461–6145 or 11/461–8962,* FAX *11/462–1112. 8 rooms. No credit cards.*

$ **Roop Nivas Palace.** A mix of Rajput and European architecture, this former palace turned Heritage Hotel is on the outskirts of one of the most interesting Shekhawati villages. Although the hotel is far from grand, the owners—descendants of the former thakur—aim to please. The rooms, which contain Victorian furniture, are modest but clean; the dining room is Rajput-quaint, and the grounds are lovely. ☎ *Nawalgarh, Jhunjhunu district, Shekhawati 333702, Rajasthan,* ☎ *15941/22008, 141/46949, or 141/351511. 25 rooms, 1 suite. Restaurant, bar, pool, billiards. No credit cards.*

Arriving and Departing

Hire a car from a licensed operator (*see* Chapter 4, Delhi, *or* the Gold Guide).

RAJASTHAN ESSENTIALS

Arriving and Departing

If your time is limited, the best way to see Rajasthan is to fly into one or more of its major cities (Jaipur, Jodhpur, and Udaipur) and make excursions from them.

By Hired Car with Driver

Delhi is about 261 kilometers (162 miles) from Jaipur, 602 kilometers (373 miles) from Jodhpur, 897 kilometers (556 miles) from Jaisalmer, and 658 kilometers (408 miles) from Udaipur. It is safest to travel only during daylight. The roads in Rajasthan are not in good shape, and the going is slow. When calculating driving time, plan to cover 40 to 50 kilometers (25–31 miles) per hour at most. Traveling by car does provide an opportunity to see the Indian countryside and glimpse village life. Hire a car with driver from a government-licensed operator (*see* Travel Agencies, *below*; *in* Chapter 4, Delhi; *in* Chapter 6, Agra, Khajuraho, Varanasi, *and in* the Gold Guide). A car with driver should cost about Rs. 8 to Rs. 10 per kilometer.

By Plane

Rajasthan has domestic airports at Jaipur, Jodhpur, and Udaipur. Each airport in Rajasthan is a short drive from the city.

Indian Airlines (☎ 141 in Delhi, 11/329–5121 from elsewhere) has daily flights between Jaipur, Udaipur, as well as between these cities and Jodhpur, Delhi, Bombay, and Aurangabad, but getting bookings can be difficult, so reserve in advance or through a travel agent. Also check with your travel agent about flights by private domestic carriers to and around Rajasthan.

By Train

At press time, Rajasthan was in the process of converting all its lines to broad gauge, a change that was expected to improve the railway service in the state greatly. However, this conversion has also changed most of the train routes and schedules; call the local office of the Rajasthan Tourism Development Corporation (RTDC) (Jaipur, ☎ 141/

376362; Delhi, ☎ 11/389525 or 11/383837) for updated information on trains going your way.

Getting Around

How you decide to travel in Rajasthan depends on your budget and your time. It's a big state with large stretches of territory between the most popular destinations. If your time and money are in short supply, just see one city and its surrounding area. Don't try to rush through the entire state.

By Hired Car with Driver

This is the best way to visit Rajasthan, especially if you move at a leisurely pace. A stop in a traditional village that is off the well-trod path or an extended stay in a Heritage Hotel could turn into the highlight of your trip. Hire a car from a recognized agent (*see* travel agents listed under cities *above, or* the Gold Guide).

Lodging

Home Stays

The Rajasthan Tourism Development Corporation (RTDC) (Jaipur, ☎ 141/376362; Delhi, ☎ 11/389525 or 11/383837) has developed a network of paying guest accommodations that enables tourists to stay in private homes during their visit. Though these homes lack the facilities of hotels, they are an authentic and much cheaper option. The RTDC has a paying-guest directory that describes the accommodations, prices, and so on.

Sports

Many hotels can arrange a round of golf for you on local courses.

See Chapter 2, Special-Interest Travel in India, for information on safaris and other activities in Rajasthan.

Important Addresses and Numbers

Changing Money

Most Western-style hotels have foreign-exchange facilities for their guests. You can also change money at branches of the **State Bank of India.**

Emergencies

For any emergency, contact your hotel or the East West Clinic (*see* Chapter 4, Delhi).

Travel Agencies

See also travel agents listed under cities *above*. Many tour operators offer trips to this part of India (*see* Tour Operators *in* the Gold Guide, *and* Chapter 2, Special-Interest Travel in India). These travel agencies can help with bookings and supply cars with drivers. The American Express representative is **TGS Tours and Travels** (Tholia Circle, Mirza Ismail Rd., Jaipur, ☎ 141/367735; Chetak Circle, Udaipur, ☎ 294/29661).

Visitor Information

Government tourist reception centers can be a good source of information in Rajasthan: Jaipur (Paryatan Bhawan, Govt. Hostel Campus, ☎ 141/376362 or 141/370180), Jaisalmer (Hotel Moomal, ☎ 2992/52392), Jodhpur (Hotel Ghoomar, High Court Rd., ☎ 291/44010), Udaipur (Shastri Circle, Udaipur, ☎ 294/29535).

6 Agra, Khajuraho, Varanasi

Sacred Temples, Tombs, and Ghats

These three destinations, which form a triangle southeast of Delhi, provide insight into India's spirituality and offer a glimpse of the country's stellar monuments. Agra, dusty and crowded, offers the glorious Taj Mahal and exquisite, jewel-like smaller tombs. Southeast of Agra, in the sleepy village of Khajuraho, are some of India's finest Hindu temples. Crowds of Hindus descend on the holy city of Varanasi, northeast of Khajuraho, to purify themselves in the Sacred River Ganga, or Ganges.

THE CITIES OF AGRA, KHAJURAHO, AND VARANASI offer three perspectives of North India's colorful history and varied cultures. Agra, in the state of Uttar Pradesh, was once the seat of Mogul power in India. Dominated by Muslim influences in culture, art, architecture, and cuisine, it's a testament to the poetry and opulence of Mogul rule in India. In the northern part of the central Indian state of Madhya Pradesh, Khajuraho is purely pre-Mogul. The temples of this small village celebrate the many Hindu gods and goddesses and the vibrancy of life in ancient India. In many ways, Varanasi, in Uttar Pradesh and one of India's oldest and Hinduism's holiest cities, is the antithesis of Khajuraho. Where temples in tiny Khajuraho celebrate life in all its many forms, Varanasi is a crowded city filled with pilgrims hoping to shed their ties to this world and achieve salvation in the next. Together, these three cities provide an intriguing glimpse of Indian culture.

Agra, Khajuraho, and Varanasi form an inverted isosceles triangle in Northeastern India with Khajuraho at the tip and Agra and Varanasi on the base about 350 miles apart. They are well connected to one another by air and road. Agra is closest to Delhi and makes a convenient starting point from which you can hop to Khajuraho (a 35-minute flight) and then Varanasi (40 minutes by plane) and then back to Delhi. Each of these cities can be seen in a day, though that's rushing it. If you're flying, you can probably see them in five days, but if you're going by road, plan on at least a week.

AGRA

By Smita Patel

The 200-kilometer (124-mile) journey from Delhi to Agra follows the royal road the Mogul emperors established in the 16th and 17th centuries, when their capital alternated between these two cities. Under the Mogul emperor Akbar (1542–1605) and his successors, Jahangir and Shah Jahan, Agra flourished, but after the disintegration of their empire, which began with Shah Jahan's son Aurangzeb (1618–1707), the city passed from one invader to another before the British took charge early in the 19th century. The British, particularly Governor General Lord Curzon (in office 1898–1905), did much to halt and repair the damage done to the forts and palaces by raiders and vandals.

Today, Agra is crowded and dirty: and unfortunately some of the Mogul buildings remain irrevocably scarred. Other monuments, however, are strewn like pearls in ashes and evoke that glorious period in Indian history when Agra was the center of the Mogul empire, and the empire itself was the focus of political, cultural, and artistic evolution.

Opening times and admission fees (especially those of the Taj Mahal) change constantly in Agra; check in advance with the Uttar Pradesh State Tourist Office or your hotel. As you must remove your shoes at all tombs and mosques, you might carry along old socks to slip on if you don't want to go around barefoot.

Exploring

★ **Agra Fort.** The architecture of this fort reflects the creative brilliance of Akbar, his son Jahangir, and his grandson Shah Jahan. The fort was built by Akbar for security. Its roughly triangular shape is encircled by a massive wall 2½ kilometers (1½ miles) long and 21 meters (69 feet) high. With the Yamuna River running at its base, the fort was also protected with a moat and another wall, making it a daunting barrier to anyone trying to reach the treasures within. Today, entrance is easy through the Amar Singh Gate.

To the north of this entrance is the largest private residence, the **Jahangiri Mahal**, built for Akbar's son Jahangir. Akbar's own palace, closer to the entrance, is in ruins. Jahangir's palace, measuring 75 by 90 meters (250 by 300 feet), blends Hindu architecture with Central Asian influences imported by the Moguls. The central court of the palace is lined by two-story facades with remnants of the rich gilded decorations that once covered much of the structure. Next to his devotion to architecture and the arts, Jahangir's greatest loves were wine and his Persian-born wife Nur Jahan, who, failing to persuade him to pay attention to his empire, did it for him. A strong-willed woman, she made short shrift of all rivals. Often she just dropped them into a pit that conveniently emptied into the Yamuna River (the grim underground chambers near this pit are still intact).

After Jahangir's death in 1628, Shah Jahan (whose mother was one of Jahangir's other wives) assumed the throne and started his own buildings inside the fort, often tearing down those built by his father and grandfather to make room for his own. The **Shahjahani Mahal** is actually the remodeled northern section of Jahangiri Mahal. From the tapering tower gallery, Shah Jahan watched elephant fights. In tranquil moments, he received instruction from a Hindu holy man who was carried up in a litter. Shah Jahan outdid himself in the **Khas Mahal** (Special Palace), built in 1637: three pavilions overlooking the Yamuna, with a fountain tank opposite the central pavilion. The white marble central pavilion follows the Mogul pattern in style: three arches on each side, five in front, and two turrets rising out of the roof. A second pavilion is of white marble and was supposedly decorated with gold leaf, while the third is made with red stone. They are said to have housed Shah Jahan's two daughters. In one part of the Khas Mahal, a staircase leads down to the "air-conditioned" quarters of the palace, cool underground rooms that were probably used during the summers.

On the northeastern end of the Khas Mahal courtyard stands the **Sheesh Mahal** (Palace of Mirrors), built in 1637. This was the bath of the private palace and the dressing room of the harem; each of the two chambers contained a bathing tank that was once fed by marble channels. In front is the Anguri Bagh (Vineyard Garden).

To the empire's citizens and to the European emissaries who came to see this powerful monarch, the most impressive part of the fort was the **Diwan-i-Am** (Hall of Public Audience), set within the large quadrangle. The huge, low structure rests on a 4-foot-high platform, with nine cusped Mogul arches held aloft by rows of slender supporting pillars. Scholars disagree over who the builder was—Akbar, Jahangir, or Shah Jahan, but they all accept that only Shah Jahan had the creative vision to produce the stunning throne room, with its inlaid mosaics a marvel of Mogul art. Here, the emperor sat and dispensed justice to all his subjects. Below the throne, his *wazir* (prime minister) sat on a small platform with a silver railing.

The emperor received foreign ambassadors or dignitaries in the **Diwan-i-Khas** (Hall of Private Audience), built by Shah Jahan in 1636–37 due east of the Diwan-i-Am. Outside this structure is the marble throne terrace, with its pair of black and white thrones. The black throne, carved from a single block of marble, overlooks the Yamuna. The white throne was made of several marble blocks. The inscription indicates it was used by Shah Jahan, while the black throne had been his father's seat of power.

Near the Diwan-i-Khas is the tall, octagonal **Musamman Burj** (tower), built by Shah Jahan for Mumtaz Mahal, his favorite wife, who is buried in the Taj Mahal. Delicate marble lattices enabled the ladies of the court to gaze out, unseen. In the center of the tower is a beautifully carved fountain. It is thought that Shah Jahan spent his last seven years here, a prisoner of his son, Aurangzeb, and cared for only by his daughter Jahan Ara.

Northeast of the Diwan-i-Khas is the white marble **Nagina Masjid**, a private mosque raised by Shah Jahan with typical cusped arches. Walled in on three sides, it has a marble courtyard for worshippers and three graceful domes. Nearby is the lovely **Moti Masjid**, a perfectly proportioned pearl mosque built in white marble by Shah Jahan. *(At press time it was undergoing renovation and closed to the public.) Yamuna Kinara Rd., near Nehru Park.* ☞ *Rs. 10.50.* ۞ *7–6.*

Itmad-ud-Daulat's Tomb. The empress Nur Jahan built this small but elegant tomb for her father, a Persian nobleman who became Jahangir's chief minister. One of Agra's most beautiful monuments, it was supposedly built by workers from Iran (then Persia). The tomb incorporates much Persian brown and yellow marble and shows the first use of Persian-style marble inlay in India. With its red sandstone gate and minarets, it was a precursor to and probably an inspiration for the Taj Mahal. *About 5 km (3 mi) north of Taj Mahal on left bank of Yamuna River.* ☞ *Rs. 10.50, Fri. free.* ۞ *6–6.*

★ **Sikandra.** This tomb, with its hybrid air, was started by the great emperor Akbar in 1602 and completed after his death by his son Jahangir. With its rough red sandstone topped with smooth white marble and its graceful minarets surrounding a typically Hindu courtyard, this monument is an eclectic blend of cultures and styles. It's an appropriate epitaph for the emperor who united the country to the extent of trying to create a new faith, *Din-i-Illahi* (religion of God), which was an amalgamation of the major religions. Much of the gold work that once adorned this tomb was destroyed during the 18th century by Jat raiders (who invaded Agra after the fall of the Mogul empire), though some of it was partially restored by the British. In a domed chamber three stories high, the crypt is inscribed with the 99 names attributed to Allah, plus the phrases *Allah-o-Akbar* (God is Great) at the head, and *Jalla Jalalahu* (Great is His Glory) at the foot. *10 km (6 mi) north of Agra, along Great Trunk Rd. to Delhi.* ☞ *Rs. 10.50, Fri. free.* ۞ *6–5:30.*

★ **Taj Mahal.** It's beautiful, yes! But what makes this marble monument so endearing is its haunting tale of love and loss. Arjuman Banu, the niece of Jahangir's wife Nur Jahan, supposedly captured the heart of the young Shah Jahan the minute he saw her. In 1612, at the age of 21, she married him and became his Mumtaz Mahal (the Exalted of the Palace) and Mumtazul-Zamani (the Distinguished of the Age). Numerous tales recall her generosity and her wisdom, both as a household manager and as an adviser to her husband, but even these qualities were diminished by the love that bound her to Shah Jahan. She bore him 14 children, and it was in childbirth that she died in 1630 while accompanying her husband on a military campaign. On her deathbed, it is said, she begged the king to build a monument so beautiful that the world would never forget their love. Shattered by her death, legend claims, Shah Jahan locked himself in his private chambers for a month, and when he finally emerged, his hair was white. Six months after his wife's death, a huge procession brought her body to Agra, where Shah Jahan began to honor his wife's request.

Although no one knows who drew up the actual plans, Shah Jahan's chief architect, Ustad Ahmad Lahori, was involved with the construction, which began in 1632; so were skilled craftsmen from Persia, Turkey, France, and Italy. Shah Jahan put an army of 20,000 laborers to work, building a new village (Taj Ganj, which still stands) to house them as they spent 17 years creating the white marble tomb. On the banks of the Yamuna River, visible from the Agra Fort, the Taj was completed on the exact anniversary of Mumtaz Mahal's death. Shah Jahan's plans to build an identical tomb for himself in black marble were ruined by his son Aurangzeb, who (not unlike his forebears) imprisoned his father in the Agra Fort and took over the throne. The great emperor spent his last years locked in one of his own creations, gazing across the Yamuna at his wife's final resting place.

The Taj Mahal is built on two bases, one of sandstone and, above it, a marble platform measuring 97 meters (313 feet) square and worked into a black-and-white chessboard design. A slender marble minaret stands at each corner of the platform; these towers blend so well into the general composition that it's hard to believe their 40-meter (130-foot) height. Each one is also constructed at a slight tilt away from the tomb (so that, in case of an earth tremor, they'd fall away from the building).

Inside the mausoleum, the easy curves of pointed Mogul arches on the facade highlight the building's square corners. The tomb's entrance is an archway inscribed with verses from the Quran. Though the arch soars more than 90 feet high, all the lettering looks the same size. Inside, notice the tiny, intricate flowers—the detailed stonework on each petal and leaf. The work is so fine that not even a magnifying glass reveals the tiny breaks between the stones. Yet a single one-inch flower on the queen's tomb contains 60 separate pieces. Shine a flashlight and see the delicate stones' translucence. Feel the perfectly smooth surfaces. Directly under the high curve of the marble dome (which is actually a dome within the larger dome you see outside) lie the tombs of Mumtaz Mahal and Shah Jahan. A marble screen carved from a single block of stone, whose latticework is as intricate as lace, surrounds the tombs. In the center of the enclosure behind the screen, diminishing rectangles lead up to what looks like a coffin. In fact, both Mumtaz Mahal and Shah Jahan are buried in a crypt below these tombs in obedience to the Islamic tradition that no one should walk upon their graves. After his death, Shah Jahan was buried next to his wife by his son Aurangzeb, upsetting the perfect symmetry, most likely a money-saving measure that is an ironic postscript to the munificence of Shah Jahan. But it may be fitting that he lies for eternity next to his favorite wife, and the romantically inclined give Aurangzeb credit for bringing the two together. Mumtaz Mahal's tomb bears this Persian inscription: "The illustrious sepulcher of Arjuman Banu Begum, called Mumtaz Mahal. God is everlasting, God is sufficient. He knoweth what is concealed and what is manifest. He is merciful and compassionate. Nearer unto him are those who say: Our Lord is God." The emperor's epitaph reads: "The illustrious sepulcher of His Exalted Majesty Shah Jahan, the Valiant King, whose dwelling is in the starry Heaven. He traveled from this transient world to the World of Eternity on the 28th night of the month of Rajab in the year of 1076 of the Hegira [February 1, 1666]."

The best time to see the Taj is early morning when the pale rays of the sun give a soft pastel luster to the marble. Don't visit the Taj on Fridays; it's free, and the crowds are awful.

The **Taj Mahal Museum** stands near the mosque on the grounds of the Taj. Though small, it contains interesting memorabilia from the Mogul period and historical background about the Taj Mahal, as well as paintings of the famous couple. *Taj Rd., Taj Ganj.* ☞ *Taj Mahal: Rs. 100 (sunrise–8 and 4–7), Rs. 10.50 (8–4), both including museum entry; free Fri.* ☉ *Taj Mahal daily, museum Sat.–Thurs. 8–5.*

Shopping

In Agra, look for good bargains in hand-knotted carpets and dhurries, precious and semiprecious stones, inlaid marble work, and brass statues. Beware of taxi drivers and touts who want to take you to "bargains"; they often receive huge commissions from shopkeepers, which you end up paying. Also beware of soapstone masquerading as marble. This softer, cheaper stone is a convincing substitute, but you can tell by scraping the item with your fingernail. Marble won't scrape.

Chirali (Fatehabad Rd., near Hotel Amar, ☎ 562/56217) sells precious and semiprecious stones, beautiful *zari* (embroidery work), and custom-made jewelry. **Cottage Industry** (18 Munro Rd., ☎ 562/360417) offers good dhurries and carpets. **Ganesha** (18 Munro Rd., ☎ 562/353421) has brass, copper, and bronze curios. **Jewel Palace** (62 Pratappura) sells good precious and semiprecious stones; it also designs jewelry to order. **Oswal Emporium** (30 Munro Rd., ☎ 562/363240) has excellent marble inlaid items.

Dining

In Agra you can treat yourself to celebrated Mughlai (Mogul) cuisine. Here you will find kebabs spiced with garlic and ginger and rich curries with spices such as cardamom and cloves. Most restaurants are open from 7 to 10 for breakfast, noon to 3 for lunch, and 7:30 to 11 for dinner.

Beware of cab drivers and guides who want to take you to an "excellent" restaurant. Most of them get hefty commissions; they're perfectly capable of telling you that the place you request serves terrible food or has closed down if your choice doesn't cough up a commission.

For price categories, *see* the chart for Other Areas *in* On the Road with Fodor's.

What to Wear

Casual clothing is acceptable in Agra, but respect the city's conservative Muslim influences: women should avoid short shorts or tank tops.

$$$ **Bagh-e-Bahar.** This Continental restaurant/coffee shop is decorated in soft pastels and offers a view of gardens through its large windows. A live band plays during lunch and dinner, and there's a small dance floor. The Continental cuisine doesn't taste like it's out of a curry pot, and there is a well-stocked buffet. ✕ *Welcomgroup Mughal Sheraton, Taj Ganj,* ☎ *562/361701. Dinner reservations advised. AE, DC, MC, V.*

$$$ **Mahjong Room.** Enjoy excellent Chinese dishes in an intimate, dimly
★ lit, wood-paneled restaurant with red-and-green linen and Chinese lanterns. Try the tangy hot and sour soup and the spicy chili chicken. The restaurant, which overlooks the hotel gardens and courtyard, offers no-smoking tables. ✕ *Welcomgroup Mughal Sheraton, Taj Ganj,* ☎ *562/361701. Dinner reservations advised. AE, DC, MC, V.*

$$$ **Mogul Room.** This elegant rooftop restaurant is decorated in pinks and
★ reds, with a twinkling "star" ceiling. At night enjoy live performances
of Indian *ghazals* (Mogul-inspired romantic songs). You can choose
from good Indian, Chinese, and Continental cuisines. Try the chicken
steak or the fish and chips. For dessert, have the *shahi tukra* (toast of
kings), a rich, bread-based pudding. ✕ *Clarks Shiraz, 54 Taj Rd.,* ☎
562/72421. Reservations advised. AE, DC, MC, V.

$$$ **Nauratna.** Named for the "nine jewels" (ministers) of Akbar's court,
this intimate restaurant has Mogul decor, with expanses of marble, and
the color purple (the emperor's favorite) dominates. The Mughlai cuisine is similar to what the emperor himself ate. Try their *biriyanis* (meat
and rice), the quintessential Mughlai dish. Also try the excellent kebabs. During the evening, expect live performances of Indian ghazals.
✕ *Welcomgroup Mughal Sheraton, Taj Ganj,* ☎ *562/361701. Dinner
reservations advised. AE, DC, MC, V.*

$$ **Sonam.** The flower-filled garden of this restaurant is ideal for lunch
★ on a winter afternoon. A converted wine cellar, it has a spacious, cen-
trally air-conditioned dining room and a fireplace. The menu carries
good Indian, Chinese, and Continental fare. Try the hot and sour soup
or the spicy chicken *tikka* (chicken marinated in yogurt and baked),
with coriander and garlic chutney for starters. Also try *handi ghost,* a
spicy mutton curry served in a pot over a small coal stove. This is also
Agra's only nonhotel restaurant with a licensed bar. ✕ *51 Taj Rd., Agra
Cantonment,* ☎ *562/368633. AE, MC, V.*

$ **Dasaprakash Restaurant.** A far cry from the traditional cuisine of
★ Agra, the light and spicy south Indian dishes served here make a nice
change from rich Mughlai fare. With its Formica tables and fake
Tiffany lamps, this restaurant resembles an American pizza joint, but
the food is excellent, and the service is fast. Be sure to try the crisp *aplam*
(fried wafers) and the *rasam* (thin, spicy lentil soup), as well as fluffy
idlis (steamed rice cakes) and crisp *dosas* (crisp rice crépes). The restau-
rant also has an exotic selection of fresh juices and a great dessert menu
with all sorts of ice creams and floats. ✕ *Meher Cinema Complex, No.
1 (5 min from Taj Mahal, near Hotel Agra Ashok), Gwalior Rd., Agra
Cantonment,* ☎ *562/363368. DC, MC, V.*

Lodging

Unless mentioned otherwise, hotels have central air-conditioning, and
rooms have cable TV, bathrooms with showers, and room service.

For price categories, *see* the chart for Major Cities *in* On the Road with
Fodor's.

$$$$ **Taj View Hotel.** This Western-style Taj group hotel lacks architectural
inspiration but offers good service and spacious, modern rooms. It also
has the best views of the Taj Mahal of any hotel. ☎ *Fatehabad Rd.,
Agra 282001, Uttar Pradesh,* ☎ *562/361172,* FAX *562/361179. 100
rooms, 5 suites. Restaurant, bar, coffee shop, pool, health club, bad-
minton, baby-sitting, business services, meeting rooms, travel services.
AE, DC, MC, V.*

$$$$ **Welcomgroup Mughal Sheraton.** Winner of the Aga Khan Award for
★ excellence in architecture, this stunning brick and marble hotel is
Agra's class act. It has huge, landscaped gardens and even a minilake.
The spacious rooms have low-key modern decor, with soft white walls
accented by handsome dark wood trim. You can request an Indian-
feature room if you want ethnic fabrics and furniture. Some rooms offer
a view of the Taj. ☎ *Taj Ganj, Agra 282001, Uttar Pradesh,* ☎ *562/
361701,* FAX *562/361730. 300 rooms, 12 suites. 5 restaurants, bar, no-*

smoking rooms, pool, miniature golf, 2 tennis courts, croquet, health club, boating, dance club, astrologer, snake charmer, business services, travel services. AE, DC, MC, V.

$$$ **Clarks Shiraz.** This Western-style highrise, set on 8 acres with extensive gardens, evokes the 1960s, not the Mogul age. The comfortable rooms have subdued contemporary decor. The odd-number rooms offer a distant view of the Taj. The newer tower rooms are more spacious and offer a better view. Also expect an evening barbecue on the beautifully lighted lawn. ☎ *54 Taj Rd., Agra 282001, Uttar Pradesh,* ☎ *562/361421,* FAX *562/361428. 237 rooms, 2 suites. 4 restaurants, bar, pool, golf privileges, miniature golf, croquet, baby-sitting, business services, meeting room, travel services. AE, DC, MC, V.*

$$$ **Hotel Agra Ashok.** This attractive Western-style hotel is also inspired by Mogul architecture: lots of marble, lattice trim, and an interior water fountain. Spacious rooms have modern decor. Some rooms offer a view of the Taj. ☎ *6B, The Mall, Agra 282001, Uttar Pradesh,* ☎ *562/361620. 55 rooms, 2 suites. 2 restaurants, bar, coffee shop, pool, baby-sitting, business services, travel services. AE, DC, MC, V.*

$$$ **Novotel Agra.** This new Oberoi hotel, built around a lovely garden court-
★   yard with stone pathways, fountains, a sandstone pavilion, and an outdoor pool, is one of Agra's best values. It's simple, clean, and elegant, with excellent service. The rooms have subdued modern decor, individually controlled air-conditioning, and tile floors. ☎ *Taj Nagri Scheme, Fatehabad Rd., Agra 282001, Uttar Pradesh,* ☎ *562/368282,* FAX *562/360217. 139 rooms. Restaurant, bar, no-smoking rooms, pool, barbershop, beauty salon, badminton, volleyball, bookstore, travel services. AE, DC, MC, V.*

$$ **Hotel Mumtaz.** Under renovation at press time, this Western-style hotel has a spacious lobby with a fountain and will offer simply decorated modern rooms. ☎ *Fatehabad Rd., Agra 282001, Uttar Pradesh,* ☎ *562/64771. 100 rooms, 3 suites. Restaurant, bar, coffee shop, pool, health club, baby-sitting, meeting room, travel services. AE, DC, MC, V.*

$ **New Bakshi House.** If you'd like to stay in a typical Indian middle-class neighborhood, this guest house is perfect. The two-story house has a homey feel and is decorated with all sorts of mementos, including the owner's collection of old maps. Each room is cozy and clean. Air-conditioned rooms cost more, but they're still inexpensive. You can choose home-cooked meals from an Indian or a Continental menu. ☎ *5 Laxman Nagar, Agra 282001, Uttar Pradesh,* ☎ *562/368159 or 562/ 363991,* FAX *562/361146. 7 rooms. Dining room, travel services. No credit cards.*

Excursion to Fatehpur Sikri

★   **Fatehpur Sikri.** After a 16th-century mystic, Salim Chisti, blessed the Mogul Emperor Akbar with a much-wanted male heir, Akbar built his capital in the mystic's tiny community, Sikri, 37 kilometers (24 miles) southwest of Agra. Akbar constructed his city, which had a circumference of about 12 kilometers (7 miles), on a rocky ridge (after slicing off the top) that overlooked the village of Sikri. Three sides of the city were enclosed within massive walls; the fourth was protected by a lake. A cluster of royal dwellings tops the ridge. When Elizabethan Englishmen came to Fatehpur Sikri in 1583 to meet the great emperor Akbar, they were amazed to see a city that exceeded London in both population and grandeur. They lost count of the rubies, diamonds, and plush silks. Today the structures are intact, but the city is silent and deserted, a beautiful relic of its glorious past. Akbar ruled here for only 15 years before mov-

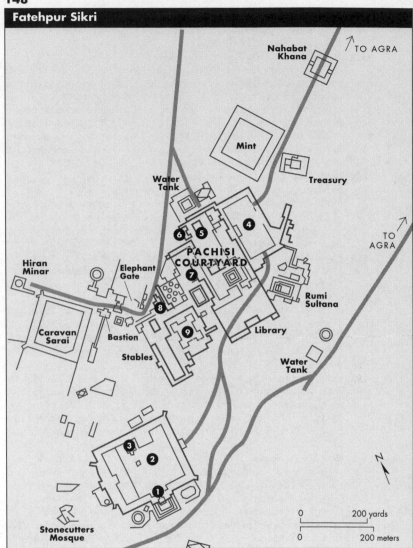

Ankh Michauli, **6**
Buland Darwaza, **1**
Diwan-i-Am, **4**
Diwan-i-Khas, **5**
Jama Masjid, **2**
Jodh Bai's Palace, **9**
Nagina Mosque, **8**
Panch Mahal, **7**
Salim Chisti's
Tomb, **3**

ing his capital—perhaps in pursuit of water—to Lahore (now in Pakistan) and eventually back to Agra. Fatehpur Sikri's elegant blend of cultures and styles still reflects his foresight and wisdom.

❶ The **Buland Darwaza** (Victory Gateway) rises above the palace complex. Akbar built the triumphant portal, which sums up Mogul power, after he conquered Gujarat. Its dimensions are in keeping with its purpose: 42 meters (134 feet) high over a base of steps that climb another 11 meters (34 feet). Beware of the bees that have their own fortifications here and the badgering, phony guides.

❷ Beyond the Buland Darwaza you will find the **Jama Masjid** (Imperial Mosque) to your right. It was built around 1571 and designed to hold 10,000 worshipers. Note the deliberate use of Hindu elements in the design (especially the decorations on the pillars)—more examples of Akbar's wish for religious harmony so frequently mirrored in his architecture. In the mosque's courtyard (opposite the Buland Darwaza)
❸ lies **Salim Chisti's tomb,** surrounded by walls of marble lace. People of all faiths come here and tie strings on the marble as they ask the saint for the same blessing he bestowed on Akbar. From here you can cross the courtyard and exit through the King's Gate (once reserved for Akbar) and pass through a parking lot to the main palace complex.

❹ The **Diwan-i-Am** (Hall of Public Audience) is more than 92 meters (350 feet) long. It consists of cloisters surrounding a courtyard that contains the Hall of Judgment. Here, Akbar sat on a throne flanked by marble screens and handed down his decisions as the chief justice of his subjects. Those condemned to die were reportedly impaled, hanged, or trampled under the feet of an elephant. Akbar also played *pachisi* (an early form of Parcheesi) with slave girls as living pieces in the courtyard behind the Diwan-i-Am.

❺ Inside the **Diwan-i-Khas** (Hall of Private Audience), which looks like a two-story building with domed cupolas at each corner, is the room where, elevated on a stone column topped with a lotus flower, Akbar sat and held discussions with his ministers, the "nine jewels," who each occupied a window seat.

❻ Near the Diwan-i-Khas is a small platform topped with a *chattri* (umbrella) for Akbar's royal astrologer. Close by is the **Ankh Michauli** (blindman's bluff). Akbar was reported to love playing the game with his harem inside this building. Fantasy and whimsy prevail in the decorative stone monsters who allegedly kept thieves from the crown jewels believed to have been kept in secret niches carved into the walls.

❼ Just opposite the giant chessboard rises the five-story **Panch Mahal,** each floor smaller than the one below. This pavilion, the highest structure in the palace, is a combination of primarily Hindu and Buddhist architecture. Akbar probably sought shelter here from the afternoon
❽ sun. Behind this structure is the small **Nagina Mosque** used by the court ladies.

❾ **Jodh Bai's Palace,** built for Akbar's Hindu wife, Jodh Bai, once again blends Muslim and Hindu architecture: Mogul domes extend above the palace, but the carvings inside and the courtyard are Hindu. Upstairs, walled in by a red sandstone screen, is the Hawa Maha (Palace of the Winds), the coolest vantage point from which the ladies of the court could peek outside unseen.

Other royal structures include **Akbar's chambers,** behind a square fountain with a central platform where the court musician, Tansen, sat and sang for the emperor. Near the fountain a small room with zigzag patterns along its walls is thought to be part of Akbar's Turkish wife's living quarters.

Getting There

Fatehpur Sikri is 37 kilometers (27 miles) southeast of Agra. You can reach it with one of the daily tours from Agra (*see* Guided Tours *in* Agra Essentials, *below*) or by car. Hire a car from one of the recommended travel agencies listed *below.*

Dining and Lodging

Few people choose to stay in Fatehpur Sikri; it can be seen in about three hours, and it's close enough to Agra to be done as a day trip. It's also only half an hour from the Keoladeo Bird sanctuary in Bharatpur and can easily be combined with a trip there (*see* Chapter 2, Special-Interest Travel in India).

$ Gulistan Tourist Complex. Run by Uttar Pradesh State Tourism Development Corporation, this small hotel among spacious gardens makes a convenient lunch stop on a day trip to Fatehpur Sikri. ⌺ *Fatehpur Sikri,* ☎ *5619/2490. 24 rooms. Restaurant.*

Agra Essentials

Arriving and Departing

BY CAR

Agra is 200 kilometers (124 miles) south of Delhi, over roads made by the Mogul emperors to connect their two capitals. The roads are good, but don't expect to travel much above 50 kilometers (31 miles) per hour. The best route is probably by the Mathura Road, via Faridabad, Vrindavan, and Mathura.

BY PLANE

Kheria Airport is roughly 7 kilometers (4 miles) from the Taj Mahal. **Indian Airlines** (☎ 562/361053 or 562/361421) flies daily between Agra and Delhi, Khajuraho, and Varanasi. Contact your travel agent for other domestic carriers that may have flights into Agra.

Between the Airport and Center City. You can get a fixed-rate taxi (Rs. 75) or auto rickshaw (Rs. 50) from the airport to the city center. Inquire at your hotel about the airport shuttle that picks passengers up from some hotels.

BY TRAIN

Air-conditioned coaches run daily on the Delhi-Agra-Gwalior-Jhansi-Bhopal route (☎ 562/72511 for inquiries and 562/63787 for reservations) of the **Shatabdi Express.** The second-best train is the **Taj Express.** In winter, trains may actually be a more reliable way to get to Agra from Delhi than planes because the Delhi airport is often plagued by fog-caused delays.

Getting Around

BY AUTO RICKSHAW

You can hire an auto rickshaw for a half day (Rs. 75) or a full day (Rs. 150).

BY BICYCLE RICKSHAW

This pleasant option should cost no more than Rs. 20 per hour.

BY HIRED CAR WITH DRIVER

Hire a car with driver only from a tour operator or travel agency mentioned in the Gold Guide (*see above*). Prices generally range between Rs. 4 and Rs. 8 per kilometer. A non-air-conditioned car for two hours or 20 kilometers should cost about Rs. 80, the minimum charge.

A non-air-conditioned car for 8 hours or 100 kilometers should cost about Rs. 400. For overnight excursions, also figure on a Rs. 100 halt charge. **Budget Rent-a-Car** has an office in the Hotel Mumtaz (Fatehabad Rd. ☎ 361771). In the peak season, book a rented car with driver in advance.

BY TAXI
If the driver says his meter is broken, set the rate before you depart. Someone at your hotel should be able to help you.

Guided Tours
Uttar Pradesh State Road Transport Corporation (96 Gwalior Rd., ☎ 72206, and Platform No. 1, near enquiry window, Agra Cantonment. Railway Station) offers a daily bus tour with a guide of Fatehpur Sikri, Agra Fort, and Taj Mahal for Rs. 100 per person. Excellent guides are available from the **Take-A-Guide Office** (opposite Hotel Taj View, Fatehabad Rd.). For up to four persons, full-day charges are Rs. 100. The office is open daily 9 to 6.

Opening and Closing Times
Most offices are open from 10 to 5 with a lunch break from 1:30 to 2.

Important Addresses and Numbers
CHANGING MONEY
Besides your hotel, which is the easiest and most convenient, you can change money at the State Bank of India (Mahatma Gandhi Rd., Rakabganj, ☎ 562/26322) or the Canera Bank (Sadar Bazaar).

EMERGENCIES
For any emergency, contact your hotel, your embassy in Delhi, or East West Clinic (*see* Chapter 4, Delhi).

VISITOR INFORMATION
The **Uttar Pradesh State Tourist Office** (64 Taj Rd., ☎ 562/360517) is open Monday through Saturday 10 to 5 and closed Sunday and the second Saturday of each month. **The Uttar Pradesh State Tourism Development Corporation** (Tourist Bungalow, near the Raja Mandi Station, ☎ 562/351720) arranges tours and car hires. It's open 10 to 5 and closed Sundays. **The Government of India Tourist Office** (191, The Mall, ☎ 562/363959 or 562/363377) is open Monday through Friday 9 to 5:30 and Saturday 9 to 1.

KHAJURAHO

By Smita Patel Mountains in the Chattarpur district of Madhya Pradesh surround the small village of Khajuraho. It is so rural that it's hard to imagine Khajuraho was once the religious capital of the Chandella dynasty (at its height during the 10th–14th century), one of the most powerful Rajput dynasties of Central India. The only significant river is some distance away, and the village seems far removed from any substantial economic activity. Yet this is where the Chandellas placed 85 temples. Today, its 22 remaining temples give us a glimpse of a golden time when art and devotion were at their peak.

During their rule, India was the Asian Eldorado. People were rich, the land was fertile, life brimmed with pleasure. Purdah (the seclusion of women introduced by the Moguls) hadn't yet cast its inhibiting pall over joy. Everyone lived the 10th-century-style good time, trooping off to fairs, feasts, hunts, dramas, music, and dances. This untroubled abundance provided the perfect climate for creativity, with temple-building emerging as the major form of expression. No strict boundaries ex-

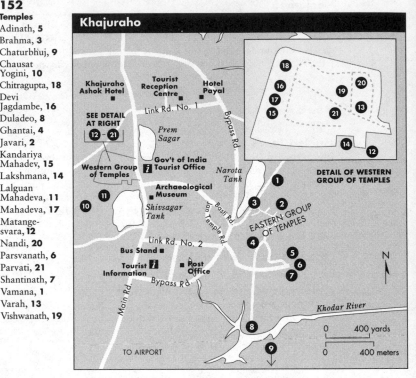

isted between sacred and profane. Shiva, Vishnu, Brahma, and the Jains'
saints were all lavishly honored. Despite the interest in heaven, the real
focus was earthbound, rooted in the facts of life. Here, portrayed with
no false modesty and no sense of prudery, virile men and voluptuous
women, immortalized in stone, cavort in the most intimate and erotic
postures. To call these sculptures pornography is irrelevant. Khajuraho
represents the best of Hindu sculpture: sinuous, twisting forms—
human and divine—throbbing with life, tension, and conflict.

The Chandella dynasty reigned for five centuries until it succumbed
to invaders of a different moral outlook. In 1100, Mahmud the Turk
began a holy war against the "idolaters" of India. By 1200, the sultans of Delhi ruled over the once-glorious Chandella domain.

★ The **temples of Khajuraho** have more to offer than their erotic sculptures. The soaring towers on these temples, rising like the Himalayas,
represent the builders' attempts to reach upward, out of the material
world, to *moksha,* the final release from the cycle of rebirth. An example of the vibrancy of Hinduism, the temples are actually architectural symbols of the philosophy and religion of the people who built
them. They also represent central-Indian temple architecture at its
best, while the combination of structure and sculpture gives them a
unique sense of completeness and exuberance.

Of the 85 original temples, 22 remain; all but two were made from
sandstone mined from the banks of the River Ken, 30 kilometers (19
miles) away. The stone blocks were first carved, and then the interlocking
pieces were assembled to form a temple. Though each temple is different, they are all built on exact principles of architecture that dictate
shape, form, and even direction.

The *sikharas* (spires) are meant to resemble the peaks of the Himalayas, the abode of Lord Shiva. Starting with the smallest sikhara over the entrance, each successive spire rises higher than the one before, like a range of mountains, which, as they soar upward to the heavens, invite the viewer to reach toward the highest human potential.

The temples all contain the essential elements of a high raised platform, an *ardh-mandapa* (entrance porch), a *mandapa* (portico), an *antrala* (vestibule), and a *garba-griha* (sanctum). Some of the larger temples also include a walkway around the inner sanctum, a *mahamandapa* (hall), and subsidiary shrines on each corner of the temple platform, making it a complete *panchayatana* (five-shrine complex).

A number of sculptural motifs run through the temples, including the pantheon of gods and goddesses, such as the directional gods, which have an assigned position on each temple. The elephant-headed Ganesh faces north; Yama, the god of death, and his mount, the male buffalo, face south. The two damsels who guard the entrance to the sanctum are the rivers Ganges and Yamuna. Other sculptures include the *apsaras* (heavenly maidens), found mainly inside the temples, and the Atlaslike *kichakas,* who support the temple ceilings on their shoulders. Many sculptures simply reflect everyday activities, such as a dancing class. The sultry *nayikas* display various human emotions, and the *mithunas* are amorous couples.

No one knows for sure why erotic sculptures are so important here, though many explanations have been offered. One theory, rooted in legend, says the founder of the Chandella dynasty was born of an illicit union between his mother and the moon god, which resulted in her ostracism. When he grew up to become a mighty king, so the legend goes, his mother begged him to show the world the beauty and divinity of lovemaking. Others suggest that the sculptures reflect the influence of a tantric cult that believed the way to heaven was by satisfying the appetites. Still others argue that sex has been used as a metaphor: The carnal and bestial sex generally shown near the base of the temples represents uncontrolled human appetites, while the couples deeply engrossed in each another and oblivious to everything else represent a bliss that is divine and the closest humans can approach to God.

Numbers in the margin correspond to points of interest on the Khajuraho map.

Exploring

The best way to see Khajuraho is to hire a guide (especially for the Western Group of temples) and to visit the Western Group in the first rays of the morning sun, follow them with the Eastern Group, see the museum in the afternoon, and make it to the Chaturbhuj temple in the Southern Group in time for sunset.

Eastern Temple Group. This temple group includes three Hindu and three Jain temples; their proximity attests to the religious tolerance of the times in general and of the Chandella rulers in particular. The **Vamana Temple** is northernmost and is dedicated to Vishnu's dwarf incarnation. The idol in the sanctum, however, looks more like a tall, sly child. The sanctum walls show total tolerance, featuring most of the major gods and goddesses. Vishnu appears in many of his forms, including the Buddha, his ninth incarnation. Outside, two tiers of sculpture are concerned mainly with the nymphs of paradise, who strike charming poses under their private awnings. The small, well-proportioned **Javari Temple,** just to the south, is of the simplified three-shrine design. The two main exterior bands bear hosts of heavenly maidens.

❸ The granite and sandstone **Brahma Temple** opposite is among the earliest (c. AD 900). It differs in design from most of the other temples, particularly in the combination of materials and the shape of its sikhara. The temple even contains a shivlingam (phallus-shape stone) which suggests it was originally dedicated to Shiva.

❹ The Jain complex of the Eastern Group lies to the south (just beyond the Khajuraho village), beginning with a little gem, the **Ghantai.** All that's left of this temple are its pillars festooned with carvings of pearls and bells. Adorning the entrance are an eight-armed Jain goddess riding the mythical bird Garuda and a relief illustrating the 16 dreams of the mother of Mahavira, the greatest religious figure in Jainism and a contemporary of the Buddha.

❺ The 11th-century **Adinath Temple,** a minor shrine, is east of Ghantai. Its porch and the statue of Tirthankara (perfect soul) Adinatha are modern additions. Built at the beginning of the Chandellas' decline, the temple is smaller, but the sikhara and its base are richly carved.

❻ The **Parsvanath Temple** to the south, the largest and finest of the Jain complex, contains some of the best sculpture in Khajuraho. Statues of flying angels and sloe-eyed beauties who are occupied with children, cosmetics, and flowers adorn the outer walls. The stone conveys even the texture of the thin garments they wear. The fourth temple in this
❼ cluster, the modern **Shantinath,** contains some ancient Jain sculpture.

❽ **Southern Group.** Of the two temples in this group, **Duladeo Temple,** south of the Ghantai Jain Temple, though built in the customary five-shrine style, looks flatter and more massive than the typical Khajuraho shrines. One of the last temples erected in Khajuraho, dated to the 12th century, the Duladeo Temple lacks the usual ambulatory passage and crowning lotus-shape finials. It has some vibrant sculptures, but many of its sculptures are clichéd and overornamented. Here, too, in this temple dedicated to Shiva, eroticism works its way in, though the erotic figures are discreetly placed.

❾ The small, 12th-century **Chaturbhuj Temple,** nearly 3 kilometers (2 miles) south of Duladeo, has an attractive, colonnaded entrance and a feeling of verticality. It enshrines an impressive four-handed image of Shiva. The exterior sculpture, with a few exceptions, falls short of the Khajuraho mark (a sign of the declining fortunes of the empire), but this temple offers the best place to see the sunset.

❿ **Western Group of Temples.** The first three temples are considered part of the Western Group, but are actually outside the enclosure that surrounds the rest of the group. The **Chausat Yogini Temple,** on the west side of the Shivsager Tank, a small artificial lake, is the oldest temple at Khajuraho, possibly built as early as AD 820. Because it is dedicated to Kali, its name, *Chausat* (meaning 64), was chosen to signify the number of nymphs who serve this fierce goddess of wrath. The temple was built of granite (all the others are a pale, warm-toned sandstone) and is the only one oriented northeast–southwest instead of the usual north–south. It was originally surrounded by 64 roofed cells, for the figures of Kali's attendants, of which only 35 remain.

⓫ The **Lalguan Mahadeva** stands about ½ kilometer (⅓ mile) from the Chausath Yogini. This Shiva temple is in ruins, and the original portico is missing, but it is of historical interest because it was built of both granite and sandstone and represents the transition from Chausath Yogini to the later temples. Just outside the boundary of the Western Group of temples is the **Matangesvara Temple,** the only temple still in use, where worship takes place in the morning and afternoon. The lack of ornamentation, its square construction, and its simpler floor plan date it to the early 10th century. The temple has oriel windows, a projecting portico, and a ceiling of overlapping concentric circles. An enormous lingam, nearly 3 meters (8½ feet) tall, is enshrined in the sanctum.

As you enter the temple complex, you will find the **Varah Temple** (circa AD 900–925) to your right. It is dedicated to Vishnu's Varaha-Avatar, or Boar Incarnation, which he took to rescue the earth after it had been hidden in the slush at the bottom of the sea by a demon. All of creation is displayed on the massive and beautifully polished sides of a sculpture depicting the boar. The ceiling represents a lotus in relief.

Behind the Varah temple stands the **Lakshmana Temple,** dedicated to Vishnu, and the only complete temple remaining. The ceiling of the hall is charmingly carved in shell and floral motifs. The lintel over the entrance to the main shrine shows Lakshmi, goddess of wealth and consort of Vishnu, with Brahma, Lord of Creation (on her left) and Shiva, Lord of Destruction (on her right). A frieze above the lintel depicts the planets. The relief on the doorway illustrates the scene of the gods and demons churning the ocean to obtain a pitcher of miraculous nectar from the bottom. The wall of the sanctum is carved with scenes from the legend of Krishna (one of Vishnu's incarnations). The idol in the sanctum with two pairs of arms and three heads represents the same god in his lion and boar incarnations. The outside of this temple is a metaphor for human life and the quest for salvation. At the base are some of Khajuraho's most famous erotic sculptures: scenes of bestiality and sex at its most carnal, interspersed with scenes of war and gluttony. The carvings, too, are rough. Higher on the temple wall, the carvings become more refined, war is replaced with art and culture, and lust is replaced with love.

The **Kandariya Mahadev,** west of the Lakshmana temple, is the largest and most evolved, in terms of the blending of architecture and sculpture, of all the Khajuraho temples and one of the finest in India. North of Chausat Yogini, and probably built around AD 1020, it follows the five-shrine design. Dedicated to Shiva, it has an inner sanctum that houses a marble lingam with a 4-foot circumference. The rich carving of the interior includes two beautiful *toranas* (arched doorways). Outside, the three bands of sculpture around the sanctum and transept bring to life the whole galaxy of Hindu gods and goddesses, mithunas, celestial handmaidens, and lions. A total of 872 statues—226 inside and 646 outside—have been counted. Notice that the figures in this temple are taller and slimmer and the main sikhara is actually made up of smaller ones that seem to reach ever higher.

The **Devi Jagdambe Temple** was originally dedicated to Vishnu (indicated by a sculpture of him located prominently over the sanctum's doorway). It is now dedicated to Parvati, Shiva's consort. Because the image is black, a color associated with Kali, goddess of wrath and an avatar of Parvati, it is also known as the Kali Temple. From the inside, its three-shrine design makes it seem shaped like a cross. The third band of sculpture has a series of erotic mithuna themes. The ceilings are similar to those of the Kandariya Temple, and the three-headed, eight-armed statue of Shiva is one of the best cult images at Khajuraho.

The small, mostly ruined **Mahadeva Temple,** shares its platform with the Kandariya and the Devi Jagdambe. Now dedicated to Shiva, it may originally have been a subsidiary to the Kandaria Mahadev temple, probably dedicated to Shiva's consort. In the portico stands a remarkable statue of a man caressing a mythical horned lion.

18 The **Chitragupta Temple** lies slightly north of the Devi Jagdambe and resembles it in construction. It faces east toward the rising sun in honor of its presiding deity, Surya, the sun god. The temple cell contains Surya's 5-foot-high image with his chariot and seven horses that carry him across the sky. Surya is also depicted above the doorway. In the central niche to the south of the sanctum is an image of Vishnu with 11 heads; his own face is in the center, and the other heads represent his 10 (9 past and 1 future) incarnations. A profusion of sculpture—scenes of animal combat, royal processions, masons at work, and joyous dances—depict the lavish country life of the Chandellas.

19 20 The **Vishwanath** and **Nandi** temples face one another on a common terrace to the east of the Chitragupta and Devi Jagdambe temples. There are two staircases, the northern flanked by a pair of lions and the southern by a pair of elephants. The Vishwanath probably preceded the Kandariya, but here two of the original corner shrines remain. On the outer wall of the corridor surrounding the cells is an impressive image of Brahma, the three-headed Lord of Creation, and his consort, Saraswati. On all the walls, the form of the woman dominates, portrayed in all her daily 10th-century occupations: writing a letter, holding her baby, studying her reflection in a mirror, applying makeup, or playing music. The nymphs of paradise are voluptuous and provocative; the erotic scenes, robust. An inscription states that the temple was built by Chandella King Dhanga in 1002. A simpler, extra shrine (the Nandi Temple) houses a statue of the god's mount, the massive and richly harnessed sacred bull Nandi, carved from a single piece of stone.

21 The small and heavily rebuilt **Parvati Temple**, near Vishwanath, was originally dedicated to Vishnu. The present idol is that of the goddess Gauri standing on her mount, the iguana.

Across the street from the Matangesvara Temple, the **Archaeological Museum** contains some exquisite carvings and sculptures recovered by archaeologists. The three galleries attempt to put the various sculptures into context according to the deities they represent. *Western Group entrance: off Main Rd., opposite State Bank of India.* ☛ *Western Group Rs. 1 (including museum entry).* ☉ *Western Group sunrise–sunset, museum Sat.–Thurs. 10–5.*

TIME OUT **Restaurant Lal Bungalow,** a small red house opposite the Western Group of temples, is a great place to stop for a cup of tea or a snack. Its owner, one of the most respected guides in Khajuraho, known as *Mama* (uncle) by the locals, will discuss the temples with you.

Dining

For price categories, *see* the chart for Other Areas *in* On the Road with Fodor's.

$$$ **Apsara.** This pleasant restaurant has teak lattice screens and silk bird paintings. The chef prepares good Indian and Continental dishes. Try the tandoori kebabs or the *korma* (vegetables cooked in a creamy onion and tomato curry). ✗ *Jass Oberoi,* ☎ 76861/2085. *Dinner reservations advised. AE, DC, MC, V.*

$$$ **Bhoj Bundela.** This small restaurant, decorated in shades of gold, has tile floors, cane furniture, and elegant plants everywhere. The menu features Indian and Continental fare, and the chef is creative. Try the vegetable-coriander soup and the chicken *hara masala* (chicken with green spices). ✕ *Clarks Bundela,* ☎ *76861/2364. Dinner reservations advised. AE, DC, MC, V.*

$$ **Gautama.** This Indian-specialty restaurant is spacious and pleasant. Try the chicken stuffed with spinach in a fenugreek sauce and the stuffed potatoes in a butter masala sauce. ✕ *Holiday Inn Khajuraho,* ☎ *76861/2178. AE, DC, MC, V.*

$ **Mediterraneo.** You can eat either on the rooftop or in a small dining room downstairs in this Italian restaurant. It doesn't have a single frill, but the kitchen is spotless, and the chef is from Italy. Try pizza or one of the many pasta dishes. ✕ *Jain Temple Rd., Khajuraho,* ☎ *76861/2340. Reservations advised. Rupees only.*

$ **Raja Cafe, Swiss Restaurant.** This little restaurant is a popular meeting place for guides. You can eat on the roof, in the courtyard, or in the small dining room. The restaurant is pretty basic, but its Continental food is popular. Try the chicken pancake béchamel (chicken in white sauce served in a crêpe). ✕ *Khajuraho, no* ☎. *Rupees only.*

Lodging

For price categories, *see* the chart for Other Areas *in* On the Road with Fodor's.

$$$ **Clarks Bundela.** This white, two-story hotel is a recent addition to the small but growing number of hotels in this tiny village. Well illuminated, it has abundant marble, which gives it a generally cool effect. The rooms are Western-style comfortable with French doors and balconies. ⌂ *Chatarpur district, Khajuraho, Madhya Pradesh, 471606,* ☎ *76861/2364 or 76861/2365,* ℻ *76861/2359. 45 rooms, 2 suites. Restaurant, bar, travel services. AE, DC, MC, V.*

$$$ **Holiday Inn Khajuraho.** From the outside this hotel looks more like an
★ American condominium complex than a hotel, but its interior, with plenty of marble, chandeliers, and curving staircases, is surprisingly elegant. The Western-style rooms are decorated in soft cream shades and have large bay windows. Some rooms have temple views. The suites are decorated along cultural themes. ⌂ *Airport Rd., Khajuraho 471606, Madhya Pradesh,* ☎ *76861/2178,* ℻ *76861/2300; reserve through Suite 7-B, Girdhar Apartments, 28 Feroz Shah Rd., New Delhi 110001,* ☎ *11/3755501,* ℻ *11/3739260. 56 rooms, 8 suites. 2 restaurants, bar, coffee shop, pool, beauty salon, 1 tennis court, health club, jogging, Ping-Pong, baby-sitting, meeting room. AE, DC, MC, V.*

$$$ **Hotel Chandella.** This elegant hotel is set around a lovely pool and surrounded by gardens. The rooms are Western style and comfortable and have balconies or patios. ⌂ *Chatarpur district, Khajuraho 471606, Madhya Pradesh,* ☎ *76861/2054,* ℻ *76861/2095. 102 rooms, 6 suites. 3 restaurants, bar, coffee shop, pool, miniature golf, health club. AE, DC, MC, V.*

$$$ **Jass Oberoi.** The main motifs in this hotel are white marble and plants in brass pots. Just a kilometer (½ mile) from the Western Group of temples, the two-story hotel has comfortable Western-style rooms with balconies offering views of either the pool or the hills. ⌂ *Chatarpur district, Khajuraho 471606, Madhya Pradesh,* ☎ *76861/2085 or 76861/2086,* ℻ *76861/2088. 94 rooms, 2 suites. Restaurant, bar, pool, tennis court, health club, travel services. AE, DC, MC, V.*

$$ **Hotel Khajuraho Ashok.** At this Western-style hotel, some rooms offer a good view of the temples. All the rooms have twin beds. ⌂ *Khajuraho 471606, Madhya Pradesh,* ☎ *76861/2024,* ℻ *76861/2042. 38 rooms. Restaurant, bar, coffee shop, pool, Ping-Pong. AE, MC, V.*

$$ **Ken River Lodge.** Near Panna National Park, 27 kilometers (17 miles) from Khajuraho, the lodge offers village-style mud huts and spacious tents, all with running hot and cold water and private baths and showers. The restaurant is a platform built on tree limbs on the banks of the Ken River. ⌨ *Madla Village, Panna district; reserve through Ken River Lodge, c/o Pro-Host, A/C-456 Vasant Kunj, New Delhi 110070, ☎ 11/689–3027 or 11/689–2764, FAX 11/689–3027. 4 cottages, 4 tents. Restaurant, beach, boating, fishing. No credit cards.*

$ **Hotel Jhankar.** This new one-story MPSTDC hotel offers spacious, clean rooms with modern decor. Some rooms are air-conditioned; others have fans. ⌨ *Airport Rd., Khajuraho 471606, ☎ 76861/2063; reservations, MPSTDC, 4th Floor, Gangotri, T. T. Nagar, Bhopal 462003, Madhya Pradesh, ☎ 755/554340. 19 rooms. Restaurant. MC, V.*

$ **Hotel Payal.** This hotel, run by the Madhya Pradesh State Tourism Development Corporation (MPSTDC) has rooms set around small courtyards. The accommodations are simple but clean, and the service is friendly and helpful. Most rooms are air-conditioned; the rest have fans. The Indian and Chinese restaurant has very good food and is a popular meeting place for locals. ⌨ *Khajuraho; reserve through MPSTDC, 4th Floor, Gangotri, T. T. Nagar, Bhopal 462003, Madhya Pradesh, ☎ 755/554340. 25 rooms. Restaurant, travel services. AE, DC, MC, V.*

The Arts

Khajuraho has an annual dance festival (MPSTDC ☎ 76861/2051) set against the backdrop of the temples. Don't miss this superb event if your trip is planned anywhere around the beginning of March.

Excursions

If you have the time, stay an extra day and explore and picnic in the beautiful country around Khajuraho.

Khajuraho Village. This typical traditional Indian village has small streets crammed with animals and bicycles and is backed by the distant mountains.

★ **Gharial Sanctuary.** For a slightly longer excursion, bike or drive to the nearby Ken River sanctuary, 28 kilometers (17 miles) away, which was set up to protect the slender-snouted crocodile and has some lovely waterfalls. ☉ *Sunrise–sunset.*

★ **Panna National Park.** Here you can see the elusive tiger and a host of other wildlife. It is only 31 kilometers (19 miles) from Khajuraho and is still relatively undisturbed by visitors. ☉ *Sunrise–sunset.*

Khajuraho Essentials

Arriving and Departing

BY CAR

Madhya Pradesh is one of the most scenic states to drive through. Khajuraho is 395 kilometers (223 miles) southeast of Agra. You can tailor a delightful trip covering Agra, Orchha, and Khajuraho over four or five days. Hire a car in Delhi or Agra from one of the tour operators or travel agencies mentioned in the Gold Guide (*see above*).

BY PLANE

Indian Airlines (☎ 76861/2035, airport ☎ 76861/2036) flies daily between Delhi, Agra, Khajuraho, and Varanasi.

From the Airport to Town. The airport is 5 kilometers (3 miles) from Khajuraho; the taxi ride costs about Rs. 50.

BY TRAIN

The MPSTDC has a daily air-conditioned deluxe coach that runs from the Jhansi (*see* Agra Essentials, *above*) railway station to Khajuraho.

Getting Around

Most places in Khajuraho are within walking distance of one another.

BY BICYCLE

You can rent a bicycle across from the bus stand, behind the museum, or from one of the hotels. It should cost about Rs. 10 per day and is probably the best way to get around Khajuraho.

BY BICYCLE RICKSHAW

Bicycle rickshaws are expensive here, with fares starting around Rs. 30. But this is a pleasant way to get around, especially to the outlying temples. Negotiate the rates (you can get an estimate from the Government of India Tourist Office, ☎ 76861/2047).

BY HIRED CAR WITH DRIVER

A car may be convenient if you want to go out of Khajuraho or can't walk the two miles to the most distant temples. A non-air-conditioned car should cost about Rs. 175 for two hours or 30 kilometers. Hire a car with driver through your hotel, the Khajuraho Regional MPSTDC office (☎ 76861/2051), or one of these travel agencies: **Touraids** (☎ 76861/2060), **Travel Bureau** (76861/2037), or **Khajuraho Tours** (76861/2033).

BY TAXI

You can hire a taxi for about Rs. 4 per kilometer.

Guided Tours

Licensed guides who speak excellent English can be hired through the **Government of India Tourist Office** (Opposite the Western Group, ☎ 76861/2047).

Important Addresses and Numbers

CHANGING MONEY

Most Western-style hotels have foreign-exchange counters for their guests. The **State Bank of India** (☎ 76861/2173) is opposite the entrance to the Western Group of temples.

EMERGENCIES

For any emergency, contact your hotel, your embassy in Delhi, or the East West Clinic (*see* Chapter 4, Delhi).

VISITOR INFORMATION

The **Madhya Pradesh State Tourism Development Corporation (MPSTDC)** (Gangotri, 4th Floor, T. T. Nagar, Bhopal 462003, ☎ 755/553006 or 11/3321187 in New Delhi) is one of the better organized and more helpful tourist offices in India. Its staff can help you plan your itinerary, reserve rooms in any of the MPSTDC facilities, and advise you on other travel arrangements, such as hiring cars. The **Khajuraho Regional MPSTDC** office (Tourist Bungalow Complex, Khajuraho 471606, ☎ 76861/2051 or 76861/2221) is open Monday through Saturday 10 to 5. The **Government of India Tourist Office** (opposite the Western Group of temples, ☎ 76861/2047) in Khajuraho is a good place to get maps and other information and to hire guides. It's open 9 to 5:30 Monday through Friday and 8 to 12:30 on Saturdays.

VARANASI

By Vikram
Singh

Varanasi, or Kashi ("resplendent with divine light"), as it was called in the 12th century BC, has been the religious capital of Hinduism through all recorded time. No one knows the date of Varanasi's founding, but when the historic Buddha, Siddhartha Gautama, came here around 500 BC, he encountered an ancient and developed settlement. Contemporary with Babylon, Nineveh, and Thebes, Varanasi is one the world's oldest cities.

Every devout Hindu wants to visit Varanasi to purify body and soul in the Ganges, to shed all sin, and, if possible, to die here in old age and find release from the cycle of rebirth. Descending from the Himalayas on its long trek to the Bay of Bengal, the Ganga (the Ganges) is believed by Hindus to hold the power of salvation in each drop. Pilgrims seek that salvation along the length of the river, but the holiest site is Varanasi. Every year, the city welcomes millions of pilgrims for whom these waters—fouled by the pollution of humans, living and dead— remain pristine enough to cleanse the soul.

The old city, which has 1 million inhabitants, is a maze of streets and alleys, hiding a disorderly array of at least 2,000 temples and shrines. Domes, minarets, pinnacles, towers, and derelict 18th-century palaces dominate the sacred left bank of the river. The streets are noisy and rife with color. The air hangs heavy, as if in collaboration with the clang of temple gongs and bells. Some houses have simply decorated entrances; other buildings are ornate with Indian-style gingerbread on balconies and verandas. You'll see marriage and funeral processions and cows munching on garlands destined for the gods, and you'll be hounded by phony guides and assertive hawkers.

Despite the variety of religious shrines, Varanasi is essentially a temple city dedicated to Shiva. According to legend, the Ganges was created when the river goddess Ganga, whose waters purified everything they touched, was ordered to descend to Earth to redeem the souls of some humans of great merit. Because the gods feared that the force of her waters crashing down would damage the Earth, Shiva caught the goddess in his hair, making her flow more gently.

Numbers in the margin correspond to points of interest on the Varanasi map.

Exploring

The old city of Varanasi rests on the west bank of the Ganges; *ghats* (wide stone stairways down to the water) stretch along the river from Ram Ghat in the north to the university area in the south, across from Ram Nagar Fort. The city itself spreads out behind the ghats, with the hotels in the cantonment area about 20 minutes by rickshaw from the river.

❶ Durga Temple. Dedicated to Durga, Shiva's consort, this 18th-century shrine stands due west of Asi Ghat. The sikhara (spire) is formed on top of five lower spires—a convergence that is a visual symbol of the belief that all five elements of the world merge with the supreme. Durga is also called the Monkey Temple; the pests are everywhere, and they'll steal anything. *Durgakund Rd.*

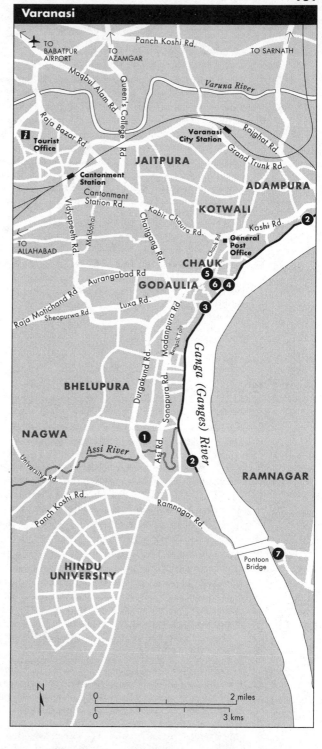

Dashashwamedh Ghat, **3**
Durga Temple, **1**
Ghats, **2**
Gyanpavi Mosque, **5**
Kashi Vishwanath Temple, **6**
Manikarnika Ghat, **4**
Ram Nagar Fort and Palace, **7**

Varanasi

TO BABATPUR AIRPORT

TO AZAMGAR

Panch Koshi Rd.

TO SARNATH

Maqbul Alam Rd.

Queen's College Rd.

Varuna River

Raja Bazar Rd.

Tourist Office

Varanasi City Station

Rajghat Rd.

Cantonment Station

Cantonment Station Rd.

Grand Trunk Rd.

JAITPURA

ADAMPURA

Vidyapeeth Rd.

Maldahai

Kabir Chaura Rd.

KOTWALI

Kashi Rd.

Chaitganj Rd.

Chauk Rd.

CHAUK

TO ALLAHABAD

General Post Office

Aurangabad Rd

GODAULIA

Raja Motichand Rd.

Sheopurwa Rd.

Luxa Rd.

Madanpura Rd.

Bengali Tola

Ganga (Ganges) River

BHELUPURA

Durgakund Rd.

Sonapura Rd.

NAGWA

Assi River

Asi Rd.

University Rd.

RAMNAGAR

Panch Koshi Rd.

Ramnagar Rd.

Pontoon Bridge

HINDU UNIVERSITY

N

0   2 miles
0   3 kms

★ ❷ **Ghats.** Along a 7-kilometer (4-mile) stretch of the Ganges, you see ghats (wide stairways that lead down to the sacred river). About 70 sets of these stone steps wed the great Hindu metropolis to the Ganges. The numerous lingams (phallus-shaped stones) remind pilgrims that they are under Shiva's care here. The best time to visit the ghats is at early dawn, when a solemn multitude of people and even animals—lit by the sun's first rays—all move in one direction, bent on immersion in the holy stream. If you decide to hire a boat, which is not expensive,

❸ go to the **Dashashwamedh Ghat,** the main ghat as you head from the Godowlia (the main traffic circle in the Chowk district) down to the water. As you float on the river, you'll see young men performing vigorous hatha yoga exercises; older men sitting cross-legged in the lotus position, eyes closed in deep meditation; and Brahmin priests offering prayers while sitting under huge umbrellas. Devotees drink from the polluted water. A carcass may even float by. Women glide in and out of saris with such finesse that they reveal nothing, and you don't even think about averting your eyes. Others beat and swoosh linen against the stone, purifying the clothes they wear.

❹ Thin blue smoke twists up to the sky from fires on the **Manikarnika Ghat,** the chief cremation center of Varanasi (the smaller cremation ghat is called Harish Chandra Ghat). Corpses wrapped in silk or linen—traditionally white for men and red for women—are carried on bamboo stretchers to the smoking pyres, where they are deposited and wait their turn. First, they are immersed in the Ganga and then, after a short wait, are placed on the pyre for the ritual that precedes the cremation. These funeral ghats cannot be photographed, but you are allowed to watch.

❺ **Gyanvapi and Alamgir mosques.** In the 17th century the Mogul emperor Aurangzeb pulled down the Visheswara Temple and erected the Gyanvapi Mosque on the site. The foundation and the rear of the mosque still reveal parts of the original temple. The tallest of its minarets, which dominated the skyline of the holy city, collapsed during a flood in 1948. North of the Gyanvapi Mosque, and also on the river, is another of Aurangzeb's creations, the Alamgir Mosque, an odd blend of Hindu and Muslim designs. Aurangzeb destroyed the 17th-century Beni Madhav ka Darera, which was dedicated to Vishnu, and built this mosque with an odd fusion of Hindu (lower portions and wall) and Muslim (upper portion) designs. Head toward Ganges and Ram Ghat on Aurangabad Rd., take last left before river; Alamgir is on right.

❻ **Kashi Vishwanath Temple.** Dedicated to Shiva, this shrine in the old city is set back from the Ganges between the Dashashwamedh and Manikarnika ghats. The most sacred shrine in Varanasi, off-limits to non-Hindus, it is best seen from the top floor of the house opposite (pay a small fee to the owner). You'll see men and women making offerings to the lingam in the inner shine. The present temple was built by Rani Ahalyabai of Indore in 1776 near the site of the original shrine, which had been destroyed by Aurangzeb. The spire, covered in gold plate, was a gift from the maharaja Ranjit Singh in 1835.

★ ❼ **Ram Nagar Fort and Palace.** On the opposite side of the Ganges is the residential palace of the former maharaja of Varanasi. Within, the **Durbar Hall** (Public Audience Chamber) and the **Royal Museum** have collections of palanquins, furniture, arms, weapons, and costumes that are open to the public. The palace was built to resist the floods of the monsoon, which play havoc with the city side of the river. ☞ Rs. 5. ⊘ Daily 9–noon and 2–3.

Dining and Lodging

Varanasi has abundant food for the soul, but not so much for the palate. The hotels offer decent if uninspired Indian, Chinese, and Continental cuisines. Hotel pools are all outdoors. For price categories, *see* the charts for Major Cities *in* On the Road with Fodor's.

$$$ **Clark's Varanasi.** This modern hotel offers attractive rooms with light, cheery decor; the best overlook the pool or the lawn. Indian classical dance and musical performances can be arranged. ☎ *The Mall, Varanasi 221002, Uttar Pradesh,* ☎ *542/42401,* ℻ *542/42947. 140 rooms. Restaurant, bar, pool, travel services. AE, DC, MC, V.*

$$$ **Hotel Hindusthan International.** This property built at the end of the 1980s is closer to the ghats than Varanasi's top hotels, but it is smaller and books a large number of groups, so you may have trouble reserving a room. ☎ *C-21/3 Maldahai, Varanasi 221002, Uttar Pradesh,* ☎ *542/ 57075,* ℻ *542/55030. 51 rooms. Restaurant, bar, pool. AE, MC, V.*

$$$ **Hotel Taj Ganges.** This Western-style highrise has a lavish lobby and spacious modern rooms, but it lacks the expected Taj hotel-chain class. The best rooms have a view of the swimming pool. ☎ *Nadesar Palace Grounds, Raja Bazar Rd., Varanasi 221002, Uttar Pradesh,* ☎ *542/ 42481,* ℻ *542/322067. 130 rooms. 2 restaurants, bar, pool, tennis court, travel services. AE, DC, MC, V.*

$$$ **Hotel Varanasi Ashok.** A long, landscaped driveway leads up to this multistory Western-style hotel with a personal feel just outside the madness of downtown Varanasi. Rooms have simple, contemporary furnishings and balconies, with the best rooms overlooking the pool. ☎ *The Mall, Varanasi 221002, Uttar Pradesh,* ☎ *542/46020,* ℻ *542/42141. 84 rooms, 3 suites. Restaurant, bar, pool, travel services. AE, DC, MC, V.*

$ **Best Western Ideal Hotel.** The salmon-pink-and-white exterior of this hotel built in 1994 opens into a spacious white marble lobby. The rooms are large and actually nicer than those of many more expensive hotels. ☎ *The Mall, Varanasi 221002, Uttar Pradesh,* ☎ *542/42591,* ℻ *542/ 385785. 40 rooms, 4 suites. Restaurant, bar, travel services, airport shuttle.*

$ **Hotel de Paris.** Set on pretty grounds, this old, rambling bungalow with a handsome cream-and-pink exterior is an elegant relic of the British cantonment. Bedrooms are spacious and simple; some are air-conditioned. Classical Indian dance and music performances and astrology readings can be arranged. ☎ *15 The Mall, Varanasi 221002, Uttar Pradesh,* ☎ *542/46601,* ℻ *542/348520. 50 rooms with bath. Restaurant, bar, travel services. AE, DC, V.*

Excursion to Sarnath

★ **Sarnath.** This town, 11 kilometers (6 miles) from Varanasi, is the historic center of the Buddhist world. At the deer park in Sarnath, Siddhartha Gautama preached his first sermon more than 2,500 years ago. Here, he revealed his Eightfold Path leading to the end of sorrow and the attainment of inner peace, enlightenment, and ultimate nirvana. Here, he established his doctrine of the Middle Way, the golden path lying between asceticism and self-indulgence.

Two hundred years later, in the mid-3rd century BC, Ashoka—the Mauryan emperor who was the greatest convert to Buddhism—arrived. In Sarnath, he built several stupas (shrines) and a pillar with a lion capital that symbolizes the ideals of peace and righteousness, which was adopted by India as the state emblem. By the 4th century AD, Sarnath reached its zenith under the Gupta dynasty. The 12th century marked

Sarnath's decline, when the devout Queen Kumaradevi built a large monastery—the final tribute before Varanasi rulers dismantled the stupas for building materials. The decay continued until 1836, when Sir Alexander Cunningham started extensive excavations. First, a stone slab was discovered with an inscription of the Buddhist creed; then numerous other relics were found. It was only then that the Western world realized that the Buddha had been an actual person and not simply a mythical figure.

Ashoka Pillar. One of Ashoka's famous pillars stands in front of the main stupa (shrine), where Ashoka used to sit in meditation. The pillar is one of many inscribed monuments that Ashoka erected throughout his empire. *North of museum on Ashoka Rd.*

Chankama. Buddha paced this sacred promenade while preaching.

Chaukhandi Stupa. In the 16th century, the Muslim Emperor Akbar built a brick tower on top of this 5th-century stupa to commemorate his father's visit some years earlier. *Just south of Sarnath Archaeological Museum.*

Deer Park. Before you leave Sarnath, walk north from Dhamek Stupa into the deer park and buy carrots (Rs. 1) to feed the deer. Legend has it that Buddha was once incarnated as the King of the Deer here.

Dhamekh Stupa. Built around AD 500, this is one of the five great remaining monuments. It is the largest survivor, with geometric ornaments on its walls, and is thought to mark the place where the Buddha set the Wheel of Law in motion, although excavations have unearthed the remains of an even earlier stupa of Mauryan bricks of the Gupta period (200 BC). *Northwest of Sarnath Archaeological Museum.*

Dharamrjika Stupa. Set up by Ashoka to contain the bodily relics of the Buddha, it now lies basically in ruins.

Mulagandha Kuti Vihari. Near the Dhamekh Stupa, and joining the old foundations of seven monasteries, is a temple built in 1931. Its walls are decorated with frescoes depicting scenes of the Buddha's life, painted by a Japanese artist, Kosetsu Nosu. The temple also contains a fine collection of Buddhist relics and a collection of rare Buddhist literature. On the anniversary of the temple's foundation—the first full moon in November—an assembly of monks and lay devotees from all parts of Asia come together.

Sarnath Archaeological Museum. This excellent museum houses the original of Ashoka's lion pillar, among other relics of the period. *Ashoka Marg at Dharmapal Marg,* ☎ *542/385002.* ☛ *50 paise.* ⊙ *Sat.–Thurs. 10–5.*

Getting There

A taxi from Varanasi will drop you in Sarnath for Rs. 50; it will wait for you about three hours for Rs. 200. Rickshaws will take you on the long haul for about Rs. 100 (round-trip).

Varanasi Essentials

Arriving and Departing

BY CAR
If you come by car, you'll be using National Highway (NH) 2 or NH 56 from the northwest, NH 29 from Gorakhpur in the north, NH 2 from Calcutta, or NH 30 and NH 2 from Patna.

BY PLANE

Regular service connects Varanasi with such cities as Delhi, Bhubaneswar, Kathmandu, and Bombay. **Indian Airlines** (☏ 542/43746 or 542/43832).

Between the Airport and Center City. The airport is about 45 minutes by car from most hotels. A taxi costs about Rs. 200 to the cantonment and Rs. 250 into town; the airport shuttle is Rs. 40.

BY TRAIN

Several trains a day come to Varanasi from both Calcutta and Delhi. At Varanasi Junction station, people will immediately try to get you in a taxi. If you take one, be aware that the 5- to 10-minute ride into the cantonment (where the best hotels are) costs Rs. 100 or more. If you don't have much luggage, an auto rickshaw should cost around Rs. 10.

Getting Around

BY AUTO RICKSHAW

Auto rickshaws are a fast way to scoot through the crowded streets. Ask at your hotel or the tourist office for the going rate per kilometer and set the fare in advance.

BY BICYCLE RICKSHAW

Distances are long, so a bike rickshaw isn't actually money-saving; it just feels right. A trip from the cantonment to the ghats should cost about Rs. 30. If you hire a rickshaw for the day, negotiate in advance and expect to pay at least Rs. 100 for the service.

BY BOAT

The price should be between Rs. 40 and Rs. 60 an hour. So many touts will pounce on you that you can haggle and go with the best bargain. A boat from the main ghats to Ram Nagar Fort *should* cost you about Rs. 150, round-trip.

BY HIRED CAR WITH DRIVER

Hire a taxi from your hotel or either the Government of India or UP Government tourist office (*see* Visitor Information, *below*). A three- to four-hour car excursion should cost Rs. 200 to Rs. 300.

BY TAXI

For the most part, taxis here are not metered and are overpriced. You're probably better off with a hired car for any long trips.

Guided Tours

Both the Government of India and the UP Government tourist offices (*see* Visitor Information, *below*) conduct tours and provide information on other tours.

Important Addresses and Numbers

CHANGING MONEY

Your hotel will change money for you, or you can go to the **State Bank** (Hotel de Paris), open weekdays 10 to 2 and Saturdays 10 to 12.

EMERGENCIES

For any emergency, contact your hotel, your embassy in Delhi, or the East West Clinic (*see* Chapter 4, Delhi).

VISITOR INFORMATION

The **Government of India Tourist Office** (15 B, The Mall, ☏ 0545/43744) in the cantonment is open Monday through Saturday, 10 to 5; it also has an information desk at the airport. The best information at the **Uttar Pradesh (UP) Government Tourist Office** (Parade Kothi, opposite train station, ☏ 0545/43486) is in Hindi, but the staff can still help you out. The UP tourist office also has a desk at the train station.

ELSEWHERE IN THE REGION

Gwalior and Orchha

Agra's neighboring cities to the south can boast their own rich histories and collection of assorted of monuments.

Gwalior

Now a bustling commercial city, Gwalior traces its history back to a legend: A chieftain named Suraj Sen was cured of leprosy by the hermit-saint Gwalipa. On the hermit's advice, Suraj Sen founded his city here and named it for his benefactor. After that, Gwalior changed hands numerous times, each dynasty leaving its own mark on the city.

Gwalior Fort. Set on a high, rocky plateau, this huge structure, with its 3-kilometer- (2-mile-) long, 11-meter- (35-foot-) high wall, dominates the skyline. Considered invincible, but often captured, this fort achieved its greatest glory under the Tomar rulers of the 14th century. The main palace, **Man Mandir,** was once resplendent in gold and mosaic tiles. Take a flashlight and explore the underground dungeons where the Moguls, after capturing the fort in Akbar's time, kept their prisoners. Don't miss the beautifully carved 11th-century **Sas-Bahu** and the 9th-century **Teli ka Mandir** temples. The state museum in the **Gurjari Mahal** at the base of the fort has an excellent collection of sculptures and archaeological treasures dating as far back as the 2nd century BC. Ask to see the statue of the goddess Shalbhanjika, an exquisite miniature, which is kept in the curator's custody. *Gwalior Rd.,* ☎ *751/8641.* ☛ *Fort Rs. 1., museum Rs. 2.* ⊙ *Fort sunrise–sunset, museum Tues.–Sun. 10–5.*

Jai Vilas Palace and Museum. Belonging to the Scindias, the rulers of Gwalior until independence, the palace is an opulent structure with Tuscan and Corinthian architecture. In the massive **Durbar Hall** (Public Audience Hall; still in use by the family) the ceiling is gilded and hung with enormous chandeliers. In the dining room below you can see the crystal train that carried liqueurs along the maharaja's banquet table. *Jayandra Gang, Lashkar,* ☎ *751/23453.* ☛ *Rs. 30.* ⊙ *Tues.–Sun. 10–5.*

Orchha

Orchha, 119 kilometers (74 miles) southeast of Gwalior, is a sleepy village of palaces, the one place in the world where the Hindu god Rama is considered king. In the 16th and 17th centuries the Bundela rulers built huge palaces and temples here on the banks of the Betwa River. Then, for unknown reasons, they abandoned Orchha. Today it is little more than a village crowded with remnants of Bundela splendor.

There is no established tourist track, making it a great place to poke around. Take a flashlight so you can explore the underground rooms and passageways that riddle the ground below the town. Most of the sites can be seen at any time, but some are open only from 10 to 5; inquire at the Sheesh Mahal hotel (☎ 224).

Cenotaphs. Along the banks of the Betwa River, you can see 14 sandstone structures built in honor of the former rulers. *Next to Kanchana Ghat.*

Chaturbhuj Temple. Built in the 16th century to house the idol of the Hindu god Rama, it stands desolate because worshipers believed that the idol refused to be moved from the queen's palace, now the Ram Raja Temple (*see below*). *In town below fort.*

Dinman Hardaul's Palace. At this palace, you'll find some interesting underground rooms. The palace's **Phool Bagh** gardens have an ancient, intricate watering system. *In town below fort.*

Laxminarayan temple. This 17th-century mix of temple and fort architecture has vibrant murals on the walls and ceilings and offers lovely views of the surrounding country from its upper terrace. *½ km (⅓ mi) west of town.*

Ram Raja Temple. This massive pink palace-turned-temple is one of the only places in India where Rama is worshipped as a king, rather than as a god. *In town.*

Sheesh Mahal Fort-Palace Complex. At the end of a winding road just above the town, this impressive installation is approached by a multi-arched bridge. Among the structures here is the 16th-century **Raj Mahal** (royal palace), which has beautiful murals. The 17th-century three-story **Jahangir Mahal,** a palace blending Hindu and Mogul themes, was built especially to honor the visit of the Mogul emperor Jahangir. The **Rai Praveen Mahal,** a two-story brick palace named for the consort of Bundela king Indramani, has more readily accessible underground rooms. You can pick up an excellent self-guided audio tour of the complex at the Sheesh Mahal, the hotel (run by the Madhya Pradesh State Tourism Development Corporation, MPSTDC) located in the palace. *At top of winding road from town.*

Dining and Lodging

For price categories, *see* the charts for Other Areas *in* On the Road with Fodor's.

GWALIOR

$$$ Welcomgroup Usha Kiran Palace. Now a Heritage Hotel, this white palace, trimmed with filigreed sandstone, has served as both a royal guest house and a royal residence. Stand in the passageway and look out through the stone screen over the beautifully designed lawns and you will see the view granted the women of the royal family. The hotel exudes a gentle, old-time ambience. The Western-style rooms aren't opulent, but they're comfortable. Be sure to take a ride in the maharaja's buggy. ⌂ *Jayendraganj, Lashkar, Gwalior 474009, Madhya Pradesh,* ☎ *751/323993,* 🅵🅰🆇 *751/321103. 30 rooms, 10 suites. Restaurant, bar, indoor pool, badminton, croquet, horseback riding, billiards, meeting rooms. AE, DC, MC, V.*

$ MPSTDC Hotel Tansen. This white, two-story hotel is surrounded by pleasant lawns. The air-conditioned rooms have TVs, and the rooms without TVs have fans. This hotel isn't luxurious, but it's clean, and the staff is very friendly. Opt for a suite; the decorations, carpeting, and furniture tend to be better. ⌂ *6 Gandhi Rd., Gwalior 474009, Madhya Pradesh,* ☎ *751/340371. 36 rooms, 12 suites. Restaurant, bar, meeting room. MC, V.*

ORCHHA

Note: Because Orchha is under "Ram Rajya" (Lord Rama's rule), alcohol is forbidden in the city.

$ Betwa Cottages. These charming cottages, on the banks of the Betwa River, are newly built. They even have exhaust fans in the bathrooms. Each cottage has a little lawn outside, and the immaculate rooms have huge windows and are pleasantly furnished with comfortable beds and rugs on the floor. Some rooms are air-conditioned; the rest have fans. The chef in the hotel restaurant prepares excellent kebabs and Chinese food. ☎ *Orchha; reserve through MPSTDC, Gangotri, 4th Floor, T. T. Nagar, Bhopal 462003, ☎ 755/554340. 10 rooms. Restaurant. MC, V.*

$ **Sheesh Mahal.** This seven-room hotel, run by MPSTDC, is actually part of the fort-palace complex. It's a great way to experience Orchha's past. The rooms are simply furnished, but they are clean. Ask for room number 1, huge and regally decorated, which has a bathroom the size of many regular hotel rooms. There are no phones, TVs, or air-conditioning (you don't need air-conditioning here until March), but the rooms have fans. ☎ *Orchha; reserve through MPSTDC, Gangotri, 4th Floor, T. T. Nagar, Bhopal 462003, ☎ 755/554340. 8 rooms. Restaurant. MC, V.*

Getting There

A one-hour trip links Agra and Gwalior (120 kilometers/75 miles) on the daily Shatabdi Express. A 16-kilometer (10-mile) taxi ride takes you to Orchha.

Visitor Information

Gwalior and Orchha are both in Madhya Pradesh; contact the MPSTDC (☎ 755/554340 in Bhopal and 11/552384 in Delhi) for more information.

7 Calcutta

Calcutta is India's best city for walkers, with streets that tell stories. Old mansions, dripping with moss and spotted with mildew, remind us of the city's affluent history of cultures and people—Armenians, Bengalis, British, and Marwari merchants from Rajasthan. Vast bazaars reveal clues to today's Bengali culture, and pavement dwellers show the daily rhythm and rigors of their own difficult lives.

By Vikram
Singh

NOTHING CAN PREPARE A VISITOR for Calcutta. As the home of Mother Theresa and the birthplace of an empire, as a playground for the rich and a haven for the destitute, as a wellspring of creative energy and a center for Marxist agitation, Calcutta almost dares people to make sense of it. Whether it repels you or seduces you, Calcutta will impress itself upon you. To understand India today and learn from it, a visit to Calcutta is vital.

In 1690, Job Charnock, an agent for the East India Company, leased the villages of Sutanati, Gobindpur, and Kalikutta and formed a trading post to supply his company. Legend has it that Charnock had won the hearts of Bengalis when he married a local widow, thus saving her from *sati* (the custom that calls for a woman to throw herself on her husband's funeral pyre). Within a few years Charnock's son-in-law, Charles Eyre, acquired the land rights to the area for Rs. 1,300 from Sabarna Roy Choudhury, a local landowner. Through Charnock's venture, the British gained a foothold in what had been the Sultanate of Delhi under the Moguls, and the directors of the East India Company became Indian *zamindars* (landowners) for the first time. It was here, as traders and landowners, that British entrepreneurs and adventurers began what would amount to the conquest of India and the establishment of the British Raj. More than any other city in India, Calcutta is tied to the evolution and disintegration of the British presence.

The Bengali people—animated, laconic, intellectual, spirited, argumentative, anarchic, imaginative, and creative—have dominated the city and made it the soul of India for over 150 years. They were among the first to react to the intellectual and political stimuli of the West and have produced many of India's most respected filmmakers, writers, scientists, musicians, dancers, and philosophers. Having embraced 19th-century European humanism, Bengalis like Rabindranath Tagore and others revived their indigenous culture and made the first organized efforts to oust the British. Emotions here ran high early on, and agitation in Bengal broke away from Gandhian politics to choose terrorism—one reason the British moved their capital from Calcutta to Delhi in 1911.

Calcutta remained cosmopolitan and prosperous throughout the British period. But after Independence, it became a city of refugees, severed from one of its main sources of production: East Bengal. With partition, the world's center of jute processing and distribution (Calcutta) was separated from its production center (the eastern Bengali hinterland). For Calcutta and the new East Pakistan, partition was equivalent to separating the fingers of an industry from the thumb. In addition, natural disasters—normally cyclones and droughts but also, as in 1937, earthquakes—had often sent millions to the city in search of shelter, sustenance, and survival. But beginning with 4 million refugees after partition in 1947, politics added to the pressure. Conflict with China and Pakistan sent in millions more throughout the 1960s, and Pakistan's 1971 military crackdown alone brought 10 million temporary refugees to the city. By the 1970s, many saw Calcutta as the ultimate urban disaster. Riddled with disease and squalor, plagued by garbage and decay, the heart of the British Raj, the Paris of Asia, had quickly and dramatically collapsed. Or had it? Calcutta's entire metropolitan district covers over 426 square kilometers (264 square miles) and is home to over 12 million people. It comprises two municipal corporation areas (Calcutta and Howrah), 32 municipalities, 62 nonmunicipal urban centers, and over 500 villages, and it has not collapsed. As one local put it, "Calcutta is full of challenges, but there is hope and even fun in meeting those challenges." The city remains open, smiling, hopeful, and thoughtful. Amid the squalor there is dignity, and amid the crises there are ideas.

Numbers in the margin correspond to points of interest on the Calcutta map.

EXPLORING

Calcutta and Howrah (also known as Haora) straddle the Hooghly River, Calcutta on the east side, Howrah on the west. In Calcutta, the Howrah Bridge spills into Bara Bazaar, the vibrant wholesale market area that anchors the city's commerce. North Calcutta includes Bara Bazaar and the Calcutta University and extends to the distant neighborhood of Chitpur and the Jain Temple in Tala. The heart of Central Calcutta remains B. B. D. Bagh (Binoy-Badel-Dinesh Bagh, formerly Dalhousie Square), where commerce and government have been concentrated since British times. Central Calcutta also holds the expansive park, Maidan, the crowded bazaar at New Market, and the posh shops and restaurants on Park Street. At the south end of the Maidan you find the Victoria Memorial and Calcutta's racecourse. South Calcutta has the National Library and zoo in Alipore and the temple of Kali in Kalighat.

North Calcutta

The streets in northern Calcutta are more crowded and narrower than those elsewhere in the city. This is where the Indians lived while the British spread their estates east and south of Fort William and Dalhousie Square.

★ ❾ **College Street.** In the animated area around Calcutta University, the sidewalks of College Street are littered with bookstalls in which you may find nothing but can possibly discover something to treasure. The establishments here, such as the **Indian Coffee House** (15 Bankin Chatterjee St.), are crowded every night with students and intellectuals.

★ ❶ **Dakshineshwar Kali Temple.** Far to the north, this 19th-century complex with 13 temples is a major pilgrimage site to which devotees continue to flock to see the temples of Shiva, Kali, Radha, and Krishna. It was here that Ramakrishna received the spiritual vision that led him to renounce his Brahmin caste and preach the unity of all religious faiths and altruism for all people. His most famous disciple, Swami Vivekananda, went on to be a major force in the intellectual and spiritual growth of Calcutta and founded the Ramakrishna Mission, headquartered in the Belur Math *(see below)*. Ramakrishna's room here is a museum. *P.W.D. Rd., near Vivekananda Bridge.* ✹ *Dawn–10 PM.*

★ ❻ **Howrah Bridge.** The web of girders stretches 465 meters (1,500 feet) over the Hooghly. Its eight lanes of chaotic traffic include all manner of transportation—rickshaws, cars, scooters, bicycles, pushcarts, and animal-drawn carts—and bear 2 million people each day. The bridge seems more like a crowded bazaar than the main link between Howrah and Calcutta. Coming from the railway station, Howrah Bridge dumps you just north of Bara Bazaar (wholesale markets) in the old heart of Calcutta.

❸ **Kumartuli.** In this area countless potters work to create the millions of clay images that serve as idols for Calcutta's never-ending festival season. *Chitpur Rd.*

172

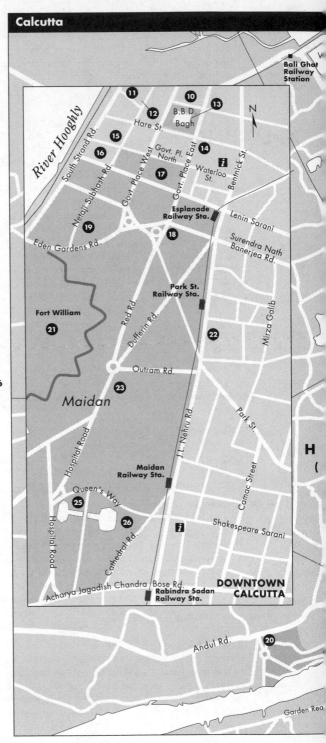

Calcutta

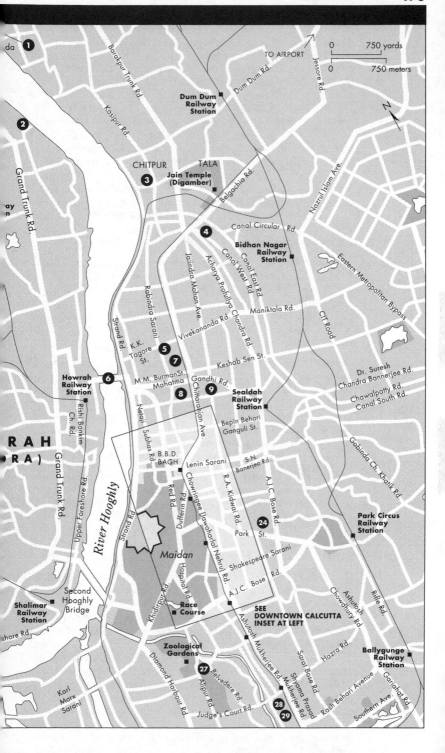

TO AIRPORT

0   750 yards

0   750 meters

**Dum Dum
Railway
Station**

Dum Dum Rd.

Baratpur Trunk Rd.

Kasipur Rd.

Grand Trunk Rd.

Jessore Rd.

Nazrul Islam Ave.

CHITPUR   TALA

**Jain Temple
(Digamber)**

Belgachia Rd.

Canal Circular Rd.

**Bidhan Nagar
Railway
Station**

Eastern Metropolitan Bypass

Canal East Rd.

Canal West Rd.

Acharya Profulla Chandra Rd.

Jatindra Mohan Ave.

Rabindra Sarani

Vivekananda Rd.

Maniktala Rd.

CIT Road

K.K.
Tagore
St.

M.M. Burman St.
Mahatma

Keshab Sen St.

Gandhi Rd.

Chittaranjan Ave.

Dr. Suresh
Chandra Bannerjee Rd.

Chawalpatty Rd.
Canal South Rd.

**Howrah
Railway
Station**

Strand Rd.

Rishi Bankim Ch. Rd.

**Sealdah
Railway
Station**

Bepin Behari
Ganguli St.

Gobinda Ch. Khalik Rd.

R A H

(R A)

Netaji Subhas Rd.

B.B.D.
BAGH

Lenin Sarani

S.N.
Banerjea Rd.

R.A. Kidwai Rd.

A.J.C. Bose Rd.

Grand Trunk Rd.

Upper Foreshore Rd.

River Hooghly

Strand Rd.

Red Rd.

Dufferin Rd.

Chowringee (Jawaharlal Nehru) Rd.

Park St.

Shakespeare Sarani

**Park Circus
Railway
Station**

**Shalimar
Railway
Station**

Second
Hooghly
Bridge

Maidan

Hospital Rd.

Khidirpur Rd.

A.J.C. Bose Rd.

**SEE
DOWNTOWN CALCUTTA
INSET AT LEFT**

Ashutosh
Chowdhury Rd.

Rifle Rd.

shore Rd.

Karl
Marx
Sarani

**Race
Course**

**Zoological
Gardens**

Diamond Harbour Rd.

Alipur Rd.

Belvedere Rd.

Judge's Court Rd.

Ashutosh Mukherjee Rd.

Sarat Bose Rd.

Shyama Prasad Mukherjee Rd.

Hazra Rd.

Rash Behari Avenue

Southern Ave.

Gariahat Rd.

**Ballygunge
Railway
Station**

★ ❼ **The Marble Palace.** One of the strangest buildings in Calcutta was the inspiration of Raja Rajendra Mullick Bahadur, a member of Bengal's landed gentry. Mullick constructed the palace in 1855, making lavish use of Italian marble. It's set behind a spacious lawn cluttered with sculptures that pay homage to Christopher Columbus, the Buddha, animals, Jesus Christ and the Virgin Mary, and Hindu gods. A large tank or pool near a small granite bungalow where Mullick's descendants still live, is home to ducks, peacocks, and ostriches. The palace has an interior courtyard, complete with a throne room where a peacock often struts around the seat of honor. The upstairs rooms are downright baroque. Enormous paintings and mirrors cover the walls, gigantic chandeliers hang from the ceilings, and hundreds of statues and oriental urns populate the rooms. Even lamps are detailed creations, especially those on the staircases, where enormous metal women are entwined in trees with a light bulb on each branch. Movie producers use the palace for Hindi films. *46 Muktaram Basu St., off Chittaranjan Ave.* ☛ *Free (you must get a pass from the West Bengal Tourist Office 24 hours in advance; tip your guide).* ⊙ *Tues., Wed., and Fri.–Sun. 10–4.*

★ ❽ **Nakhoda Mosque.** The massive red sandstone mosque, which can hold 10,000 worshipers, was built in 1926 as a copy of Akbar's tomb in Agra. Each floor has a prayer hall. From the top there is an excellent view of Calcutta. The streets below the mosque are crowded with stalls selling everything from paperback editions of the Quran to greasy kebabs. *Mahatma Gandhi Rd. and Rabindra Sarani.* ☛ *Free.* ⊙ *Daily sunrise–8 PM.*

★ ❹ **Paresnath Temple.** This Jain temple built in 1867 and dedicated to Sitalnathji, the 10th of the 24 *tirhankaras* (perfect souls), is a flamboyant structure filled with mirror-inlay pillars, stained-glass windows, marble floors in a floral design, a gilded dome, and chandeliers from 19th-century Paris and Brussels. In the garden are blocks of glass mosaics with European figures and statues covered with silver paint. It is an unusual place of honor for the ascetic Jains. *Badridas Temple St., near Raja Dinendra St.* ⊙ *Daily sunrise–noon and 3–7.*

★ ❺ **Rabindra Bharati University Museum.** Within the walls of Rabindranath Tagore's home, the university now fosters cultural activities. The complex holds a wealth of memorabilia as well. It was once the nerve center of Calcutta's intellectual activity. *6/4 Dwarkanath Tagore La.,* ☎ *33/239–6601.* ☛ *Free.* ⊙ *Weekdays 10–5, Sat. 10–1:30.*

Central Calcutta and the Maidan

The British first built Fort William in the middle of a dense jungle. When disagreements led the local Bengali ruler, Siraj ud-Daula, to attack and destroy the original fort, the British response was a quick decisive battle led by Robert Clive. Following the Battle of Plassey, which trasformed the British from traders into a ruling presence in 1757, the forest was cut down in order to provide a clear line for cannon fire should there be an attack. It is really from the year 1757 that modern Calcutta traces its history and from the new, inpenetrable Fort William (completed in 1773) that the city began its explosive growth. Starting just north of the fort, Central Calcutta became the commercial and political heart of the city. It is here that the British conducted business and here that they built their stately homes. The immense area cleared for British cannons is now Calcutta's 3-square-kilometer (1-square-mile) park, the Maidan. Central Calcutta today includes the entire Maidan, B. B. D. Bagh, and most of the commercial and residental areas east of the giant park.

★ **B. B. D. Bagh (formerly Dalhousie Square).** South of the Hooghly along
⑬ Netaji Subhash Road, around the **Lal Dighee** (red tank)—so named for
the color it turns around Holi, the festival of colors—are some of the
finest examples of Victorian architecture in Calcutta. For the most part,
the buildings are still offices (government or otherwise) and most interesting from the outside, even when admisssion is permitted. On the
⑩ north side of the square you find the **Writers' Building,** a dramatically
baroque set of bureaucratic offices. The original "writers" were the clerks
⑫ of the British East India Company. To the west is the **General Post Office** (GPO), its massive white Corinthian columns resting on the site of
the original Fort William, where the British were attacked in 1756 and
many officers imprisoned in the infamous "black hole of Calcutta." Next
⑪ door is the redbrick **Collectorate,** Calcutta's oldest public building. In
⑭ the northeast corner is **St. Andrew's Church,** built in 1818. Farther south
⑮ you come to **St. John's Church,** in which Charnock's mausoleum is found.
If the church is locked, you can call the vicar (☎ 33/248–3439). Con-
⑯ ⑰ tinue south from the square to reach the **High Court Building** and **Raj
Bhavan,** which is home to the Governor of West Bengal.

⑲ **Eden Gardens.** In the northwest corner of the Maidan, these gardens
are often crowded, but you can visit the picturesque Burmese Pagoda
and just relax for a while. If you head along Strand Avenue toward the
Hooghly from here, it is easy to get a brief, refreshing boat ride. As
you walk, boatmen will certainly approach you offering a "romantic"
ride. Be careful, as the boats are often quite rickety, and pay about Rs.
50 for a half hour. ☛ *Free.* ⊙ *24 hours.*

㉑ **Fort William.** The irregular octagon south of the Eden Gardens is surrounded by a moat almost 16 meters (50 feet) wide. Begun in 1757
after Robert Clive's victory at Plassey over Siraj ud-Daula, this fort was
meant to prevent any future attacks. The walls of the fort, as well as
the barracks, stables, and Church of St. Peter, have survived to this day
chiefly because the fort has never been attacked. The Indian government still uses the fort, and much of it is closed to the public.

★ ㉓ **Maidan.** Known as Calcutta's green lung, the expansive park is dotted with some of the city's most exciting attractions and is highly
prized by its citizens. Calcuttans are justifiably proud to have a clean,
open space for the public in the center of their concrete jungle. The
entire area came into existence when forests were cleared to give Fort
William a clear line of fire. It streches from the High Court in the north
(just south of B. B. D. Bagh) to the race course in the south (just north
of Alipore) and from the Hoogly River in the west to Jawaharlal Nehru
Road and the shops of Park Street in the east.

⑱ **Ochterlony Monument** (Sahid Minar). On the north end of the Maidan
stands the 49-meter (148-foot) high pillar commemorating Sir David
Ochterlony's victories in Nepal. The impressive monument has a rather
curious design: its base is Egyptian, the column is Syrian, and the
cupola is Turkish. Origins aside, it has been the site of many political
rallies and student demonstrations during Calcutta's turbulent post-
Independence history. *J. L. Nehru Rd., near Esplanade metro entrance.*

㉖ **St. Paul's Cathedral.** Built in 1847, it now has a steeple modeled after
the one at Canterbury Cathedral; previous steeples were destroyed by
earthquakes. Florentine frescoes, the stained-glass western window, and
a gold communion plate presented by Queen Victoria are of special
interest. *Cathdral Rd., east of Victoria Memorial,* ☎ *33/244–5756.*
⊙ *Sunrise–sunset.*

★ ㉕ **Victoria Memorial.** Red Road cuts south through the Maidan to this building, conceived in 1901 by Lord Curzon and constructed over a 20-year period. Designed in a mixture of Italian Renaissance and Saracenic architectural styles and surrounded by spacious gardens within the Maidan, this greatest symbol of the British Raj houses a collection of artifacts illustrating British roots in India. It includes Queen Victoria's writing desk and piano, Indian miniature paintings, watercolors, and Persian books. Today the white marble, streaked by pollution, and the grim statue of Queen Victoria out front seem to illustrate the decline of the Raj. *Queen's Way,* ☎ *33/248–5142.* ☞ *Rs. 2.* ☉ *Tues.—Sun. 10–4:30. Cameras and electronic equipment must be left in checkroom. Sound-and-light show Tues.–Sun. 7:15 and 8:15.*

Chowringhee and Park Street

★ The north may be the heart of intellectual Calcutta, but in the era of business-friendly communist governments, the slick commercial area east of the Maidan is the city's spinal cord. **Chowringhee,** now Jawaharlal (or J. L.) Nehru Road, runs along the Maidan, and Park Street intersects it halfway. Together, they mark the modern social center of Calcutta, with upscale boutiques, classy hotels, and many, many restaurants.

㉒ **Indian Museum.** India's oldest museum has one of the largest and most comprehensive collections in Asia. Known locally as *Jadu Ghar,* the "House of Magic," the museum has 36 galleries and one of the best natural-history collections in the world. The archaeology section has a representative collection of antiquities from prehistoric times to the Mogul period, including relics from Mohenjodaro and Harappa, the oldest excavated Indus Valley civilizations. The southern wing includes the Bharhut and Gandhara rooms (Indian art from the 2nd century BC to the 5th century AD), the Gupta and Medieval galleries, and the Mogul gallery.

The museum also houses the largest collection of Indian coins in the world. To see this display, get permission from the museum information desk. Gems and jewelry are also on display. The art section on the first floor has a good collection of textiles, carpets, wood, papiermâché, and terra-cotta pottery. A gallery on the third floor contains exquisite Persian miniatures, Indian paintings, and Tibetan monastery banners. The anthropology section on the first floor is devoted to cultural anthropology, but the museum plans to establish India's first comprehensive physical anthropology exhibit soon. Some interesting specimens on display are an Egyptian mummy donated in 1880 by an English seaman, a fossilized 200-million-year-old tree trunk, the lower jaw of a 26-meter (84-foot whale) and meteorites dating back 50,000 years. *27 J. L. Nehru Rd.,* ☎ *33/249–9853.* ☞ *Rs. 1 (free Fri.).* ☉ *Sept.–Apr., Tues.–Sun. 10–4:30; May–Aug., Tues.–Sun. 11–5.*

㉔ **South Park Street Cemetery.** On graves and memorials here you find a repository of British imperial history. People who lived as a part of the Raj from 1767 on are buried in this cemetery, and in the records of their lives you see the trials and triumphs of the building of an empire. *Park St. at Rawdon St., no* ☎. ☉ *Sunrise–sunset.*

Southern Calcutta

Calcutta's rich and powerful moved consistently south as the city grew more and more crowded and unpleasant. Here you find an interesting mix of large colonial homes, modern hotels and businesses, open space, and some crowded temple areas.

★ ㉙ **Kalighat Kali Temple.** Built in 1809, the Kali is one of Hinduism's renowned pilgrimage sites, containing shrines to Shiva, Krishna, and Kali, the patron goddess of Calcutta. Human sacrifices were reputed to be common in the last century, but only goats are slaughtered now and offered to Kali with Ganges water and *bhang* (an uncultivated hemp). As with many temples, technically only Hindus are allowed in the inner sanctum. *Kalighat Rd. (from Taj Bengal: south on Belvedere Rd., left on Judge's Court Rd,, right on Kalighat Rd.), no ☎. ☉ Daily sunrise–sunset.*

㉗ **National Library.** The massive Renaissance-style building houses miles of books and very pleasant reading rooms. The rare books section contains some particularly significant works, adding to the importance of this 2-million-volume library. *Belvedere, Alipore, ☎ 33/245–5381. ☉ Weekdays 9–8, weekends 10–6.*

㉘ **Nirmal Hirday** (Pure Heart). Mother Theresa's first home for the dying is now one among 300 affiliated organizations worldwide that take care of people in the most dire need. At the headquarters of the **Missionaries of Charity** (54A A. J. C. Bose Rd., formerly Lower Circular Rd., ☎ 33/244–7115) you can learn about Mother Theresa's work. She does grant audiences, but it can be inspiring just to see the joy among the people in one of the homes or refuges. *Next to Kali Temple.*

Howrah

Across the Hooghly from the old part of Calcutta, the Howrah district, which houses the massive train station, is a constantly expanding suburb.

★ ❷ **Belur Math Shrine.** This is the headquarters of the Ramakrishna Mission, a reform movement inspired by Ramakrishna Paramahansa, who died in 1886. Having forsaken his high-caste Brahmin heritage, he preached the unity of religious faiths and an adherence to altruistic values for all people. His disciple, Swami Vivekananda, established the mission in 1898. The Belur Math Shrine resembles a church, a temple, or a mosque, depending on the angle from which it is viewed. *Belur Rd., Howrah (2 km south of Vivekananda Bridge), no ☎. ☉ Daily 6:30–noon and 3:30–7:30.*

★ ⑳ **Indian Botanical Gardens.** Across the New Bridge (also known as the second Howrah Bridge, or officially, the Vidyasagar Setu) in Howrah are the massive Botanical Gardens, first opened in 1786. Darjeeling and Assam teas, both treasured the world over, were developed here. The banyan tree here is over 400 meters in circumference, among the world's largest. The gardens are so huge that you can even relax on Sundays. *Between Andul Rd. and Kurz Ave., Shibpur, Howrah, ☎ 33/660–3235. ☛ Free. ☉ Daily 1 hour after sunrise–1 hour before sunset.*

Off the Beaten Path

If you're an early riser, the historic northern part of Calcutta offers a few unusual morning activities. Just below and south of the Hooghly

★ Bridge along the waterfront is the **wholesale flower market.** Years of discarded vegetation make a soft green-and-brown carpet from which rickety stalls rise and onto which the colorful merchandise flows. Flowers are everywhere: on the ground, on people's heads, in carts and trucks, and on display. A tremendous bouquet will cost a few rupees. But get here early, while the bridge is still shrouded by mist and the representatives of florists and hotels, alongside people in charge of weddings and funerals, are carting away the fragrant stock. By 7 AM things start winding down, and by eight you may as well sleep in. If you managed the flower market early enough, there may still be time to visit what's left of the old Chinatown, north of Lal Bazar. Again, between 6 AM and 8 AM, the **Chinese market** is alive, supplying Calcutta's restaurants for the day. At this time the people with business here all enjoy breakfast: hot soup, dumplings (often filled with pork), and noodles. Breakfast on the street is a unique and tasty adventure. Think twice about the pork, though, especially if your stomach's not hardened yet.

★ An evening stroll on **Strand Road** along the Hooghly, especially near the New Bridge, is another simple delight in Calcutta. At sunset, the river and city look magical; it becomes a different town altogether.

SHOPPING

Some of the most interesting crafts in West Bengal are brightly painted terra-cotta figurines and bas-reliefs, as well as other pottery items. *Dokra* are cast figures made of clay and metal. Shells, bell metal, and soapstone are other mediums used frequently to make popular trinkets and figurines in Bengal. All sorts of textiles are available throughout Calcutta's bazaars and shops.

Shopping in bazaars around Calcutta is an adventure and a test of your ability to shake off touts. Part of **New Market** (officially called Sir Stuart Hogg Market, 19 Lindsay St., off J. L. Nehru Rd. behind the Oberoi Grand), which is over 110 years old, houses about 2,500 stores under one roof, selling cotton saris, Bankura clay horses, Malda brassware, leather from Shantiniketan, silk from Murshidabad, khadi cloth, poultry, cheeses, nuts, and other foods.

Head up Rabindra Sarani from Lal Bazar Road near the West Bengal tourist office, and you'll soon enter an Islamic world and shoppers' paradise. Women walk by in *burkas* (long tent-shaped robes), their eyes barely visible behind spiderlike veils. Men sit on elevated platforms selling Bengali *kurtas* (shirts) and pants, and colorful *lungis* and white *dhotis* (both wraps worn by men). Stands sell vials of perfume created from the essence of flowers. This street continues to be interesting all the way to Chitpur Road.

On or near Chitpur Road, you'll find potters and shops that make musical instruments. To the east is **Bowbazar,** home to Calcutta's jewelers.

Calcutta's Sunday auctions take place along Russell Street. A trip to the oldest auction house, the **Russell Exchange** (12C Russell St., ☎ 33/249–8974), or any of its neighbors will certainly be entertaining. For curios in a hurry, head to **Central Cottage Industries** (7 J. L. Nehru Rd.). The **Handloom House** (2 Lindsay St.) and **Manjusha** (7/1D Lindsay St.) sell all manner of textiles. The best bookstore in Calcutta is **Oxford Bookstore–Gallery** (17 Park St., ☎ 33/297–8509).

The following are some of Calcutta's better boutiques: **Ritu's** (46A Rafi Hamed Kidwai Rd., formerly Wellesley St.), **Esperance** (3A Judge's Court Rd., ☎ 33/479–3284), **Studio Appareli** (Park Center, 1st Floor, Park St.), **Zenon** (1st Floor, 113 Park St., ☎ 33/295405), **Kalyani** (238A A. J. C. Bose Rd., ☎ 33/403467), and **Espee Boutique** (37 Theatre Rd. ☎ 33/404393) all have fine creations for women. **Monapali** and the **Silk Route** (15 Loudon St., ☎ 33/406103) are two designer boutiques, under the same management, with lovely collections of saris and *salwar kameez* (the long, loose-fitting blouse and trousers popular throughout India) in cotton, satin, and silk. Designs are inspired by the Orient and enhanced with Indian motifs and artwork: batik, embroidery, *zardozi* (gold threading), handpainting.

SPORTS

Calcutta still puts class first when it comes to sports. The **Royal Calcutta Golf Club** (120 Deshpran Sahmal Rd., ☎ 33/473–2316) caters to the elite. For horse racing, the **Royal Calcutta Turf Club** (RCTC, 11 Russell St., ☎ 33/249–1109) has an old-world air of sophistication. Whether you want to watch or play, you can get information about cricket from the **Calcutta Cricket and Football Club** (19/1 Gurusaday Rd., ☎ 33/475–8721) and about polo from the **Calcutta Polo Club** (51 J. L. Nehru Rd., ☎ 33/242–2031.

DINING

Calcutta has a tradition of restaurants like no other Indian city. Recently, this has come to include some better sources for delicious Bengali cuisine, noticeably absent from most restaurants in the city. Two popular Bengali dishes are *macheer jhol* (fish stew) and *chingri malai* curry (prawns brilliantly cooked in coconut and spices). Thursdays in Calcutta are "dry" and meatless—no alcohol or red meat is served in most establishments. Calcutta-Mughlai describes the unique cuisine that has developed here since the influx of the Moguls in the 16th century. This is the most common type of food in Calcutta today; it's what you find in carts and stalls around the city. Staples include *champ* (chicken or mutton slowly cooked in large, thick-cast open pans), *biriyanis* (meat and rice dishes), and tandoori items, none of which resemble their namesakes in places like Oudh or Hyderabad. From vendors, the chief item is the now-ubiquitous Nizam, or Calcutta, roll, in which seasoned meats and chutneys are wrapped in thick *parathas* (rich Indian breads) with onions and sometimes even eggs. Not to be missed are Bengali sweets, which fill the life of every native. Sweet shops can be found everywhere, and the variety—from *payash* (a rice pudding called Kheer in north India) to *gokul pitha* (coconut cakes in syrup)—is truly tempting.

Many people say Calcutta's best Chinese food is found in the Chinese-populated leather-tanning area of Tangra, about a half-hour drive from the city center. If you decide to come here, you'll experience a side of Calcutta much rougher around the edges than even Howrah Station. Try **Ka Foo Lok**, **Kim Ling** or one of the many unnamed eateries.

For price categories, *see* the chart for Major Cities *in* On the Road with Fodor's.

What to Wear

Even in the finer restaurants, neat and tidy casual wear will stand you in good stead. During the day and at less expensive restaurants, shorts are even okay, but remember that in India shorts remain an eccentricity associated with foreigners.

Bengali

$$$$ **Aheli.** This newcomer is Calcutta's first upscale Bengali restaurant, and not surprisingly, it draws a crowd. In the intimate terra-cotta dining area, you can enjoy traditional Bengali delicacies like *maacher sorse paturi* (fish cooked with mustard paste) and chingri malai curry (prawns curried in coconut milk). ✗ *Quality Inn, 12 J. L. Nehru Rd.,* ☎ *33/243–0222. Dinner reservations advised. AE, DC, MC, V.*

Calcutta Dining and Lodging

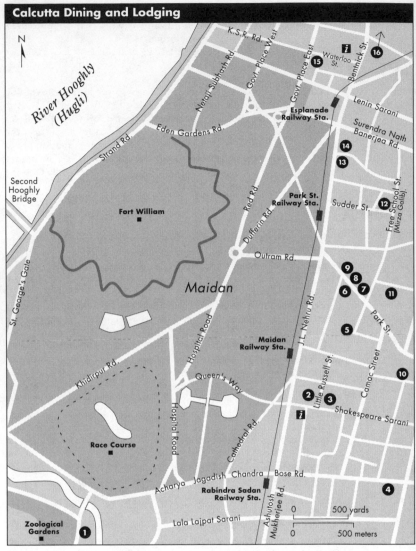

Dining
Aheli, **14**
Amber, **15**
Bar-B-Q, **8**
Blue Fox, **7**
Kebab e que, **2**
Ming Court, **13**
Moghul Room, **13**
Pemyangtse, **10**
Peter Cat, **6**
Saruchi, **11**
Shenaz, **5**
Sonorgaon, **1**
Zen, **9**

Lodging
Best Western
Kenilworth, **3**
Fairlawn Hotel, **12**
Hotel Airport
Ashok, **16**
Hotel Hindustan
International, **4**
Oberoi Grand, **13**
Park Hotel, **9**
Quality Inn, **14**
Taj Bengal, **1**

Reality check. Call home.

—— *AT&T USADirect® and World Connect®. The fast, easy way to call most anywhere.* ——

Take out AT&T Calling Card or your local calling card.** Lift phone. Dial AT&T Access Number for country you're calling from. Connect to English-speaking operator or voice prompt. Reach the States or over 200 countries. Talk. Say goodbye. Hang up. Resume vacation.

American Samoa	633 2-USA	Korea	009-11
Australia	1800-881-011	Macao ■	0800-111
Cambodia ■	1800-881-001	Malaysia*	800-0011
China, PRC♦♦♦	10811	Micronesia ■	288
Cook Islands ■	09-111	New Zealand	000-911
Fiji ■	004-890-1001	Palau ■	02288
Guam	018-872	Philippines*	105-11
Hong Kong	800-1111	Saipan†	235-2872
India♦	000-117	Singapore	800-0111-111
Indonesia†	001-801-10	South Africa	0-800-99-0123
Japan*■	0039-111	Sri Lanka	430-430

Taiwan*	0080-10288-0
Thailand♦	0019-991-1111

AT&T
Your True Choice

For a free wallet sized card of all AT&T Access Numbers, call: 1-800-241-5555.

All the best trips start with **Fodor's**.

$$ **Saruchi.** Popular and informal, this unpretentious restaurant, with
★ overhead fans and rows of tables, serves a Bengali menu of fish and
prawns. For years it was the only real restaurant to do so. The menu
changes daily, depending on the catch. ✗ *89 Elliot Rd.,* ☎ *33/249–
3292. No reservations. No credit cards.*

Cafés and Bakeries

Kathleen's (12 Mirza Ghalib St., ☎ 33/244–8614) has branches all
over the city, including one at 1 A. J. C. Bose Road. Every branch serves
excellent pastries as well as good tandoori items. The **Atrium** (in the
Park Hotel, *see below*) is the best new café around. It serves fresh, cre-
ative deserts and real cappuccino, and it is the *only* place in town that
even attempts Mexican food. Among the other bakeries that crowd the
city are **Upper Crust** (☎ 33/479–3667) and **Monginis,** which have out-
lets all over town, and **Flurry's** (18 Park St.).

Chinese and Southeast Asian

$$$$ **Ming Court.** In this restaurant, elegance reigns supreme, with deep red
pillars, silk-brocade robes framed on cool gray walls, and soft lighting.
The Chinese cuisine, with a Szechuan emphasis, is equally refined. Try
the prawns with oyster sauce or chicken in garlic sauce. ✗ *Oberoi Grand,*
☎ *33/249–2323. Dinner reservations advised. AE, DC, MC, V.*

$$$$ **Zen.** Art Deco meets postmodern in the sleek lines of this new South-
east Asian restaurant that serves dishes from throughout the region.
The Thai green curry and Indonesian specialties are unlikely to be on
any other menu in India. ✗ *Park Hotel,* ☎ *33/249–7336. Dinner reser-
vations advised. AF, DC, MC, V.*

$$$ **Bar-B-Q.** Another locally favorite restaurant, it has an unexpected mix
of German-chalet and Chinese decor. Bar-B-Q serves Cantonese and
Szechuan dishes. Try the crisp fried chicken served with a mild "surprise" sauce or the boneless chili chicken. ✗ *43 Park St.,* ☎ *33/299916.
Weekend reservations advised. AE, DC, MC, V.*

Indian and Multicuisine

$$ **Moghul Room.** Sleek, modern decor formed in marble is warmed by
Indian ghazals (Mogul-inspired romantic songs) nightly. The Indian cui-
sine, with an emphasis on Mughlai dishes, is superb. ✗ *Oberoi Grand,*
☎ *249–2323. Dinner reservations advised. AE, DC, MC, V.*

$$ **Sonorgaon.** The name of this restaurant means "golden village," and the
restaurant itself is a replica of a rural home, complete with a courtyard,
a well, a stringed cot mounted on the wall, and ethnic curios hung here
and there. The cuisine is Indian. Popular dishes include *kakori* kebab
(minced lamb kebab) and *murg Wajid Ali* (stuffed, pounded chicken breast
marinated in saffron and cooked in a mildly spicy sauce). ✗ *Taj Bengal, Alipur,* ☎ *33/248–3939. Reservations advised. AE, DC, MC, V.*

$ **Amber.** Upstairs with subdued lighting, this restaurant serves Continental
and Indian cuisine, including especially tasty Mughlai and tandoori dishes.
✗ *11 Waterloo St.,* ☎ *33/248–3018. Reservations advised. AE, DC.*

$ **Blue Fox.** This Calcutta landmark, popular with the smart set, is spa-
cious, with high ceilings and quiet decor in which to enjoy excellent
Indian and Continental dishes. The sizzlers and crab or lobster ther-
midor are excellent. ✗ *55 Park St.,* ☎ *33/249–7948. Reservations advised. DC.*

$ **Kebab e que.** In an outdoor courtyard with its own waterfall, this is
the best place in town for kebabs. Several varieties are served, and you

can watch the grills in action. ✕ *Hotel Astor, 15 Shakespeare Sarani,* ☎ *33/242–9957. AE, MC, V.*

$ **Peter Cat.** In this intimate restaurant, with white stucco walls, Tiffany-
★ style lamps, and soft lighting, you can enjoy good Continental and Indian dishes, especially tandoori. ✕ *18 Park St.,* ☎ *33/249–8841.
Dinner reservations advised. DC, V.*

$ **Shenaz.** This dark and crowded restaurant and bar serves delicious Pun-
★ jabi specialties and Mughlai food. The decor is from the fuzzy checker-
board period (you'll understand when you see it). Try any of the
kebabs or tandoori with some miniature naan (round flat bread). ✕
2-A Middleton Row, off Park St., ☎ *33/247–0686. AE, DC, MC, V.*

Tibetan

$ **Pemyangtse.** If you're not heading to Sikkim, try some food here. This
restaurant serves *momos* (tibetan dumplings) and *thugpa* (noodle soup)
daily. ✕ *1 Mehar Ali Rd.,* ☎ *33/404470. No credit cards.*

LODGING

Unless it's otherwise mentioned, hotels have central air-conditioning,
room service, and foreign-exchange facilities, and rooms have cable
TV and bathrooms with tubs. All swimming pools are outdoors. In addition, some luxury hotels have exclusive floors with special privileges
or facilities designed for the business traveler (*see* Special Hints for Business Travelers *in* Chapter 3, Business Travel in India).

For price categories, *see* the chart for Major Cities *in* On the Road with
Fodor's.

$$$$ **Oberoi Grand.** Impeccably maintained at the height of elegance, this
★ Victorian landmark in the center of town has a glowing white exterior and rich marble and dark wood interior. The rooms lack any
sense of antiquity, but they are spacious, with wall-to-wall carpeting
and modern bathrooms. The best rooms overlook the interior courtyard and swimming pool. ⌘ *15 J. L. Nehru Rd., Calcutta 700013,* ☎
33/249–2323, 🖷 *33/249–1217. 221 rooms, 11 suites. 3 restaurants,
bar, pool, sauna, health club, nightclub, business center, travel services.
AE, DC, MC, V.*

$$$$ **Taj Bengal.** Calcutta's new hotel is a fusion of modern India and its
cultural heritage. On the fringe of the city center, the Taj Bengal overlooks the Victoria Memorial Hall. You walk into an enormous atrium
lobby with a soft green stained glass ceiling eight floors overhead. Palm
trees reach up to the first open corridor, which wraps around the interior. Striking modern Indian art and artifacts or antiques are show-
cased everywhere. Unfortunately, the good-size bedrooms have classic
Western furnishings that eliminate the feeling of being in India once
the door is closed. ⌘ *34-B Bellvedere Rd., Alipur, Calcutta 700027,
West Bengal,* ☎ *33/248–3939,* 🖷 *33/248–1766. 228 rooms, 16 suites.
3 restaurants, bar, pool, health club, nightclub, business center, travel
services. AE, DC, MC, V.*

$$$ **Hotel Airport Ashok.** This modern hotel with pleasant rooms is primarily
for the traveler with just an overnight stop. Though clean and fresh,
the high-rise offers little excitment and is far from Calcutta's attrac-
tions. ⌘ *Calcutta Airport, Calcutta 700052,* ☎ *33/552–9111,* 🖷
*33/552–9137. 149 rooms, 9 suites. 2 restaurants, bar, pool, beauty salon,
business center, travel services. AE, DC, MC, V.*

$$$ **Hotel Hindustan International.** A completely renovated hotel, the HHI
provides modern rooms within its plain white walls. The best rooms

overlook the pool, but many have a good view of the city. ☎ *235/1 A. J. C. Bose Rd., Calcutta 700020,* ☎ *33/247–2394,* FAX *33/247–2824. 212 rooms, 12 suites. 3 restaurants, bar, pool, spa, health club, nightclub, business center, travel services. AE, DC, MC, V.*

$$$ **Park Hotel.** Inspired renovations have turned this hotel into one of the
★ best in Calcutta. In the long, white building in the thick of things on Park Street, everything has been designed with care. The lobby sparkles with mirrors and cut-glass chandeliers against rich wood and marble; the restaurants and café are full of creativity in everything from daring decor (black art-deco in Zen) to simple things like serving cappuccino. The comfortably furnished rooms are small, but the great location makes up for it. ☎ *17 Park St., Calcutta 700016,* ☎ *33/249–7336,* FAX *33/249–7343. 155 rooms, 10 suites. 2 restaurants, bar, pool, nightclub, business center, travel services. AE, DC, MC, V.*

$$ **Best Western Kenilworth.** Popular with repeat visitors to Calcutta, this hotel, with pretty gardens, has two attractive wings—one new in 1995 and the other refurbished. The common rooms are filled with marble and cheerful furnishings. The rooms are comfortable and spacious with standard anonymous decor. Continental breakfast is included. ☎ *1–2 Little Russell St., Calcutta 700071,* ☎ *33/242–8394,* FAX *33/ 242–5136. 110 rooms. 2 restaurants, bar, bookstore, business center, travel services. AE, DC, MC, V.*

$$ **Quality Inn.** Along one of the crowded streets near the Grand Hotel and New Market, this hotel has somewhat cramped rooms with decor long overdue for a facelift. Its best feature is the Bengali-specialty restaurant, Aheli. ☎ *15 J. L. Nehru Rd., Calcutta 700013, West Bengal,* ☎ *33/2430301,* FAX *33/2486650. 123 rooms. 3 restaurants, bar, health club, business center. AE, DC, MC, V.*

$ **Fairlawn Hotel.** If you want old-fashioned charm, stay in this Calcutta
★ landmark, built in 1801. The small hotel has great ambience, with memorabilia cluttering the walls. The rooms have chintz bedspreads and old-style tubs. In the hot months, ask for an air-conditioned room. Here you can feel as if you were living in the Raj. Meals are included. ☎ *13/A Sudder St., Calcutta 700013,* ☎ *33/245–1510,* FAX *33/244–1835. 20 rooms. Restaurant. AE, MC, V.*

THE ARTS AND NIGHTLIFE

The Arts

Calcutta is India's deepest well of creative energy. Artists here live in the inspiring shadow of greats, such as Rabindranath Tagore and Satyajit Ray; fortunately, this has not intimidated contemporary artists. To find out what is going on, check *Calcutta this Fortnight,* available from the West Bengal Tourist Office (*see* Visitor Information *in* Calcutta Essentials, *below*). Other sources include "City Watch" on page 3 of the *Statesman* and the *Sunday Telegraph's* magazine section. Check *Calcutta: Gateway to the East* for comprehensive listings.

English-language theater productions are regularly put on by the **British Council** (☎ 33/242–5478). Many auditoriums in town have regular performances of music, dance, and theater—the most Bengali of the performing arts. Venues include the **Academy of Fine Arts Auditorium** (Cathedral Rd., ☎ 33/242–1205), **Kalamandir** (48 Shakespeare Sarani, ☎ 33/247–9086), and **Rabindra Sadan** (Cathedral Rd., ☎ 33/248–9936). Many movie theaters around New Market feature regular English-language films. Generally, the tourist office is your best bet concerning current performances.

Galleries worth visiting in Calcutta include the **Academy of Fine Arts** (*see above*), the **Birla Academy of Art and Culture** (108–109 Southern Ave., ☎ 33/762843), **Chitrakoot Art Gallery** (55 Gariahat Rd., ☎ 33/475–6587), **Artage** (6/1A Palm Ave., ☎ 33/247–3284), and **Galerie 88** (28B Shakespeare Sarani, ☎ 33/247–2274).

Nightlife

Calcutta nightlife is making a comeback after 20 years of tight governmental regulation. Thus, although bars and clubs in hotels are still the best by far, unlike most Indian cities, Calcutta has a tradition to build on.

Bars and Lounges

The most attractive places to enjoy a nightcap are the Oberoi Grand and the Taj Bengal. The Pub at the Park Hotel is one of the few places where you'll find decent beer on tap; it makes a pleasant afternoon watering hole. The bar at the Fairlawn Hotel draws an interesting crowd and is much more social. Bars stay open until 11 PM or midnight and are closed on Thursday.

Discos

The dance clubs in Calcutta are technically open only to members and hotel guests, but you can get in either for a cover charge or a smile, depending on the doorman. the **Pink Elephant** (Oberoi Grand, ☎ 33/249–2323) is the oldest. **Someplace Else** (in the Pub at the Park Hotel, ☎ 33/249–7336) is new and small. **Incognito** (Taj Bengal, ☎ 33/248–3939) has a dance floor encased in glass. **Anticlock** (HHI, ☎ 33/247–2394) is the best. They all share such features as over-priced drinks, a high potential for asphyxiation on the cramped dance floors, and Indian interpretations of western pop music.

CALCUTTA ESSENTIALS

Arriving and Departing

By Car

People driving into Calcutta come from the southwest by National Highway (NH) 6, from the northwest by NH 2, or from the north along NH 34, which stretches into Sikkim and Darjeeling. NH 36 reaches Calcutta from Bangladesh.

By Plane

All international and domestic airlines use **Dum Dum Airport,** 15 kilometers (9 miles) from the city. Domestic service in India is changing rapidly; check with your travel agent for carriers other than **Indian Airlines** (☎ 33/260810).

BETWEEN THE AIRPORT AND CENTER CITY

When you leave the airport baggage claim area, you'll find counters where you can get free airport **shuttle** service to and from your hotel. A **taxi** downtown will take about 40 minutes and cost you around Rs. 300; use the prepaid taxi counter outside the baggage claim/customs. The **airport coach** (Rs. 50) goes to most of the better hotels and the city center; its counter is near the baggage-claim area.

By Train

An incredible number of trains roll into and out of **Howrah Junction** (1 block south of west end of Howrah Bridge, ☎ 33/220–3545 to 3554 or simply 131), which is divided into the neighboring old and new Howrah stations, every day from all over India. In Howrah Junction, a permanent population resides on the platforms among the ferocious crowds of travelers, vendors, and coolies; indeed, "platform children" attend school between the tracks at Howrah, taught to read and write by volunteers. The main reservation office (6 Failie Pl., ☎ 33/220–6811) has a foreign tourist office upstairs, open daily 9–1 and 1:30–4; buying tickets here (in foreign currency or with a valid encashment certificate for rupees) is a breeze. There are also ticket offices on the first floor of Howrah Station and second floor of New Howrah Station and in Kolighat (14 Strand Rd., ☎ 33/220–3496; first-class bookings) and Rajbindra Sadan (61 J. L. Nehru Rd., ☎ 33/247–2143). Only trains to and from northern destinations like Darjeeling use **Sealdah Station** (east end of Bepin Behari Ganguly St., ☎ 33/350–3535 or 33/350–3496), which has ticket sales on the first floor.

Getting Around

Despite its congestion, Calcutta is a fairly manageable city. The majority of Calcuttans rely on buses, trams, and the spotless metro. You will probably rely mostly on taxis, rickshaws, and your feet (the bus system is indecipherable, the rickety trams are good only for an early morning ride, and the metro is somewhat limited). Calcutta is not a good city for driving. Take a cab to or from the area you're visiting, and once there, rely on your feet or a sturdy rickshaw.

Many streets in Calcutta have been renamed in a rather haphazard way. Though some maps and street signs have only the new names, you're more likely to see just the old or both. Taxis and rickshaws use the names interchangeably, but, unsurprisingly, old names are still favored, as most of the new names are ridiculously long and obscure. The most important name changes are: Chowringhee Road is now Jawaharlal Nehru (J. L. Nehru) Road; Ballygunge Circular is now Pramathesh Barua Sarani; Bowbazar is now B. B. Ganguly Street; Harington Street is now Ho Chi Minh Sarani (and, in a poetic, Calcuttan manner, home of the U.S. and U.K. consulates; Lansdowne Road is now Sarat Bose Road; Lower Circular Road is now A. J. C. Bose Road; Rippon Street is now Muzaffar Ahmed Street; and Theater Road is now Shakespeare Sarani; a complete list is available at the Government of India tourist office or in *Calcutta: Gateway to the East*. In response to the painful traffic situation, authorities have made many roads in Calcutta one way and then the other way and then two ways at various times throughout the day and week.

By Auto Rickshaw
Auto rickshaws are cheaper than taxis, but they're not as easy to find in the city center. In heavy traffic they can be more efficient (and more filthy) alternatives.

By Hired Car with Driver
You can hire a car and driver from one of the travel agencies listed below or from the following car rental companies: **Travel Cars** (Queens Mansion, Garage No. 8, Park St., ☎ 33/249–4970), **Time Cabs** (13 Carmac St., ☎ 33/247–9574), or **Wenz** (in the Oberoi Grand, ☎ 33/278926). Expect to pay Rs. 400 to Rs. 600 for half a day (four hours) and 80 kilometers (50 miles), with an hourly and per-kilometer rate afterward. If you plan to do a lot in a little time, hiring a car can be useful, but just using taxis can work out to be less expensive and you do not need to find parking or to remember where you left your car (and driver).

By Rickshaw

Calcutta is the last city on earth to use enormous Chinese-style rickshaws pulled by men on foot. At least 1 million people depend on the hard-earned wages of these men for what little daily sustenance and shelter they get. Many pullers say they wouldn't trade positions with cycle-rickshaw wallahs and their debilitating saddles for anything. If you ever get the chance to pull a rickshaw, you will be horrified at how difficult it is, even when the rickshaw is empty. With that in mind, use these vehicles, don't rush your driver, and expect to pay a little more. The driver deserves it. (Nonetheless, negotiate ahead of time.)

By Subway

Calcutta's metro system, which has been evolving over the past 20 years, is clean and efficient. Only the central part of the system is complete, from Tollygunge to Central Station in Tiretta. Eventually, it will connect Dum Dum Airport with downtown. Tickets cost Rs. 2 to Rs. 3 and are available from machines and windows in every station. The metro runs daily until 9 PM and is crowded only at rush hour.

By Taxi

Taxis in Calcutta are less expensive than in the rest of India, and the meters are accurately calibrated. Assuming you don't get driven five times around the Maidan, the fare should be just. Traffic, unfortunately, plagues Calcutta, and at rush hour you may just want to find a sweet shop and wait until it's over.

Guided Tours

Orientation

The tourist offices *(see* Visitor Information, *below)* and any of the travel agents *(see above)* can arrange guided tours, both government and private.

Special-Interest

The most interesting tours in Calcutta are the walking tours of various neighborhoods given by the **Foundation for Conservation and Research of Urban Traditional Architecture** (CRUTA, 67B Beadon St., Calcutta 700006, ☏ 33/306127). Contact CRUTA in advance to arrange a tour.

Important Addresses and Numbers

Changing Money

American Express (21 Old Court House St., ☏ 33/248–4464); **Thomas Cook** (Chitrakoot Bldg., 230A A. J. C. Bose Rd., ☏ 33/247–5378). You can also cash traveler's checks at these banks: **Bank of America** (8 India Exchange Pl., ☏ 33/262352), Citibank (Tata Center, 43 J. L. Nehru Rd., ☏ 33/299220), **ANZ Grindlays Bank** (19 Netaji Subhas Rd., ☏ 33/242–8346), and the **State Bank of India** (33 J. L. Nehru Rd., ☏ 33/402430).

Consulates

United Kingdom. 1 Ho Chi Minh Sarani, Calcutta 700071, ☏ 33/242–5171, FAX 33/242–3435. **United States.** 5/1 Ho Chi Minh Sarani, Calcutta 700071, ☏ 33/242–3611, FAX 33/242–2335.

Emergencies

For any emergency contact your hotel, consulate, or the East West Clinic *(see* Chapter 4, Delhi).

Post Offices

General Post Office (1 Kolighat St., in B. B. D. Bagh; central branch, 8 Red Cross Sarani). Most hotels have mailing facilities and many sell stamps; it's best to take your mail to the post office and have the stamps canceled in front of you.

Travel Agencies

These agencies can help with bookings and supply cars with drivers: **American Express** (21 Old Court House St., ☎ 33/248–4464), **Thomas Cook** (Chitrakoot Bldg., 230A A. J. C. Bose Rd., ☎ 33/247–5378), **Ashok Travel and Tours** (c/o Government of India Tourist Office, 4 Shakespeare Sarani, ☎ 33/440901; Ashok Hotel, ☎ 33/552–9111), **Mercury Travels** (46-C J. L. Nehru Rd., ☎ 33/443555; Oberoi Grand, ☎ 33/249–2323).

Visitor Information

The **West Bengal Tourist Office** (3/2 B. B. D. Bagh East, Calcutta 700071, ☎ 33/248–8271; also counters at the airport and railroad station) is open Monday through Saturday, 10 to 5. The **Government of India Regional Tourist Office** (4 Shakespeare Sarani, Calcutta 700071, ☎ 33/242–1402) is extremely well equipped to help baffled travelers in Calcutta. Information is also available from the **Calcutta Information Centre** (1/1 Acharya Jagadish Chandra Bose Rd., Calcutta 700020, ☎ 33/248–1451).

Publications. Calcutta is overflowing with books, magazines, and pamphlets to make your stay easier. Try to find *Calcutta: Gateway to the East* (published by Travel House, Rs. 40), which describes the city in detail. Look for the free "Calcutta this Fortnight"—which lists cultural events, exhibitions, and tours—at the tourist offices.

8 Bhubaneswar

Bhubaneswar, capital of the eastern state of Orissa, is an easy-going temple city with 500 ancient shrines. Tiny and reasonably peaceful, it is also a town of artisans. On palm-sheltered side streets sculptors chisel statues from stone and weavers create silk or cotton hand-loomed fabrics.

THE CITY OF BHUBANESWAR, and all Orissa, a coastal state in eastern India south of West Bengal, is a tangibly religious place. Orissa was once a center of Buddhist learning and propagation, but changes in ruling dynasties brought changes in religion, moving away from Buddhism first to Jainism (circa 1st century BC) and then to Hinduism. It is now one of Hinduism's most active pilgrimage sites. In the temple cities of Bhubaneswar, Puri, and Konark, you can see the unusual Orissan temple architecture, with its strange shapes and fabulous and often erotic sculptures, which reached its peak in the 10th century. The Orissan temples, especially in Bhubaneswar, represent a coherent development of the Nagara style of Indo-Aryan architecture. Beyond the hundreds of distinctive temples, signs of religion appear everywhere. From village huts to taxis to five-star hotels, the smiling face of Lord Jagganath, an avatar of Krishna and Orissa's main god, appears everywhere.

The Orissan temple consists almost entirely of a vaulting spire thrusting upward among much lower turrets that seem like mere surface decorations. The temple contains the *jagamohan* (porch), which is usually square with a pyramidal roof and, immediately following the jagamohan, the *deul* (the cube-shape inner apartment that enshrines the deity and supports the soaring tower). Sometimes one or two more halls—the *natmandir* (dancing hall) and the *bhogmandir* (hall of offerings)—are set in front of the porch.

The architecture may seem heavy, but the sculpture on these temples is graceful, animated, often unashamedly erotic, and steeped in mythology. Most temples have a sacred tank in their yards in which worshippers bathe themselves for religious cleansing.

Orissa is also known as Utkala—"land of arts and crafts"—a title that holds true today, as you can see a fantastic variety of distinctive crafts wherever you go, from the gaily colored appliqué umbrellas of Pipli to twisted brass-wire *dhokra* figures made by the tribal people.

The countryside is lush with rice-paddy fields so green they seem to glow, as well as coconut, mango, banana, and cashew trees. These verdant stretches are punctuated with tiny villages of mud huts with thatched roofs, their dry brown walls decorated with traditional white paintings.

A final note: The coastal town of Puri is a heavily visited destination containing one of Hinduism's holiest sites, the Jagganath Temple—vast and beautiful, but strictly off-limits to non-Hindus, who can glimpse it only from a distance. (Even the late Prime Minister Indira Gandhi, who married a non-Hindu, was denied entrance.) Because accommodations and restaurants are of limited quality and the town's important sights are inaccessible, we do not include a more detailed section on Puri in this book. Puri can be rewarding to non-Hindu travelers who are studying Hinduism or who are members of the Hare Krishna sect and to young foreigners who come to do easily accessible drugs on the beach. It is also popular with people interested in witnessing Rath Yatra, the midsummer Car Festival, one of the most spectacular of India's temple fairs, attracting crushing hordes throughout its duration. Although Puri is also touted as a beach destination, it is not recommended if you prefer clean, uncrowded beaches.

Whether you're at the airport in Bhubaneswar or on a dirt path in a tiny artisan's village, keep in mind that Orissa is still one of India's less-

Bhubaneswar and Vicinity

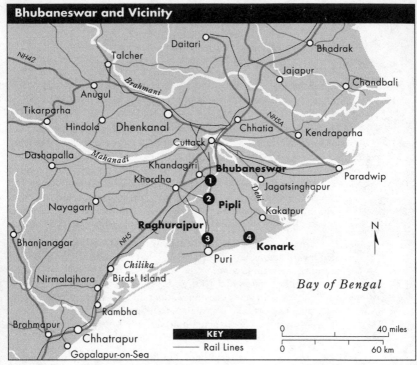

developed spots in terms of infrastructure and tourism facilities. Be patient and settle into a slower pace.

Numbers in the margin correspond to points of interest on the Bhubaneswar and Vicinity map.

EXPLORING

❶ Bhubaneswar, Orissa's capital, is known as India's city of temples. At one time, there were some 7,000 temples; today, only a fraction survive, but they still total over 400, in various stages of preservation. Unfortunately, the greatest of the city's temples, the Lingaraj, is off-limits to non-Hindus. Its huge tower is visible from miles away, but the closest foreigners will get to it is a viewing stand erected during the period of the Raj when Lord Curzon, the British viceroy, visited the temple.

Bhubaneswar's main temples are clustered in the old town within about 3 kilometers (1½ miles) of one another. If you enjoy walking, you can get around on foot. If you're not with a hired car and driver, bicycle rickshaws are a pleasant way to travel from temple to temple. Dhauli, however, is a bit farther out and up a hill, and is best reached by a taxi or hired car.

Upon entering one of Bhubaneswar's lovely temples, you may be harassed for money by the temple's priest, who will follow you around, grumbling, with a dog-eared notebook (a phony donation register) scribbled with names of foreign tourists and the amounts they've allegedly donated—with an extra zero tacked on the end to deceive you. The money is usually pocketed for the priest's own use, rather than for preserving the temple, but it's sometimes worth giving Rs. 10 or less to avoid the unpleasantness of being tailed by a cranky priest.

Consult the map for temple locations. admission is free; donations are solicited. The temples are open daily, sunrise to sunset; entrance into the inner sanctums of active temples may be restricted for half an hour or so during offering times (early morning, around noon, and late afternoon).

Bindusagar. The largest of Bhubaneswar's sacred tanks, in which worhippers religiously cleanse themselves, is surrounded by a stone embankment and was the central point around which Bhubaneswar's multitude of temples was built. Pilgrims believe that it is filled with water from every sacred stream and tank in India and can therefore wash away sins. *North of Lingaraj Temple.*

Brahmeswar Temple. The exterior of this 11th-century temple is sumptuously carved with scrolls of monkeys, swans, and deer; figures of gods and goddesses; and religious scenes. Over the entrance is a row of similar figures representing the nine planets. If you're lucky, you'll be shown around by a squat priest who will lecture to you intensely, almost aggressively, about the temple's carvings and their dizzyingly complicated symbolic significance in Hinduism. (He'll expect a tip.)

★ **Dhauli.** It was from the top of this hill, a few kilometers outside Bhubaneswar, that India's legendary king, Ashoka the Great, looked down, in 272 BC, over the verdant countryside littered with bodies after a giant battle. Overcome with horror, Ashoka underwent a transformation and, then and there, abandoned his warring drive to conquer and converted to the spirituality of Buddhism. He then began to propagate Buddhism throughout Orissa and India. The spot of Ashoka's vantage point and conversion is marked by the carving of the head and forelegs of an elephant emerging from a rock—said to be the oldest rock-cut sculpture in India (3rd century BC)—symbolizing the birth of Buddha and the emergence of Buddhism. Here, also carved into the stone, are the Ashokan edicts in which the once-ruthless warrior declared that all men are his children.

A bit farther up the hill is the **Shanti Stupa,** a Buddhist peace pagoda built jointly by Japanese and Indian Buddhist groups in 1972. Visible from most points in Bhubaneswar, the striking, white-domed building, topped with several umbrella-like protrusions, resembles a massive alien crustacean from below; from closer up, one senses how beautiful and peaceful it is. The view from here is lovely, of the Daya River curving through the green rice paddies and cashew trees.

Lingaraj Temple Complex. This giant 11th-century shrine is considered by religious devotees and art historians alike to be the ultimate in Orissan temple architecture. It is a world in itself, set in a huge walled compound, teeming with activity, that holds some 100 smaller votive shrines. Unfortunately, it is strictly off-limits to non-Hindus. The closest you'll get (if you're not Hindu) is the small, raised platform 100 yards away, from where you can strain to view its profuse exterior carvings, representing a high point of Hindu decorative art. Unfortunately, however, you are too far away to see the details. Dating from about 1050, the Lingaraj Temple originally consisted only of the porch and shrine; the dancing hall and the hall of offerings were added about 100 years later. The *vimana* (curvilinear tower), built without mortar, soars to a height of 45 meters (147 feet). Note: many enterprising locals post themselves at the foot of the platform stairs with a phony guest registry notebook and demand a donation for climbing the stairs. The money will not go toward the temple, let alone the stairs, but into their pockets. Nondonors are likely to be harassed.

★ **Mukteswar Temple.** Bhubaneswar's smallest temple was built in the 10th century. Its earthy red sandstone body is encrusted with intricate carvings, from emaciated, crouching sadhus (Hindu holy men) to voluptuous, buxom women bedecked with jewels. On the left side of the entrance, the statues of bearers grimace under the temple's monumental weight, which they've borne for 10 centuries. The Mukteswar's most distinctive feature is its *torana*, a thick-pillared, arched gateway draped with carved strings of beads and ornamented with statues of smiling women in languorous positions. This torana shows the influence of Buddhist architecture. Beyond it, set back in a shady yard, stands the **Kedareswar Temple,** with its 8-foot-high statue of Hanuman, the monkey god.

Parasurasameswara Temple. Built in AD 650, this small temple is the oldest of those remaining in Bhubaneswar and a perfect example of the pre-10th-century Orissan temple style—a high spire curving up to a point over the sanctum, which houses the deity, and the pyramid-covered jagamohan, where people sit and pray. The exterior is covered with wonderful carvings of Ganesh the elephant god and other deities and ornamentations.

★ **Rajarani Temple.** Standing by itself in green rice fields, set far in from the road, this 11th-century temple is perhaps the most harmoniously proportioned one in the city and definitely the most peaceful. The Orissan king who created the Rajarani died before its finishing touch—namely, a deity—was placed, leaving its sanctum sanctorum eternally godless, yet filled with a vacant peace. As a result, there are no aggressive priests. The temple's carvings are lovely, with dragons tucked into cracks, enchanting erotic couples, and beautiful women smiling with a distinctly nonstony warmth. A small tip to the gardener-caretaker will also get you inside.

Tribal Museum. This small, informal museum, run by the state's tribal research institute, provides a glimpse into the traditions and daily practices of many of Orissa's 62 tribes. Set back in a garden, several thatched-roof huts, constructed in various tribal styles, house jewelry, ornaments, weapons, figurines, dresses, and other tribal objects—many still in use today, but some already phased out of daily tribal life as the modern world seeps in. *Tribal Research and Training Institute, National Hwy. No. 5, CRPF Sq.,* ☎ *0674/403649.* ☛ *Free.* ☉ *Mon.–Sat. 10–5; closed 2nd Sat. of month.*

Vaital Temple. This 8th-century structure, near the Bindusagar tank, is one of the area's earlier temples. Unlike others in Bhubaneswar, it is devoted to tantric goddesses, and its two-story, barrel-shape roof shows the influence of south Indian architecture.

TIME OUT After temple touring, for a cheap, filling snack with an interesting twist, take a taxi or rickshaw to the massively popular **Guvinda Restaurant** (Iskon Temple, National Hwy. No. 5, near Oberoi Hotel, ☎ 674/404283), the International Hare Krishna temple's in-house eatery, known for its simple, hygienic, strictly vegetarian meals (Rs. 10) served on metal *thali* trays. Remember that it's a religious place, not a bona fide restaurant: leave your shoes at the entrance gate and prepare to eat with your hands.

SHOPPING

Bhubaneswar's main shopping area is **Capital Market,** along the central stretch of Raj Path (a road). Several good fabric and handicrafts shops, including the two government emporiums, are in the **Tower Market** shopping complex off the eastern side of Raj Path. All along Raj Path are small stalls selling everything from bananas to bedcovers—mostly wares for local shoppers. Most stalls are open every day from around 6 AM to 10 PM.

Handicrafts

Kalamandir (3 Western Tower Market Bldg., ☎ 0674/407483) is one of eastern India's largest fabric and clothing shops, where you'll find traditional Orissan texiles, as well as a variety from all over India. **Kalinga Art Palace** (Plot 2132/4323, Nageswar Tangi, ☎ 0674/51454) specializes in tribal artwork, with a distinctively large and good quality collection of brass-wire dhokra objects, both new and antique. **Odissika** (265 Lewis Rd., ☎ 0674/412982, 0674/480412) stocks a good variety of stone carvings, terra-cotta objects, dhokra, and a host of other authentic Orissan handicrafts. **Orissan State Handloom Weaver's Cooperative Society (Boyanika)** (Western Tower Market Bldg., Hall 2, Ashok Nagar, no phone) has lovely saris, bedcovers, and fabrics in many different Orissan styles and textures. **Sudarshan Arts and Crafts Village** (CB–5, Nayapalli, ☎ 0674/402052) is a working stone-carving teaching center where you can stroll through the small yard and watch young artisans squatting in the shade chiseling their creations out of 10 different types of stone. **Utkalika** (Orissa State Handicrafts Emporium, Eastern Tower Market Bldg., Ashok Nagar, ☎ 0674/400187), the government's fixed-price emporium, sells a great selection of every type of Orissan handicraft.

DINING

For price categories, *see* the Chart for Other Areas *in* On the Road with Fodor's.

$$ Chandini. Its name means canopy, and in this elegant restaurant, an
★ antique chandini is suspended from the center of the ceiling. Paintings of Rajput heroes adorn the walls, along with old daggers. *Jharokahs* (carved stone Indian bay-window frames) are mounted on the walls. The kitchen serves delicious, somewhat small, portions of Indian cuisine, from tangy, light tandoori items to richly gravied meats. Try the traditional Orissan *dahi machli* (Bay of Bengal fish cooked in creamy curd sauce). ✗ *Oberoi Hotel, Nayapalli,* ☎ *0674/440890. Reservations advised. AE, DC, MC, V.*

$$ Executive-Swosti. This dark, cozy restaurant is a great place to sample traditional Orissan fare. With a few hours' advance notice, the chef will prepare specialties such as *santula* (mixed vegetables in coconut sauce) and *dahi machli* (boneless fish fillets in rich curd gravy). For dessert, a rich square of *gajor ka halwa* (carrot halva) is buttery, sweet, and divine. Brown leather and mirrors create a dark '80s ambience, but it's brightened by green-and-white gingham linens and friendly service. The kitchen also serves Chinese and Continental food. ✗ *Best Western Swosti, 103 Janpath,* ☎ *0674/404395. Dinner reservations advised. AE, MC, V.*

$ Cooks' Kitchen. Two young locals decided to open this very simple second-floor eatery based on the tremendous popularity of their tiny fast-food stand downstairs. The good selection of Indian and Chinese food includes *paneer pasanda* (chunks of meaty curd with a zesty stuffing and a thick, tomato sauce). ✗ *260 Bapuji Nagar,* ☎ *0674/400025. No credit cards.*

$ Dawat. Once your eyes adjust to the darkness, you'll find yourself in a small dining room with white stucco walls and royal blue tablecloths. Locals and tourists like Dawat for its slightly more upscale atmosphere (by Bhubaneswar standards) and for its Chinese food and good, reasonably priced Indian fare. Try vegetable *dopiaza,* a spicy mix of fresh vegetables cooked so they're still slightly firm. ✗ *620 Sahid Nagar,* ☎ *0674/407027. MC.*

$ Hare Krishna Restaurant. You won't find any onions, garlic, or oil in the tasty fare served at this popular, second-floor restaurant, which observes the strictest culinary vegetarian rules of the Hare Krishna sect. Cool (it's known for its good air-conditioning) and decidedly dark, the dining room has dark-mirrored walls and barely lit lamps. A single green bulb spotlights the charming fountain at the front of the room—a sculpture of Shiva emerging from rocky Mt. Kailash with the River Ganga (Ganges) flowing out of his hair. Try "Keshaba's favorite" (vegetables sautéed in spicy tomato gravy) or *"Makhan chor* delight" (grated cheese and carrots simmered in a mild tomato gravy). Finish with *kheer* (sweet rice and milk pudding). ✗ *Lalchand Market Complex, Station Sq.,* ☎ *0674/403188. No credit cards.*

$ Venus Inn. In this age-old popular upstairs dining hall, the menu offers an endless variety of *dosas* (south Indian stuffed crêpes) and *uttappams* (south Indian-style pizzas). Try the *rawa masala sada* dosa, stuffed with a slightly salty and sweet grain mixture or butter coconut uttappam, an Orissan specialty. A small, dark room filled with blue Formica-topped tables, this eatery is best suited for a quick, hearty lunch or snack, rather than a lingering, main-event dinner. ✗ *217 Bapuji Nagar,* ☎ *0674/401738. No credit cards.*

LODGING

Bhubaneswar's two best, and most recently built, hotels are significantly better than the others. For price categories, *see* the chart for Other Areas *in* On the Road with Fodor's.

$$$ Mayfair Gardens. Opened in spring 1995, the newest of Bhubaneswar's hotels is also among the best. Impressively designed to feel like an elegant garden, the three-story beige stucco building is fronted by stately pillars and a large terrace topped with a profusion of magenta bougainvillea. The lobby and hallways, lined with windows, are sunny and filled with leafy plants in terra-cotta pots. The contemporary rooms are done up with Orissan-print bedspreads in dark greens and maroons. ⌕ *Janpath, Bhubaneswar 751001, Orissa,* ☎ *0674/405412,* ℻ *0674/400053. 77 rooms, 3 suites. Restaurant, bar, coffee shop, pool, beauty salon, sauna, exercise room, dry cleaning, laundry service, business services, meeting rooms, travel services. AE, DC, MC, V.*

$$$ Oberoi. The lobby's lights are tucked inside huge brass temple bells in
★ this handsome two-story hotel. A balcony, guarded by carved temple lions, is mounted atop exquisite sandstone pillars. Even at full occupancy, the public areas feel bathed in a hushed quiet, with a peaceful air of cool calm. The rooms, overlooking either the pool or extensive landscaped gardens, have attractive modern teak furnishings, complemented with lovely Orissan hand-loomed fabrics, brass lamps, and framed prints of Bhubaneswar's temples. Special, unusual offerings include a jogging path that winds through the grounds and, for night movers, two floodlit tennis courts and a pool with no designated closing time. ⌕ *Nyapalli, Bhubaneswar 751013, Orissa,* ☎ *0674/56116,* ℻ *0674/56269. 64 rooms, 6 suites. 2 restaurants, bar, pool, 2 tennis courts, jogging,*

shops, baby-sitting, dry cleaning, laundry service, business services, meeting rooms, travel services. AE, DC, MC, V.

$ **Best Western Swosti.** A well-run, friendly hotel, the Swosti offers efficient, courteous service and reasonable rates. The cozy lobby is decorated with Orissan *pata chitra* (exquisitely detailed, fine-lined religious paintings on specially prepared cloth, using only vegetable and natural dyes). The hotel is right on one of Bhubaneswar's main thoroughfares, close to the train station; for maximum quiet, ask for a room in the back. All the good-size rooms are clean, with plain, contemporary decor; most have bathtubs. ☎ *103 Janpath, Bhubaneswar 751001, Orissa,* ☎ *0674/404178 or 0674/404397,* ℻ *0674/407524. 53 rooms, 3 suites. 2 restaurants, bar, patisserie, laundry service, meeting rooms, travel services. AE, DC, MC, V.*

$ **Hotel Kalinga Ashok.** The lobby of this government-operated hotel is full of appealing Orissan touches, including a miniature replica of Konark's chariot temple (*see* Konark, *below*) tucked in the corner. Room furnishings and decor are slightly worn but comfortable, with dark-colored carpeting and coordinating drapes and bedspreads with large floral designs. ☎ *Gautam Nagar, Bhubaneswar 751014, Orissa,* ☎ *0674/53318 or 0674/53830,* ℻ *0674/410745. 58 rooms, 6 suites. 2 restaurants, bar, laundry service, meeting rooms, travel services. AE, DC, MC, V.*

$ **Hotel Prachi.** This boxy, three-story hotel's modest rooms lack its lobby's Orissan touches and instead have simple Western, slightly worn decor of dark wood furniture and plain carpeting in pea green or orange-brown. Ask for a room overlooking the pool and for a bathroom with a tub, if that's your preference. ☎ *6 Janpath, Bhubaneswar 751001, Orissa,* ☎ *674/402467,* ℻ *674/403287. 48 rooms. Restaurant, 2 bars, pool, beauty salon, exercise room, laundry service, meeting rooms, travel services. AE, DC, MC, V.*

THE ARTS AND NIGHTLIFE

The Arts

Odissi, the classical dance form of Orissa, is perhaps the most lyrical style of Indian dance, flowing with graceful gestures and postures. When you see a performance, it's as if the lovely sculpted dancers on the Sun Temple at Konark (*see* Excursions from Bhubaneswar, *below*) have suddenly come to life. In addition to classical Odissi dance, folk dances and tribal dances are still performed during festival times throughout Orissa. There aren't yet any regular cultural performances, however. For information, contact the Orissa Department of Tourism (*see* Bhubaneswar Essentials, *below*) or the College of Dance, Drama, and Music, near Rabindra Mandap.

Nightlife

Most people congregate in hotel bars for a nightcap or a post-temple-touring beer. The bars at the Oberoi and the Best Western Swosti are the best bets.

EXCURSIONS FROM BHUBANESWAR

Konark

❹ The sleepy beach town of **Konark** is home to one of India's most fab-
★ ulous temples—the **Sun Temple** or "Black Pagoda," so named because

of the dark patina that has covered it over the centuries. Legend shrouds the Sun Temple. Constructed in the shape of the sun god's chariot in the 13th century by King Narasimha, probably as much as a monument to himself as to honor Surya, the sun god, it is an architectural and engineering wondery. Today, only half the main temple and the audience hall approximate the Sun Temple's original shape. The temple once consisted of a dancing hall, an audience hall, and a tremendous tower that soared to 69 meters (227 feet) high but had fallen to ruin by 1869. Then the audience hall had to be filled with stone slabs and sealed off to prevent its collapse. The temple's location on sand, near the sea, which has since receded 3 kilometers (2 miles) from the site, is majestic; but the salty air and the softness of the sand dunes have taken their toll.

The Sun Temple is constructed in the form of a chariot with 24 wheels pulled by seven straining horses. Every surface of it is intricately carved with some of the most fantastic sculpture to be seen in India. Platforms, horses, colossal mythical animals, whimsical depictions of daily life, war, trade, erotic sculptures of amorous dalliances—the panoply of a culture's finest instincts: its imagination, mythology, history, and knowledge of the life cycle. Each structural feature of the temple has a hidden meaning. The seven horses of the chariot represent the seven days of the week, the 24 wheels are the 24 fortnights of the Indian year, and the eight spokes of each wheel are the eight *pahars* into which the ancients divided day and night.

Try to arrive between 7 and 8 AM, before the busloads of pilgrims and other tourists. The Archaeological Survey of India provides a guide service, but ask to see the guide's identification badge, as many less-informed freelance guides are eager to take you around. *64 km (40 mi) southeast of Bhubaneswar.* ☛ *Free.* ☉ *Daily sunrise–sunset.*

Arriving and Departing

Konark is 64 kilometers (40 miles) from Bhubaneswar. It's best and most convenient to go by hired car with a driver, so that you can gaze out at Orissa's verdant, rolling countryside and colorful people and have the freedom to stop in villages like Pipli (*see below*) along the way. The trip takes about 1½ hours. Any of the tour operators and travel agencies in Bhubaneswar (*see* Bhubaneswar Essentials, *below*) can arrange the trip for you.

Visitor Information

A tourist information officer at the **Yatri Nivas** (☎ 67581/8820), the new Orissa Tourism Development Corporation (OTDC) guest house just before the temple, is on duty Monday through Saturday, 10 to 5 (closed second Saturday of the month), but the guest house staff can help travelers 24 hours a day. At the entrance to the temple site, you can hire a tour guide from the Archaeological Survey of India to show you around (check his or her ID). The going rate is only Rs. 20 per person.

Pipli

❷ The little village of **Pipli** 16 kilometers (10 miles) southeast of Bhubaneswar is famous throughout India for its brightly colored appliqué work. Dozens of shops line both sides of its street, each crammed with piles of cheery wall hangings, bedspreads, lamp shades, bags, beach umbrellas, and more in patchworks of bright greens, yellows, blues, and reds. You can watch the village artisans at work sewing in some of the shops.

Raghurajpur

★ ❸ One "must-see" village is **Raghurajpur,** about 44 kilometers (27 miles) from Bhubaneswar heading south toward Puri (just under a two-hour drive). In this idyllic village set back from the main road, every dwelling is owned by an artisan. The art you discover—stone and wood carvings, pata chitra, *tala patra* (intricately etched and painted artwork on palm leaves)—is worthy of a visit. If you're interested, the artists will demonstrate how they create their crafts. The pata chitra artists, for example, show you how they do everything from scratch—from the preparatory rubbing of a specially prepared cloth with tamarind-seed gum and stones to making razor-fine strokes of color with natural dyes made from plants and crushed stones. Even here, prices are raised for tourists, but they can be brought down to lower than you'd pay anywhere else. Bargain: it's not rude; they expect it. Expect to pay in rupees. Most artisans accept customers daily from around 9 to 6, with a lunch break between 1 and 3.

TIME OUT For a bite to eat before heading back to Bhubaneswar, you can go to one of the hotel restaurants in Puri, just 12 kilometers (10 miles) down the road. Those in the **Mayfair Beach Resort** (Chakratirtha Rd., ☎ 6752/24041) and the **Hans Coco Palms Hotel** (Swargadwar Gourbarsahi, ☎ 6752/2638) stand out.

BHUBANESWAR ESSENTIALS

Arriving and Departing

By Plane
Bhubaneswar Airport is about 5 kilometers (3 miles) from the center of town. At press time (summer 1995), only **Indian Airlines** (☎ 674/406472, 674/400533; airport ☎ 674/401084) was operating flights to Bhubaneswar from Delhi, Calcutta, and Hyderabad.

Between the Airport and Center City. The trip into town takes about 15 to 20 minutes. Most hotels offer free **shuttle** service if they're informed of your flight information in advance.

White Ambassador **tourist taxis** wait outside the terminal. Fares are theoretically fixed, but be sure to agree on a fee before setting out. The fare to a central hotel should be around Rs. 75; to the Oberoi, slightly farther, about Rs. 110.

Getting Around

Hiring a car and driver for a half or full day is inexpensive and the most convenient way to get around the city; you'll avoid the hassles of haggling over fares with taxi or rickshaw drivers.

By Auto Rickshaw
Auto rickshaws are cheaper and slower than taxis, but quicker through heavy traffic. The same fare rules apply as for taxis.

By Bicycle Rickshaw
For short distances, bicycle rickshaws can be fun, a delightfully Indian way to go. Negotiate a fare with your pedaler before he pushes off; keep in mind that these men work hard for the money.

By Hired Car with Driver
You can hire a car and driver from a travel agency (*see below*). Four hours of local sightseeing will cost about Rs. 180 with a non-air-conditioned

Ambassador car and around Rs. 600 with an air-conditioned car. For short excursions covering over 10 kilometers (6 miles) per hour, figure about Rs. 3 per kilometer (Rs. 7 for a car with air-conditioning), with a halt charge of Rs. 10 per hour.

By Taxi

Taxis in Orissa don't have meters, so you have to bargain for every ride. Ask your hotel for the appropriate taxi fare and then negotiate.

Guided Tours

Private Guides

The best way to get the most out of your sightseeing is to hire a private tourist guide. The most knowledgeable and English-proficient guides are those trained by the Government of India Tourist Office. You can hire one from the OTDC or the Government of India Tourist Office (*see* Visitor Information, *below*) for around Rs. 250 per half day and Rs. 500 for a full day (eight hours). An additional charge of Rs. 800 for food and accommodations is levied for overnight stays.

Special-Interest Tours

A number of travel agents operate tours of various fascinating tribal areas in Orissa, as well as to villages that are famous for their crafts. *See* Tour Operators *in* Chapter 2, Special-Interest Travel in India.

Shopping

Orissa is renowned for its ancient handicraft tradition.

Look for pata chitra (finely wrought temple paintings); tala patra (palm leaf art); dhokra (adorable primitive animal and human figures of twisted brass wires made by tribal families); *tarkashi* (exquisite silver filigree jewelery and objects, created mostly in Cuttack, north of Bhubaneswar); and gaily colored appliqué work from the village of Pipli. Shopping can mean great sidetrips into the beautiful hidden Orissan villages that are home to master craftsmen. (*See* Excursions, *above*.)

As in most of India, tourists are subject to grossly inflated prices—even in remote artisan villages. Start bargaining at half the original price and you may end up with a 30% to 40% "discount." Although initially it may seem inappropriate, even rude, to start bargaining over unique pieces of art that venerable old artisans display for you in their huts, don't worry; it's expected. In Pipli, competition drops the rate of initial price inflation. Here, you'll only need to baragain over 5% to 10%. If you shy away from haggling, you can find good artifacts at fixed rates at the government emporiums.

Dining

In Bhubaneswar and Orissa's other towns and resort areas, expect good food at low prices and only basic, simple-looking restaurants. You'll find fresh seafood and a profusion of excellent vegetables, which benefit from Orissa's mineral-rich soils. Unfortunately, you won't find many restaurants serving large varieties of traditional Orissan food. Most places listed above, however, offer some Orissan specialties, which are definitely worth sampling. Look for curries prepared with coconut milk, creamy gravies made with curd, and delicious *baigan* (eggplant) and *bhindi* (okra) vegetable dishes.

What to Wear
Casual, neat clothing is appropriate for Bhubaneswar restaurants.

Lodging

For the time being, travelers can enjoy lower lodging rates in Bhubaneswar and environs than in more heavily traveled parts of India.
Unless otherwise mentioned, hotels have central air-conditioning, room
service, doctors on call, and foreign-exchange facilities, and rooms have
cable TV and bathrooms with tubs.

Important Addresses and Numbers

Changing Money
Most Western-style hotels have foreign-exchange facilities for their guests.
You can also cash traveler's checks at the various national banks in
Bhubaneswar. Try the main branch of the **State Bank of India** (near
Market Building). Banking hours are Monday through Friday, 10 to
2, and sometimes Saturday 10 to noon.

Emergencies
For any emergency, contact your hotel, embassy, or the East West
Clinic (*see* Chapter 5, Delhi). Police, ☎ 100; fire, ☎ 101; ambulance,
☎ 102.

Travel Agencies
Many tour operators offer trips to this part of India (*see* Tour Operators *in* the Gold Guide *and* Chapter 2, Special-Interest Travel in India).
These travel agencies can help with bookings and supply cars with drivers.
The **Orissa Tourism Development Corporation** (OTDC, Panthanivas,
Old Block, Lewis Rd., ☎ 674/412449), has reliable cars and drivers
and conducts several good sightseeing tours of Bhubaneswar and the
whole region, all at reasonable rates. **Swosti Travels** (103 Janpath, ☎
674/407470 or 674/408738, FAX 674/407524) is a well-established
local company with strong experience in the region. Also try **Mercury
Travels** (in the Oberoi Hotel, Nayapalli, ☎ 674/440890), **Sita World
Travels** (14a Bapuji Nagar, Janpath, ☎ 674/404408), or **Discover Tours**
(463 Lewis Rd., ☎ 674/57377).

Visitor Information
The Orissa Department of Tourism (5 Jayadev Marg, near Panthanivas, Bhubaneswar 751002, ☎ 0674/50099; Bhubaneswar airport, ☎
0674/404006; railroad station, ☎ 0674/404715) is the best source of
information on the state. The main office is open Monday through Saturday, 10 to 5 (closed second Sat. of month). **The Government of India
Tourist Office** (B-21, B. J. B. Nagar, Kalpana Area, Bhubaneswar
751014, ☎ 0674/412203; Bhubaneswar airport, no ☎) is also helpful and is open Monday through Friday 10 to 5.

9 Tamil Nadu

Madras, capital of Tamil Nadu and fourth-largest city in India, sits on the Bay of Bengal. At the temple cities of Tiruchirapalli and Madurai, where the devout crowd the enormous shrines, you can see the fascinating rituals of Hindu temple life. You can relax at beach resorts south of Madras in Mamallapuram, with its historic cave carvings and a shore temple.

THE DIFFERENCE BETWEEN SOUTH INDIA and the rest of the country is much greater than a few degrees on a thermometer. The south has been relatively unaffected by the waves of invasion that shaped India for centuries, even though it was the starting point of the last invasion of all—that of the Europeans. Alien empire builders either never reached the south or had spent their fury and zeal by the time they did. Thus, 5,000 years of Dravidian history have been little influenced by people from distant lands. The result is a fascinating survival of ancient India—and in many respects Hinduism—in its purest form. Nowhere else is classical dancing performed on the scale of the Bharata Natyam dance in Madras and other, smaller cities. Nowhere else can you experience the spiritual exuberance of ancient Hinduism as you can in Madurai or Tiruchirapalli (Trichy). The temples of South India have massive *gopura* (towers), and some—especially the more recent ones—have color combinations that outdo Miami Beach. The ancient temples that punctuate the tropical landscape are clear expressions of traditional India.

The village life you see while traveling through Tamil Nadu has also undergone little change. Before the temples were built, after they began to crumble, and through their restoration, the villagers and farmers of Tamil Nadu have been raising rice, drinking tender coconut water, threshing their grain—though only recently under the wheels of passing cars and trucks—bearing their harvest to market, and reverently worshipping the gods. Every morning you will also see *kolams* or *rangolis* (colorful drawings) on the ground or pavement in front of each dwelling. At dawn the woman of the house uses white or colored powder to create these lovely geometric or floral designs. Traditionally, the powder is made from rice and the design is eaten by insects or birds. In this way the woman pleases the gods by starting her day with an act of charity.

Tamil Nadu is a vast, tropical state that stretches from the Bay of Bengal and Indian Ocean over a coastal alluvial plain, with stands of coconut and banana, to fertile plains. In the west rise the Western Ghats, and the north is dominated by the lush and rugged Nilgiri Hills. The state's cities are crowded, sprawling, and not pretty, but they are in many ways the heart of the Tamil people, and in ways more profound still, the soul of India. For this land—though often portrayed as a place of demons and ape-men in Aryan-Hindu mythology—is the deepest root of Hinduism. The elemental components of modern Hinduism are here in the rituals and beliefs of ancient Dravidian society.

Numbers in the margin correspond to points of interest on the Tamil Nadu, Madras, and Mamallapuram maps.

MADRAS

Traditions are still seen even in the quiet neighborhoods of Madras. This is not to say that Madras is unaffected by the pace of change in India. It is growing more prosperous (and crowded and dirty), but while the Dravidian people embrace progress, they seem quietly and forcefully to resist any change to their basic nature. Madras insists on remaining the port town it has been since the British came, though now there's a movement underway to destroy British monuments.

In spite of its large population—currently over 4 million—Madras has a gentle pace and is made for people-watching. Having carried a civilization for thousands of years, the people here are more comfortable

Tamil Nadu

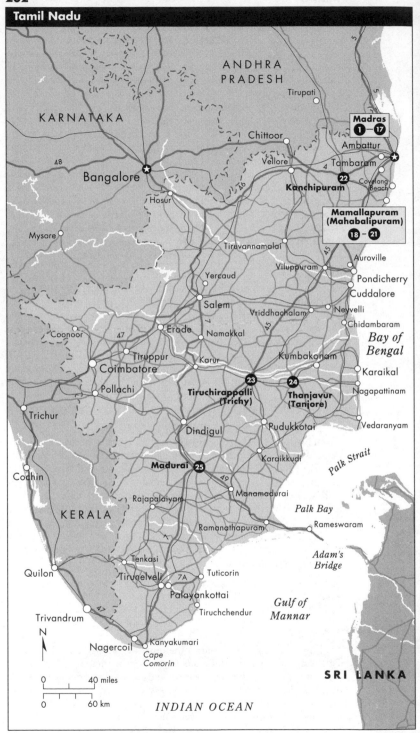

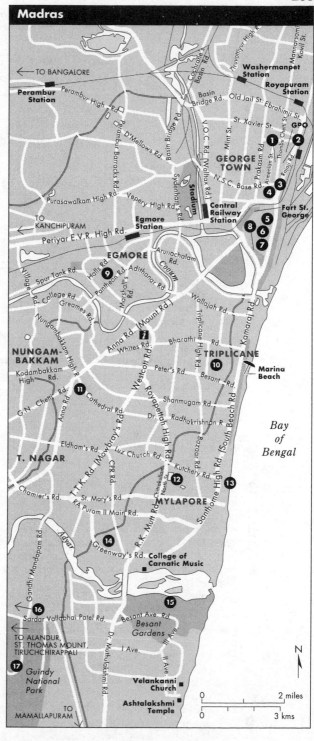

Madras

in their cultural identity than are most of their northern counterparts. Their finely tuned cultural heritage stresses artistic expressions of Hindu life—where the mundane and the sacred are constantly intertwined. Unfortunately, the complications of modern times are beginning to make Madras dirty and congested like its larger sisters—Bombay, Calcutta, and Delhi.

Exploring

This city began in the north, growing outward from Fort St. George. North of the Fort is the old commercial district. Central Madras is dominated by more modern throughfares and more recent shopping areas. As the city grew, the British made their homes farther south, where you find elegant residential neighborhoods and such diversions as the race track.

Northern Madras

★ **Fort St. George.** In 1639, 25 years before the British reached Bombay and 50 years before they arrived in Calcutta, the raja of Chandragiri gave Francis Day a lease to open a trading post for the British East India Company on the site of Madras, then known as Madraspatram. The following year, work began on Fort St. George, which was finished in 1653. From this stronghold, Britain held Madras until India achieved independence, except for a two-year period beginning in 1746, when Joseph-François Dupleix took it for France. Fort St. George is tightly interwoven with the swashbuckling story of the struggle for India in the 18th century. Robert Clive arrived here in 1743 as a modest clerk for the East India Company. When Fort St. George surrendered to the French, he escaped and became an officer in the company's army. By the time he was 30, he had become governor of Madras and was well launched on his meteoric career, which saw him preserve India for Britain only to die by his own hand in disgrace back in his native England.

Modern Madras has grown around Fort St. George, and the old fortress ❻ now houses the **Tamil Nadu State Legislature** and other government offices. The fort's 6-meter (20-foot) walls still guard the center of Madras and its busy commercial artery, Anna Salai (Mount Road). In- ❽ side the walls, you can stroll through the pages of history. **Clive's house** is here, and Colonel Arthur Wellesley, who later became the duke of Wellington, lived in another old house within the fort. Visit the old- ❼ est Anglican church in India, **St. Mary's Church,** consecrated in 1680. The roof and walls of St. Mary's are 5 feet thick and bombproof, which probably explains why the French ransacked the interior and sacrile- ❺ giously turned the building into a military fortification. Finally, the **Fort Museum,** once used as an exchange by the merchants of the East India Company, contains many relics from precolonial days. *S. Beach Rd.* ☺ *Museum Sat.–Thur. 10–5.*

★ **George Town.** North of the fort stands the original Madras. Streets here still bear such names as China Bazaar Road, Portuguese Church Street, and Armenian Street, all reminiscent of Madras's four-century history as a center of international trade. Popham's Broadway (now Praksam Road) was Madras's main commercial street into the early 20th century and forms the western side of the massive shopping area between Rajaji Salai and Broadway north of N. S. C. Bose Road. On ★ ❶ Armenia Street, notice the fine old **Armenian Church,** originally built in 1629. It subsequently became the cornerstone of the influential Armenian community. While you're here, don't miss the wholesale haven ❸ of **Evening Bazaar** (also called Parrys—pronounced Paris—after the former British confectionery factory that made Parry Sweets). A spanking-new building at the corner of N. S. C. Bose Road and Rajaji Salai holds new wholesale emporiums under a proud blue "Parrys" sign, but the district's soul remains in narrow, produce-filled streets where color, scent, and humanity swarm together like a living kaleidoscope. The odors change from street to street. Countless open stalls selling fruit, vegetables, pastries, flowers, colorful paper ornaments, and bangles—a thoroughly fascinating bustle of bartering and noise. Be prepared for the crowds, though. All Madras seems to be here, and getting in with a car at rush hour can be a long, hot, and uncomfortable process. North on Rajaji Salai from N. S. C. Bose Road is **Burma Bazar,** the once-shady domain of blackmarketers. In the now-sanctioned stalls here, you'll find everything not yet on the general Indian market. Whether it's for shampoo or a VCR, be sure to haggle.

★ **❹ The High Court.** This mammoth Indo-Saracenic judicial complex is just north of the fort. Within the red sandstone walls and under towering domes and minarets is a labyrinth of corridors as dumbfounding as the justice system itself. Fifty meters (164 feet) high, the central tower here served as a lighthouse. You can visit the courts; court number 13 has the finest decoration inside. *Just north of Fort across Muthuswamy Iyer Rd.* ☉ *Mon.–Sat. 10–5. Guided tours, Rs. 10, Mon.–Sat. 10:30– 1:45 and 2:30–4:30.*

Central Madras

The more prosperous residents of Madras have generally moved southward, and here you find some of the finest Indo-Saracenic architecture in the city. You find new shops, old mosques, and crowded bazaars in the heart of Madras, as well as the university and the National Museum. The eastern edge is bordered by a fairly clean stretch of Marina Beach, where you'll see makeshift villages crowding the sand and water buffaloes being bathed in the ocean. The Chepauk district is home to historic Madras University. Farther south in Triplicane you find Parthasarathi Temple. Anna Salai (previously Mount Rd.) is increasingly considered the center of Madras. Shopping opportunities abound here, as do small, cheap, and good places to eat. In the Egmore district you find the National Museum. Nungambakkam, south of Egmore, was the poshest residential area for Europeans (and later upper-class Indians) to live. Massive old homes are now interspersed with expensive boutiques and hotels, but the area remains as fashionable as ever.

❾ National Museum and Art Gallery. Established in 1857, this institution contains an extensive all-around art collection. Hindu, Buddhist, and Jain sculptures have been gathered from all over the south. Metalwork, in the form of south Indian lamps; objects of worship; weapons; and images in bronze are scattered through the vast complex. A singular Chola-period bronze of Nataraja-Shiva in the cosmic dance pose, a beautifully executed two-foot-high statue, seeming constantly in motion, that has rightfully become the best-recognized symbol of Indian art around the world. The contents of the Arms Gallery are mostly from the palace at Thanjavur and Fort St. George. The Bronze Gallery contains some of the best of India's ancient icons and some excellent modern bronzes. *Pantheon Rd., Egmore.* ☛ *Free; Rs. 10 for still and Rs. 50 for video cameras.* ☉ *Sat.–Thurs. 9–5.*

TIME OUT Alsa Mall, near the National Gallery, has a downstairs **Hot Bread Bakers and Confectioners** (149 Montieth Rd., ☎ 44/866724) and adjoining coffee shop.

❿ Parthasarathy Temple. Originally constructed by the Pallavas in the 8th century, this temple is dedicated to Vishnu. It was rebuilt by the

Vijayanagar kings in the 17th century. After passing under the brilliantly colored gopuram, you enter a courtyard with several beautifully carved shrines. Even the streets around the temple are sprinkled with colored powders, idols, flowers, and other articles of Hindu worship. Non-Hindus can enter only the courtyard. *Peter's Rd., Triplicane.* ⊘ *Daily 6:30–noon and 4–8.*

⑪ St. George's Cathedral. Built as an Anglican church in 1816, the cathedral is now almost invisible in the commercial sprawl off Anna Salai. Hidden behind the modern U.S. consulate and information center, the white colonial church has a 40-meter (130-foot) spire. *Cathedral Rd.* ⊘ *Daily 8–6.*

Southern Madras

South of the T. Nagar district, the city quiets down. The area around and south of the Adyar River has wide, tree-lined streets, open spaces, and many of the city's quieter centers for learning. Toward the airport lies St. Thomas Mount, where St. Thomas—credited with building seven churches along the Indian coast—was supposedly lanced to death in AD 72.

★ **⑬ Basilica of San Thome Cathedral.** St. Thomas is thought to be entombed inside this handsome neo-Gothic structure with elegant arches and a 56-meter (180-foot) steeple, built in 1895. The Portuguese form of its name dates from the 16th century, when the original church was built. Inside is an unusual image of Christ standing on a lotus flower (a typical Hindu pose). *End of Kutchery Rd., Mylapore.*

⑮ Besant Gardens. Near the coast you find the serene plantings that surround the world headquarters of the Theosophical Society. Within the gardens are shrines of several faiths. The buildings include a museum and the Adyar Library for people interested in learning about theosophists. *Theosophical Society Headquarters, Besant Ave.,* ☎ *44/413528.* ⊘ *Weekdays 8–11 and 2–5, Sat. 8–11.*

⑯ Church of Our Lady of Expectation. This 16th-century church, on St. Thomas Mount, is set in the foundation of a church said to have been built by St. Thomas. Legends claim that Thomas the Apostle ("Doubting Thomas") came to this part of India from Palestine and was martyred while praying in front of a cross engraved in stone here. Now installed behind the church's high altar, this so-called **Bleeding Stone** is believed to shed blood on December 18 (the day of St. Thomas's death). *Great Mount, Alandur.*

⑫ Kapaleeswarar Temple. This grand temple dating from the 13th century is dedicated to a manifestation of Shiva. Rebuilt in the 16th century, the shrine is alive with brightly colored, typically Dravidian sculptures. It offers an impressive contrast to European cathedral architecture. Non-Hindus can enter only the courtyard. *Between Chitrakullam North St. and Kutchery Rd., Mylapore.* ⊘ *Daily 5–noon and 4–8:30.*

★ **⑰ Madras Snake Park and Conservation Center.** In the Guindy National Deer Park, this center was founded by Romulus Whitaker, an American conservationist who settled in India in the 1970s. While the deer park itself was recently closed to the public because of security problems, the snake park gives visitors a chance to see, photograph, and touch the common snakes of India (over 500 species), as well as alligators, monitor lizards, chameleons, and tortoises. More than half a million people visit the park each year, and their entrance fees help cover the cost of maintenance and fund various wildlife projects and rele-

vant surveys. *Guindy National Deer Park, Sardar Vallabhai Patel Rd.
and Gandhi Mandapram Rd.* ☛ *Rs. 2; still cameras Rs. 5; video cameras Rs. 50.* ☉ *Daily 9–6; hourly demonstrations.*

★ ⑭ **The Study.** The Krishnamurthi Foundation of India has set up this center in which people can immerse themselves in the teachings of J. Krishnamurthi (1895–1986). As a young boy in Andhra Pradesh,
Krishnamurthi was chosen by the Theosophical Society as the future
World Teacher. Krishnamurthi traveled the world teaching about the
human condition and developing his ideas about truth. Aside from all
his written work, the Study has a large library of his audiotapes and
video cassettes, as well as some other philosophical writings. Accommodations are possible for serious students of Krishnamurthi. *Vasanta
Vihar, 64 Greenways Rd., Madras 600028,* ☎ *44/493–7803.* ☉ *Tues.–
Sun. 10–1 and 2–7.*

TIME OUT Nala Sweets (1 Cathedral Rd.) has a quiet old-time ambience and good
Indian snacks and sweets, including ice cream. At the popular **Wood-
land's Drive-In Restaurant** (29/30 Cathedral Rd.) you don't drive in, but
you do choose among numerous eating halls surrounded by gardens,
where you can order Indian sweets and snacks.

Shopping

The bustling fruit and vegetable market, **Jam Bazaar** (junction of Py-
croft's and Triplican roads) holds mountains of fruits in narrow, colorful lanes. **Evening Bazaar** (also called Parrys; near Broadway and N.
S. C. Bose Rd.) consists of wholesale markets. Best visited at night, **Burma
Bazaar** (running north along Rajaji Salai from the eastern end of N.
S. C. Bose Rd.) was once the center of Madras's black market; come
here for anything that's tough to find in India. Finally, **Pondy Bazaar**
(T. Nagar) features a bit of everything, including some excellent silk
stores. If something strikes your fancy, haggle.

Madras's best shops (most of which take some credit cards) include
the following: **Alison's Fabrics** (43 College Rd., ☎ 44/826–3358), at
the end of a long drive, has excellent handwoven silks and cottons, along
with a large array of handicrafts, dhurries, and leather goods. **Aparna
Art Gallery** (5 Bawa Rowther Rd.; Rayala Bldg., 781 Anna Salai) has
a good selection of old and new curios in wood and bronze, Tanjore
and Mysore paintings, and miniatures. **G. R. Thanga Maligai** (104
Usman Rd., T. Nagar, no ☎) has excellent gold and silver jewelry. **Nalli
Chinnasami Chetty** (opposite Panagal Park, T. Nagar, ☎ 44/434–
4115) has two floors filled with silks (including the beautiful Kanchipuram silk), hand-loomed fabrics, and patrons. **Poompuhar Sales and Show
Room** (818 Anna Salai, ☎ 44/852–0624), a government-run emporium, has a good selection of Tamil Nadu handicrafts: brass, wood,
papier-mâché sculptures, and hand-loomed fabrics. **Shilpi** (Shop 1,
Gee Gee Minar Bldg., 23 College Rd.) sells exquisite hand-loomed fabrics by the meter and clothing made of hand-loomed fabric. **Shreenivas Silks and Sarees** (77 Sri Thyagaraya Rd., Pondy Bazaar, T. Nagar,
☎ 44/828–4758) has fabulous Kanchipuram silks.

Sports

Horse Racing

West of Guindy National Deer Park you'll find the racecourse. Ask the
Government of India tourist office (or your consulate) if you're interested
in attending the races or other events at the elitist Madras Riders' Club.

Dining

Until recently, the best dining in Madras was in the luxury hotels. For price categories, *see* the chart for Major Cities *in* On the Road with Fodor's.

$$$ Dakshin. This handsome restaurant, with Tanjore paintings, south Indian statues, and brass lanterns shaped like temple bells, focuses on the cuisine of India's southern states. Meals are served on banana leaves set in silver *thali* trays (platters filled with individual portions of numerous dishes), and an Indian flutist plays nightly. The nonvegetarian or vegetarian thali gives a taste of all the cuisine, or try Tamil Nadu's *daskshin yera* (fried prawns marinated in ginger, chili, and garlic) or Andhra Pradesh's spicy *mirupakaikodi* (sautéed chili chicken). ✗ *Welcomgroup Park Sheraton Hotel and Towers, T. T. K. Rd.,* ☎ *44/499–4101. Reservations advised. AE, DC, MC, V.*

$$$ Golden Dragon. Oriental elegance sets the tone of this intimate Chinese restaurant: Brass lanterns hang from the ceiling, and dragon murals adorn the walls. Try fish in hot tomato sauce, stir-fried lobster with garlic and scallions, or Cantonese stir-fried shredded lamb. ✗ *Taj Coromandel Hotel, 17 Nungambakkam High Rd.,* ☎ *44/827–2827. Reservations advised. AE, DC, MC, V.*

$$$ Other Room. Thousands of seashells hang from this restaurant's ceiling, and mirrors decorate its walls. Nightly except Wednesday, a Western rock band entertains, and you can dance. At lunch, enjoy a good buffet or order à la carte from the Continental and Indian menu. Try the lobster thermidor, chateaubriand, or *sikandri raan* (spicy leg of lamb cooked in a tandoor). ✗ *Ambassador Pallava, 53 Montieth Rd.,* ☎ *44/826–8584. Reservations advised. AE, DC, MC, V.*

$$$ Peshwari. Its Pathan decor—rough stone walls, copper plates, and soft lighting—is handsome. The Indian northwest frontier cuisine, with an emphasis on tandoori, is good. Try the tasty *murgh malai kabab* (boneless chicken kebabas marinated in cheese, cream, and lime juice) or *kadak seekh reshmi* (crisp rolled chicken cooked over a grill). ✗ *Welcomgroup Chola Sheraton, 10 Cathedral Rd.,* ☎ *44/828–0101. Reservations advised. AE, DC, MC, V.*

$$$ Rain Tree. In a garden with delicate lights strung through the trees, this restaurant offers a Bharata Natyam dance recital and/or an Indian flute performance (check for times). Along with the show, enjoy Tamil Nadu *chettinad* cuisine served on a banana leaf set in a copper plate. Try *vathal kozhambu* (sun-ripened berries cooked in a spicy chettinad gravy) or *yera varuwal* (prawns marinated in chettinad masala, then deep fried). ✗ *Taj Hotel Connemara, Binnys Rd.,* ☎ *44/826–0123. Reservations advised. AE, DC, MC, V.*

$$$ Shanghai. Pretty upholstered chairs, lacquered black lattices, paintings of emperors, and a good view of an enclosed interior garden and water cascade add up to an appealing ambience for Chinese fare. Try the spicy king prawns sautéed in *sambal* (chili paste mixed with fruit jam) or the mildly spicy chicken served in lotus leaves. ✗ *Oberoi Trident Hotel, 1/24 G. S. T. Rd. (near airport),* ☎ *44/234–4747. Reservations advised. AE, DC, MC, V.*

$$ Cascade. Run by a professor, this restaurant, with its chipped marble fountain and white-and-silver-blue decor sets the standard for Madras restaurants. Quiet Chinese music accompanies tasty Chinese, Malaysian, Japanese, or Thai cuisine. Try Phuket fish (fried sailfish fillet with garlic and chili paste), chili crab, or Szechuan *sapo* (prawns, chicken, fish, or lamb marinated in five-spice powder, then cooked and served in a sapo dish). Don't overorder; the portions are large. ✗ *Kakani Tow-*

ers, *K. N. K. Rd., near Taj Cormandel Hotel,* ☎ *44/472514. Reservations advised. AE, DC, MC, V.*

$$ **Copper Chimney.** The newest branch of this successful Bombay establishment has sprung up in Madras. The standard Copper Chimney fare remains—unique Indian creations based on Mughlai standards. From the tandoor, try a fish *tikka*, which comes light and flaky out of the clay oven. Also good is *bhagani bahar* (spicy chicken barbecued in mint). ✕ *74 Cathdral Rd.,* ☎ *44/827–5770. Reservations advised. AE, MC, V.*

$$ **Residency.** Wrought-iron gates lead into this elegant restaurant with a mirrored ceiling, lace curtains bordered by heavy drapes, and rich red-and-green decor. The chef prepares tasty Chinese, Indian, and Continental dishes. At lunch, there's a buffet; at night, expect a Western dance band and an à la carte menu. Try the good butter chicken, spicy chili chicken, or pepper steak. ✕ *Welcomgroup Park Sheraton Hotel and Towers, T. T. K. Rd.,* ☎ *44/499–4101. Reservations advised. AE, DC, MC, V.*

$–$$ **AVM Dasa.** This spacious informal restaurant, with a high ceiling, an attractive cedar gazebo, lattice screens, and Tiffany-style lamps, is cosmopolitan chic. The food—both Indian and Continental—is tasty vegetarian. At lunch, a rusty and charming pianist plays Western standards. ✕ *806 Anna Salai, no* ☎. *DC, V.*

$ **Amaravathi Hotel.** An older restaurant, it has four small rooms with booths and tables and usually a crowd who come for the excellent Andhra Pradesh–style cuisine. House favorites are spicy chicken Amaravathi or the "vegetable meal" served on a banana leaf. ✕ *1 Cathedral Rd., opposite Music Academy,* ☎ *44/476416. Rupees only.*

$ **Hotel Hari Nivas.** This Madras institution is in an old hotel in a crowded bazaar. Have fun while you eat vegetarian Indian food served on a banana leaf (the set meal) or on a metal thali if it's a snack. For snacks, you can eat in a fan-cooled cafeteria or in an air-conditioned side room with an illuminated shrine to Krishna. Set meals are served in an air-conditioned room with a shrine to the owner. ✕ *168 Thambu Chetty St., near High Court Building,* ☎ *44/582121. No credit cards.*

Lodging

The best places to stay in Madras are still the larger hotels, which offer standard services and standard prices for clean, modern rooms. All pools are outdoors. For price categories, *see* the chart for Major Cities *in* On the Road with Fodor's.

$$$$ **Taj Coromandel Hotel.** This central luxury high-rise has a dramatic mar-
★ ble lobby with teak pillars and teak set into the ceiling. The rooms are elegant though standard, done in soft greens and blues with rich wood accents. ⌂ *17 Nungambakkam High Rd., Madras 600034, Tamil Nadu,* ☎ *44/827–2827,* FAX *44/825–7104. 240 rooms. 3 restaurants, bar, no-smoking floor, pool, health club, business services, travel services. AE, DC, MC, V.*

$$$–$$$$ **Welcomgroup Park Sheraton Hotel and Towers.** A modern monolith in the center of town, it has a lavish and spacious marble lobby. The rooms are done in soft hues, including satin print curtains and bedspreads. The rooms in the towers are more elegant. ⌂ *T. T. K. Rd., Madras 600018, Tamil Nadu,* ☎ *44/499–4101,* FAX *44/499–7101. 302 rooms, 20 suites. 3 restaurants, bar, pool, health club, nightclub, business services, travel services. AE, DC, MC, V.*

$$$ **Oberoi Trident Hotel.** Near the airport and 10 kilometers (6 miles) from the city, this modern hotel has an attractive lobby with an interior garden and water cascade. The spacious rooms' decor elegantly incorporates Indian fabrics. The best rooms overlook the pool. ⊡ *1/24 G. S. T. Rd., Madras, Tamil Nadu,* ☎ *44/234–4747,* ℻ *44/234–6699. 162 rooms. 2 restaurants, bar, pool, health club, business services, travel services, airport shuttle, AE, DC, MC, V.*

$$$ **Taj Fisherman's Cove.** This luxury resort, on a cove 32 kilometers (20 miles) from Madras, offers modern rooms in a high-rise or in cottages privately nestled in a grove. Most rooms overlook the sea. Guests have access to a full array of water sports. ⊡ *Chingleput district, Madras 603112, Tamil Nadu,* ☎ *4113/44304,* ℻ *4113/44303. 70 rooms. 2 restaurants, 2 bars, pool, tennis court, baby-sitting, travel services. AE, DC, MC, V.*

$$$ **Taj Hotel Connemara.** The city's prettiest Western-style hotel maintains its old elegance. Though it is in the center, the lovely lobby, numerous quiet lounges, and the garden areas feel distant from central Madras. The old wing has deluxe rooms with contemporary furnishings. The best rooms in this class have private terraces leading to the pool. Standard doubles (in the new wing) are also attractive. Ask for a river view. ⊡ *Binnys Rd., Madras 600002, Tamil Nadu,* ☎ *44/826–0123,* ℻ *44/ 825–7361. 150 rooms, 12 suites. 2 restaurants, bar, pool, baby-sitting, business services, travel services. AE, DC, MC, V.*

$$$ **Welcomgroup Chola Sheraton.** One of the earlier luxury hotels, the Chola Sheraton has a large marble lobby with a sunken lounge area and spacious, modern rooms still suitable for most visiting VIPs. Its central location makes it convenient. ⊡ *10 Cathedral Rd., Madras 600086, Tamil Nadu,* ☎ *44/828–0101,* ℻ *44/827–8779. 100 rooms, 12 suites. 2 restaurants, bar, pool, health club, dance club, business services, travel services. AE, DC, MC, V.*

$$ **Ambassador Pallava.** This Western-style hotel offers spacious rooms with reasonably modern decor. The Pallava also tries to impress with grand halls and a spacious entrance, but it's a bit dingier than its newer counterparts. The best rooms have balconies that overlook the pool. ⊡ *53 Montieth Rd., Madras 600008, Tamil Nadu,* ☎ *44/855– 4476,* ℻ *855–4492. 120 rooms. 2 restaurants, bar, pool, health club, business services, travel services. AE, DC, MC, V.*

$–$$ **Quality Inn Aruna.** The marble lobby of this new hotel is open and com-
★ fortable. The tastefully decorated rooms are a good size. The best overlook the pool and have a nice view of Madras. The Jewel in the Crown Indian Restaurant serves excellent meals at a reasonable price. Live classical Indian music accompanies dinner. Breakfast is included in the rate. ⊡ *144 Sterling Rd., Madras 600034, Tamil Nadu,* ☎ *44/ 825–9090,* ℻ *44/825–8282. 94 rooms. Restaurant, patisserie, bar, pool, health club. AE, DC, MC, V.*

The Arts

The day's outlook in terms of music, dance, and drama can always be found on page 3 of the *Hindu;* the newspaper's "Friday Review" section lists the coming week's events under the heading "In the City." Madras is a center for the fine arts; you shouldn't leave it without seeing a performance of the *Bharata Natyam*—considered by many to be the purest and most beautiful classical dance form in India. Check the *Hindu* or call the Government of India Tourist Office (☎ 44/852–4785), which keeps a list of current cultural events. The following theaters and halls also present cultural events with some frequency: **Kalaivanar Arangam** (Government Estate, Wallaja Rd., ☎ 44/565669); **Rajah Annamalai Hall** (Esplanade, ☎ 44/561425); **Rani Seethai Hall** (603 Anna Salai, ☎ 44/474863), and the **Music Academy** (115 E. Mowbray's

Rd., ☎ 475619). Another option is to view a dance class at one of Madras's many schools for the performing arts; try **Khalakshetra** (Tiruvanmiyur, ☎ 44/4911169) or the **Kuchupudi Art Academy** (105 Greenways Rd., ☎ 44/4937260). The Government of India tourist office can tell you about several other venues for various dance forms.

Nightlife

Madras's best bars are in the luxury hotels; they're generally open 11–11. Dancing in Madras is almost an impossiblity, and the bars are far from exciting. All this dreariness is the legacy of prohibition in an anti-alcohol state. Some hotels are in the beginning stages of planning discos. For now, your best nighttime bet here is something cultural.

Madras Essentials

Arriving and Departing
See Tamil Nadu Essentials, *below.*

Getting Around
As in much of India, many street names in Madras have recently been changed from their colonial designations. Mount Road, the city's main thoroughfare, is now called Anna Salai after C. N. Annadurai, leader of Tamil Nadu's grassroots movement to Dravidian power, who was popularly known as *Anna* (Elder Brother). South Beach Road is now Kamaraj Salai, Poonamallee High Road is Periyar E.V.R. Salai, North Beach Road is Rajaji Salai, and Popham's Broadway is now Praksam Road. Fortunately for the easily confused traveler, the colonial and indigenous names remain essentially interchangeable.

See also Tamil Nadu Essentials, *below.*

Visitor Information
See Tamil Nadu Essentials, *below.*

Publications. The monthlies *Hallo! Madras* and *Madras this Month* are handy booklets with information on hotels, restaurants, sights, travel agencies, airlines, events, and more. Both are available free at the Government of India tourist office or for Rs. 5 to Rs. 10 at train stations and most local bookstores. Page 3 of the *Hindu* lists the day's music, dance, and drama events, and every Friday the paper publishes "In the City" detailing the coming week. *Sura's Madras* (Rs. 22 at most bookstalls or the train station) has a map and provides all the basic information plus a detailed section on bus routes.

KANCHIPURAM AND MAMALLAPURAM

Here you see the glorious past of great dynasties—Pallava, Chola, Vijayanagar—who for centuries were affected by internal conflict and external trade but never northern invasion. The dynasties merely jostled each other, building ever greater shrines to their developing and intertwining sets of deities. The Pallava emperors (circa AD 630 to 850) built important ports like Mamallapuram, which have been left deserted with the passage of time. Though Kanchipuram is a major pilgrimage town, the temples here seem like echoes of the past.

Mamallapuram

★ **Mamallapuram,** 59 kilometers (37 miles) south of Madras, is the former main harbor and naval base of the Pallava emperors. Although the reign of the Pallavas waned some 1,200 years ago, their contributions still stand on and near the shore of the "city of the seven pagodas," its European designation. Tiny Mamallapuram, with its under-5,000 population, offers a breathtaking display of masterful sculpture carved from solid rock. In fact, the Pallavas developed four distinct kinds of sculpture: *rathas* (chariot-shaped temples), bas-relief sculptural panels, rock-cut caves, and freestanding temples. In Mamallapuram humans worked nature into sublime art. Today, they fight nature as it tries to reclaim the artisans' vision with salt spray and rising ocean levels.

From the center of town (the bus stand), the shore temple is due west (at the shore), the five rathas are about 1 kilometer (½ mile) south, and the bas-relief is just a couple of blocks east.

Exploring

⑳ Bas-Relief. Mamallapuram's most astounding display of artistry is the "Penance of Arjuna," the world's largest bas-relief and a masterpiece of composition, carved on two gigantic side-by-side boulders, each some 31 meters (100 feet) long with an average height of 16 meters (50 feet). This bas-relief, with its nearly 100 figures of gods, demigods, people, animals, and birds—almost every real and mythological form of creation—is filled with vitality. The most prominent of its myriad characters is the group of elephants, one of them five meters (17 feet) long, and the emaciated figure thought to represent Arjuna, a major character in the Hindu epic the *Mahabharata,* standing on one leg and doing penance as he prays to Lord Shiva for a powerful weapon to destroy his enemies.

★ ⑱ The Five Rathas. The so-called pagodas of Mamallapuram are actually 7th-century rathas, although to a Western eye they resemble small pyramid-shape temples cut off by flat roofs. The walls of these freestanding monolithic temples—each chiseled from a single rock—are a picture book of Hindu mythology. Also known as the Pancha Pandava Rathas, after the heroes of the Hindu epic the *Mahabharata,* the rathas are dedicated to Durga, Shiva, Vishnu, and Indra. They are not overpowering in size and are well proportioned even though they are all unfinished, lacking finials. Near these delicate temples, life-size stone statues of an elephant, a lion, and a bull stand guard.

⑲ Rock-Cut Caves. In the nine rock-cut caves scattered around the site, you'll find some of India's most animated Hindu sculptures. Visit the 7th-century Mahishasura Mandapa and see the sculptural relief of the goddess Durga riding a lion in her struggle against evil, which is represented by the image of Mahishasura, the buffalo-headed demon. Another bas-relief shows the god Vishnu in his cosmic sleep, lying on the coils of a serpent. Pastoral scenes from the life of Krishna are carved into the Krishna Mandapa cave temple.

㉑ Shore Temple. On the shore of the Bay of Bengal stands a temple built by King Rajashimha in the 8th century. With two shrines—one to Vishnu and the other to Shiva—it is a good example of the first phase of Dravidian temple architecture. Surrounded by a row of bulls carved from solid rock, the Shore Temple stands with its back to the sea, rising up against blue waters with a white wreath of foam. There were once two or three more temples along the shore nearby, a total a seven along all Tamil Nadu, but only this one has withstood time and the sea for 12 centuries.

Dining

At Mamallapuram, the best food is from the sea. Inexpensive and good restaurants abound in town, and some beach-resort restaurants offer a unique atmosphere along with the fresh seafood.

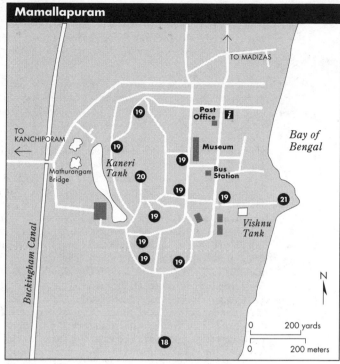

Mamallapuram

For price categories, *see* the chart for Other Areas *in* On the Road with
Fodor's.

$–$$ **Ideal Beach Resort.** Eat Indian, Continental, or especially good Sri Lankan
items in the pretty garden or in a simple interior restaurant with Sri
Lankan murals and sculptures. Try the Sri Lankan rice and curry or
Sri Lankan fish curry and follow it with *vatil appam* (custard). ✗ ☎
4113/2240. AE, DC, MC, V.

★ $ **Pumpernickel Bakery.** This rooftop café, run by a German who has
lived in South Asia for over 20 years, offers treats such as genuine cap-
puccino. The fresh breads, pastries, and juices are delicious. ✗ *Uma
Lodge (from post office, walk north on main road, take first right).*
No ☎. No credit cards. Closed May–Oct.

$ **Seafront Restaurant and Whispering Woods.** The Seafront has a lively
atmosphere under a thatch roof on the beach near the small outdoor
dance floor of the Silver Sands hotel. Open flames light the romantic
Whispering Woods, which has tables in a pine grove out of sight—but
not sound—of the beach. Both places serve Chinese, Continental, and
Indian dishes, including fresh seafood. ✗ *Silver Sands, Mamallapuram,*
☎ *4113/2228. AE, DC, MC, V.*

$ **Sunrise Restaurant.** Set in a cozy thatched hut, with no ocean view but
good tropical breezes, this restaurant serves Indian, Continental, and
Chinese cuisine. Try fish steak, steamed with tomato, garlic, and butter, or grilled lobster or jumbo prawns. ✗ *Beach Rd., no ☎. No credit
cards.*

Lodging

The lodging options here vary widely. Buildings in town are more likely
guest houses than not, and many people choose to stay here for weeks
or months at a time. Two people can find a wonderful room (normally

in a small, residential guest house, rather than a hotel) for Rs. 100 to Rs. 200 a day, including meals, if they look around. The "lodges" (small hotels) are often clean though generic and are always cheap. For price categories, *see* the chart for Other Areas *in* On the Road with Fodor's.

$$ Temple Bay Ashok Beach Resort. Overlooking the ocean, this complex offers rooms in the main building and in cottages (two doubles per unit). The rooms and cottages vary greatly in quality and character. The newer cottages are more sterile but also boast nicer facilities. Some redecorated rooms are elegant and luxurious. Ask to look around and pick what suits you. The restaurant serves a variety of cuisines. ⊞ *ITDC (India Tourism Development Corporation) Shore Cottages, Mamallapuram 603104, Tamil Nadu,* ☎ *4113/2251,* ℻ *4113/2257. 16 rooms, 35 cottages. Restaurant, bar, pool, tennis court, beach, travel services. AE, DC, MC, V.*

$ Ideal Beach Resort. The personalized Ideal has a Sri Lankan touch in its lush green gardens decorated with sculptures. The best rooms are upstairs in two-story, air-conditioned cottages, with clean modest decor and verandas offering an ocean view. The restaurant offers a variety of cuisines. ⊞ *Mamallapuram 603104, Tamil Nadu,* ☎ *4113/2240,* ℻ *4113/2243. 25 cottages. Restaurant, pool, beach, travel services. AE, DC, MC, V.*

$ Silver Sands. This secluded beach resort has a whimsical ethnic decor that creates a charming rustic ambience and rooms to fit every style and budget. The air-conditioned villas have beach views, TVs, and music systems. One villa has its own interior swimming pool; another has a private sun deck. Air-conditioned beach-front rooms have sitting rooms with swings and verandas overlooking the ocean. Deluxe air-conditioned rooms lack an ocean view but have a sitting room with a swing and light, tropical decor. The standard air-conditioned rooms have interior swings but no sea view. The restaurants are open-air and serve a variety of cuisines. ⊞ *Mamallapuram 603104, Tamil Nadu,* ☎ *4113/ 42228,* ℻ *4113/42280; reservations also through Transit House, 26 Venkatraman St., T. Nagar, Madras 600017,* ☎ *44/828–1346. 75 rooms. 2 restaurants, 2 bars, miniature golf, beach, fishing, bicycles, dance club, travel services. Off-season discount May–Oct. AE, DC, MC, V.*

Excursions

On your way to Mamallapuram from Madras, stop at the **Cholamandal Artists Village** (about 20 km, or 12 mi, south of Madras; follow signs off the Madras–Mamallapuram Rd.; no ☎). It is home to several artisans who display and sell their work (batik, pottery, sculpture, and painting) daily from 6 AM to 8 PM. About 34 kilometers (21 miles) south of Madras is another of American conservationist Romulus

★ Whittaker's projects, the **Madras Crocodile Bank** (Vadanemeli, Madras 603104, ☎ 4124/332; open daily 8–5:30), founded with help from the World Wildlife Fund in 1975. The original stock here has produced over 6,000 crocodiles and been vital in saving the species in India.

If popular Mamallapuram is ever too crowded, some good bicycle-trip (or car-trip) destinations include the peaceful excavated rathas at **Tiger Cave,** 5 kilometers (3 miles) north of town, and the hilltop temples of **Tirukkalukundram,** about 16 kilometers (10 miles) west of Mamallapuram through lush fields of rice. If you're driving, 14 additional kilometers (9 miles) will bring you back to the coast at **Sadras** (about 10 km/6 mi south of Mamallapuram). Here near the ocean you'll find a ruined 17th-century Dutch fort and cemetery.

Mamallapuram Essentials

ARRIVING AND DEPARTING

Hire a car from Madras to get here. The state tourist office (*see* Tamil Nadu Essentials, *below*) arranges cars.

GETTING AROUND

Mamallapuram is a comfortable and manageable little village. The sites are a few kilometers apart, so you may want to rent a bicycle from any of the shops along East Raja Street (the main road).

VISITOR INFORMATION

The tourist office (East Raja St.; ⊘ Daily 10–5:30) is on the left as you enter town from the north.

Kanchipuram

㉒ **Kanchipuram,** the Pallavas' capital, is one of India's seven holiest cities. Called "the Golden City of 1,000 Temples," it is currently a bustling village in which locals are outnumbered by tourists and pilgrims drawn to the astounding array of shrines—there are still at least 124. Sacred to both Shiva and Vishnu (it's often called Shiva Vishnu Kanchi), Kanchipuram is a stop for Hindus making their pilgrimage to the seven holy cities (the other six are Haridwar, Ujjain, Varanasi, Mathura,
★ Ayodhya, and Dwarka). The **temples** here (whether Pallava, Chola, or Vijayanagar) were built by kings who patronized not only architecture and sculpture but all the arts, making Kanchipuram into one of India's greatest centers of learning. Hindu and Buddhist philosophies flourished here side by side.

By wandering around, you are likely to find unexpected treats and adventures among this city's temples. Be sure to carry plenty of change (for beggars, priests, and self-appointed tour guides) and some candy to give to children. Aside from this *baksheesh* (tipping), some temples have small fees of a few rupees (ranging from entrance fees to fees for cameras). Though most temples are closed daily from 12:30 to 4, the degree of closure varies; some temples shut down completely while others close just their Hindu-only inner sanctums.

Exploring

Ekambareswara Temple. Although it was originally constructed before the mid-9th century by the Pallavas, this temple's most significant feature—its 61-meter (200-foot) gopuram (tower entrance), with more than 10 stories of intricate sculpture—was the result of a 16th-century addition by the Vijayanagar kings. Recently renovated, this temple is dedicated to Shiva, who appears in the form of earth, one of Hinduism's five sacred elements. Inside the courtyard is a mango tree said to be 3,500 years old. Each of its four main branches is said to bear fruit with a different taste representing one of the four Hindu Vedas (sacred texts). Of the original 1,000 pillars that once stood in the *mandapa* (portico), fewer than 600 remain. *Between W. and N. Mada Sts. in northwest part of town.*

Kailasanatha Temple. King Rajashimha built this oldest (and possibly most beautiful) of Kanchipuram's temples in the early 8th century. The sandstone work of this temple, dedicated to Shiva, is the finest example of Pallava architecture. The shrines are adorned with extraordinary sculptures—a big Nandi bull (Shiva's vehicle) on a raised platform, other Nandi bulls everywhere, and innumerable images of Shiva—as well as many lovely paintings on the walls. Unusual tiny shrines surround the courtyard, each with its own pillared pavilion and uncomfortable resting space—58 exquisite monuments to fastidious labor and devotion. *1.5 km (1 mi) west of town center; follow Putleri St.*

Sri Kamakshi Temple. In the heart of the old town, the gold-plated go-porum of this temple is dedicated to the goddess Kamakshi (Parvati). At the annual winter **car festival** (generally in February or March), numerous small deities from nearby temples are pulled by wooden temple cars in a procession here. *Odai St.*

Vaikunthaperumal Temple. Built by King Nandivarman in the 8th century, this temple, with its three-story *vimana* (tower over the central shrine), is dedicated to Vishnu, who is shown repeatedly— sitting, standing, and reclining—the figures often appearing one above another. The sculptured panels of the mandapa recount the history of the Pallavas, including their battles with the Chalyukas. Such nonreligious subject matter in a temple was unusual at that time. In many ways, this temple, with its colonnade of lion pillars, marks a new stage in the development of Dravidian architecture (the thousand-pillar halls were yet to come). *1 km (½ mi) southwest of train station.*

Varadaraja Temple. The 31-meter (100-foot) goporum here was originally built in the 11th century but was renovated by the Vijayanagar kings 500 years later. Also known as the Devarajaswamy Temple, this edifice is dedicated to Vishnu, and its 100-pillar mandapa—all of it exquisitely carved—is one of the best. Here you can see a massive chain carved from one stone, as well as the handsome pillars standing in the courtyard. *3 km (2 mi) southeast of town; follow Gandhi Rd.*

Shopping
This city of weavers makes some of India's finest silk, but be sure to buy from government-approved shops. **Shreenivas Silk House** (17-A, T. K. Nambi St.) is one of the best and sells hand-spun, hand-loomed, and hand-printed silk and cotton by the meter, as well as ready-made clothes, silk ties, and scarves.

Dining and Lodging
Accommodations here are aimed more at pilgrims than tourists, and there is no real restaurant scene. Food options are basically the *dhabas* (snack shops) all around town where you can get a cheap thali. There are numerous guest houses.

For price categories, *see* the charts for Other Areas *in* On the Road with Fodor's.

$ **Hotel Tamilnadu.** The government-run hotel is near the train station and has clean, modestly furnished rooms and a decent restaurant. ⌨ *Kamatchi Sannathi St., Kanchipuram 631502, Tamil Nadu,* ☎ *4112/22553,* ℻ *4112/22552. 23 rooms. No credit cards.*

Kanchipuram Essentials
ARRIVING AND DEPARTING
From Mamallapuram it's an easy 64-kilometer (40-mile) trip inland by hired car to Kanchipuram.

GETTING AROUND
It is easiest to appreciate Kanchipuram from a bicycle or bicycle rickshaw; set the rate for a rickshaw (around Rs. 70 for the day) in advance.

VISITOR INFORMATION
There is no tourist office in town; check the Tamil Nadu Tourism Development Corporation in Madras (*see* Visitor Information *in* Tamil Nadu Essentials, *below*) before your trip.

MADURAI

㉕ **Madurai** is said to have been bathed in nectar that fell from Shiva's hair, and it is undoubtedly the capital of religion in Tamil Nadu. The old town of Madurai lies south of the Vaigai River. The area is bordered by North, East, and South Veli Streets and the railroad tracks (on the west side). Within this square is a perpetual state of chaotic activity centered on Meenakshi Temple. Known as the "city of festivals," Madurai seems to celebrate just about every day. Trumpets, drums, and religious chanting constantly fill the air but do not seem to disturb pilgrims who are taking a quick snooze under shady arcades.

Exploring

★ **Meenakshi Temple.** Shiva and his consort, Meenakshi, are honored in Madurai's greatest landmark. A virtual city within a city, the complex includes a **bazaar** that bustles from dawn to nightfall. This is the first major Indian temple whose towers are being restored to their original polychrome colors. Concrete moldings and bright fresh paint have replaced the gentle pastels and crumbling stones of weathered Hindu sculpture. Now the hundreds of leering deities from the Hindu pantheon are something you'll not forget in a hurry.

Although there are four entrances to the Meenakshi Temple, enter through the **eastern gopuram.** In the mural on the upper right in the entrance mandapa, painted in 1923, the Indian artist included an image of Mahatma Gandhi. When the British insisted on its removal, the artist turned Gandhi into a holy man with long hair, using watercolor that eventually disappeared, revealing Gandhi as a young man—hands held together in the traditional *namaste* greeting.

The swirling life of the Meenakshi Temple never seems to stop. Although nonbelievers are denied access to the two sanctuaries where Meenakshi and Shiva, in his incarnation as Sundereswarar, are enshrined, they can visit the rest of the temple quite freely. Hindus have no common worship and perform the *puja* (worship of the gods) either themselves or through the mediation of a priest.

The high point of the Meenakshi Temple is its **Hall of a Thousand Pillars.** This hall (with 985 pillars), built around 1560, is as great a work of structural engineering as it is of art. The ornately carved pillars are a picture book in stone that run the gamut of human expression, from stateliness and grace to lusty humor and ribaldry. The **Meenakshi Temple Art Museum,** inside the 1,000-pillar hall, contains temple art and architecture. The temple also contains a hall known as the **Kambatti Mandapa,** where Shiva is represented in all his various manifestations on sculptured pillars.

Throughout the day worshipers pour oil on minor gods, deposit flower offerings, and go through pujas in front of their deities. The temple is closed to devotees from 12:30 to 4—a time when visitors are allowed to take photographs for Rs. 10. The temple is peaceful and moving at this time. During the closing ceremony every evening, an image of Shiva is carried from near the eastern gopuram into Meenakshi's chambers for the night. *Between N., S., E., and W. Chithirai Sts, no ☏. ☯ Daily 4:30 AM–12:30 PM and 4 PM–9:30 PM. Photography permitted 12:30–4. ☛ Museum Rs. 3. ☯ Museum 6–8.*

Teppakkulam Tank. This lovely tank, with an island temple, lies 5 kilometers (3 miles) east of Madurai, far from the hubbub of town. A visit is most worthwhile during the Float Festival in January and February, when images of deities are carried on rafts through the water.

Tirumala Nayak Mahal. Built by Thirumalai Nayak, this Indo-Saracenic palace has a curved dome that soars without any visible support. Though it is mostly in ruins, restoration work promises to bring back some of the 17th-century grandeur. Every evening an excellent sound-and-light show dramatizes the city's past. *1 km (⅔ mi) from Meenakshi Temple,* ☎ *0452/26945.* ☛ *Palace Rs. 2, English-language sound-and-light show Rs. 2–Rs. 3.* ☉ *Palace daily 9–1 and 2–5, show 6:45.*

Shopping

Shops full of carvings, textiles, and brasswork fill the streets around Meenakshi Temple, particularly Town Hall Road and Masi Street. The **Handloom Society Hall** (24 W. Chitrai St.) has excellent hand-loomed cottons.

Dining

It isn't difficult to find a decent restaurant in sprawling Madurai, especially in the center of town around the temple.

For price categories, *see* the chart for Other Areas *in* On the Road with Fodor's.

$ **New Arya Bhavan.** A few blocks west of the temple, at this popular, air-conditioned eatery, you can also have delicious vegetarian fare (north and south Indian) in the garden, or head next door to **Arya Bhavan by Night,** which serves south Indian specialties from 4 PM to 2 AM. ✕ *241-A W. Masi St.,* ☎ *452/34577. No credit cards.*

Lodging

There are many hotels on the west side of the town center, but nicer hotels lie across the river to the north. All pools are outdoors.

For price categories, *see* the chart for Other Areas *in* On the Road with Fodor's.

$$$ **Taj Garden Retreat.** Home to officers of the Madurai courts for 100 years, this elegant old British estate overlooks all Madurai from a secluded hilltop. The rooms in the original bungalow have the most character: Rich hardwood floors continue out of the rooms onto a breezy colonial veranda. All the buildings maintain an elegant colonial feel. The restaurant serves Indian and Continental cuisines. 🏨 *Pasumalai Hill, Madurai 625004, Tamil Nadu,* ☎ *452/601020,* 📠 *452/604004. 34 rooms. Restaurant, bar, pool, tennis court. AE, DC, MC, V.*

$$ **Hotel Madurai Ashok.** The rooms in this two-story bungalow are spacious and clean, though the decor remains Brady-Bunch plush. A lovely lawn and pool enhance the sprawling building's exterior. 🏨 *Alagarkoil Rd., Madurai 625002, Tamil Nadu,* ☎ *452/42531,* 📠 *452/42530. 43 rooms. Restaurant, bar, pool. AE, DC, MC, V.*

Madurai Essentials

Arriving and Departing

The day-long drive from Madras to Madurai along NH 5 takes you through many of Tamil Nadu's village areas.

Visitor Information

The main **tourist office** (W. Veli St., ☎ 452/22957) is open Monday through Saturday 10 to 5:30 and Sunday 10 to 1. There are branches at the airport and the train station.

TIRUCHIRAPALLI (TRICHY)

㉓ **Tiruchirapalli** (Trichy) is a historic seat of power and bears the scars of conflict alongside its religious wonders. Trichy is a living temple city. More than in any other of the sacred towns you visit, the people here worship and the temples function. The town is spread out, but the incredible, vibrant religious life deserves some time. About 1½ kilometers (1 mile) north of the hotel area by the river you find the "heart" of town under the Rock Fort. The other temples are north of the river another 2 kilometers (1 mile).

Exploring

Chinna and Big bazaars. At the base of the Rock Fort, Chinna Bazaar, the Big Bazaar, and interesting narrow side streets make up the heart of the Old City. Both bazaars sell almost everything but specialize in the various tools of worship. You'll share the streets with crowds of people and the typical Indian array of animals, including donkeys. Temple ceremonies and festivals often spill onto the streets down here, giving you a show to enjoy with your "yard of coffee" (so named for the way it is poured at a yard's length from the cup).

★ **Rock Fort.** The military and architectural heart of Trichy is its startling Rock Fort, rising 83 meters (272 feet) above the city on the banks of the Cauvery River. Cut into the rock, 437 steps lead up to a temple dedicated to Lord Vinayaka (closed to non-Hindus) and the summit. Along the way are various landings and shrines: an ancient temple dedicated to Ganesh (the elephant god), a Shiva temple (also off-limits to non-Hindus), and cave temples cut into the rock. Finally, at the top, you are rewarded with a breathtaking view of the massive city below and the rich countryside surrounding it. To the north, the Srirangam temples rise dramatically out of the fields and riverbeds.

Srirangam. The glory of religious India explodes in Srirangam, an island between the Cauvery and its tributary, the Kollidam. Here, worshipers of Vishnu come to one of India's largest temples dedicated to
★ their god—the **Sri Ranganathaswamy Temple,** built between the 14th and 17th centuries. The town of Srirangam and most of its people exist within the seven sets of walls and 22 gopurams of their 156-acre temple. The temple itself really begins when you reach the mandapa behind the fourth wall, with its 940 remaining pillars. The tallest tower is just now nearing completion. This is very much a "living temple," especially in January when pilgrims from all over India come for the Vaikunta Ekadasi festival. During the celebrations, Heaven's Gate is opened, and the idol of Ranganatha is brought into the mandapa from the inner shrine under a golden dome. This temple also houses a beautiful collection of jewelry.

Thiruvanaikkaval. About 6 kilometers (3½ miles) east of Srirangam is another shrine to Shiva, named for a legendary elephant that worshipped the lingam. In the Mambukeswaram pagoda the lingam is submerged in water, one of the five elements that Shiva represents. The architecture of this temple, with five walls and seven gopurams, is among the finest Dravidian work still in existence.

TIME OUT In Chinna Bazaar, relax at **Sree Renga Bhavan** or **Vasantha Bhavan**—two enjoyable sidewalk *bhavans*—and have delicious coffee and memorable snacks.

Shopping

The best shopping here is among the shops in the Chinna and Big bazaars, below the Rock Fort. You'll find some brilliant wood and clay toys, traditional products of the region.

Dining

For price categories, *see* the chart for Other Areas *in* On the Road with Fodor's.

$ **Amaravathi.** Chinese and Indian cuisine are served in a dimly lit tropical setting of green-and-white lattice work. ✗ *13-D Williams Rd., Cantonment,* ☎ *431/460936. No credit cards.*

$ **Woodlands.** Here you can have Indian and Continental cuisine at reasonable prices. The best bet is the thali. ✗ *Femina Hotel, 14-C Williams Rd., Cantonment,* ☎ *431/461551. AE, DC, MC, V.*

Lodging

The hotels are concentrated in the southern cantonment area, also called Junction (for the Trichy Junction Railway Station).

For price categories, *see* the chart for Other Areas *in* On the Road with Fodor's.

$$ **Femina.** This central hotel has a bright, wide-open marble lobby and clean, comfortable rooms. The best rooms have a stunning temple view. The restaurant is vegetarian. ☷ *14-C Williams Rd., Cantonment, Tiruchirapalli 620001, Tamil Nadu,* ☎ *0431/461551,* ℻ *0431/460615. 130 rooms. Restaurant, travel services. AE, DC, MC, V.*

$$ **Hotel Sangam.** This newly renovated Western-style hotel, set on a lawn, offers rooms with modern (circa 1975) decor. The best rooms overlook the pool. ☷ *Collectors Office Rd., Tiruchirapalli 620001, Tamil Nadu,* ☎ *431/464700,* ℻ *431/461779. 60 rooms. Restaurant, bar, coffee shop, pool, health club, travel services. AE, DC, MC, V.*

$$ **Jenny's Residency.** This high-rise hotel is somewhere between cheap and elegant. The marble lobby has crystal chandeliers, but the ceiling is dirty and cracked in places. The best rooms are spacious and well furnished, but the worst are cramped and noisy. Extensive renovation now underway should raise the standard throughout. The newer suites already look good. A new bar and a poolside coffee shop were well on the way to completion at press time. One restaurant serves Chinese and the other serves a variety of cuisines. ☷ *3/14 McDonald's Rd., Tiruchirapalli 62001, Tamil Nadu,* ☎ *0431/461301,* ℻ *0431/461451. 120 rooms, 65 with shower, 55 with bath, 13 suites. 2 restaraunts, bar, pool, health club, travel services. AE, DC, MC, V.*

Excursion to Thanjavur

㉔ **Thanjavur** (once known as Tanjore), capital of the Chola Empire from the 10th to the 14th centuries, lies at the foot of one of India's greatest temples. A Chola king, Raja Raja Chola, who ruled from 985 to 1016, built this one among the empire's 74 temples.

★ **Brahadeeswarar Temple.** Dedicated to Shiva, with a soaring vimana (tower) over the inner sanctum. On the dome of this 62-meter (203-

foot) vimana rests a single block of granite weighing 80 tons. The enormous hulk was inched up to the top along an inclined plane that began in a village 6 kilometers (3¾ miles) away, a technique used by the Egyptians to build the pyramids.

The main shrine of the temple, at the end of a paved courtyard, houses a huge lingam. As you near the inner shrine (technically, only Hindus are allowed *inside* the inner sanctum) of Brahadeeswarar, you will encounter India's second largest Nandi bull statue. The god Shiva's mount in this case is 5 meters (16 feet) of black granite. Other sculptures inside the temple draw on Vishnu and Buddhism, as well as Shiva, for their subjects. The walls of the inner courtyard of the temple are covered with excellent frescoes of the Chola and Nayak periods. For a long time, the earlier and more interesting Chola frescoes lay hidden under the upper layer of the Nayak paintings. Only when a modern archaeologist was able to expose the bottom layer did art historians realize the existence of a school of painting in the Chola period comparable to the frescoes in the Ajanta cave shrines. *W. Main Rd. at S. Rampart St., no* ☎. ☛ *Free.* ۞ *6–noon and 4–8:30.*

The Palace. Partly in ruins, this mid-16th-century Nayak palace is one of the fort's central buildings. Within the complex is the **The Raja Raja Museum and Art Gallery,** which holds ancient Chola statues in bronze and granite. Also among the palace buildings is the **Saraswati Mahal Library,** which has a collection of books in many languages as well as 8,000 rare palm-leaf and paper manuscripts in Indian and European languages. *E. Raja St., no* ☎. ۞ *Museum and Art Gallery: Sat–Thurs. 9–1 and 3–6; Library Thurs.–Tues. 10–1 and 2–5.*

Shopping

R. Govindarajan (31 Kuthiraikatti St., Karantha, ☎ 4362/20282) has a large selection of Tanjore paintings, brass and copper artifacts, wood carvings, and glass.

Dining and Lodging

Small vegetarian restaurants are easy to find, especially along Ghandiji Road. For price categories, *see* the chart for Other Areas *in* On the Road with Fodor's.

$ **Hotel Parisutham.** Set on a pleasant lawn, this hotel has attractive modern rooms with fans or air-conditioning. ⌸ *55 G. A. Canal Rd., Thanjavur 613001, Tamil Nadu,* ☎ *4362/21466. 42 rooms. Restaurant, bar, business services, travel services. AE, DC, MC, V.*

$ **Hotel Tamilnadu.** This government-run hotel has simple Western-style decor; the fan-cooled rooms are clean. The best rooms open onto an upstairs veranda overlooking an interior courtyard. ⌸ *Gandhi Rd., Thanjavur 613001, Tamil Nadu,* ☎ *4362/21421. 31 rooms. Restaurant, bar. Rupees only.*

Thanjavur Essentials

ARRIVING AND DEPARTING

The best way to reach Thanjavur is by road from Trichy, 55 kilometers (34 miles) west. There are regular trains from Thanjavur to Madras (9 hours), Madurai (6 hours), and Trichy (2 hours).

VISITOR INFORMATION

The **tourist office** (Hotel Tamilnadu complex, Gandhi Rd.) is open Tuesday through Sunday, 10 to 1 and 2 to 5.

Tiruchirapalli Essentials

Arriving and Departing

The **Tiruchirapalli Airport** is 8 kilometers (5 miles) from the city center. Indian Airlines (Dindigul Rd., ☎ 431/25202) has regular flights to Madras and Madurai.

Getting Around

Scooters and taxis will do, but if you can find them, rickshaws are a great form of transportation in this sprawling but relaxed town.

Visitor Information

The **tourist office** (1 Williams Rd., in Hotel Tamilnadu complex, ☎ 431/25336; counters at train station, airport) is open Monday through Saturday 10:30 to 5:30.

TAMIL NADU ESSENTIALS

Arriving and Departing

By Hired Car with Driver

Madras is linked to the north by National Highway 5 (NH 5), to the west by NH 4, and to the south by NH 45. Getting here by car is most feasible from Bangalore, 334 kilometers (207 miles) to the west. Otherwise, air or rail is preferable.

By Plane

The domestic and international terminals of Madras's Meenambakkam Airport are about 16 kilometers (10 miles) from the city center. Madras has regular service from major international carriers (*see* Important Contacts A to Z *in* the Gold Guide). Domestic service is provided by **Indian Airlines** (☎ 44/825–1677 or 44/827–7977 or 140); check with your travel agent for the current status and schedules of other domestic carriers.

BETWEEN THE AIRPORT AND CENTER CITY

A shuttle to the major hotels costs Rs. 50. Hired cars are available through prepaid booths just past the baggage claim areas. The ride will cost around Rs. 300.

By Train

Trains to and from the north and west generally use Madras Central Station (Wall Tax Rd., ☎ 132 or 44/563535). The best way to book trains is through the foreign tourist quota available at the Indrail office on the second floor of Central Station's new building (open 10–5; if you don't have a valid encashment certificate with your rupees, tickets must be purchased in dollars or sterling—you need your passport). All the regular booking offices are open daily 7:30 to 1 and 1:30 to 7 (morning only Sun.).

Getting Around

By Auto Rickshaw

In congested cities and small towns this is the fastest, most economical way to get around. Figure Rs. 5 for the first kilometer and Rs. 1.75 per additional kilometer.

By Bicycle Rickshaw

In temple cities and villages, this is a leisurely, pleasant, and cheap way to travel. But remember that pedaling in the heat is rough. Set the fare in advance and be a little generous; these people work hard.

By Car
NH 7 (from Bangalore) and NH 45 (from Madras) are the state's major north–south arteries. East–west roads include NH 4 (Madras–Bangalore), NH 46 (Vellore–Bangalore), NH 47 (Salem–Coimbatore), and NH 49 (Madurai east to the coast and west into Kerala). In any kind of metered transit, it is wise to use a map to familiarize yourself with the shortest route to your destination. This is best done *before* you get in the scooter or taxi, but even with your driver staring at you in the rearview mirror, a little map work helps keep you from being taken advantage of. In smaller destinations (which often have unmetered vehicles), always set the fare in advance. Hire a car from a government-licensed operator (*see* Travel Agencies, *below*). Figure about Rs. 3 to Rs. 7 per kilometer and a halt charge of Rs. 100 per night. In the city, a car of your own is a headache. Instead, rely on some combination of public transit, scooters, rickshaw, taxis, and your feet.

By Plane
At press time you could get flights from Madras to Coimbatore, Madurai, and Trichy. Check with your travel agent for airlines and schedules.

By Taxi
This is a good way to see sights within major cities. A taxi should cost about Rs. 7 for the first kilometer and Rs. 2 per additional kilometer. Make sure the driver uses his meter or set the fare in advance.

By Train
Several trains a day leave Madras Egmore station (☎ 44/563545) for destinations throughout Tamil Nadu, including Trichy, Madurai, and Rameshwaram. (*See also* Arriving and Departing by Train, *above*).

Dining

In addition to the restaurants listed here, if you see a crowded local restaurant, its popularity is an indication that the food is good. If you look around, it is still possible to eat a satisfactory meal for Rs. 30 or less. When pressed, the staff members at your hotel are bound to have some recommendations in addition to their own restaurant.

Lodging

Except for resorts in areas like Mamallapuram, hotels in Madras and other Tamil Nadu towns are standard. Unless otherwise indicated, hotels have central air-conditioning, and rooms have cable TV, bathrooms with tubs, and room service. In addition, many luxury hotels have exclusive floors with special privileges or facilities designed for the business traveler (*see* Special Hints for Business Travelers *in* Chapter 3, Business Travel in India), and many have 24-hour coffee shops.

Important Addresses and Numbers

Changing Money
In Madras, **American Express** (G-17 Spencer Plaza, Anna Salai, ☎ 44/825–7640) is open daily 9:30–7:30. Both the **Thomas Cook** offices (112 Nungambakkam High Rd., ☎ 44/827–5052, and 20 Rajaji Salai, ☎ 44/534097) are open daily 9:30–8. In other cities, head for a branch of the State Bank of India or change money in your hotel.

Consulates
United Kingdom (24 Anderson Rd., Madras 600006, ☎ 44/827–3136. ☉ Weekdays 8:30–4). **United States** (220 Anna Salai, Madras 600006, ☎ 44/827–3040. ☉ Weekdays 8:30–5:15).

Emergencies

For any emergency contact your hotel, consulate, or the East West Clinic (*see* Chapter 4, Delhi).

Travel Agencies

American Express (G-17 Spencer Plaza, Anna Salai, Madras, ☎ 44/825–7640) is open daily 9:30 to 6 for non-card members and until 7:30 for card members. **Ashok Travel and Tours** (29 Victoria Crescent at C-in-C Rd., Madras, ☎ 44/827–8884) is open Monday through Saturday 10 to 5:30. **Tamil Nadu Tourism Development Corporation** (143 Anna Salai, Madras, ☎ 44/849803) is open weekdays 9:45 to 6. **Thomas Cook** (112 Nungambakkam High Rd., ☎ 44/827–5052, and 20 Rajaji Salai, ☎ 044/534097) is open Monday through Saturday 9:30 to 6.

Visitor Information

The **Government of India Tourist Office** (154 Anna Salai, on corner opposite Spencer's, Madras 600002, ☎ 44/8524785, and at airport's domestic and international terminals) has a knowledgeable staff and an astoundingly comprehensive computer database. It is open weekdays 9 to 5:45 and Saturday 9 to 1 and is closed Sunday. Just down the road is the **Tamil Nadu Tourism Development Corporation** (143 Anna Salai, ☎ 44/830498) where you can get information and book guided tours or private cars through approved travel agents. The **India Tourist Development Corporation** (ITDC, 29 Victoria Crescent at C-in-C Rd., ☎ 044/8278884) arranges excursions throughout the state. If you plan to visit any restricted areas or need your visa extended, you should head for the **Foreigners' Regional Registration Office** (Sastri Bhavan Annexe Bldg., Haddows Rd., ☎ 44/827–8210).

10 Kerala

The best way to explore this southern state is slowly, from the deck of an indigenous boat as it moves through picturesque backwater canals past palm-shrouded fishing villages. Cochin, the state's port city, is congested, but its historic district sells good curios. Kerala's excellent game park, Lake Periyar, is best visited by boat to sight wildlife, especially elephants. Finally, you can enjoy a secluded beach resort set in a cove on the Arabian Sea near Kovalam, a few kilometers south of the small capital of Trivandrum.

By Vikram
Singh

KERALA, A TROPICAL PARADISE in the south between the Western Ghats and the Arabian Sea, is
one of India's most progressive states. Kerala's
natural wealth has made it remarkably cosmopolitan, with a heritage
of 3,000 years of relations with the rest of the world. Phoenicians, Arabs,
Jews, Chinese, and Europeans came in droves, attracted by the region's
valuable cash crops: tea, rubber, cashews, teak, and a wide assortment
of spices—most notably pepper (Kerala's "black gold") and cardamom.
Yet life moves at a leisurely pace in this part of the world, where rice
and coconut are abundant and the daily catches of fishermen are rich
and bountiful.

Kerala didn't exist as a state until 1956. Since then, however, it has
achieved a name for itself, becoming the first place in the world to adopt
a communist government in a free election: a political event that caused
tremendous discussion and speculation, as Keralans are also the most
highly educated population in India. With a literacy rate of well over
90% (against a national level of 52%), Keralans—men dressed in pristine white *dhotis* (wraps) and women in brightly colored saris—walk
with pride in the shade of their black umbrellas. Although the com-
munists have now fallen from power, they are still influential.

Although Kerala's ethnic makeup is similar to that of the rest of India,
its historical ties have resulted in a unique culture. For nearly three centuries before 1795, when the British finally established a firm grip on
the area, a procession of Portuguese, Dutch, Arab, and Jewish traders
used every means possible—from signing treaties with the local rulers
and chieftains to fighting it out among themselves—to secure Kerala's
profits.

With the exception of Cochin, Kerala's attractions are most definitely
rural: pristine beaches dripping with coconuts (*see* Chapter 2, Special-
Interest Travel in India) and fishing boats laden with bountiful catches;
exotic wildlife and a landscape that is as confusing as it is beautiful; a
cultural tradition that combines ayurvedic health treatments with
snakeboat races and Carnatic music with the Kathakali dance; and 12
wildlife sanctuaries and two national parks, including the renowned
Periyar Wildlife Preserve near Thekkady (*see* Chapter 2, Special-Interest
Travel in India).

*Numbers in the margin correspond to points of interest on the Kerala
map.*

COCHIN

❶ Cochin is one of those rare places where the 20th century and ancient
civilizations thrive side by side. A Jewish synagogue, Portuguese
churches, Dutch buildings, a couple of mosques and Hindu temples,
and Chinese fishing nets all share the city.

Modern Cochin (a name used to describe a cluster of islands and
towns, including the mainland, Ernakulam) is one of the largest ports
on India's west coast, handling over 5 million tons of cargo a year. But
the cargo of spices, coffee, and coir has not changed for centuries. The
streets behind the docks that are Cochin's heart are still lined with old
merchant houses, godowns (warehouses), and open courtyards heaped
with betel nuts, ginger, peppercorns, and coir.

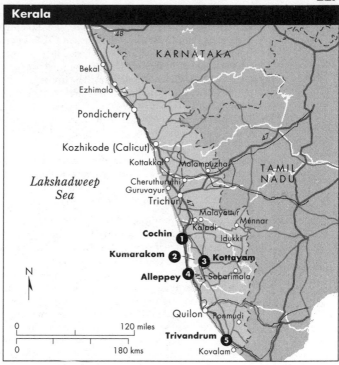

Kerala

KARNATAKA

Bekal
Ezhimala
Pondicherry
Kozhikode (Calicut)
Kottakkal
Malampuzha
Lakshadweep Sea
Cheruthuruthi
Guruvayur
Trichur
TAMIL NADU
Malayattur
Kaladi
Munnar
Cochin ❶
Idukki
Kumarakom ❷
❸ **Kottayam**
Alleppey ❹
Sabarimala
Quilon
Ponmudi
N
Trivandrum ❺
Kovalam

0 ————— 120 miles
0 ————— 180 kms

Exploring

Three miles from the harbor—but linked by bridges and ferries—lies Ernakulam, once the capital of the former state of Cochin and now its commercial center. Coir magnates, who often have their business on Gundu Island, primarily live in the residential quarter of Fort Cochin, where their pseudo-Tudor houses are reminiscent of the British and London—except for the coconut palms and sunshine. Bolghatty Island, north of Ernakulam, is the most beautiful of all the islands, and its colonial mansion, formerly used by the Dutch governor and later by the British Resident, is now a hotel. Mattancherry, or Jew Town, southwest of the harbor, is the home of the dwindling Jewish community, and along with Fort Cochin, the historic center of the city.

Dutch Palace. Built by the Portuguese in the middle of the 16th century, the structure was taken over in 1663 by the Dutch, who added some improvements before presenting it to the rajas of Cochin. The rajas, in turn, made more improvements, notably some of the best **mythological murals** in India, particularly in the bed chambers. In one room, you can see the entire story of the *Ramayana* on the walls. The palace also contains a rare example of traditional Keralan flooring, which looks like polished black marble but is actually a subtle mix of burned coconut shells, charcoal, lime, plant juices, and egg whites. On display in the coronation hall are many of the Cochin rajas' artifacts. *Palace Rd., Mattancherry, no ☎.* ☛ *Free.* ☺ *Sat.–Thurs. 10–5.*

★ **Fort Cochin.** The northern tip of the Mattancherry peninsula is believed to be the oldest European settlement in India. It first saw the Portuguese flag in 1500; Vasco da Gama arrived in Cochin in 1502. The following year, Alfonso de Albuquerque came with half a dozen ships bearing settlers and built the fort. He also brought five friars, who built the first European church in India in 1510, still standing in Fort Cochin as **St. Francis Church.** Da Gama returned in 1524 as Portuguese viceroy of the Indies. He died here and was buried in St. Francis Church. You can still visit his gravestone, but his remains were shipped back to Portugal in 1538 (he's buried in Lisbon). The history of the church reflects the colonial struggle for India. It was Dutch Reform from 1664 to 1804 and Anglican from 1804 to 1947; now it's part of the Church of South India. The church contains Dutch gravestones and has the *Doep Boek,* a register of baptisms and marriages from 1751 to 1894. You can look at a photographic reproduction of the vital statistics (the original is too fragile). St. Francis is a sedate church in the Spanish style, not nearly as flamboyant as the **Santa Cruz Cathedral** in Fort Cochin, which verges on the gaudy. The Santa Cruz was completed in 1904. *Parade Rd. and Rampath Rd. Churches open sunrise–sunset.*

★ **Mattancherry.** The first migration of Jews to Kerala supposedly took place in the 6th century BC, followed by a much larger wave in the 1st century AD, when Jews fleeing Roman persecution in Jerusalem came and settled at Craganore. In the 4th century, the local king promised the Jews perpetual protection, and the Jewish colony flourished, serving as a haven to Jews from the Middle East and, in later centuries, Europe. When the Portuguese leader Albuquerque discovered the Jews near Cochin, however, he requested permission from his king to "exterminate them one by one" and destroyed their city at Craganore. Muslim anti-Semitism flared up, as well. The Jews rebuilt in Mattancherry but were only able to live without fear once the Dutch had taken control in 1663. Very few of the "white Jews" of Cochin remain today: most of the youth has left India for Israel.

Parishith Thampuran Museum. Also known as the Cochin Museum, this museum holds artifacts from the royal family, many 19th-century paintings and sculptures, and some beautiful old murals. The ajoining art gallery holds contemporary works by local Indian artists. *D. H. Rd., Ernakulam,* ☎ *484/36907.* ☛ *Rs. 5.* ☺ *Tues.–Sun. 9:30–12:30 and 3–5.*

★ **Synagogue.** This imposing structure was built in 1568 when the Jews settled in Mattancherry after their expulsion from Craganore. It was considerably embellished in the mid-18th century by Ezekiel Rahabi, who built a clock tower and paved the floor of the synagogue with hand-painted willow-pattern tiles (each one different) brought from China. Its most important relics are the impressive copper plates recording King Bhaskara Ravi Varma's 4th-century decree that guaranteed the Jewish settlers domain over Craganore. Indeed, the entire synagogue is beautiful, and the elder loves to show his visitors around. *Mattancherry.* ☛ *Rs. 1.* ☺ *Sun.–Fri. 10–noon and 3–5. Closed Jewish holidays.*

Shopping

Antiques and Handicrafts
Try **Cochin Gallery** (C. C. 6/116 Jew Town Rd., ☎ 484/228199) for various collectables. **Indian Arts and Curios** (Jew Town Rd.) is the oldest and most reliable shop on this curios- and antiques-laden street; its two outlets are filled with brass and wood items and Tanjore glass paintings. **Kairali** (M. G. Rd., Ernakulam, ☎ 484/354407) is a government shop with a good collection of Kerala handicrafts and curios. **Surabhi** (M. G. Rd., Ernakulam, no ☎), run by the state's Handicrafts Cooperative Society, has a strong selection of locally made products. Be aware that "antique" can be a suspect term in all stores.

Dining

Seafood is plentiful, fresh, and delicious. While exploring near the Chinese fishing nets, you can buy a freshly caught fish and have it fried up for about Rs. 10 at one of the small stalls near the vendors.

For price categories, *see* the chart for Other Areas *in* On the Road with Fodor's.

$$$ Jade Pavilion. An interior Oriental pavilion, exotic wall mural, and brass lanterns create an elegant, romantic atmosphere. From the extensive Chinese menu, try lobster *sing-tu* style (spicy lobster cooked in chili and oyster sauce), tiger prawns in garlic sauce, or tasty steamed fish. ✗ *Taj Malabar Hotel, Willingdon Island,* ☏ *484/666811. Reservations advised. AE, DC, MC, V.*

$$$ Rice Boats. Eat inside a traditional Kerala wooden boat under a woven bamboo awning. The lighting is subdued, and oars and bamboo hats adorn the walls. The chef prepares seafood specialties, including *karimeen grandeur* (fresh local sea fish marinated in subtle spices and fried), and lobster and prawn dishes. ✗ *Taj Malabar Hotel, Willingdon Island,* ☏ *484/666811. Reservations advised. AE, DC, MC, V.*

$$ Fort Cochin. The bamboo and traditional furnishings give this outdoor
★ restaurant the feel of a Kerala-style cottage. The day's catch is wheeled before you in a wooden cart, and your choice is cooked to your specifications—from simply grilled to exquisitely curried. ✗ *Casino Hotel, Willingdon Island,* ☏ *484/666811. Reservations advised. AE, DC, MC, V. No lunch.*

$ Fry's Village Restaurant. This simple restaurant—four plain pavilions with bamboo curtains—screens out the city's bustle. It serves typical Kerala set meals (thalis) at lunch, including various specialties like molly (fillet in a sweet green curry with coconuts) or the inexpensive *kadala* (Kerala plain curry) with *puttu* (steamed rice and coconut cake) for under Rs. 10. Fry's is very popular with locals; expect a crowd. ✗ *Chittoor Rd., next to Mymoon Cinema,* ☏ *484/353983. No credit cards.*

$ Pandhal. This modern multicuisine restaurant with rough white stucco walls, a pine ceiling, and a quiet waterfall, serves a variety of seafood and Indian dishes, but the Chinese cuisine and steaks are especially popular. It is crowded in the evenings. ✗ *M. G. Rd., opposite Grand Hotel,* ☏ *484/367759. Dinner reservations advised. AE, DC, MC, V.*

Lodging

Though they are are in a city of unique charm, the hotels in Cochin offer only a standard level of comfort, style, and service. What most distinguishes them is the quality of the view.

For price categories, *see* the chart for Other Areas *in* On the Road with Fodor's.

$$$$ Bolgatty Palace Hotel. Set in 15 acres of gardens on the southern tip of long, narrow Bolgatty Island, this government-run hotel was once the seat of the British Residents. Built in 1744 by the Dutch, the old stone building retains its 18th-century charm on the outside. The interior is adequate, but rooms are quite small unless you get a suite. Although it is lovely being on the island, a steady stream of families and newlyweds keeps the grounds far from peaceful. Several cottages are available, but you are better off in the historic (and better kept) main building. ⌑ *Bolgatty Island, 5 min by ferry from High Court Jetty,* ☏ *484/355003 or 354879. 11 rooms. Restaurant, beer garden, travel services. AE, V.*

$$–$$$ **Taj Malabar Hotel.** This luxury resort, on the tip of Willingdon Island,
★   offers elegance, privacy, and fantastic sea views. The hotel blends
carved dark wood and Kerala-style furnishings with more modern
tiles and brass. If you want antiquity and handsome, older furnishings,
ask for a room with wooden floors in the old wing. Rooms in the new
wing have modern decor and spectacular views from the higher floors.
The best rooms have a seaside view; the others overlook gardens. ▦
Willingdon Island, Cochin 682009, Kerala, ☎ *484/666811,* ℻ *484/
668297. 99 rooms, 9 suites. 3 restaurants, bar, pool, travel services.
AE, DC, MC, V.*

$$ **Casino Hotel.** This handsome Western-style hotel offers excellent value
and privacy. Its lobby is cozy, with cane furnishings. The spacious rooms
have elegant, modern decor. The best rooms overlook the lawn and
pool. ▦ *Willingdon Island, Cochin 682003, Kerala,* ☎ *484/668221,*
℻ *484/668001. 50 rooms with bath, 20 with shower, 1 suite. 2 restau-
rants, bar, travel services. AE, DC, MC, V.*

$$ **Taj Residency.** Opened in 1994, this downtown hotel caters to Cochin's
ever-growing community of business travelers. Rooms in the beauti-
fully refurbished building are small, but the harbor and sea views are
spectacular. A new floor catering exclusively to business travelers is
planned for 1996. ▦ *Shanmugham Rd., Ernakulam 682031, Kerala,*
☎ *484/371471,* ℻ *484/371481. 109 rooms with shower, 12 suites.
Restaurant, bar, coffee shop, business services. AE, DC, MC, V.*

$ **Avenue Regent.** This high-rise hotel in the heart of the city has art deco
touches in its lobby: red bands around the ceiling molding and in the
floor pattern. Contemporary rooms are spacious. Its business services
make this hotel good for the corporate traveler. ▦ *M. G. Rd., Cochin
682016, Kerala,* ☎ *484/353003,* ℻ *484/370129. 53 rooms with bath.
Restaurant, bar, business services, travel services. AE, DC, MC, V.*

$ **Best Western Viceroy.** On its own private island, this new hotel offers
palm-fringed serenity and convenience. Rooms are comfortably furnished in standard, unremarkable colors and wood accents. It's good
for business travelers who want to avoid staying in crowded Ernakulam. ▦ *Silver Sand Island, Cochin 682016, Kerala,* ☎ *484/318357,*
℻ *484/318358. 76 rooms. Restaurant, bar, pool, health club, business
services, travel services. AE, DC, MC, V.*

The Arts

Vijnana Kala Vedi Cultural Center (Tarayil Mukku Junction, Aranmula
689533, between Cochin and Trivandrum, ☎ 4731/2552, ℻ 4731/
2783), established by a Frenchwoman in 1971, is dedicated to preserving
the arts and heritage of Kerala. People from all over the world come
to live and study here with experienced masters in a simple, village atmosphere. Students can enroll for as little as one week (space permitting). You can also stay overnight just to visit.

Dance

Many companies in Cochin offer performances of Kerala's unique
dance form, the 400-year-old Kathakali (*Katha* means "story" and *kali*
means "play"), in which a story is told through dancing, pantomime,
and music. Many centers offer a two-hour performance that includes
an opportunity to watch the application of the elaborate makeup. The
best performances are at the **See India Foundation** (Kalthil Parambil
La., ☎ 484/369471), where the director offers clear and lively explanations to his audience before every 6:45 PM show. Performances at
the **Cochin Cultural Center** (Manikath Rd, ☎ 484/367866) are also clearly
explained and begin at 7 PM. Makeup application—amazing in itself—
can be seen at either center from 6 PM onward.

Martial Arts

Practitioners of Kerala's traditional martial art form, Kalarippayattu, can be observed at **Arjuna Kalari Samgham** (Puthiya Rd. Junction, ☎ 484/360980; daily 5–9AM and 5–9PM), and at the **E. N. S. Kalari Centre** (Nettoor, Ernakulam, ☎ 484/805682; Mon.–Sat. 6 PM–7 PM, Sun. 3 PM–7 PM.).

Nightlife

The hotels have bars, and rules are less strict here than elsewhere, but a night out means catching a performance. There are no nightclubs. Beer, however, is very cheap.

Cochin Essentials

Arriving and Departing

BY PLANE

The tiny airport is on Willingdon Island. *See* Arriving and Departing by Plane *in* Kerala Essentials, *below.*

Between the Airport and Center City. The airport is served by taxis. A cab to your hotel will cost anywhere from Rs. 60 (on Willingdon) to Rs. 100 (in Ernakulam or Mattancherry).

Getting Around

BY AUTO RICKSHAW

This is a convenient, quick way to travel. Figure Rs. 4 for the first kilometer and Rs. 2 per additional kilometer. Set the fare in advance on meterless auto rickshaws.

BY BICYCLE RICKSHAW

An enjoyable way to travel, it should be cheaper than an auto rickshaw. But remember, the driver works hard for his money, and distances can be considerable. Set your fare in advance.

BY BOAT

Within Cochin, ferries and private boats ply between the fort, Willingdon Island, and Ernakulam throughout the day. Getting across by ferry costs only a few rupees; on private boats, be sure to set the rate in advance.

BY TAXI

This is a good option for destinations in and around the city. Figure about Rs. 7 for the first kilometer and Rs. 4 per additional kilometer. Ask at either tourist office for current legal rates.

Guided Tours

The **Government of India Tourist Office** (*see* Visitor Information *in* Kerala Essentials, *below*) in Cochin can supply guides for walking tours of the city. Four hours for one to four people will cost around Rs. 60. The **Kerala Tourism Development Corporation** (KTDC, *see* Visitor Information *in* Kerala Essentials, *below*) conducts two inexpensive boat sightseeing tours of Cochin a day. The 3½-hour tours depart at 9 AM and 2 PM from the Boat Jetty.

Important Addresses and Numbers

CHANGING MONEY

Most Western-style hotels have foreign-exchange services. **Thomas Cook** (M. G. Rd., Ernakulam, ☎ 484/373819) offers good rates. **The Bank of India** (Shanmugham Rd. and Willingdon Island), and **ANZ Grindlays** (Willingdon Island) will cash traveler's checks and exchange money, as will any branch of the State Bank of India.

VISITOR INFORMATION

Kerala State Tourist Information Center, Kerala Tourism Development Corporation (KTDC), and the **Government of India Tourist Office** (*see* Visitor Information *in* Kerala Essentials, *below*) all can help with information and tours within Cochin.

CENTRAL KERALA

Between Cochin and Quilon to the south is the immense labyrinth of waterways called *kayals* through which much of the life of the people of Kerala, the Malayali, has historically flowed. From the vastness of Vembanad Lake to quiet waterways just large enough for a canoe, the backwaters have carried Kerala's products—mostly coconut-based—from the village to the market for centuries.

Exploring

A backwater cruise through the region's inland waterways provides a window on the Malayalis' unique traditional life. Several agencies operate such tours. The tours can be two- or three- hour journeys through shady and sheltered villages or lengthy, hot adventures (Quilon to Alleppey is a popular 8-hour journey; *see* Getting Around *in* Central Kerala Essentials, *below*). Private travel agents and even the KTDC are eager to hook people up with private boat trips through these waters (*see* Visitor Information *and* Travel Agencies *in* Kerala Essentials, *below*).

❹ Alleppey. This waterborne industrial city has canals teeming with country boats. It offers a special treat on or around the second Saturday in August. Throngs of supporters line the shore to watch the annual **Nehru Cup** snakeboat race, which starts with a water procession and concludes in dramatic fashion as the boats (manned by as many as 100 rowers) vie for the trophy. Alleppey is also a good place to get the boat to Quilon and then southward to Trivandrum or Kovalam.

❸ Kottayam. This pleasant town, just inland from Alleppey, has a number of old Christian churches established by missionaries for whom it was long a base. It is also a good place to buy provisions (including beer) for trips to the Periyar Wildlife Sanctuary (*see* Chapter 2, Special-Interest Travel in India).

❷ Kumarakom. A trip to this tiny, rapidly developing paradise 16 kilometers (10 miles) west of Kottayam on the shores of Vembanad Lake is generally centered around a stay at either the historic Taj Garden Retreat or the secluded Coconut Lagoon (*see* Lodging, *below*). The waterways quickly become twisting village "lanes," which are fascinating to explore by canoe. The lake offers opportunities for plenty of water-based recreation (happily, motor sports have been limited so far).

Lodging

Of the towns mentioned, only Kumarakom stands out as a place to spend some time.

For price categories, *see* the chart for Other Areas *in* On the Road with Fodor's.

$$$ Coconut Lagoon. Accessible only by boat, this new resort is one of south India's best. Hotel boats ferry guests between the secluded lagoon on the shores of Lake Vembanad and two pick-up points along a nearby river. The grounds are criss-crossed with canals and footbridges, and guests can choose between two types of cottage. The smaller are air-conditioned and have open-to-the-sky bathrooms, complete with a live banana tree. Other cottages are actually reconstructed traditional homes in which the breeze keeps you cool. The large, curving pool is a masterpiece set by the lake under swaying palm trees. The open-air restaurant overlooks the water and serves mouth-watering buffets. ⊞ *Kumarakom, Kotayam 686563, Kerala,* ☎ *48/192491. 23 cottages. Restaurant, pool, massage, spa, travel services. AE, DC, MC, V.*

$$$ **Taj Garden Retreat** Completed in 1891, the main building of this resort is an old colonial dream house. Large rooms with high ceilings open onto broad, dark-wood verandas. Built by the son of an English missionary, the house looks over a man-made lake and speaks volumes about the elegant life of plantation owners. The property opened as a Taj hotel in 1994. Much of the produce is grown in the hotel's extensive gardens, geese live next to the small private lake, and guests have access to Lake Vembanad. ⊞ *1/404 Kumarakom, Kottayam 686583, Kerala,* ☎ *48/ 192377. 6 rooms. Restaurant, travel services. AE, DC, MC, V.*

Central Kerala Essentials

Arriving and Departing

Getting to the backwaters of Kerala is easiest by car from Cochin, where you will find travel agents and the tourist office to help you plan your itinerary. If you're planing to visit either of the resorts in Kumarakom (*see above*), their sister hotel in Cochin (Casino Hotel) will help make arrangements as well.

Getting Around

BY BOAT

The **Alleppey Tourism Development Cooperative** (ATDC; *see* Guided Tours, *below*) runs daily trips between Alleppey and Quilon (8 hrs, Rs. 100). Boats in both directions leave at 10:30 AM. Boats also link Allepey with Kottayam and Changanacherry.

Guided Tours

The **Alleppey Tourism Development Cooperative** (ATDC, Karthika Tourist Home, near Alleppey Bus Station, ☎ 477/3462 or 477/2554) conducts several backwater tours in addition to the Quilon–Alleppey run. Private companies, the KTDC, and the Tourist Desk (*see* Visitor Information *in* Kerala Essentials, *below*) operate short (half-day) backwater tours for around Rs. 100 to Rs. 400.

Visitor Information

The **Alleppey Tourism Development Cooperative** (ATDC, Karthika Tourist Home, near Alleppey Bus Station, ☎ 477/3462 or 477/2554) provides complete information. The tourist offices in Cochin and Trivandrum can also help.

TRIVANDRUM (THIRUVANANTHAPURAM)

❺ The quiet capital city of the Raja of Travancore since 1750, **Trivandrum** now fills the same role for the state of Kerala. Built on seven low hills and cleansed by ocean breezes, Trivandrum is surprisingly calm and pleasant. Its few sights and quiet lanes (outside the center) make it a good place to spend a day. Most travelers soon head for the irresistible beaches of Kovalam, 16 kilometers (10 miles) south (*see* Chapter 2, Special-Interest Travel in India).

Exploring

Padmanabhaswamy Temple. Trivandrum's main architectural land-mark, dedicated to Vishnu, is a handsome example of south Indian tem-ple architecture, with an impressive seven-story *gopuram* (tower). The date of its construction is uncertain, although one legend traces it to 3000 BC. What is known, however, is that it was built by 4,000 ma-sons, 6,000 laborers, and 100 elephants in six months. In the main court-yard, the **Kulasekhar Mandapam,** there is some intricate granite sculpture; more can be appreciated on nearly 400 pillars supporting the temple corridor. Technically, the entire complex is open only to Hin-dus, and even they must be properly dressed. The temple keeps erratic hours. *M. G. Rd. at Chali Bazaar,* ☎ *471/450233.* ☉ *Sunrise–12:30 and 4:30–9:30.*

Museum and Art Gallery Complex. In a beautiful 80-acre park at the north end of M. G. Road, you'll find a number of attractions. The **Napier Museum,** with its Cubist pattern of gables, has a marvelous collection of local arts and crafts. The **Sri Chitra Art Gallery** has an eclectic col-lection of paintings, including works of the Rajput, Mogul, and Tan-jore schools; copies of the Ajanta and Sigirya frescoes; and works from China, Japan, Tibet, and Bali, along with canvases by modern Indian painters. A **zoo** and an **aquarium,** are also within the grounds. *Museum Rd.,* ☎ *471/436275.* ☛ *Museum and gallery free, zoo and aquarium Rs. 2.* ☉ *Thurs.–Tues. 10–5, Wed. 1–4:45. Zoo and aquar-ium Tues.–Sun. 9–4:45.*

Shopping

Gifts Corner (M. G. Rd., ☎ 471/73196) has both new and antique trea-sures to uncover. The **SMSM Handicrafts Emporium** (behind the Secre-tariate, ☎ 471/331668) sells curios and handicrafts.

Sports

Kovalam, 16 kilometers (10 miles) south of Trivandrum, has some of the finest beaches in southern India; *see* Beaches *in* Chapter 2, Special-Interest Travel in India.

Trivandrum Essentials

Arriving and Departing
BY PLANE
Trivandrum's small, confusing airport is 6 kilometers (3¾ miles) from the city center. (*See* Arriving and Departing by Plane *in* Kerala Essen-tials, *below*).

Between the Airport and Center City. Taxis charge about Rs. 50. Traf-fic can be heavy.

Visitor Information
The **KTDC** (Station Rd. or Mascot Square, Thiruvananthapuram 695033, ☎ 471/75031, and at the airport; open weekdays 10–5) offers advice and literature. The **Tourist Information Center** (Park View, across from the museum, ☎ 471/62574) is also a good source.

KERALA ESSENTIALS

Arriving and Departing

By Car

Years of communist rule did not make Kerala's roads any better than those in the rest of India. Nonetheless, it is a beautiful state to drive through. If you are coming from Tamil Nadu, the scenic drive from Madurai along the Madurai–Kottayam Road is well worthwhile. NH 47 runs from central Tamil Nadu (Salem) to Cochin through some beautiful country before heading down the coast to Kanya Kumari (Cape Comorin). NH 17 runs down the coast form Mangalore to Cochin. Traffic is generally fine outside the cities.

By Plane

All flights to the region arrive at either Cochin or Trivandrum, which are served by **Air India** (☎ 484/351299) and **Singapore Airlines** (☎ 484/367911). **Indian Airlines** (☎ 484/353901) serves domesic routes; contact your travel agent or the Government of India tourist office in your home country for the current schedules of other domestic carriers.

Getting Around

By Boat

The backwaters of Kerala are Venice on an immense scale. Even with roads, rail travel, and airplanes, these ancient waterways are still used for some long-distance transport and commuting (*see* Central Kerala Essentials, *above*).

By Car

By hired car with driver is the best way to get around Kerala. Figure about Rs. 4–5 per kilometer and a halt charge of Rs. 100 per night. Hire a car from a government-approved travel agency (*see* Guided Tours, *below*) and be sure to shop around. The coastal highway (NH 47 south of Trichur, NH 17 north) will serve most of your needs. Roads to the interior ghats (mountains) are often breathtaking as the landscape changes from the brilliant green of the paddy fields to the rich shades of the tea plantations and the mountain jungle. The journey from Trivandrum to Cochin takes about six hours.

By Plane

Indian Airlines flies between Cochin and Trivandrum every Wednesday, Friday, and Sunday.

Guided Tours

The **KTDC** (*see* Visitor Information, *below*) has a series of specialty tours with names like "Age Halt" for revitalization and "Soul Stir" on the pilgrim trail through Kerala's sacred shrines. The tours (7–14 days) cost around $100 to $500. Private tour operators all now offer dozens of unique tour programs.

Travel Agencies

Many tour operators offer trips to this part of India (*see* Tour Operators *in* the Gold Guide *and* Chapter 2, Special-Interest Travel in India). These travel agencies can help with bookings and supply cars with drivers. **Sita Travels** (Tharakan Building, M. G. Rd., Ravipuram, Ernakulam, Cochin, Kerala, ☎ 484/361101) and **Travel Corporation of India** (Telstar Building, M. G. Rd., Ernakulam, Cochin, ☎ 484/351646) can help you arrange a trip. The best travel agency in Kerala is the **Great India Tour Company** (head office, Mullassery Towers, Vanross Junction,

Trivandrum, 695039, ☎ 471/331516, 🗚 471/330579); it has offices in Cochin (1st Floor, "Pithuru Smarana," Srikandath Rd., Ravipuram, Cochin 682016, ☎ 484/369246, 🗚 484/351–328) and throughout south India.

Dining

Kerala is home to many of the world's most treasured spices and, of course, seafood. You can find delicious creations in almost every town.

What to Wear
Casual wear is generally acceptable.

Lodging

Unless otherwise mentioned, hotels have central air-conditioning, room service, and foreign-exchange facilities, and rooms have cable TVs and bathrooms with tubs. Also, unless noted, *ayurvedic treatment* means that full treatment—massage, diet, and medicine—is available; *yoga* and *meditation* include instruction; and hotel beaches are private. Some luxury hotels have exclusive floors with special privileges or facilities designed for the business traveler (*see* Special Hints for Business Travelers *in* Chapter 3, Business Travel in India). Most hotels in Kerala have significant off-season discounts—often up to 75%.

The Arts

Some 50 classical, folk, and tribal dance forms can be seen throughout Kerala. Many are unique to a particular caste and even to one particular temple, and, not surprisingly, they have not gained the same popularity as Kerala's most famous dance form, Kathakali. Mohiniyattam is a beautiful dance that lies somewhere between Kathakali and Bharatnatyam. Padayani is a colorful re-creation of Kali's victory march after vanquishing Darika. It takes place during festivals at many southern temples. Pulikali (or Kaduvakali) brings men, brightly painted as green, yellow, orange, and red striped tigers, into the streets in Trichur and Palghat districts. For details on what dances may be performed while you're in town, talk to the tourist office or the Tourist Desk in Cochin (*see* Visitor Information, *below*).

Important Addresses and Numbers

Changing Money
Most Western-style hotels have foreign-exchange facilities for their guests.

Emergencies
For all emergencies, turn to your hotel, or the East West Clinic (*see* Emergencies *in* Chapter 4, Delhi).

Telephones
All telephone numbers in Cochin were scheduled to change in 1996; check with the KTDC in Cochin (*see below*) for the current status.

Visitor Information
The best source of information on Kerala is the **Tourist Desk** (Main Boat Jetty, Ernakulam, Cochin 682011, no ☎), a privately run, non-profit organization that conducts boat tours and provides straightforward information on the whole state. **Kerala State Tourist Information Center** (Old Collectorate, Park Ave., Ernakulam 682001, no ☎; open weekdays 10–5 and alternating Sat. 10–5, closed Sun.) has information on the state. The **Kerala Tourism Development Corporation** (KTDC, Tourist Reception Center, Shanmugham Rd., Ernakulam 682001, ☎

484/353234; open daily 8–6) provides information and handles book-ings for its own vehicles, boats, accommodations, and tours. The **Government of India Tourist Office** (Willingdon Office, ☎ 484/668352; open weekdays 9–5:30, Sat. 9–1) does the same.

PUBLICATIONS

Festivals of Kerala (Rs. 100), an invaluable book published by the Tourist Desk, not only details festivals, but describes all the dance forms, boat races, temples, and regions of Kerala. The JAICO pamphlet (Rs. 2) and "Kerala A to Z" (Rs. 10) are also useful.

11 Karnataka

Outside Karnataka's tropical capital, Bangalore, village life transports you to an earlier time. Mysore is a city of palaces; the former maharaja's palace is an architectural tour de force. Near Mysore are Belur and Halebid villages, with their meticulously wrought 12th-century temples. Karnataka also has one of India's most enjoyable game parks, the Nagarhole Wildlife Sanctuary.

By Julie Tomasz

WITHIN THE BORDERS OF KARNATAKA (formerly Mysore), you can find the most colorful and fascinating aspects of India, plus an occasional high level of comfort that can be Oriental-sumptuous and Occidental-efficient. Karnataka, the size of New England, probably has had a civilization as long as any place on earth. Scattered throughout the state in such places as Belur, Halebid, and Hampi, you'll find some of the best religious monuments in India.

The 42 million people of Karnataka, called Kannadigas after their language, known as Kannada, are sinewy and robust. In villages, colorfully dressed women wait patiently with their jugs at the well, which is also the social center. The men, often scantily dressed in *lungi* (colorful skirtlike wraps) or *dhotis* (white skirtlike wraps) work in the fields, walking slowly behind buffalo dragging plows that have not changed much in 3,000 years. The climate here makes it possible to live perpetually outdoors—the huts in the villages are often of rudimentary construction, and people frequently set up their beds outside.

The simplicity of the countryside is one extreme balanced by another: the grand palaces and formal gardens of Mysore, the cosmopolitan young city life of Bangalore, the splendor of such festivals as Dussehra, and the relics of centuries of royal living—Hindu and Muslim.

For wildlife, you can spend a few days on safari in Nagarhole National Park (*see* Chapter 2, Special-Interest Travel in India), finding both excitement and natural tranquility.

While Bangalore and Mysore are well connected by express trains, the advantage of traveling by car is that generally wherever you go, the Karnataka countryside along the way is lovely, verdant with palms and rice paddies, brightened with colorfully dressed women washing clothes in the roadside streams. For timid passengers and backseat drivers, however, there is the disadvantage of an occasionally alarming experience, as you roar through curves marked with skull and crossbones signs warning "accident zone," past giant buses, plodding oxcarts, and men pushing bicycles laden with coconut bunches.

If you have extra time, stop in the small town of Sravanabelagola, about 84 kilometers (52 miles) north of Mysore, to view the colossal monolithic statue of the Jain saint Gommateshwara, carved in AD 981 and alleged to be one of the largest monolithic statues in the world. Towering 18 meters (58 feet) high, stark naked, with 8-meter (26-foot) wide shoulders, 3-meter (10-foot) feet, and other similarly massive endowments, he is at once imposing and soothing.

BANGALORE

Bangalore is a relatively new city; at the end of the sixteenth century, nothing was here but a mud fort and a small bull temple, both built by the chieftain who founded Bangalore, Kempe Gowda. Today, Bangalore is the capital of the state and the fastest growing city in India, with explosively booming businesses—particularly in the computer industry—affording it the nickname, "India's Silicon Valley." With the city and suburbs well planned in advance—unlike many other Indian cities—it feels orderly, serene. As a result, Bangalore's population is rapidly increasing as people flee the urban-jungle atmosphere and ex-orbitant prices of cities like Bombay.

It's an increasingly snazzy city, where you'll find such Western-style commercial elements as bookstore cafés, trendy boutiques, and nearly 200 pubs where beer is drunk with gusto.

Numbers in the margin correspond to points of interest on the Bangalore map.

Exploring

It's hard to spend more than half a day seeing the bona fide sights of Bangalore. You can give ample time to soaking in this bright city's fresh, cosmopolitan feel by browsing and buying in the new shops, trying out some of the excellent restaurants, and having a beer or two at a pub (or two) at night.

4 **Bull Temple.** This small temple houses the enormous 1786 monolith of Nandi—the sacred Hindu bull, vehicle of Lord Shiva. The temple's front yard bustles with activity—peddlers sell coconuts, bananas, and jasmine blossoms for offerings. Don't be alarmed if a woman sitting on the pavement suddenly yanks out a live cobra from a straw basket in front of her, taunting it to fan out its collar; for a few rupees, you can snap a photo of the angry creature from as close (or as far) as you wish. Inside, Nandi lies in his traditional position, legs tucked underneath him, leaning lightly to one side. Nandi's hefty black bulk is beautifully carved with ornamental bells and glistens with coconut oil regularly applied by priests to keep the stone moist. *Bull Temple Rd.* ☛ *Free.* ☉ *Daily 6 AM–8 PM.*

3 **Lal Bagh Botanical Gardens.** This 220-acre park is one of the remaining reasons for Bangalore's increasingly obscure nickname, "the Garden City." Closed to auto traffic, it is laced with pedestrian paths through more than 100 types of trees and thousands of varieties of plants and flowers from all over the world. From October through December, most of the flora are in their fullest bloom. Some trees, like the venerable 200-year-old elephant tree near the western gate entrance, date from the time of Tipu Sultan, who continued to develop the park in the late 18th century after the death of his father, Hyder Ali, who designed the grounds in 1760. Marking the heart of Lal Bagh is the **Rose Garden,** a square, fenced-in plot blooming with some 150 different kinds of roses. Just beyond, near the north gate entrance, is the **Glass House,** a cross-shaped pavilion modeled after London's Crystal Palace and built in 1881. Twice a year, around Independence Day (August 15) and Republic Day (January 15), week-long Bangalore flower shows are held here. ☏ *80/602231.* ☛ *Free; during flower shows, Rs. 3.* ☉ *Daily sunrise–sunset.*

2 **Tipu's Palace.** Tipu Sultan built this wooden summer palace for himself in 1789. It is a replica of his summer palace in Srirangapatana but lacks the elaborate fresco painting inside. The building now houses a modest photo exhibit about Tipu and his era. *Albert Victor Rd.* ☉ *Daily 8–5:30.* ☛ *Free.*

1 **Vidhana Soudha.** Bangalore's most beautiful building is a relatively recent addition to the city, built between 1954 and 1958 to house the state legislature and secretariat. The sprawling, sandy-colored granite structure was designed in the Indo-Dravidian style, studded with pillars and carved ledges, with a central dome crowned with a golden four-headed lion, emblem of the great 3rd-century BC Buddhist king, Ashoka.

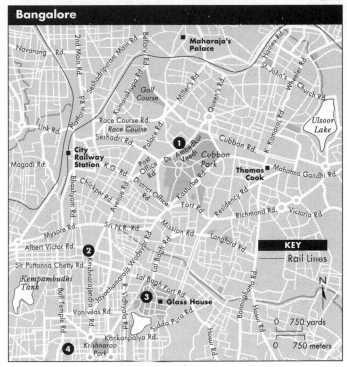

Bangalore

The building's interior is off-limits to visitors. Facing the Vidhana head-on across the street is another of Bangalore's attractive public buildings, the multipillar, redbrick High Court of Karnataka, originally built in 1885 as the seat of the former English government. *Dr. Ambedkar Veedi Rd.*

TIME OUT For a truly ethnic experience, go to **Arya Bhavan Sweets** (K. G. Circle, ☎ 80/287–1175), a bustling stand-up joint that each morning prepares fresh Indian sweets that sell out by the time it closes. Try the *kesari peda* or *dudh peda*—sweets made from sugary milk paste.

Shopping

Bangalore's main shopping pockets are along **M. G. Road,** where you'll find government shops and some giant silk emporiums; **Brigade Road,** lined with flashier shops, foreign boutiques, and a number of multilevel shopping arcades; and **Commmercial Street,** a narrow, more eclectic shopping area packed with old and new shops selling everything from suitcase locks to Kashmiri hats to precious jewelry.

Antiques and Handicrafts

Cauvery (49 M. G. Rd., ☎ 80/558–1118) is a state-run, fixed-price store that sells all the products made in Karnataka: sandalwood handicrafts, terra-cotta pots, carved rosewood furniture, silk, leather work, jute products, lacquered toys, *bidri* wares (decorative black-and-silver-color metal wares), embossed bronze, soaps, perfumes, incense, and sachets. **Central Cottage Industries Emporium** (144 M. G. Rd., ☎ 80/558–4083 or 80/558–4084), which sells authentic handicrafts from all over India, is part of the nationwide government chain of fixed-price cottage industries stores. **Natesan's Antiqarts** (64 M. G. Rd., ☎

80/558–8344) sells an unusual collection of high-quality stone, bronze, and wood antiquities; old paintings; and exquisite new artifacts; plus silver jewelry and precious stones.

Silks

A number of giant silk emporiums on M. G. Road sell top-quality Karnataka silk products, from solid-colored material by the meter to bright, ornately handblocked saris and scarves. **Deepam Silk International** (M. G. Rd., ☎ 80/558–8760) has been in business for nearly 25 years. **Karnataka Silk Industries Corporation Showroom** (Leo Complex, Residency Rd. Cross, off M. G. Rd., ☎ 80/582118; also at Gupta Market, K. G. Rd., ☎ 80/262077), a fixed-price government shop, sells silks hot off the government silk looms in Mysore. **Lakshmi Silks** (144 M. G. Rd., below Central Cottage Industries Emporium, ☎ 80/558–2129) has a full collection of excellent silks. **Nalli Silks Arcade** (21/24 M. G. Rd., ☎ 80/558–3178) sells silks of all sorts, as well as some cotton clothing.

Sports

Golf

The Bangalore Golf Club (2 Sankey Rd., ☎ 80/225–7121), designed by the British in 1876, has a lovely 18-hole course open to nonmembers. Call ahead to reserve your game.

Health Clubs

Facilities, including swimming pools, at the **Holiday Inn** and the **Taj Residency** hotels (*see* Lodging, *below*) are open to nonguests for around Rs. 200 per day.

Horse Racing

Thoroughbred racing is a major sport in Karnataka. The **Bangalore Turf Club** (1 Race Course Rd., ☎ 80/226–2391) goes into high gear mid-May through the end of July and November through March, holding races Saturday and Sunday afternoons.

Dining

Bangalore has an up-and-coming restaurant scene, growing more and more cosmopolitan by the month. Chinese and other Asian restaurants abound, and Italian, American, and other ethnic eateries are springing up quickly. Although the scene is changing, many of the best restaurants are still to be found in the major hotels. Consult your hotel concierge for the latest hot spots.

For price categories, *see* the chart for Major Cities *in* On the Road with Fodor's.

What to Wear

Casual clothes are acceptable at all restaurants, but it's best to keep it neat and scale it up slightly for Bangalore's fancier hotel eating places.

$$$$ **Dum Pukht.** This posh restaurant is the second of only two establishments in India serving Nawab of Avadh cuisine, slow-cooked in traditional sealed containers. Specialties include *subz purdah* (vegetable and pineapple casserole baked in puff pastry); *kakori* (finely minced mutton spiced with cloves and cinnamon and grilled on a skewer); and the 100-layer *lachchedor paratha* bread. Arched ceilings and white pillars frame the elegant room, and the unusual menu made of ivory silk is brought to you literally on a silver platter. ✗ *Welcomgroup Wind-*

sor Manor, 25 Sankey Rd., ☎ *80/2269898. Reservations advised. AE, DC, MC, V.*

$$$ Karavalli. In the parking lot behind the Taj Gateway Hotel, this top restaurant has tables on a shady terrace walled in by hedges and in an adjoining cottage. Waiters wear dhotis, and south Indian classical music sets the tone. The menu offers coastal cuisines from Goa, Kerala, and Karnataka's Mangalore. Two regional specialties are *kori gassi* (chicken pieces simmered in coconut gravy) served with *neer dosa* (Karnataka-style crépe), and *kane bezule* (fish marinated in ground Mangalorean spices, then deep-fried). Save room (lots) for *bibinca*, the sinfully rich Goan coconut and butter dessert. ✕ *Taj Gateway Hotel, 66 Residency Rd.,* ☎ *80/558–4545. Dinner reservations advised. AE, DC, MC, V.*

$$$ Paradise Island. This open-air restaurant in a British gazebo, sur-
★ rounded by water and lush plantings, opened in 1989 as India's first Thai restaurant. It has evolved to include Chinese, Japanese, Singaporean, and other Asian cuisines, with the emphasis remaining on Thai. Specialties include *som tam* (spicy-salty-sweet raw papaya salad tossed with peanut sauce) and *hormok* (curried prawns or fish steamed and served wrapped in banana leaves). Try to save room for the coconut ice cream and coconut pancakes topped with orange sauce. ✕ *Taj West End Hotel, Race Course Rd.,* ☎ *80/226–9281. Dinner reservations advised. AE, DC, MC, V.*

$$$ Tandoor. The extensive menu offers cuisine from all over the sub-
★ continent, with a focus on tandoor items, which you can watch being skewered and cooked by white-capped chefs through a large window into the kitchen. Particularly good are the chicken *seekh kabab* and the fish *tikka*. Ivory walls and pillars ornamented with gold trim, dimmed glass-bead chandeliers, and tables with red roses in silver vases create an ambience of Indian elegance. ✕ *28 M. G. Rd.,* ☎ *80/558– 4620. Reservations advised. AE, DC, MC, V.*

$$ Ebony. This popular rooftop restaurant sits unsuperstitiously on the 13th floor of an M. G. Road hotel. Tables on two outdoor terraces offer lovely views of Bangalore and are in high demand in the evenings, when the south-Indian sun cools down and the city lights come on. The Ebony chef specializes in Parsee cuisine, unusual in Bangalore, and also cooks good north and south Indian and Continental fare. On Saturdays, you can sample unusual, spicy Balti food from the Indian-Afghan border. ✕ *Ivory Tower Hotel, 13th Floor, 84 M. G. Rd.,* ☎ *80/558– 9333. Dinner reservations advised. AE, DC, MC, V.*

$$ Nagarjuna Savoy. Indian food from the Andhra region is the specialty of this classy, modern restaurant, the upscale sister of the original Nagarjuna eatery next door. Zesty-sweet chicken, mutton, and vegetable *biriyani* dishes are served on plates, not plantain leaves—less authentic, but a good option if you are wary of eating with your hands. The dining room is decorated with brass and copper masks and framed primitive-art prints. ✕ *45/3 Residency Rd.,* ☎ *80/558–7775. AE, DC, MC, V.*

$$ Only Place. From its humble beginnings in 1965 as a joint where
★ American Peace Corps volunteers could get a wholesome taste from home and muse about life with the kind and colorful owner, Haroon, The Only Place has grown to become a Bangalore institution. Today, Haroon still puts out what could easily be the best American-style food in India. Best of all are his steaks—thick, tender, and impeccably fresh. Haroon himself now supplies the American embassy and consulates, as well as other western foreign missions throughout India, with all of

their beef. ✕ *158 Brigade Rd., in Mota Royal Arcade,* ☎ *80/558–8678. AE, DC, MC, V.*

$ **Chung Wah.** Modern Oriental decor—wooden latticework, Chinese fans and paintings on the wall, and lanterns—defines this cozy, popular restaurant, which offers most of China's cuisines. Two favorite dishes are *huli* chicken (fried, sliced chicken simmered with soy sauce and onions) and deboned pomfret with a choice of mild-to-spicy sauces. ✕ *45/1 Residency Rd.,* ☎ *80/558–2662. Dinner reservations advised. AE, MC, V.*

$ **Mavalli Tiffin Rooms.** For Indian vegetarian food, visit this bustling Ban-
★ galore institution, established in 1924. The front rooms, with ceiling fans, are crowded with marble tables. The small back room is air-con-ditioned. You won't find better dosas (Indian-style stuffed crêpes), and you can't beat the price. You can also enjoy great desserts and su-perb coffee. Expect to wait a long time for a table; but once the dhoti-clad bearer takes your order, it's fast service all the way. ✕ *Lalbagh Rd.,* ☎ *80/220022. No credit cards.*

Lodging

Bangalore is experiencing a lodging boom, with dozens of good, new, business traveler–geared hotels going up in the city's prime commer-cial centers. Competition is stiff, keeping the majority of the hotels in the moderate price range.

For price categories, *see* the chart for Major Cities *in* On the Road with Fodor's.

$$$–$$$$ **Welcomgroup Windsor Manor Sheraton and Towers.** Bangalore's pret-tiest hotel is recently built. The exterior is striking white, with arched windows and wrought-iron ornaments. The lobby has a marble foun-tain beneath a domed skylight and massive teak pillars. The smaller Towers atrium lobby area gleams with polished marble and brass; it is the entrance to an opulently exclusive 5-story business traveler wing, offering sleek contemporary rooms and services such as voice-mail, in-room fax machines, and private butler service. Handsome Manor rooms in the original wing have modern furnishings with endearing Victorian touches. ⊞ *25 Sankey Rd., Bangalore 560052, Karnataka,* ☎ *80/226–9898,* 𝖥𝖠𝖷 *80/226–4941. Manor: 88 rooms, 12 suites. Tow-ers: 139 rooms, 1 suite. 2 restaurants, bar, coffee shop, pool, health club, dry cleaning, laundry service, business services, travel services. AE, DC, MC, V.*

$$$ **Oberoi.** Slick, elegant, and well run, this young hotel has a stunning
★ lobby with a green marble floor, a central fountain, and a bank of win-dows overlooking a landscaped garden dominated by a gorgeous blos-soming rain tree and a small waterfall cascading into a fish-filled lotus pond. The spacious rooms have polished green marble entryways; pri-vate balconies; handsome teak-and-brass furnishings, accented with ei-ther light blue or mauve pink; and shuttered teak sliding doors on the balcony window. Each floor has a private butler. ⊞ *37/39 M. G. Rd., Bangalore 560001, Karnataka,* ☎ *80/558–5858,* 𝖥𝖠𝖷 *80/558–5960. 130 rooms, 9 suites. 2 restaurants, bar, outdoor pool, barber shop, hair salon, health club, laundry service and dry cleaning, business services, meet-ing rooms, travel services, airport shuttle. AE, DC, MC, V.*

$$$ **Taj West End.** Over a century old, it has an exterior and public rooms
★ that are decidedly Victorian. The setting is tropical, with 20 acres of lush gardens. Most of the rooms have elegant contemporary decor, with brass lamps and teak or solid cane furniture. Slightly more expensive "Old World" rooms have a turn-of-the-century ambience, with ma-hogany writing desks and brass four-poster beds. The best rooms in

the main building are on the second floor opening onto a veranda overlooking the pool. ⊡ *23 Race Course Rd., Bangalore 560001, Karnataka, ☎ 80/225–9281, FAX 80/220–0010. 131 rooms, 9 suites. 3 restaurants, 2 bars, pastry shop, outdoor pool, sauna, 2 tennis courts, exercise room, baby-sitting, laundry service and dry cleaning, business services, travel services. AE, DC, MC, V.*

$$ **Central Park.** Tucked behind a large commercial complex, this 10-story high-rise is one of Bangalore's newer business hotels. From the small lobby, glass-backed elevators afford a view of the city as you rise to your floor. The rooms are small with standard contemporary furnishings and a few tartan-plaid details. For about $5 more, "Park Chamber" rooms on separate executive floors are slightly larger and better appointed and include breakfast—a good value. ⊡ *47 Dickenson Rd., Bangalore 560042, Karnataka, ☎ 80/558–4242, FAX 80/558–8594. 126 rooms, 4 suites. Restaurant, bar, coffee shop, patisserie, book store, business services, meeting rooms, travel services. AE, DC, MC, V.*

$$ **Holiday Inn Bangalore.** The enormous atrium lobby of this modern high-rise sparkles with white marble and shiny brass carriage lamps. The hallways and rooms, however, are surprisingly dark and less showy. The modern room decor includes burnt-orange carpeting, dark floral-print upholstered chairs and an ottoman, and lighter floral drapes and bedspreads. Gradual renovations are under way; you're best off requesting a recently renovated room. ⊡ *28 Sankey Rd., Bangalore 560052, Karnataka, ☎ 80/226–2233, FAX 80/226–7676. 196 rooms, 30 suites. Restaurant, bar, coffee shop, pool, beauty salon, sauna, steam bath, tennis court, exercise room, baby-sitting, laundry service, business services, meeting rooms, travel services. AE, DC, MC, V.*

$$ **Hotel Ashok.** Built in 1971 in the park where Mahatma Gandhi once meditated, this hotel has a small memorial to Gandhi on the extensive grounds behind it. The rooms look fresh, with blue-gray and pale green decor and light-painted wood furnishings. The small marble lobby has low ceilings and comfortable wicker chairs. The best rooms overlook the pool. ⊡ *Kumara Krupa, High Grounds, Bangalore 560001, Karnataka, ☎ 80/226–9462, FAX 80/225–0033. 164 rooms, 17 suites. 2 restaurants, coffee shop, bar, pool, tennis court, beauty salon, exercise room, dry cleaning, laundry service, meeting rooms, travel services. AE, DC, MC, V.*

$$ **Taj Gateway Hotel.** For similarly moderate prices, this Western-style Taj property offers rooms of more reliable quality than do its peers among the new, lower-mid-range business hotels. Public areas and rooms are decorated with framed abstract prints; rooms have modern wood and wicker furniture and pale blue carpeting. Only suites have bathtubs. ⊡ *66 Residency Rd., Bangalore 560025, Karnataka, ☎ 80/558–4545, FAX 80/558–4030. 94 rooms with shower, 4 suites. 3 restaurants, bar, pool, exercise room, laundry service, business services, travel services. AE, DC, MC, V.*

$$ **Taj Residency.** This 10-story high-rise hotel has been around for over 10 years. The white marble lobby is busy and spacious, and the rooms are furnished with teak contemporary basics in blue-and-green patterns. Ask for a recently renovated room on an upper floor with a lake view. ⊡ *41/3 M. G. Rd., Bangalore 560001, Karnataka, ☎ 80/558–4444, FAX 80/558–4748. 157 rooms, 5 suites. 2 restaurants, bar, coffee shop, patisserie, pool, exercise room, book store, baby-sitting, business services, meeting rooms, travel services. AE, DC, MC, V.*

$ **Hotel Cauvery Continental.** Built in the early 1970s, this boxy cement hotel, set back from the main road, provides impressively clean, low-frills accommodations. The rooms are small and worn looking, with dated

1970s decor and simple wood furniture. The small white-tile bathrooms have only open showers. The more recently renovated "deluxe" rooms are only minimally different—a shower curtain in the bathroom and a fresher paint job—but are worth the extra few dollars. You can request an air-conditioned room. ⊞ *11/37 Cunningham Rd., Bangalore 560052, Karnataka,* ☎ *80/225–6966,* 𝔽𝔸𝕏 *80/226–0920. 54 rooms with shower, 2 suites. 2 restaurants, bar, beauty salon, playground, laundry service and dry cleaning, meeting room, travel services. AE, DC, MC, V.*

$ **Quality Inn Kensington Terrace.** Opened in spring 1995, this property is the first in India to install an interactive television system that provides quick information ranging from what sights to visit in town to the status of your hotel bill. The rooms are on the small side and unobtrusively furnished with the basics, with dark green and brown fabrics. Breakfast is included in the room rates. ⊞ *Kensington Rd., off M. G. Rd., Bangalore 560042, Karnataka,* ☎ *80/559–4666,* 𝔽𝔸𝕏 *80/ 559–4029. 98 rooms, 10 suites. Restaurant, bar, coffee shop, pool, exercise room, laundry service, business services, meeting rooms, travel services. AE, DC, MC, V.*

The Arts

Your best source of information about cultural happenings in Bangalore is the "In the City Today" column, usually on page 3, of the *Deccan Herald,* Bangalore's daily newspaper. Other sources are posters, the Karnataka Department of Tourism, the free "Bangalore this Fortnight" pamphlet (*see* Visitor Information, *below*), and your hotel information staff.

Music, Dance, and Drama

Bangalore has a number of venues for classical Indian dance and music, as well as plays, which are sometimes performed in English: **Chowdiah Memorial Hall** (Gayathri Devi Park Extension, 16th Cross, Malleswaram, ☎ 80/225–8762), **Sri Puttanachetty Town Hall** (Sri Narasimharaja Circle, J. C. Rd., ☎ 80/222–1270), **Ravindra Kalakshetra** (Jayachamarachendra Rd., ☎ 80/222–1271), and the **Dr. Narasimaiah Kalakshetra** (Jayanagar, 7th Block, ☎ 80/649684). The **Yavanika State Youth Center** hosts free Indian classical music and dance peformances and other cultural happenings nearly every evening.

Nightlife

Bangalore is famous in India for its pubs. Over the last several years, nearly 200 have sprung up throughout the city, providing a variety of places for people of all types and trades to meet over beers or other drinks and listen to music. Recently the government has attempted to curb students' alcohol consumption by forcing pubs to close for a few hours in the afternoons, as well as to shut down by 10:30 or 11 PM sharp. Further governmental regulations to prevent prostitution and go-go club scenes prohibit the combination of dancing, alcohol, and women in the same establishment, except for a few major hotels with special permits. Live bands are also outlawed. This all may change, but it's at the whim of the government.

The atmosphere in all Bangalore's pubs is casual, upbeat, and decidedly friendly. Music, played by a D.J., tends to be very loud, despite the fact that there's usually no dancing. Weekends, particularly Saturday, are the most popular nights to go pubbing; expect large crowds.

Bars and Pubs

Black Cadillac (50 Residency Rd., Mohan Towers, ☎ 80/221–6148) attracts a slightly corporate, upscale crowd inside on red-upholstered stools at tables with psychedelic, swirly-painted tops or out in the back yard, with store awnings, yellow-striped curbs, and painted street scenes. **Downtown** (41-42 Residency Rd., ☎ 80/558–2050) is the most spacious pub in town, with a particularly friendly and hospitable atmosphere, with low, raftered ceilings, wood paneling, and swivel chairs; the owner trains his bartenders to do magic tricks. **The Jockey Club** (Taj Residency, 41/3 M. G. Rd., ☎ 80/558–4444), is a small, posh bar and restaurant where white-gloved waiters serve you beer in silver steins, amid richly carved teak walls, Belgian mirrors, and subdued light from dimmed lanterns. **NASA** (1-A Church St., ☎ 80/558–6512) has the look and feel of a space shuttle; you duck through an oval door into two oblong, oval-shaped rooms decorated in metallic silver and black. At the **Polo Bar** (The Oberoi, 37/39 M. G. Rd., ☎ 80/558–5858) stained-glass windows and beautiful views of the lush Oberoi garden and cascading waterfall provide a peaceful setting. **The Pub World** (65 Residency Rd., Laxmi Plaza, ☎ 80/558–5206), true to its name, has polished wood, shiny brass fixtures, a low ceiling with wooden rafters, and glasses hanging from racks above the bar.

Discos

On weekends only, the elegant **Midnight Express** (in Welcomgroup Windsor Manor Hotel) dims its chandeliers, turns on the strobe lights, and goes disco.

Bangalore Essentials

Arriving and Departing

BY PLANE

The airport in Bangalore serves **Indian Airlines** flights from Bombay, Madras, Delhi, Ahmedabad, Calcutta, Cochin, Goa, Hyderabad, and other points in India. Check with your travel agent for current schedules of other domestic airlines.

Between the Airport and Center City. Two pre-paid taxi counters compete in the arrivals hall. The Karnataka state government outfit's rates are slightly lower than its neighbor's. With either one, the fare to a central major hotel will run about Rs. 100. A fleet of metered taxis is in the parking lot at the arrivals hall exit; the same journey with one of them should cost about Rs. 85, but it's best to agree on a price before you begin. An **auto rickshaw** ride into the city (approximately Rs. 70) is best if you have very little luggage and are not in a hurry.

BY TRAIN

The **Bangalore City Railway Station** (☎ 131, general inquiries; 132, reservations; 133, recorded information; 134, after-hours arrivals and departures information) reservations office is open Monday through Saturday 8 to 2 and 2:15 to 8, Sunday 8 to 2. Counter 14 on the ground floor is reserved exclusively for foreign tourists, senior citizens, people with disabilities, and freedom fighters.

Getting Around

BY TAXI

You can't hail a metered taxi on the street in Bangalore; you'll find these taxis only at the train and bus stations and at the airport. Have your hotel call one.

Guided Tours

The transport wing of the **Karnataka State Tourism Development Corporation** (*see* Visitor Information *in* Karnataka Essentials, *below*) is widely used for its sightseeing tours and car-hiring service. **Ambassador Travel Services** (76 Mission Rd., Kasturi Complex, 2nd Floor, ☎ 80/224–1516, 80/222–1342) has reliably good cars and drivers at moderate rates. The American Express travel services representative is **Marco Polo Travel and Tours** (*see* Changing Money, *below*). **Thomas Cook** (*see* Changing Money, *below*) also has an office here. **Travel Corporation of India** (9 Residency Rd., Richmond Circle, ☎ 80/221–2990, 80/221–2826) is also known as TCI. **Clipper Holidays** (Suite 406, Regency Enclave, Magrath Rd., ☎ 80/221–7054, ⨍Ⱥ⨯ 80/227–7052) has special-interest tours. **Mercury Travels Ltd.** (70/1 Infantry Rd., ☎ 80/559–1641 through 1643) also offers tours.

Important Addresses and Numbers

CHANGING MONEY

You can cash traveler's checks at **Thomas Cook** (55 M. G. Rd., ☎ 80/558–6742) and **Marco Polo Travel and Tours** (Janardhan Towers, 2 Residency Rd., Bangalore, ☎ 80/223–6671). Most banks also exchange foreign currency and cash traveler's checks. Try **ANZ Grindlays Bank** (Raheja Towers 26/27, 1 M. G. Rd., ☎ 80/558–7684). The **State Bank of Mysore** has a branch in the airport arrivals area.

24-HOUR PHARMACIES

Al-Siddique Pharma Centre (K. R. Rd., opposite Jamia Masijd, near City Market, ☎ 80/605–491); and **Janata Bazaar** (in Victoria Hospital, ☎ 80/225-9268 or 80/226–3495) are open 24 hours.

VISITOR INFORMATION

Karnataka Department of Tourism (K. G. Rd., Cauvery Bhavan, F Block, 1st Floor, ☎ 80/221–5489; and 9 St. Marks Rd., ☎ 80/223–6854) is your best source of information about Bangalore (*see* Visitor Information *in* Karnataka Essentials, *below*).

Available in most hotels, *Bangalore this Fortnight* is a free, biweekly publication full of listings on shops, restaurants, hotels, and other useful tourist information, including local events. *The Explorer's Sourcebook: Bangalore* (spring 1995) is a privately published insider's guide to the city sold in many hotel bookstores. The most complete map of Bangalore is the red "A Road Guide to Bangalore," part of the TTK Discover India Series, available in most Indian bookstores.

MYSORE

Mysore, no longer the official capital of Karnataka, survives as the principal residence of the former royal family and is called the "City of Palaces." When you see what the maharajas accomplished in the way of public service, you will understand why the current one was appointed the first governor of Karnataka.

Mysore's main attraction is the Maharaja's Palace, which you can explore in a few hours. If you can arrange to stay in the Lalitha Mahal Palace (*see* Lodging, *below*), that alone will almost be worth the trip. An evening visit to Brindavan Gardens is a good way to glimpse the culture's kitschy but charming fascination with colored musical fountains.

In contrast to its opulent origins, there's nothing flashy or fancy in Mysore, at least not in the modern, commercial sense. Although there aren't many places to wine and dine and far more dozing cows than boutiques line the streets, this is where you'll find India's richest silks spun with real gold and other elements of an age-old spirit of elegance that endures even as it deteriorates over the years.

Numbers in the margin correspond to points of interest on the Mysore map.

Exploring

❶ **Brindavan Gardens.** Nineteen kilometers (12 miles) northwest of Mysore (about a half-hour's drive), this vast, terraced garden, extending out from the side of one of India's largest dams, is the pride of the city and a tourist magnet. The park is rigidly laid out and carefully manicured, laced with long symmetrical paths and scores of fountains spouting streams of water into coordinated arcs and swirls. Exposed metal pipes and concrete curbs give it an artificial feel, but the profusion of fragrant flowers and welcome lack of honking cars and cows make it a comparatively peaceful place to stroll. Hordes of people flock here to see the "Musical Dancing Fountain" show at the far end of the gardens as water sprays and spouts into the air, just slightly out of sync with the recorded pop-classical Indian music and the pulsing colored lights. *19 km (12 mi) northwest of Mysore, Krishnaraja Sagar Rd.* ☛ *Rs. 5; camera fee, Rs. 10.* ☉ *Gardens daily; fountain show weekdays 7–7:55 PM, weekends 8–8:55 PM.*

❻ **Chamundi Hill.** Steps to the top of this hill, with its panoramic view of Mysore, take you past a 5-meter (16-foot) stone **Nandi** (Shiva's holy bull). From here and on the way up the hill, Mysore looks its best. The **Sri Chamundeswari Temple** on the summit is dedicated to the royal Wadiyar family's titular deity, the goddess Chamundi, who is an avatar of Parvati (Shiva's consort). The base of the temple, dates from the 12th century; the ornately sculptured pyramidal tower was constructed in the 1800s. As it is still an active religious site, the entire area surrounding the structure teems with beggars and peddlers. The temple's inner entrances are manned by aggressive priests hassling tourists into buying flower offerings and *bindis* (forehead dots), applied by a fat thumb right between your eyes. Tuesdays and Fridays, auspicious days, are more crowded than others. Near the temple is the giant statue of the demon **Mahishasura** (Mysore is named for him), who was killed by the goddess Chamundi, bringing peace to the country. *Southeast Mysore, 2.4 km (1.5 mi) south of Lalitha Mahal Palace Hotel.* ☉ *Temple daily 6:30–12:30 and 4–8:30.*

❺ **Government Silk Weaving Factory.** The late maharaja created this factory in 1932 to obtain the finest hand-loomed silks for himself and his royal family—and for some profitable exportation. Today, run by the Karnataka Silk Industries Corporation, the slightly dilapidated factory continues to produce the sumptuous Mysore silks coveted by women throughout India. From simple cocoons to crepe de chines, chiffons, and other regal fabrics, the spinning, soaking, weaving, and dyeing are all done here. Accompanied by a factory official, visitors can stroll through the numerous giant workrooms busy with whirring spooling machines and complex clanking mechanical looms, and witness the transformation of hundreds of hair-thin, colorless threads into a maharani-perfect sari. Ask to see the work stations where real gold threads are woven into elaborate *zari* borders. Bring your wallet for a post-tour spree at the factory showroom, where the selection and prices are great. *Mananthody Rd.,* ☎ *821/21803.* ☛ *Free.* ☉ *Mon.–Sat. (except 2nd Sat. of month) 10:30–5. No cameras.*

250

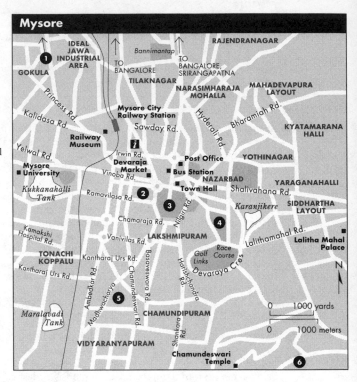

★ ❸ **Mysore Palace.** By far the most impressive Mysore building is the maharaja's palace, set on 73 acres, a massive edifice that took 15 years to build (starting in 1897). The palace, one of the largest in India, is in the Indo-Saracenic style—a gigantic synthesis of Hindu and Islamic architecture. The main rooms and halls are a profusion of domes, arches, turrets, and colonnades, all lavishly carved, etched, or painted, with few surfaces spared. The halls and pavilions glitter with unabashed opulence—giant brass elephant gates; silver-plated doors encrusted with patterns and figures; richly carved teak ceilings; ivory gods and goddesses; a 280-kilogram (616-pound) solid-gold *howda* (elephant throne). The cavernous **Kalyana Mandap** (Marriage Hall), where the women sat behind screened balconies, exudes royal wealth, with turquoise-painted cast-iron pillars soaring up to a translucent dome of Scottish stained glass with brilliantly colored peacocks and flowers. A massive brass Czechoslovakian chandelier hangs far below, above a floor of colorful English tiles. The impressive **Durbar Hall,** where public gatherings were held, is an elegant preservation of history, with white Italian marble floors inlaid with semi-precious stones. The present-day maharaja (technically a prince—son of the last maharaja, who died in 1974) lives in a private wing at the rear of the palace, which is owned by him but maintained by the Karnataka State Government. You can visit the small **Residential Museum,** which exhibits the prince's private collection of artwork and artifacts illustrating royal life of the past. For the optimal palace experience, time your visit to coincide with the annual **Dussehra Festival** in September or October (*see* Festivals and Seasonal Events *in* Chapter 1, Destination India). On Sundays from 7 to 8 PM and on holidays, the palace is illuminated with thousands of tiny lights that turn it into a glittering statement of wealth. *Mysore Palace,* ☎ *821/22672.* ☛ *Palace Rs. 5, museum Rs. 5, guide service free.* ☺

Palace daily 10–5, museum daily 10:30–6:30. No shoes or cameras allowed in palace.

❷ **Sri Jayachamarajendra Art Gallery.** Housed in the tired, 150-year-old Jaganmohan Palace, this slightly run-down museum exhibits paintings from various schools and periods of Indian art, beautiful antique inlaid furniture, antique sandalwood and ivory carvings, and a large variety of other decorative pieces. Some displays are truly eclectic, such as a set of carved ivory vegetables and the amazing "rice paintings"— portraits painted on single rice grains. *Jaganmohan Palace,* ☏ *821/23693.* ☛ *Rs. 3, guide service free.* ☉ *Daily 8:30–5. No cameras.*

❹ **The Zoological Garden.** In this 250-acre park, you'll encounter white tigers, giraffes, African elephants, and a variety of other animals from all over the world. One quirk of this zoo is that it is subject to labor disputes between opposing staff labor unions, which have on more than one occasion resulted in one of the groups' secretly releasing a panther or a pair of pythons to cause trouble. Watch where you step! *Indiranagar,* ☏ *821/20302.* ☛ *Rs. 8 adults, Rs. 2 children.* ☉ *Mon.–Thurs., weekends 8:30–5:30.*

Shopping

Mysore is famous for its exquisite silks and fragrant jasmine, as well as for its sandalwood products—oils, incense sticks, soaps, and carvings—and rosewood inlay work. The main shopping area is along **Sayaji Rao Road,** beginning at K. R. Circle in the center of town. Here you'll find a plethora of silk emporiums and shops of all kinds. Most shops are closed Sunday.

Markets
Devaraja Market (Devaraja Urs Rd.; open daily 6 AM–9 PM) is a bustling, old indoor fruit-and-vegetable and flower market, where you can immerse yourself in the vibrant colors and smells of Karnataka's bounteous produce.

Antiques and Handicrafts
Cauvery Art and Crafts Emporium (Sayaji Rao Rd., ☏ 821/52158) is the fixed-price, government showroom for sandalwood carvings, rosewood figurines, brassware, and other Karnataka handicrafts. **Mysore Crafts Emporium** (70-D Devaraja Urs Rd., ☏ 821/30294), the largest handicrafts showroom in Mysore, has a good selection of very reasonably priced local sandalwood and rosewood products, as well as crafts from other regions of India.

Silks
Karnataka Silk Industries Corporation (Government Silk Weaving Factory Complex, Mananthody Rd., ☏ 821/21803; Mysore center, Visveshwaraiah Bhavan, K. R. Circle, ☏ 821/22658; Mysore Zoo, Zoo Complex, Indiranagar, ☏ 821/25502), the state body that runs the government silk factory (*see* Exploring, *above*), has several fixed-price showrooms where you can buy or just admire the profusion of silks created at the factory. The factory complex has a "seconds" showroom where imperfect silks with barely noticeable flaws are sold at up to 40% off.

Sports

Health Clubs
The **Quality Inn Southern Star** hotel's (*see* Lodging, *below*) mediocre health club charges guests and non-guests about Rs. 70 a day to use the facilities.

Horse Racing

The Mysore Race Club (Race Course Rd., ☎ 821/521675) is the scene of the action from August through October, with races about twice a week.

Dining

In Mysore there is a dearth of dining options for the cautious Westerner. For the most part, you'll find good food in the hotels. For price categories, *see* the chart for Other Areas *in* On the Road with Fodor's.

$$$ **Lalitha Mahal Palace Hotel Restaurant.** Here, you'll dine in the maharaja's cavernous former ballroom—a tour de force of Italian baroque-regal with stained-glass domes and sky-blue walls enhanced by ornate white plaster moldings and pillars. Try the Mysore *thali* (assorted regional dishes served on a platter) or the mutton *ulathiyathu* (mutton cooked with coconut, red chili, and curry). There's a flutist at lunch and a sitarist or vina player at dinner. ✕ *T. Narsipur Rd.,* ☎ *821/27650. Dinner reservations advised. AE, DC, MC, V.*

$$ **Gardenia.** The Quality Inn's restaurant has a contemporary Indian look, with upholstered rattan chairs, and brass candle-lanterns on the tables at night. The kitchen serves mostly north Indian fare, with some Chinese and Continental options. The Tandoori items are delicious; try *malai murgh tikka* (tender, boneless chicken chunks seasoned with Mughlai masala spices) with some *paneer kulcha* (bread stuffed with cottage cheese and masala spices). ✕ *Quality Inn Southern Star, 13–14 Vinoba Rd.,* ☎ *821/27217. AE, DC, MC, V.*

$$ **Ilapur.** Specializing in spicy Andhra region foods, this clean, fresh restaurant serves good biriyani dishes—chicken, mutton, or vegetable—as well as various curries, north Indian tandoori items, and an economical vegetable thali; Chinese fare is slightly more expensive. The decor is contemporary, with plastic plants and several colorful paintings of Lord Krishna. ✕ *2721/1 Sri Harsha Rd.,* ☎ *821/32878. AE, MC, V.*

$ **Jewel Rock.** Candlelight and red-checked linens create a cozily romantic atmosphere at this multicuisine restaurant. Chinese dishes, including nonspicy chicken in wine sauce (not on the menu) and sliced lamb with chilies, are the most popular. ✕ *Hotel Maurya Palace, 2-3-7 Sri Harsha Rd.,* ☎ *821/35912. AE, DC, MC, V.*

Lodging

Mysore has a few excellent hotels with very moderate rates.

For price categories, *see* the chart for Other Areas *in* On the Road with Fodor's.

$$$ **Lalitha Mahal Palace Hotel.** Just outside the city center, this gleaming
★ white 1920s palace of the former maharajah is now a sumptuous hotel. Its interior is Italian baroque. Public areas are lavishly trimmed with ornate plaster moldings, huge pillars, and gorgeous domes; broad marble staircases rise and curve majestically up through the three floors. The best rooms are in the original structure and have appealing but not necessarily grand Victorian furnishings. The suites are palatial, favored by film stars, Arabian sheiks, and honeymooners. The rooms in the new wing have a contemporary decor. Staying here is a delightful and unique experience, but not without occasional reminders of the palace's age: hot water and air-conditioning are not totally reliable. ⌗ *T. Narsipur Rd., Mysore 570011, Karnataka,* ☎ *821/27650,* ☒ *821/33398. 45 rooms, 10 suites. Restaurant, bar, pool, beauty*

salon, 2 tennis courts, health club, billiards, baby-sitting, meeting rooms, travel services, helipad. AE, DC, MC, V.

$$ **Quality Inn Southern Star.** Opened in 1985, India's first Quality Inn
★ property may also be the best. The large renovated rooms are done up with floral drapes and bedspreads and coordinating light pastel carpeting; unrenovated rooms are much darker with dated '80s decor. The cozy back lawn is surrounded by high hedges, making it feel removed from the busy city road out front; children love the cage of chattering parakeets and the tame white rabbits that hop lazily around the pool. ⊞ 13–14 Vinoba Rd., Mysore 570005, Karnataka, ☎ 821/27217, ⅢX 821/521689. 71 rooms, 1 suite. 2 restaurants, bar, pool, barbershop, beauty salon, health club, laundry service, meeting rooms, travel services. AE, DC, MC, V.

$ **Hotel Metropole.** This lovely old 1920s British bungalow, a guest house of the former maharaja, is low on frills but faultlessly maintained. All rooms face the busy main road and can be noisy. The best rooms are on the upper floor of a sweeping veranda with rattan furniture and potted plants. The furnishings are basic but charming, evoking the 1940s; all beds come with romantic mosquito-net curtains. You can ask for air conditioning. ⊞ 5 Jhansi Lakshmibai Rd., Mysore 570005, Karnataka, ☎ 821/20681 or 821/20871, ⅢX 821/31869. 16 rooms, 4 suites. Restaurant, bar, laundry service, travel services. AE, DC, MC, V.

$ **Kings Kourt Hotel.** This three-story hotel is clean and new but lacks charm and historic appeal. The top two floors, added in 1991, have midsize rooms with modern furnishings in dark red and black, and small bathrooms. The rear-facing rooms are quieter. ⊞ Jhansi Lakshmibai Rd., Mysore 570001, Karnataka, ☎ 821/25250, ⅢX 821/563131. 58 rooms, 2 suites. Restaurant, bar, laundry service, meeting room, business services, travel services. AE, DC, MC, V.

The Arts

To find out what's on in Mysore, your best bet is to check with the Karnataka Department of Tourism (KDT) and look for posters around town.

Music, Dance, and Theater
Kalamandir Auditorium (Vinoba Rd., ☎ 821/28185), hosts drama, dance, ballet, folklore, and classical Indian music productions. Admission is usually free, or a nominal sum. Cultural performances are sometimes also held at the **Jaganmohan Palace** (☎ 821/23693) and the **Mysore Palace** (☎ 821/22672). The Karnataka State Government's culture department organizes various events, sometimes in nearby villages. Contact the Karnataka Department of Tourism (see Important Addresses and Numbers, below) for further information.

Nightlife

In Mysore, you can have a drink at a hotel bar or lounge.

Bars
The Lalitha Mahal Palace Hotel (see Lodging, above) has a good bar with comfortable Victorian furnishings and a casual ambience. It's worth having a drink here to see the majestic building. **The Derby** (Quality Inn Southern Star, see Lodging, above), has an equestrian motif, complete with saddles for bar stools and staff dressed in jockey outfits.

Mysore Essentials

Arriving and Departing

BY TRAIN

The **Mysore Railway Station Enquiry and Reservation Office** (☎ 821/520100 or 821/37300) is open Monday through Saturday 8 to 2 and 2:15 to 8 and Sunday 8 to 2.

Getting Around

In Mysore, with luck, you can flag down vacant taxis on the street; otherwise, you can pick one up at one of the taxi stands throughout the city, or your hotel can get one for you. The meter rate is Rs. 60 for the first 5 kilometers (3 miles).

Guided Tours

SPECIAL-INTEREST

Clipper Holidays (Suite 406, Regency Enclave, Magrath Rd., Bangalore 560025, ☎ 80/221–7054, FAX 80/227–7052) will arrange for a minimum of 15 people at a time to have dinnner with the maharaja of Mysore at his own palace in Mysore.

Important Addresses and Numbers

TRAVEL AGENTS

The following organizations can book accommodations, arrange sightseeing tours, provide a car and driver, and so on:

The transport division of the **Karnataka State Tourism Development Corporation** (*see* Visitor Information, *below*), **Siddharta Tours & Travels** (Hotel Siddharta, 73/1 Guest House Rd., Nazarbad, ☎ 821/34155 or 821/30555; Lalitha Mahal Palace Hotel, ☎ 821/35702), and **Seagull Travels** (Quality Inn Southern Star, ☎ 821/27217 or 821/27266).

VISITOR INFORMATION

The **Karnataka Department of Tourism** (Old Exhibition Bldgs., Irwin Rd., ☎ 821/22096, 821/31061), open Monday through Saturday, 10 to 1:30 and 2:15 to 5:30, can provide you with brochures, maps, and other useful information about Mysore and all Karnataka. The transport wing of the **Karnataka State Tourism Development Corporation** (KSTDC, Yathrinivas Bldg. 10/4 Kasturba Rd., ☎ 80/221–2901, 221–2902; airport, ☎ 80/526–8012; railway station, ☎ 80/287–0068) can give information and bookings for sightseeing tours, hotels, car hires, and more. The main office is open daily 7 AM to 8 PM.

Belur and Halebid

Once flourishing cities of the 12th-century Hoysala dynasty, Belur and Halebid are now just fading rural villages, but each houses some of the finest examples of stone carving to be found in southern India.

An otherwise unexceptional town, Hassan is the gateway to the temples at Belur and Halebid, each about 35 kilometers (22 miles) away, in a triangle. As good lodging options are still few and far between in Belur and Halebid, most visitors spend a night or two in Hassan and explore the region from here.

To get the most out of these temples, hire a guide to show you around (*see* Visitor Information, *below*). As you must remove your shoes before entering the temples, bring socks along on your visits; the stones can be painfully hot in the midday sun, particularly at Belur.

Belur

In the midst of lush tropical landscape, the old city of Belur is dusty and run down. The town has only one reminder of its once-splendid time.

Temple of Lord Channakeshava. Still a functioning temple dedicated to this Vishnu incarnate, it stands almost as perfectly preserved as it did the day it was completed. Started in 1016 by the Hoysala king Vishnuvardhana, it was completed 101 years later. Legend claims that when Muslim conquerors came to Belur to destroy the temple, they left it alone, awed by its magnificence.

Carved of soapstone, the Belur temple is designed in a star shape, to allow for a maximum carving surface area, with a total of 32 corners. The squat temple, flat on top, sits on a platform of the same shape. To its left is a small prototype, built just before it was. Some 10,000 impossibly intricate sculptures ornament every possible surface. Everywhere is a profusion of gods and goddesses in all their varied aspects and incarnations and scenes from the great Indian religious epic, the *Ramayana,* as well as hunters, dancers, musicians, and beautiful women dressing and adorning themselves.

In the center of the temple, the domed ceiling is supported by four pillars surmounted by sculptures of beautiful women—voluptuous, full-breasted, and full-hipped, taking any number of graceful poses beneath the intricately pierced, scrolled, and scalloped stone canopies. The carving is so detailed that some of the stone bangles the women wear can be moved.

South of the main temple, a smaller shrine, the **Channigaraya Temple** is worth a good look. The other remaining Hoysala temple, **Viranarayana,** has rows of very fine images on its outer walls. ☛ *Free, guide Rs. 25 for 2 people.* ⊙ *Daily 8 AM–8:30 PM; inner sanctums closed daily 1–3 and 5–6.*

Halebid

Near Belur is a sister temple at **Halebid,** a tiny rural village that was once the capital of the Hoysala kingdom.

★ **Hoysaleswara Temple.** Dedicated to the Hindu Lord Shiva, this temple was started after the one at Belur in 1121 by the same king. It was left uncompleted after 190 years of labor because attacks on it by the Delhi sultanates had leveled the once pyramid-peaked roof. It, too, follows a star-shape plan, but it is a double-shrine temple, with two of everything created—one for the king and one for the queen. At Halebid, with some 20,000 statues, the sculptors' virtuosity reaches its peak. The figures are carved so intricately that they appear to have been etched. You can see the taut fibers of the cord from which a drum hangs, feel the weight of the jewel beads dangling from a dancer's neck, sense the swinging of the bells around elephant-god Ganesh's arms.

The breathtaking friezes wrap all the way around the temples; first comes a row of elephants for stability, then one of lordly lions for courage, then convoluting scrolls of swift horses, and a row of fairly graphic sex lessons. Above more scroll work are scenes from the religious epics that not only present philosophical ideas but mirror the living conditions of the time. The largest frieze is also the most exuberant; here are the *apsaras* ("celestial maidens"), clothed in jewels, with bracelets on each arm—sometimes they have as many as six arms.

Behind the queen's shrine (the one closest to the entrance), the giant sculpture of Nandi the bull, Shiva's vehicle, is treasured as the "best bull in India," with beautifully smooth features and a polished belly that almost seems to breathe.

The smaller **Kedareswara Temple** a few minutes' walk down the road bears more exquisite carving. The lovely friezes are similar to those of the other temples and are executed with equal finesse. Here also stand two relatively unadorned early **Jain temples**; their finely polished black pillars reflect like mirrors. On a low hill next to a lake, this is an attractive, peaceful spot in its own right.

A small **museum** next to the Hoysaleswara Temple exhibits various statues and brass and copper figures excavated from the surrounding area. ☞ *Free.* ☉ *Temples daily sunrise–sunset, museum Sat.–Thurs. 10–5.*

Dining and Lodging

For price categories, *see* the charts for Other Areas *in* On the Road with Fodor's.

$$ **Hotel Hassan Ashok.** The best lodging option in Hassan, this three-story modern hotel is about half an hour's drive from either Belur or Halebid. Rooms are reasonably priced and low on frills, with worn modern decor. Some rooms are air-conditioned. The restaurant serves good Indian and Continental cuisine. Try a thali (spicy south Indian or milder Punjabi, with or without meat). *Rasam,* a typical South Indian lentil soup, is a spicy way to start your meal. ☒ *Bangalore–Mangalore Rd., Hassan 673201, Karnataka,* ☎ *8172/68731,* FAX *08172/67154. 45 rooms, 1 suite. Restaurant, bar, laundry service, meeting room. AE, DC, MC, V.*

Visitor Information

BELUR

The small **reception center** (☎ 8233/2218) immediately inside the temple yard entrance offers information Monday through Saturday, 8:30 to 5:30, and sometimes on Sunday. The **Tourist Information Center** (Hotel Mayura Velapuri, Temple Rd., Belur, ☎ 8233/2209) is a three-minute walk from the temple entrance; its hours are the same as those of the reception center. Government-approved guides, available at the temple entrance, can tour you through the sights for about Rs. 25 (for one or two people).

HASSAN

The **Karnataka Department of Tourism** (KDT, Vartha Bhavan, B. M. Rd., Hassan, ☎ 8172/68862) maintains an information office, open Monday through Saturday, 10 to 5:30 (closed 2nd Sat. of month), where you can get guidance in planning your trip to Belur and Halebid.

KARNATAKA ESSENTIALS

Arriving and Departing

By Car

National highways connect Bangalore to Madras (about 290 km, or 180 mi) and the Kerala coast (about 370 km, or 230 mi), as well as to points much farther away.

By Plane

All flights to the region operate out of the airport in Bangalore, 140 kilometers (90 miles) northeast of Mysore, and 240 kilometers (150 miles) from Nagarhole National Park (Kabini River Lodge). **Indian Airlines** flies from Bombay, Madras, Delhi, Ahmedabad, Calcutta, Cochin,

Goa, Hyderabad, and other points in India. Check with your travel agent for current schedules of other domestic airlines.

BETWEEN THE AIRPORT AND ELSEWHERE
If you want to avoid Bangalore, you can book a car and driver at the KSTDC counter (*see* Visitor Information, *below*) at the airport and be off to Mysore or beyond straight from there. Taxis and car services will also take you long distances, but you're likely be significantly overcharged. For rates for hiring cars and drivers, *see* Getting Around by Car, *below*.

By Train
The superfast new Shatabdi Express runs between Mysore and Madras via Bangalore.

Getting Around

By Auto Rickshaw
In congested cities, the "three-wheeler" is a convenient, quick way to travel short distances. Figure approximately Rs. 5 for the first kilometer and Rs. 2.50 per additional kilometer. The final fare will be a certain percentage more than that shown on the meter; the driver should show you a tariff card with the latest conversions. Insist that the driver start the meter before departing. To avoid being cheated when the meter is in use, set the fare in advance. You can also often hire an auto rickshaw for the entire day (about eight hours) for around Rs. 150; bargain with the driver, and don't pay until you've finished the day.

By Car
The best way to see beautiful Karnataka is to hire a car and driver. For journeys outside city limits, figure about Rs. 3.50 per kilometer (the minimum distance is 250 km/155 mi) plus a halt charge of Rs. 75 per night to feed and shelter the driver. Flat rates for hiring a car and driver just to get around in Bangalore or Mysore run approximately Rs. 450 for an eight-hour day, plus Rs. 30 for each additional hour. Hire a car from an agency listed under Tour Operators *in* the Gold Guide; KSTDC's rates are slightly lower than those of private companies. Driving a car on your own is not recommended for most foreign travelers because traffic and road conditions vary greatly but are consistently hazardous if you're unfamiliar with the area.

By Taxi
In the main cities, regular taxis charge according to their meters, more or less (usually more), with an initial charge of about Rs. 60 for the first 5 kilometers. As a tourist, you are vulnerable to being overcharged; it's best to agree on a price with the driver before setting out.

By Train
Numerous express trains run from Bangalore to Mysore. The fully air-conditioned, more expensive Shatabdi Express runs from Mysore to Madras every afternoon except Tuesday (Rs. 400 full trip). (*See also* Bangalore Essentials *and* Mysore Essentials, *above*.)

Guided Tours

Orientation
The **KSTDC** (*see* Visitor Information, *below*) offers several full-and half-day bus tours of major sights in Karnataka. These tours are inexpensive and fairly low-frills, usually on aging buses, but they provide a compact, well-rounded look at what's important.

Private Guides

The **Government of India Tourist Office** (*see* Visitor Information, *below*) trains and approves all official tour guides. By Western standards, the rates are low (about Rs. 450 per eight-hour day or Rs. 900 per day for a trip outside the city), and the guides are informative and helpful. You can hire one directly or through almost all travel agents and tour operators (*see* Chapter 2, Special-Interest Travel in India).

Special-Interest

Clipper Holidays (Suite 406, Regency Enclave, Magrath Rd., Bangalore 560025, ☎ 80/221–7054, FAX 80/227–7052) offers general-interest tours, special-interest tours, and treks of various lengths.

Shopping

The old skills of Karnakata's artisans still flourish. You can find exquisite hand-loomed silk fabrics, intricately inlaid rosewood furniture, and smooth sandalwood carvings, as well as sandalwood incense sticks, oils, and soaps, which make great, easy-to-carry gifts. Bangalore also has shops that sell curios. If you're not in a fixed-price government shop, bargain hard and remember "old" is often no more than 24 hours old.

Sports

Fishing

Avid anglers can spend a few days at the **Cauvery Fishing Camp** on the banks of the Cauvery River near Bhimeswari, 100 kilometers (60 miles) south of Bangalore and 75 kilometers (46 miles) east of Mysore, where they can hook mammoth mahseer fish weighing upward of 50 pounds, as well as smaller Carnatic carp, pink carp, and the good old catfish. (*See also* Chapter 2, Special-Interest Travel in India.)

Health Clubs

Many hotels have fitness centers with weight-training equipment, swimming pools, saunas, steam rooms, and Jacuzzis.

Dining

In contrast to Bangalore's up-and-coming restaurant scene, dining-out options in the rest of Karnataka are significantly fewer, with good food but limited menus. As Karnataka is in the south, you'll almost always find tasty, predominantly vegetarian regional favorites such as *dosas* Indian-style stuffed crepes and *idli* (steamed rice cakes), served with coconut chutney and other condiments.

What to Wear

Casual clothes are acceptable for dining out throughout the state; it doesn't hurt, however, to scale it up slightly for Bangalore's fancier hotel restaurants.

Lodging

Options in Karnataka, outside Bangalore, are few and far between. Unless otherwise indicated, hotels have central air-conditioning, room service, doctors on call, and foreign-exchange facilities, and rooms have cable TVs and bathrooms with tubs. In addition, many luxury hotels have exclusive floors with special privileges or facilities designed for the business traveler (*see* Special Hints for Business Travelers *in* Chapter 3, Business Travel in India).

The Arts

Karnataka has a rich ancient tradition of folk drama and dance, as well as a colorful present-day scene of classical music and dance from throughout India. In Bangalore and Mysore, performances are frequent—often daily—in high tourist season (December through March) and during major festivals. During other months, there's usually something cultural brewing on weekends. More touristy restaurants sometimes have live music and even dance performances during dinner.

Some events require advance ticket purchases, but most are free. For those events that do require them, tickets (about Rs. 5–Rs. 10, depending on the event) can usually be purchased at the venues.

Important Addresses and Numbers

Changing Money

Most Western-style hotels have foreign-exchange facilities for their guests. Also, the main branches of the **State Bank of India** (generally open Mon.–Fri. 10–1), found in most cities, exchange currency and frequently cash traveler's checks.

Emergencies

Police, ☎ 100; fire, ☎ 101; ambulance, ☎ 102. For all emergencies, turn to your hotel, consulate, or the East West Clinic (*see* Emergencies *in* Chapter 4, Delhi).

Telephone Directory Assistance

Telephone numbers throughout the state are changing rapidly, in no particularly logical fashion. Dial 197 for directory assistance.

Travel Agencies

Many tour operators offer trips to this part of India (*see* Tour Operators *in* the Gold Guide *and in* Chapter 2, Special-Interest Travel in India).

Visitor Information

The **Karnataka Department of Tourism** (KDT, in Bangalore, K. G. Rd., Cauvery Bhavan, F Block, 1st Floor, ☎ 80/221–5489, and 9 St. Marks Rd., ☎ 80/223–6854) is your best source of information about Bangalore and Karnataka. The offices are open Monday through Saturday 10 to 5:30 (closed 2nd Sat. of month). The transport wing of the **Karnataka State Tourism Development Corporation** (KSTDC, in Bangalore, 10/4 Kasturba Rd., ☎ 80/221–2901 or 80-221–2902; airport, ☎ 80/526–8012; railway station, ☎ 80/287–0068), provides information and bookings for its state-run hotels, tours, and car rentals. The main office hours are Monday through Saturday 10 to 5:30 (closed 2nd Sat. of month). For information about wildlife reserves in Karnataka, visit the KTD's separate wing, **Jungle Lodges & Resorts Limited** (Shrungar Shopping Centre, 2nd Floor, M. G. Rd., Bangalore, ☎ 80/559–7021), open Monday through Friday 10 to 5:30 and Saturday 10 to 1:30 (closed 2nd Sat. of month). The **Government of India Tourist Office** (KFC Bldg., 48 Church St., Bangalore, ☎ 80/558–5417) also provides useful information about the region and arranges private guides. The office is open Monday through Friday 10 to 5 and Saturday 10 to 1:30 (closed 2nd Sat. of month).

12 Bombay and the Ellora and Ajanta Caves

Bombay is urbane and jazzy and as hip as India gets. But beneath its Westernized exterior, Indian preferences still reign.

RAZZLE-DAZZLE INDIAN STYLE—that's Bombay, the country's trendiest city. The capital of Maharashtra rests on the Arabian Sea, an island set off from By Julie Tomasz   the rest of India by a winding creek. Its superb harbor provides the city with the country's busiest port. Its airport is also India's most active for international arrivals and departures. And Bombay is not only the financial hub of India, it is one of the largest manufacturing centers in the East.

Bombay is a city unto itself and hits you with an intensity all its own. It's distinctly tropical, with pockets of palm trees and warm, salty breezes that keep you aware of the Arabian Sea. Its weathered Victorian mansions, some still privately owned, and grand public buildings, many beautifully lit at night, stand as a lingering reminder of the days of the British Raj. Bombay's culture is new, vibrant, and often aggressive, reflecting the affluence and energy of a busy city of 10 million people.

Initially Bombay consisted of seven marshland islands, given in 1661 to King Charles II of England as part of a dowry upon his marrying Portuguese Princess Catherine de Braganza. Although Bombay was technically within the territory of a young Marathi leader, Shivaji, the British established a fort and trading post that grew quickly in size and strength. It endured only occasional raids by Shivaji, who was too busy warring with the Mogul emperor Aurangzeb to take over.

After many years of intrigue, betrayals, and mismanagement, the territory Shivaji had governed fell under British rule. Soon, land reclamation joined the seven small islands into one, grafting together modern-day, multifarious Bombay. The pride of the British in Bombay and their power over the western region are symbolized in the city's most celebrated landmark, near Shivaji's statue: the Gateway of India, built to commemorate George V's visit in 1911.

The Bombay you see today is a city of mind-boggling contrasts—sometimes charming, sometimes deeply disturbing. As your airplane descends toward the runway, your first view of Bombay is of vast stretches of slums, stacked and piled onto each other like cardboard boxes—only a fleeting glimpse of the staggering poverty that coexists with Bombay's other side, the dazzling, flashy wealth encountered in a trendy boutique or a five-star deluxe hotel. In the neighborhoods of Churchgate or Nariman Point, Bombay's slick hotel and business centers, a fleet of dark-suited businessmen may breeze by on the way to a meeting while, just behind them, a naked little girl with matted hair scavenges in the gutter.

But Bombay can be as much fun as it is disturbingly eye-opening. You can feast in fabulous restaurants, sunbathe poolside at luxurious hotels, bargain like crazy in the mayhem of a street bazaar, browse in an exclusive boutique, stroll at sunset along Marine Drive's waterfront promenade, get lost in the carvings of the 7th-century Elephanta Caves, take a horse and buggy spin around the stately old Gothic and Victorian buildings, or watch the sun rise over the Gateway to India.

EXPLORING

There's plenty to see in Bombay, but it is not only in the traditional visiting of museums and other bona fide tourist sights. Much of experiencing Bombay is in eating, shopping, and wandering through its strikingly different neighborhoods, immersing oneself in the pulsing life and soaking up the less tangible essences that blend and clash to make Bombay the unique city that it is.

Churchate and **Nariman Point** are the business and hotel centers, with all the major bank and airline headquarters clustered in skyscrapers on Nariman Point. The district referred to as **Fort,** which includes Bombay's hub, Flora Fountain (now called Hutatma Chowk), is the city's commercial heart, with busy, narrow streets lined with small shops and office buildings, as well as a number of colleges and other schools. Farther up, **Kemp's Corner** is a trendy new, chic area popular for expensive boutiques, exclusive restaurants, and high-priced living. An older expensive residential neighborhood is **Malabar Hill,** lovely, leafy, and breezy, with the fine old stone mansions of wealthy industrialists. If you enjoy shopping and people-watching, go to one of Bombay's chaotic bazaar areas, such as **Chor Bazaar** or the **Zaveri** (Jewelry) **Bazaar.** More recently, Bombay's suburbs have seen explosive development in business and in residential neighborhoods, as more and more people move out of Bombay center to escape its soaring real estate prices and simple lack of space. **Juhu Beach** is a popular suburb between Bombay and the airports about 20 kilometers (12 miles) from Bombay center. It's on the Arabian Sea coast and has a number of beaches and resorts; unfortunately, the beaches are polluted and unsafe for swimming, and the whole area has become a somewhat crowded, dirty, honky-tonk resort.

Numbers in the margin correspond to points of interest on the Bombay map.

★ ❽ **Bombay's Bazaars.** Early one morning, visit the **Mahatma Jyotiba Phule Market** (formerly Crawford Market; Dadabhoy Naoroji Rd. and L. Tilak Rd.) and walk through Bombay's fresh-produce emporiums. If it's late spring or early summer, treat yourself to a delicious Alphonzo mango, a food worthy of the gods. From here, wander into nearby
❼ **Zaveri** and **Dagina** bazaars, Bombay's crowded jewelry markets, where shops are filled with fabulous gold and silver in every conceivable de-
❷ sign. North of here, **Chor Bazaar,** which means thieves' bazaar, is a narrow thoroughfare lined with stores crammed with antiques—clocks, old phonographs, brass, and glassware. At all the bazaars, be sure to keep your eyes and hands on your wallet. (*See also* Shopping, *below.*)

★ ⓭ **Elephanta Caves.** Exactly who carved the 7th-century cave temples on Elephanta Island, originally called Gharapuri, is not known. It is known, however, that the Portuguese renamed the island Elephanta after they found a large stone elephant near the landing place. (The figure collapsed in 1814 and was subsequently moved to Victoria Gardens and reassembled.) Shortly before the time of the caves temples' creation Bombay had experienced the golden age of the late Guptas, during which the talents of artists had free scope. Sanskrit had been finely polished, and Kalidasa and other writers—under the Court's liberal patronage—had helped to bring about a revival of Hindu beliefs. It is the worship of Shiva, or Shaivism, that inspired the building of these temples.

The outside of the main cave consists of a columned veranda 9 meters (30 feet) wide and four meters (6 feet) deep, approached by steps flanked by sculptured elephants. The entire temple is 40 meters (130 feet) square, carved out of the basalt hillside. The main sculpture area is on the southern wall at the back. The central recess in the hall contains the most outstanding sculpture, the unusual Mahesamurti, the Great Lord Shiva, a 6-meter (18-foot) triple image. The three faces represent three aspects of Shiva: as the creator (on the right), the preserver (in the center), and the destroyer (on the left).

Other sculptures at the doorways and on side panels show Shiva's usefulness. Shiva brought the river Ganga (Ganges) down to Earth—the story says—letting it trickle through his matted hair. He is also depicted as Yogisvara, lord of Yogis, seated on a lotus, and as Nataraja, the multiarm cosmic dancer. The beauty of this sculpture lies in the grace, balance, and sense of relaxation conveyed in spite of the multiple actions.

The trip takes about one hour each way. The Maharashtra Tourism Development Corporation (MTDC, *see* Visitor Information *in* Bombay Essentials, *below*) offers an excellent tour every day. *9 nautical mi from Gateway to India in Bombay. Regular motor launches depart daily every 30 minutes, 8–2:30 from Gateway to India and 1–5 from Elephanta Island. Round-trip fare: approximately Rs. 40 adults, Rs. 25 children under 7. Air-conditioned catamarans depart daily at 10 AM from Gateway and 2 PM from Elephanta. Round-trip fare: approximately Rs. 110 adults, Rs. 70 children under 8.*

★ ⑱ **Gateway to India.** Bombay's landmark monument, an elegant 26-meter (85-foot) stone archway, was hastily erected as a symbol of welcome to Queen Mary and King George V of England on their visit to India in 1911. In the years following, artisans added decorative carvings and lovely *zaroka* work (window carvings), completing it in 1923. The monument is surrounded by throngs of people selling postcards, shoe shines, and souvenirs and is the launching point for boats going to Elephanta Island and other smaller islands. This is also where the *Queen Elizabeth 2* and other luxury liners dock on their cruises. The majestic Taj Mahal Hotel, built before the Gateway to India, in 1904, stands just behind it.

❶ **Haji Ali Shrine.** Set far out on a rocky jetty jutting into the Arabian Sea, this striking white shrine was built in honor of the Muslim saint, Haji Ali, who drowned here some 500 years ago while on a pilgrimage to Mecca. When a coffin containing his mortal remains floated and came to rest on a rocky bed in the sea, devotees constructed the tomb and mosque at this spot. The shrine is reached by a long walkway just above the water, lined with destitute families and beggars ravaged by leprosy all writhing, chanting, and calling out to you as you make your way down—a deeply discomfiting experience not for the fragile hearted, but one that is unfortunately quintessentially Bombay. Inside, the shrine is full of colored-mirror mosaics and crowded with worshippers praying over the casket, which is covered with wilted flower garlands. Men and women must enter at separate doorways. *End of causeway, off Lala Lajpatrai Marg, near Mahalaxmi Race Course. Approachable only at low tide.*

❹ **Hanging Gardens.** Perched at the top of Malabar Hill, on its western side, just opposite the Kamala Nehru Park (*see below*), these terraced gardens, also known as Ferozeshah Mehta Gardens, provide lovely sunset views over the Arabian Sea. The park was laid out in the early 1880s over Bombay's main reservoir, some say to cover the water from the potentially contaminating activity of the nearby Towers of Silence (*see below*). *B. G. Kher Marg, Malabar Hill.* ☉ *Daily 6 AM–9 PM.*

❶⑯ **Jehangir Art Gallery.** Bombay's main art gallery, just next to the Prince of Wales Museum (*see below*), displays changing exhibits by well-known Indian artists. There's plenty of art to be seen outside as well, as the plaza in front of the building is full of artists offering their works for

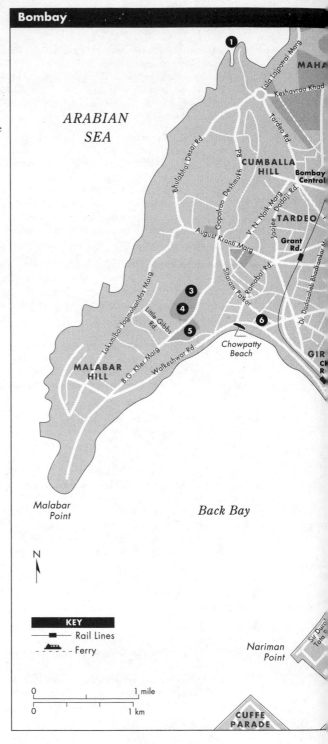

Bombay

ARABIAN
SEA

MAHA

Lala Lajpatrai Marg

Keshavrao Khad

Tardeo Rd.

**CUMBALLA
HILL**

**Bombay
Central**

Bhulabhai Desai Rd.

Gopalrao Deshmukh

V. N. Naik Marg

Jaolee Dadaji Rd.

TARDEO

August Kranti Marg

Ramabai Rd.

Dr. Dadasaheb Bhadkamkar M.

**Grant
Rd.**

Laxmibai Jagmohandas Marg

Little Gibbs
Rd.

Sitaram Patkar

3

4

5

6

B. G. Kher Marg

Wolkeshwar Rd.

**MALABAR
HILL**

*Chowpatty
Beach*

**GIR
CH
R**

*Malabar
Point*

Back Bay

N

KEY
━━■━━ Rail Lines
┄┄🚢┄ Ferry

*Nariman
Point*

Sir Dura
Tata

0   1 mile
0   1 km

**CUFFE
PARADE**

sale and their talents for commission assignments. *M. G. Rd., Fort,* ☎ *22/243989.* ☛ *Free.* ☉ *Daily 11–7.*

⑤ Kamala Nehru Park. On the eastern side of the top of lovely, residential Malabar Hill, this small park is primarily a children's playground, but it offers gorgeous panoramic views of the city below. From the special viewpoint clearing, you can see all of Marine Drive and the Bombay skyline, from Chowpatty Beach to Colaba Point. Try to come up after dark to see why Marine Drive, sparkling with lights, is known as the Queen's Necklace. *B. G. Kher Marg, Malabar Hill.* ☉ *Daily 6 AM–9 PM.*

⑥ Mani Bhavan. This charming, three-story Gujarati house, painted brown and yellow, in a lovely, tree-shaded Parsi neighborhood on Malabar Hill was the home of Mahatma Gandhi from 1917 to 1934. Now overseen and maintained by the Gandhi Institute, it houses a library and small museum about Gandhi's life and work. You can visit Gandhi's room, where his simple belongings are displayed, including his original copies of the Bible, the Quran, and the Bhagvad Ghita. *19 Laburnam Rd., Malabar Hill,* ☎ *22/363–4864.* ☛ *Rs. 3 donation suggested.* ☉ *Daily 9:30–6.*

⑰ Prince of Wales Museum. The Prince of Wales Museum, the city's finest Victorian building, completed in 1911, is named for Britain's King George, who laid the cornerstone in 1905. Bombay's principal museum is divided into three sections: art, archaeology, and natural history. The picture gallery contains, in addition to ancient Indian paintings, works by European and contemporary Indian artists and copies of magnificent cave temple paintings from Ajanta. *M. G. Rd.,* ☎ *22/244519.* ☛ *Rs. 3.* ☉ *Tues.–Sun. 10:30–6.*

③ Towers of Silence. This is the place where Bombay's Parsi community—the last surviving community following the Zoroastrian religion—dispose of their dead. Bearers carry the corpse to the top of one of the towering cylindrical bastions, where it is laid out and left to be devoured by waiting vultures and decomposed by the elements. The Towers are surrounded by a small park and concealed by high walls, strictly off-limits to all, even to the relatives of the deceased, who sit and meditate in the park. Although you cannot see any part of the towers themselves, you can occasionally see the vultures flying above during the body-deposition time—usually in the morning and late afternoon. There is a model of the Towers of Silence in the Prince of Wales Museum (*see above*). *B. G. Kher Marg, Malabar Hill.*

Other Landmarks

Bombay has a large collection of buildings and monuments known for their grand Gothic and Victorian architecture. They are beautifully flood-
⑪ lit at night. **Flora Fountain** stands at a major five-way intersection and marks the heart of Fort, Bombay's commercial neighborhood. The ornately sculpted stone fountain was created as a memorial to one of Bombay's early governors. The square in which it stands is named Hutatma Chowk (Martyr's Square) in honor of those who died in the violence during the establishment of the state of Maharashtra. It is now also a
⑭ popular hot spot for political and apolitical rallies. The attractive **High Court** (K. B. Patil Marg) was built in early Gothic style in 1878. Elegant carvings and statues representing Justice and Mercy decorate the
⑨ facade. The **Municipal Corporation Building** (Dr. Dadabhai Navroji Marg), constructed in 1893 in an imposing V-shape early-Gothic style,
⑮ has Indian motifs crowned by a large dome. The **Rajabhai Clocktower**

(K. B. Patil Marg), the 79-meter (260-foot) tower of Bombay University, is built in 19th-century Gothic style. The **Royal Asiatic Society** building (Horniman Circle), formerly the Town Hall, houses one of the oldest and largest libraries in the city. The floodlighting makes the vast flight of stone stairs leading up to the entrance a popular studying place at night. **Victoria Terminus** (Dr. Dadabhai Naoroji Marg), built by the British in 1888, is one of the city's busiest train stations and one of the largest buildings in Bombay. The structure combines Indian and Gothic architecture and bears a life-size statue of Queen Victoria on its imposing dome.

TIME OUT **Cafe Samovar,** in the Jehangir Art Gallery *(see above),* is a popular, artsy place for a quick snack or a drink.

SHOPPING

From exclusive air-conditioned boutiques to gregarious street bazaars, Bombay has everything to keep a serious shopper riveted for days. In addition to the neighborhoods around Colaba Causeway and Flora Fountain, Kemp's Corner and Breach Candy are the current trendy shopping areas—very chic and very pricey. The arcades of five-star hotels—those at the Oberoi and the Taj Mahal are particularly good—offer a little bit of everything for a lot more than anywhere else, but the merchandise is beautiful and the atmosphere unhurried and climate controlled. For lower prices and a more vibrant atmosphere, throw yourself into the middle of one of Bombay's famous bazaar areas. Once you've exhausted Bombay proper, you can venture out to the suburbs, where prices can be lower. Linking Road in **Bandra** is a trendy place to shop, and **Juhu Beach's** main strip, Juhu Road, is lined with boutiques, art galleries, and varied shops. Important note: each neighborhood has a different day of closure for shops. In Colaba, up to Worli, shops are closed Sunday; in Worli, up to Bandra, they are closed Monday; and in Bandra, up to the suburbs, they are closed Thursday. Throughout the city, many shops are closed on Sunday.

Bazaars and Markets

Chor Bazaar (Mutton St., near Kutbi Masjid) is a bustling flea market where you can find exactly what you don't need but have to have—old phonographs, broken nautical instruments, dusty chandeliers, and brass objects, from junky knickknacks to valuable antiques and curios. Keep an eye on your purse or wallet and come relaxed—it can be chaotic. **Fashion Street** (M. G. Rd., opposite Bombay Gymkhana) is a cotton bargain basement in a row of stalls, with mounds of colorful, cheap clothing and textiles. **Zaveri Bazaar** (near V. Vallabh Chowk) is the place to go for diamond, gold, and silver *zaveri* (jewelry). The chaotic streets are lined with tiny, decades-old family jewelry businesses, into which you can duck and sip a customary cup of tea or coffee while the salesperson shows you the merchandise. Most shops are authentic, but beware of false silver; it's difficult to catch.

Specialty Stores

Art and Antiques
A. K. Essajee (Suleman Chambers, Side St., opposite Cottage Industry, ☎ 22/202–1071) sells handsome old and new Indian curios and handicrafts: carved doors and chairs, old perfume bottles, jewelry, Rajasthani chests, Tanjore and Mysore paintings, old silver jewelry, silver, bronze, and Islamic artifacts. **Natesans Antiquarts Ltd.** (Jehangir Art

Gallery, basement, Fort, ☎ 22/285–2700; Taj Intercontinental Hotel, ☎ 22/202–4165), which has branches in many Indian cities, sells magnificent curios, subcontinental antiquities, wood carvings, sculptures, and paintings, even registered national monuments (not exportable!), plus wonderful new artifacts. **Phillips Antiques** (Madam Cama Rd., opposite Regal Cinema, ☎ 22/202–0564) has the best old prints, engravings, and maps in Bombay. It also sells many possessions left behind by the British—Staffordshire and East India Company china, old jewelry, crystal, lacquerware, and sterling silver.

Clothing
Charagh Din (64 Wodehouse Rd., Colaba, ☎ 22/218–1375) is one of the best-known Indian brand names for top-quality, pure silk shirts in a tremendous variety of styles and patterns, with prices ranging anywhere from $10 to $60. **Ensemble** (Great Western Bldg., 130/132 Shahid Bhagat Singh Marg, Bombay, ☎ 22/287–2883), a pricey boutique near the Taj Mahal hotel, has exclusive *salwar kameez* (2-piece outfit of long, loose pants tapered at the ankle and long-sleeved, long, loose-fitting tunic) for women, *kurtas* (collarless or small-ridge collared shirts) for men, western fashions, saris, and lovely costume jewelry, all by high-profile Indian designers. Ask to see the rare *banarasi* silk saris, in rich colors woven with real gold and silver thread. **Ravissant** (Kemp's Corner, ☎ 22/364–0845, 22/368–0277) was India's first haute couture salon, selling its exclusive-label women's and men's clothing in exquisite patterns and fabrics, from rich silks to feather-light moiré. The store also sells unique silver housewares and jewelry. **Vama** (72 Peddar Rd., ☎ 22/387–1450) looks like another Benetton and Lacoste outlet at first glance, but it also has racks and glass counters full of gorgeous, high-fashion Indian women's and men's wear. Ask to see the nearly sacred *paithani* saris, hand-woven of silk and real gold-and-silver thread, in brilliant colors with gorgeous border designs.

Handicrafts
Central Cottage Industries Emporium (Apollo Bunder, Colaba, ☎ 22/202–2491) is packed with textiles, carvings, and myriad other traditional Indian handicrafts from regions all over the country. This is the place to go for the souvenirs you forgot to buy on your previous stop. **The World Trade Center** (Cuffe Parade, ☎ 22/218–9191), at the southern tip of Bombay, is where you'll find government handicrafts emporia and boutiques from most states in India, all under one air-conditioned roof. Fixed prices provide a respite from the usual haggling in shops and on the street. **Gangotri** (☎ 22/218–8191) sells lovely stone and wood carvings from Uttar Pradesh. The regal Mysore silks are at **Mysore Sales International** (☎ 22/218–6283). You can find Maharashtra's own crafts at **Trimourti** (☎ 22/218–6283).

Jewelry
Tribhovandas Bhimji Zaveri (241–43 Zaveri Bazaar, ☎ 22/342–5001) is the largest jewelry showroom in India, with five floors of gorgeous 18-, 22-, and 24-karat gold, diamond, and silver jewelry. In business for some 130 years, this venerable store is known for its authenticity and reliable quality.

Leather
The **Oberoi Hotel's** (Oberoi Towers, Nariman Point, ☎ 22/202–5757) posh, extensive shopping arcade has over 75 pricey boutiques to keep your wallet slim, with a particularly wide variety of leather shops stocking stylish goods at prices that are still lower than those in the Western shopping world.

SPORTS AND FITNESS

Cricket

Wankhede Stadium in Churchgate hosts Bombay's major domestic and international cricket matches. In season, October through March, there is usually play several times a week. Tickets, ranging from Rs. 50 to Rs. 400, can be bought through the **Bombay Cricket Association** (D. Rd., Churchgate, ☎ 22/206–7795, 22/206–7820).

Golf

The Willingdon Sports Club (K. Khadye Marg, ☎ 22/494–5754) has Bombay's only 18-hole golf course. Nonmembers can usually play as "guests" of the secretary; just call ahead to arrange it.

Horse Racing

Bombay's **Mahalaxmi Race Course** (Mahalaxmi, near the Nehru Planetarium, ☎ 22/307–1409) is one of the finest in the East. The racing season is usually November to the end of April, with races on Thursdays and Sundays.

Sailing

Members of any yachting association affiliated with the **Royal Bombay Yacht Club** (Apollo Bunder, Bombay 400039, Maharashtra, ☎ 22/202–1880) can charter a boat for local sailing.

DINING

In Bombay, you can expect great meals and a wide choice of cuisines: Continental, Chinese, and numerous regional Indian dishes. You may also encounter some Parsi items, cooked without onions, garlic, and other ingredients banned for Parsi religious reasons. Many restaurants tend to be pricey by Indian standards, but some tasty bargains will leave you and your wallet quite satisfied. While we include only our selection of the best restaurants, many hotels also have good restaurants. Although very popular among foreigners, buffet meals can sometimes be risky, when the food has been sitting out too long. If you're a die-hard buffet diner, just make sure the food you select is steaming hot and well cooked.

For price categories, *see* the chart for Major Cities *in* On the Road with Fodor's.

WHAT TO WEAR
With just a few exceptions (noted below), you can dress casually for dining at most Bombay restaurants. Keep in mind, however, that the city can be quite cosmopolitan, and even tourists are expected to look neat and respectable. The more expensive the restaurant, the better off you are scaling your dress up a notch or two.

$$$$ **Mewar.** The *gumbaz* (domes) and *jhakoras* (windows) are covered with embroidered silk, paintings of Rajasthani maharajas adorn the walls, and live music is performed all evening except Tuesday. In this regal ambience, the cuisine is Indian. Try *jhinga pardanashin* (prawns with mustard seed cooked in a coconut shell), or a *thali* (assorted dishes served on a platter). ✕ *Oberoi Towers, Nariman Point,* ☎ *22/202–4343. Reservations advised. AE, DC, MC, V.*

Downtown Bombay Dining and Lodging

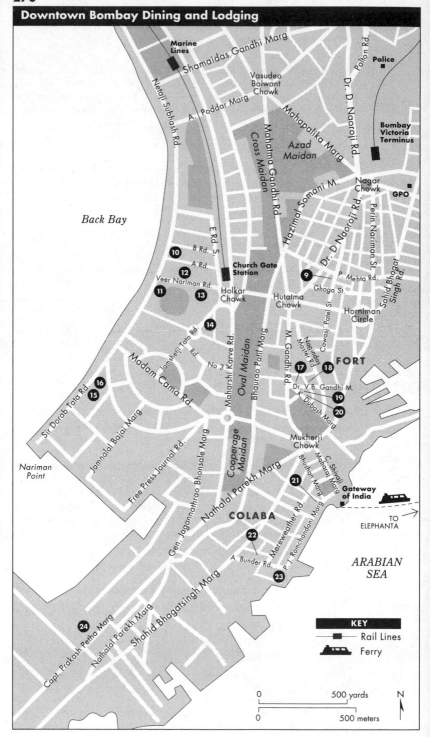

Marine Lines

Shamaidas Gandhi Marg

Vasudeo Balwant Chowk

Netaji Subhash Rd.

A. Poddar Marg

Mahapalika Marg

Mahatma Gandhi Rd.

Cross Maidan

Azad Maidan

Hazimal Somani M.

Dr. D. Naoroji Rd.

Palon Rd.

Police

Bombay Victoria Terminus

Nagar Chowk

GPO

Back Bay

E Rd. S.

B Rd.

A Rd.

Veer Nariman Rd.

Church Gate Station

Holkar Chowk

Hutatma Chowk

Perin Nariman St.

Sahid Bhagat Singh Rd.

P. Mehta Rd.

Ghoga St.

Horniman Circle

⑩

⑫

⑪

⑬

⑨

⑭

Jamshetji Tata Rd.

Rd.

No 3 Rd.

Maharshi Karve Rd.

Oval Maidan

Bhaurao Patil Marg

M. Gandhi Rd.

Nanabas Master Rd.

Cowasji Patel St.

FORT

Madam Cama Rd.

⑯

⑮

Sir Dorab Tata Rd.

⑰ ⑱

Dr. V.B. Gandhi M.

⑲

⑳

Dubash Marg

Jamnalal Bajaj Marg

Free Press Journal Rd.

Gen. Jagamnathrao Bhonsole Marg

Nathalal Parekh Marg

Cooperage Maidan

Mukherji Chowk

Nariman Point

C. Shivaji Maharaj Marg

Bhuslan Marg

Gateway of India

TO ELEPHANTA

㉑

COLABA

Mereweather Rd.

A. Bunder Rd.

P. J. Ramchandani Marg

㉒

㉓

ARABIAN SEA

㉔

Capt. Prakash Petha Marg

Nathalal Parekh Marg

Shahid Bhagatsingh Marg

KEY

Rail Lines

Ferry

0 · · · 500 yards

0 · · · 500 meters

N

Dining

Chetana, **20**
China Garden, **8**
Gaylord
Restaurant, **13**
Goa Portuguese, **6**
Khyber Restaurant, **17**
Mahesh Lunch
Home, **9**
Mewar, **16**
Rajmudra, **7**
Sheetal Samudra, **5**
The Society, **12**
Thai Pavilion, **24**
Trishna, **18**
Wayside Inn, **19**
Zodiac Grill, **21**

Lodging

Ambassador Hotel, **12**
Fariyas Hotel, **23**
Holiday Inn, **3**
Hotel Godwin, **22**
Leela Kempinski, **1**
Nataraj, **10**
Oberoi, **15**
Oberoi Towers, **16**
Ramada Palm Grove, **4**
Ritz Hotel, **14**
Sea Green, **11**
Sun 'n' Sand, **2**
The Taj Mahal
Hotel, **21**

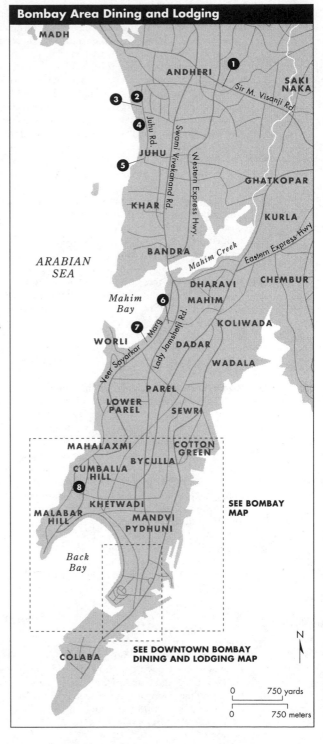

Bombay Area Dining and Lodging

$$$$
★ **Thai Pavilion.** A Thai woman kneels on banana leaves carving flower blooms out of carrots and watermelons as you enter this elegant restaurant. The small dining room is tastefully decorated with teak-inlaid surfaces, candles, and orchids. The Thai chef's cuisine, served in unusually generous portions, is exceptional. Start with a clay crock of *tom yum koong,* a spicy prawn soup aromatic with lemongrass and fiery with chilies (not for the faint-of-palate), and some *kai haw bai toey* (sweet marinated chicken chunks wrapped in pandanus, or screw pine, leaves—don't eat them), then steamed and deep-fried. Knowledgeable, attentive waiters also provide fantastic service. ✕ *Hotel President, 90 Cuffe Parade, Colaba,* ☎ *22/215–0808, ext. 5621. Reservations advised. AE, DC, MC, V.*

$$$$ Zodiac Grill. This Continental-cuisine restaurant, in the legendary Taj Mahal Hotel, is Western-style elegant, with subdued lighting, handsome chandeliers, captains in black jackets, and waiters in black or white (including white gloves). Specialties include lobster chambery (lobster pieces cooked inside puff pastry with a mustard-cream sauce) and Camembert *dariole* (cheese soufflé). Save room for the creamy Kahlua mousse. ✕ *Taj Mahal Hotel, Apollo Bunder,* ☎ *22/202–3366. Reservations required. Jacket and tie. AE, DC, MC, V.*

$$$ Gaylord Restaurant. This 40-year-old restaurant, which serves Continental and Indian cuisines, has an Anglo ambience: upholstered chairs, Victorian mirrors, small crystal lamps, marble floors, and a handsome upstairs balcony. Try the lobster Newburg or *murg makhani* (boneless chicken cooked in tomato curry with cream). Gaylord's also has café seating out front and an excellent bakery. ✕ *Mayfair Bldg., Veer Nariman Rd., Churchgate,* ☎ *22/282–1259. Reservations advised indoors. AE, DC, MC, V.*

$$$
★ **Khyber Restaurant.** Named for the mountain pass between Afghanistan and northwestern India, this is one of Bombay's most attractive and popular restaurants, with three floors of delightful rooms done up in a northwest frontier decor—all white marble floors, terra-cotta urns, carved stone pillars, low wooden rafters, and handsome fresco murals by local artists. The waiters, dressed in Pathan tribal garb, serve delicious kebabs, rotis, and other north Indian food. Try the pomfret green *masala* (fried pomfret stuffed with tangy green chutney and scallions) and Khyber *raan* for two (leg of lamb marinated overnight, then roasted in a clay oven). Reserve a table—Khyber is always packed. ✕ *145 M. G. Rd., Fort,* ☎ *22/273–227 or 22/273–228. Reservations advised. AE, DC, MC, V.*

$$$ Society. If you're in the mood for Continental and nouvelle cuisine and want a good steak, visit this elegant Victorian restaurant, with mirrors and handsome ivory-and-blue decor. The best steak, "à la Fernandes," named after a former maitre d', is richly seasoned with cinnamon, spices, and cream and cooked and flambéed at your table. ✕ *Ambassador Hotel, Veer Nariman Rd., Churchgate,* ☎ *22/2041131. Reservations advised.*

$$ Chetana. Rajasthani decor—hand-blocked fabrics on the ceiling and traditional *toranas* (ornamental carvings above temple entrances) on the walls—provides a cozy ambience in which to enjoy tasty vegetarian Rajasthani and Gujarati thali at lunch and delicious Rajasthani cuisine at dinner. Sample some Rajasthani *dal bati* (lentils), *kadhi* (curd curry), and mint *raita* (curd and mint salad). The service is great. ✕ *34 K. Dubash Marg, Kala Ghoda,* ☎ *22/222514. Reservations advised. No credit cards.*

$$
★ **China Garden.** There hasn't been an unreserved table at this restaurant in Kemp's Corner since it opened in 1984. The dining room resembles a flashy, somewhat kitschy hotel lobby—two levels of white

marble, glass, and fountains, with waterfalls streaming down the walls. Bustling with Bombay's trendiest young fashionables, VIPs, and film stars, it's a real scene, but not pretentious, probably due to owner and Chinese master chef Nelson Wang's outgoing friendliness. The extensive menu offers a pan-Asian selection of seafood, vegetarian, and meat dishes, including bird's nest soup, Thai prawn curry, and cook-it-yourself Chinese fondue. ✕ *O. M. Chambers, 123 A. K. Marg, Kemp's Corner,* ☎ *22/363–0841 or 22/363–0842. Reservations required. AE, DC, MC, V.*

$$ Goa Portuguese. Designed like a modern Goan cottage, this charming, popular restaurant serves such Goan dishes as spicy *rechia* fish (pomfret stuffed with red Goan masala) and prawn *balchao* with *pao* (pickled prawns prepared in curry with palm vinegar). Wash it all down with some potent *feni* liquor. Every night from 9 o'clock on you're serenaded with live Goan music. ✕ *Kataria Rd., opposite Mahim Head Post Office, Mahim district,* ☎ *22/444–0202 or 22/451–633. Reservations advised. AE, DC, MC, V.*

$$ Rajmudra. The name of this elegant restaurant means "seal of the king," and teakwood antiques, rich tapestries, silk organza draperies, and dark wood carvings create an opulent royal Mogul ambience to match. On the outskirts of Bombay, Rajmudra is the best restaurant you'll find between the suburbs and city center. The kitchen serves Continental, Chinese, and Mughlai Indian cuisine, with a few Punjabi dishes as well. Tandoori and *paneer* (curd) dishes are favorites; try the *kaju* paneer *khorma* (cooked with cashew nuts in white gravy). Musicians singing *ghazals* (Mogul-inspired romantic songs) entertain from 8 o'clock every night but Monday. ✕ *Kohinoor Corner, Veer Savarkar Marg, Prabhadevi,* ☎ *22/422–6743. AE, DC, MC, V.*

$$ Sheetal Samudra. Film stars, tourists, foreign businesspeople, and
★ sundry gourmands regularly make the one-hour trip out of Bombay center to dine at the city's best suburban restaurant, right on the main road between Bombay and Juhu Beach. Decor is unexceptional contemporary, but the cuisine—Punjabi and Chinese, with an accent on fresh seafood—is creative and delicious. Try the prawns in buttery, mild crab sauce or the boneless fish with cool, creamy gravy made with ground lettuce leaves. Live crabs, sold by weight, are cooked any way you choose. Waiters, dressed in black vests and red bow ties, are skilled and attentive. ✕ *Unity Compound, Juhu Tara Rd., Juhu,* ☎ *22/612–2973. Reservations advised. AE, DC, MC, V.*

$ Mahesh Lunch Home. At first glance, this simple, two-level eatery,
★ tucked humbly on a narrow street, may not seem like much—just another lunch place bustling with barefoot waiters. However, this unlikely spot serves what may be Bombay's best, freshest seafood, personally picked at the fish market every morning for the last 17 years by its owner, Mr. Karkerah. Local office workers, bankers, five-star hoteliers, suburban families, and cricket and film stars in the know come here for giant portions of exquisite crab and *rawas* (pomfret) tandoori dishes, all succulently tender and light, essentially oil-free, and seasoned with tangy tandoori spices. ✕ *8-B Cawasji Patel St., Fort,* ☎ *22/287–0938. Reservations advised. AE, DC, MC, V.*

$ Trishna. At the end of the 1980s, this small, side-street restaurant near busy M. G. Road was another neighborhood lunch place. Today, it has been "discovered," and trendy yuppies and film stars crowd into its rows of benches and tables alongside Trishna's loyal regulars, all coming to devour fresh seafood, as well as Indian and Chinese vegetarian and nonvegetarian dishes. Squid or oyster chili garlic, and salt-and-pepper butter crab are among the favorites. Ask the waiter to show you the live crab before it's cooked; its giant, snapping claws will dispel every skeptic's doubts about its freshness. ✕ *7 Rope Walk La., next to Commerce House, Fort,* ☎ *22/272–176. Reservations advised. AE, DC, MC, V.*

$ **Wayside Inn.** Plants lined up at open windows, red-and-white checked tablecloths, whirring overhead fans, and the owner's collection of crockery and mugs on walls and in sideboards create an inviting, casual atmosphere at this over-60-year-old establishment. On Tuesday, Thursday, and Saturday, enjoy Parsi cuisine, such as *dhansak* (brown rice cooked with meat or chicken and ground vegetables) or pomfret stuffed with chutney and cooked in a banana leaf. On other days, try Continental fare or the popular pomfret and chips. ✕ *38 K. Dubash Marg, Kala Ghoda district,* ☎ *22/284–4324. No credit cards.*

LODGING

For price categories, *see* the chart for Major Cities *in* On the Road with Fodor's.

Unless it's indicated otherwise, hotels have central air-conditioning, room service, doctors on call, and foreign-exchange facilities, and rooms have cable TVs and bathrooms with tubs. In addition, many luxury hotels have exclusive floors with special privileges or facilities designed for the business traveler (*see* Special Hints for Business Travelers *in* Chapter 3, Business Travel in India).

$$$$ **Leela Kempinski.** Close to the airports and 25 kilometers (16 miles) from the city, this stylish, extremely posh hotel has become the stopover hub for high-powered businesspeople, airline employees, and foreign tourists, who check in and out at all hours of the day and night. Its airport location is less convenient if you want to spend a few days sightseeing or doing business in Bombay proper. While the Leela's alleged 110% occupancy rate detracts from its level of personalized service, all else is superior five-star deluxe. Rooms are spacious, immaculate and sumptuous, with plush carpeting and armchairs in shades of white and ivory and exquisitely comfortable beds. Outside, 11 acres of beautifully maintained gardens include lotus pools and a small waterfall. ▦ *Sahar, Bombay 400059, Maharashtra,* ☎ *22/836–3636,* ⨎ *22/836– 0606. 425 rooms, 32 suites. 4 restaurants, 2 bars, pool, steam room, 2 tennis courts, health club, business services, meeting rooms, travel services, airport shuttle. AE, DC, MC, V.*

$$$$ **Oberoi.** This elegant sky-rise in the heart of Bombay's business dis-
★ trict focuses on upscale business travelers. From service to decor, everything about it is sleek and efficient. Each floor is staffed with a butler to provide personalized assistance, and all contemporary rooms have small separate dressing and luggage areas to allow for clutter-free in-room meetings. Complimetary personalized stationery in the rooms, and a superior business center are extra touches. If you don't mind spending a bit more, ask for a room with a view of the Arabian Sea. ▦ *Nariman Point, Bombay 400021, Maharashtra,* ☎ *22/202–5757,* ⨎ *22/204–3282. 350 rooms, 22 suites. 3 restaurants, bar, pool, barbershop, beauty salon, sauna, Turkish bath, health club, dry cleaning, laundry service, business services, meeting rooms, travel services. AE, DC, MC, V.*

$$$$ **Oberoi Towers.** This 35-story high-rise is geared for the business traveler but hosts a mixed clientele of both tourists and executives. True to the Oberoi chain's characteristic efficiency, this hotel runs like a well-tuned instrument. Rooms are modern and elegant with pastel-patterned coordinating bedspreads and draperies, brass-framed prints

of Indian monuments, and smooth, contemporary wood furniture. High-floor, sea-facing rooms have stunning views. ☒ *Nariman Point, Bombay 400021, Maharashtra,* ☎ *22/202–4343,* FAX *22/204–3282. 546 rooms, 54 suites. 5 restaurants, 2 bars, sauna, health club, disco, meeting rooms. AE, DC, MC, V.*

$$$$ **Taj Mahal Hotel.** J. R. Tata, the Indian magnate, is responsible for the
★ creation of this first Taj hotel, a Victorian extravaganza built in 1903. It faces the Arabian Sea and the Gateway to India. In its heyday, the Taj rivaled the Raffles in Singapore and received a host of luminaries, including Mark Twain. The hotel's stone exterior is stunning: Rows of jutting balconies on upper floors reinforce symmetrical lines. The large central dome is echoed in the smaller circular corner towers. A 19-story new wing, called the Intercontinental, built in the 1970s, towers next to its elegant sister. In the old wing, elevators and a majestic staircase lead to interior verandas that retain their Victorian character. Lower, harbor-facing rooms can be noisy, so ask for an upper room with the same view. They have high ceilings, pastel prints, and various styles of furnishings, including appealing cane furniture. Rooms in the Intercontinental, slightly less expensive, are spacious, with contemporary decor. ☒ *Apollo Bunder, Bombay 400039, Maharashtra,* ☎ *22/202–3366,* FAX *22/287–2711. 610 rooms, 40 suites. 3 restaurants, 4 bars, coffee shop, patisserie, pool, barbershop, beauty salon, health club, disco, baby-sitting, dry cleaning, laundry service, business services, meeting rooms, travel services. AE, DC, MC, V.*

$$$ **Ambassador.** Once a residential building, this 1940s 9-story hotel in the heart of Bombay is less sleek in service and appearance than its downtown counterparts but offers a bit more old-fashioned personality. Rooms are simply furnished in a functional modern style, all with the Ambassador chain's signature brass knocker on their doors. The Ambassador is topped with India's first revolving restaurant, offering gorgeous views over the city and the Arabian Sea. ☒ *Veer Nariman Rd., Churchgate, Bombay 400020, Maharashtra,* ☎ *22/204–1131,* FAX *22/ 204–0004. 123 rooms, 4 suites. 3 restaurants, bar, coffee shop, dry cleaning, laundry service, travel services. AE, DC, MC, V.*

$$$ **Holiday Inn.** This Juhu Beach Western-style high-rise, built in the mid-1970s, underwent major renovations in the mid-1990s, adding special executive floors and revamping the restaurants. The lobby is spacious, and modern rooms are uniformly decorated with standard contemporary furniture and coordinating pastel wall-to-wall carpeting and fabrics. The best standard rooms offer a limited view of the beach; only deluxe rooms directly face the sea. ☒ *Balraj Sahani Marg, Juhu Beach, Bombay 400049, Maharashtra,* ☎ *22/620–4444,* FAX *22/620–4452. 174 rooms, 16 suites. 2 restaurants, bar, coffee shop, pool, health club, dry cleaning, laundry service, business services, meeting rooms, travel services. AE, DC, MC, V.*

$$ **Fariyas Hotel.** With a cool, gleaming marble lobby full of glass chandeliers and brass and carved wood details, this 1970s hotel looks newer and better than ever. But behind shining new wood doors, many rooms are in noticeably shabby shape: lumpy beds and outdated sparkly metallic floral bedspreads and curtains. Executive rooms, about $10 more than a standard double, are significantly better, with new contemporary furnishings and wall-to-wall carpets. Its central location—half a block from the eastern shore in trendy Colaba, near the Gateway to India—and range of facilities make the Fariyas among the best buys in its price range. ☒ *25, Off Arthur Bunder Rd., Colaba, Bombay, 400005, Maharashtra,* ☎ *22/204–2911,* FAX *22/283–4992. 74 rooms with shower, 2 suites with tub, 2 suites with shower. Restaurant, bar, pool, meeting rooms. AE, DC, MC, V.*

$$ Nataraj. There's no sign out front, but you can recognize this seven-story hotel from the two cast-iron dragons guarding the lobby's entrance. On central Marine Drive, the Nataraj is blessed with views of the Arabian Sea; this location, rather than the rooms, is the bulk of what you pay for. Standard rooms are small but fresh and clean; bathrooms are roomy. Avoid interior-facing and unrenovated rooms. For a step up, request a pricier deluxe suite—a spacious, elegant apartment filled with unusual Indian antique furniture and rugs. ⌘ *135 Netaji Subhash Rd., Bombay 400020, Maharashtra,* ☎ *22/204–4161,* ℻ *22/204–3864. 69 rooms, 6 suites. Restaurant, bar, bookstore, disco, travel services. AE, DC, MC, V.*

$$ Ramada Palm Grove. The long lobby of this Western-style high-rise in Juhu Beach is lined with marble and etched glass. The rooms are fairly large, each with a small sitting area and subdued contemporary decor in shades of mauve and green. The best standard rooms offer a limited view of the beach; only deluxe suites and executive salons face the sea directly. A modest-size pool in a small enclosure behind the hotel is a pleasant if slightly cramped place to unwind. ⌘ *Juhu Beach, Bombay 400049, Maharashtra,* ☎ *22/611–2323,* ℻ *22/611–3682. 112 rooms, 2 suites. Restaurant, bar, pool, beauty salon, health club, windsurfing, business services, meeting rooms, travel services. AE, DC, MC, V.*

$$ Ritz Hotel. The small lobby and white-with-green-trim exterior of this 1930s-vintage hotel are in better shape than those of the nearby Nataraj (*see above*), and the location is central but more peaceful—on a tree-lined side street just off Marine Drive. The rooms, however, fall slightly behind, with simple furniture and worn fabrics. White stone and tile bathrooms are clean and have small baskets of toiletries; the water heater, or "geyser," must be switched on manually 30 minutes before you use the hot water. Some rooms have pleasant balconies. ⌘ *5 Jamshedij Tata Rd., Bombay 400020, Maharashtra,* ☎ *22/285–0500 or 22/283–7623,* ℻ *22/285–0494. 66 rooms, 6 suites. 2 restaurants, coffee shop, dry cleaning, laundry service, meeting room, travel services. AE, DC, MC, V.*

$$ Sun 'n' Sand. You'll find a tangibly friendly and relaxing ambience at this experienced 1963 hotel in Juhu Beach. A small circular driveway curves up to the intimate lobby, which leads out to a lovely garden terrace and pool overlooking the beach. The rooms have basic, modern decor that is in the process of being refurbished. Ask for a recently renovated room with a partial beach view; the more expensive rooms directly face the sea. ⌘ *39 Juhu Beach, Juhu, Bombay 400049, Maharashtra,* ☎ *22/620–1811,* ℻ *22/620–2170. 108 rooms, 12 suites. 2 restaurants, bar, pool, health club, travel services. AE, DC, MC, V.*

$ Hotel Godwin. On a small side street in Colaba, minutes from major sights and shops, this nine-story hotel is a good, low-frills bargain. Rooms are fairly small, with outdated dark wood and faux-leather furnishings. Most bathrooms do not have separate shower stalls—only shower curtains. Most rooms have window air-conditioning units; several are centrally air-conditioned. Request an upper room with a good, though distant, view of the Taj Mahal Hotel and Gateway to India. ⌘ *Jasmine Bldg., 41 Garden Rd., Colaba, Bombay 400039, Maharashtra,* ☎ *22/287–2050,* ℻ *22/287–1592. 42 rooms with shower, 5 with bath; 2 suites with shower, 1 with bath. Restaurant, lounge, laundry. AE, DC, MC, V.*

$ Sea Green. This friendly, five-story hotel is indeed a faded green, weathered by the Arabian Sea (and pollution) over its more than 50 years of housing guests on Marine Drive. Given its city-central location, the Sea Green is a good bargain if you don't mind its lack of facilities and its worn look. Narrow halls open onto surprisingly large rooms, with window air-conditioners and clean but institutional furnishings, such as metal wardrobes and turquoise vinyl 1970s couches. Bathrooms have only open showers—without tubs or shower stalls. All rooms but one have small balconies. A pantry serves beverages and simple breakfasts. ⌘ *145 Marine Dr., Bombay 400020, Maharashtra,* ☎ *and fax 22/282–2294 or 22/282–2363. 30 rooms with shower, 4 suites with shower. Coin laundry. AE, DC, MC, V.*

THE ARTS AND NIGHTLIFE

The Arts

The best source of information is the Government of India Tourist Office's fortnightly culture calendar, "Programme of Dance, Music and Drama," free at GITO offices. The daily *Times of India* newspaper usually lists the day's films, concerts, and other events on the last two or three pages. Program information and details usually appear on the **MTDC**'s city guide programs, shown regularly on hotels' in-house TV stations. Also, the **National Center for the Performing Arts** (NCPA; ☎ 22/283–3737 or 22/283–3838) posts its upcoming performance schedule on the program bulletin board at the center's main entrance and by the entrances to the Tata and Experimental theaters. Many performances at the NCPA are open to members only. To become a member—the cost is very low—contact the NCPA office. Other performance tickets in Bombay are usually very inexpensive (from entirely free to Rs. 200) and can be purchased from venue box offices and from the ticket counter at Rhythm House Private Ltd. (40 K. Dubash Marg, Rampart Row, ☎ 22/284–2835, 22/284–2940), one of Bombay's main music stores, where you can find out what's happening as well as purchase tickets for most events.

Dance

Tanjore Restaurant (Taj Mahal Hotel, ☎ 22/364–3805) doubles as a dance venue, where local performers present a classical Indian dance demonstration with explanation on Tuesday, Thursday, and Saturday from 5:30 to 6:30 PM (check the time of performance with the hotel concierge). Later performances are also held for dinner guests. The **NCPA** complex (*see above*) also houses the **Godrej Dance Academy Theater**, a main venue for classical Indian dance performances as well as workshops and master classes, and the **Drama Opera Arts Complex**, a 1,000-seat auditorium planned as Bombay's ballet and opera theater.

Film

Bombay, a.k.a. "Bollywood," is the center of the Indian film industry, the largest film producer in the world. Unfortunately, most of the epic, musical Indian films shown in movie theaters are not in English. The **Regal Cinema** (opposite Prince of Wales Museum, Colaba) and **Eros Cinema** (Maharshi Karve Rd., Churchgate), however, usually show current English-language movies. Interesting art films are sometimes shown at the **Nehru Center Auditorium** (*see above*) in Worli, and at the **National Center for the Performing Arts** (*see above*).

Music and Theater

The **NCPA** (Nariman Point, box office ☎ 22/283–4678) complex includes the **Tata Theater**, a grand 1,000-seat auditorium. It regularly hosts drama performances, often in English, and classical concerts by major Indian and international musicians. **Little Theater** is the NCPA's smallest theater; it hosts many small-scale plays and chamber music recitals. **Experimental Theater**, with 300 seats, is usually used for avant-garde drama and occasionally for concerts and small-scale dance performances. **The Nehru Center Auditorium** (Dr. Annie Besant Rd., Worli, ☎ 22/492–8237) is Bombay's second major venue, where theater, music, and dance performances are regularly held.

Nightlife

From couples strolling on the breezy, moonlit promenade around the Gateway to India to trendy young partiers on the pounding dance floor at the Cyclone disco, Bombay does not fade away at night.

Because of astronomical real estate prices and bullying by racketeers, few private groups can afford to start up their own clubs or bars. As a result, the nightspots that can and do exist in Bombay city are those in established hotels and restaurants. The rest are pushed to the wealthy suburbs, like Juhu and Bandra, where the nightlife scene thrives on suburbia's young nouveau riche clientele, as well as Bombay city folks who are willing to make the long trip for a good night out.

Note: Many clubs and bars have strange "couples" policies, whereby a lone man is not permitted to enter without a woman—a circuitous attempt to prevent brawls, pick-up scenes, and possibly prostitution. To avoid an unpleasant encounter at the door, check with your hotel staff before you head out on the prowl with a group of men or innocently alone. Clubs also tend to have a membership policy by which they screen out would-be troublemakers. Dress nicely (apparently troublemakers don't)—jackets for men—and you will probably be favored with a distant nod of approval at the door. As crazy as it sounds, an advance call to the nightclub from your hotel concierge could make your entry smoother. Most nightspots, even the pubs that would otherwise have atmospheres conducive to cozy talks over beers, tend to have extremely loud music. If you're going out with someone with whom you'd like to converse beyond a few shouts over blaring rock music, opt for the more reserved hotel bars and lounges.

Revelry usually peaks Thursday through Sunday nights, with primarily an "older" late-20s to mid-30s crowd on Sundays. Some places collect a nominal cover charge at the door.

As in all metropolises, the reign of a Bombay nightspot can be ephemeral. Consult a young hotel employee for the latest on what and when is "in."

Bars and Lounges

The Ambassador Hotel (Churchgate, ☎ 22/204–1131) rooftop garden bar is lovely for a quiet drink with a gorgeous view of the city and the Arabian Sea; it's often booked for private parties, so call ahead to avoid disappointment. The **Bay View Bar** (The Oberoi, Nariman Point, ☎ 22/202–5757) faces the Arabian Sea; it's elegant and more reserved than many of its peers and has a dance floor and a live band. The **London Pub** (by Chowpatty Beach) organizes theme parties as often as its staff can come up with an excuse for one; it's a tiny place, with a small open loft upstairs, but people dance to the loud music wherever there's room.

The Tavern (Fariyas Hotel, 25, Off Arthur Bunder Rd., Colaba, ☎ 22/204–2911), a friendly, small, dark room with wooden rafters, has high tables and stools and no membership policy; talking is difficult over the very loud pop and rock music.

Clubs and Discos

The Cellar (The Oberoi Towers, Nariman Point, ☎ 22/202–4343) is indeed a basement, but a classy one, with rough stone walls and wood floors; tables on one side face the small but jam-packed dance floor on the other. **Cyclone** (Leela Kempinski Hotel, Sahar, ☎ 22/836–3636), which admits only hotel guests, members, and invitees, outdoes every disco in town with its flashing electronic gadgetry, sophisticated sound system, and posh decor (ask your concierge for help getting in). **1900s** (Taj Mahal Hotel, Apollo Bunder, ☎ 22/202–3366), primarily for hotel guests, is an upmarket club with a high-tech, Gotham City theme—full of metal girders and waiters dressed like the Joker's henchmen. Trendy Bombay socialites of all ages pack the small, very dark **Piano Bar** (China Garden restaurant, O. M. Chambers, 123 A. K. Marg, Kemp's Corner, ☎ 22/363–0841), especially on Friday night (men arriving alone will have a difficult time being admitted; if possible, come as a couple and have your hotel concierge call ahead for an invitation). At **Razzberry Rhinoceros** (Juhu Hotel, Juhu Rd., Juhu Beach, ☎ 22/614–6140) the feel is young and casual, the look rustic, and the music loud rock and pop or jazz. **R. G.'s** (135 Nataraj Hotel, Netaji Subhash Rd., Marine Dr., ☎ 22/204–4161) is a pop-art themed disco; you can either sit at low, round tables and stools off to the side or jump into the strobe lights on the central dance floor (you're more likely to get in if your hotel arranges it for you in advance). At **Wig Wam** (18/B Juhu Tara Rd., Juhu, ☎ 22/614–8754), one of the most popular spots in the suburbs, wood floors, tree-stump stools, and Native American prints provide a rustic, mellow decor.

Horse and Buggy Ride

For a quick tour of Bombay's illuminated sights by night, hop in one of the horse-drawn buggies parked at Nariman Point next to the Oberoi Towers, at the northern end of Marine Drive, or at the Gateway to India. Neither carriages nor horses are in particularly good shape, let alone elegant, but if you don't require luxury, it can be an enjoyable the jaunt. A loop taking in the Gateway to India, the Rajabhai Clocktower, and other key sights takes about one hour and should cost under Rs. 100 (agree on the price ahead of time).

EXCURSIONS

The Retreat

For price category, *see* the chart for Major Cities *in* On the Road with Fodor's.

$$ **Retreat.** The pampering and relaxation you'll find at this elegant yet
★ friendly beach resort makes it well worth the 2½-hour drive from Bombay. By the time you are sipping your complimentary cold welcome coconut water, garnished with a giant fuchsia hibiscus bloom, the stress of the city fades far away. Although the ruggedly beautiful ocean beach is not safe for swimming, guests can soak in the outdoor Jacuzzi or bathe in the 8,000-square-foot, semicircular swimming pool—Bombay's largest—complete with a waterfall, a small island, and a bar in the pool. Paths wind down to the sandy beach through beautifully landscaped grounds, past towering palms strung with hammocks and alive with chattering parrots. Inside, rooms are spacious and stylishly contemporary in cool, light colors: white walls; pale lilac or blue carpeting; and coordinating pastel draperies, spreads, and upholsteries. Request an ocean view. ☒ *Erangal Beach, Madh-Marve Rd., Malad (West), Bombay 400061, Maharashtra,* ☎ *22/882–5335,* ℻ *22/882–*

5171. 137 rooms, 7 suites. 3 restaurants, bar, coffee shop, pool, billiards, baby-sitting, laundry service, business services, meeting rooms.
AE, DC, MC, V.

Ellora and Ajanta Caves

Dating back over 2,000 years, the cave temples of Ajanta and Ellora
rank among the wonders of the ancient world. Here, over a period of
700 years—between the 2nd century BC and the 5th century AD—great
armies of monks and craftsmen carved cathedrals, monasteries, and
whole cities of frescoed, sculptured halls into the solid rock faces.
Working with simple chisels and hammers and an ingenious system of
reflecting mirrors to provide light, they cut away hundreds of thousands of tons of rock to create the cave temples. The precision of their
planning, their knowledge of rock formations, and the delicacy and
profusion of their art have created masterpieces that are truly unique
wonders of the world, driven by a religious fervor and sustained by a
sacred patience beyond the grasp of modern humanity. Between them,
the cave temples span three great religions—Buddhism, Hinduism,
and Jainism.

The city of Aurangabad, with several excellent hotels and a growing
number of good restaurants, is used as the gateway to Ellora and
Ajanta and can serve as your base city from which to visit the cave temples, about 30 kilometers (18 miles) and 100 kilometers (62 miles) away
respectively. Far from simply a "gateway," Aurangabad itself has a number of fascinating ancient sites, such as the imposing **Daulatabad Fort,**
surrounded by seven giant walls over 5 kilometers (3 miles) long, built
in 1187 by the then Hindu king. Another interesting sight is the **Bibi-
ka-Maqbara,** also known as the mini Taj Mahal, which you can usually see from the plane as you approach the city. It is a pale but nobly
attempted imitation of the original Taj Mahal, built by the last of the
six great Mogul emperors, Aurangzeb, founder of Aurangabad and son
of the Taj Mahal's creator, Shah Jahan.

For optimum absorption of the vast and phenomenal caves, we suggest that you allow one full day for each visit.

Ajanta Caves

It is believed that a band of wandering Buddhist monks first came here
in the 2nd century BC searching for a place to meditate during the monsoons. Ajanta was ideal—peaceful and remote from civilization. The
setting was spectacular: a sharp, wide horseshoe-shape gorge that fell
steeply to a wild mountain stream flowing through the jungle below.
The monks began carving crude caves into this rock face for themselves,
and a new temple form was born.

Over seven centuries, the cave temples of Ajanta evolved into a work
of splendid art. Structural engineers are awestruck by the sheer brilliance of these ancient masters who, undaunted by the limitations of
seemingly crude implements, materials, and labor, created this marvel
of art and architectural splendor. In all, 29 caves were carved, 15 of
which were left unfinished; some of them were *viharas* (monasteries)—
complete with hard stone pillars carved onto the monks' stone beds—
others, *chaityas* (Buddhist cathedrals). All of them were intricately and
profusely decorated with sculptures and murals depicting the many incarnations of Buddha.

During the decline of Buddhism, the monk-artists abandoned their work,
and the temples were swallowed up by the jungle. A thousand years
later, in 1819, Britisher John Smith was tiger hunting on a bluff nearby

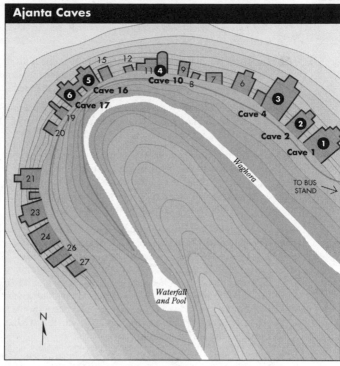

Ajanta Caves

during dry season and noticed the soaring arch of what is now dubbed Cave 10 peeking out from the thinned greenery; he subsequently unveiled the masterpieces to the modern world.

At both Ellora and Ajanta, monumental facades and statues were chipped out of solid, hard rock, but at Ajanta, an added dimension survived the centuries, expressed in India's most remarkable examples of cave paintings. Onto a carefully prepared plaster of clay, cow dung, chopped rice husks, and lime spread onto the rough rock walls, the monks devotedly painted their works with only natural local pigments: red ocher, burnt brick, copper oxide, lampblack, and dust from green rocks that had been crushed.

The Ajanta caves are like chapters of a splendid epic in visual form, recalling the life of the Buddha and illustrating tales from Buddhist *jatakas* (fables). As the artists lovingly told the story of the Buddha, they portrayed the life and civilization they knew. The total effect is that of a magic carpet transporting you back into a drama played by nobles, wise men, and commoners. When the electric spotlights flicker onto the paintings, the figures seem to come alive.

Opinions vary as to the most exquisite of the Ajanta caves. The best paintings are generally considered to be found in Caves 1, 2, 16, 17, and 19, and the best sculptures in Caves 1, 4, 17, 19, and 26. (The caves are numbered from west to east, not in chronological order.)

Numbers in the margin correspond to points of interest on the Ajanta Caves map.

❶ Most popular are the paintings in **Cave 1,** of the Bodhisattva Avalokitesvara and Bodhisattva Padmapani. Padmapani, or the "one with the lotus in his hand," is considered to be the alter ego of the Lord Buddha who assumed the duties of the Buddha when he disappeared. Padmapani is depicted with his sinuous-hipped wife, one of the most widely reproduced figures of Ajanta.

② **Cave 2** is remarkable for its ceiling decorations and its murals relating the birth of the Buddha. For its sheer exuberance and joie de vivre, the painting in Cave 2 of women on a swing is judged the best.

③ In **Cave 4,** sculpture is the main interest. It is the largest vihara in Ajanta and depicts a man and a woman fleeing from a mad elephant and a man giving up his resistance to a tempting woman.

④ The earliest cave is **Cave 10,** a chaitya dating from 200 BC filled with Buddhas and dominated by an enormous stupa. However, it is only from AD 100 that the exquisite brush-and-line work begins. In breathtaking detail, the Shadanta Jataka, a legend about the Buddha, is depicted on the wall in a continuous panel.

The mystical heights attained by the artist-monks reach their zenith in **⑤** **Caves 16** and **17,** where the viewer is released from the bonds of time and space. Here one is faced by a continuous narrative that spreads horizontally and vertically, evolving into a panoramic whole—at once logical and stunning. One painting here is riveting; known as "The Dying Princess," it is believed to represent Sundari, the wife of the Buddha's half-brother, Nanda, who left her to become a monk. There is an excellent view of the river from Cave 16, which may have been the entrance to the entire series of caves.

⑥ **Cave 17** possesses the greatest number of pictures undamaged by time. Luscious heavenly damsels fly effortlessly overhead, a prince makes love to a princess, and the Buddha tames a raging elephant. Other favorite paintings include the scene of a woman applying lipstick and of a princess performing *sringar* (her toilet).

A number of unfinished caves were abandoned mysteriously, but even these are worth a visit. A steep climb of 100 steps takes you to them. You may also take the bridle path, a gentler ascent, with a crescent pathway running alongside the caves. From here, there is a magnificent view of the ravines of the Waghura River. *100 km (62 mi) northeast of Aurangabad.* ☛ *50 paises adults, children under 15 free; video-camera fee Rs. 25.* ⊙ *Daily 9–5:30.*

Ellora Caves

In the 7th century, for some inexplicable reason, the focus of activity shifted from Ajanta to a site 123 kilometers (76 miles) to the southwest (only 30 kilometers or 18 miles from Aurangabad)—a place known today as Ellora. The cave temples of Ellora, unlike those at Ajanta, are not solely Buddhist. Instead, they trace the course of religious development in India—through the decline of Buddhism in the latter half of the 8th century, the Hindu renaissance that followed the return of the Gupta dynasty, and the Jain resurgence between the 9th and 11th centuries. Of the 34 caves, the 12 to the south are Buddhist, the 17 in the center are Hindu, and the 5 to the north are Jain.

At Ellora, the focus is on sculpture, which covers the walls in an exquisitely ornate mass. In the Buddhist caves, the carvings present a serene reflection of the Buddhist philosophy. But in the subsequent Hindu caves, they acquire a certain exuberance, a throbbing vitality. Gods and demons do fearful battle, Lord Shiva angrily flails his eight arms, elephants rampage, eagles swoop, and lovers intertwine.

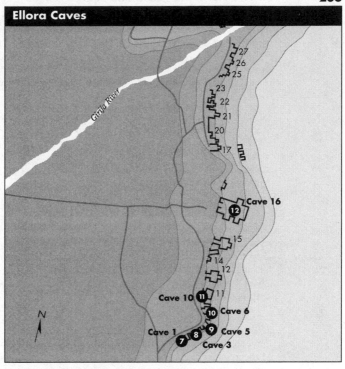

Ellora Caves

Unlike Ajanta, where the temples were chopped out of a steep cliff, the caves at Ellora were dug into the slope of a hill in a north–south direction (they face the west and could receive the light of the setting sun).

Numbers in the margin correspond to points of interest on the Ellora Caves map.

❼ ❽ **Cave 1** (two stories) and **Cave 3** (three stories) are remarkable for having more than one floor. The two caves form a monastery behind an open courtyard; the facade looms nearly 15 meters (50 feet) high. Although this facade is simple, the interior is lavish. This block of rock was gouged into a ground-floor hall, a shrine on the story above it, and another hall on the top story with a gallery of Buddhas seated under trees and parasols.

❾ The largest of the Buddhist caves is **Cave 5,** 36 meters by 17 meters (117 feet by 56 feet). It was probably used as a classroom for young monks, and its roof appears to be supported by 24 pillars. Working their way down, sculptors first "built" the roof before they "erected" the pillars.

❿ **Cave 6** contains a statue of the Hindu goddess of learning, Saraswati, **⓫** in the company of Buddhist figures. **Cave 10** is the "Carpenter's Cave," where Hinduism and Buddhism meet again. Here, the stonecutters reproduced the timbered roofs of their day over a richly decorated facade that imitates masonry work. Inside this chaitya, the only Buddhist chapel at Ellora, the main work of art is a huge image of Buddha.

The immediate successors to the Buddhist caves are the Hindu caves, and a step inside them is enough to pull the visitor up short. It's another world—another universe—in which the calm contemplation of the seated Buddhas gives way to the dynamic cosmology of Hinduism, in which mythical gods seemingly come alive from stone. These sculptures are estimated to have been created around the 7th and 8th centuries. They depict goddesses at battle; Shiva flailing the air with his eight arms; elephants big as life groaning under their burdens; boars, eagles, peacocks, and monkeys prancing around what has suddenly turned into a zoo; and lovers striking poses that leave the imagination somewhere far behind.

Ellora is dominated by the mammoth **Kailasa** temple complex, or ⑫ **Cave 16.** Dedicated to Shiva, the complex is a replica of his legendary abode at Mount Kailasa in the Tibetan Himalayas. The world's largest monolithic structure, approximately twice the area of the Parthenon in Greece and 1½ times as high, the Kailasa reveals the genius, daring, and skill of its artisans.

To create the complex, an army of stonecutters started at the top of the cliff, where they removed 930,000 cubic meters (3 million cubic feet) of rock to create a vast pit with a freestanding rock left in the center. Out of this single slab, 86 meters (276 feet) long and 48 meters (154 feet) wide, they created Shiva's abode, which includes the main temple, a series of smaller shrines, and galleries (small rooms) built into a wall that encloses the entire complex. Nearly every surface is exquisitely sculpted with epic themes.

Around the courtyard numerous friezes illustrate the legends of Shiva and stories from the great Hindu epics, the Mahabharata and the Ramayana. One interesting panel on the eastern wall relates the origin of the symbol for Shiva, the lingam or phallus. Another frieze on the outer wall of the main sanctuary in the southern side of the courtyard shows the demon Ravana shaking Mount Kailasa, a story from the Ramayana.

TIME OUT **Ellora Restaurant** (parking lot, Ellora Caves) is a great spot for a cold drink and a hot *samosa*. The outdoor patio is very pleasant, with fruit trees (home to many monkeys) and floods of pink bougainvillea flowers spilling down the arbor.

Dining

For price categories, *see* the chart for Other Areas *in* On the Road with Fodor's.

$$$ **Madhuban.** A central white marble fountain; dark wood tables; and
★ burgundy, ivory, and gold fabrics set a regal Mughal ambience at this top restaurant. One wall of windows opens onto lovely tropical trees and flowers, and another opens into the busy kitchen, where you can watch chefs in tall, stiff white hats skewering meats for the tandoor oven. The menu also includes some Chinese and Continental dishes, as well as a popular buffet lunch. ✕ *Welcomgroup Rama International Hotel, R-3 Chikalthana,* ☎ *2432/85441. AE, DC, MC, V.*

$$ **Angeethi.** Named for a traditional Indian cooking vessel, this cozy, dark restaurant serves Punjabi, Continental, and Chinese fare, with a special knack for tandoori items. Other specialties include Afghani kebab masala (boneless chicken pieces in sweet, white cashew nut gravy) and the two-person *sikendari raan* (a large leg of goat marinated in rum and spices and seared in a tandoor oven). The service is friendly and efficient. ✕ *Mehar Chambers 6, Vidya Nagar, Jalna Rd.,* ☎ *2432/20966. Reservations advised. AE, DC, MC, V. Closed daily 3–7.*

$ Tandoor Restaurant and Bar. Tandoor's kitchen creates some of the best vegetarian and nonvegetarian Indian and Chinese food in town. Try the mixed tandoori sizzler, a variety of kebabs and *naan* (bread) or the "special vegetable" served in white peanut sauce. The decor runs to Egyptian prints and statuary hung on greenish-brown tile walls. With only 16 tables, packed close together, the room tends to fill up quickly. ✕ *Shyam Chambers, Bansilal Nagar, Station Rd.,* ☎ *2432/28482. Reservations advised. AE, DC, MC, V. Closed daily 4–6:30.*

$ Woodlands. Carnivores can move on: This primarily south Indian eatery is strictly vegetarian, offering tasty *dosas* (stuffed Indian crepes) and tangy *paneer makhanwala* (curd steaks spiced with chili), as well as thali options and a few Punjabi dishes. Decorated with a Madras elephant mural, Rajasthani metalwork chairs, and a plethora of brass figures and bells, it feels festive. A glass window into the kitchen lets you watch the chefs at work. ✕ *Akashay Deep Plaza, near Cidco Bus Stand, Jalna Rd.,* ☎ *2432/82822. DC, MC, V. Closed daily 3:30–7.*

Lodging

For price categories, *see* the chart for Other Areas *in* On the Road with Fodor's.

Unless it's otherwise indicated, hotels have central air-conditioning, room service, doctors on call, and foreign-exchange facilities, and rooms have cable TVs and bathrooms with tubs.

$$$ Welcomgroup Rama International. ★ A long driveway takes you away from the main road through spacious grounds to this attractive two-story hotel with red bands of elephants chiseled on its bleached-white facade. The efficient and genuinely friendly staff provide personalized service of the highest level and a warm and intimate, smaller-hotel atmosphere. Standard rooms are spacious and comfortably elegant, all with views onto the verdant garden of palms and bright flower beds. Corner suites are like vast living rooms. The exclusive Rama Chambers wing on the second floor provides larger rooms for business travelers and a variety of special extras. ☒ *R-3 Chikalthana, Aurangabad 431210, Maharashtra,* ☎ *2432/85441,* ℻ *2432/84768. 97 rooms, 3 suites. Restaurant, bar, coffee shop, pool, barber shop, beauty salon, massage, sauna, steam room, miniature golf, 2 tennis courts, croquet, exercise room, Ping-Pong, astrologer, dry cleaning, laundry service, business services, meeting room, travel services. AE, DC, MC, V.*

$$ Ambassador Ajanta. Just next door to its rival, the Rama, this five-story marble hotel sits amid sweeping lawns, well-kept flower beds, and towering trees alive with birdsong. Filled with brass goddesses, marble elephants, wood carvings, and myriad other Indian antiques, the Ajanta is a haven of dark, Indian elegance—a welcome change from the uninspired decor of many Western-style hotels. The rooms have garden-view windows and more authentic Indian decorative details. Don't miss a dip in the pool, where you can imbibe midstroke at the sunken bar at the shallow end. ☒ *Jalna Rd., CIDCO, Aurangabad 431003, Maharashtra,* ☎ *2432/85211 or 2432/85212,* ℻ *2432/84367. 76 rooms with bath, 20 suites. Restaurant, bar, pool, tennis court, badminton, dry cleaning, laundry service, business services, meeting rooms, travel services. AE, DC, MC, V.*

$$ Taj Residency. ★ Inside and out, this gleaming Mogul palace is bright white marble and stone with gold accents. Windows and doors arch to regal Mogul points, and the grand dome over the lobby is hand-painted in bright yellow-and-white traditional Jaipuri patterns. Rooms have brand-new smooth teak furniture with matching headboards and mirror frames. All rooms open onto the garden and have balconies or patios, most equipped with a teak swing. Stone paths wind through five acres of beautifully landscaped lawns, flower beds, and blossoming hedges. The staff consists primarily of young students from the Indian Institute of Hotel Management, just next door. ⊠ *8-N-12 CIDCO, Aurangabad 431003, Maharashtra,* ☎ *2432/33501 or 2432/33502,* FAX *2432/31223. 40 rooms. Restaurant, pool, exercise room, dry cleaning, laundry service, business services, meeting room, travel services. AE, DC, MC, V.*

$ **Hotel President Park.** All curves and semicircles, the attractive contemporary building was designed to embrace the central garden, to afford every room a view of the swimming pool. Rooms have semicircular balconies or patios and teak-trimmed furniture, dark-toned fabrics, and brass fixtures. Bathrooms are on the small side. ⊠ *R 7/2, Chikalthana, Airport Rd., Aurangabad 431210, Maharashtra,* ☎ *2432/84601 or 2432/84602,* FAX *2432/84823. 56 rooms, 4 suites. Restaurant, bar, coffee shop, pool, sauna, steam room, tennis court, exercise room, dry cleaning, laundry service, meeting room, business services, meeting room, travel services. AE, DC, MC, V.*

$ **Hotel Windsor Castle.** This small, five-story pale-pink brick hotel opened in late 1994. The decor is consistently bold: Through teak-framed glass doors with elephant carvings, one enters the tiny lobby where electric purple, red, and black modular couches and chairs stand on red marble floors. A diminutive elevator opens onto pale-red marble halls covered with unevenly cut turquoise carpeting. Rooms are clean and functional but quite small and unusually polyhedric, with simple, modern furniture and clashing curtains and upholstery. Only 12 rooms have air-conditioning. ⊠ *Opposite CIDCO Office, Jalgaon Rd., Aurangabad 431003, Maharashtra,* ☎ *2432/84818 or 2432/84177,* FAX *2432/24925. 43 rooms, 2 suites. Restaurant, bar, coffee shop, meeting rooms. AE, DC, MC, V.*

The Arts and Nightlife

The Ellora Dance Festival, held annually in March, draws top classical Indian dancers and musicians from around the country to perform outdoors against the magical backdrop of the Ellora Caves. The **Ambassador Ajanta**'s restaurant offers live ghazal music on Friday and Saturday nights.

Ajanta and Ellora Caves Essentials

ARRIVING AND DEPARTING

By Plane. Aurangabad and Bombay are only about 45 minutes apart by air. **Indian Airlines** (☎ 2432/85421 or 24864; at the airport, ☎ 2432/82111 or 2432/85780) flies regularly. Check with your travel agent for the current status and schedules of other domestic airlines.

GUIDED TOURS

The **Government of India Tourist Office** (*see* Visitor Information, *below*) in Aurangabad oversees about 40 expert, polite, multilingual tour guides who can be hired through its office, the MTDC office, also in Aurangabad (*see* Visitor Information, *below*), and more or less all travel agents. For one- to four-person parties, fees are Rs. 200 per half day (four hours) and Rs. 300 for a full day (up to eight hours). An extra Rs. 225 is charged for any trips that entail traveling more than 100 kilometers (60 miles); for example, a full-day guided trip to Ajanta caves would run around Rs. 525. It's best to book ahead. **Archaeological Survey** guides can be hired without prearrangement at the sites as well, often at a lower rate, but there's no guarantee one will be available when you want one.

Once you have a guide, your best bet for transportation is to hire a car and driver. A full-day trip with air-conditioned car and driver may cost around Rs. 800 to Ajanta and around Rs. 600 to Ellora. Ask your hotel travel desk to arrange it, or try one of these agencies: **Classic Travel Related Services** (MTDC Holiday Resort, Station Rd., Aurangabad, ☎ 2432/35598) or **Aurangabad Tours and Travels** (a.k.a. Aurangabad Transport Syndicate, in Welcomgroup Rama Hotel, Airport Rd., Aurangabad, ☎ 2432/82423).

IMPORTANT ADDRESSES AND NUMBERS

Changing Money. Hotels can change money only for their guests. **Classic Travel Related Services** (at MTDC Holiday Resort, Station Rd., Aurangabad, ☎ 2432/35598) is scheduled to become the first licensed exchange office in 1996. These banks in Aurangabad also change currency: **State Bank of India** (Kranti Chowk, ☎ 2432/31872 or 31386; ☉ Mon.–Fri. 10–2, Sat. 10–noon) and the bank in **Hotel Aurangabad Ashok** (Dr. Rajendra Prasad Marg, ☎ 2432/31426 or 31427; ☉ Mon.–Fri. 1–5, Sat. noon–2).

Visitor Information. The **Government of India Tourist Office** (Krishna Vilas, Station Rd., Aurangabad, ☎ 2432/31217), across the street from the train station, provides a warm and informative welcome to Aurangabad; it is open Monday through Saturday, 8:30 to 6, holidays until 1:30. The **MTDC** (Maharashtra Tourism Development Corporation, in the MTDC Holiday Resort, Station Rd., Aurangabad, ☎ 2432/31198, 2432/31513, or 2432/34259) is extremely helpful; it operates daily from 7 AM to 8 PM; its airport counter is open with flight arrivals. In addition, most hotels have travel desks and informed concierges who can help with basic tourist information.

BOMBAY ESSENTIALS

Arriving and Departing

By Boat

Damania Airways (17 Nehru Rd., Vakala, Santa Cruz, ☎ 22/610–2525) runs daily (weather permitting) catamaran service between Bombay and Panaji, Goa, that departs at 7 AM from the ferry wharf. The journey takes about seven hours and costs Rs. 900 for second-class seats and Rs. 1,100 for first-class seats.

By Car

Fairly good roads connect Bombay to most major cities and tourist areas. Although using a hired car and driver affords you the chance to watch the often beautiful surroundings whiz by, it can also be a slow, noisy, frequently hair-raising experience. If you have the time and the nerves for it, you'll experience what many people miss when they fly. Some distances from Bombay are: Pune, 162 kilometers (101 miles); Panaji (Goa), 597 kilometers (373 miles); Ahmedabad, 545 kilometers (341 miles); Hyderabad, 711 kilometers (444 miles).

By Catamaran

In 1995, **Damania Shipping (India) Ltd.** (Shed No. 2, New Ferry Wharf, Mallet Bunder Rd., Bombay 400009, ☎ 22/374–3737) began overnight catamaran service between Bombay and Goa.

By Plane

Bombay's **international airport** (☎ 22/836–6767) is at Sahar, 30 kilometers (18 miles) from the city center. The **domestic airport** (☎ 22/611–2850) is at Santa Cruz, 26 kilometers (15½ miles) from the city center. Reconfirm your flight at least 72 hours before departure and arrive at the airport at least 60 minutes before the scheduled takeoff for domestic flights and 2 hours before international flights; Delta Airlines and some others require you to arrive 3 hours before takeoff. Convenient for long delays or layovers, both airports have 24-hour business centers available to major credit-card holders.

Delta Airlines (☎ 22/202–9020) has flights to and from Bombay every day via its Frankfurt hub. Other international carriers serving Bombay include **Air India** (☎ 22/202–4142), **Air Canada** (☎ 22/202–7632), and **British Airways** (☎ 22/202-1314). Domestic carriers include **Indian Airlines** (☎ 22/202–3031 or 287–6161) and a number of new airlines; check with your travel agent for carriers and schedules.

BETWEEN THE AIRPORTS AND CENTER CITY

The trip should take about 30 minutes if you arrive before 9 AM or after 8 PM. At other times, traffic near the city center can increase the trip time to more than an hour. Most hotels provide complimentary airport transfers if you are staying in a suite or on an exclusive floor (*see* Special Hints for Business Travelers *in* Chapter 3, Business Travel in India). All hotels, however, will provide airport transfers for about Rs. 200 to Rs. 300, depending on their location.

Each airport has a **prepaid taxi service.** Head to the prepaid taxi counter (outside either the baggage or the customs area). Your destination and amount of luggage determine the rate; Rs. 450 should get you to the center of the city from either airport. Once you get into a taxi (black with a yellow top), don't give the driver the payment slip until you reach your destination. If the driver demands more rupees, complain to the hotel doorman. A regular metered taxi from the international airport to the city center should cost about Rs. 200 and from the domestic airport, about Rs. 150.

By Train

Bombay has two train stations: **Victoria Terminus Station** (Fort, ☎ 134 or 22/262–3535), hub of India's Central Railway line, and **Bombay Central Station** (☎ 131 or 22/493–3535), hub of India's Western Railway line. *Be sure to go to the right train station;* check before you set out. To avoid the pandemonium at the stations, have a travel agent take care of your ticket booking; it will cost you more but will save time and stress. If you do it yourself, head for the tourist counter established especially for foreign tourists. For more information and recommended trains, *see* the Gold Guide.

Getting Around

Usually, having a car and driver for a day is most convenient. Within certain areas, however—in the bazaars, for example—it's easier and more fun to explore on foot.

By Auto Rickshaw

Auto rickshaws are permitted only in Bombay's suburbs, where they can be flagged down on the street. The charge is about Rs. 2.50 for the first kilometer and Rs. 1.20 per additional kilometer. As with the taxis (*see below*), insist on the meter and ask to see the tariff card.

By Hired Car with Driver

Having a car at your disposal eliminates the hassle of hailing taxis and haggling over fares. Contact the travel agencies listed below or your hotel travel desk. Rates vary; you'll probably pay more if you use your hotel desk. You'll get lower-end rates from the India Tourism Development Corporation (*see* Ashok Travels and Tours, *below*): with a non-air-conditioned Ambassador, Rs. 500 for a half day and Rs. 650 for a full day; with air-conditioning, the fees are Rs. 800 and Rs. 1,000, respectively. Higher tariffs apply for Toyotas, Mercedeses, and other "luxury" cars.

By Hydrofoil

In 1995, swift, air-conditioned hydrofoil service was introduced to connect Bombay with points in the suburbs. Contact the MTDC office for its current schedules.

By Taxi

Yellow-top black taxis can be flagged down anywhere in the city. Insist that the driver turn on the meter, a rusty mechanical contraption on the hood of the car, before going. As taxi-meter development cannot keep up with the rising costs of fuel, the latest, raised fares must be computed by some arithmetic, based on what the meter reads. Drivers are required to show you their revised tariff cards for easy reference, but they sometimes conveniently misplace them. At press time (summer 1995), final fares were 9.5 times the amount shown on the meter, based on roughly Rs. 9 for the first kilometer and Rs. 2.5 for each additional kilometer. Ask your hotel clerk what the going rates are.

Guided Tours

The **Government of India Tourist Office** (*see* Visitor Information, *below*) trains and oversees knowledgeable, multilingual tour guides, available directly from the GITO or through nearly all travel agencies and tourist offices. Rates run approximately Rs. 200 per half day for groups of one to four people, Rs. 300 for a full, eight-hour day. Additional fees are applied for trips beyond 100 kilometers and for those involving overnight stays.

Important Addresses and Numbers

Changing Money

Most Western-style hotels have foreign-exchange facilities for their guests. **American Express Travel Services** (*see above*) is open daily 9:30 to 7:30. **Thomas Cook India, Ltd.** (*see above*) is open Monday–Saturday 9:30–6. You can also cash traveler's checks at **Citibank** (Sakhar Bhavan, ☎ 22/202–8765), **ANZ Grindlays** (90 M. G. Rd., ☎ 22/265–0162), and **State Bank of India** (Madame Cama Rd., ☎ 22/202–2426). Most banks are open Monday–Friday 10–1.

Consulates

The **U.S. Consulate** (Lincoln House, 78 Bhulabhai Desai Rd., ☎ 22/363–3611) is open Monday–Friday 8:30–11:30 AM; the staff is on duty until 5 PM in case of emergencies. The **Canadian Consulate** (41–42 Makers Chambers VI, 4th Floor, Nariman Point, ☎ 22/287–6027) is open Monday–Friday 9–1 and 2–5:30. The **British Consulate** (Makers Chambers IV, 1st Floor, Nariman Point, ☎ 22/283–2330) is open Monday–Friday 8–11:30 AM.

Emergencies
Police, ☎ 100; **fire,** ☎ 101; **ambulance,** ☎ 102.

Most hotels have house physicians and dentists on call. Your consulate will also give you the name of a reputable doctor or dentist, or contact the East West Clinic (*see* Emergencies *in* Chapter 4, Delhi).

English-Language Bookstores
Many bookstores have English-language sections, and most hotels have small bookshops, but Bombay's best selection is at **Strand Book Stall** (Dhannur Sir P. M. Rd., Fort, ☎ 22/266–1994 or 22/266–1719), which offers good discounts and is open Monday–Saturday 10–7 and Sunday 10–1.

Late-Night Pharmacies
Most hotels have pharmacies that are open daily until about 9 PM. **Royal Chemists** (opposite Wadia Hospital, A. D. Rd., Vishwas Niwas Bldg. 8, Shop 3, Parel district, ☎ 22/411–5028) is open 24 hours.

Travel Agencies
These travel agencies are best bets for helping with bookings and supplying cars with driver: **American Express** (Regal Cinema Bldg, Chhatrapati Shivaji Maharaj Rd., Colaba, ☎ 22/204–6361 or 22/204–8291), **Ashoka Travels** (Kothari Mansion, 9 Parekh St., opposite Girgaon Court, ☎ 22/385–7622 or 22/387–8639), **Cox & Kings** (Grindlays Bank Bldg., 22/270–272 D. N. Rd., ☎ 22/204–3065), **Makson Auto Hirers** (5 Sagar Kunj, 78 Napeansea Rd., Bombay 400006, ☎ 22/361–6762), and **Thomas Cook India, Ltd.** (Thomas Cook Bldg., D. N. Rd., Fort, ☎ 22/204–8556). The transport department of the **India Tourism Development Corporation** (ITDC, 11th Floor, Nirmal Bldg., Nariman Point, ☎ 22/202–3343 or 22/202–6679) is also helpful with travel arrangements.

Visitor Information
You cannot count on hotels to stock general tourist information, such as maps and brochures. The **Government of India Tourist Office** (123 Maharishi Karve Rd., Churchgate, Bombay 400020, ☎ 22/203–3144), by Churchgate Railway Station, has useful material and is open Monday–Friday 8:30–6 and Saturday and holidays until 2. The **Maharashtra Tourism Development Corporation** (MTDC, Tours Division, opposite L.I.C. Bldg., Madame Cama Rd., Bombay 400020, ☎ 22/202–6713 or 202–7762) is open daily 8–8. Both have counters at the airports; the MTDC also has counters at Victoria Railway Station and the Gateway of India. At the airport, try the MTDC's multimedia, computerized, **interactive information machine**—the first of its kind in India—next to the MTDC counter in the baggage carousel area at the domestic terminal (and soon at the international terminal).

13 Portraits of India

The Religions of India

Further Reading and Viewing

Dining Glossary

THE RELIGIONS OF INDIA

INDIA IS THE BIRTHPLACE of Hinduism, Buddhism, Jainism, and Sikhism; these religions, as well as Islam, have left their mark on the landscape. The power of faith finds expression in the country's art and architecture, in many festivals, and in the daily activities of millions of devotees.

Buddhism

Siddhartha Gautama was born into a princely family in Lumbini, along the Indian and Nepalese border, around 563 BC. He renounced his privileged status—an act called the Great Renunciation—lived as an ascetic, and then entered a lengthy meditation that led to his Great Enlightenment.

Transformed, Siddhartha went to Sarnath, near Varanasi in India, and preached his revolutionary sermon on the dharma (truth), also called "The Setting in Motion of the Wheel of Truth or Law." His discourse set forth his Four Noble Truths, which define the essence of Buddhism: (1) Life is connected to suffering, (2) a suffering that arises from greed, insatiable desires, and man's self-centered nature; (3) once man understands the cause of his suffering, he can overcome it by following (4) the Eightfold Path.

The Eightfold Path includes right views and right aspirations, which lead to wisdom. Right speech, right behavior, right means of livelihood, and right efforts to follow the path to salvation relate to proper and intelligent conduct. Right meditation and right contemplation bring nirvana (supreme bliss).

Siddhartha Gautama became the Buddha (Enlightened One), or Sakyamuni (Lion of the Sakya clan), and his faith became Theravada Buddhism, a religion of compassion and reason in which idols were not worshipped. His followers did not consider Sakyamuni the founder of Buddhism, but simply the historic Buddha of their time.

In the 1st century AD, a second school, Mahayana Buddhism, was formed, which introduced the concept of the bodhisattva—the enlightened being who postpones his own nirvana to help others. Unlike Theravadians, who prayed only before symbols, such as the Buddha's empty throne or his footprints, Mahayanists also worshipped before depictions of the various Buddhas, other gods and goddesses, and revered bodhisattvas. Over time, Mahayana Buddhism divided into subsects, including Nyingmapa, Kargyu, Sakya, and Gelug. The Gelug achieved spiritual preeminence in Tibet. Their leader, His Holiness the Dalai Lama, is considered the God King of Tibet and is currently living in exile in Dharamsala, India.

Pantheon

Once you know the symbols that identify the more popular members of the pantheon, they're easy to recognize.

Adibuddha (Original or Supreme Buddha) is considered infinite or abstract: without beginning or end. Still, he is often depicted in human form, sitting in the lotus (cross-legged) position with his arms crossed. One hand holds a *vajra* (thunderbolt: symbol of the ultimate reality); the other hand holds the *ghanta* (bell: symbol of wisdom). His body is usually blue.

The Five Dhyani (Cosmic) Buddhas, which emanated from the Adibuddha, represent the top tier of the Mahayana pantheon and embody the five elements of the cosmos (earth, water, fire, air, and ether). They are always shown in a meditation pose. **Vairocana** (Buddha of Resplendent Light or the Buddha Supreme and Eternal) is also known as Buddha in the Center. Both hands appear in front of his chest in an image of a preacher who is "Turning the Wheel of Truth." His color is white, his symbol is the wheel, his element is ether, and his vehicle is the lion. **Amitabha** (Buddha of Boundless Light) is also known as Buddha of the West. Both hands usually rest on his lap. His color is red, his symbol is the lotus, his element is water, and his vehicle is the peacock. **Aksobhya** (Undisturbed Buddha) is also known as Buddha of the East. The fingers of his right hand usually touch the earth. His color is blue, his symbol is the thunderbolt, his element is air, and his vehicle is the elephant. **Ratansambhava** (Jewel Being or Buddha of Precious Birth) is also known as Buddha of the South. His right hand is held low, palm open in a gesture of giving. His color is yellow, his symbol is the jewel, his element is fire, and his vehicle is the horse. **Amoghasiddhi** (Buddha of Infallible Power) is also known as the Buddha of the North. He holds his right hand up in a gesture of fearlessness, which also offers a blessing of confidence. His color is green, his symbol is the double thunderbolt, his element is earth, and his vehicle is Garuda (half-man and half-bird).

Sakyamuni (Historic Buddha) has a third eye symbolizing wisdom and usually sits on a lotus throne. His body is gold, his earlobes are long, a protuberance atop his head is a symbol of his enlightenment, and he wears monastic garb. His hands gesture one of three ways: His right hand may touch the earth, signifying his realization of spiritual discovery; both hands may be in his lap, palms turned upward as in meditation; or both hands may be near his chest, symbolic of the delivery of his sermon: "The Wheel of Truth."

Bodhisattvas

Maitreya (Future Buddha) usually appears with one hand held to his chest in the gesture of a preacher delivering "The Wheel of Truth," while the other hand holds a jug of water. His color is yellow, and he usually sits with his feet resting on a flowering lotus.

Avolokitesvara (Buddha of Compassion) has up to 11 heads and 1,000 arms and signifies compassion and wisdom. When he is portrayed with four heads, he is seated in the lotus position; when he appears with his 11 heads, he is standing. One hand holds a *mala* (set of rosary beads) and another carries a lotus. All Dalai Lamas are considered his incarnation.

Manjushri (Buddha of Transcendent Wisdom) appears with a sword held high in one hand, symbolizing his power to cut through ignorance. His other hand carries a book on a lotus, symbolic of wisdom.

Vajrapani (Buddha of Rain or Power) is blue, appears either seated or standing, and wears a serpent around his neck. In his most ferocious aspect, he carries a thunderbolt; in other depictions, he holds a lotus as well.

Amitayus (Buddha of Eternal Life) is bright red, appears seated in meditation in the lotus position, and carries a vase of ambrosia, symbolic of long life.

Buddhist Saktis (Female Goddesses)

Green Tara (Green Savioress) is the patron goddess of Tibet and Avalokitesvara's consort. She sits on a lotus throne and holds a lotus in each hand.

White Tara (White Savioress) is also Avalokitesvara's consort. She usually sits in the lotus position, with her right hand outstretched in a gesture of charity and her left hand holding a lotus in full bloom.

Nagarjuna and Padmasambhava

Nagarjuna, the founder of the Mahayana School of Buddhism, usually wears a crown with seven snakes and monastic garb and looks like the Buddha with long earlobes. His hands are normally held palm to palm to his breast in the gesture of a preacher.

Padmasambhava (Guru Rimpoche, or Lotus Born), the Indian mystic who brought Buddhism to Tibet, appears in royal robes, including the red cap of the Nyingma sect, and sits on an open lotus. His right hand carries the thunderbolt; his left hand holds a *patra* (begging bowl), and tucked in his arm is his *khatvanga* (magic tantric stick), which cuts through evil and ignorance.

Important Symbols

Om Mani Padme Hum is a mantra (invocation) that means "Hail to the Jewel in the Lotus," reminding the devotee of the Four Noble Truths. The **lotus,** usually shown as the throne of the enlightened, grows out of mud to reveal its purity and beauty above water. *Om* also represents the realm of the gods; *Mani,* the world of nongods; *Padme,* the lotus, or Buddha; and *Hum,* the life-forms lost in purgatory. Reciting this mantra helps the devotee rise above imperfection and end the cycle of rebirths.

Mani walls (low stone walls), inscribed with "Om Mani Padme Hum," guard

Buddhist villages in the spiritual sense and protect them and crops by diverting the runoff from heavy rains. When a Buddhist passes a mani wall, he repeats the mantra and keeps the wall to his right, believing it a sacrilege to do otherwise.

Stupas (receptacles of offerings) are tall hemispheres made of stone and clay, built near monasteries or villages. Eight early stupas are said to contain the divided ashes of the Buddha. Subsequent stupas hold the remains of sacred lamas or commemorate an event in the Buddha's life. If you see five steps built into the central mound, they stand for the elements that form the cosmos (earth, water, fire, air, ether) or the Five Cosmic Buddhas (see above). The 13 rings that often lead to a depiction of the moon and sun represent the Path to Enlightenment, frequently symbolized by an uppermost small circle.

Prayer Wheels are prayer-inscribed cylinders that contain paper or cloth strips—each one inscribed with "Om Mani Padme Hum." When the prayer wheel is rotated—always clockwise out of respect for the Buddha—it sends the mantra to heaven.

The **Wheel of Life,** which the Buddha traced for his disciples, appears in most monasteries and represents a visual microcosm of Buddhism. The central image is a large circle, or wheel, divided into six sections, with a small interior circle and a larger circle around the rim. Often the wheel is held by Shindje, the Lord of Death, whose presence is a reminder of mortality. The interior circle shows the symbols of the root of suffering: a cock (lust), a pig (ignorance), and a snake (lack of compassion). The six sections inside the large circle describe the stations of life that come with rebirth. The bottom half portrays the three lowest forms: animals, ghosts, and the tormented in purgatory. The upper half reveals the inhabitants of the three worthiest realms: the deities; the *ashuras* (fallen deities), who long to rejoin the deities; and the mortals who hope for ascension. The band around this circle depicts allegories of human faults or conditions that humans must overcome. A blind person represents ignorance, the monkey represents consciousness, and a woman in labor represents birth, to name a few.

Thang-kas (religious scrolls) appear in monasteries or private shrines. These detailed paintings on cloth show deities, the mandala *(see definition, below),* or the Wheel of Life, and are an aid to meditation. The entire painting is often enclosed in a silk brocade border, called its door.

Mandalas, created in sand paintings or thang-kas, are a geometric rendering of the dwelling of the god, who resides within a circle that is set inside a square with four entrances, one on each side. During meditation, Buddhists gaze at the mandala to help achieve union with the divine.

Musical instruments, used during chanting, are also symbolic. The strident sound of 12-foot trumpets represents the cosmos and the thump of kettle drums suggests the unending cycle of life and rebirth.

Eight Auspicious Signs

The **Jewelled Parasol** protects the mind from evil influences. The **Golden Fish** represent humans' rescue from the ocean of misery and is a symbol of spiritual happiness and wealth. The **Conch Shell** proclaims the glory of those who have achieved Enlightenment. (Before the Historic Buddha preached his first sermon, he blew on a conch shell.) The **Holy Vase** represents spiritual wealth and eternal bliss. The **Sacred Lotus** reaffirms the pledge to attain purity and salvation. The **Knot of Eternity,** which has no beginning or end, stands for the Four Noble Truths and eternity. The **Banner of Victory,** which is used in rituals and processions, proclaims the victory of the Four Noble Truths over evil. The **Eight-Spoked Wheel of Truth** symbolizes the Eightfold Path that leads to nirvana.

Hinduism

Hinduism, with its megafamily of gods and goddesses, extends back at least three millennia. Like Buddhists, Hindus believe in reincarnation. Hindus also share the Buddhist goal: *moksha* or liberation from the endless cycle of rebirth. Hinduism also espouses a similar relationship between dharma (truth) and karma (action). If one fulfills one's assigned duty and moral obligation to society, one will be rewarded in the next life.

Sacrifice is an essential part of dharma. An offering to a god blesses the worshipper in return. Sacrifice also calls for the sacrifice of one's individuality, which the Hindu believes frees the *atman* (universal consciousness) and allows the realization of moksha. This theory explains an important ritual attached to cremation: The head of the deceased is ignited first to free the atman for the journey that will, it is hoped, end in unity with Brahma *(see Hindu Pantheon, below)*.

Devout Hindus also practice yoga, which they consider an indispensable expression of faith. Yoga (which literally means "union") is a series of complex mental and physical exercises that rid the practitioner of all thought, so he or she can experience a sense of detachment from the realities of the physical world.

Strictures underlying dharma and karma also help to explain the tolerance of the caste system that divided all Hindus into four segregated rankings: Brahmans (priests), Ksatriyas (nobles and warriors), Vaisyas (tradesmen), and Shudras (menial laborers). Panchamas (the filth), more commonly known as "Untouchables," fell outside the system. A member of one of the castes who accidentally touched a Panchama was considered polluted until he went through purification rites.

To most Westerners, the caste system seems like fuel for revolution. But within Hindu society, even those who sat on the lowest rung accepted their fate, seeing it as a direct result of their karma. If they followed the laws of truth and action, properly fulfilling their assigned duties, they could hope for a better next life. Centuries passed before the Untouchables found a way back from exclusion. The catalyst was Mahatma Gandhi. Through his efforts, the caste system was abolished in 1947—abolished by law, that is. Practically speaking, it still regulates much of Hindu behavior.

Hindu Temples

As in Buddhism, the Hindu temple is filled with symbols of belief. Before the structure is built, a priest traces a mandala, which represents the cosmos and determines the placement of all rooms and icons. The center of the temple, called the inner sanctum, represents the egg or womb from which all life originates. This is where the sacred deity resides. The *vimana* (spire) is directly over the inner sanctum. It draws the attention of the devout to the heavenly realm and its connection with the sacred deity.

Many festivals take place in the temple's *mandapa* (a front porch that may be an elaborate pillared pavilion or a simple overhang). Water is the agent of purification. Ideally, a temple is constructed near a river or lake, but if no natural water source is available, a large tank is often built, with steps around it. Before the devout Hindu worships, he takes a ritual dip to rid himself of impurities. Daily *darshan* or viewing of the idol—usually performed at sunrise, noon, sunset, and midnight—is imbued with sacred traditions. Ancient rituals combine into an elaborate pageantry, with a touching gentleness toward the god's idol.

Before the priest enters the temple, he takes his sacred dip. The actual darshan begins with the clanging of a bell to ward off any evil presence and to awaken the sleeping deity. Burning camphor sweetens the air as the priest recites mantras and blesses the idol with oils and sandalwood paste. Next, the deity receives offerings of incense (an aroma favored by the gods), vermilion powder, flowers, and decorative platters of food. Lamps of ghee (clarified butter) and more camphor are waved before the idol; then the priest blesses the devotees, and the door to the inner sanctum is often closed to let the deity return to its sleeping state.

Hindu Pantheon

The Hindu pantheon is dominated by three gods—Brahma, Shiva, and Vishnu—along with their numerous avatars (incarnations). **Brahma,** the Creator of the World and the Progenitor of All Living Things, has four heads and four arms, each one holding sway over a quarter of the universe. The four heads also signify the four Vedas, the most sacred Hindu holy books, which put forth the concept of rebirth. Brahma is the god of wisdom; the rosary that he counts in one hand represents time, and his lotus seat represents the earth. Brahma's vehicle is the swan, symbol of the freedom that comes with knowledge. His consort is Sarasvati, the goddess of learning. Unlike Shiva and Vishnu, Brahma has no avatars.

Shiva is the god of destruction—destruction that gives rise to creation, just as the seedling tears apart the seed. This is why Shiva is also called the god of creation and sexual power and is often worshipped in the form of a lingam (phallic symbol). Images of Shiva have distinctive elements, like the third eye in the middle of his forehead, the tiger skins wrapped around his loins, and the serpents coiled around his body. Shiva often carries a weapon, a trident, or a bowl fashioned from a human skull. Cosmic Shiva, a common manifestation of Shiva, shows him as a dancer with four hands poised and surrounded by a ring, which represents the Earth. Since one foot holds down Apasmara, the demon of ignorance, his dance ensures perpetual creation. His mount, Nandi, the sacred bull, usually guards the entrance to a Shiva temple. Priests who pray to Shiva have three horizontal stripes painted on their foreheads.

Shiva's consort is the most powerful Hindu goddess. With each avatar she assumes, her name and image change. When she is benevolent **Parvati,** she's beautiful and sexy. As **Durga,** the goddess of battle, she holds weapons of retribution in each of 10 hands. As **Kali,** the terrible black goddess who conquered time, she wears a necklace of skulls and dangles her red tongue. Devotees must appease her with sacrifices. These sacrifices were formerly humans, but now she accepts considerably less.

Ganesh, Shiva and Parvati's son, is the popular god of wealth and good fortune. As he is also the remover of obstacles, this god is normally worshipped before the start of any journey or ritual. Ganesh has the head of an elephant because, one legend claims, Shiva, unaware that he had a son, returned from a trip just after Parvati told Ganesh to guard the house while she slept. When Shiva approached, Ganesh blocked the entrance. Shiva lopped off his head. When he discovered Ganesh was his son, he ordered his servants to go to the forest and take the head of the first creature they saw—it was an elephant.

The preserver of the universe, **Vishnu,** has nine known avatars; a 10th is prophesied. Each successive avatar reflects a step up the evolutionary cycle, beginning with the fish and moving up to the ninth, Buddha, accepted by the all-embracing Hindus as a figure in their own pantheon. Vishnu's most popular incarnations are Rama and Krishna, the sixth and seventh, respectively, who are the two gods that embody humanity. Vishnu priests have three vertical stripes painted on their foreheads.

Vishnu appears with four arms that signify the four cardinal directions and his command over the realms they encompass. In one hand, he carries the lotus, the symbol of the universe. The conch shell, which he holds in his second hand, represents the evolutionary nature of all existence. A wheel in his third hand refers to the rotation of the Earth, with each spoke honoring a specific season of the year. In his fourth hand, Vishnu often holds a weapon to protect him from demons. A common image of Vishnu has him lying on a bed of coils formed by his serpent, Ananta, who symbolizes time. Creation will begin when Vishnu wakes up. Vishnu has two consorts: **Bhudevi,** the goddess of Earth, and **Lakshmi,** the goddess of wealth and prosperity, who rose from the foam of the ocean like Venus. Lakshmi assumes a different name with each of Vishnu's avatars. When Vishnu is Rama, she's Sita; when he's Krishna, she's Radha.

Rama, the hero of the Hindu epic, *Ramayana,* slew the 10-headed demon, Ravana, who had kidnapped Sita. This episode, including Sita's rescue by Hanuman, the monkey god and Rama's faithful servant, is celebrated during Dussehra, one of India's most festive holidays. Krishna, a central figure in another great Hindu epic, *Mahabharata,* is a playful boy god. He plays the flute, has a weakness for teasing young girls, and is colored blue. An embodiment of a human love that has the power to destroy all pain, Krishna represents the ideal man and lover.

Jainism

The origins of Jainism (the name comes from the word *jina,* or victor) go back more than 2,500 years. Jainism became a powerful sect during the time of Parsvanatha, the 23rd Tirthankara (perfect soul), who lived in the 8th century BC, when Hindu Brahmins dominated much of Indian society. Jains (followers of the victor) revere 24 Tirthankaras, who were former disciples that devotees believe achieved spiritual victory and attained moksha, or liberation from the cycle of rebirth.

The 23rd Tirthankara, Parsvanatha, who was a prince, renounced his wealth to become an ascetic who advocated honesty, respect for all life in the belief that every creature has a soul, and *ahimsa* (nonviolence) and abhorred any form of theft and the ownership of property. The 24th Tirthankara was Mahavira (Great Hero), who lived in 6th century BC around the time of the historic Buddha. Mahavira also became a monk and eventually shed his clothes as a sign of devotion and absolute self-denial. Indeed, he advocated a life of poverty, although he realized that his example would be difficult to follow.

In 300 BC, the original Jain sacred scriptures were finally committed to writing. Jainism also split into two sects: Svetambaras, who wear white clothes, and Digambaras, who practice nudity and believe that women cannot achieve moksha until they are reborn as men. Women, according to Digambaras, are the greatest source of earthly temptation.

Jains reject the existence of a supreme being and divide the universe into three worlds, which, in turn, are divided into numerous levels. The Jain goal, however, is to follow the model of the 24 Tirthankaras. Devotees want to cross the river and obtain freedom for the soul from all three realms.

The Jain cosmology is a common motif in religious paintings. The lower world, which normally looks like truncated pyramids, represents various infernos occupied by mortals who have sinned. The middle world, which resembles a disc, contains all nonliving matter and lifeforms, including human beings who are struggling through the cycle of rebirth and striving for liberation. The upper world, which is often drum shaped with a bulging middle, is the realm of the gods and spirits. Some paintings also take the shape of the Cosmic Man: the truncated pyramids are turned into legs, the disc becomes the waist, and the upper world extends up from the abdomen. When gods are depicted in the cosmos, their visible serenity increases as they move up each level within the upper world.

The restrictions of Jainism are severe. Jains are supposed to avoid all occupations that involve the destruction of any lifeform. Consequently, many Jains are members of the trading community, and few are farmers. Jains are not permitted to eat meat or eggs, and many of them even shun vegetables and edible roots that grow underground for fear of ingesting infinitesimally small creatures. They must also take 12 vows that include the practice of *ahimsa* (nonviolence) and meditation, restrictions on the acquisition of wealth and unnecessary belongings, and the commitment to spend some time as a monk or nun.

An important Jain symbol is the swastika, with each appendage representing the four possible stages of birth: life in hell, life as an insect, human life, and life as a god or demon. The three dots on top of the swastika stand for right faith, right knowledge, and right conduct. The half moon above the dots stands for moksha: the ultimate Jain goal. Jain temples are often exquisitely adorned, as another important vow instructs devotees to contribute generously to the construction and maintenance of temples and animal hospitals. The Charity Bird Hospital in Delhi is a remarkable example of this instruction.

Images of the 24 Tirthankaras, depicted as ascetics with or without clothes, embellish most Jain temples. Parsvanatha is blue and usually appears with a snake. Mahavira is golden and usually appears with a lion.

Islam

"There is no God but Allah, and Mohammed is His Prophet." This, the *shahadah* (religious creed) and the most important pillar of the Islamic faith, originated with Mohammed (his name means "highly praised"), who was born about AD 571 in the Arabian town of Mecca. A series of revelations from Allah, passed on through the Angel Gabriel, instructed Mohammed to preach against the paganism practiced by the Meccans. Initially, Mohammed saw himself as a social reformer who advocated a virtuous life in a city where virtue had vanished. The Meccans, however, saw him as a menace and a threat and forced him to flee to Yathrib (present-day Medina).

This move in AD 622, which Muslims now call *hijra*, marks the beginning of the Islamic era—an era in which Mohammed established the concept of Islam, which means "submission" and "peace," as a way of life that dictated the proper behavior of the individual. By the time Mohammed died in AD 632, the inhabitants of a large expanse of Arabia stretching from Persia to the Pyrenees and from Samarkand (in Uzbekistan) to the Sahara had converted to Islam.

With the death of Mohammed, his father-in-law, Abu Bakr, one of the first converts to Islam, became the next ruler and was called caliph (successor of the Prophet). In AD 656, during the reign of the fourth caliph, Ali, who was the Prophet's nephew and the husband of his daughter Fatima, civil war broke out. Ali moved his capital to Mesopotamia, where he was murdered by Muslim dissidents.

Ali's death signaled the beginning of a period of religious dissension between the traditionalists, Sunnis, who followed the orthodox teaching and example of the Prophet, and Ali's supporters, who claimed Ali's right to the caliphate based on his descent from the Prophet. In time, Ali's supporters broke away from the Sunnis and formed a sect known as the Shias or Shiites (the party of Ali).

Originally political in nature, the differences between the Sunnis and Shiites took on theological overtones. The Sunnis retained the doctrine of leadership by consensus. After Syrians massacred Hussain, Ali's son, at Karbala in Iraq, the Shiites strengthened their resolve that only Mohammed's rightful heirs should rule. They modified the shahadah: "There is no god but Allah; Mohammed is the Prophet of God, and Ali is the Saint of God."

Islam demands submission to God—a God who is invisible, yet omnipresent. To represent him in any form is a sin, which explains the absence of icons in mosques and tombs. Every bit of decorative touch, often fashioned out of myriad tiny gems, is limited to inscriptions of the holy scripture, the Quran, and the names of Mohammed and his important followers.

Muslims believe that Allah (God) existed throughout time, but humans had strayed from his true teaching until Mohammed set them straight. Islam has concepts similar to those of Judaism or Christianity: guardian angels, the day of judgment, the general resurrection, heaven and hell, and the eternal life of the soul. Muslims are also instructed to follow a strict code of ethical conduct that encourages generosity, tolerance, and respect and forbids adultery, gambling, usury, and the consumption of pork and alcohol.

Other duties of Muslims form the five pillars of the faith: the recitation of the shahadah; *salat* (daily prayer); *zakat* (almsgiving); *siyam* (fasting); and *haj* (pilgrimage). The believer must pray to Allah five times daily, with each occasion preceded by a ritual washing of the hands, feet, neck, and head. Whenever possible, men pray at a mosque under a prayer leader; this is obligatory on Fridays. Women may also attend public worship but are segregated from the men.

The ninth month of the Muslim calendar, Ramadan, when Mohammed received his revelations, is a month of obligatory fasting from sunrise to sunset for all but the weak, pregnant women, and young children. During this period of abstinence, drinking, smoking, and sexual intercourse are also prohibited.

During his life, a Muslim is supposed to make the haj to the Great Mosque in Mecca to participate in 10 days of special rites, held during the 12th month of the lunar calendar. While on the haj, the pilgrim wears an *ihram* (seamless white robe) that symbolizes equality and devotion to Allah and abstains from sexual relations, shaving, and cutting his hair and nails. The returning pilgrim is entitled to the honorific "hajji" before his name and a turban carved on his tombstone.

The word *mosque,* or *majid,* means "a place of prostration." It is generally square in shape; constructed from stone, clay, or brick; and has an open courtyard surrounded with *madrasas* (cloisters) for students who are studying the Quran. After the muezzin (crier) sings the call for prayer from the minaret (tower), the faithful line up in rows behind the imam (one who has studied the Quran). The imam stands in the sacred part of the majid facing the *mihrab* (a niche in the wall that indicates the direction of Mecca). When the imam prays, the mihrab—an ingenious amplifier—bounces the imam's voice back to the devotees. Only prayers are heard and prostrations are made; ceremonies connected with birth, marriage, and death occur elsewhere.

Sikhism

Guru Nanak, the founder of Sikhism, was born into a Hindu family in 1469 when the Lodi sultanate, a Muslim dynasty from Afghanistan, ruled over his north Indian homeland. From an early age, he railed against the caste system, the corruption of Hindu priests, their superstitious beliefs, and their unwieldy family of gods. He also abhorred the advent of Muslim persecution. His anger led to his new theology, which included the belief in one god, and his title of guru (*gu:* one who drives away darkness and *ru:* preaches enlightenment).

Nanak's view of Sikhism, recorded in the Adi Granth (Sikh holy book), upheld the Islamic idea that the goal of religion was the union with God, who dwelled within the soul. Through meditation and dharma (Hindu concepts), he believed, devotees could rid themselves of impurities, free themselves from the endless cycle of rebirth, and attain eternal bliss. For Hindus at the bottom of society, Sikhism offered equality and tolerance. They gladly converted and became Sikhs (disciples).

During the early years of the Mogul Empire, Sikhism flourished without interference until Emperor Jehangir assumed the throne. Jehangir resented the Sikh view of Islam and ultimately tortured and murdered the fifth guru. When Aurangzeb, the next emperor, revealed his own ruthless intolerance, Gobind Singh, the 10th and final guru, forged the Sikhs into a martial community that he called the *khalsa,* which means the pure. Gobind Singh instructed every Sikh man to observe and wear the five *kakkari* (visible symbols): *kesh* (uncut hair and beard); *kachh* (boxer shorts); *kara* (a steel bangle); *kanga* (a wooden comb); and *kirpan* (a dagger). All Sikh men also assumed the surname Singh, meaning "lion" (though not all Singhs are Sikh), and Sikh women adopted the name Kaur, meaning "lioness" or "princess." Members of the khalsa were to follow a strict code of conduct that forbade the use of alcohol and tobacco and advocated a life of meditation and courage.

— by Kathleen Cox

FURTHER READING AND VIEWING

Books

The classic work on early Indian history is A. L. Basham's *The Wonder that Was India*. In *The Discovery of India,* by Jawaharlal Nehru (if you've never read Nehru, you're in for a treat), Nehru's sense of his country's history is passionate and poetic. *India Britannica,* by Geoffrey Moorhouse, is an entertaining and informative history of British rule in India. *Freedom at Midnight,* by Larry Collins and Dominique Lapierre, is a spellbinding account of India's break from Britain. *City of Joy,* by the same authors, gives a powerful view of Calcutta. *Portrait of India,* by Ved Mehta, and *India: A Million Mutinies Now,* by V. S. Naipal, offer two thought-provoking views of contemporary India. *The Speaking Tree,* by Richard Lannoy, is an excellent introduction to Indian culture. *Myths and Symbols in Indian Art and Civilization,* by Heinrich Zimmer (completed and edited by Joseph Campbell), is required reading for the art or mythology lover. *Gods, Demons, and Others,* by R. K. Narayan, retells the Hindu myths. *Hinduism,* by K. M. Sen, offers insights into this religion. *Freedom in Exile* is the stunning autobiography of the Dalai Lama. *Tales of India* and *Kim,* by Rudyard Kipling, are light reading from one who knew India intimately. *Midnight's Children,* by Salman Rushdie, is a fabulous novel woven around India after independence. Rushdie's newest Bombay-centered epic, *The Moor's Last Sigh,* has raised the hackles of some Indians who see Hindu slurs between its lines. The *Raj Quartet* by Paul Scott will get you in the mood for your trip. Rabindranath Tagore, a Nobel laureate (1913) and one of India's foremost modern poets, can be read in translation in books such as *The Crescent Moon* (1913) and *Collected Poems and Plays* (1936, 1973).

Films

For a sense of Indian history and society and some views of the country, try screening a film or video before you go.

The prolific Indian film industry has produced a wealth of historical and adventure movies, as well as some of the great international classic films. *Aan* (1952), directed by Mehboob, a story of royalty tamed by peasants, is a prime example of Indian costume melodrama. *Pather Panchali* (1955), *Aparajito* (1956), and *The World of Apu* (1959), written and directed by India's premier filmmaker, Satyajit Ray, are a powerful film trilogy that depicts tragedy and poverty in the life of a child in modern Varanasi. *Shakespeare Wallah* (1965), written by Ruth Prawer Jhabvala and James Ivory and directed by Ivory, focuses on a group of English actors on tour in India. *Heat and Dust* (1982), also written by Ruth Prawer Jhabvala and directed by Ivory, re-creates India's past through letters discovered by the protagonist.

Films set in India by Western directors are numerous. *Elephant Boy* (1937) is a flawed documentary drama about a boy elephant keeper who helps conservationists. *The River* (1951), directed by Jean Renoir, follows a group of English people living beside the Ganges. *Phantom India,* directed by Louis Malle, is an epic documentary of life in India. *City of Joy* (1982) is based on the Collins/Lapierre book *(see* Books, *above).* The award-winning *Gandhi* (1982), directed by Richard Attenborough, traces the life of the leader of India's independence movement. In *A Passage to India* (1984), based on the E. M. Forster novel and directed by David Lean, the conflict between Indians and the English under the Raj is played out through the story of a man accused of rape. *The Jewel in the Crown* (1984), a TV series based on Paul Scott's *Raj Quartet (see* Books, *above),* is an epic of Britain's last years of power in India, involving a romance between a British woman and an Indian man. *Salaam Bombay* (1988), directed by Mira Nair, is a fictionalized account of the life of Bombay's slum children.

DINING GLOSSARY

Because India is a land of many languages and cuisines, you may not find these dishes on every menu. The spelling of items can also vary.

General Terms
Dum pukht: aromatic dishes that are sealed and slow-cooked
Kadhai: foods prepared in an iron pot similar to a wok
Katoris: small metal bowls with food items placed on the *thali* (*see below*)
Tandoori: foods cooked in a clay oven fired by charcoal
Thali: a large round metal platter

Beverages
Chai: tea
Feni: Goan cashew-nut liquor
Lassi: cold yogurt and milk drink
Masala chai: spicy tea with whole cardamom, clove, and cinnamon
Nimbu pani: lemonade
Paan liqueur: Sikkimese betel-nut liqueur

Dairy Products
Dahi: yogurt
Ghee: clarified butter
Paneer: Indian-style cottage cheese

Vegetables and Grains
Aloo: potato
Baigan: eggplant
Bhindi: okra
Chawal: rice
Chenna: chickpeas
Chutney: pickled relishes
Dal: cooked lentil preparations
Gobi: cauliflower
Mattar: peas
Piaz: onion
Raita: chopped vegetables mixed with yoghurt
Saag: spinach; also called **palak**
Sabzi: vegetables; also called **subzi**

Seafood and Meat
Gosht: mutton or lamb
Jhinghe: prawn; also called **jhinga**
Muchli: fish
Murgh: chicken

Breads
Aloo paratha: potato-filled *paratha* (*see below*).
Chapatti: unleavened gheeless bread cooked in an iron pan
Kulcha: *naan* (*see below*) stuffed with herbs and onions
Naan: slightly leavened bread prepared in a tandoori
Pappad: fried thin wafer made with bread and pepper; also called **pappadam**
Paratha: shallow-fried unleavened bread made with ghee
Pudina paratha: paratha with mint
Puri: deep-fried puffed bread

Popular Main Dishes

Biriyani: rice cooked with meat or vegetables
Kofta: spicy meat or vegetable balls
Korma: braised meat or vegetable preparation
Murgh reshmi: spicy minced chicken roll
Pillau: spiced rice with meat or vegetables
Raan: roast lamb or mutton with spices
Roghan gosht: lamb with yogurt
Shaan-e-murgh: chicken breast stuffed with paneer
Shami kebab: deep-fried ground meat patty
Tikka: skewered and barbecued chunks of meat, vegetables, or cheese

Desserts

Barfi: supersweet milk sweetmeats
Falooda: transparent vermicelli that often comes with *kulfi* (*see below*).
Firni: sweet ground-rice pudding with pistachios
Gulab jamun: fried cream cheese and milk balls
Kheer: thick creamy rice pudding with almonds
Kulfi: Indian ice cream
Rasgullah: syrupy sweet cream cheese balls

Snacks

Aloo tikki: fried potato patties
Bhajii: vegetables fritters
Chaat: cold spicy fruit or vegetable salad
Dosa: enormous, fried, crepe-style pancake
Idli: steamed rice cakes
Masala dosa: potato-stuffed dosa
Pakoras: deep-fried vegetable fritters
Sambhar: spicy sauce served with dosa and idli
Samosa: deep-fried pastry stuffed with meat or vegetables

Digestive

Paan: betel leaf filled with lime paste, crushed betel nut, sweet and aromatic spices, and sometimes a narcotic

Tibetan Dishes and Drinks

Chang: wine made from distilled barley or rice
Kothay: fried dumplings
Momo: steamed dumplings
Thukpa: hearty noodle soup

INDEX

NOTES

NOTES

NOTES

NOTES

NOTES

NOTES

NOTES

NOTES

NOTES

NOTES

Fodor's Travel Publications

Available at bookstores everywhere, or call 1–800–533–6478, 24 hours a day.

Gold Guides
U.S.

Alaska

Arizona

Boston

California

Cape Cod, Martha's Vineyard, Nantucket

The Carolinas & the Georgia Coast

Chicago

Colorado

Florida

Hawaii

Las Vegas, Reno, Tahoe

Los Angeles

Maine, Vermont, New Hampshire

Maui

Miami & the Keys

New England

New Orleans

New York City

Pacific North Coast

Philadelphia & the Pennsylvania Dutch Country

The Rockies

San Diego

San Francisco

Santa Fe, Taos, Albuquerque

Seattle & Vancouver

The South

U.S. & British Virgin Islands

USA

Virginia & Maryland

Waikiki

Washington, D.C.

Foreign

Australia & New Zealand

Austria

The Bahamas

Bermuda

Budapest

Canada

Cancún, Cozumel, Yucatán Peninsula

Caribbean

China

Costa Rica, Belize, Guatemala

Cuba

The Czech Republic & Slovakia

Eastern Europe

Egypt

Europe

Florence, Tuscany & Umbria

France

Germany

Great Britain

Greece

Hong Kong

India

Ireland

Israel

Italy

Japan

Kenya & Tanzania

Korea

London

Madrid & Barcelona

Mexico

Montréal & Québec City

Moscow, St. Petersburg, Kiev

The Netherlands, Belgium & Luxembourg

New Zealand

Norway

Nova Scotia, New Brunswick, Prince Edward Island

Paris

Portugal

Provence & the Riviera

Scandinavia

Scotland

Singapore

South Africa

South America

Southeast Asia

Spain

Sweden

Switzerland

Thailand

Tokyo

Toronto

Turkey

Vienna & the Danube

Fodor's Special-Interest Guides

Branson

Caribbean Ports of Call

The Complete Guide to America's National Parks

Condé Nast Traveler Caribbean Resort and Cruise Ship Finder

Cruises and Ports of Call

Fodor's London Companion

France by Train

Halliday's New England Food Explorer

Healthy Escapes

Italy by Train

Kodak Guide to Shooting Great Travel Pictures

Shadow Traffic's New York Shortcuts and Traffic Tips

Sunday in New York

Sunday in San Francisco

Walt Disney World, Universal Studios and Orlando

Walt Disney World for Adults

Where Should We Take the Kids? California

Where Should We Take the Kids? Family Adventures

Where Should We Take the Kids? Northeast

Special Series

Affordables
Caribbean
Europe
Florida
France
Germany
Great Britain
Italy
London
Paris

Fodor's Bed & Breakfasts and Country Inns
America's Best B&Bs
California's Best B&Bs
Canada's Great Country Inns
Cottages, B&Bs and Country Inns of England and Wales
The Mid-Atlantic's Best B&Bs
New England's Best B&Bs
The Pacific Northwest's Best B&Bs
The South's Best B&Bs
The Southwest's Best B&Bs
The Upper Great Lakes' Best B&Bs

The Berkeley Guides
California
Central America
Eastern Europe
Europe
France
Germany & Austria
Great Britain & Ireland
Italy
London
Mexico
Pacific Northwest & Alaska
Paris
San Francisco

Compass American Guides
Arizona
Canada
Chicago
Colorado
Hawaii
Idaho
Hollywood
Las Vegas
Maine
Manhattan
Montana
New Mexico
New Orleans
Oregon
San Francisco
Santa Fe
South Carolina
South Dakota
Southwest
Texas
Utah
Virginia
Washington
Wine Country
Wisconsin
Wyoming

Fodor's Citypacks
Atlanta
Hong Kong
London
New York City
Paris
Rome
San Francisco
Washington, D.C.

Fodor's Español
California
Caribe Occidental
Caribe Oriental
Gran Bretaña
Londres
Mexico

Nueva York
Paris

Fodor's Exploring Guides
Australia
Boston & New England
Britain
California
Caribbean
China
Egypt
Florence & Tuscany
Florida
France
Germany
Ireland
Israel
Italy
Japan
London
Mexico
Moscow & St. Petersburg
New York City
Paris
Prague
Provence
Rome
San Francisco
Scotland
Singapore & Malaysia
Spain
Thailand
Turkey
Venice

Fodor's Flashmaps
Boston
New York
San Francisco
Washington, D.C.

Fodor's Pocket Guides
Acapulco
Atlanta
Barbados

Jamaica
London
New York City
Paris
Prague
Puerto Rico
Rome
San Francisco
Washington, D.C.

Rivages Guides
Bed and Breakfasts of Character and Charm in France
Hotels and Country Inns of Character and Charm in France
Hotels and Country Inns of Character and Charm in Italy

Short Escapes
Country Getaways in Britain
Country Getaways in France
Country Getaways in New England
Country Getaways Near New York City

Fodor's Sports
Golf Digest's Best Places to Play
Skiing USA
USA Today The Complete Four Sport Stadium Guide

Fodor's Vacation Planners
Great American Learning Vacations
Great American Sports & Adventure Vacations
Great American Vacations
National Parks and Seashores of the East
National Parks of the West